To Brenda

No. 1 Volunt

Happy Birthday 2001

Love Jan. Don

THE VOLUNTEERS

THE VOLUNTEERS

How ordinary Australians
brought about the extraordinary
success of the Sydney 2000 Games

MAX WALKER
AND GERRY GLEESON

A Sue Hines Book
Allen & Unwin

First published in 2001

Allen & Unwin
83 Alexander Street
Crows Nest NSW 2065
Australia
Phone: (61 2) 8425 0100
Fax: (61 2) 9906 2218
Email: info@allenandunwin.com
Web: www.allenandunwin.com

National Library of Australia
Cataloguing-in-Publication entry:

Walker, Max, 1948- .
The volunteers: how ordinary Australians brought about the extraordinary success of the Sydney Games.

ISBN 1 86508 568 5.

1. Olympic Games (27th :, 2000 : Sydney, N.S.W.). 2. Volunteers - Australia. I. Gleeson, Gerry. II. Title.

361.370994

Cover and text design by Phil Campbell
Typeset by J & M Typesetting
Printed in Australia by Griffin Press

10 9 8 7 6 5 4 3 2 1

Australia made a great success of the Sydney 2000 Games. Our leaders did a fine job of securing the event and the world's best athletes put on a great show, but in the end it was the people who made it work.

This book is dedicated to you, the volunteers who went the extra mile for the XXVII Olympiad, and kept on smiling.

CONTENTS

CITIUS · ALTIUS · FORTIUS

INTERNATIONAL OLYMPIC COMMITTEE

THE PRESIDENT

Message From the IOC President

The Olympic Movement thrives on volunteerism. All of us have a passionate love for sport that drives us to work for its development. The members of the IOC, in fact, volunteer their time to promote Olympism and to ensure the regular celebration of the Olympic Games. The Games, however, could not flourish without the added energies of the tens of thousands of volunteers who support the operations of the organizing committee.

In Sydney, one of the truly great performances was turned in by the volunteers. Their work and dedication helped make the 2000 Olympic Games the best Games in Olympic history. Everywhere I went, I saw smiling, helpful volunteers ensuring everyone's needs were well taken care of. They were the best hosts the Olympic Movement could have hoped for.

This book is full of voices praising their good work. I resoundingly add mine. To the volunteers of Sydney 2000, I say, « Aussie, Aussie, Aussie ! »

Best regards,

CHÂTEAU DE VIDY, CASE POSTALE 356, 1001 LAUSANNE, SWITZERLAND

THE TWO OF US

"At the 2000 Olympic Games Australia staged an event that shattered all previous attendance records. Crucial to this success was the indefatigable spirit of the volunteers and they have been universally acclaimed for their effort. This recognition, unlike that of the single-minded performance-focused athletes, was not because these incredibly generous people sought it. This book is a celebration of this spirit, this expression of true Aussie character, sense of humour and the ability to do what had to be done … with a genuine smile.

What was the catalyst for the book?

It became a reality because of a phone call between two ageing footballers, Gerry Gleeson and myself. We'd both pulled on the red and blue guernsey for the Melbourne Football Club … we had a fair amount of shared history between us. We'd both been recruited as 18-year-olds, Gerry from Berrigan in NSW in 1953, and me from Hobart in 1967. The same man had spotted both of us, all those years apart – Jim Cardwell, the club secretary. We both made it to the final training list after a few practice matches. We were both coached by Norm Smith, recently voted coach of the century. We both played in the ruck. And there the similarities stopped. Gerry played in the Melbourne teams that made it to seven Grand Finals, including five Premiership teams. Unfortunately I never played with 17 players who were good enough to earn me the honour of doing the victory lap on that last Saturday in September.

Football talent oozed out of the Gleeson genes, it seems. Gerry's brother Brian won the 1957 Brownlow Medal playing for St Kilda, for the best and fairest player in the league. One of Gerry's mates, Tony 'Ocka' O'Callaghan, reckons the family should have won the double that year – Brian the fairest, and Gerry the dirtiest! I'm told by those who know that Gerry became quite a different person when he crossed the boundary line. Gerry's penchant for a descriptive phrase got him into trouble more than a few times, earning him the honour of being the first league player to be rubbed out in a practice match. Apparently he described the umpire as a %#@&*#! idiot, thinking that anything goes in a practice match. But they'd changed the rules at the start of the season, and Gerry reckons they forgot to tell him, and anyway, the umpy deserved it – that's my man's story and he's sticking to it.

Sorry, I've gone off the track again. But that's what it's like when Gerry and I catch up. A lot of common ground, a good place for a conversation to start.

So Gerry rings me up out of the blue, and eventually says, 'You know, I was a volunteer at the Sydney Olympics ... had a fantastic time ... great people ... unforgettable sights ... great stories ... I reckon I've got an idea for a book!' His enthusiasm is contagious (I could see how he made a great vollie). I agree ... all those stories ... yes, it's a wonderful idea for a book. And then:

'You've written a few books, Max, you know what you're doing, and we were both ruckmen ...' Yes, Gerry, you've got my ear. We're on the same page. After I put down the receiver, my mind started spinning at the enormous diversity of stories potentially on offer. But there was no way we could ring 50,000 people ... what if they all wanted to relate their story ... scary!

Gerry got that part organised. He discussed the logistics with TAFE NSW, who had had the task of training 50 000 personnel prior to the big event. Without their support, the process of contacting the volunteers to get their stories would have been even more daunting. And people gave their stories so willingly, just as they had given their time.

I love telling and listening to stories. Maybe it's a legacy from my late dad, Big Max. As an adolescent, I was privy to story telling at its best – across the front bar at the Empire Hotel in North Hobart. Dad was the proprietor and I reckon he sold a lot of beer on his ability to colour, stretch and tamper with the truth. 'Never let the facts get in the way of a good story!' he used to say. His audience would always agree, thirsty for more. 'One for the footpath …' This was my first place of learning, the old institute of experience, Dad used to call it.

Gerry could relate similar stories of outstanding story telling in the main bar of the Royal Hotel in Berrigan, NSW. So with our combined passion for stories, and the fact that we knew where each other had come from, we started this amazing journey, a journey that involved a lot of talking to a lot of people. Everywhere we went, people would tell us about more people they knew who had volunteered. 'You should talk to Bill', or 'Betty's got a few stories for you', it seemed like everyone knew a volunteer.

We had some very enjoyable times in our travels. At the start of the 2001 footy season the Sydney Swans celebrated their twentieth year of life in coat hanger city. The club paid tribute to the volunteers' efforts by inviting them to go to the match for free if they were wearing their uniform. Gerry and I attended this Swans celebration for the footy … and we thought we'd pick up a story or two for this book.

Gerry was resplendent in his official issue white hat, and brightly coloured vollie shirt. As each group entered the ground and made their way towards the grandstand, Gerry and I greeted them like a couple of pollies on the campaign trail. We handed out leaflets and explained what we had in mind.

We didn't get to the grandstand to watch the game until ten minutes into the second quarter … but the delay was worth it. To hear first-hand all those stories, to feel all that enthusiasm for what they did … that's when we knew we were on a winner and could create a fascinating read.

So, the book became a collection of stories, with people telling it the way it happened to them, in their own voices. It was our job to find those stories, through lots of phone calls, faxes, emails and chance meetings. In the years to come, this book will provide a unique oral history of the most dynamic sporting event ever held in Australia.

Over to you, Gerry, I'll take a breather.

Before the Games, Australia sent representatives to the Atlanta Olympics to observe and work with volunteers. The feedback was that volunteers would not make a great contribution. But they didn't realise then that an autocratic management style doesn't fit well with most Australians. The clue is communication. Just show them the task and they will get it done. Australians showed they don't need a rigid structure to perform. No matter where you were, the uniform conveyed to people you were available for duty.

The diversity of age and cultural background among the volunteers was extraordinary but still everyone melded in together. You realise how different people can be but also learn how close they can be. Natural leadership qualities floated to the surface and teams worked harmoniously and efficiently within an informal structure.

The Olympic volunteers had no political agenda. They were there to do a job the best way possible. We were family. Amongst ourselves we exchanged stories. Talk about writing a book on the experiences of the volunteers was often raised. I was driven mad by Dennis Robertson (in another life he works as a fireman in Sydney) who urged me to do something. He motivated me and it was only when I'd talked to Max that I finally realised it could happen. Well, Dennis has managed to get a book out of me, but I didn't get the story he promised out of Dennis!

Between us, Max and I were a great team. People bowl up to Max and will tell him anything. And I'd been there on the inside. So thanks to all of you who put pen to paper for us. We've tried to cover a wide range of experiences and to include as many of you as space would permit. We like to think we've chosen the best bits of your stories … if we'd included everything we'd have filled fifty books, and we're taking it one at a time. And special thanks to ALL the volunteers, whether you're in the book or not. You gave your time to showcasing Australia at the Games and this is your book too. ”

Max & Gerry

ABBREVIATIONS

ALO	Athlete Liaison Officer
AOC	Australian Olympic Committee
HAAC	Homebush Athlete Accreditation Centre
IOC	International Olympic Committee
NBA	National Broadcast Authority
	National Basketball Association
NBC	National Broadcast Centre
NBL	National Basketball League
NOC	National Olympic Committee
ORTA	Olympic Roads & Traffic Authority
OVIPR	Olympic Volunteers in Policing Road Events
SES	State Emergency Service
SOCOG	Sydney Organising Committee of the Olympic Games
SOP	Sydney Olympic Park
SSM	Spectator Services Manager
TLO	Team Liaison Officer
TOC	Tasmanian Olympic Council
UDAC	Uniform Distribution and Accreditation Centre
VCC	Venue Command Centre
VTM	Venue Training Manager
WPV	Water Polo Venue

SPECIAL TERMS

mag and bag at the entrance to every venue, bags were passed through a magnetic metal detector, and accreditation passes were checked
vollie shorthand for volunteer … nothing to do with tennis!
'Aussie Aussie Aussie Oi Oi Oi' the special Olympic anthem

SLEEVE COLOURS

A volunteer could be identified according to their area of service by the plain sleeve colour of their uniform. For example, if a vollie was called a 'yellow sleeve' it meant they were working in Spectator Services.

YELLOW	Spectator Services
PURPLE	Transport
RED	Medical
LIGHT GREEN	Security
DARK BLUE	Games Services
LIGHT BLUE	Logistics
DARK GREEN	Technical Officials

STATS

Official training numbers were provided by TAFE NSW. Please note that the other statistics are unofficial, and are intended only to give a broad look at who the volunteers were and where they came from.

HOW MANY VOLUNTEERS WERE THERE?
47,000 Olympic volunteers were trained and worked at the Olympic Games. A further 14,000 were trained specifically for the Paralympic Games. Many volunteers worked at both. Around 12,500 volunteers were trained for participation as performers and back stage people at the Opening and Closing Ceremonies of the Olympic Games. These people did not need to go through the TAFE NSW training, and therefore do not always appear in the official figures. They were trained by the 'show people' – the artistic directors and production managers.

WHERE DID THEY COME FROM?
About 78% of volunteers came from New South Wales, followed by 8% from Victoria and Tasmania, 6% from Queensland, 3% from Australian Capital Territory, 3% from South Australia and the Northern Territory and 2% from Western Australia. There were more volunteers from the USA than from any country outside Australia.

WERE THEY MOSTLY MALE OR FEMALE?
52% of volunteers were female, 48% were male.

HOW OLD WERE THEY?
13% of volunteers were aged between 50 and 59.
20% of volunteers were aged between 40 and 49.
15% of volunteers were aged between 30 and 39.
23% of volunteers were aged between 20 and 29.

CONTRIBUTORS

The following athletes and members of the Olympic community have generously contributed stories and tributes to the volunteers.

John BERTRAND
Raelene BOYLE
Peter BROCK
Priya COOPER
Dr Ken CRICHTON
Herb ELLIOT
Tim FISCHER
Andrew GAZE
Lindsay GAZE
Kevan GOSPER
Grant HACKETT
Geoffrey J. HENKE
Sandy HOLLWAY
Daniel KOWALSKI
John LANDY
Laurie LAWRENCE
Michael McLEAN
Clare MITCHELL-TAVERNER
Alan PATCHING
Kieren PERKINS
Geoff POLLARD
Cst. Duncan POUND
Nikki WEBSTER
Leon WIEGARD

Other contributors are the SOCOG employees, artistic directors, production managers, TAFE trainers, attachés and former Olympians who experienced first-hand the generous spirit of the vollies they worked with at the Games. Of course, the main contributors are the 250 volunteers whose stories appear on these pages. Please see the Volunteers Honour Roll starting on page 263 where these names appear in bold.

 This symbol denotes an Olympian, past or present.

Part 1

THE WINNER IS SYDNEY

" From the moment in September 1993 when Olympic president Juan Antonio Samaranch announced to the world that 'SID-IN-EE' would host the 2000 Olympic Games, Australia was immersed in an incredible outpouring of emotion and national pride. Darling Harbour became an uninhibited sea of humanity. On the other side of the world, the Premier of New South Wales, John Fahey, and his dedicated Olympic bid team leaped into the air. An unbridled clench-fisted punch of the air symbolised this momentous victory.

Not since John Bertrand had skippered *Australia II* to that memorable America's Cup victory way back in 1983 had everyone so unashamedly celebrated a win. With great leadership, courage and innovative design *Australia II* did us proud, against the odds. 'We come from a land down under.' What a song! It still makes the hair on the back of my neck stand to attention when I hear that sporting anthem.

The Olympic decision was like that – a genuine reason to let go of the steering wheel. Australia and Sydney would never again be quite the same. The romantic notion of a second Olympic Games down under was now a reality, no longer a collection of individual hopes and dreams. As a nation we would come together in the spirit of collaboration. Collectively we took on ownership of the Olympic dream, but at that stage we weren't really thinking about the hundreds of thousands of human hours, paid and voluntary, that would be seamlessly stitched together by SOCOG and its organising team to create the finished product.

I looked forward to the Olympics because I love my sport. For me, the opportunity to talk sport every weekend for 15 years on Nine's Wide World of Sport was a dream come true, especially during the lead time into both the Atlanta and Sydney Games. So many Olympic athletes, swimmers, cyclists, coaches and administrators accepted our offers of make-up, coffee, lights, camera, action before a chat on the box. We talked to Cathy Freeman, always a delight – never a formal interview, more of a conversation, spontaneous and bubbly. We talked to women's hockey coach, Ric

Charlesworth. We were privy to athletes' dreams – childhood and Olympic. We talked to Kieren Perkins after winning in Atlanta, and he assured us there was one more great swim left in him – this one would be saved for Sydney and an historic third 1500m gold medal. Michael Klim wanted to make up for a personally disappointing 1996, so as a result the world records toppled between Atlanta and Sydney – body suits and controversy. He just kept swimming faster, a long long way from 'the round little fella in Speedos who first turned up at the pool'.

We even got to do a satellite hook-up with Mark Spitz when he seriously had a crack at making the USA team for Atlanta – aged 42 years. My first (and, as it turned out, only) question to Mark was, 'Don't you think at 42 years of age you're a bit optimistic about beating all the young guns?' A simple 'no' would have sufficed, but an agonisingly long 12 minutes later, Mark took his only breath. Believe me, there was no way of breaking into this one way conversation. In back-announcing the interview, I said to my broadcasting partner, 'Gee, you reckon I can talk under water with a mouthful of marbles – this fella's got me well covered!'

Rob de Castella and Steve Moneghetti, champion marathon runners, provided many words of wisdom over the years – they're both wonderful athletes and ambassadors for Australia. That's what sports people are often – wonderful ambassadors, just like all you volunteers.

Sitting in the leather swivel chair parked in front of a huge wall of television monitors week after week after week was like attending a University of Sport with an exam every Saturday and Sunday. How much research could we cram into 48 hours – that was how much notice we usually had. Then it was up to our natural curiosity about what made sports people tick, what made them laugh, what made them vulnerable, who might their competition be – and frame all this into a sense of history and present day happenings. Just like the Games themselves there was always plenty to talk about.

So, while I was hanging on every word in the time leading up to the Olympics, Gerry watched proceedings from a different vantage point.

You'd better tell that story, Gerry.

1956 was a very significant year for me, as well as for Melbourne and Australia. I was part of the Demons premiership team, playing in front of 120,000 people on the hallowed turf and six weeks later the Melbourne Olympics took place on the same ground at the MCG. I was a very contented young ruckman sitting in the new grandstand watching a different group of champions compete for their ultimate prize. It was so exciting being there. It was that great year of 1956 that made me put my hand up to volunteer.

I thought we had a good chance of getting the Games. I've lived in Sydney for over 25 years, so I knew it was a great town and that they'd do a good job. I'd kept tabs on what was going on from the start when Nick Greiner, Premier of NSW at the time, announced that Sydney was going to make a serious attempt to stage the 2000 Olympic Games. My whole being was filled with joy and anticipation just at the possibility! The feeling prior to the final announcement was 'very hopeful' but there was no certainty. When Samaranch revealed to the world that 'SID-IN-EE' would host the 2000 Olympic Games, I saw it on telly at home, I saw John Fahey leap with joy and simultaneously made my decision that I would be involved somehow – I'd get my life organised and find the necessary time.

I didn't want to miss out on anything, you see. That's a real Australian thing, I reckon. So I just followed the normal procedure to volunteer and got accepted. I was all psyched up for it, and then I nearly didn't make it because my body packed up.

Dr Con Reed and I play golf together, and he'd witnessed my physical deterioration. He put me through a barrage of tests and then brought me in to his rooms for the results:

'Do you want the good news or the bad news first?'

'Give me the good news,' I said.

'Well you have a motor in you as good as someone 20 years younger.'

I said, 'That's good, continue.'

He went on. 'Your body is completely stuffed. We've never seen so much trauma, there's even a crack in your spine that was never reported and it's healed itself. I know you played a tough game of football, but there must be more to this than meets the eye.'

(Well, I did train on a broken leg once.)

So I told him about shearing and throwing bags of wheat around at the age of 15 and how my mother told me not to lift heavy things. He said, 'You should have listened to your mother.' Then I told him of my years in a management consultancy, pounding along concrete footpaths in sandshoes early in the morning so I could be intelligent for my power breakfasts with the Young Turks, after dinner with the Big Boss the night before.

I agreed to have a series of operations, first a double hernia, then right and left hip reconstructions. Between Con and Dr Barbara Fisher I was in good hands, and recovered so well I was able to carry out 13 shifts as a volunteer, which was a pretty normal involvement.

I didn't care what I ended up doing as a volunteer. Because of my management background I could have done back room strategic planning work, but I wanted to be where the people were. So I was assigned to Spectator Services (yellow sleeves), located at the Superdome.

I witnessed first-hand the magnificent job TAFE NSW did with training. This was such a good start, I knew everything would go well. ”

Max & Gerry

When Sydney won the 2000 Games, my wife, Dorothy, and I decided we both wanted to help so we put our hands up to be volunteers. We're both retired. I'd carried the torch in 1956, and women weren't eligible then, so Dorothy hadn't been as involved. We met in Murrumburrah, western NSW, in 1952. She was in town from Sydney visiting the man she was going to marry. But then she met me on the main street. She was the best girl in the town, and we got married three months later.

Sometimes, getting up early as a volunteer is exhausting but when the sun comes up in Sydney you feel just great. It's a fabulous feeling to think you can be part of helping out, that you will be the face of the Olympics, showcasing your country to the world. Volunteers, after all, are what visitors will remember more than anything else.

NORM WILLIAMS, *Pioneer volunteer*
PROSPECT NSW

> “Norm and Dorothy Williams are a unique Olympic double. They both carried an Olympic torch in the same country, 44 years apart. Norm was a torchbearer for the 1956 Melbourne Olympic Games, and Dorothy carried the torch on a leg of the Sydney 2000 Olympic Games Torch Relay. Dorothy and Norm started as 'pioneer volunteers' six years before the big event, contributing well over 3000 volunteer hours – an extraordinary effort in anyone's book. Before the Games, they answered thousands of phone calls and letters, working in the city every Wednesday. They road-tested uniforms, took part in practice events, did anything and everything. Then during the Games they personally welcomed athletes and members of the Olympic family to the Village, and worked in Spectator Services.”
>
> **Max**

'And the winner is Sydney.'
That was it for me! My goal was to be part of it.

KATHY PAYNE, *Spectator Services*
DUBBO NSW

On 23 September 1993, at the unholy hour of 4.30 a.m., on the foldout couch with my daughter April and the announcement of 'Sydney', I made the decision to be there no matter what, and that my family would be part of this magnificent event in 2000.

TERESA REID, *MOST Team*
SEYMOUR VIC

In 1956 I was a child living on a sheep property in central Victoria. Dad took me to see the Olympic torch changing hands from one runner to the next at Tatura, near Shepparton, and I was struck with Olympic fever. I can still remember the atmosphere of enthusiasm and excitement. Dad had told me that this was a once in a lifetime experience and I promised myself that if the Olympics ever returned to Australia I would make sure I played a greater part than merely being an onlooker at the torch relay!

CAROLYN BYRNE, *Accreditation*
HIGHFIELDS QLD

The flagship of the volunteer training program developed by TAFE NSW was the orientation training session. This was a one and a half hour session delivered to all volunteers in 52 sessions around Australia. It ranged from an extravaganza delivered to 3000 volunteers at the Darling Harbour Convention Centre to a more intimate affair with 200 volunteers in Adelaide. The content was the same and the mode of presentation was as sophisticated as was possible at the range of venues selected.

The dedication to a top quality product by the TAFE NSW team was unbelievable. Over the 52 sessions a relatively small team of approximately 20 TAFE NSW staff were rostered to meet and greet the volunteers, hand out their training material (folder, video and 'Go' passport) and even take part in a fashion parade of the volunteer uniform.

From the first fairly nerve-racking parade at Darling Harbour when the training program was launched to approximately 3000 people including the Minister for Education and various other officials, the parade developed and gained a life of its own for the TAFE NSW models.

It became a joke and a competition between we models to see who could get the biggest round of applause. Would it be the security volunteer with the big 'stop' movement? How about the ORTA volunteer 'driving' the cars, the medical volunteers 'taking a pulse' or the Spectator Services volunteer offering a helping hand with directions? We all tried to get the audience involved and clapping as we tried to outdo each other.

Our initial embarrassment in taking to the catwalk in front of thousands of people ended in a great sense of camaraderie and fun – and pride in the level of dedication and professionalism of our team.

A great deal of planning, development and organisation went into bringing the Orientation Training session to fruition and it was without doubt an incredibly successful training session, achieving a good balance between information, inspiration … and fun!

JANET CHESTER, *Orientation Trainer for TAFE*
SYDNEY NSW

THE SCENE:
Darling Harbour Convention Centre, six weeks before the Opening Ceremony of the Sydney 2000 Olympic Games.

THE EVENT:
The official launch of the TAFE NSW training program for volunteers, with over 3000 volunteers in attendance and a cast of dignitaries including the Minister for Education and the chairperson of the local Aboriginal Land Council and a strong media contingent ready to beam the event across the world.

THE ACTION:
Eight minutes before the launch is due to start, the volunteers are sitting expectantly in their seats, clutching their 120-page training manual, video and training passport. The official party is about to move into the auditorium and the technical crew is all in place. Ruth Constantine, stage manager for all of the 48 sessions that will be delivered across the country, gives the call for the aboriginal dance group who will open the proceedings to move to their positions. Two of the group move on to the stage. Where are the other three? Messages start flying across the intercom system and the TAFE NSW crew is put on high alert: find the other three dancers!

David Riordan, manager of the TAFE NSW training unit, is engaged in polite conversation with his boss Janet Stewart and SOCOG's Workforce training manager Claire Houston. It's my job to gently break the news to him that with six minutes to go, we are missing over half of the opening act.

David has been working 20-hour days for the last two weeks and what little colour he still has in his face quickly disappears. 'Where are the ones who are here?' he rasps. 'In the dressing room,' I reply. 'Quick, take me to them,' and with that we're off down the escalator. Now I should point out that I had never actually been to the dressing rooms in the Darling Harbour Convention Centre, but with unbounding confidence and a fair degree of panic I led the way.

What followed was a scene straight out of the movie, *This is Spinal Tap*.

Open the first door leading off from the foyer … a cloakroom. Take the next door … the security manager's office. Try another one … a very long corridor that we charge down with David pleading with me to convince him that this is the right direction. Three bends and two doors later, we reach a very dark area surrounded by ceiling-high black curtains. On the other side of those curtains are the 3000 volunteers.

In the meantime, the rest of the dance group have calmly made their way into the Convention Centre, met up with their fellow performers and are doing some final stretches before they take their position on stage. Unaware of all of this, David and I retrace our steps and find ourselves in the loading dock … one minute before the scheduled start. His face is a mixture of despair, panic and homicidal tendencies towards his so-called guide!

We manage to get back to the main foyer, just in time for David to fall in with the official party as it makes its way into the auditorium. A quickly whispered 'They're here!' from David's deputy Janet Chester and the show goes on. The dance group sets just the right mood and the whole launch and first training session goes off without a hitch.

The only thing I have noticed since that particular day is that David no longer asks me for directions … to anywhere!

PETER HOLDEN, *TAFE Olympic and Paralympic Unit*
SYDNEY NSW

" I remember my orientation session at Darling Harbour. Near the end of the presentation, the facilitator said, 'Stand up those who were not born in Australia.' A large number of the 3000 present stood up. Then followed 'Stand up those whose parents weren't born in Australia', and finally 'Stand up those whose grandparents weren't born in Australia.' Needless to say, by the end not many of us were still in our seats. Someone close to me yelled out, 'Must be all the convicts are sitting down.' We laughed. I love it when people tell stories that are a joke on themselves. It's part of the Aussie culture. "

Gerry

We used to have to go and train to be team leaders from 4 p.m. till 10 p.m. This particular night, some people from the university came in, and put us in groups and then asked us questions.

One of the questions was: 'What would you do if you were a team leader for the Olympics, and one of the people in your team was making passionate love to one of the other volunteers?' She asked my group and I answered, 'Well, if it wasn't my husband I'd say "Go for your life!"'

I think that might have taken a few points off me!

DOROTHY WILLIAMS, *Pioneer volunteer*
PROSPECT NSW

I entered the Australian Olympic Headquarters offices with a real spring in my step. 'I'd like to see Herb,' I ventured politely to the immaculately dressed smiling receptionist, who, incidentally, amazed me as she effortlessly answered a constant barrage of phone calls.

'Australian Olympic Committee, can I help you?' … and … 'One moment please I'll transfer you now.' She did this as well as juggling visitors who regularly entered the swinging glass doors. In the midst of this hive of office activity a young woman who I'd never met before burst through the door, spied me, grabbed my arm, looked intently into my eyes and exclaimed, 'Laurie! Just the man I want to see. Don't go away,' and she disappeared as quickly as she appeared.

The busy receptionist's eyes twinkled over the top of her glasses. She continued her work on the phone but was still alive to all that was happening around her.

'Who's she?'

'Jodie Smith. Great kid. She's in charge of issuing team uniforms … Australian Olympic Committee, can I help you?'

I'd called into the AOC offices to see Herb Elliot about clarifying certain duties he wanted the ALOs to perform during the Sydney Olympics, as these Sydney Games would be a major contributor to the sporting social and cultural history of Australia. They would also be a lot of fun not only for all the marvellous volunteers but also particularly for the ALOs. The ALOs were six people: Dawn Fraser, John Bertrand, Peter Brock, Robyn Maher (a three-time Olympian and bronze medallist), Megan Marcks (an Olympic gold medallist in Atlanta), and myself who had been chosen to assist all the competitors on our team. It would be Australia's largest Olympic team ever and strict planning and preparation were underway to make it the best ever. In Herb's words at an athlete liaison officers planning luncheon we attended in Sydney, our job was to 'unite, relax and inspire the team'.

Herb appeared. 'Come in Laurie.' I obeyed and followed. Jodie flung open the glass door and called again, 'Don't you leave without seeing me.'

'I dare not – I'm scared of women; I'm controlled by four at home,' I replied and kept following Herb.

After Herb had briefed me on specific duties in the Village I headed out of the AOC offices. Jodie collared me at the door. She had two big suitcases chock-full of Olympic gear as well as a large duffle bag on wheels and a knapsack. I had never seen so much Aussie gear. Home Olympics had certainly brought out the goodies.

'Don't worry if they don't fit. Bring them all to the Village and we can change them at University of Western Sydney when you pick up the rest of the gear,' she said.

'There's more?' I asked incredulously.

'Yes! Opening and Closing Ceremony gear.'

'What's it look like?'

'Great! But it's a big secret! Don't forget.'

I struggled out of the AOC offices laden with goodies.

Six weeks later, laden with these same goodies I cabbed it to the security gate outside the Olympic Village. Before I knew it two young policemen marched out of the security tent and went to work. One opened the cab door while the other helped the cabby unload. Five-star service and security in an Olympic Village; I felt really comfortable, I felt at ease, I felt at home. These were my fifth Olympic Games and I'd never been treated like this before.

'This is going to be one great Olympics,' I thought to myself.

'We'll put these through the security scan in double-quick time for you, Lozza,' called the beefy young constable.

'You just make sure you look after our boys and girls,' added the other as he lifted my bags up to be x-rayed.

'Where's the Aussie section from here?' I asked.

'Straight up the hill, turn right and it's about 50 metres on your left, but it's going to be a bit of a struggle with those bags.'

'I'll manage,' I replied.

'Blue! You throw Lozza's bags on the back of the trike and take them up for him. We can't have him getting a hernia before the Games begin,' he said.

Before I knew it I was in a mini Olympic parade following the two burly NSW police security. As we trundled up the hill scores of volunteers, dressed in their familiar blue on blue shirts, smiled, waved and welcomed with a good old Aussie 'G'day.' I felt completely at home.

This was just the start of an easy atmosphere of friendliness, helpfulness, and cooperation that was created by a team of volunteers that were the best ever at any Olympic Games I have ever attended.

'When's Kieren come in?' screamed one volunteer as we paraded past.

'The swimmers arrive next week; they're in Melbourne at the moment in final preparation mode,' I replied.

'Give him our best,' screamed another, 'We'll be cheerin' for Kieren!'

'We'll be cheerin' them all,' screamed yet another.

'I can't wait to see the clash between Perkins and Hackett ... Kieren will win, won't he? ... What's the inside mail? We don't carry everyone's bags in you know but if ya can't do it for the Aussies in your own country there's something wrong,' blurted the young policeman in one breath.

This was one time I felt comfortable answering a policeman's questions.

'Both are looking terrific at this stage of their preparation ... Both coaches are confident ... Hackett is hungry ... He's desperate to be taken seriously ... I would never bet against Kieren though ... My advice to you is don't have a bet,' I said with authority. I'd seen too many upsets in my coaching career to think that anyone had a mortgage on a race. This, after all, was the Olympics and many athletes had spent their whole lives working for this moment.

We arrived at the Aussie section of the Olympic Village.

'I'll just slip into admin and find out where I'm sleeping,' I said.

'We'll wait,' answered Blue.

'No, you go. Just leave my gear there.'

'No way, we'll wait. We've brought you this far, we'll see out our mission,' insisted Blue.

Within five minutes I was in the demountable accommodation chosen specifically for us by the AOC. Even though this wasn't the most luxurious accommodation available to us in the Village it was chosen because it was within easy walking distance to the dining hall and transport. I've never known an athlete that doesn't want to be close to food. It also featured a large central grassy square, which affectionately became known as 'Kangaroo Square'. It was here that we organised our team barbeques, had team bonding concerts, brought in celebrities, put up the portable coffee shop manned by volunteers, welcomed the rowers back into the Village after they had finished competition at Penrith, had Prime Minister Howard present medals to the swimmers who swam heats of relays but not finals, gathered for team sorties to the various sporting venues to support and cheer our teammates.

The boys in blue unloaded my gear on the verandah of the demountable. This was to be my home for the next 20 days. I pulled my bags through the sliding glass doors into a long lounge room. A TV set dominated the entrance. It sat in front of a small table and chairs, and a sink, small fridge and lounge at the far end of the room completed the furnishings. I struggled left through a narrow passageway into the sleeping quarters. A longer passageway that extended left and right had five small rooms on one side and three bathrooms, toilets and washbasins on the other. I shouldered open my bedroom door into a tiny room that contained a lowboy, a chest of drawers and a bedside table that separated two single beds. An immaculately dressed, fit-looking middle-aged man with a bristly moustache lay on the right-hand, bed legs crossed and hands cradled under the back of his head. He was first in and had marked his territory.

'Hi, I'm Geoff. I guess we're roommates for the next 20 days. I might warn you I snore.'

'Me too,' I replied easily.

He smiled and I knew I had a roommate with whom I would be comfortable.

He sat up, we shook hands and so started 20 days that are indelibly etched into my memory bank.

'What's the Village like?' I asked.

'First impressions: food's great, Village volunteers unbelievable – nothing too much trouble, friendly but not intrusive or pushy. There's a group across the road that mans laundromats 24 hours a day.'

'You're kidding! They do your washing?'

'Yep. Put it in at night, pick it up clean in the morning.'

'That's great. If they can keep that up they just might be our trump card in lifting our medal count.'

'What do you mean?'

'Well I reckon we all have our parts to play if the team is to be successful. You know the old saying … if you surround yourself with nine losers you'll be the tenth. We need these people. We need them to be positive and to help create that friendly stress-free environment that will give our athletes the opportunity to perform at their best.'

This they did. They performed well beyond the call of duty; the friendly faces in the food hall who greeted you with a smile and a 'G'day' as you entered and a friendly 'See ya later' as you left; the hundreds that lined the road cheering and clapping as their team marched in full regalia to the flag-raising ceremony in the Village: the volunteers in the tunnel, who would not see the Opening Ceremony, but deafened us with their roar of approval as we paraded behind Andrew Gaze, our flag bearer. They stood on rubbish bins and sat on each other's shoulders to cheer themselves hoarse as we moved slowly through the bowels of the stadium into the arena for the Opening Ceremony. They sent goosebumps surging through our bodies even before we entered the stadium.

This was the start of 16 great days of Olympic competition made even more memorable by the volunteers. And each of them has their stories …

LAURIE LAWRENCE, *Athlete Liaison Officer*
Master Coach at the AIS, International Hall of Fame Honoree
GOLD COAST QLD

As a youngster growing up in the 70s, Australian Rules football and cricket were the only sporting choices for most schoolboys. To have a passion for basketball was to be very different. But when you are born with a father who has played basketball in three Olympics and coached in a further four, I guess I had no choice but to be different.

It was sometimes tough during those vulnerable pubescent years to deal with the ridicule of your mates during recess and lunch breaks, who couldn't understand what you were doing shooting baskets on the netball rings which were normally reserved for the girls. Initially, I think it was the intrinsic enjoyment of the game that drove me there, but ultimately it was the dream to compete at the Olympic Games that kept me there.

The passion for the Games took some time to develop. I can remember as a youngster having Mum dress me up to go to the airport to see Dad off to the Olympic Games. At the time I was oblivious to the significance of the occasion. I also remember hearing about some of the interesting stories of the games, like in Montreal when Eddie Palaubinskus was the leading scorer for the tournament, or great team performances, or special moments like the Opening Ceremony. But I can also recall being confused hearing the stories of how 11 Israeli athletes were killed in Munich, and trying to understand why the African nations boycotted the Montreal games and the Americans in Moscow.

It was not until Moscow in 1980 that I became committed to the dream of competing at the Olympic Games. I remember it was a school day but Mum had woken me and my sister up especially early in the hope that we could catch a glimpse of Dad during Australia's game against Italy. Much of our interest in the team's performance had waned because Australia had already lost to Cuba in its opening game and to advance to the final rounds it had to beat either Cuba or Italy and Italy was one of the favourites to win the gold medal. Because it was generally regarded that Australia had no chance against the Italians it was unlikely that much, if any, of the game would make the telecast. We watched and waited until finally they said they were crossing to the basketball. There were about seven minutes remaining in the game and Australia had a narrow lead. I can't recall exactly what happened but I remember seeing Phil Smyth, who was having an outstanding game, get knocked out by a cheap shot from one of the Italians which forced him to the bench, but he returned to the game for the final few minutes. I also remember Ian Davies hitting a jump shot from just over the centre line.

The images that have remained permanently fixed in my head were those of the diminutive Phil Smyth dribbling around, weaving in and out of the Italian opponents for the final 20 seconds of the game to secure a seven-point victory for the Aussies. And as the final siren sounded the cameras flashing towards the Australians' bench and seeing my father jumping as high as he could with fists raised. I had never before seen him show such emotion. Then backup point guard Gordie Macloud, who had not seen a second of action, came running over to give my dad a bear hug followed by the rest of the team.

These moments were my first cognitive impressions of the Olympic Games and remain some of my most memorable Olympic experiences. When I reflect back on my own playing career, the impact and inspiration I derived from them shaped many of my desires and ambitions.

During my time as a participant in the last five Olympic games, Australian teams have been involved in similar victories at each event. Some of the most memorable were in Seoul, Atlanta and Sydney where we qualified for the medal play-offs. In Seoul it was against Spain, in Atlanta it was against Croatia and in Sydney it was against Russia. In all these games they were against opponents that we had never beaten before in the history of international competition.

As a participant, these were all career highlights and I

feel extraordinarily privileged to have had those opportunities. But there is much more to an Olympic experience than an athletic challenge. In Sydney my role and responsibilities were extended way beyond my participation in the basketball competition, when I was given the honour of being flag bearer and team captain of the Australian Olympic team.

Elite sport is an obsessively goal-oriented endeavor, but not in my wildest dreams did I ever envisage carrying the Australian flag and leading an Australian team into an Olympic Opening Ceremony. Even though Sydney was going to be my fifth Games and I had been mentioned as a potential candidate in the media during the lead-up, I never realistically believed that I would receive that honor.

As incredible as it was – to be the first Australian athlete to walk out in front of 120,000 people, in your home country, in the most important sporting event in the world – the events that preceded that occasion are equally, if not more, memorable.

I was informed that I was going to be the flag bearer a few days before the Opening Ceremony. The Opening Ceremony was on the Friday and we arrived into the Village on the Monday. Part of the procedure when teams arrived in the Village was that they had to be available for an arrival press conference, which for us was held first thing Tuesday morning. As the captain of the basketball team I had to attend and Mark Bradtke was selected to join me. The chef de mission of the Australian team, John Coates, hosted these press conferences and he was also the sole person responsible for selecting Australia's flag bearer.

The press conference lasted about half an hour but Mark and I had to spend a little extra time to do a couple of one-on-one interviews after the official press conference had ended. We then headed back to our living quarters in the village and as we were walking back we ran into Mr Coates along the way. He called us over to him and asked if he could have a quick chat to us. He thanked us for our time with the press and began to talk about the Opening Ceremony and in the most nonchalant and matter of fact way he said '... and Andrew I would like you to carry the flag for the Australian team during the Opening Ceremony.' It was said in such a manner that I didn't immediately comprehend or understand exactly what he was saying. I looked at Mark and tried to steady myself, and thought, did I hear right? I had to clarify what he had just said and felt it necessary to ask one of those questions that I knew could be very embarrassing and awkward if I got the wrong response. But I tentatively interrupted Mr Coates and said, 'So you want me to carry the flag during the Opening Ceremony.' He quickly replied in the same steady tone, 'Yeah, that's right, I think you deserve that honour and ...' And from that point on, I have no recollection of what he went on to say. He probably spoke for another minute or two but once he confirmed my role as flag bearer I was overcome with a sensation of excitement and emotion that I had never before experienced. As soon as he left, I looked at Mark and the enormity of what I had just received hit us both and I broke down with tears of joy.

Through the myriad of emotions I was experiencing, one of the only things I could remember Mr Coates asking was that we keep it a secret and not to tell anyone. There was going to be an official announcement by the Prime Minister at a special function on Wednesday night and it was important that the media didn't find out until the official announcement. At the time we gladly agreed but it took only about two minutes – just enough time for us to compose ourselves – before we were both on the mobile phones to our families to let them know the news.

The most difficult challenge was going to be keeping the news from our teammates. We agreed that whatever it took, we couldn't tell anyone but our families. That night we had a practice game against Lithuania in Wollongong. The whole day I felt like I was cheating on the team by not sharing my good news.

We played the game and in 30 years of competition I had never felt more distracted and unfocused on a game of basketball. With about five minutes to go in the game I went to Mark and told him that although the consequences may be dire, I had to tell the rest of the guys in the team what was happening. Mark agreed, so I decided that I would pass on the news in the locker room at the end of the game.

Fortunately we won the game and spirits were high. Barry Barnes gave his usual post-game address and was talking about the next day's training routine and schedule. He went on to explain about a very important function that we had to attend and how it will be a special night for one Australian athlete. Just as he was saying that I interrupted him and said, 'Just on that Barry, Mark and I met with John Coates after our press conference this morning, and he told me that I got the job.' As I was saying this I was again overcome with emotion and although I had difficulty uttering the last few words, everyone knew exactly what I was telling them and the room erupted with jubilation.

I have been in the locker rooms when I was a part of NBL titles, following huge wins at the Olympics, and when the San Antonio Spurs won the NBA championship, but this was by far the greatest locker room celebration I had ever been a part of. The entire team jumped me and hugged me and to see the emotion and excitement of my teammates was even more rewarding than when I received the news myself.

The final significant moment that related to my role as flag bearer was immediately prior to the ceremony itself. All the countries participating in the Opening Ceremony assembled in the Superdome, which is about 300 metres from Stadium Australia, about four hours prior to the beginning of the march. Each country was seated in its own section of the venue and watched the ceremony on the Jumbo screens that hang from the centre of the venue. Once it was time for the athletes to begin the march procedure, each country was called to assemble on the concourse area before they began the walk over to the main venue.

The host nation is traditionally the last country to enter the arena so we were the last to be called. We also had the most people marching of any of the countries. While we were waiting I sat with my basketball teammates and when we assembled in the concourse area, it just so happened that we were at the very back of the team. It was at this point I had to farewell my basketball teammates and make my way to the front of the pack. As I began to walk through the team there was a rumbling amongst the athletes as they realised I was making my way to the front. The rumbling quickly intensified and it was like the parting of the Red Sea as a gap was made for me to walk straight up the middle of the entire team. All the athletes started cheering and yelling and I was high-fiving everyone as I made my way forward.

When I think back on it I don't necessarily think they were cheering for me the person, but more so they were cheering what I was representing. To be in such an environment with the greatest athletes the country can produce, some of whom I idolised and all of whom I respected, and here they were screaming and cheering for something I was involved in, created an atmosphere that for me will never be matched. This was unquestionably the most rewarding memory of my sporting career.

It is somewhat ironic that ever since I can remember having the ability to dream I have been completely absorbed with basketball. Yet when I think back on my Olympic experiences it is not the critical shot I may have made, or the big rebound I may have pulled down, or an unlikely defensive play that I may have executed that I remember the most. It is moments such as those in Sydney that had very little to do with playing basketball that seem to stick out the most. Sure, basketball was the vehicle that got me there but once there you come to realise there is a lot more to it. Maybe my perceptions would be completely different if I had been involved in a medal-winning team, but I doubt it.

Much has been written and said about the Sydney Games and there is little doubt in my mind that they were the greatest Games ever. The atmosphere that was created in Sydney made it the most exciting place on the planet to be. It is this type of environment where athletes have the opportunity to fulfill their potential and set new standards. Such conditions do not come about by accident. There are many people and organisations that were responsible for creating this setting.

I believe one of the most significant features and integral parts of the Games' success was the role of the volunteers. When I reflect back on my time in Sydney I am constantly humbled by the honour that was bestowed on me as the team captain and flag bearer of the team. But almost equally, I reflect back on that time as a period when it was a privilege to be an Australian. Baron Pierre de Coubertin, creator of the modern Olympic Games, said: 'The Olympic movement tends to bring together in a radiant union all the qualities which guide mankind to perfection.' No doubt that's what happened in Sydney and in my mind the catalyst was the volunteers.

ANDREW GAZE, *Captain of the Australian Basketball Team and Flag Bearer at the Opening Ceremony, Five times Olympian*
MELBOURNE VIC

When I heard Sydney had been awarded the Games, my initial euphoria changed to dismay when I thought of all the hours of televised sport my sons and husband would watch … I decided that I would be involved, but on my terms, and that meant through quilting.

DIANNE FINNEGAN, *Quilts 2000*
SYDNEY NSW

(The quilt project was named the Most Outstanding Fundraising Project for 2000 and Dianne was awarded an Australian sports medal for her contribution to fundraising for sport.)

My name is Ying Wu. I am proud of my Chinese ancestry and my Australian citizenship. I put my name down as a volunteer because I wanted to thank Australia for accepting me.

YING WU, *Dining Room Assistant*
SYDNEY NSW

We used to do these test events before the Olympics happened. At the sailing, this little old lady in a yellow jacket would come down every day, saying 'Look what you're doing to my park! This is our park, and SOCOG are ruining it!' We had to try and get on her good side, so I kept saying to her that when it finished SOCOG would have it better than it ever was. This had been going on and on, and then one day I said, 'Do you know what? You'd make a wonderful volunteer, have you ever thought of it?' I kept telling her about it, and by the end of that week we were in the good books with her and she'd bring down coffee and biscuits!

That's what being a volunteer was all about. We had to find ways to answer every question, and make the best of every situation.

DOROTHY WILLIAMS, *Pioneer volunteer*
PROSPECT NSW

I was so disappointed to miss the Melbourne Olympics in my home city in 1956. When I made my booking for an overseas trip of a lifetime I didn't realise that we would have the Games, but in those days one had to book a cabin on a ship at least three years ahead. I came home to Melbourne in 1957 and commenced to travel around Australia as I felt I did not know enough about my own country. But Sydney was as far as I got because I met my future husband! He was very wise – he taught me to drive a car while we were still engaged. Do they not say never endeavour to teach your wife to drive? He taught me well which has held me in good stead for driving with ORTA since July 1998.

MAVIS BOOTH, *Driver*
SYDNEY NSW

Can you imagine the excitement of a 60-year-old retired grazier's wife at being chosen to be a volunteer at the Olympic Games? The feeling was of complete disbelief and yet … perhaps I could still be useful and contribute something useful towards the greatest event ever to come to Sydney.

KAYE OVERTON, *Spectator Services*
DUBBO NSW

Paul was a last-minute volunteer driver. He responded when an urgent call went out for more drivers. He hadn't applied earlier because he was tied up with his own work. When the urgent message went out he paid someone to do his work and started immediately.

PAUL MITTAS, *Driver*
SYDNEY NSW

It was December 1999 when my neighbour, Johanna, asked me if I had seen the ad in *Horse Deals* requesting people to try out for displays at the Olympics. I went in search of the ad and read it carefully. Banjo, my bay Australian stock horse, fitted the description they wanted perfectly but there was no way I could commit myself to something like that, what with work and everything else. I didn't know what I was doing from one week to the next let alone nine months in advance. My husband and I both work in the film industry; we often leave home for months at a time at very short notice.

Over the next few days I kept going back to the ad and reading it. Maybe I could go along to the try-out and see what this was all about. Try-outs were being held throughout New South Wales and south-eastern Queensland from November to mid-February. The closest try-out for me would be held at Luddenham, an outer south-western suburb of Sydney at the end of January.

The try-out was a fairly easy test for Banjo. We had to ride one-handed holding a flag in the other. I found holding the flag difficult; fortunately it didn't phase Banjo. Other various exercises designed to spook the horses were carried out to test their temperaments.

A letter arrived at the end of February to say that Banjo and I had been selected and would we please attend the first training camp (we called them boot camps) to be held in Scone, in the Upper Hunter Valley of New South Wales, the second weekend of March. I couldn't believe this. We had actually been selected.

The first boot camp was a very full-on event. We were to be trained by Sergeant Don Eyb from the NSW Mounted Police. He had the task of training this group of volunteer riders, who had had no experience at anything like this. They had come from vast and varied backgrounds; most didn't know each other till they came together at that first boot camp. As time went on he became known fondly as 'The Don' and he did the most magnificent job at turning this group of people into something Australia could be so proud of.

There was a lot to do before the next boot camp to be held at the end of June: courses of vaccinations for the horses against various equine diseases; and Banjo's and my own fitness levels had to be increased. He had stood up well to the first boot camp but we had plenty of work to do before the next one. If we were still in there, that is.

A letter finally arrived: 'Please be at Scone the last weekend in June.' We were still there.

It was surprising how much we all remembered from the first camp. Even holding the flag was getting easier …

The third and final boot camp was a gruelling ten days. We went into camp on the Tuesday and the first dress rehearsal was on Saturday night. We still had not cantered the full routine or used the full-size flags; our practice ones were much smaller than the real thing.

Our first practice night at Homebush was a nerve-wracking experience. All the horses were very tense – they were in a very strange place in the middle of the night with the weirdest sights they had ever seen. The floor of the Stadium itself was covered with a coconut matting and was very uneven underfoot. Their first reaction to the floor was very hesitant but they soon got used to it. Suddenly, the music was turned up to a deafening crescendo. Banjo turned on a rodeo act, bucking and carrying on. We've blown it now; we'll be out after that performance. I was so busy trying to regain control that I didn't know that many others were having the same problems.

The big day arrived, similar to the dress rehearsal days. This time there was an extra buzz in the atmosphere, if that was possible. Everyone was running around with cameras – we hadn't been allowed to take photos up till now.

We got to the Stadium and took our places at the Voms. From where I was I could see John Williamson singing *Waltzing Matilda* and again that sea of faces. What an incredible journey we had been on over the last nine months leading to this night.

John Williamson finished and the countdown began … ten, nine, eight … that enormous crowd counting at the top of their voices. The music started and were away. Waves of horses down the length of the Stadium, split and turn, round the edge then back down the centre to form the Olympic rings, then the dash to the edge of the Stadium to change our Olympic flags for Australian ones and the singing of the national anthem. While I was standing there two Chinese gentlemen caught my eye and waved their Chinese flag furiously and I grinned back through my tears and held my Australian flag with such pride I thought I would burst. The anthem finished all too quickly. We turned and left the Stadium with our Australian flags flying proudly above us.

What a crazy idea it had been, and oh, how it had worked!

SHANE NAYLER, *Rider in Opening Ceremony*
MARAYLA NSW

The letter did arrive eventually inviting me to attend an interview, which was held at an office in East Melbourne. I sat waiting with the other applicants, all of whom were in short, short skirts and could have been my grandchildren. I began to wonder if I was past the age of volunteer acceptance!

VERENA BROWN, *Customer Service*
MELBOURNE VIC

I remember it like yesterday. I was at the under-18 selection camp at Waverley basketball stadium. It was a December day and I decided that going home early to go for a swim sounded a much better idea than sweating in a stadium. So off I went.

Halfway home on Blackburn Road my mobile rang. It was Lorraine Landon calling to see if I was interested in being a team liaison officer (TLO) at the 2000 Olympics, so as you don't get a call like that every day I turned the music off, shut the sunroof and nearly side-swiped the car next to me in order to compose myself and give Lorraine my full attention. She went on to list the responsibilities of a TLO and to be honest I was listening but I was waiting for her to finish so I could say yes in case the reception on my mobile went down. Lorraine finished and I said, 'Do you really need me to say yes?' Then I honestly thought I'd died and gone to heaven when she said, 'We would like to offer you the position of TLO to the Italian men's national basketball team'. First shock set in, then I punched the air with my fist about three times saying, 'Yeah baby' over and over in my mind. It was a good minute before Lorraine asked if I was still there. 'Yes, yes, yes,' I replied …

Well, there I was in the middle of Blackburn Road, just been offered this position and didn't know who to call and for a split second there I had to remember how to drive manual again.

I eventually made my way home and called my dad (who is a soccer, basketball, F1 Italian fan; he was also born in Italy) and told him the news. First there was silence and then the simple word 'bullshit'. I went on to explain and I think he was more excited than me! Telling my mother (who is still an Italian citizen) the news I know would have to be diplomatic as she is a bit of a serious person when it comes to work. I waited for her to come home from work; meanwhile I had friends over helping me celebrate so by the time my mum did make it home I was a little bit tipsy. She walked in the door and asked why everyone was over. I told her to sit down as I had some news. I will never forget the look on my mum's face to this day. I have not seen it again. It was a mix of looking worried, tense, happy and confused. I sat her down and before I could say anything she burst out, 'You're not pregnant.' Oh yeah, single, 24 years old, Italian upbringing … 'As if!' So, 'No,' I replied (that took the worried look off her face). 'Lorraine from SOCOG called and offered me the position of TLO with the Italian men's team.' Again, silence, then she jumps up and runs out of the room. She comes back with rash cream in her hand and said, 'Put in on now.' I just laughed as I have a tendency to not only stress but break out in a rash whilst stressing.

So like all good Italian families, off she went to ring the relatives (you don't like to rub it in!). God bless her.

ANDREA PETROCCO, *TLO to Italian Men's National Basketball Team*
MELBOURNE VIC

When I first signed up as a volunteer, my family and friends laughed at me. It was still almost two years away and I had no idea about what arrangements I would have to make for my three children. But I had made up my mind – this was something I was absolutely going to do for *me*! For 18 years I had been a wife and mother. Many of my hours had been sacrificed for them; now it was my turn.

My husband was my greatest critic (although he is a sports fanatic and great Olympic follower) – he was constantly making jokes about how I would be 'directing traffic in a dusty car park miles from the action'. Well if that was what I was going to do, then I didn't care – I was prepared to do anything. After a long wait the letter finally arrived: I was placed at the Aquatic Centre as an IBM information officer. Who's laughing now!

JOHANNA VANCE, *IBM Information*
CASULA NSW

To go to training meant catching a train or driving to Sydney and staying one or two nights with friends, attending training, and then returning home. For volunteers in the country, it usually meant giving up a full weekend for a two- to five-hour session as well as outlaying approximately $100 each time we travelled. But that was the price we knew we had to pay for the privilege of being selected as a volunteer.

FIONA HENDERSON, *Relations and Protocol*
WAGGA WAGGA NSW

" An important part of the lead up to the Games was the Torch Relay. My most emotional Olympic moment was definitely lighting the cauldron in Melbourne for the Paralympics. What an unexpected honour – a very humbling experience indeed, for a retired fast bowler.

At dawn on Thursday 5 October on the forecourt of the Parliament House in Canberra, representatives of three generations of the Ngunnawal people, the traditional inhabitants of the area, performed a smoking ceremony to protect the flame on its journey through 200 towns, with the assistance of 900 torch bearers. Prime Minister John Howard lit the flame in Canberra and handed it to Olympic tennis player David Hall. From Melbourne Airport the flame arrived at the Town Hall where it was transferred to my torch. Once ignited, the parade of host nations in ceremonial costumes snaked its way to the traffic lights at Collins Street – the boys in blue ensured we had a continuous crossing.

That walk was unlike anything else I've ever been involved in with sport. Torch at shoulder height, I was encouraged to chat to the crowd but not to let go of the precious cargo. How could I not chat and smile? I was in my element. In the past, I've walked out onto the MCG in bright light trying to adjust my eyes to cope with the immediate danger – a West Indian faster bowler on a mission to eliminate me from the battle line-up. As a footballer, I've run down the race to a thunderous roar of expectation, and burst through the banner ready for the man on man contest.

So I've floated on air before and I thought I knew what to expect, but not this time – I was definitely not in total control of my emotions as I bounced up the stairs to the elevated stage. I was pleased that my green XXXL outfit was not body hugging. Baggy is beautiful! Seated among the dignitaries was Victorian Premier, Steve Bracks. I turned to face the crowd and light the community cauldron, and my heart started to pound violently. My throat dried up. I raised the torch in my right hand before counting to three. The square was packed. My eyes welled up. Now both arms were up, like an umpire signaling a six. I couldn't help but wonder how a guy like me gets the privilege of doing this. I will never forget the spontaneous explosion of noise when I lowered the torch deep into that cauldron. My heart went out to all those Paralympians who would do Australia proud in Sydney.

After the lighting, we watched a cluster of indigenous Australians dance around a fire maker clad in red garments, decorated with body paint – a hypnotic stomp in time with banging sticks. The dignitaries spoke. I stood in the wings to one side. The voice of singer Vanessa Amorosi boomed from a bracket of massive loudspeakers as I prepared to re-light my torch from the cauldron. She serenaded everyone with the words to 'Shine', one of her many hits.

Meanwhile, I get a tap on the bum – 'On yer bike, Maxie, or we'll be late, mate.' So I dip the shiny aerodynamic torch back into the cauldron. Vanessa's words are uplifting. With almost perfect choreography I acknowledge the crowd – they cheer in delight – Vanessa continues, focused on her performance without even a change of eye line in my direction. She is totally in the moment.

Meanwhile, I'm not sure whether I'm in or out of the moment. I know I've got a serious role to play here, but my gut instinct says, 'Don't move, you'll make a fool of yourself,

Maxie.' I'm used to working on cue and to the nearest second, but this cue felt all wrong. You see, I'd been educated in a school that said boys shouldn't interrupt while someone was speaking – and I assume that applies to women singing, especially in public with TV cameras everywhere. So I hesitate.

Another tap on my rear end, this time more emphatic. 'Go, Maxie, get going!'

Well, the torch had a 10km trip ahead of it, so left foot in front of right foot – tanglefoot across the stage in the direction of the singing sensation – my legs feel like fluorescent light globes. Gee, how bad must I look? Not pretty – pretty silly – but here goes.

So as not to appear rude or unappreciative, I waltz straight up to Vanessa, who is mid-sentence. My freshly trimmed but prickly moustache poised above my puckered lips, I lurch between her and the microphone, and BANG! Connection! Then I'm outta there – down those steps real fast.

Yes, I stole a kiss on my way off stage! Incredibly, she didn't see it coming, didn't react, didn't miss a beat. And all this happened mid-sentence.

My daughters and Mum have headed for the roped off area. My wife Kerry and I share a look, a moment, a squeeze, a kiss I will never forget – public but very personal. It's not easy to see clearly as I move away – my heart strings have been tugged mighty hard. Other people are crying too. Photos were being taken every few seconds – this could be a very long first leg. An old lady gives me an Aussie flag to carry as well – as each conversation goes by I can feel that elevated flame getting heavier. I'm running out of puff and I need water.

Eventually I get on the support bus that follows the torch as it's borne towards the Royal Childrens Hospital. We stop at a primary school, where kids are pressed up against the cyclone wire. I start at one end like a kid dragging his fingers along fences on the way home from school, and I lightly touch the fingers of each child – every face is electric with excitement – youthful enthusiasm is so hard to ignore!

This part of the relay ends as Sir Gustav Nossal proudly walks the flame into the hospital's main entrance. Patients, staff and parents eagerly await their turn to triumphantly hold the symbolic flame. One kid reckons he got hold of it seven times – an Olympian in the making for sure. This hospital is a long way from the Olympics, but what spirit is here! All these kids have a special story of pain and courage and hope.

The torch relay was about people, and the Olympic spirit. It was a fitting introduction to the Games and the Paralympics, and I was honoured to be part of it at such close quarters. Talk about 'Be Inspired', the catch cry of the Paras – it was impossible not to be inspired! It was wonderful to be part of the athletes' pursuit of achievement and excellence, even in a small way. ”

Max

In 1956, I was living in Harden in country NSW, playing football when the Melbourne Olympic organisers called for volunteers who could run a mile in six minutes – the Olympic torch was coming through. Everyone who could drink a bit reckoned they could do it in six minutes, but I managed to do more than just talk, running well under the time.

I nearly didn't get to carry the torch, because there was a controversy over my 'professional' status. I used to make £6 a week and get my board at the local hotel for playing football. It wasn't a lot but people said it made me professional. Anyway, that all got sorted out, and for weeks I trained with 25 others from the area, getting the feel for running with a torch by carrying a beer bottle full of sand or a stick with a treacle tin nailed to the top.

When they put the real torch in my hand at two in the morning, it was an absolutely unbelievable feeling. Something made you feel you were representing all the people in Australia who couldn't do it. It was spiritual and exhilarating, and I felt like I could have run to Melbourne on my own.

That was 42 years ago and it was a big event. The whole town stopped and partied on through the night. When you were running, they all left the ball and came and watched you run. When the torch was 16 minutes ahead of schedule it put the whole celebration out of synch!

NORM WILLIAMS, *Pioneer volunteer*
PROSPECT NSW

My great experience was running the torch. I ran it at Wolumla, a place I'd never heard of. We went down there, it took about 4 hours to drive, and about 30 of our friends came down too. It really was the most amazing day you could have in your life.

Norm used to tell me about his 1956 torch, and I felt good for him because I'd followed him, but it was nothing like the feeling when you get that torch in your arm yourself.

I had a hill so steep you couldn't believe it. It was the biggest hill in New South Wales (well, I reckon it was anyway). I really think the torch carried me up that hill. When I got to the top I just thought, 'WOW. I've done it – I've carried the torch.'

Well, I went to bed that night and I said to my husband Norm, 'You know the closest thing to today is my wedding day.' I didn't know what to expect both times, wondered whether I'd drop my flowers, whether I'd drop the torch, but really, in the end both days were such a thrill.

So that's how I describe carrying the torch – it's the most wonderful feeling in your life, next to your wedding day.

DOROTHY WILLIAMS, *Pioneer volunteer*
PROSPECT NSW

What inspired me the most happened before the Olympics when I volunteered to drive my friend, a photographer, from Brisbane to Cairns following the Olympic torch. The tremendous involvement and spirit of all those extras needed to put on such an event was wonderful to witness. Gorgeous school kids waving flags by the side of the road with cane fields waving in the background. A young girl's running in memory of her brother; many grandmothers doing their bit as well. The young man in the wheelchair making his first steps out of it to hand on the flame. These scenes were all tremendously moving and what made me determined to volunteer as a driver for the real thing.

LORRAINE MAE, *Driver*
SYDNEY NSW

One particular story that I really loved was about a little village called Wombat, of all things. The torch was to pass right by their town on an outback road, but was not stopping. A loud protest was made, so they obligingly pulled over to the side of the road to let the entire population of 30 people see the torch. After the big occasion the town all trouped down to the local pub and celebrated – they had their big moment and they were happy! We ourselves watched it pass through Budgewoi just a block away from our home and it was great.

PAM McGLINN, *Administration Assistant*
BUDGEWOI NSW

Because I was a vollie and being reasonably young (32), SOCOG was at times offering me various jobs. Some of the offers were great but there was one I could not turn down. To be a staff member on the torch relay. My role was torch bearer shuttle bus driver (and party animal) – who could refuse that? To be involved in such a task with 160 other staff, meeting all those torch bearers and escort runners, not to mention seeing this beautiful country … there are millions of memories that will never be forgotten. Some things will stay with me for ever, certain TB or ER (torch bearers, escort runners), certain places or towns, even the shopkeepers who would give us a free drink because we let them hold a torch. The childrens' faces were the best, from them dressing up or cheering the crew along and then letting them hold the torch. The pictures are priceless. People on the side of the road cheering on the TB or ER. Most people did not know who the TB was, but still clapped and cheered all the same. True Aussie spirit.

But the most pleasing aspect about the torch relay (and Games too) was the vollies. We had two kinds: ones who would only be able to do a month and ones who helped out at the celebration sites. Our one-month vollies were great. Fresh faces, fresh ideas and great laughs to be with and because they were only there for a month, they gave it everything they had for the TB and ER, which was great for us 100-day crew, as they brought new excitement, games, songs, etc. which made it easier for some of us who were getting tired. On the road times did get tough: time deadlines, traffic, weather, and lost or late TBs and ERs. But we all pulled together as a team, got through it and had a wonderful time.

The other kind of vollie we had was the Melbourne Storm. Five fantastic girls from Melbourne made the trip even more fun, they were something else. Full of energy, song and dance, they kept the fun times going and made them last for 100 days. There was never a problem for them (maybe lack of sleep some days) always smiling, laughing, thinking up great ideas to keep the TB and ER amused on the bus before and after their run, giving them a day never to forget. For me, it was such a pleasure to be able to say the Melbourne Storm certainly made the fun times and it was great to be able to work with all of them at various stages of the relay.

While I drove, the girls would keep the spirits up for the TB or ER. On a few occasions I actually let the girls have a drive of the bus. The singing, dancing, aerobics, the party times. Some great memories never to be forgotten. At times the girls would comfort a worried or nervous or disabled TB or ER, do warm-up exercises for the cold or get everyone on the bus singing together. Great voices too. Then they would do it all again at night when the staff could let themselves relax and have a few drinks. These girls certainly made the relay for the TBs and ER and staff with their great attitude, humour and dancing skills. And to think these girls did all this as volunteers. I wish them all the best. These girls were just as special as the other 47,000 vollies.

KEVIN HUDSON, *Driver*
SYDNEY NSW

It is difficult to know where to start, because when I think about the torch relay I am filled with so many amazing memories and mixed emotions.

Basically I miss it. I miss it so much more than I could explain. The Torch relay was the most positive thing that I have ever been involved in. I have never worked so many long hours, back to back, barely having enough sleep to get out of bed the following day.

My role as Host was definitely the best position. I applied for it with four fantastic people, and we became known as the 'Melbourne Storm'. We had a connection to each other before we applied for the positions, and all thought it would be a once in a lifetime opportunity – which it definitely was. Our position was out on the road, we were the face of the torch relay in that each torch bearer had one host and driver who looked after them thought their experience with the torch. We saw the torch every day, and the unforgettable faces of those torch bearers filled with pride and overflowing with emotions.

Our job was to meet and greet the torch bearers, hand out the torches, give a 20–30 minute spiel on how to carry the torch, safety, sponsors, exchanging the flame and so on. Each time we usually had about 2–3 hours with the torch bearers, meeting and greeting, and then the famous bus ride. In this time we played a video of past torchbearers, with the great *Carry the Flame* song. We knew every word, we sang every word, sometimes with our pretend microphones, and we danced. We did this because we could. The torch relay gave us a licence to be ourselves, to be silly, to be loud, to be personable, to let our character shine. We had a licence to speak to people on the streets, even people we didn't know, especially people we didn't know! Every place we went to, people were happy to see us. There was a party at every town, whispers of when the torch is arriving, 'Did you see the torch?', 'Yes, I saw the Olympic flame.'

The people we met every day were the people who made the 3, 4, 5 or 6 a.m. starts bearable. The torch bearers were either sponsors, Olympians or community. The person who sticks in my memory the most was the young girl who had her leg and arm amputated and qualified for the Para Games in an athletic event but her event was cancelled due to lack of funding. I remember the suicide survivor who is now working with young suicidal people. I remember the bus load of torch bearers in Bacchus Marsh who were so blown away when we drove through the main road, (which was so completely taken over by 15 deep rows of people). I looked back to the busload of faces to see not one without tears in their eyes. I remember a young boy who was in a manual wheelchair, he was so determined to wheel himself with no assistance and carry the torch without a torch holder attached to the wheelchair. I remember the family of four who each had a run through an old beach town, and the buzzing electricity as they entered my bus after their run was contagious. I remember the aboriginal community in Queensland, who made a sea of hands to symbolise reconciliation.

My most special memory without a doubt would have to be the train across the Nullarbor. This experience has changed my life forever, and makes an impact on my life every time I think back to it.

We had many whistle stops during this trip, where we met with numbers of (mainly) Aboriginal people who travelled up to 500 kms to have a glimpse of the Olympic flame. The most amazing stop was Watson. There was no town, just desert for miles and miles. There were maybe 100 children, adults and elderly people, gathered in the dust, waiting for the torch. We all piled out of the train, with the amazing torch and the flame. The people were in awe, looking on at a flame that had travelled from Greece, Oceania, and half way around Australia. The torch was placed in a stand, and an unlit torch was passed around the enormous group of people, each taking their time, to hold the special torch that would at one stage carry the flame. Next, the children were divided into two groups, and took part in a relay with an unlit torch, running about 15 metres and passing the torch onto the next person. The children ranged in age from 3–18, barefoot, without a worry in the world. These children were so awestruck by this amazing torch. They were different from us, they did not wear the right labels, or have the best hairstyles, or shop at the right shops, or drive the best cars. They live a completely different life to mine, yet they were happy, and they seemed content. This experience made me take such a long hard look at myself, and the issues I have in my life, and things I get upset over, and put it all in perspective for me. I took six rolls of film this day, and cried for about three hours. Actually when I think of it, I didn't see many people during our visit to Watson that did not shed a tear. This time I spent on the train and at each whistle stop will remain in my memory forever. I will never have an opportunity like that again – I will hold this memory in my heart forever. When I look at my photos of this time, and of the torch relay as a whole, I have the warmest memories, and I laugh, and sometimes cry. I feel so sad that this experience is over, but I feel so rich in having had the once in a lifetime opportunity to share such a positive experience with so many amazing people.

Last but certainly not least, the amazing crew that made the trip. If you put a group of 150 people together, from different walks of life, different ages, home towns, interests and so on. These people have to spend 100 days together, away from their families and friends and comforts, sharing rooms, living in each others pockets, and working extremely long hours on a sometimes emotional rollercoaster. You could think that this would be a difficult task. The 150 crew on the road were the most amazing group, we all worked as a team to ensure that each and every torch bearer had the most amazing experience during their time of glory – holding the flame. Each torchbearer at that particular moment was the only person holding the Olympic flame, the same flame that was to burn brightly during the Olympic Games and we wanted them to know it.

We went to the Opening Ceremony, and cheered the sports men and women into the stadium. We were in awe of the amazing acts that were created with so much time, care and effort. And we cried as the torch was carried around the stadium, and the cauldron was lit. This was so emotional for us all. A hundred days of no sleep, meeting amazing people who had suffered the most horrible illnesses or bad luck during their life, the friendships made, the places visited, the excitement – boy, do I miss the excitement ... Everyone was happy to see us, and interested and in awe. We changed the Sydney 2000 Olympic Games. We made publicity positive after various negative events in the lead up to the relay. Everyone was skeptical … but in the end everyone loved it.

The Melbourne Storm … We are all special friends, and we always will be. We are connected by something far stronger than basic friendship and that is the power of the memories of our Olympic Torch experience. I will never forget those four girls, who I laughed with, cried with, roomed with, was silly with, depended upon, had days off with, got up at ridiculous hours of the morning with ... and the list goes on. These girls *made* the experience, as we had each other, and now we still have each other, to reminisce about the good old days with the torch.

Of the 150 on the road crew, 13 of us were voluntary which included The Melbourne Storm. I would do it again 100 times over, knowing that I wouldn't be paid, and knowing others were, as it has made me such a better person for the experience.

JULIA VAN DER LINDEN, *Torch Relay 'Melbourne Storm'*
MELBOURNE VIC

This is just a little account of some of the best moments of my experience as a 100-day volunteer on the Sydney 2000 Olympic torch relay. I was one of only five volunteers, known as the Melbourne Storm, who did the whole event, and we had the role of torch bearer shuttle hosts. This role required us to brief the torch bearers, organise their transport to and from their running positions, and make sure they had one of the most memorable days of their life.

The Sydney 2000 Olympic Torch Relay was the most amazing experience of my whole entire life. The whole event taught me so much about the hardships that some people have to endure in their lives, it taught me about Australia and demonstrated how remote some areas of our country are, and it taught me about the spirit of the people in this country when they unite in one celebration. You rarely see events these days in which everyone is truly excited, but this was one event in which people were honestly overjoyed to have us come to their community. And to think that most people only saw the actual flame for a period of about 10 to 15 seconds and were still so excited.

I feel so privileged to have met some of the people I did on the torch relay. I met young children who were nominated by their parents, community people nominated for extensive service to the community, sick or disabled people who defied the odds to live their life, community leaders, political leaders, and national sporting heroes. One of the people I met who I have so much admiration for is a lady by the name of Janine Shepherd. Janine was a promising cross-country skier when she smashed into a tree-trunk while training. The accident caused horrific damage to Janine's body, and she was lucky to survive. After the doctors told Janine she wouldn't walk again she set out on a mission to defy them, and she did. She now has three children, flies aeroplanes in her spare time, and has just started doing equestrian events. I thought Janine was one of the most amazing and inspiring people I have ever met. Just being around her I was in awe of how she has coped with such a life-changing experience, and all of the challenges that have been thrown in her path.

There were other experiences that touched your heart and made you realise the power of the flame. There were people who got out of hospital to run with flame, older members of the community such as Jack Lockett (109 years old) who united the city of Bendigo when he slowly walked down the main street, and people who were lucky enough to run with the flame in 1956 and again in 2000. A group of people who really stick out in my mind though, are the children we met while crossing the Nullarbor at a little place called Watson. One minute we were looking out the window of the Indian Pacific at dust and shrubs, the next there were about 50 cars, and a large group of people sitting in a circle waiting to see the flame. The majority of these people were Aborigines who had travelled five and a half hours, along rugged dirt tracks, with their children so that the could see the flame for 30 minutes. It was decided that we would have a mini-relay for the kids, and all of the children got to have a little run with an unlit Olympic torch. In some cases, the torch was bigger than the kids. The joy and delight on these kids' faces was something I will always remember. It is hard to believe that one little flame can inspire someone to travel that far to see it, and then make someone's day or possibly week, but that is precisely what it did.

Of the five of us who did the entire event I was the only one who then went on to do the Paralympic torch relay as well, and I was rewarded by being selected to brief the torch bearers at the Opera House when the Paralympic flame ventured there. The six torch bearers selected to run there were a disabled boy who made an inspiring speech at Sydney Town Hall after his run, Sir James Hardy, Marcia Hines, Steve Waugh, Andrew Ettinghausen and Kieren Perkins. What a daunting experience. I know people who would pay big money for five minutes of these people's time, and here I was, spending hours with these people organising them and directing them. I am still learning from my experiences on the torch relay, but the experience I am most thankful for is the chance to meet the people I did.

So many people asked me, 'How did you keep going?' For 100 days we had to be helpful, enthusiastic, excited hosts, often through times of personal hardship, illness and extreme exhaustion. The support of our amazing crew helped immensely. I have never had the pleasure of working with such professional and helpful people as I did on the torch relay. And the camaraderie amongst the crew was truly amazing. The other thing that kept us going was the flame itself. This was the first time in 44 years that this flame, and an amazing spectacular called the Olympics, was going to be in our country. And for most people it was the first chance they had to witness a torch relay. For that reason we entered into every day thinking that we had to make that day another amazing day. We were helped along by enthusiastic crowds that still amaze me with their size, and excited torch bearers, and together we put on the best torch relay ever.

LISA MEEHAN, *Torch Relay 'Melbourne Storm'*
MELBOURNE VIC

It is quite difficult sitting down and trying to write about just how amazing and indescribable an experience my volunteer work for the Sydney 2000 Olympics was. After all, if someone had said to me two years ago that the Olympics would have had any kind of impact on my life whatsoever, I would never have believed it. So to attempt to now convey to others just how truly special the Olympic Games ended up being to me is somewhat daunting and a little frightening.

I almost cannot believe that we are nearing one year since my very first taste of the 'Olympic Spirit' – in April 2000 at the torch relay test event held in NSW. As someone who rarely gets involved in community activity or follows any kind of sport at all, I could never have predicted that this four-day event was to become the first chapter of the most amazing experience of my life. For, in one of those little twists of fate that life tends to throw at us, I was to later find myself literally *living* the Olympics for the entire three months leading up to the Opening Ceremony in September.

The Sydney 2000 Olympics touched many people in many different ways and my story is just a small example of its effect on the Australian community. My volunteer position was as a torch bearer host on the shuttle buses that transported the runners all over Australia. So the stories I have to share are ones that do not involve gold medals or world records, but rather the achievements of the Australian community and the 'everyday' people that played a part in carrying the Olympic flame to Sydney for the Opening Ceremony on 15 September.

There are two elements that made the torch relay so special to me. Firstly of course a truly amazing aspect was the towns we visited and the unbelievable people that we met. It really was *the* best way to tour Australia as absolutely everyone that we encountered had big smiles on their faces. The Indian Pacific train trip across the Nullarbor was a perfect example of this. Just to see those beautiful Aboriginal children that had travelled so far in pursuit of a small glimpse of the tiny flame was mind-blowing.

However the torch relay was also special because of the bond it created between all who were involved. After all as a part of the crew that travelled with the relay for almost the entire 100 days, we did not just work with our colleagues – we lived with them for three months. Laying the foundation for some indestructible, never-ending friendships. And I think I can say with some certainty that anyone that I lived and worked with in those three phenomenal months will always remain a friend.

I feel so fortunate to have been selected as one of the torch relay team that successfully took the Olympic Spirit to many areas of our country that may otherwise have felt little or no connection to the Sydney 2000 Games. However I think that as a member of the core (100-day) crew it was often too easy for us to forget that whilst we got to live and experience the power of the flame 24 hours a day, others saw it for only three minutes or even less. It would have been easy to become complacent and almost cynical toward the event were it not for the amazement on people's faces each day the first time they saw or held a torch.

The thousands of people that we met often asked whether we were getting sick of our job – doing the same thing day in, day out – but how could we when every day brought new faces and excitement? It became (subconsciously) important to all of us that we treated each new lot of torch bearers as if they were our first. After all, how could we possibly downplay their special moment just because we were so fortunate to witness many many moments?

Personally I received the most satisfaction from the tiny little country towns where the population was low – yet seemed to double or even triple as the torch went by. Beerwah (a little town in Queensland) has a population of approximately 1500 – yet 15,000 turned out to watch the three torch bearers and escort runner that ran that day.

It was days such as these that really brought home just how much the torch relay meant to so many people. As the flame went by we witnessed the community expressing their own 'Aussieness' in many different ways. Barbeques or champagne breakfasts by the side of the road, homemade torches in the hands of not only children but also adults and, on one occasion, about eight drag queens. Australians erected huge replica torches, held signs such as, in Sydney: 'Our Brush With Flame' and in

Cherbourg: 'That's Our Mum. You Go Girl.' School children lined the streets dressed as the Olympic rings, an entire town spent a day dressed in Grecian costumes and two little girls dressed up as the torch itself.

I don't believe anyone could have predicted what a huge effect such a simple thing as 'The world's most flash cigarette lighter' (as written in one of the buses' Comment Books by one of the 11,000 torch bearers) was going to have on the community. Approximately 11,000 torch bearers literally carried the flame to Sydney but thousands of others played a part in its journey.

The effort that not only the friends and family of the torch bearers, but also the general public went to was overwhelming. I am so unbelievably lucky to have played a part in the torch relay and am still in awe of the effect it had on so many people. We were told so many times that our involvement in the torch relay was a 'once in a lifetime experience' but it is only now that the true meaning of those words are beginning to sink in.

I think one of the runners, Gabrielle Richards, probably said it the best:

'It was soooooo amazing.
It was fantastic! It was just magical!
The best thing I have ever done.
I will remember it forever and ever.'

REBECCA GRIFFITHS, *Torch Relay 'Melbourne Storm'*
MELBOURNE VIC

Monday 21 August – day 75 of the Olympic torch relay – was a special day for Olympic volunteer Robert Dickson of Uralla NSW. In late 1998 I had applied to be a volunteer for the Olympic Games, and was advised in 1999 that I had been accepted as a volunteer fleet driver to assist the Danish Olympic team.

When the planned route for the Olympic torch relay was announced, I noted that it would pass by my boyhood home, and the site of the primary school that I attended as a child in the 1940s in the district of Yarrowyck, 30 kilometres west of Armidale.

My dream was to see the torch relay stop at Yarrowyck, on a quiet country road many kilometres from any town or village.

There is a saying: 'If you can dream it, you can achieve it.' So I set my goal, to arrange for the Olympic Flame to pause at Yarrowyck, on an 80 kilometre non-stop leg of the route from Bundarra to Uralla.

In October 1999 I wrote to the organisers of the torch relay, with my request for the relay to pause at Yarrowyck. I received a very courteous reply from the person in charge, pointing out that this would not be a usual thing to happen with such a tight schedule to maintain, however Mr Doran invited me to contact him by letter, approximately six months prior to the event for a review of my request.

Further correspondence with Mr Doran in the following April was most encouraging. He advised that a short unscheduled stop could be achieved if the torch convoy was on schedule at that point of the journey. I assured him that there would be a good group of district residents on hand to welcome the relay at Yarrowyck. He sent me final details, which requested a meeting with him and his advance party, travelling one hour ahead of the main relay convoy. All was now ready for this very special event!

During the two weeks prior to 21 August I was required to be in Sydney to attend volunteer training. The final arrangements for inviting the district residents were thankfully handled by local farmer Ann Mitchell. On the big day everything went to plan. Approximately 30 people from small children to elderly folk gathered together.

To our surprise the torch relay convoy arrived ten minutes ahead of their appointed time, at 4.10 p.m., which allowed them to meet the residents. The two torches were passed around for inspection and photos, and the Miner's lamp containing the hallowed flame was brought out and shown to all.

This was indeed a very special and private viewing of the Olympic flame. Everyone present felt so privileged to have shared this unique experience. The point where the stop was made was in front of where the small school house once stood, until it closed in 1954.

For me to have achieved such an important high profile event as the Olympic torch relay, to make an eight-minute stop in a remote country district, proves 'Dreams really can come true.'

ROBERT DICKSON, *Spectator Services*
URALLA NSW

For many people, when asked what has been their life's highlight, they most probably will volunteer that it was their wedding day or the birth of their first child. For me, it was being one of the Harley Boys. Two coppers from each state were given this honour, to wear their particular uniform as the torch inched its way around Australia.

My team was a close-knit quartet, consisting of a champion fellow from Queensland named Peter, laconic Mick from the ACT, and a crazy little bloke from the Northern Territory, Deano. Together we managed to steer clear of most of the bosses, upset Harley-Davidson in Launceston, and still managed to hand-deliver that flame to the Stadium on 15 September. We also almost lost Deano during those many miles.

Out of all the vehicles in the convoy, the Harleys had the shortest fuel range by far. The solution to this problem was to use the Harleys' superior speed to forge out ahead of the convoy, fill up at the sponsor's service station, before being in position in time for the commencement of the next torch bearer stage.

Meanwhile, the average speed of the convoy was between 80 and 90 km/h ...

We had left Innisfail in northern Queensland that morning and there were quite a few long legs between fuel stops. It was a beautiful day, the temperature just right. Thankful to be away from the restrictions of the slow convoy, the four of us moved ahead, pleased to be able to stretch our tired left hands, after feathering clutches all morning during torch bearers. This particular day Pete was in front of me, and we rounded a slight bend on the bitumen. Midway through the corner I felt my bike shift outwards, and the suspension struggled with the corrugation that couldn't be seen until you hit it. I glanced in my mirrors and saw Mick having a similar fight. Deano, bringing up the rear took the corner at a slightly wider arc, and had no chance. The rear of the bike stepped out from under him, onto the soft verge. Somehow he managed to avoid a deep and sheer-walled culvert before I saw him tumbling, over and over again.

One hundred and ten metres of jetsam led to a totally destroyed Harley Davidson that had previously been subject to coat upon coat of polish every morning and night. In the trail of wreckage was a boot, a mobile phone carrying case, a Northern Territory police shoulder patch. A short distance away was our mate, unmoving but moaning softly. A jumble of radio messages, a vast collection of police vehicles, and the wonderful doctor who accompanied the relay were with us quickly. Deano was taken away in the ambulance.

The show had to go on. Unaware of the prognosis, a final town had to be covered before our relief could take over. Despite being down two bikes (Pete went with the ambulance) we still managed to smile through our tears and ensure the flame continued on its way towards Sydney.

Deano surprised everyone, with merely a broken wrist, a cracked vertebra, a loss of bark, and eternal exclusion from the Harley Davidson Admirers Club. He reunited with our team in Victoria and is one of the gutsiest people I have ever met.

The Harleys? Let me dispel a few fallacies. No, they didn't burn out a single clutch, and never looked like they would. The mechanics that accompanied the relay around Australia had a lovely time, as they were on holiday. The bikes always started first kick (or should I say, first push of the button), never broke down, overheated, or had any other problem. They braked well, accelerated hard, and were a magnificent choice for that duty.

DAVE GARDNER, *Torch Relay 'Harley Boy'*
SYDNEY NSW

Back in 1948 I was somehow able to live in the London Olympic Games camp. I remember sketching the various nationalities within their quarters and of course, catching a number of Olympic Greats in caricature. I tried to live in camp again at the 1956 Melbourne Olympic Games, but they wouldn't fall for the Olympic Act of 1948. In 1997 I managed to get to the World Championship athletics in Athens, then in 1998 covered the World Championship swimming in Perth when the Aussies broke into the world records. I have spent thousands of hours and created an enormous collection of athlete caricatures, most of them signed by the athletes themselves. In Sydney 2000 I became, no doubt, the only artist in the world to be accredited to the Olympic Games.

TONY RAFTY, *Artist and Torch Bearer, Sydney 2000 Torch Relay*
LITTLE BAY NSW

My attaché role included looking after many of the Canadian officials for the two years leading up to the Games and often I entertained them in my own home. My wife and I invited our friends over so that our visitors could meet some Australians from different walks of life. The Canadians really enjoyed it.
PETER FALK, *Attaché for Canada*
SYDNEY NSW

I was born in Japan to Vietnamese parents and have been living in Sydney since I was six years old. Though I have a foreign name, I've lived in Sydney most of my life so it's only natural that I feel more Aussie than anything else. However, the Aussie pride grew even stronger during the Olympics. I knew this country was multicultural, but to hear the 'Aussie, Aussie, Aussie!' chant in so many accents was quite touching. I am proud to be an Australian and proud to have been an Olympic volunteer ... I would have been happy with any volunteer job, but to be at the eye clinic (I am an orthoptist) *and* in the Olympic Village, that made my day, my week, my year! I'm still pinching myself!
YUMI PHAM-VU, *Eye Clinic*
SYDNEY NSW

My volunteer job was a little different. I was the first volunteer in Uniform Distribution – commencing on 3 March, entering the size details into the computer for technical officials. We went out to the Uniform Distribution and Accreditation Centre at Redfern in May. On 8 July we began distributing uniforms for staff and volunteers and this went through until 22 October. I travelled four hours every day by train and paid my own fares until mid-July, three days a week ...
PHYLLIS DAVIS, *Uniform Distribution*
UNANDERRA NSW

While sewing at Eveleigh, a group of us were working to Jenny Kee's directions making costumes for the American segment. Jenny wanted more and more sequins on a flared skirt but our supervisor said that even if we were all volunteers, we could not spend more hours on it. One Saturday after handing out costumes at Schofields, we came back to Redfern at 9 p.m., signed ourselves in, and three of us – Barbara Pamba, Gerry Hopkins and myself – sewed sequins on all night and signed ourselves out at 9.30 a.m. on Sunday morning.

IRIS GOVER, *Costume sewer and dresser for Opening and Closing Ceremonies*
SYDNEY NSW

It was preparation time for the Paralympics and we were very busy issuing accreditation passes. I was working on the first line of computers, identifying whether the volunteers or workforce personnel needed to have a photograph taken, or whether all the information was already in the computer and they just needed to have it printed out and laminated. Or maybe they had to go to the help desk if the information was incomplete.

We had a long queue of bus drivers waiting, as they had all arrived together, so we were working as fast as possible to keep the waiting time down. I had coped with quite a few when the next one in the queue came to my station. I saw he was carrying a driver's licence as had been requested, so I asked his surname.

'Birch,' he said, and as I entered it on the computer I asked his Christian name. I typed in the first three letters, which was the quickest way of bringing up the name I wanted. A whole list of name flashed on to the screen – all Birch and all Richard, as I had punched in the letters 'Ric'. As I glanced down the list of Richard John, Richard Matthew, Richard Paul etc., I asked for his middle name. He told me he had no second name, so I clicked on to the name at the end of the list – the only one without a second name and which was entered as 'Ric'. It flashed up with a photo and the message 'To be validated'. As I ticked the paper, suddenly the penny dropped.

'*The* Ric Birch,' I blurted out.

He nodded and gave me a beaming smile as he picked up the paper and shook my hand. I was so astonished I was struck dumb and didn't even take the opportunity to thank and congratulate him on that wonderful Opening Ceremony. But I think he understood, for I will always treasure the memory of that handshake.

That was my brush with fame, and I even forgot to ask for his autograph.

MURIEL HARDING, *Accreditation Officer*
SYDNEY NSW

Red hat volunteers! As a practice run for the real thing, pioneer vollies worked as information officers at the Royal Easter Show in March 1998. Left to right: Mary Wojtowyez, Dot and Norm Williams, Kathryn Bendall, Brian Reberger, Philip Rhead and Matthew Bond. *(Courtesy of Jacky Ghossein / The Sun Herald)*

As part of their pioneer duties, Dorothy and Norm Williams had to live in these trial uniforms for a month, going about their daily business as usual. On the left, Dorothy hopes her style will impress her favourite tennis player, Pat Rafter, while Norm washes the car on the right.
(Courtesy of Norm Williams) *See page 6.*

Armed and ready to go: special Olympic duo, Dorothy and Norm Williams. He holds a replica of the torch he carried in the 1956 Olympic torch relay, while she holds hers from the 2000 torch relay.
(Courtesy of Norm Williams) *See pages 30 and 31.*

Max Walker runs the Paralympic torch through the city of Melbourne. 'How does a guy like me get the privilege of doing something as great as this?'
(Courtesy of News Ltd). *See page 27.*

Village people: the athletes' quarters. Wonder what country this lot comes from? *(Courtesy of Ivan Moore)*

Service with a smile at Stadium Australia. *(Courtesy of Alan Patching)*

An ecstatic Andrew Gaze leads the Australian athletes into the Stadium at the Opening Ceremony. Signed copies of this photograph are available at www.gaze.com.au. A family heirloom in the making … *(Courtesy of Andrew Gaze)* *See page 15.*

Left: Roll up, roll up …
the best ever Olympic
Games are here!
(Courtesy of Alan Patching)

Below: The hills are
alive with the sound
of vollies.
(Courtesy of Ivan Moore)

Where's vollie? See how many volunteers you can spot in the crowd.
(Courtesy of Alan Patching)

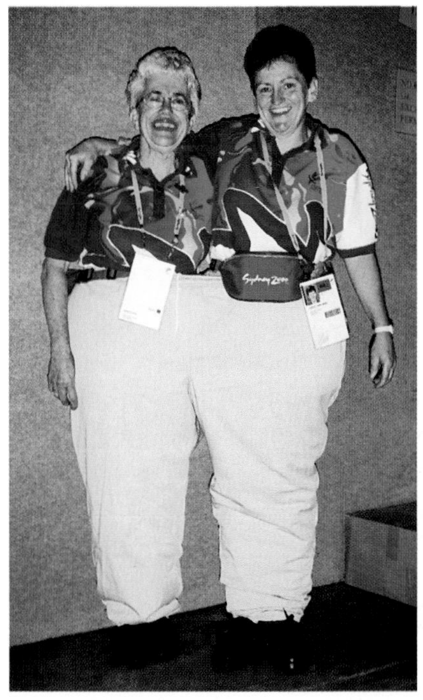

Despite the hard yakka, there was still time for some 'vollie good fun':
Left: Gwen and her mate Jodie try the size 50 volunteer trousers on for size!
(Courtesy of Gwen Cootes) *See page 98.*
Right: An old photo trick that never ceases to amuse. *(Courtesy of Alan Patching)*

Never forget that volunteering was also a serious business: Left: What are they negotiating? *(Courtesy of Alan Patching)*
Right: No caption required!
(Courtesy of Ivan Moore)

The Paralympics were an unforgettable experience for athletes and spectators, and the volunteers were a huge part of making it by far the most successful Paralympics ever.

The volunteers for the Sydney 2000 Olympic and Paralympic Games did much to give this magnificent celebration its distinctive Australian character. Their courtesy, efficiency, helpfulness and humour will long be remembered by visitors from Australia and overseas. Although most visible in Spectator Services and other 'front-of-house' roles, the volunteer contribution extended right through to vital 'back-of-house' functions in such fields as Information Technology, Medical and Language Services and Transport Operations. Not only were 47,000 Olympic and 15,000 Paralympic volunteers essential from a financial and operational point of view, but even more importantly they became ambassadors for the Games – and indeed for Australia. They did us proud. Their story is a great one and deserves to be told.

SANDY HOLLWAY, *Chief Executive Officer of SOCOG*
SYDNEY NSW

In addition to keeping the pace of the press conference acceptable for translation, my job will also include opening and closing the press conference, introducing the athletes (I can't wait for some of those Asian and eastern European names!), moderating the questions (in case one journalist gets piggy, for example) and worst case, if no one asks any questions, asking a few of my own! I also have to watch to make sure the coaches aren't translating on behalf of the athletes. We wouldn't want to miss out when some sore loser calls his coach a jerk because the coach edited it out.

SHEILA CONSAUL ('A Sheila Down Under'), *Press Conference Supervisor*
VIRGINIA USA

The experience of a lifetime was had by all SOCOG volunteers, especially the ones who really enjoyed themselves and I was one of those.

I was attached to the accreditation team at the 'meet and greet' area at Homebush Bay, where the buses from Sydney Airport arrived with people, that is, athletes, trainers, coaches and other officials who had travelled a long distance to get here.

Before the Games began, I was rostered on an evening shift on the first bank of computers. As the people arrived they wandered on past us, very tired and 'down in the dumps'.

However, part of the American swim team arrived, and as they approached us, I found a plastic lid that resembled a frisbee. I ran out to one of the other male volunteers and said, 'Here, cop this,' and with that let fly the frisbee. He charged out from behind his computer, caught it, then returned it in flight over my head, straight for some of the American swimmers, who dropped their luggage and came alive. For the next 15 or 20 minutes we had a 'frisbee Olympics' all of our own, Australia versus the United States. After much frivolity and fun, our supervisor asked us to take up our positions again at the computers. We didn't want to because we were winning and it was against Olympians, too! Sanity was restored, the American thanking us for 'A wake-up pleasure experience and a fun welcome to Sydney.'

My disappointment was that I never caught up with those Americans again, but that's what it was all about. We all had a great laugh and a fun time.

CLEVELAND DAVIES, *Accreditation Officer*
SYDNEY NSW

We were volunteers of a different kind – a primary school principal promoting the Olympics by teaching it from every aspect: historical, geographical, mathematical, social and physical – and two school secretaries who played a vital role from an administrative point of view.

The three of us were 'members' of the Sydney 2000 Olympics Club, which dealt with the provision of curriculum information for schools including the school newspaper *O News*. It was our task to distribute this information to staff and students. Our reward came in the form of three tickets to the dress rehearsal of the Opening Ceremony.

That night held much enjoyment and many highlights. It was filled with action, wonderment and talent. One of our personal highlights was to have witnessed that the age of chivalry is not dead. We were seated to the left side of the main stage and were able to see Olivia standing backstage in her glorious gown waiting for her cue. The problem was that this was an unusually cold night for Sydney and Olivia was shivering and trembling. All of a sudden a gentleman appeared, took off his jacket and placed it around Olivia's shoulders. Those who witnessed this act applauded him enthusiastically. Will he ever have that jacket dry-cleaned? We think not.

REGINA, BARB AND DEB, *Sydney 2000 Olympics Club*
MELBOURNE VIC

Speech given by Emma Pollard, Form 11, 2000

I stand here tonight as a proud member of the Sydney 2000 Olympic Games Band, one of 2000 young musicians from around the world lucky enough to be part of both the Opening and Closing Ceremonies of the Sydney 2000 Olympic Games.

Rehearsals began 26 September 1999. It was hard work and nothing could prepare me for the sheer discipline and intensity with which the band worked. Of our 292-piece band I knew one girl but friendships were to start fast and grow strongly. I was known as 'a saxophone tenor' player, one of only five girls tough enough to handle such an instrument.

Twelve months later, 1 September 2000 – a year from my application date and how fast it has gone. It felt only right that today began our two-week intensive camp with all 2000 musicians and the formation of the Olympic band, the 'Musicians of the World'.

Breakfast 6 a.m., regular rehearsal 8.30 to 5.30, dinner 6.30, followed most nights by rehearsal 7 p.m. to 10 p.m. Yes, it was intensive. Weather brought us rain, hail and shine but we continued to rehearse as the mud piles accumulated below our feet. The temperature ranged from minus nine to minus five degrees in the mornings, with evenings warranting at least seven layers of clothing.

On 9 September, life changed. What we thought hectic became wild. We were woken at 3.30 a.m. with brekky at 4 a.m. and driven to dress rehearsal. We made it to the Stadium by 10 a.m. and proceeded to rehearse until 3 p.m. Combined lunch and dinner came at 4 p.m, 12 hours after our last meal. Left to wait. Called at 6 p.m., but played at 9.30 p.m. to a crowd of over 90,000. It was a warm-up and surely a test of fitness as we lost 472 casualties that first night. We left the Stadium at 2 a.m. and were at Bathurst by 5.30 a.m. So passed the first 25-hour day.

The next five days before the Ceremony called for three more trips to Sydney, taking travelling time to a total of 40 hours. Worked consistently to improve our drill and playing standard on top of strengthening our growing friendships. Such a schedule demanded so much and it was a surprise to no one that in the three days prior to the big night 57 per cent of the band were in sick bay. Those remaining were left to rehearse and support those who were sick. I lost count of our trips to Bathurst in search of tissues and medicine. A combination of the cold and our lack of sleep and food were to blame.

It's 1 a.m., 15 September 2000 and we can't sleep. My dorm is up and we are reminiscing whilst signing assorted memorabilia … 2 a.m., 3 a.m., 3.30 a.m. and we crashed. We are woken at 7 a.m. and never before have I seen the band move faster. We arrive in Sydney at 3 p.m. and our holding zone, the baseball stadium, is a buzz of excitement. We were given dinner at 4 p.m. and left to braid hair and remove jewellery whilst listening to assorted renditions of *Aussie, Aussie, Aussie, Down Under*, and *Waltzing Matilda*. Much of that day passed in a haze. Everyone focused on the job at hand.

At 7.50 we were marched to the Stadium and there was not one face around without a smile. Friends walked hand in hand, waving at the thousands outside the Stadium. Fifteen, ten, five minutes to go and we finally felt ready.

At 8.13, we marched onto the Stadium floor to the sounds of *Eternity* and 750 tap dancers. The atmosphere was incredible, the stands without a remaining seat, and the excited squeals of my friends around me. We had been told to 'know your music well enough that you can just enjoy the moment'. That we did, heads high.

After 40 minutes, the moment had come. We began *Down Under*; the audience rose to its feet and the Australian team entered the Stadium. From that moment, I was overcome with emotion, standing directly beside the stage. Andrew Gaze passed only a metre away as we closed with *I am Australian*. Thankfully, we ran over time and before I had a chance to realise it, Olivia Newton John and John Farnham were only metres from my side as the speakers boomed *I Dare to Dream*. There was no holding back as we turned to watch. The team ran, I admit, as the Stadium became a mass of moving light. We marched off. The party began.

The fireworks were positioned perfectly so as to appear to be our fireworks. The magnitude of all we had done only became a reality as we left the Stadium and everyone's faces showed pure joy and delight. We did not sleep that night, each person trying to express what they felt. We all knew it was impossible.

Whilst the band helped to define me as a person and gave me a musical experience that will surpass all others, it is not for these reasons that I have enjoyed it so much. I have met so many amazing people as a result of the experience and I can honestly say I will know all music teachers in the state for the next 30 years. The diversity of those involved has given me a balanced and more informed look at teenage life and society as a whole. Most importantly, we have worked together for a common goal. Those from the city, country and a variety of socio-economic backgrounds have come together to show the world what we are capable of and the knowledge, experience and broader perspective of life I have gained from the experience will stay with me forever.

EMMA POLLARD, *Olympic Games Marching Band*
SYDNEY NSW

Well, the letter came – yes I was going to the Games not as a spectator, but as a valuable member of a Spectator Services Volunteer Unit.

The fact that I live over 3500 km from Sydney didn't worry me. What with 500 km riding every day, I should get there in seven days! You see, I live in Esperance WA, and I'd decided to make the trip on my Harley Davidson 883 Hugger and my boyfriend, Greg, would accompany me on his Yamaha Virago 1100. People said to me 'Why not fly over?' and my response was 'The journey of getting to and from Sydney was as much part of the excitement of the Games as actually being there.'

SUE NORWOOD, *Spectator Services*
ESPERANCE WA

During April 2000, we conducted a series of what were euphemistically called 'cast induction sessions'. The selected cast members for each segment of the Opening Ceremony were invited to Stadium

Australia for an introduction by David Atkins, and an address from each segment's director, designer and choreographer. All of us production managers were deployed to help with each other's segments in terms of formally registering the chosen cast members and explaining to them the strict requirements for their involvement (even though they weren't being paid – hilarious when you think about it). This explanation was particularly difficult with my multicultural 'Arrivals' segment, with its rich tapestry of cultural and language differences and the inevitable differences between each of those groups within communities. 'Arrivals' was the first cast induction, and as such was definitely the hardest. One particular woman caused a ruckus at the outset, protesting loudly that she did not want to dance nude, particularly in front of her children. Dancing nude was news to us! My colleague on the receiving end of the outburst stared at her in disbelief, and tried to point out that her name wasn't even on the list. I was summoned to his aid, and found that the only way to comfort the poor woman was with an old-fashioned hug, and an assurance that she would be included in the Opening Ceremony, and that she would definitely *not* be required to dance nude, and would instead be wearing a fantastic costume designed by the wonderful Jenny Kee, just like the ones displayed on the wall for all the volunteers to see.

That incident became part of our folklore. For the following six months, any of our outbursts of sheer frustration or emotion (and there were plenty) were prefaced with a loud: '*I don't want to dance nude*!'

CATHERINE FLANAGAN, *Production Manager for 'Nature' and 'Arrivals' segments in the Opening Ceremony*
SYDNEY NSW

'The Streets Where They Lived'

It was during the lead-up to those other magnificent Olympic Games – in Melbourne in 1956 – that I first became involved in the tricky business of naming Village streets. It happened during a media visit to the Heidelberg Olympic Village a couple of weeks before it was due to be opened for those Games. I was writing a sports column at the time.

We sampled the accommodation (later to become a Housing Commission complex), the food and the amenities, and they were all fine. But, wandering around the Village, I was appalled to find that all the streets had been named after battles in which Australian troops had fought.

It didn't take long to calculate that the Japanese athletes would have to walk to and from meals, six trips a day in all, along a street called Buna – celebrating a place where thousands of Japanese lives had been lost. Similarly, the Germans had to parade along Alamein Street, again commemorating the scene of great loss of life.

It all seemed a little insensitive, and I wrote a column suggesting that it was hardly appropriate in a place where young people were due to come together in a spirit of international goodwill. I proposed that it might be more fitting to have the streets named after Olympic heroes and heroines. Among the names I suggested were those of the pioneer athletes Edwin Flack, Freddie Lane, Fanny Durack and Frank Beaurepaire.

There was quite a fuss. The article was quoted in parliament, and a lot of indignant letters were sent to newspapers. Finally it was announced, on behalf of the Housing Commission, that, yes, those names would be changed. There would be a Flack Road and a Beaurepaire Street, but these were not utterly liberated times: there was still no street for Fanny Durack.

For my newspaper, Melbourne's *Sun*, it amounted to a small triumph, and I later received a journalism award for the column. When the Games were over, though, and the Olympic caravan had moved on, the street signs honouring the old athletes were all hauled down. Up went the battle names again, and they remain there today.

When John Coates asked me in October 1996 to represent the AOC on the Homebush Bay Names Committee, I had the chance to make a more permanent impact on urban geography. The brief was to make recommendations to the Olympic Co-Ordination Authority on the naming of public places, streets and roads on the Homebush Bay Olympic site. Later this was broadened to include all Olympic sites in Sydney. This voluntary task would take me three years.

The naming committee included representatives of ethnic and Aboriginal communities, historical, cultural, municipal and environmental interests, and various state road and rail authorities. I found myself working closely with SOCOG's representative, Kevin Simmonds, and quickly came to realise that – with Olympic Park, the Olympic Village and the many venues – I would have a fairly free hand.

The geography of most Olympic host cities is unmarked by the Games. Normally a huge Olympic invasion force moves in, the place becomes a major focus of world interest for a short time, then all the visitors pack up and go home. If a legacy remains, it's usually in minds rather than on maps.

This is understandable. The main streets and buildings occupied during the Games are generally established, and thus already possess names. And the villages in which athletes live are by their nature temporary strongholds, converted from some other role – often as student residences, sometimes as housing projects.

Rarely is there the opportunity for the Games to leave a physical imprint. Munich in 1972 was one city that retained Olympic links on the map after the Games moved on. At the centre of Munich Olympic Park stands Coubertinplatz, a public area serving a common forecourt to the stadium, indoor arena and swimming hall. There's also a Brundageplatz (after Avery Brundage, IOC chief in 1972) and a ring road named after Spiridon Louis, the first marathon winner.

Sydney was unlike previous host cities in one important respect. Its entire Olympic Park precinct was built in a place that had been a near-city wilderness. Homebush Bay had been home to an abattoir and brickworks, and many regarded the place as a community rubbish dump.

As the place was transformed, in the run-up to the Games, into a magnificent sports complex, parklands, a large new suburb of medium-density living and a high-technology industrial area, a lovely opportunity emerged. More than 150 streets, plazas, gardens and other features needed names. That's the reason I received a tap on the shoulder.

Using my knowledge of Olympic history, collaborating throughout with Simmonds, I submitted a series of recommendations. They needed the approval of the Olympic Co-Ordination Authority, the local Auburn municipal council and (in the case of the Athletes' Village, which was to become private housing) the developer, Mirvac. Except for a few hiccups, the system worked well.

The first names nominated were those for streets and boulevards that skirted main stadiums at Olympic Park. They celebrated our first male and female gold medallists, Edwin Flack and Fanny Durack, as well as Dawn Fraser, Shirley Strickland, Herb Elliot, Murray Rose, Marjorie Jackson, and the distinguished Paralympic athlete Kevin Coombs.

That's when we encountered our first hiccups. At the highest levels of SOCOG, it was felt that Australians generally wouldn't recognise the names of Flack and Durack. It was also felt that the use of the word 'Fanny' in a street name would invite ridicule from overseas visitors. I objected strongly to this kind of nonsense, and finally the names were approved – although some bureaucrat insisted that Fanny's street sign be given the more sedate name of Sarah, which she didn't much use.

In the Village, it was possible to honour 25 great foreign Olympians, including Jesse Owens, Abebe Bikila, Nadia Comaneci, Muhammad Ali, Carl Lewis, Kip Keino, Emil Zatopek, Vladimir Kuts, Michael Jordan, Jackie Joyner, Janet Evans, Al Oerter, Tefilio Stevenson and Alex Popov (who later observed, 'Nobody ever named a street after me in Russia, but they've done it in Sydney').

The 27 Australians who received their own streets included Freddie Lane, Bobby Pearce, Russell Mockridge, Ron Clarke, Bill Roycroft, Bill Northam, David Theile, Jon Henricks, Michael Wenden, Kieren Perkins, Snowy Baker, Frank Beaurepaire, 'Boy' Charlton, Susan O'Neill and Kathy Watt. There was also Cecil Healy, the only Australian gold medallist to have been killed in action.

Even the Olympic rings themselves got a street name: one each for the Avenue of Africa, Avenue of Asia, Avenue of the Americas, Avenue of Europe and Avenue of Oceania.

And there was a street for John Ian Wing, who made an enduring contribution to the Olympic movement when he persuaded the organisers of the 1956 Melbourne Games to make the Closing Ceremony an informal affair. It's been that way ever since, and there's a John Ian Wing Parade at Homebush Bay.

A few more hiccups occurred during this process. The developers didn't like foreign or difficult-sounding names much. This problem was resolved when we found parks and pathways to commemorate the names of such champions as Fanny Blankers-Koen, Laryssa Latynina and Louise Sauvage. The swimmer Krisztina Egerszegi had to settle for just Kristina Avenue.

After the Village was settled, the naming process continued around the venues – one of which was in fact named after the great cyclist Dunc Gray. At the equestrian centre it was possible to honour not only seven great riders, including Laurie Morgan and Neale Lavis, but also some formidable horses.

Gillian Rolton had a street named after her in the Olympic Village. But I reckon she was even more delighted when she looked one day up at a major signpost leading into that equestrian centre. It showed that Peppermint Grove, the horse she rode to gold medals in Barcelona and Atlanta, had a road of his own – forever.

HARRY GORDON *Official Historian AOC*
SYDNEY, NSW

(Harry Gordon's personal contribution to the Sydney 2000 Olympic Games was even more extraordinary than his story reveals. He nominated towns whose heritage and history entitled them to inclusion in the torch relay, and chose six Australian Olympic legends to be honoured in special issue postage stamps. Already author of *Australia and the Olympic Games*, Harry wrote major articles in many of the official programs. He produced, for no fee, the book *A Certain Passion*, which was presented to all members of the IOC, all chefs de mission, and all members of the Australian Olympic team. He worked with sculptors on a public art project in the Olympic Park complex, and took part in state and Australian Olympic Academies. In May 1999, the AOC conferred on him its highest award, the Order of Merit.)

For those who have been fortunate to visit an Olympic Village, they would recognise that the Sydney home for nearly 17,000 team members from 199 attending Olympic Countries or National Olympic Committees (NOC) was the greatest ever. This was my twelfth Olympic Games, starting from 1956 onwards, and the opportunity to live in an Olympic Village once again provided my eighth Village experience.

Without doubt the intimate and also extreme detail in setting up the Villages, and in the main the Athletes' Village, was of the highest order. The ultimate and successful operations created repeated expressions of pleasure from the many persons living in the Village, and was also acclaimed by all who had the good fortune to visit the Village. The teams lived in either established modern brick dwellings of varied designs and high quality, or in modular units, also of varied sizes. My small villa comprised a kitchen-lounge-entry area, two bedrooms and a bath-shower-toilet room. A verandah with table and chairs completed a very comfortable set-up.

The Australian team, our largest ever; including support personnel, was in excess of 800. With our extremely experienced and highly influential chef de mission, John Coates (there is none better) the team was very well set up in the Olympic Village, all living in the temporary modular villas and houses. My little villa was in immediate proximity to the Aussies. They even had their own Village Green area, which served for entertainment, including barbecues, medal victory celebrations, which all added much to the team members' Village enjoyment and comfort. Another team effort was a competition for the best decorated house – there were some great creations which the gymnasts won.

Accommodation buildings already mentioned housed 17,000 team members and a resident staff of 200. An operative voluntary staff of 7000 of whom a minimum of 4000 were in the Village at all times – they did not live in the Village. Other than the security force of 400 and a paid housekeeping staff in excess of 300, all others were again volunteers including the deputy mayors. Graham Richardson as a member of the SOCOG Executive Committee received a remuneration for that position. He did an excellent job as the mayor.

The total voluntary force for the Games was in excess of 40,000; a wonderful personal contribution; never to be beaten, I would believe.

Housekeeping

The many rooms for sleeping and administration purposes were cleaned every day, beds were made every day; sheets and pillowslips changed every four days; 34,000 of each. Towels changed every two days exchanged daily at one of the 22 Resident Centres strategically placed around the Village.

Dining Hall

Seated 6000 at any one meal; overall this huge centre served in excess of 63,000 meals each day. Chefs came in from around the world. The variety and quality of the food provided was exceptional and for the first time in Olympic Village history; regardless of the greater numbers, no queues prevailed. Volunteers manned many areas of the dining centre – doing a great job and adding to the overall success of the Village operations. The wonderful variety, quality and quantity of the food provided in the dining hall was so great it tempted a number to do unusual things. It was permissible to take items from the dining hall, fruit, etc, and there was a free

McDonalds in the dining hall. Taking a hamburger or two, or three, was fair, but when one person, checked by a voluntary supervisor, had 20, that was a bit over the top. Similarly with special biscuits and ice-creams; some were overloading with these. The point is they could come back to the dining hall as often as they wished, as some areas of this large complex operated day and night. It obviously was 'Heaven of the Food World' for a number of Village residents.

The Games overall were as President Juan A. Samaranch said: 'The best' and there is no doubt much of this can be attributed to the great work and devotion to the cause by the volunteers of which I was proud to be one.

JULIUS (JUDY) PATCHING, *Deputy Mayor of Olympic Village*
MELBOURNE VIC

Six weeks before the Olympic Games, Michael Knight called me on my mobile phone. Instantly I thought: 'What have I done wrong?!'

Michael asked me to participate in the Opening Ceremony, joining Betty Cuthbert as a torch bearer. What a privilege. But it had to be top secret – nobody could know. Ah … how could I keep this to myself? Well, I did (bar two people) and this heightened the emotional and adrenaline-filled moment of truth.

The crowd went wild. With a quiet calm I entered the Stadium and acted like a sponge, taking in the whole situation to store forever in my memory. Betty was so excited and I was honoured to be pushing her into an arena that we both loved.

Never had an Olympic Games begun with such splendour, happiness and anticipation. My only concern was for Cathy Freeman – standing there wet and cold, an image that will be everlasting in the minds of millions of people. It didn't seem to affect her performance at the Games, though!

What a champion.

What a performance.

What a legend.

What a RELIEF.

It turned into the greatest 'carnivale' of sport ever witnessed. The world had a smorgasbord of sport supported by well thought-out organisation and management.

Everything through to the 47,500 volunteers was fantastic. Sydney was resplendent.

The athletes and the organising committees made the Games but the Volunteers drove the Games with smiles and happy dispositions. These people varied in age, nationality, sex, socio-economic background and all other groups you could think of.

On one occasion I saw a volunteer on a tennis umpire-type stand dressed as a surf lifesaver with all the messages of sun protection, guiding the public to their required venues: 'And for those who wish to go to the Main Stadium, just head towards the Big Barbecue over my left shoulder – sausages will be served later.'

How wonderful. How Australian.

RAELENE BOYLE MBE, *Torchbearer, Opening Ceremony*
Triple silver medallist at Mexico and Munich Olympics, Competed at Montreal, selected for Moscow
GOLD COAST QLD

PART II

THE GAMES

“Where were you on that Friday night, 15 September, 2000? Like many millions of Australians, I stayed at home with friends and family to watch the Opening Ceremony on telly – let the Games begin!

Much had been made of the secrecy. So much build up, all that 'not knowing' had captured the nation's imagination. Whether you were at home with a bunch of mates, or were behind the scenes like Gerry, or in the audience at Stadium Australia, in the future everyone of us will have our own story to tell.

What were you doing on the night, Gerry?

I wasn't watching the Opening Ceremony, I was working at the Superdome where all the athletes assembled to take their place in the line-up. I reckon every athlete walked past me, a mere five metres away – twice! I had my own unique experience, because I saw the world twice in two hours. I saw all those different cultures at close quarters, saw their different uniforms, how they laughed, smiled, spoke to each other. I spoke to lots of them while they waited for two or three minutes – in fact I had a good chat to Andrew Gaze while he was waiting. I was really rapt watching it on video later that night, having been behind the scenes. I had such a gut feeling for all the organisers, knowing the pain of getting it all together, hoping that it came off all right. But there was nothing to worry about, Sydney did us proud.

Back to you Max.

A year down the track, if I close my eyes it all comes back into focus, like watching rushes from a movie set. 'The Man from Snowy River' – what an unexpected start. Hundreds of riders charging across the screen like drovers in the outback, proudly carrying the Aussie flag – I couldn't help myself, I broke into song: 'Under the Southern Cross I stand, a sprig of wattle in my hand, a native of this native land, Australia, you little beauty!' It was just like the old days, post Test Match celebrations. Imagine people sitting and watching in

New York, Tokyo and Bangkok – what a knockout! We clinked our glasses in acknowledgment of their extraordinary achievement. 'Cheers!' we said. 'Cheers!' echoed the kids.

Then the massive screen displaying the symbolic coat hanger bridge became visible at one end of the Stadium. And framed in naive capital letters, a huge G'DAY. And so it went on – 118,000 lucky ticket holders were there to witness what one journalist described as 'a mighty corroboree, a seven-act spectacle'.

Who will ever forget the ten-storey high Wandjina spirit figure dominating the air space in the centre of the Stadium? Haunting eyes and a smoky halo – what a mood the 'Awakenings' segment evoked from the start. My three-year-old, Isabella, thought this was a great time to start her own corroboree, stomping around the lounge room, in time to the chanting and dancing of Aboriginal and Torres Strait Islanders.

Remember the larger-than-life black picture frames connected to bodies by a neck? For once Ned Kelly outnumbered the police and the crowd loved it – and so did we.

As an architect, I've always admired corrugated iron as a building material. But in 'Tin Symphony' – tap dancing workers in harmony with industrial strength sparks on a mega scale – well, that gave the old corrugated iron a whole new dimension. Ten out of ten for that idea, guys!

But there was more and better to come – suspended in the blackness of the night, tiny 13-year-old, Nikki Webster rolled out her beach towel and applied her suntan cream. Everywhere, girls thought they could have done it too (including my nine-year-old Alexandra and her friend, Felicity – they didn't quite appreciate the height above the ground, and hours and hours of practice required).

And then there was the powerful image of Djakapurra Munyarryun, fully painted for ceremony, hand in hand with little Nikki in her floral dress, pink bows and curly hair – quite a statement.

Five time Olympian and friend Andrew Gaze led the Australian team – distinctive yellow shirt, terracotta jacket and accreditation slung round his neck, he waved to the crowd, smiling. The hair on my neck stood up as he held the Australian flag aloft in his left hand. Then moments later the gigantic wave of cloth with Olympic images projected onto it spilled down to cover all 11,000 athletes and became the new focus.

And just when you thought you'd seen and felt all there could be, there was more – what about when our great female athletes brought the torch into the arena? Shane Gould, Dawn Fraser, Raelene Boyle, Debbie Flintoff-King and Betty Cuthbert – our very best. Eyes welled up with emotion as Raelene Boyle steered the legendary Betty Cuthbert around the athletics track – a modern day chariot with pumped up tyres, the Olympic torch shedding light on their features. Every now and then, a wave – going much slower than when they had both dominated the track. Before we knew it, the torch had been handed to Cathy Freeman – where did she come from? We all had opinions, we all saw her in the athletes' march – very cleverly done.

Now we could see the contemporary architecture of the cauldron. Cathy moved up the staircase, elegant in her white body suit – the crowd roared. Inside the amphitheatre, not a dry eye, I'm told. Inside the Walker theatrette – same thing. Big boys do shed tears.

That flame had travelled 27,000 kilometres – the longest torch relay in history was now in its final moments. God-like, elevated, Cathy saluted the world with her right arm – the torch a tiny flame compared to the one that surrounded her dancing on the surface of the pool. All Aussie hearts stopped beating when that huge dish paused for too long on its skyward journey, but the relief when it moved forward – what an emotional moment. If there were any dry eyes before, there certainly weren't now!

They're all memories now, fixed forever. It's as much a part of us as knowing where you were when John F.

Kennedy was assassinated, where you were when man walked on the moon, or what you were doing when you heard the tragic news of Princess Diana's death.

Everyone at the Walkers' place that night agreed that this opening extravaganza far exceeded our expectations – but even more importantly it was entertaining, it was great fun. It appealed to little kids and big kids alike – we were all mesmerised. So much was crammed into those few hours, but it took hundreds of thousands of people hours from concept to creation to execution. Ric Birch and team – take a very big bow!

And let's not forget all those volunteers who sewed costumes, danced, rode horses, performed, all for free. Think of those hundreds of rehearsal hours – the Opening Ceremony could not have happened without you all. What a unique Australian fingerprint you gave to the Sydney Games. Sophisticated and innovative – Sydney, you got it right!

Max & Gerry ”

The most fascinating thing was how well it all went off. In our practices, we used to think 'Boy, is this *really* going to work?' and it just went off so beautifully. Sydney should be so proud of what they did – it was carried off to perfection. When the Opening was all over, four of us sat in the park outside the Stadium, and drank a bottle of champagne. We were that pleased and proud of what our city had shown the world, and that was our moment where we realised that that six years of hard work was something to be so proud of. Right at that moment it really was worth every minute of it.

DOROTHY WILLIAMS, *Pioneer volunteer*
PROSPECT NSW

Finally, the real thing started and something near to miraculous happened. Despite tough, demanding and often stressful conditions, people remained enthusiastic, happy, smiling, cooperative, committed and inclusive. The 5 a.m. wakeups, the relentless sun in the unshaded venue (with some spectators fainting and needing medical attention), the

limited food and drink intake (in case our workload did not allow us to join the long toilet queues) and the very large crowds … nothing seemed to interfere with the uplifting experience of simply being there.
AGNES WALKER, *Electronic Scoring*
CANBERRA ACT

There is no prouder moment than to witness your national team win gold at the Olympics in your own country and hearing all the crowd singing *Advance Australia Fair* in full voice. I will remember this night for the rest of my life.
BRENDEN SMALL, *Spectator Services*
MELBOURNE VIC

I caught sight of a very dapper gentleman, turned and told him he looked very smart, only to find when he faced me with a smile, it was our governor-general!
NOELINE WALK, *Spectator Services*
FRASER ISLAND QLD

To make it speedier for the ticket holders to enter the turnstiles, I was telling the patrons to have their tickets ready and have their butts facing towards the collector. I thought that was a fairly reasonable instruction. I acknowledged that the crowd was being very friendly as everyone was during the Games when they smiled and several laughed good-naturedly. It was not until the end of my shift that I realised just what I had been saying to those people. I was very careful with the way I worded my instructions from then on.
MARGARET McINROY, *Spectator Services*
BELFIELD NSW

Having had the privilege of leading six Olympic Games teams as chef de mission, I have always appreciated the value and contribution that volunteers have made to the

Olympic movement. The Sydney experience has recognised that the volunteers have played a major part in Sydney being remembered as 'the best Games ever' and I have no doubt that in future Olympic Games the precedent will be further enhanced.

GEOFFREY J. HENKE, *AO, Member of Executive Committee for Sydney 2000*
MELBOURNE VIC

... times like being on megaphone duty outside the South Stand at the end of the night's program, everybody thanking me as they make their way home, laughing, smiling, arm-in-arm, kids in strollers – taking the time to wish me goodnight.
Incredible. Thanking *me* as a volunteer for making their day! Priceless.

GRAEME LUGSDIN, *Spectator Services*
BALGOWLAH NSW

" MAX TALKS TO JOHN BERTRAND
John Bertrand unbolted America's Cup from the New York Yacht Club where it had been housed for 132 years. That was in 1983, when he skippered *Australia 11* to victory against all odds. John knows what it's like at the sharp end of his sport, technically and psychologically, and that's what made him a wonderful sounding board for Olympic athletes.
Max "

John: Herb Elliot asked me to get involved. His credibility with the athletes, no matter how long he's been retired, has always been huge and will always be. In fact, he was recently voted by an International Sport Organisation as the greatest 1500m runner in the modern Olympic era.

We were brought in to be an unemotional sounding-board for the athletes because we'd been there and done it ourselves. They needed to know how you withstand the pressure. It was a question of listening to them, understanding and not being shocked by some of their fears, which was very comforting to them. And for them to realise that some of the inadequacies and fears that they were feeling then, were the same as the ones we were feeling in our heyday. Then, as an extension to that, how we coped with the environment and how we turned this environment into success.

I was involved with the rowing team, the sailing team of course, the beach volleyball, shooting team. Some athletics.

Max: It was like ricochet city for you.

John: Exactly. At first I was asked to look after the sailing, the shooting, the soccer team and the cycling team, which I did. But then it expanded when we got our feet on the ground and we got familiar with the lay of the land. It ended up being whoever we came across who needed help.

After all those years of preparation, the global competition they'd been involved with, the effort they'd put in, the biggest thing they had to come to grips with were the consequences of winning or losing and how that could screw them up in the process. The dream of victory, the consequence of defeat in some of these cases was overwhelming for the athlete. And when they started concentrating on the consequences of winning or losing, that's when they lost the main game. So it was a question of eliminating thoughts on the consequences and concentrating on the process, and enjoying the process.

And it was good for them to know that people like myself had gone through that rationalisation. We'd had fear of failure too. They'd ask me 'How did you feel when you had to perform in that final race?' A lot of them knew about the America's Cup. They wanted to know how I handled that pressure.

Max: How did you rationalise the enormity of the task in front of you?

John: I'd been through an Olympics and had people thrust on me when it looked like I was going to do well. This was a turn-off for me, because I got there on my own merit. I had my own support team which was very very rudimentary in those days. My wife was my mentor and my closest support member. From my perspective the last thing I needed was interlopers. So my feeling was that if people like myself wanted to be of help to these athletes, it was purely on the basis that they wanted our assistance. Definitely not to thrust ourselves upon them. Let them know that we were available to be a trusted confidant if that's what they wanted. One of the most important things was to be trusted, not to divulge anything that would be embarrassing to those individuals. I think that came through and people felt they were comfortable with us. Not so much solving their problems, because we didn't have the technical expertise in their area. It was purely to say, well that's how I handled that type of scenario myself.

I've always felt the difference between winning and losing at that level is not expertise, it's lack of fear.

Max: Could you draw one or two common fears?

John: Fear of failure. It's a fishbowl environment: the Olympic Games held in your own country and everyone but everyone wants you to succeed. Then the enormity of the event, bigger than anything you've ever dreamt about. Take the volleyball. Up until now you've been touring the world, no one wants to know about you. When they scored a point overseas, people would boo and whenever they missed, people would clap. Then they come to Bondi and when they scored a goal people would cheer and when they missed – sigh. These sound effects were so foreign to them, it put them off their game.

We're not talking about motivation, we're talking about stress control. This is not a weekend event, this is the biggest show on earth. And you can't practise for that environment.

We couldn't practise for the America's Cup. We could practise every day, but you can't practise for 1000 aircraft above you, all those people watching. The chop in the water. You can't simulate it. You can only talk about it with people who have been through it before.

No one wanted to know about the shooters in Atlanta, but now everyone wants to know about them.

Max: So how did these 'sessions' actually happen?

John: Generally discussions were set up. It was steal away to a corner, have a coffee, maybe a bus ride home. We're talking about the intimacy of a mentor away from the cut and thrust of competition.

Max: You would have been aware of all the other volunteers active in the Village and been aware of the contributions they too have made.

John: Oh yes. When you talk about the highlights, for me it was the volunteers and the police. Just sensational. The coppers were very professional. They came from the toughest areas of NSW. The criteria was that they were there for high security and not for small misdemeanors. Men and women coming out of these tough areas, they'd turn a blind eye to trivia because they were interested in protecting the lives of the athletes; the rest was irrelevant. That was the right scenario. The bottom line was the quality of the police was just superb and they really got into the spirit of things. It was just a delight to see people getting paid back in terms of their service to the community.

Max: The Americans couldn't believe how so many people came out and were willing to help and guide and give, whereas back there you'd get a chit for everything, you'd expect to be paid for it, there's always a dollar in it.

John: Laurie Lawrence set up different times for the teams to practise the 'entertainment' before the Olympics started. The beach volleyball girls started to do their thing, up in front of the audience doing their dance and the water polo girls started to do their jig. It was all spontaneous.

I was able to con the coppers – all the security people around that area – to get up on stage. And they did a rendition like the Village People. All the coppers with their guns, big bazookas, the whole thing. On stage with their hobnailed boots. We had so much fun. They really got into the spirit of things. My only concern when they were doing their thing was that their bloody guns were in the way.

Max: Let's talk about individual events. I mean I watched just about as much as anyone could've possibly watched on television. And I know I could reel off my ten best moments or highlights. So how was it being privy to the inner thoughts of some of the athletes and then to watch it out there? Let's say, for example, the Cathy Freeman night. Everyone can relate to that. Where were you?

John: The Cathy moment was one of the defining moments of the Olympic Games. In terms of being in that fishbowl. She'd been the main player in the Opening Ceremony, and all the pressure was on her. The fact that she was able to produce that performance on the track was a wondrous success for her as an individual. Because if there's any person who could have dwelled on the consequences of winning or losing it would have been her. The way that young girl, that little girl, handled that was a knockout. Great athlete, great person.

It just goes to show you compete for yourself. She for one knows all the work she put into it for years and years when nobody else cared. And then you compete for your loved ones and your family and then you compete for your nation. But initially you do it because you love what you do. It's a great thing to see that young kid compete and have such enormous success despite the enormous pressure she's been under. And it was a big call. So that night was a biggie.

Max: I was interested in what you saw happen at the beach volleyball. How they changed their culture from a bronze medal in Atlanta – which was pretty good – and then to have to split and come back together and turn it into a gold culture.

John: The feeling was after Atlanta, that they had to live and breathe the sense of winning and the winning was represented to them by gold – the colour gold. So they decided in their own way to do everything they could in the environment of gold. Everything gold. They got a gold beach volleyball to train with. Gold cameras, their clock radio was gold, they had gold eiderdowns on and I'm sure they wore gold lipstick. Part of their rationalisation was that they belonged to that; they weren't comfortable with silver. And I think the real testament of that was that when they were down, other teams would have buckled (the world champions, Brazil, were leading). These girls wouldn't give in because they weren't comfortable with second place. And they went on and did the job. If ever there's a lesson to be learnt, these girls showed us if you live the dream and work the dream, then it's amazing what can happen.

Max: Apart from support and counselling, did you have other responsibilities?

John: Athletes used to receive their uniforms in a box, but Herb insisted it was a great privilege to be part of the Australian Olympic team, so we made a special presentation out of it. When each of the teams were brought in, there was a ceremony away from the Village in a lovely environment, where parents and loved ones would come and they'd be presented with their Olympic uniform. As part of the liaison team, I was privileged to present to the teams that were on our roster. I presented to the women's water polo. Well these girls showed up, the most beautiful-looking girls you've ever seen, talk about fantastic representation of Australian womanhood – strong, beautiful skin, you know, healthy kids. I remember we kicked off with *Advance Australia Fair,* and not one of them knew the words!

I can sing *God Save the Queen* because I learnt it at school. You've got to get them early, teach them at school. So the first thing I said is, when you people win your gold medal, whatever you reckon you're going to win, you've got to know the words. Really important. Because you'll look foolish!

But yeah, tough girls. They wanted it desperately, they wanted success. And listening to these girls: they'd fought their way to the Olympic Games, and they weren't going to let go without a fight. It was great. So they had resolve that stood them apart. And there was an inner-win feeling that went very deep, lit by their pride.

Max: Any stories about experiences with volunteers?

John: Oh yeah, I remember accompanying the soccer team to one of the events. Of course, there's a lot of pressure on these kids coming home from Europe. And not all were able to come. Talk about desperation to win for their country. And their dream was to win, and to see the sadness when they lost ... well, it was very heartfelt. They were saying, 'We want to prove to our fellow Australians that we are Australians. A lot of us don't have Aussie accents and we're desperate to prove that we are part of this country.' So they were really trying hard, and the fact is that logistically, it's a hard act because they can't get to know each other because it all happens so fast …

So here we are, we're in the bloody bus off to the cricket ground, one of these big matches. And part of the deal is you have the bus driver volunteer. This guy came from Queenstown and the other bloke, the navigator, he comes from Rockhampton, and he sits behind the bus driver. So off we go from Homebush out through Sydney. We don't have a lot of time. We take off at a quarter to six and I think the match is at eight o'clock. All of a sudden, it became apparent to everyone that we were on our way across the Harbour Bridge, which was entirely the wrong direction.

You should've seen the officials go into a panic as they tried to figure out how to turn a bus around on a freeway! We took a bypass off and we enter downtown Sydney, and I ring ahead and I say, 'We have a problem. Can you organise a police escort – please – to open up the traffic, close off the traffic lights to get this team to the Sydney Cricket Ground. This is head of Top Security, okay?' Every other contingency they'd thought about, but not to unclog traffic for the Australian soccer team in a bus. You see the sweat rolling down the bus driver's face. This guy died a thousand deaths. He had the weight of the nation on his shoulders ... he didn't sign up for that. The navigator was speechless, he'd lost all control: what was up, what was down on this map? We had the head coach, the goalie and the top scorer all trying to decipher the Gregorys. Huddled around the driver and the navigator trying to figure out how in the hell we were going to get to the SCG to play the big match.

Well this call comes through from the cops: they can't organise it quickly enough. They've got things going on, robberies etc and 10,000 police out at Homebush, so the police force was stretched. So they say good luck.

Eventually we figured it out. The driver was so relieved when we drove in. Needless to say the boys got there on time. They didn't win the match but they had one hell of a bus ride.

Then there was this volunteer bus driver. I asked him how he got involved and he said, 'I got a distress call. I own a bus company up in Mackay and they were running out of people who could drive a bus so I got on a plane and here I am.' Here's the boss of a company and he's driving a bus.

Another time I was going from the Village via the canteen to our promotion area. A lovely lady, a volunteer, had such a serene smile. I said, 'How did you get involved with this?' She said, 'Well, I'm dying of cancer and I figured I want to put in before I go.' Just blew me away. This girl, she says,

'I am so happy doing this. I come from Adelaide and I feel really proud to be involved.' And I said, 'Well what can I say?' and she said, 'You don't have to say anything. I just feel very privileged and I'm just having so much fun. I've met so many people, everyone's so friendly. It's such an honour to be involved in it.'

And I thought that put things into perspective.

JOHN BERTRAND, AM, *Athlete Liaison Officer*
Bronze Medallist in Yachting at Montreal 1976
MELBOURNE VIC

I will never forget asking my supervisor on my first day if I could walk around the park to familiarise myself with the location and they asked me if I could ride a bike. I said I had not ridden a bike for 30 years. They told me it was just like riding a bike – you never forget! They were right. So off I went at 56 years of age, riding around Olympic Park on a state-of-the-art Harley Davidson pushbike. I felt like a kid again.

KAY SYLVESTER, *Logistics*
SYDNEY NSW

Ninety seconds of today's showjumping paid me back a hundredfold for the 18 days of volunteer work.

Yes, we won gold! 'Aussie Aussie Aussie, Hoy Hoy Hoy' is the new catchcry at the equestrian.

MAUREEN TREVANION, *Loss Investigator*
CANBERRA ACT

As a member of the Executive Corporate Committee of the NSW Olympic Committee, for every Olympic Games since 1980, I was invited by John Coates, AOC Chairman, to submit my name as an attaché volunteer, during the Sydney Olympics. Imagine my surprise that Barbados, subject to that country's approval, would be the proposed appointment. Unbelievable!

The reception and reaction shown by the chef de mission and the team members was so spontaneous and warming, it reminded me vividly of the wonderful relationship Australia shared with the West Indies cricket team, during the famous tied Test Series 1960–61. As a player, it was wonderful to be caught up in the unsolicited spirit of fair play and friendship.

Once the Games began, many visitors came to the Village to meet the team, including the Barbados sports minister and director of sport, but easily the most moving and memorable visit was the day Sir Garfield Sobers dropped by. As one of cricket's greatest ever all-rounders entered the team lounge area, they rose as one and bowed to His Excellency … the title he is known by for his standing in Barbados. To be recognised and revered by his peers from the Olympic sports was truly a moment to treasure.

The team also had its ups and downs, even before the Games competition commenced – Milton Brown succumbed to chicken pox. The entire team underwent a thorough medical test. It was like drawing a line in the sand … those that had contracted chicken pox and those that had not. Fortunately, only Milton Brown showed the symptoms and the patient had to be quarantined away from the rest of the team. But the Olympic Medical Group ruled he had to be kept within the Barbados specified accommodation. This obviously caused a lot of anxiety. The team doctor, Lou Harper, did a superb job in helping the runner's recovery. Despite this period of sickness, Milton was determined to compete. He hadn't travelled halfway around the globe just to lie in bed counting his spots and feeling sorry, while watching everyone else compete for Olympic medals, on a television set.

So, after his 'exile' he had only three days of lead-up training, but nevertheless he courageously took his place in the 400m heat. Incredibly, this was a shocker of a night. A nasty Sydney southerly storm engulfed Stadium Australia. Apart from being cold, he also drew a fellow named Michael Johnson, who went on to predictably win the gold medal.

Initially everything was just fine, with a massive wind behind him at the start, but by the time he turned into the straight for a big finish, in his words, 'I was hit by a double-decker bus, man!' He was totally overrun by the field, to finish last. But, to see him that night, you would have thought he'd won, sporting the biggest of smiles, after receiving his competitor's medal. The guts Milton showed, just to get to the line, after what he went through, makes one think his day of glory will become a reality one day in the future.

On a personal note, I took my grandson Mitchell (aged eight) to the Athletes' Village. First, we visited the Barbados area, where he met most of the team, including the charismatic Obadele Thompson. He was impressed! Next, down by bus to the dining area, he keenly grabbed a tray of goodies and sat down. The next minute, a couple of athletes moved into eat, two seats away. Mitchell grabbed me by the arm. 'Pa ... it's Matt Shirvington!' That was the start of a marvellous day for him. He was quickly identifying so many of the Olympic stars. Mitchell is his school's under-ten cross-country champ, so who knows what lies ahead in the year 2016 or 2020 …!

Finally, I would love to pay a tribute to all of those wonderful men and women, who so selflessly gave of their time and skills, to make the Olympic experience even better. To each of you, thank you and congratulations!

Every day so much to smile about.

ALAN DAVIDSON, *Attaché to Barbados and former Australian Test Cricketer*
SYDNEY NSW

I remember the first day that I walked into the Sydney 2000 Olympic Village as a member of the Australian Olympic team. Just after I walked through the gate after passing muster at the security checks were all these people looking at me and smiling. I thought my fly must have been undone. But after a quick and surreptitious (I think) inspection, and finding all in order I realised that these people were SOCOG volunteers and that they were making me feel welcome. They persisted with this infectious friendliness right through the entire Games at all venues and created an atmosphere that will be remembered by all of our visitors. They were wonderful. Congratulations to them and to the people who trained them.

HERB ELLIOT, *Director of Athlete and Corporate Relations*
Winner of 1500m Gold Medal at Rome Olympics, 1960
MELBOURNE VIC

My story involves two Olympics: Melbourne in 1956, as a 14-year-old Boy Scout volunteer, and Sydney 2000, as a recently retired AFL coach.

In 1956 I had the privilege of being a telegram delivery boy at the

Village at Heidelberg. Each morning I ran telegrams to a variety of athletes from a variety of countries. It allowed me to meet first-hand many of the great Olympians, one of which was Rafer Johnson, the champion decathalete from the USA. Each afternoon I went to the MCG and watched the athletics. I was fortunate enough to see some of the most exciting events – Cuthbert's 100m, Kuts' 10,000m, Richards' pole vault, Delaney's 1500m, Dumas's high jump and Johnson's decathlon. The memories have remained vividly with me over the past 40-odd years.

Midway through 2000 I received a phone call from Volley Devitt, an unknown name to me. Through council records she traced me as the current owner of her original family home in Hawthorn. I was fascinated to learn that when she was 17 years old, her family provided six weeks accommodation for Rafer Johnson's mother prior to, during and after the Games in Melbourne.

Volley met and dated Rafer following visits to see his mum in Hawthorn. After one such night out they returned to her home in the early hours of the morning to find no means of public transport to get back to the Village. Undeterred, Rafer ran the eight kilometres back to Heidelberg using a rough map provided by Volley. This during the period he was competing in the most arduous of all Olympic events …

DAVID PARKIN *AFL Premiership Player and Coach*
MELBOURNE VIC

My first drug test was as an 18-year-old after winning a gold medal on the pommel horse at the 1990 Commonwealth Games in Auckland. I was on a high! I felt invincible! That was until a short man in black-rimmed glasses approached me: 'Brennon Dowrick, you have been selected for a drug test. I am your chaperone. From now until the test is completed I will not leave your side.'

Fair enough. Eager to prove my drug-free status I followed him to the testing compound. After an explanation of the test procedure, I settled down with a few mates to rehydrate ourselves. After a litre of water, one mate went in to be tested, only to return with an empty beaker.

'What happened?' I asked.

'I don't know – stage fright!' he replied.

I decided to drink another litre of water – just to be sure I could go! My mate went for his second go, only to return with a half-full beaker. In drug testing you must produce a minimum sample – now I was really worried. So just to be safe, I drank a third litre of water. Busting to go, I decided now was the time. I had a look at the tiny beaker and back at my three empty bottles of water and wondered how I was going to stop the flow once it started.

Once in the testing area, my chaperone asked my to drop my pants to my ankles '… it's so I can make sure you aren't concealing any tubes.' Feeling a little nervous now I obliged. I was ready to perform my duty when the chaperone bent down to my hip level. And I am not boasting when I say this, a quick swivel of the hips and I would have hit him in the eye! Starting to sweat, and not producing anything. I thought I might be able to relax myself if made conversation.

'So mate, are you enjoying the Games?'

'Oh yes,' he replied, 'I am really enjoying watching all the athletes.'

Oh dear.

I tried again: 'So, bit of a bummer you got stuck with this job!'

'Oh no,' he said, 'I volunteered!'

That was it, I was out the door with my empty beaker to join my mates. Another two litres of water and I was finally able to complete my test. I retired 43 drug tests later. No test was ever as stressful as that first one.

BRENNON DOWRICK,
Olympic Gymnast at Barcelona 1992 and Atlanta 1996
SYDNEY NSW

In particular, it was the spectators' faces that I would watch as they entered the Stadium for the first time. I would see hundreds of faces light up each day as they saw the field and the inside stands. I remember one group of people from Wagga arrived as soon as the gates had opened (two hours before the session was scheduled to start) and proceeded to use an entire roll of film before the event even began!

SARAH BOERSON, *Spectator Services*
CLEVELAND QLD

… the Japanese tourist who fell and broke both wrists, but sat through the football game prior to seeking medical attention. That's what I call real dedication to his team!

FELICITY WAY, *Press Help Desk*
CANBERRA ACT

Some of the most memorable experiences include: witnessing the transformation of the Olympic Village to the Paralympic Village – the buses and walkers being replaced by wheelchairs, skateboards and prostheses ... seeing an ambulant Paralympian leading four visually-impaired athletes to lunch ... seeing a Paralympian with no hands completely dress himself ... passing the Paralympic Service Centre with its rows of legs, arms and wheelchairs.
MARGARET SHARPE, *Masseur*
PARADISE POINT QLD

After an eight-hour shift day (it was a long day), someone said to me it was wasting time to do this without pay, but I do not think of it that way because I had learned something each day, met some new friends and I was very overjoyed, overjoyed at being part of the biggest Games, in Sydney. It was a good memory for me in my life.
JENNY KE, *Officer Accreditation*
SYDNEY NSW

After receiving our medical assistance an American gentleman swapped a USA band-aid for an Aussie one. I'm sure you have all heard of the pin-swapping but this must be the only band-aid swap of the Games.
MARIA GODWELL, *Spectator Medical Services*
PERTH WA

... nothing could have stopped the crowd of volunteers that flocked to the stands to watch Australia take gold. The majority of staff had left their post and cheered Simon Fairweather to his victory including myself. Just about every other location in the Archery Park was deserted. If anyone threatened us to stop watching and return to duties we all replied with the same quote: 'What are you going to do? Sack me?!'
LISA GYECSEK, *Risk Manager*
SYDNEY NSW

On our way back Ray suggested that as our Mexican team shirts had fooled the kids we could have a bit of fun with our fellow volunteers so we put it to the test! Ray speaks Spanish and we approached a married couple and he went into action and asked for directions to the tennis – after a few minutes of hand waving and complete frustration, I could not keep a straight face and so gave the game away. Our next victim was a younger girl who had plenty of patience and made us both smile with her remarks, 'Sorry you pair of buggers, I can't speak your lingo, where do you come from anyway?' After proudly displaying our Mexican emblems, Ray came out with, 'Thanks luv, you volunteers are doing a bloody good job.' I'm sorry to say I can't print what she called us, we parted friends and all had a good laugh. Three more times we played the practical jokers and did not get caught out once – by now I had learnt not to laugh. We were called a couple of Bs a few times and I think the ones who were not sure if they were part of a joke were too polite to tell us where to go, but everyone eventually took it in fun – the way it was meant to be.

LEN RILEY, *Field of Play and Swiss Timing*
SYDNEY NSW

Being on at night meant going literally anywhere. After dutifully learning the official Olympic routes, we instead spent the night searching for restaurants, private houses, party sites etc., as long as it seemed to fit the general criteria of being unknown or extremely difficult to find. At times we were flagged down by someone wanting a taxi, quite prepared to pay for the privilege of driving with us and arriving at their destination slower than walking there!

CORRYN ANDERSON, *Driver*
SYDNEY NSW

My favourite time was when I was able to bring my eight-year-old daughter to Sydney during the Para's. I took her to several events and was able to smuggle her into several parties the Aussie team had and into the Aussie team party after the Closing Ceremony. As I teach disabled kids to ride horses she had had an association with the disabled and was keen to see the Para's, so it was a real buzz to see her mixing with all the athletes, people who she had only seen on TV or newspapers. And here she was amongst them, laughing and playing games with them.

KEN WHITE, *Driver*
NAROOMA NSW

Then there was the time when a small group of us after work, unable to get into the Main Stadium because our IDs didn't allow it, got on our motorised buggies and drove through the tunnel, put on our 'work' faces and zoomed straight into the Stadium. We then got into the lift and went up to the VIP's area and sat with 'Bob and Blanche' to watch the track and field finals. All part of a hard day's work (after an eight-hour shift we needed it!).
JUDY KOHN, *Training venue for Track and Field*
MELBOURNE VIC

One of the more interesting incidents I 'investigated' was the disappearance of 20 lambs from Fairfield City Farm. They were in a paddock under the control of SOCOG when it happened. Anyway they were long gone by the time I heard about it. Someone's roast dinner I suspect.
MAUREEN TREVANION, *Loss Investigator*
CANBERRA ACT

It was my involvement with the 'unknown' athletes that gave me the most pleasure. I encountered many such athletes during my six shifts at the Olympic Village. For example, I treated the first athlete ever to compete for Eritrea, the women's 1500m gold medallist from Algeria and a 100m sprinter who didn't qualify but was only one of two athletes from Chad (the other was his sister).
KYLIE BRADFORD, *Physiotherapist*
BRISBANE QLD

Whilst escorting a party of three to the car park pickup point, the lady mentioned she was a gymnast and said, 'Did you know the elder fellow you were talking to was a 100m gold medallist from the Ukraine at Munich in 1972?' Well, I couldn't resist and challenged him to a mock sprint in the covered car park.
RICK PATZOLD, *Protocol Assistant*
MITTAGONG NSW

Paralympics: not the parallel games but rather the essence of true sportsmanship and unity.

CLEOPATRA SCLAVOS, *Physiotherapist*
SYDNEY NSW

I realised I was standing right outside the dressing room for the USA football team. A few of them started kicking a ball around, then they asked if I wanted to join in, so we were all kicking the ball around for a minute before they had to go back into their dressing room!

NATALIE WINSLADE, *Spectator Services*
CANBERRA ACT

The emotions these athletes were feeling at the time were extreme. When we approached them, they had just completed an event that culminated many years of intense preparation. There were tears of joy and tears of despair. It seemed the only emotion matching the level of exuberance after winning a gold medal was the intensity of the devastation after losing one as the favourite.

KEVIN MURPHY, *Doping Control Escort*
SYDNEY NSW

The athletes came on buses. When they got to the Superdome they were given muffins and bottles of water to see them through the time until they left for the Main Stadium. The lack of coffee puzzled some nationalities. Incredibly, the most popular area was the smoking area!

JEANETTE SHARP, *Spectator Services*
SYDNEY NSW

In 1956 I was an 18-year-old apprentice working at Jolimont Railway Yards just across the road from the MCG – venue for the Olympic Games.

With the Olympics coming to Australia again, I was never going to make it as a team member, so I showed the ad in the paper requesting volunteers to my wife, Joan. She has a sister and husband, Helen and John, living in Sydney. And we had a caravan.

'What about we fill this form out and see what happens? We'll do our bit for the country if we get the nod.'

That was October '98. I explained I had a sporting administration background, with Hawthorn and Melbourne football clubs. We had to attend a training session so we drove up and back to Sydney in one weekend. Finally they notified us that we would be working in the main dining room. You couldn't get anywhere better for seeing the athletes' point of view.

As the Games got near, I was also 'randomly' offered the job of on-field marshall for the Opening and Closing Ceremonies. This meant another trip to Sydney.

'Don't they realise some of us have to work for a living!' I said to Joan.

Anyway, it happened to coincide with Hawthorn Football Club's game against the Swans in Sydney, so I was able to watch the game as a board member of Hawthorn Football Club and do my interview at the same time.

Opening night was the fifteenth. Now, at this stage Hawthorn was sailing along with a possibility of getting into the finals. Remember, the Grand Final was held earlier because of the Olympics – the first Saturday in September, not the last! This meant rehearsals were scheduled for Sunday, the day after the Grand Final. North Melbourne made the decision for us. We departed in the second weekend of finals, well short of a flag!

Our relatives have a very small terrace house in Mosman, with a narrow lane at the rear. Luckily our caravan managed to fit, ever so tightly, into their rear car park. That's where we lived for the next five weeks. We worked afternoon shifts, which didn't finish until 11 p.m. The only downside to our location was Spencer, the garbage man, on Monday mornings: beep beep beep at 5 o'clock. Next, the rubbish bins would be up-ended almost through our window. Not much later, the recycle man, then the newspaper pick-up! Wonderful, after arriving home at 12.30 in the morning.

Joan and I were sort of host and hostess in the dining room at the Athletes' Village. We were encouraged not to talk to the athletes. If they wanted to talk to you, sure, but definitely don't hassle them for autographs, or photographs. Peter Brock walked past one day and I said: 'Go

Pies Go!' He didn't know me, but he was great. 'Yeah man!' I was just a guy in a funny white hat.

The dining room was a hands-free zone which meant no bags – they had to be locked away, or stored in shelves. This caused a bit of tension. Early in the first week the atmosphere was very stiff and rigid. You'd say 'Hello' to hundreds of athletes every day. They'd just walk through the door, brutally focused. You might get a nod from some, others would ignore you. It was hard to know if they understood English or not. It was quite a tense period, but as the Games progressed and elimination happened and relaxation started to appear, it became an entirely different environment to work in. Klim, Thorpe, Perkins were very focused. I didn't go near them. You could sort of see them saying through their body language: 'Give me space. Please give me space!' Pat Rafter and Leyton Hewitt were lots of fun. The swimming, cycling and athletics teams all ate together – they enjoyed a lot of laughs.

Most athletes ate in groups, different people, different cultures. Some always looked down, never spoke, others laughed a lot and we soon got to know each other ... slowly! It was like Coles Cafeteria, with thousands of seats. Many of the police, security and volunteers also ate in a specified area without the range of wonderful healthy food. But it was surprising how many police, in particular, broke ranks to move into where the athletes chose their food. Predictably, the magnet was the 'Big Mac' counter. Yes, 'The Golden Arches' were even available to athletes! Everything was free: fruit, fish, pasta, orange juice, etc. But the police and the army guys overlooked the roast beef and chicken for a Big Mac and chips.

There was a stall with a qualified nutrition person, a dietitian. Everything was labelled: the protein content, fat content, everything you wanted to know. If a swimmer, say, was looking for some specific food type, they only needed to ask and, in a matter of minutes, it would be cleared and sitting on their tray. Several teams made separate arrangements for special preparation of foods: e.g. an eye fillet cooked this way with eight eggs sunny-side up. Anything was possible.

It didn't sit very comfortably with me, but as volunteers, we were also asked to take on the role of a 'policeman'. We had to ensure that athletes were not taking unacceptable amounts of food out of the dining room. If a big guy's had his meal and you spotted him walking out with two Big Macs, cheese and biscuits or ice-cream well, that was okay. But, if somebody walked out with a plate of roast beef, we had to be a bit careful. There was a concern that some of the poorer athletes might take stuff back to their room and there is no refrigeration. It goes off and they eat it and we're accused of serving contaminated food in the dining room. We had to use our discretion a bit.

Nevertheless, I tended to turn a blind eye, because I felt that it wasn't really my job to tell somebody, 'You aren't allowed to leave with the food on that plate!' Very awkward, uncomfortable position to be placed in. The supervisors were all paid, even though they had volunteers' uniforms on. I used to say, 'Listen, c'mon, this is your job. I'm not going to make a mongrel of myself!'

Disappointingly, we hooked up the caravan and set off for Melbourne the day after the Closing Ceremony, which meant we missed the Volunteer Tribute March through the streets of Sydney. But the sign on the rear of the van said it all for Joan and I:

GOODBYE SYDNEY and THANKS
TWO MELBOURNE VOLUNTEERS

All the way to Melbourne, people on the streets would wave and cheer, cars would toot their horns in recognition. I guess being volunteers to the greatest sporting event on the planet, we could ask no more.

Yes, Joan and I would do it all again. Now where can I learn the Greek language inside four years?

IVAN AND JOAN MOORE, *Athletes' Dining Room Hosts*
MELBOURNE VIC

My role was medal/flower bearer for the medal ceremonies, and also to supervise the transport and security of the medals and flowers from the time we picked them up at SOCOG Headquarters until the medals went around the athletes' necks and the Olympic flowers into their hands.

The Australian water polo women had fought hard and long to have their sport admitted to the Olympics, so when they made it into the final against America there was much excitement amongst my team, as we were rostered to perform the medal ceremony. When Australia won the game in such a dramatic fashion (scored the winning goal in the last ten seconds) the excitement 'Back of House' had reached a fever pitch and my brave girls were becoming more than a little nervous.

The only hitch to the ceremony came when, after the entry of the athletes to the medal podium poolside, the camera crews closed ranks, blocking the only path for the medal/flower bearers to reach the podium with the most important part of the ceremony (outside the athletes), the medals. Luckily I had anticipated the problem and having sprinted ahead of the girls was able to manhandle the camera people out of the way to allow the girls through.

The ceremony was very special and most of the medal/flower bearers were unable to control their emotions, with the tears flowing freely.

PHILLIP DRYDEN, *Medal Supervisor*
LISMORE NSW

I traded pins until I was blue in the face meeting some of the neatest people and athletes around. The sad part was watching the poorer athletes sell their participant medals and uniforms ... 'A hundred dollars is a few months' salary where I come from – can't eat souvenirs!' as one athlete told me.

PAT HASSETT, *Spectator Services*
INDIANA USA

China had a seven-foot five-inch player. He stopped to talk to me. I am five-foot five-inches tall and got a cramp in my neck looking up at him. I asked him what the weather was like up there. He jokingly said 'snowing'. We both laughed. He was the tallest basketball player at the Olympics.

PHILIP CRONIN, *Spectator Services*
EASTWOOD NSW

I was fortunate enough to speak not only to spectators but also with Olympians before and after their heats. The gratitude they had towards volunteers and the compliments we received by both swimmers and spectators is something that made me float on air.

NICOLE STEFANO, *Spectator Services*
MELBOURNE VIC

One day I had to climb an umpire's chair and use a megaphone to tell 20,000 people where the bus stops (if my friends could see me now, I thought!).
GAYNOR STANFORD, *Spectator Services*
MELBOURNE VIC

While riding on the train you could see the cauldron with the flame burning so brightly which for me was quite inspirational; it put a lump in my throat. Also going to work was made easier by wearing our fabulous uniforms – so colourful and made us stand out. I loved it.
GAIL ROMARI, *Spectator Services*
LALOR VIC

When Simon Fairweather won the gold medal for Australia it was the most fantastic feeling that I think I will ever experience. I had met Simon on several occasions, so to have him standing eight feet in front of me, shooting the final arrows to win gold, sent a special tingle up my spine. It is a feeling that is very hard to describe. I was having trouble even talking.
JOHN SUTHERN, *Archery Results Commentary*
CANBERRA ACT

Briefly, Max, I retired from the NSW Police Force in 1997. An early retirement owing to injuries I suffered whilst in Vietnam. I am now 52 years young!

I volunteered to be a driver during the Olympics as I felt I should help out, plus the fact that I thought it would be an experience to remember. I didn't realise how much of an experience I would be in for.

Whilst doing my driver training, I was asked if I would volunteer to be a 'tour guide' for other drivers. This entailed taking the drivers out to all the Olympic venues to familiarise them with the particular routes they must take. As Olympic drivers, there were designated routes to all the venues whilst in official vehicles. As a result of the tours I conducted, I was then asked to volunteer to take the 'envoys' on the same tour. The envoys were a hand-picked group of 30 drivers who were attached to the Australian Olympic team. Their role was to ferry the athletes to various venues and basically be available to them at all times. Rob Thornton (the operations director for the AOT) is the guy who hand-picked the envoys. Whilst on the coach, Rob explained to me the role of the envoy and what a select group they were. With my background, I had the front to question Rob as to why I was not one of the hand-picked envoys. Rob didn't say a lot during the course of the day. Probably thought what a hide I had. He asked me a lot of questions about myself, particularly my background.

At the end of the day, Rob asked me: if he could get a release from the ORTA drivers, would I be prepared to work with his group? If so, he had a particular job in mind. Later in the week he phoned me to say that the release had been arranged and would I meet him in town. That is the beginning of my allocation to John Coates. I met John in town and apparently the chemistry was OK and I was confirmed as his driver.

For the next 12 months, two days a week, I continued to act as tour guide for the ORTA drivers.

There was a strict stipulation during the Olympics that drivers were to work no more than 12 hours per shift and no more than five shifts per week.

On 17 August, I rocked in to the Olympic Village where John handed me the keys to his nice new Caprice. Accommodation was arranged for me at the Olympic support unit at the old Westmead Boys Home, about five minutes from the Olympic Village. A rather apt place for me to stay, so some of my mates and family say. This was done as I live at Grose Vale, some 60 minutes travel from the Village. Coatesy said this was so that I could get some rest. I didn't know what I was in for.

For the first three or four days, I didn't have to start until 9 a.m. And then the crunch came. 'See you at 5.45 tomorrow morning, Neal,' said John. 'That's OK,' said I.

I must not have heard him say, 'For the next 33 days.'

From that day on it was go, go, go. Meetings in at the Regent Hotel, city, every morning. Then out to all the various venues. Back at the Village by about 4 p.m. Wow, I thought, the first day!

'Have a rest for half an hour, Neal. Then we are off to Admiralty House for dinner with the PM.'

'You beauty,' I said to myself 'Dinner with the PM.' How stupid of me.

When we got there, Coatesy said, 'Grab yourself a decent bite and put it on my tab. See you back here at 10 p.m.' What a let down. It wasn't, really, as I didn't expect to dine with the PM. So I had two curry pies and peas at Harry De Wheels. I paid him back.

Before I went home he gave me a copy of his diary for the duration. I wiped the sweat off my brow. However, I was ready for it. With the exception of one or two nights, the earliest we finished was 10.40 p.m. We had some extremely long days, Max.

When my first five days were up after performing 12-hour shifts, Coatesy asked me if I wanted a couple of days off. By the tone of his voice, I could tell that he wanted me to stay on.

'You're not taking this car off me,' I said.

'I was hoping you'd say that,' he replied.

That was the start of 37 long days in my life as a volunteer. I went home and saw my family only once in that time.

Let me tell you how family-orientated John Coates is, Max. My daughter was off to Europe during the Games and asked me if I would see her off at the airport. My itinerary did not allow this, I indicated. During my conversations with Coatesy, families came up, the very same day Alanna was flying out of the country.

'I'll just make a few alterations to my diary and go to the soccer in Melbourne tonight, Neal,' he said. 'That way, you can drop me off at the airport, then go to see your daughter off and spend the night at home. But, I am back in Sydney at 7 a.m. You'll have a long drive, mate.'

I had the extreme honour of accompanying Coatesy to all the gold medal winning events, as well as many others, including the Opening and Closing Ceremonies. He did not treat me as a driver. I was his maaaaaaaaaaate. Everywhere we went, he introduced me to the dignitaries to whom he spoke. Not as his driver but just as Neal.

Talk about having a big head. It was nearly as big then as when I spoke to one 'Tangles' on the evening of 15 May. 'Was that *the* Mr Walker, Dad?' asked one of my daughters.

Norman May (Nugget) is a very personal friend of John's. With all the crap going on about Olympic personnel carrying the torch, John, being the person he is and one to stay out of the limelight, gave his torch relay spot to Nugget. We had to see him carrying the torch so off we went to Chatswood to watch. When Nugget finally handed the torch over to John's wife, Pauline, sweat was pissing out of him, his face was the colour of a well-versed drunk and his legs were like jelly. He had to sit down on the sidewalk and take a rest. 'How is it, Nugget?' asked John. 'Don't do that to me again, Coatesy,' said Nugget.

One of the brighter moments of the Games was when the Aussie water polo team took on the Russians. Peter Montgomery, one of John's team managers and a former Olympian water polo player, told me to have a very close look at the girls as their cossie tops were often ripped off during the game. Too true. After a while, instead of replacing the cossies, they just kept on with the game with the attention of the crowd placed squarely on the boobs and not the ball or the clock. All OK. We won and went on to win the gold medal. That was one hell of a night, Max. By the time the girls had finished rejoicing, it was well after 11 p.m. As the girls train at the Ryde pool, their drinking hole is the Gladesville Hotel.

'How do you feel about a trip to Gladesville?' asked Coatesy.

'No problems, maaaaaate,' said I.

Needless to say, the pub, which is capable of holding about 300 people, was jam-packed with about six or seven hundred. 'I'll just have a couple with "my girls",' he said. We left the pub at 3.30 a.m. By the time I had him back to the Village it was just on 4 a.m. 'Have a sleep-in this morning. See you at 6 a.m., maaaaaaate.'

'That's great,' I said. It's amazing how good that extra 15 minutes was.

I had initially signed on to do the Paralympics as well but one might guess that I was absolutely stuffed by then and I had to knock them back, unfortunately.

As the Olympics drew to a close, times became sadder by the hour. My last official job with John was to attend the athletes concert at the Capitol theatre. All the envoys were invited to attend. However, Max, I indicated to John that I would wait in the car, as it was not my place. A lot of toing and froing was had before I finally won and stayed in the car. Thank God. I slept in a No Stopping Zone for two hours. The first time I had a sleep on the job. It was really sad, Max. Our intentions were to drive John back to the Village and say goodbye to him, there. When John walked out of the Capitol with the PM, he ushered him to his car. He paused for a moment, just prior to opening the door for John Howard, walked over to me and gave me the biggest cuddle I have ever had. If it wasn't serious it would be funny. Well, I guess it was funny. There was Coatesy, all five foot nothing of him, standing on the footpath giving this big guy, six foot two and standing on the roadway, an almighty cuddle. The PM walked over and said to me, 'Great job, Neal.' Well, talk about a big head. Coatesy gave me a cab charge and told me to get a few beers on the way home. One hundred and sixty-three dollars later, I was half pissed on six beers by the time I got home. I can tell you that the welcome mat was not out. The old story: even the dog had a go at me.

Max, I didn't get to meet too many other drivers as I was not prepared to tell them what a ball I was having. Some of the poor buggers were sitting around for the whole shift. When they saw my car, with all the numerous authority stickers on it, they would ask me was I driving the queen. 'Nah. Just washing the car,' I would say.

I had such an adrenaline rush that I was able to keep the hours I did. I was honoured to work for the 'Boss' of the Olympics, a man with no power pushes. A man who did not want publicity. A quiet achiever, I would call him, plus a very knowledgeable one.

Performing my duties at the Olympics is one that I will *never* forget, let alone being the 'Boss's' driver. I had the privilege of meeting many VIPs including the PM and his wife. Sat next to Princess Anne and her army of security men; Anita Keating, what a wonderful lady she is. I had the absolute pleasure of meeting our athletes of the past. The likes of Laurie Lawrence, what a wag he is; Dawn Fraser, one of the boys she is. John Bertrand and Peter Brock were there to psych up the athletes. Then there was Herb Elliot, John Konrads and of course Marlene Mathews: a graceful lady. Our sportsmen and women of today: I could name nearly all of them but would not want to sound like a name dropper. I have done a bit of that already but only to tell you how honoured I was to obtain the position I did and meet that many people, who 'yesterday' were unknowns, apart from their names, to a layman like myself.

One of the great feelings after the Games was the volunteers' parade in Sydney. I met many of the drivers whom I had the pleasure of showing around the sites. They knew what I had done and were very envious. Nevertheless, we got on well and had a great barbecue after the parade. I even carried Fatso the wombat.

Many memories, Max, which I will never forget, and mementos, too. Even an athlete's doona which was given to me and now lies proudly on my daughter's bed.

Max, this is a fairly lengthy overview. The intention was not to make it too long. However, I had many aspects to cover. So, belt it around as much as you like and remember what my dear old dad said: N.B.A.B. … 'Never Bullshit a Bullshitter'. Use it if you like at any stage.

Best of luck with the book, Tangles, and thank you for asking me for my input. My kids are stoked.

Fondest Regards,

NEAL CREMEN, *Driver*
SYDNEY NSW

My ears twitched with the media passengers, hoping to catch a hint as to who was going to light the Olympic flame. One unusual trip was with an immaculately dressed naval officer who directed me to a shopping centre to buy an ironing board and iron so he could press the flags that were to be raised at the winners' presentation ceremony.

KATHLEEN HAMEY, *Driver Taxi Service*
SYDNEY NSW

I was surprised when my supervisor for the evening sat us down to list our names. When he got to me and saw my name tag, he said, 'Are you Bob Grant from Scotch College?' – 'Yes,' I replied.

'The Olympic javelin thrower?' – 'Yes.'

'The Housemaster of Mackie Boarding House?' – 'Yes.'

'The Housemaster who gave me two of the best?!'

What could I say but sorry and, 'Did you deserve it?'

'Yes,' he said to my relief. 'You'd already warned me three times.'

It had certainly done him no harm for he is a fine and successful man. I was pleased to see him again.

BOB GRANT, *Spectator Services*
Javelin Thrower at 1956 Melbourne Olympics
MELBOURNE VIC

As the Games were environmentally friendly, rubbish was of a big concern. In the dining room we had designated bins for compostable rubbish, hard rubbish, bottles and liquids. It was our responsibility to watch and check athletes. We made it fun, even giving awards for the best teams. Canada, Holland and New Zealand seemed to score regularly! One morning the Aussie tennis team approached with their trays and I commented,'They *should* know which bins are which.' Patrick Rafter proceeded to tip all his into the compostable bin. I gave him a motherly reprimand: 'Patrick, you know better than that!' Whereby he put his arm around me and said,'Sorry, I won't do it again.' Being a keen tennis fan, that made my day! Mark Phillipousus arrived later. 'Slept in again,' he said, but he coped with the appropriate bins very well.

JOAN GRANT, *Dining Hall Assistant*
MELBOURNE VIC

Lots of funny things happened around the Village. Everyone decorated their houses with flags, banners and good luck messages. I think the Aussies won. There was even a Sydney Harbour Bridge made out of tin foil along the front of one house, complete with Opera House and boats in the harbour. The British team brought their own telephone box and Canadians brought their mascot, Bruce the Moose, all 220 kilos of him. Bruce the Moose disappeared from the roof of their headquarters. A ransom note was delivered and the NSW police turned the site into a crime scene. Bruce was returned the night of the Opening Ceremony by a forklift.

MARION GOODING, *Information Station*
WHITTINGTON VIC

… it was also quite fun to eat your meals at the staff dining hall because it's just below the weightlifting competition and when they drop the bar the room shakes. Hold on to your forks (which, by the way, are made of recyclable corn starch – I guess if you get really hungry you can eat them too!).

SHEILA CONSAUL ('A Sheila Down Under'), *Press Conference Supervisor*
VIRGINIA USA

As I drove north along the Hume Highway with my boats, heading towards Sydney and the Paralympics, I was pretty excited. It was the last day of the Olympics and I had timed my drive so as to arrive just before the Closing Ceremony, so I could watch the fireworks on the harbour with friends I was staying with in Mosman. It was the culmination of a fantastic two weeks which I'd spent glued to the television. Not out of laziness – it was just that the Olympics were so inspirational. Now it was our turn. This was my first Paralympics, and given that this was the first time sailing was included as a full medal sport I was unbelievably proud to be part of Australia's first-ever Paralympic sailing team. Two gold medals were up for grabs in the Paralympics, which we were hoping to put next to the two golds, a silver and a bronze won by the Australian Olympic sailing team.

Our first contact with the volunteers was at the airport, the day after I arrived. We had to pick up the guys from Western Australia and all their gear and also get our accreditation organised. The volunteers were easy to pick – their uniform had become so familiar during television coverage of the Olympics, we had no trouble identifying them. Despite the warnings of more seasoned Paralympians, accreditation was so easy – a check on who we were and then bingo, we had our ID around our necks. The volunteers couldn't have been more helpful which was indeed a sign of things to come.

After accreditation came the interesting job of getting eight guys, three wheelchairs and two motorised scooters into a 4WD and a station wagon. Oh, and not to mention luggage, sails and all the other gear sailors trudge around with. The sails were tied down to the roof of my wagon, the straps running over the roof and through the windows and tightened. Somehow or other we managed to get everyone and everything in okay and off we went to our hotel. I'm not quite sure what the hotel staff thought as we parked in the driveway and extricated everyone and the gear out of the cars. Eventually we got everything sorted and we all got settled in our rooms ready for action the next day.

Normally when we go sailing there is hardly anyone around to either help or watch us. Suddenly it was full-on: at the Rushcutters Bay sailing venue we were going though metal detectors and security checks, and there were volunteer officials and helpers everywhere. Being part of the Aussie team was great – the volunteers made a special fuss of us, and there was lots of friendly banter between us and the security people.

At first all the attention from the volunteer helpers was a bit much and I actually thought there were too many people around, as we normally manage without a lot of help except from our coach. However, we quickly got used to being pampered! In fact, it was great just knowing there were people around to do anything for us. A lot of the volunteers were known to us because they'd been interested in disabled sailing for some time and we'd met them at other sailing events, and we were pretty happy they were there as they had had lots of experience with guys in wheelchairs. I could see a lot of the international competitors were really grateful for their help as some had come with very small teams.

The water police were the friendliest guys there, I think. They were desperate to get hold of some of our clothing – any of it, really. You wouldn't believe what they offered to swap with us. Mind you, I don't blame them: we got beautiful sailing gear, courtesy of Musto and Nike, and the feeling of wearing the Australian coat-of-arms and the motto 'Australian Paralympic Team, Sydney 2000' is something I can't really describe.

One of the special things about the Paralympics for me was that my wife was a volunteer at the sailing venue, in the media team. Like all the volunteers who came from places other than Sydney, she had to find and pay for her own accommodation, but she loved it. We couldn't spend much time together, but we have sailed and campaigned together for the past three years so it was great to share part of the Paralympics experience with her.

When the Australian team won gold in the three-person sailing event on the final day of Paralympic sailing, it was a special moment for every Australian at Rushcutters Bay. The best thing about the medal ceremony was that it was held at the sailing venue, so all the volunteers who had put in so many long days – in rain, wind and sun – could watch the Aussies get up and receive their gold medals. And then everyone could join in the barbecue and drinks afterwards. It was the most wonderful experience.

For me, there were two great things about the Paralympic volunteers. The first thing was that they'd volunteered at all, giving up their holidays or free time, paying their own way, and doing their jobs with the greatest of good grace and professionalism. The second was that they'd chosen to do this for the 'poor cousin', the Paralympics. Some had relatives or friends or acquaintances in the Games, but many had no connection other than a feeling that they were doing good. And they did.

MICHAEL McLEAN, *Paralympic Sailing Team, Gold Medallist at Sydney 2000*
MELBOURNE VIC

There was only one complaint from the athletes and that was there was no facility to get their legs waxed!

SENTA TAFT-HENDRY, *International Information*
NEWCASTLE NSW

I worked as a massage therapist in the Village and I was amazed at the variety of people who came in, chatted and gave us pins and gifts. I couldn't believe athletes were so impressed with my work they wanted to see me again. That is what made the Games for me: everyone got on so well and if you were walking through the Village and you saw an athlete you worked on, you would say hello.

NATALIE COLEMAN, *Massage Therapist*
ASPENDALE VIC

On the way back I tried to communicate with him, but I couldn't. I asked other drivers if they spoke Italian, but they didn't. I think he understood what I was trying to do because he started to write me little notes. Turns out he could write English but not speak it!

AMANDA DENGATE, *Driver*
SYDNEY NSW

When the athletes arrived from the Village, together with a small group of volunteers, I was there to greet and direct them to the Stadium. As the American team alighted from their bus, one young sportsman gave me his camera and said, 'Would you please take my photo with the Williams sisters?' Here was I, completely starstruck, shaking the hands of some of the world's best athletes and it was obvious that many of these athletes who were representing their country as members of their Olympic team, were just as starstruck as I was.

WENDY FAZIO, *Spectator Services*
SYDNEY NSW

One day at the Uniform Distribution and Accreditation Centre, Jodie and I thought we would try on the size 50 trousers, and guess what? They fitted the two of us in together – one woman in each leg! Everyone giggled at us. Everyone was getting up to something …

GWEN COOTES, *Uniform Distribution*
PEAKHURST NSW

I was a team leader at the baseball and I got a call over on my two-way saying there were two people down the bottom near the coffee shop without accreditation. They wanted me to go down and sort it out.

So off I went, and said, 'Where is your accreditation?'

'We haven't got any,' they said.

'So how did you get in?' I asked.

There was a chap with them and he said, 'I bought them in.'

'Actually, we're Bat Men,' they said.

To which I replied, 'I don't care if you're SUPERMEN, you still cannot be in here without accreditation!'

The bloke with me laughed, and explained to me later that the so-called bat men were the people who looked after the players' bats. I just thought they were pulling my leg, so it really backfired on me. But you have to laugh, and we had some very funny times.

DOROTHY WILLIAMS, *Pioneer volunteer*
PROSPECT NSW

The best job that the volunteers in my area got was the 'seat minding job'. To watch any match you needed an official access pass to the spectator areas. Our only 'official ticket' was to mind two rows of seats behind the cameramen in the grandstands. The rationale was that these tickets weren't sold and the rowdiest fans would gather in these seats and 'overly support their team', disrupting the cameramen. We had to keep them clear, but at the same time they were our free ticket to Olympic basketball. So fans would ask, but no, those seats were not available! We would talk to people in the stands who would tell us how great all the volunteers were, but no one was getting those seats!

We looked after those seats like no one else ever has before in the true spirit of Olympic volunteering and in doing so we saw every men's and women's basketball team play.

ANTHONY DE JONG, *Venue Assistant*
MELBOURNE VIC

One morning I picked up a male passenger and his son from the back entrance of the Regent Hotel. He told me he was an American IOC official and had a big, soft bag with him. He asked me to drive him to an address on Argyle Street. I thought he would be looking for the touristy end but no, he wanted somewhere further along. He could not explain to me exactly where he wanted to go and looked a little embarrassed. Finally he made me stop outside a laundromat called Wash on the Rocks. He got out of the car mumbling something about not everybody being able to afford to have their laundry done at the Regent! It just goes to show that not all IOC officials had a free-wheeling expense account.

IAN KEITH, *Driver*
SYDNEY NSW

Early in the morning the police, with their dogs, would check under tables and the surrounding area for explosives. One Sunday morning before 6 a.m., as we were preparing for the passengers on the first flight in for the day, there was a policewoman checking under the tables. Someone asked, 'Where's the dog?'

'It's too early for him,' she said. It appears even the dogs could sleep in on Sunday.

RALPH TOPLIS, *Accreditation and Security*
LINDFIELD NSW

We have been involved in sport all our lives and we love the Olympics. We were lucky enough to be at the Opening Ceremony in our home town Melbourne in 1956. In fact, we were so close to the flame, we saw Ron Clarke flinch as he lit it. When SOCOG called for volunteers we applied right away because we felt it would be wonderful to be involved in such a great event, and we wanted to do anything we could to help Australia stage a successful Games. None of this Melbourne versus Sydney nonsense for us.

THOROLD MERRETT, *Spectator Services*
MELBOURNE VIC

(Thorold played for the 'Pies from 1950–1960, playing in two VFL Premierships and was wingman in Collingwood's Team of the Century.)

I experienced such an incredible sense of joy, of pride and of gratitude for the opportunity I was being given to sing the Olympic hymn in its native Greek language at the Opening Ceremony as a member of the Greek Orthodox Archdiocese of Australia. Standing up there on stage, I don't think I have ever trembled as much. My sister, who was next to me, linked her pinkie finger around mine and I could feel her shaking with nervous anticipation …

ANDREANA ANGELOS, *Singer at the Opening Ceremony*
SYDNEY NSW

I picked up officials from the Wentworth Hotel (husband and wife). They were from Spain and I drove them to the Stadium. On the way they asked me if the traffic was always this bad? I said, 'It's quiet at the moment.' We were approaching the Anzac bridge and as we were going over I told them it was named the Anzac Bridge but the Aussies have nicknamed it 'Madonna's Bra'. The lady said, 'Does Madonna know about this?' I said, 'If she doesn't know now she will soon because everyone will tell her.'

HENRY PITTMAN, *Driver*
ENGADINE NSW

At the Paralympics it was more interesting because they have a different attitude towards sport and life in general. Watching a game of goal ball (which I have never heard of before) telling the spectators to sit down, be quiet and wait till the game had finished was a challenge. It is the only sport I believe where the spectators have to be absolutely silent during the game.

MIRIAM MYERS, *Spectator Services*
BEROWRA NSW

I was stationed in a first-aid room at Olympic Stadium during the Paralympics when I was called to a casualty sitting 19 rows back at the finish line where a series of track finals were being run. Quick assessment determined stabilisation and extrication using the available personnel. Via the venue command centre, two red-sleeved nurses came and the medicab sent for. An off-duty purple-sleeved volunteer fetched the folding-chair for the first-aid room and a yellow-sleeved male volunteer and male police officer offered their help and awaited instructions. The casualty was on the way to the medical centre within 15 minutes of the initial assessment due to the teamwork of complete strangers.

ALISON REEVES, *St John Ambulance*
SYDNEY NSW

A visitor complained quite vocally to me and surrounding patrons that the walk from the station to the archery was far too long – about three kilometres. I happened to notice the date on his ticket, which was hanging

around his neck. Yes, you guessed it, he was there on the wrong day. Needless to say, he then left quietly, feeling a little embarrassed I'm sure.
BOB HOOTON, *Spectator Services*
EAGLEVALE NSW

If you have never been to a shooting complex (and we hadn't) then go to this one – it has the most amazing equipment and technology … We were fortunate to watch our country win the gold and silver medal and we also had our photo taken with Michael Diamond. As each of the athletes left the competition venue and came down the ramp, we got them to sign our outdoor table. The medal winners put a circle and the type of medal they won next to their names and the others signed it with their name and country. We also included a portion for all the volunteers to sign. This table was raffled at our farewell function and the proceeds donated to charity.
PAM CORNISH, *Shooting Venue Assistant*
ASHCROFT NSW

At Blacktown Olympic Centre, a top-of-the-line Alpha arrived at the access gates, a young volunteer lady driver at the wheel. She was dropping off an Italian diplomat to watch the baseball. He had the right passes but the young lady had none. To the rescue the police: park your car over there and I'll try to get a day pass for you. A while later he returned with the goods, which put a big smile on her face. She thanked him, hopped into the Alpha and tramped it – BANG – straight in the side of the police car. The same poor bloke who did her the good deed.

Her response was, 'Must be in the wrong gear.'
DENIS BROPHY, *Spectator Services*
SEVEN HILLS NSW

I was just directing people on level one, not far from a long, long, queue of ladies waiting for the loo. Now to help out and give some of them less waiting time, I said it would be okay if they used the physically impaired toilet; as long as the green bar was showing on the door lock it would be okay. While saying this I was opening the door for the first one ... only to find that there was already a lady inside! Seated! Who hadn't locked the door. Very quickly and very red-faced, I apologised profusely and closed the door!

DON BOWN, *Spectator Services*
SYDNEY NSW

We had access to all areas including press areas. Half-jokingly I said to the head of Language Interpretation, 'If you need a Dutch interpretor I would be happy to help'. She said all the Dutch spoke English but that she would keep it in mind. Soon after, the Dutch woman cyclist, Leontien Zijlaard, won the individual pursuit and broke the world record – the first world record to go at the new Dunc Velodrome. I was minding my own business at the press conference when the first question was fielded by a European journo in Dutch. Leontien answered in Dutch. Immediately an English journo asked what had been said and there was some pandemonium among the English-speaking reporters. The language services girl grabbed me and said, 'Quick, get up there on stage and sit next to Leontien. There's a microphone for you.' Fortunately the translation went well. The French interpreter had a much tougher time of it.

TONY ADRIAANSEN, *Spectator Services*
LINDFIELD NSW

As a member of the 2000 Australian Olympic team I was not only proud of the whole team's performance but I was proud of the whole country as it was everyone that made these Olympics the most successful ever. Without a doubt though the Games would not have been what they are without the volunteers. In a word these guys were amazing.

It wasn't until halfway through the Games that I realised how much these people had sacrificed to be a part of the Olympic spirit and I am extremely grateful they did because they made the experience that much more enjoyable.

Their enthusiasm and passionate interest was contagious and what made me even prouder was the way they cared not just about the hometown kids but all the athletes of the world. Walking around talking to the athletes from other countries and sports it was great to hear them say how much they appreciated the volunteers.

Like everyone involved with the Olympics we all have our favourite volunteer stories. Some of mine include one gentleman who asked me to sign his autograph book which had the autographs of the 1956 Australian Olympic swim team. Or there were the two young girls on our door in the dining hall, who whenever they were on and I came up with my bag they put it in the same spot so it could never get mixed up!

Without a doubt, Ernie, one of the car drivers, was my favourite volunteer. He gave me a lift, once from the Village to the city and then back again. I remember walking out to the bus terminal and was going to get on a bus and catch it into the city. I was going out to dinner with a good friend on the American swim team, Kristy Kowal. Cool to get a car ride. So I walked up to the car depot and just asked jokingly and got a lift. It was so cool, and it was so much easier than the bus/train option.

After Ernie dropped us off he said call him and he may be able to bring us back to the Village but could not promise anything. After a really nice dinner overlooking the Harbour Bridge we were walking towards the train station and I thought what the heck I'll call him as it was raining. Luckily for us, Ernie was in the city, came and got us and drove us back to the Village, dropping us as close to the entrance as he could. It was a really fun, entertaining and educational drive to Homebush. I asked Ernie what I could do for him and he gave me an accreditation he wanted Grant Hackett to sign as he had already got Kieren Perkins to sign it. I finally found Grant on the last day and got him to sign the accreditation but by this stage I had misplaced Ernie's phone number in my bombsite of a bedroom. So to Ernie if you are reading this, thank you and I am sorry I never got your accreditation back to you!

To all the volunteers, thank you for being a part of my dream, you made all the sacrifices and hard times worthwhile.

DANIEL KOWALSKI, *Swimmer*
Silver and Bronze Medallist, Atlanta 1996 and
Gold Medallist Sydney 2000 for 4 x 200m freestyle relay
MELBOURNE VIC

One event that did involve us during the competition was the hurdle event. Because it was part of 'the show' a great deal of rehearsal went into coordinating the setting-up and removal of the hurdles. Timing was critical. I can honestly say I was a member of the unofficial 'Stadium Australia Olympic driving team', as the trolleys which held the hurdles were pulled by battery powered, fully enclosed bubble carts. During rehearsal on the day before competition started, on one of our many runs, the audio people in the Stadium played the tune *Baby Elephant Walk*, much to the amusement of the hurdle crew.

DENNIS LORENZIN, *Equipment Attendant*
ADELAIDE SA

I enjoyed every single working day but especially on 20 September – my most memorable time – the night Japan played against Brazil. Both teams were desperate to win to get through to the finals, both teams' supporters had reputations for their fanatical enthusiasm. Five thousand three hundred Japanese fans came in 160 buses that night. Half of them arrived on the day and left after the match returning to Japan. They called the tour 'three days no night accommodation tour'.

HATSUE CAVANAGH, *Spectator Services*
NAGASAKI JAPAN

The people of Sydney were fantastic (I come from the bush of Canberra). Each morning on the way to the Darling Harbour depot, I would stop at a small takeaway shop for an orange juice and paper. The owners, on seeing my volunteer uniform, would ensure I received first service and sometimes a free snack. Upon completion of work, some days I would drop into a small club in Regent Street Redfern and after two days found it difficult to buy a drink as the locals were only too keen to know about the volunteering and thank me for participating in 'their' Games.

GEOFF SULLIVAN, *Driver*
CANBERRA ACT

Both on and off the playing field, Australian sport, and tennis in particular, was primarily developed through a huge network of unpaid volunteers at club, association, state, national and international level.

Professionalism in sport on the playing field, including Open tennis, has seen some of the key volunteer positions replaced by professional administrators, officials and coaches, but the role of volunteers remains paramount.

Nothing demonstrates this more than the Sydney Olympic Games where the volunteers literally 'stole the show' and ensured that volunteerism, which was in danger of dying, will endure for at least another generation.

GEOFF POLLARD, *President of Tennis Australia*
MELBOURNE VIC

During the second day working at the men's triathlon, walking across the Domain on my way to catch the train back to Katoomba, an Irish guy and his partner asked me where the boxing was on. I said, 'At Darling Harbour.' As I had finished my shift and they were not from Sydney, I said, 'Follow me, and I will take you there, not a problem.' As I weaved my way through Sydney streets, I gathered another three people who asked where the boxing was held: again I said, 'Follow me.' It was great just to help others. After making it to the boxing, I turned around after a 'thank you' from all of them and headed back on my long journey to Katoomba for a sleep before the next rise at 3 a.m.

GRANT SMITH, *Spectator Services*
MELBOURNE VIC

On the very last day of the Paralympic Games, my roster finished at 4 p.m., and I had to catch the 6.40 p.m. plane back to Brisbane, so I didn't have time to change. I caught the train to the airport and joined the check-in queue. As I still had my uniform on, I was being asked for directions. Even at the airport check-in counter, a lady wanted to know how to use her electronic ticketing card and asked me for directions. Once a volunteer, always a volunteer.

THERESE CHAPPELL, *Staff Administration & Presentation Assistant*
BRISBANE QLD

In 1999 I was contracted by TAFE to train ORTA (transport) volunteers in the principles of customer service, cultural diversity, etc. After a few sessions of telling these lovely people how to be nice to people – as if they didn't already know – I decided to be a transport volunteer myself. Not only did this have a positive effect on the training sessions when the participants found out I was 'one of them' but I wouldn't have missed being a volunteer for anything! I worked for three weeks at the Sydney Olympic Village as an NOC driver for the Swaziland team and loved every minute of my Olympic experience. I have no idea whether I practised what I'd preached – all I know is – I had a ball and so did the Swazis!

JOY NASON, *Driver*
SYDNEY NSW

Quilters around Australia made and donated 650 patchwork quilts. They were hung at Sydney Olympic Park, and sold during the Games. Over $500,000 was raised and donated to the Paralympics. Themes were Olympic, Paralympic, and Australian flora and fauna, landscapes and scenes of Sydney. I met a man looking at one particular quilt. He said it was the second-last one his wife had made. I asked about the last one she made. 'It was on her coffin,' he replied. Such was the love and devotion that these women showed, spending so many hours sewing for such a good cause.

JUDY MCMAHON, *Spectator Services*
SYDNEY NSW

Some foreign journalists at the Velodrome considered me a story rather than the other way around. Whilst checking media accreditation, one reporter began to laugh and point me out to his colleagues. Within 30 seconds the group of about ten were giggling like school kids, lifting my accreditation, nodding at me and shaking my hand. I laughed with them because I'm Tracy Chapman. I only wish I could sing.

TRACY-JANE CHAPMAN, *Spectator Services*
BRISBANE QLD

Whilst I enjoyed the Olympics it was agreed with my fellow volunteers that the Paralympic experience was far more rewarding simply because of the closer contact with athletes. We encountered all levels of disability from wheelchair, limb loss, cerebral palsy and blind athletes requiring differing levels of assistance. We were required to ask, 'How may I help you?' Some needed no help, others required to be led out to the blocks and held steady for the start. With others we carried arms or legs or pushed wheelchairs to collect them at the other end of the pool after their event and assisted them back to the change rooms.

BARRIE DAWSON, *Multiple Roles at Aquatic Centre*
SYDNEY NSW

There were about seven or eight charter boats in our group and they were all fishing vessels. The drivers were all game fishermen and knew each other quite well. They were in frequent radio contact and used to chat away to one another on the radio. At the beginning of the Games they did not know a lot about sailing and didn't know one class from another. By the end of the Games they were certainly more aware of sailing but I am not sure they were ever going to be converts from game fishing to sailing. One day I heard one of them say over the radio to another: 'I am not sure whether I'll take up sailing or knitting when I retire.' That said it all.

IAN KINGSFORD SMITH, *Sailing Event Adviser*
SYDNEY NSW

The contrast in events was enormous. Where the swimming and water polo events commanded the ear-piercing shrieks of the crowd, the diving

and synchronised swimming events produced a hush to the point where you could hear a pin drop. We moved from high excitement to still-life …
GRAHAM BEATSON, *Safety Officer*
HEATHCOTE NSW

I spent some time on the entrance door as a ticket taker where we had some funny experiences. We had Chelsea Clinton, Nick Greiner, Ernie Dingo, Darryl Somers and one particular evening when the seating was restricted, a gent came through and wanted to bring some friends in. One of our vollies, who we christened 'Hitler', refused his entry and we had to call security, who sorted it out. At this precise moment a gent appeared at my door with his wife. He had the right accreditation, but he also needed to have a ticket. It was Sandy Hollway. I said, 'I hope you have the right ticket,' and he said, 'Yes'. Don't know what I would have done really if he had not. He just smiled and told us what a great job we were doing.
MAURYA ROBSON, *Spectator Services*
SYDNEY NSW

" Being on television every weekend for a decade and a half talking sport means that in quite a few households many parents have seen more of me than they have of their kids. Five hours on Saturday arvo and a couple more on Sunday morning. I know a few people who used to set their clocks by the start of 'Wide World of Sport'.

This all means I've got a recognisable head! Five broken noses, droopy moustache and a slow Tasmanian drawl, and I'm a big bloke … it's difficult to disguise me. Programs like 'Fast Forward', 'Rubbery Figures' and Billie Birmingham's 'Twelfth Man' have had enormous fun sending up yours truly over the years. Call it notoriety, call it fame … it all goes with the space. Ask any Olympian who is even half successful about being recognised. Public exposure goes with the territory of representing your country.

There have been some wonderful moments of recognition for me. This is the sort of thing that happens to me: I'm having a coffee in the Qantas Club Lounge. A man in a white coat pushing a trolley of dirty plates, cups and saucers looks at me long and hard before coming out with:

'So, how's yer fishin' goin'?'

I say, 'Not that good, but I hope to get a bite next week on Hamilton Island.'

Then he goes, 'I don't really like fish, all them bones, they get stuck in yer neck. Nah, I don't eat fish. Horrible stuff!'

I say, 'Yeah, nothing quite like a fish bone jammed in your throat. I only eat fillets.'

He smiles back … we like each other.

'But ya know,' he continues, 'I really like yer show. Even if yer not catchin' fish, it's good fun!'

'Thanks, mate,' I say, collecting the praise on behalf of Rex Hunt, the one with the fishing show. I don't really look like Rexie, but we're both big blokes, and we're both on the telly, and the main thing is that this bloke liked us!

My wife is used to this kind of scenario, although I had plenty of explaining to do in the beginning.

Way back in 1975 after the Ashes tour of England, a man asked for my autograph on the steps of the Vatican … almost a religious experience. And occasionally I've been mistaken for Prince Charles … maybe it's the ears like open doors of an old Volkswagen Beetle or something. And sometimes I'm Dennis Lillee in the eye of the beholder … at least we both played cricket! But by far the hardest ones to deal with are the 'Remember me?' ones: 'I met you at half-time in the dressing room of the Melbourne vs. Essendon game at the MCG in 1971, remember?' Or, 'Remember you were telling me about your boxer, and I had one too?' All too hard for an has-been fast bowler, so I just smile and nod.

Most people approach me because they feel comfortable. After all, I've spent all that time in their lounge rooms, haven't I? But sometimes it can all backfire, as Gerry has witnessed. Over to you Gerry …

Yes, I remember when Max and I ran into each other in the Ansett Golden Wing Lounge in Melbourne a few years back. Of course we had just enough time for a quick drink, so I got the drink while Max got his bags organised. By the time I got back with the drinks someone else was also at our table. This bloke joined in our conversation, called us both by our names, and quickly became a real pest. He controlled the conversation, so much so that we couldn't have our usual quick catch-up.

My plane was leaving first so I left saying to myself, 'Who *is* that dill Max's got himself mixed up with?' Then, a couple of months later I ran into Max again at an airport, this time in Sydney, and as usual we were in bit of a hurry. I said something to him about his dopey mate, and Max said, 'I thought he was *your* dopey mate!'

I now understand how that happens. The day Max and I went to the Swans match in Sydney to meet volunteers and collect stories for this book, everyone wanted to say hello to him, as if they knew him. He patiently signed shaved heads, backs and a range of clothing. That's what it's like when you've got a famous mug.

Thanks, Gerry, I do remember that incorrigible mate of yours … Look, seriously folks, the volunteers told us lots of stories about the famous people they recognised, but let's not forget that they were extremely recognisable too. They had the uniform, and that uniform meant 'How can I help you?' and they handled their 'fame' with endless good humour and goodwill, even though there were times when I'm sure they were tired and didn't feel like smiling. ”

Max & Gerry

After working for the Homebush Arrivals and Accreditation Centre for athletes and their coaches, I volunteered at the Regent and Wentworth Hotels. There I was responsible for meeting, greeting and accrediting members of the International Olympic Committees and their guests. It was during this time I had the unique experience of meeting, greeting and accrediting Mohammed Ali …

VERA FOLEY, *Accreditation*
MILSONS POINT NSW

At the hockey we had Prime Minister Howard and his wife visit regularly, the Queen of Spain and her entourage, Prince William of Orange in the Netherlands (he was only young and a handsome young man), not to forget Princess Anne – she's looking more mature these days!
VIC HARRIS, *Transport Supervisor*
DIANELLA WA

I also did ten days for the Paralympic Games. I didn't want to do it, but how could I do one and not the other … and I loved it more than the first Games. I was out in the common Domain mostly, directing people to the venues and telling them which ones had seating as the venues were filling all over the complex. It was terrific. The school kids were just fantastic: patriotic and dressed for it. One day I was very busy: people milling around asking directions. I was a new girl here learning fast, when I heard a voice I recognised asking me if the basketball venue was full. It was Lindy Chamberlain-Creighton. We got talking and she stayed with me for almost half an hour helping me direct people – she knew more about the place than I did!
MARCIA CARR, *Spectator Services*
ROSELANDS NSW

On the last day of competition, we were waiting for our car at the front of the hotel and I spied Alex Popov standing nearby also waiting for a car. When our car arrived we got in and I was busy talking to my delegate and his wife when I heard my door open. I quickly turned around to see Alex Popov shutting my door with a big smile on his face. Yes, I had not shut it properly and he had noticed. His words were: 'We cannot have you falling our of your car in Sydney' with a very charming smile. I thanked him and we all had a good laugh.

Fancy, saved by Alex Popov and he was soooooo gorgeous. What a way to meet him!
JANE COX, *IOC Relations and Protocol*
TORQUAY VIC

During my normal spectator host duties, over a few days, I came in contact with the young Jordanian horse-riding team. On a daily basis I talked with a gorgeous young woman and we took a photograph together. After a few days I found out the young woman was Princess Haya of Jordan. I could not see her after that to give her a photo and give her my apologies for not addressing her as Your Highness. If I am lucky I may send her a copy of the book with her name in it!

JOSEPH KALENDERIAN, *Spectator Host*
SYDNEY NSW

I thoroughly enjoyed my experience as a driver, which led me to meet all sorts of people from all parts of the world. I drove all over Sydney and the suburbs and had a ball. One exciting meeting was with a Dr Norbert Muller, a Professor from Germany who was a member of the IOC Commission for Culture and Olympic Education and a member of the National Olympic Committee. I became his trusted driver on a few occasions and had the pleasure to share breakfast on the top deck with his wife and daughter. I felt so special and enjoyed every moment of it. I now know how the *Titanic* would have looked like with its splendour and glory: the view of the harbour was just breathtaking as was the ten-course breakfast and the impeccable service.

KRYSTYNA LETTE, *Driver*
TOONGABBIE NSW

The moments, though small and brief, did come thick and fast. Seating the King and Queen of Spain, helping Shirley Strickland, finding results of events for Princess Anne, colouring in with Mr Samaranch's grandchildren, finding a light for a prince's ciggie (he may not want his country mentioned as he was away from the crowds while doing this), helping Dawn Fraser find a particular venue, escorting Mr Kissinger, congratulating Pieter van den Hoogenband and being thanked personally, including a photo with his arms around us, by Prime Minister John Howard.

NICHOLE CAMPBELL, *Protocol Attendant*
BRISBANE QLD

As I left the confines of Darling Harbour, a chap flagged me down and asked if I was going anywhere near a railway station. He introduced himself as Joe Bugner which wasn't necessary as I recognised him as the former heavyweight boxing champion. He was trying to get to North Sydney and as I was heading across the Harbour Bridge on my way home, I said to get in. When I told him I'd been driving an IOC delegate around Hunter Valley wineries all day, he said he'd actually owned a winery at one time. Anyway, I dropped him off at his hotel and he was very grateful. His parting remark was that if I ever saw him in a pub and he did not buy me a beer, I could smack him in the mouth. Having shaken his enormous hand, my chicken instinct suggested I would not be taking him up on his offer!

ROB CAPON, *Driver*
SYDNEY NSW

I was always checking my team and making sure they had water and sunscreen. I was never on one spot at one time for more than ten minutes. I went home to my family and told them all I did all day was talk, which they said I am very good at. I talked to my team and talked to the public about softball or to tourists about Sydney. I loved every minute of it. I met fabulous people and had a ball.

MONIKA WEBB, *Supervisor Spectator Services*
SEVEN HILLS NSW

With all the great experiences I had, one in particular sticks in my mind. I was on access duty at a gate at the back of the Hockey Centre. It was dark, chilly and raining. I couldn't see the game but I could hear the crowd roar and feel the rain falling on my wet-weather gear. My job was to make sure only personnel with accurate access passes could get by me through the gate. I felt very needed and very much an important, though small, link in the large chain that held this great event together.

Athens here I come! (Hey, how long would it take me to ride my motorbike there, I wonder?)

SUE NORWOOD, *Spectator Services*
ESPERANCE WA

I recall one day hearing the exasperated pleas of a Cuban athlete who was attempting to explain to a bewildered volunteer in Spanish and French that he needed to be at a meeting with his team president inside the venue. The volunteer, not understanding the request, refused entry. The athlete was utterly frustrated. Being of Italian background and with a basic grasp of French I offered to serve as interpreter and we were soon both inside searching for the president. The event concluded and spectators began flocking out of the venue when suddenly the athlete came face to face with the president! He was tremendously grateful to me. He reached into his pocket to grab a pin, but finding nothing, opted to give me a great big hug and a kiss!

MATILDA DI CERTO, *Spectator Services*
MARSFIELD NSW

The next day I was given a Vectra station wagon to drive, a very nice car, only the indicators were on the left-hand side of the steering wheel. You had to push it up for right and down for left. I had a very clean windscreen during that shift.

LYNETTE SCHUCK, *Driver*
NEWCASTLE NSW

The Mongolian contingent arrived and before they could be shown around, the coach headed for the change rooms/toilets and with a determined expression walked straight into the female change area! The sound of hysteria immediately emanated from inside and those outside started shouting and laughing as well. A significant period of time elapsed as the noises of objection continued and then the coach emerged with exactly the same expression – no sense of embarrassment, no sense of confusion, as if nothing untoward had happened. He didn't even try to look for the male change rooms. Goodness knows what he did in there!

JOHN BOUTAGY, *Training Venue Assistant*
SYDNEY NSW

During one of my shifts doing 'mag and bag', a guy came through, setting off the alarms. He took a few coins out of his pocket and went through a second time. Again he set off the alarms. He then took a metal object out of his pocket. By this time the police and my colleagues were watching to see what I would do next. On the third attempt the man pulled up his trouser leg and said, 'Could this be the problem?' He had a metal artificial leg. Everyone was in fits of laughter including the man. They got me *big* time.

PAMELLA RICHARDSON, *OVIP*
SYDNEY NSW

Most popular saying from SES OVIPs at the Paralympic Games: 'Wheelchairs lane one, school students lanes one and two, general public – for your own protection – lanes three and four.'

Sydney people seem obsessed with mobile phones. At Darling Harbour we found five (yes, five) in one handbag. When asked, the lady explained: one for her (okay), one for her husband (with her, okay), one each for her two daughters (not with her!), and a spare one in case she couldn't be contacted on the other four. The really crazy thing was that once inside the venue, she had to turn them all off!

PAT JOHNSON, *SES*
SYDNEY NSW

(In May 2001 Pat Johnson was awarded a Volunteer Emergency Service Scholarship by the Attorney General's Department to assist her to visit the Metropolitan Disaster Centre in Tokyo. She was one of four to be rewarded for outstanding commitment to the State Emergency Service.)

When a country arrived they were first bussed into the accreditation area and met by a big welcoming party and then escorted to the Village. After a Polish welcome, a Polish athlete said, 'I left my 'orse at accreditation.' They rang accreditation and asked if there was a stray horse there. The answer was, 'No, but we have some oars.'

LYNETTE GREGORY, *Village Management*
SYDNEY NSW

A teacher took the children on an excursion to the Paralympics. Children saw a young man in a wheelchair and rushed up and asked him for his autograph. He said, 'I can't, I'm not a Paralympian.' They stopped for a bit, then said, 'That doesn't matter, we still want your autograph' …

There was a story told by an Australian medico: A South African Paralympian was complaining about the fact that the team had been banned from going to the Lidcome pub. The medico asked, 'What are they doing that for?' The guy replied, 'Some of our athletes are coming back a bit blind and legless!'

DR LOUISE MAZZAROLI, *ORTA*
SYDNEY NSW

As I was hurrying in my Olympic uniform to the transport terminal at 4.40 a.m. (still dark), a police car stopped beside me and its occupants wished me a good morning. I had never experienced such a friendly greeting from members of the police force in my 40 years of living in the area.

WALTER KORABELNIKOFF, *Navigator/Interpretor/Spectator Services*
SYDNEY NSW

As venue staffing manager, I took it upon myself to spend a great part of each day ensuring the happiness of our volunteers (some 3000 in the Superdome). This included greeting them upon check-in and circulating throughout the venue to speak to them. I also distributed lollies. It only took about three days before I was referred to throughout the venue as 'The Lolly Man' – a name that was to stay with me for the entire event.

HEINZ GERSTL, *Venue Staffing Manager*
SYDNEY NSW

Did we get busy? We coped with wave after wave after wave of people – up to 2500 people arriving every 2.5 minutes. One morning by 10 a.m., 30,000 people had passed through one large tent at the 'overflow'. On our busiest day, during the 7.30 a.m. to 3.30 p.m. shift, we put enough people through the gates to fill Stadium Australia twice and keep all the other venues at Homebush full.

Did we meet anyone famous? It's hard to say because all we saw was the bottom of bags. The most common item found was a pocket or paring knife for cutting apples and oranges. The hardest item to get people to surrender would have been glass bottles containing beverages. The strangest item without doubt was a kerosene lantern. Why anybody would bring this to the Olympics we are still trying to work out. Most mobile phones on a single person was three (this was not uncommon). We could have retired if we were given $1 for every mobile phone we saw!

JOHN RICHARDSON, *Spectator Services*
SYDNEY NSW

THE THINGS YOU FIND OUT AT AN OLYMPIC GAMES!

Did you know that using Australian toilet paper is 'World's best practice'? Mexican TV presenter Eugenio Gonzalez discovered this and took a roll along to the Main Stadium to prove it. Each night, Eugenio contributed 'two or three comedy snippets' to his Mexico City audience estimated variously at between ten and 15 million viewers. To the backdrop of the huge evening athletics crowd, he did a stand-up in the media seating area. Rubbing the toilet roll across his cheek (the one on his face), Eugenio declared Sydney toilet paper to be 'the softest, and the strongest – it doesn't tear' he had encountered in a lifetime of international travel. Applauded by a fascinated media audience, he took a bow – and the toilet paper home to Mexico City.

JOHN 'FITZIE' FITZGERALD, *Olympic Public Relations*
MELBOURNE VIC

My most memorable moment at the Paralympics occurred in the Athletes' Stadium when it was filled to the brim with excited school children. A boy of about 18 was running in an 800 metres heat. He had no arms and came last in the race. As soon as the race finished a large group of children ran from their seats requesting the autograph of this young man. He gladly responded signing with a pen in his mouth. His parents, from South Africa, had also been watching the race from the stands and came rushing down to video this very special moment. This hadn't happened at any other event they had attended with 'Richard' and it was a very special and proud moment that touched not only theirs but all our hearts.

DENISE GRIBBLE, *VIP Liaison Officer*
SYDNEY NSW

One of the most quizzical experiences for me was when a sprinter was assigned to me. He could barely understand or speak English, so I gesticulated and spoke in broken English requesting he remove his shirt, trousers and shoes and lie face down on the massage table – a standard procedure – while I waited outside the curtained cubicle.

After a few minutes I re-entered, only to find him sitting on the massage table stark naked! After quelling my initial shock, I gestured for him to lie face down and discreetly covered him with a towel. At that moment a million questions raced through my dismayed head! Do they have professional massage in his country? ... If they do, surely it wasn't performed totally unclothed? ... Or maybe it was? ... If they don't, did he misunderstand my instructions regarding undressing?

I allowed my mind to rest and proceeded with the massage, opening my heart to the humanness of the experience. Here we were, two people from totally different cultural backgrounds, where things were clearly not quite the same. But essentially we were humans, so I embraced our differences and gave him the best massage I could.

CLARE SARANDIS, *Massage Therapist*
MELBOURNE VIC

About two or three days before the official opening the chef de mission of Malawi (a small East African nation) came in to see what we were about. Jerome Mvubu is an engaging type with a big happy smile. He is a short and round, very black African with a university degree and a golf handicap of 17. My real life occupation as a golf tour operator involves taking tours to South Africa twice a year. Probably because of this background we naturally gravitated together so I asked him if he would like to have a game of golf while in Australia. He was enthusiastic about the idea so we made arrangements to go to Riverside Oaks on the following Monday. He told me later he couldn't sleep for excitement for two days prior to the day and bought a new set of clubs for the occasion.

The day was such a success I invited my new friend to my home club, Wakehurst, for the following Wednesday competition. This also turned out to be a great day but for totally different reasons. The word got around the club that I had an Olympic representative from Africa as a guest and the members were unbelievably friendly. More than once players wandered over from adjoining fairways to say hello and welcome

Jerome to Wakehurst and Australia. In the clubhouse after the game he was made to feel like 'one of the boys'. Their response to an overseas visitor totally blew away any preconceived notions of racial prejudice that we might have had and it made me very proud to be an Australian and associated with these ordinary blokes from Wakehurst. I thought their behaviour exemplified the Olympic tradition in its pure form and the natural friendliness of Australians.

BOB GILL, *Resident Centre Assistant*
SYDNEY NSW

We were working in Residence 5 at the Village. It was like a hotel foyer – they had a lounge in there and that's where all the athletes in that residence came to of a night. There were people from all different teams, and we had to answer all sorts of questions. There was this one chap (this was in the Paras) who came to me and said (quietly) what sounded like, 'You got condo?' And I went, 'What?' and he said, 'Condo.' And I thought, 'No, I'm hearing things here,' so I said, 'Look, sorry, but I really can't understand what you're saying,' so he said loudly, 'YOU GOT CONDOM?' And I went (high-pitched squeak) 'Ooooh, *condom*!' So I said to my husband, 'Norm would you take him down to the Polyclinic to the doctor to get an extra condom, please?' And as he left, (he was in a wheelchair, with no legs) one of the other athletes said, 'Well, something's working, isn't it!'

DOROTHY WILLIAMS, *Pioneer volunteer*
PROSPECT NSW

Come August 2000 and after countless training sessions and site visits it was time to collect my uniform and accreditation, which proved it was all real and not just a beautiful dream. Then the nerves set in: what will I do after the Games are over? I had never had something to look forward to for so long. As a T1 relief, everything started very slowly, and that was evidently a common thing amongst transport volunteers. 'Oh well, I was sure it would get busier.' Did it ever …

As I walked through Darling Harbour every morning and evening after a 12-hour-plus shift, I could not keep the smile off my face, I was so proud to be wearing my uniform and being asked for directions to venues or other localities in the city I grew up in ...

My wife and I were generously given two tickets to the Closing Ceremony from someone I had driven for one day. Oh what a wonderful world! I had tears in my eyes when the F-111 swept over us and the cauldron, and stole the flame that Australians had taken to be their own ...

The emotions came to a head on the day Sydney turned out to thank the volunteers. I now have some idea of how our servicemen and women feel when they walk down George Street on ANZAC Day. The volunteers' march proved what Aussies felt for the volunteers, for what we had done was just incredible.

GRANT BAKER, *Driver*
NEWCASTLE NSW

A very tall Kenyan dressed in a colourful toga and matching fez arrived at the Homebush Arrivals and Accreditation Centre. He stood out like a sore thumb.

What appeared very odd (and certainly didn't go with his general attire) was a rather battered-looking briefcase that he clutched to his side. While waiting, he commented on the efficiency of the process involved in producing the valid pass, the effectiveness of the laminating and the practical and pleasing look of the final product. 'The Germans were the first to use the laminating process for producing passes, you know,' he commented, and pointed out that here in Australia we had obviously perfected and streamlined the process.

He singled me out and continued, 'You seem to be a person that can appreciate what I'm saying,' and he invited me to sit next to him.

'This is a bag full of Olympic history,' he said as he opened his bag and dipped inside. It was like taking a trip back in time. Out came a very crudely laminated pass with what looked like a shoelace for a lanyard. This was the German pass. He assured me that this was an improvement on the one issued earlier which consisted of a rectangular booklet and was easily lost or mislaid. You guessed it, he substantiated his statement by extracting an example from his briefcase. Yes, he had them all, going back over 40 years.

There were also illustrated publications of him as a young man: first as an athlete, progressing through to team coach, team manager and finally chef de mission.

He was a very interesting personality and it certainly broadened my historical knowledge about this side of the Olympics.

Just another bonus to being an Olympic and Paralympic volunteer.

FRANK COLLISON, *Accreditation*
SYDNEY NSW

I worked on all the seating levels at the Aquatic Centre and it was a different atmosphere from the bottom to the top. The bottom was freezing cold and the spectators were more controlled with their applause etc., but when the swimmers, especially in the finals, dived into the pool and came up to start their strokes, all those strokes at once, you could feel their power – you could feel it in your chest. The top row of seats was very high (which some people found distressing) and very hot yet it still had a wonderful view. Here the atmosphere was electric. The stamping, yelling and chanting was more like a rock concert. As Australia came to the finish line the noise was tremendous – you could yell as loud as you liked and not hear it above the crowd. I know, I tried it. What a great feeling!

MARIA GODWELL, *St John Ambulance*
PERTH WA

Early one evening I was wending my weary way home from a day in the Village, taking the path from Edgecliff railway station. As I passed the local bowling club I was literally swept off my feet by a gentleman who insisted I come have a drink with his friends on the balcony of the club. He said, 'You look so exhausted. You volunteers do a wonderful job.'

After a great deal of persuasion I had to agree because he actually carried me to the balcony. I made him ring my husband on my mobile phone to tell him that I was kidnapped and no ransom was to be paid. It was all done in good humour. My kidnapper introduced himself on the phone and to his great surprise he found that my husband was in school with his best mate. I am not often, and certainly never ostentatiously, patriotic, but on this occasion, as one of thousands of volunteers, I admit that it made me happy to be seen doing Australia proud.

SENTA TAFT-HENDRY, *International Information*
NEWCASTLE NSW

The athletics events were amazing. This was the brilliant thing about being a volunteer – your job was basically done by the time the events started, and I got to see quite a lot of the events, and for free! How many people can say that they got to see Cathy Freeman win her gold medal from an empty corporate suite on Level 3 – one of the prime viewing positions in the Stadium worth a minimum of $2.3 million each? Or be standing at the long jump pit when Jai Taurima won his silver medal? I was on a meal break when Tatiana won her silver, and I was standing at the start of the 200m finals. I sang *Advance Australia Fair* with the rest of the crowd when Louise Sauvage won her gold and took Shane Gould's ticket one day too. But I also endured many days under the hot sun, long nights when I would be standing for eight hours, and wheeling people around all corners of the Olympic Park precinct. It wasn't always fun and games, but the good always outweighed the bad and I would never swap those experiences for anything.

MICHELLE GAVRANICH, *Spectator Services*
WANNEROO WA

A sheer delight was experienced when being stationed at the car park for people with a disability: we saw and felt a gold medal! We had noticed a lady going past carrying a medal presentation bouquet and when we asked if we could photograph it, she said, 'Would you like to see the gold medal also?' The person then said that her daughter had won it that morning. Not knowing who her daughter was, we were curious and it was only then that we learnt her daughter was Siobhan Paton. Mrs Paton then placed the medal around the neck of a little boy who was disabled and who was passing by at that time with his family. The sheer delight shown by the parents was very heartwarming as Mrs Paton said, 'This is what Siobhan wants to do, work with children who are disabled.'

BARBARA FIRTH, *Spectator Services*
MORDIALLOC VIC

It was a wonderful experience speaking to so many people from so many countries. One American gentleman was amazed he had been to four Games and could not get over how 20 million got the Games so right when 200 million got Atlanta so wrong. He loved everything about our country; he even wanted to take me home with him. I told him to look around him – I could not leave this lovely country and also my husband would not like it.

At the Paralympics I was working at the tennis and I had the pleasure of working with and around players and saw their joys and sorrows. There was one male player silently sitting alone, tears running down his cheeks, he was so disappointed over his loss. I dried his tears, put my arms around him (at my age I can put my arms around anyone without causing a stir) telling him that is what his mum would be doing if she was here and how proud she was having an Olympian for a son. After a chat he was smiling again. The Para players were an inspiration to all.

MARY BUGGY, *Spectator Service*
SYDNEY NSW

Yep, volunteers were everywhere. They were always smiling and polite. Especially the happy chappy sitting on a high chair directing the hundreds of people to their destination at Olympic park. 'Hello, ladies and gentlemen,' he said, 'when you reach the top of this rise you will find everything you ever wanted in this life and then you will have only another nine kilometres to walk to the train or bus.'

... Who could ever forget the sensational Opening Ceremony? And what could have been more moving than seeing North Korea and South Korea teams marching into the Olympic arena together? It reminded everyone, I think, that the things which unite nations are far greater than those which divide them.

NOLA KENNY, *IBM Info Team*
ADELAIDE SA

When Kuwait played, the Kuwaiti sheik watched his beloved soccer team play. Every time Kuwait scored a goal, the sheik would rise joyously with his two bodyguards on either side. When Japan played Brazil, 5000 Japanese flew direct from Japan, watched their beloved soccer team lose 1–0 to Brazil, then flew back to Japan straight after the game.

The Brazilians were the most vocal. All the fans were up in the top section. One guy beat a drum while the rest danced and sang. The Brazilian fans jumped up and down. They made the top section sway so much, the police had to evacuate the people underneath. The Brazilians even got the entire Gabba doing the Mexican wave.

BRAD CAHOON, *Spectator Services*
BRISBANE QLD

I was assigned to the stables as a general aid to the grooms, keeping the area clean, etc. In other words I scooped poop. For anyone who doesn't know horses they poop copiously and indiscriminately, even outside the athletes' lounge! When I was told that foreign royalty were visiting one day I knew I would have to be extra vigilant and at the ready with my fork and wheelbarrow.

My first attempt to help a groom was to paint her charge's hooves black. I did a good job and she asked me to paint another horse. Alas, I was clumsy with the tin and spilt a lot over myself and new uniform. I was a big mess. Would it ever come out? That night I scrubbed and scrubbed and soaked my uniform and me in Napisan. Thank goodness for a second set of everything. The stains faded over time, but no more hoof blacking for me!

CLARE HANSON, *Stable Assistant*
MISSISSIPI USA

The next player's appearance was totally unexpected. Andrew Gaze made his way out of the players' tunnel and slowly walked towards the reserved seating area. The crowd started cheering and applauding until the room echoed as one. Andrew turned to look courtside as if to see what was happening in the game to cause such a reaction. As Andrew turned back towards me I indicated that the crowd was cheering for him.

I will never forget the look of humility on Andrew's face. He smiled and waved to the crowd and you could see the look of surprise on his face. I felt proud to be an Australian and a volunteer because of the reaction of Andrew Gaze. He did not come to courtside looking for attention and showed dignity when he received it. To me he demonstrated what the Games were all about and I believe many of the spectators that day saw this too.

MARK GREGORY CROSS, *Team Leader Spectator Services*
SYDNEY NSW

At the Olympic Village, when it had only two days to finish winding down, Dorothy and I had dinner in the Food Hall with the greatest 10,000 metre athlete in the world. He has never been beaten, and has a smile as big as the Sydney Harbour Bridge – Haile Gebrselassie of Ethiopia. He told us, 'What Australia has done in staging the 2000 Olympics will take the rest of the world 50 years to do.' And then he remarked, 'I doubt then if it will be as good.' He then graciously gave us his autograph.

NORM WILLIAMS, *Pioneer volunteer*
PROSPECT NSW

(Haile Gebrselassie was awarded a silver Olympic Order from IOC president Juan Antonio Samaranch in June 2001. This honour is given to those who have achieved 'remarkable merit in the sports world, or have rendered outstanding services to the Olympic cause, either through personal achievement or to the development of sport'. Our Cathy Freeman was among the ten athletes who received this special award.)

Imagine if you can (or have had the unfortunate experience) a late Saturday night in a busy, inner city casualty department with:

a very overweight male with a suspected heart attack;
a young woman with severe abdominal pain;
two over-excited kids that have thrown up all over themselves;
a screaming toddler with something pushed up his bleeding nose;
a woman with a severe migraine;
a little boy having an asthma attack.

All routine, except yourself and the doctor are working out of a broom cupboard under the main stairs with only one narrow bed to rest or examine everyone on!

JUDITH MATERNA, *Spectator Care Nurse*
BUNDEENA NSW

I was sitting outside with one of the other female escorts, Hayley, when the far door of the corridor opened and in walked two males. Hayley said to me, 'Hey, that looks like that guy off TV' and as they approached us we realised it was Laurie Lawrence and a friend. They walked up to us and then Laurie, taking our accreditation in his hands and reading our names said, 'Hi Julie, Hi Hayley!' Our supervisor then came out and I introduced Laurie to him as they shook hands. I asked Laurie if he had any badges to swap and he said he had always had the one badge and just kept swapping it, so I scored an Athletics Australia badge off Laurie and he scored a Queensland taekwondo badge. It was a great honour to meet such a great man.

Not long after this, the escorts were sitting outside the referees' lounge when the door down the corridor opened again and in walked a scruffy good-looking fellow, and my friend Kate said, 'Well I have to get a photo of this.' I thought well just because this guy has green and gold war paint on, why get a photo? As he approached I realised to my embarrassment that it was Peter Brock, lost and looking for Laurie Lawrence to go and cheer on Lauren Burns in her great gold medal win.

JULIE DAVIDSON, *Official Services Attendant*
BRISBANE QLD

I had a ball. I got to be involved with all the athletes but especially the Cuban team. I know two languages because I'm from a Spanish background and I told the Cubans I would help any way I could so that's how my involvement with them started.

The coach came to me needing to hire a bike so he could follow his crews around the course. All the regatta bikes were already being used so I lent him my family's own bikes. After that I helped the Cuban men's C2 crew celebrate their silver medal and showed them the sites of Penrith.

When one of the silver medallists came up to me and said, 'Where's your wife? I want to give her something,' I went and got her and he gave her the bouquet of flowers he was given when he won the silver medal.

RAY GUARROCHENA, *Field Marshall*
PENRITH NSW

We didn't only come into contact with Olympic people. Our uniform made us quite prominent and members of the public constantly approached us. They seem to think that because we were in uniform we must know everything – about the terminal and everything that goes on inside and outside it, about the Games event program, about

Games ticketing, about transport, about accommodation; you name it, they asked us about it!

We hadn't expected this secondary part of our work to be so extensive, and I and many others went to some lengths to keep abreast of developments during the Games, particularly on ticketing issues and where the shortest queues for tickets were. Our venue operation manager was not keen on us spending time with members of the public but we could hardly not do so, and providing we weren't busy with Olympic family, we saw it all as part of the general PR for the Sydney Olympic Games. Even standing at an arrival gate as passengers came off a flight I regarded as part of the Games, particularly in the week leading up to the opening. You could see from the expressions of people arriving from interstate that our presence in our Olympic uniform was a bit of a thrill. 'Yes, wow! This really is the Olympic City, the Games really are on!' they seem to be saying.

FAIRLIE CLIFTON, *Airport Relations and Protocol*
SYDNEY NSW

Following completion of the Olympic Games I also volunteered for service at the Paralympic Games. For this event I was co-opted to assist with photographing officials and others for identity passes.

Some high-profile local identities were processed with ease but one woman, who must remain nameless, decided that the Paralympic photo taken was less flattering than that which she had been given four weeks earlier for the Olympics. She, in umbrage, 'took the matter further', however, the senior official decided that the current photo was a good likeness and would stand. It can only be concluded that four weeks at the 2000 Sydney Olympics had aged the lady far more than she believed.

HEATHER PAGE, *Driver*
SYDNEY NSW

Allow me to share some of my moments as I wear with pride the blue shirt uniform of a venue assistant. I worked in the Superdome, during the artistic gymnastics, 13 shifts straight.

First I was amazed at the sacrifices many of my team had made to get to the Olympics: most were from interstate. Our team included Victorians, Queenslanders (Townsville) and one chap from South Australia. All had used their annual leave to come to work at the Olympics.

Every one of the volunteers in the team got on well, 'rolled with the punches' so to speak, as our duties and rosters were advised. No one thought themselves too important to do their assigned tasks. Everyone has an infectiously positive attitude to what was happening and a 'can do' resolve.

People at the events and within Olympic Park were happy. They would stop and chat to strangers. There was no sense of 'stranger danger'. I felt safe in the big crowds and I felt safe as one or two of us left the Olympics to catch a train after midnight.

Speaking of trains, one night at Concord West station it was extremely busy. I looked like missing the train due to crowding in all carriages. What happened? The driver opened his cab door and invited me to ride with him.

DARYL OSBORNE, *Results Printing and Distribution*
SYDNEY NSW

With the Paralympics, the tickets people bought were day passes and that meant that you could go to any event you liked but not many people realised that so our Shooting Centre didn't get too busy. So we started to try to guess how many people would come through the gates each day. It wasn't until Monday, the fifth day, that we got 1000 people so we decided to give that person a prize. We waited till nearly 1 p.m. that day. I was at the front access point with security with my radio and was told by my supervisor that the minute that they get off the bus I was to call Command Centre and let them know.

It was a young boy of 13 years in a wheelchair with his aunt and we gave him a bag of anything of interest we could find with pins, brochures, a Lizzie pass, a Paralympic cap, a Lizzie toy. We presented him with an Aussie gold rosette and the bag and he started to cry and so did we. You could almost see his chest swell he was so proud. You had to be there to feel the emotion involved because with being the Paralympics and our most important customer was a 13-year-old boy who was a paraplegic.

To me and everyone else there that boy and everyone in his position made us feel that we did the right thing by volunteering to help do anything we could to make it a time they would not forget anytime soon.

NORMA DUNCUM, *MOST Team*
SYDNEY NSW

The most unforgettable experience that I had is when I worked with the Spectator Services as host during my free time with the ceremonies. I was assigned at Kronos Hill to direct the flow of people coming in and going out of the north sector of the Olympic venue. It was three o'clock in the afternoon. Our leader, who has the radio communication, went to check people at the other side of the hill. An old woman suffered from hypoglycaemia (she was diabetic) while ascending to the top of the hill. She fell to the ground and her companion requested help from us. What I did was to look for a St John Ambulance paramedic. I sped down the hill zigzagging against the flow of people exiting the venue. I found the paramedic and we ran ascending the hill. The hardest thing to do during this emergency is to run ascending the hill opposing the flow of people entering the venue. I am praising God; the diabetic woman was given the first aid she needed.

Some Olympians at that time were running for gold but when I ran back and forth on the hill, I ran not for gold but for life. I have not received gold from the Olympics but I received the trophy and medal of joy for saving a life.

DELMAR GABRIEL, *Props Assistant / Spectator Services*
SYDNEY NSW

First day on the job I met and interviewed Peter Brock. I was a volunteer with the Olympic and later the Paralympic News Service. I was hoping to meet some famous athletes in the course of my work, but when I discovered I was covering sports such as badminton, handball and volleyball my hopes of meeting an Ian Thorpe or Cathy Freeman died. Nevertheless I was excited to be 'bringing you the Games!'

So on my first day, basically as a practice story my venue editor tells me to go and watch a practice session of the Australian men's handball team. Having never seen the sport and barely knowing it exists at all, I figured this would be a good chance to see what it's all about before I have to write sports reviews of it. I walk into the practice court looking to speak to a coach or the captain and on the sideline I see a familiar face – from TV. Shocked and stunned I blurt out, 'Hey, you're Peter Brock! What are you doing here?' Realising I've just sounded like a complete fool and possibly been insulting I quickly whipped out a pad and pen, explaining that I'm with the Olympic News Service, and continued questioning.

Turns out he was there to act as a sports motivator. The Australian Olympic team had retired sports legends who have won a lot of accolades in their chosen sport to contribute in the lead-up to the Games with motivating our athletes and sharing some of their wisdom on winning and how to do it from their own experiences. I interviewed him, raced back to the newsroom to write it up and then a few days later saw an article in the *Sydney Morning Herald* along similar lines. So what I think happened is that someone from the *Sydney Morning Herald* saw my story on the Olympic wire and went along to the next Australian Men's Handball practice match to get a story on how Peter Brock was helping them prepare for the Games. A story that I found! It was a good way to start my Olympic experience …

… My next brush with fame was far less rewarding. I was one of the main reporters for the badminton, a sport that had a very small profile in Australia and one I knew very little about. However, I can now say that I've interviewed the current world champion, the Sydney medal winners, past Olympic medal winners, and the up and coming stars. The problem was that when I was interviewing these people I had almost no idea what I was doing and most of them didn't speak English! Trying to interview someone about a sport you know almost nothing about, interviewing through a translator and talking to the world champ who is idolised in their own country can be embarrassing. It would be like trying to interview Steve Waugh having never seen a game of cricket, having no idea as to the rules or the international success of the Australian team, and not speaking his language. Fun! Sure was challenging, but hey it's an experience you don't get every day …

… There were so many highlights. Being able to see sports such as sitting fencing, sitting volleyball or wheelchair rugby – that game is insane! Being able to chat with a Hungarian rhythmic gymnast about her sport and listening to her gripe about the fickleness of the sport and how at 22 she was the oldest competitor and a bit bitter that this would be her last Olympics. Being on a train back into the city and hearing the announcer say, 'Next stop Redfern, and it's just in that the Australian women's water polo team just won gold,' and participating in the random cheering that erupted on the train. Just being in Sydney at that time; the vibe of the place was fantastic. Being able to get off a train at Central at 11 at night to walk across the road, sit in the park and listen to Vince Jones for an hour or two. I absolutely loved it all, though I barely slept for 16 days.

TIM WINTON-BROWN, *News Service*
SYDNEY NSW

I was one of six medal escorts escorting medal winners onto the pool deck to receive their medals and flowers. We led the blind out to the dais watching that they were in the right place and didn't fall. After presentation we escorted them around in front of media and spectators, then out and back to where we started. Same with wheelchairs – if the athletes needed to be pushed we did that for them. Escorting Chinese and Japanese winners who had no arms and very little or no shoulders was very heartbreaking for us. The presenters weren't sure where to put their flowers during the medal presentation ceremony. We pointed to their chin. Us escorts then held the flowers until we walked to the media box where we would place the flowers under their chin for photos and a wave to the spectators. That is one thing I won't forget for a while. It was very hard not to cry sometimes.

LAURETTE BROWN, *Medal Escort*
SYDNEY NSW

For two weeks Sydney was the friendliest place I've known. While wearing my uniform everyone wanted to talk to me, and after the first day I forgot to be nervous. People wanted to talk, and take countless photos of me and videos as well. Children walked past and shyly waved to me like I was famous. And indeed I felt famous. I even managed to learn a lot about Sydney and pass on interesting information to people when they asked.

My work friends and I developed entertaining aerobic routines to liven up our job of pointing out directions to people. We sang and danced and waved streamers around (in green and gold of course) to give our directions. Then we had to repeat this for the videos! Somewhere out in the world right now I'm wiggling my butt on someone's TV! And to top all this off I met the Paddle Pop Lion and he asked me out. And every day I lost my voice from too much talking.

Are you feeling Olympic today? This was a saying we had each day: were we in the right mood to give ourselves and others a good Olympic day? YES.

LISA SIMCOX, *Spectator Services*
MELBOURNE VIC

When Sydney first won the Games, my dream was to be at the Opening Ceremony. To me, that was the ultimate ticket. I applied for four tickets for me, my husband Dan, and two children: Eliot, 12, and Olivia, 5. I was bitterly disappointed when we missed out in the ballot. As the Games drew closer, I received my volunteer roster. I quickly opened it to see that my third shift was the Opening Ceremony! My heart slipped. I knew I was not in the Stadium, but I lived in hope.

On my first shift, a training session of gymnastics, I had an opportunity at a meal break to ask a team leader about our role in the Opening Ceremony. She told me that our job was to marshall the athletes and organise them to parade into the Stadium. She assured me our job would end at the front door of the Superdome. It sounded exciting and it was, but it still wasn't going to get me into the Ceremony.

Opening Ceremony night arrived. By now I had made friends with fellow volunteers and we basically had a three-hour party with the athletes. I was looking after Canada and some of the 'B' countries who were a patchwork of colourful uniforms. We had a ball as the athletes amused themselves playing cards, pin-trading, playing catch, videoing each other – anything to break the boredom of waiting. The Australians were the worst behaved.

As my teams left early, some of us decided to go down to the Australian section. Here we were mingling with Mark Phillipousis, Nova Peris, Mark Woodford, Kieren Perkins and many more. I was tempted to ask for autographs, but I didn't want to lose my 'job'. I was chatting to Steve Moneghetti, who was standing next to a very serious Cathy Freeman, when the scoreboard flashed 'Australia'. I politely asked Steve and Cathy to move out and wished them well. Most of the volunteers moved up to the foyer to cheer them out of the Superdome. I had tears in my eyes as they streamed past, 'high-fiving' us as they went.

Our shift was over. As we emerged from the staff exit, we could hear the crowd and see the lights. We were standing just below the cauldron.

One volunteer said she was going to race to the train and would be home in time to see the cauldron lighting on TV. A few others were heading for one of the huge screens in Olympic Park to watch it there.

This was my last chance! I looked up at the cauldron, took a deep breath and headed for one of the Stadium gates. The first guard volunteer was a low-ranking one like me. He apologised but was not prepared to risk his 'job' to let me in. The second one was the same, but just then, her team leader came along and asked what the problem was. She must have seen the tired, pleading look in my eyes, as she led me by the hand and walked me up the ramp, just as the cheer went up for Australia. She whispered to me, 'You've never seen me before in your life.' I nodded and looked around and realised I was right next to the stage. I found a spare seat and spent the next hour mesmerised.

When I realised Cathy Freeman was going to light the cauldron I let out a shriek! I had been standing next to her only an hour earlier. She showed no sign of what was to come. No wonder she was so serious! I was so close to the action I could feel the heat of the fire and hear the whirr of cogs when the raising of the cauldron hit a minor glitch. When it was all over I found a discarded yellow suitcase and filed out with the crowd. I saw the team leader who had let me in and mouthed the words 'Thank you' as I passed her.

LIANE (LEA) SIMPSON, *Spectator Services*
SYDNEY NSW

I was working the afternoon shift for the Paralympic Games, and I was asked to drive to Rushcutters Bay where the sailing was being held. After waiting my turn to join the queue to pick up passengers to take them to their destination, I was approached by the load zone operator with my instructions. Destination read: Long Bay Gaol. My immediate thought was they have made a mistake. When I queried this, they said no, George – your passenger – is ready to go. George had bags and what appeared to be musical instruments with him and he piled them all into the back seat with him, preferring not to put anything into the boot.

Now, being inquisitive as any female can be, I asked George why he wants me to drive him to Long Bay Gaol. He replied, back home, (he lives on a small island off the north of America), he hooked into the internet saying he is a minister of religion and will be in Sydney for the Paralympics and was there anyone in the area who would like to have him give a service at their church? The only reply he received was from the chaplain from the gaol, hence the visit.

George asked if he could tune in his instruments while I was driving and would I mind? No, of course not. After they were tuned in, George started singing. He had a beautiful voice, a soothing voice that one could listen to quite easily, a soul or blues type. I mentioned one of my favourite songs was *Amazing Grace*, and I'm sure he would do it justice. So, *Amazing Grace* it was. Nana Mouskouri you have competition. After George's rendition of the song, which was sung with great feeling, I felt it deserved some applause. Now, at this stage we were stopped at traffic lights on Anzac Parade, Friday afternoon, peak hour, and I burst into hearty clapping. After I settled down, I looked around me and all the other drivers, some with passengers, were giving me very strange looks. It was worth it as George made me feel good just by listening to him. George continued to sing for the rest of the journey, which wasn't long enough.

On our arrival at Long Bay, I parked the car and proceeded to the gatehouse where the guard approached me saying, 'You've got the wrong address, you must be lost.' To which I replied, 'No, I have a minister of religion who has been invited to do a service here tonight.' The Chaplain was summoned and George, luggage and instruments were unloaded. When the inmates saw the Paralympic accredited car, they were wondering who the visiting Olympian was!

MARY LUNN, *Driver*
SYDNEY NSW

When I look back at my experiences throughout the Games, apart from the actual competition and the ceremonies, the work of the volunteers really did stand out.

Everywhere I went I was met by a friendly, welcoming volunteer. They drove us to the pool, checked our accreditation, served us our meals and even kept us all up to date with the medal count.

Personally, I am very thankful to the volunteers at the Aquatic Centre who, together with team management, facilitated a meeting between my family and I halfway through the first week of the Games. As you can imagine, security was pretty tight and the fact that so many people went out of their way to ensure that the meeting took place really meant a lot to my family and I.

To each and every volunteer at the Sydney 2000 Olympic Games, I personally would like to thank you for your time, your enthusiasm and your patience during this truly memorable event in Australia's history.

GRANT HACKETT, *Swimmer*
Gold Medallist 1500m at Sydney 2000
MELBOURNE VIC

Day one: a mate and myself were in the Village looking towards the Stadium, thinking what lay ahead, just as the sun was rising over the horizon, when a couple of Yanks walked up and gave us a 'Gad-day mate.' After some small talk the first Yank said, 'Look bud, we can run across the grass, climb the fence, swim the swamp and we will be over at the Stadium.'

I said, 'Bad move pals, the swamp has got a big mother of a crocodile in it.' They said, 'What's a crocodile man?' I replied, 'I think you call them alligators.'

The look on their faces. Gotchya.

We also told them not to leave their washing on the line overnight.

'Why not, man?' they replied. We said, 'Koalas will rip them to shreds.'

The first Yank says, 'I've seen those koalas, they're cute and cuddly.' I said, 'Yeah, the ones in the zoos are but you should see the wild ones!'

The Aussie boxing team had the Yanks looking for 'hop snakes'. You know, they're the ones that roll up like a tyre, roll after you and get alongside you, let their tail go and bite off your ankle …

BRIAN (SNOWY) MARSHALL, *Driver*
SYDNEY NSW

I was given an urgent pickup to take a group from The Exhibition Centre to the Entertainment Centre in the name of NSHAN MUNCHYAN, ARMENIA. It looked easy as you could walk the distance in five minutes. I was confronted by one huge and one not-so-huge man babbling frantically in their language. They squeezed into my Commodore which now looked like a sardine can. The smaller one pointed to his watch and said, 'Medal time now', or that's what it sounded like. I pulled into a one-way street (the wrong way to my destination, of course), crossed a flyover and then into another one-way street. The air-conditioning was going flatchat but they had all the windows down and were shouting and whistling at any blonde female that vaguely resembled a human being. At Goulbourn Street I was confronted by a police blockade, but managed to squeeze through a gap. Suddenly, like in a Hollywood movie, we were surrounded by police on foot.

A very polite police lady said to me, 'You can't go this way, everything is blocked.'

I replied, 'Gold medal event! Got to be at the Entertainment Centre two minutes ago.' She said, 'Do a U-ie, up Goulbourn, right at George, second right, second right.' I said, 'But there are no right-turn streets!' She quickly replied, 'No worries, there are cops everywhere, I'll get the message though to let you drive on.' What a great Olympic spirit she displayed. Thanks to her quick thinking, we arrived at the Entertainment Centre promptly after passing the beautiful Cuban female volleyball team. From the cheers and whistles I was afraid that my Armenians were going to defect to Cuba on the spot, and I probably would have joined them. In the middle of all this chaos, I had passed my 1956 Melbourne Olympics autograph book to my passengers, but only the smaller one wrote in it '1993 Vorld Chempion Nshan Munchyan, Armenia, 48'. So I had a world champion boxer and whistler in my car – what an experience …

WAYNE WATKINS, *Driver*
WATERLOO NSW

It was the wee hours of the morning when I recall hearing that 'Sydernee' was going to host the 2000 Olympic Games. I knew from that moment I was going to be involved in some way. I decided that my position was going to be as a volunteer so I submitted my application along with 50,000 others. I applied for a specialist position so when the request came to me to apply as a National Olympic Committee Assistant (described as 'the ultimate insider's position') how could I refuse? I sent in my resume and flew to Sydney for the big interview.

'Congratulations,' the letter said. 'You have been successful.' Yippee! I was delighted but my bank balance frowned as I knew I had just made a hefty financial commitment as well as my time. I live in Adelaide, so I flew to Sydney at least 11 times (I've lost count) for training on a monthly basis.

[NB: Natasha spent over $8000 on costs to participate as a volunteer]

I was assigned to the Nigerian Olympic team (made up of 91 athletes and 45 officials) which ended up winning three silver medals – two in athletics and one in weightlifting. I was an official Nigerian team member and when the team won silver, I felt like I had won silver too! It was an amazing experience.

I will never forget the main dining hall where I spent so much of my time, the seven-foot, five-inch Chinese athlete, the flags of the world flying high, the golf buggies hooning around the Village, the 100m finals, sitting next to Cathy Freeman and seeing her win gold in the 400m, the men's 1500m freestyle, the Opening and Closing Ceremonies, riding a giant licorice-allsort shoe, standing on a giant thong, the Nigerian team and most important, the laughs we had.

NATASHA MALANI, *NOC Assistant to Nigerian Team*
ADELAIDE SA

One day during the Paralympics, I was walking to the International Village section of the complex. I was strolling along by myself when I entered the American housing area. A lady was in her motorised wheelchair and she was coming up the driveway to her housing as I was going in the opposite direction about 20 metres away. The lady started screaming at the top of her voice: 'Ma'am, help me! Help me, Ma'am!'

I thought she was yelling to someone else nearby but then I realised I was the only person around and she was in fact yelling to me. I crossed the street and the lady breathlessly asked me to get her bum-bag off her chair for her. I rummaged through the different bags hanging off the handles of her chair. I found the bum-bag and brought it around to her, placing it on the armrest.

Suddenly the lady screamed as the chair bolted forward. I had inadvertently rested the bum-bag against the drive lever and thrown the chair into gear. I apologised to the lady as she came to a stop and found that I had given her the wrong bag. 'It's inside my backpack! The bum-bag in my backpack! Quick!' I frantically rummaged through her backpack and was relieved to locate the much-needed bum-bag. I started to open it, asking her what she needed and thinking it was some sort of necessary medication. She told me it was cigarettes. So I proceeded to open the Benson & Hedges, passed her a cigarette and lit it for her. I'd made her day and she was most grateful. She wished me to have a good day and rolled off down the footpath.

DI LARKIN, *Technical Official*
WODONGA VIC

My daughter, Jasmine (14), was part of a huge historic event that made me so very proud of her and the many thousands like her. My husband and I were chaperones for a very small contingent from Swansea High School (two hours north of Sydney). She was ecstatic when she found out she would be performing in the Opening Ceremony. Then came the news that no teacher from her school could take time off for only four students. So we became chaperones, driving at least a dozen times to Sydney, waiting and waiting all day for a rehearsal, if any! Three rehearsals were at a place I called 'Hell' – hot, dirty, smelly and ugly! An old unused airport hangar at Quaker's Hill. Children waited all day in a hot circus tent or outside in the stifling heat …

There were many things I thought were such a big ask of these young people but to their credit did they grumble or complain as we adults do? They accepted it gracefully: laughing, talking, making new friends, seeing things as they were. After all, this was the entertainment industry and things don't always go to plan. They knew they were involved in something they would never forget. They were tired but they did what they were told. They were amazing; they deserved gold medals!

JULIET PASCOE, *Chaperone for Swansea High*
SUMMERLAND NSW

My billets were the greatest. Night time was the best. They all reckoned they were being spoilt – good food and overalls washed. Dinner about 8 p.m., and still talking at the table at 10.30 p.m. about the day's events – while I washed and ironed. These nightly talks were great, especially hearing about where they were during events. Standing on corners near brothels and gay bars – this was new to most of them, as being country boys, they didn't see it like we do. Residents offered them drinks, food and toilet facilities. They couldn't believe how friendly people were and the great conversations they had.

Early morning was a sight. Not good early risers, but they would eventually get moving. I made sure they packed enough coffee, fruit and chocolates for the long day ahead. The main joke was the 'magic' bowl of confectionary that never emptied as I would always refill it after they'd gone. They were a great bunch of guys and I was sorry to see them go.

PAMELLA RICHARDSON, *OVIP*
SYDNEY NSW

As I cannot run out of sight on a dark night, cannot swim more than one lap, or shoot straight or ride a horse very well, don't have an ATP ranking that rates with Rafter, Hewitt or the two Woodies and cricket is not an Olympic sport, common sense told me that the only way to achieve selection was to be a volunteer.

I requested a job in the Athletes' Village as I wanted to serve the athletes directly if possible, but behind the scenes. At the time, our son had a friend in charge of providing logistical support to every team and that sounded okay to me.

Some highlights for me were the performance of the Australian athletes, watching the raising of the Australian flag as our team was officially welcomed and the opportunity to join with the Australian team at their open air team concerts organised by Laurie Lawrence during the preparation week.

We found out that some of the athletes are natural, talented entertainers while some will need to stick to their chosen sport or profession! However, it was a lot of fun, which I am sure went a long way towards building up team spirit in that nervous pre-Games period.

On two occasions I had a wonderful spiritual experience in joining with a few athletes from different countries in a church service in the International Plaza. Just to be able to share a common faith and to shake hands in the sign of peace with people from completely different cultures was wonderful. The athletes were from the USA, China, Argentina, Germany and one young male athlete from East Timor who was at both services. He recognised me at the second service and, although we could not carry on a conversation because he could not speak English, there was an invisible bond which, to me, epitomised these Olympic Games.

Why did I want to be a volunteer? For a large part of my sporting life I was supported by so many people who volunteered to do all they could so that I had an opportunity to represent first my town, my state and then my country. This was an opportunity for me to give something back, although in a very small way, to the people of Australia for the privilege I had been given. It was also my small attempt to show the world that we in Australia could provide an efficient world sporting event and be friendly and helpful hosts at the same time.

RICK McCOSKER, *Logistical Support*
Former Australian Cricketer
NEWCASTLE NSW

September 16, the first day of hockey competition in the Sydney 2000 games. I was in a team of six and rostered on the first game and it was great as I felt that experiencing the first match was special. We arrived at the result operator office early and prepared for the match. After several weekends of training and waiting, the time has finally arrived and we are excited and a little nervous. The result manager was particularly anxious and made doubly sure that we were ready and prepared for any eventuality. Well, the teams Korea and Argentina were out on the pitch doing their last-minute preparations and were watching and making predictions of what the score might be. The first match promptly started at 8.30 a.m. and we were off. About five minutes into the game I thought of experimenting with some keys on the keyboard. I pressed a combination and to my horror the computer program for recording results just stopped and would not work. Pressing any key just produced a beep from the computer. Well I called the technicians and they were frantic, as they could not understand what happened. It took about 20 minutes before the computer was restored to working order. Meanwhile we recorded everything from the match by hand and when there was a break in play, copied the manual details into the computer system. My teammates were not too concerned, they just took the hiccup in their stride and thought Murphy's Law had struck again. However, this time Murphy was my finger! We thought it was funny and had a good laugh, which actually settled our nerves. The result manager did not think so at the time. After that everything went fairly smoothly.

DESMOND WONG, *Result Operator*
ILLAWONG NSW

The Paralympic Games were more relaxed and casual, quite a different feel to the Olympics. A highlight for me was access monitoring over at the warm-up track – SIAC. I volunteered for this happily as this was the place to see the athletes up close, get a photo or two and an autograph, if they were happy to do so (although we were told not to ask). I was on the gate with two volunteer security ladies and we were enjoying chatting and sharing Olympic stories. A wheelchair athlete arrived with his family. He was Santiago Sanz with the Spanish team. Talking later with the only English speaking member of the family we found that one brother was the mechanic for chair repairs, one brother was his coach, one his manager, his mother proudly brushed Santiago's long, thick hair into a pony tail, and his father was the proudest supporter at the Games! Santiago asked for my help to get his racing chair across to the lift and through the building to the track. The lightness of the chair surprised me – it felt as if it would blow away in any breeze. As he was to race in about two hours we three volunteers 'adopted' him, and were able to time our tea break to watch his 1500m race from the staff canteen. Needles to say we had a few puzzled stares from our colleagues as we shouted encouragement to 'our' Santiago in a race that starred an Australian! He came third so we clapped and cheered with excitement. His family came back to the gate to meet him and we all proudly congratulated him and looked at his bronze medal and took lots of photos. Again the next day everything stopped whilst I watched his 3000m race on TV. I clapped, encouraged and cheered in the quieter arena of my home. 'Our' Santiago looked very happy with his gold medal!

SUE BENTLEY-JOHNSTON, *Spectator Services*
SYDNEY NSW

I loved it all (except the food and the requisite one-size-fits-all vollie trousers). But some moments still blaze like beacons in my personal standout catalogue. Like the night I was standing waiting to catch a pithy quote or two from the Italian women's team foilists competing in their final bout for the gold medal. There she was right beside me, my all-time media idol, Italian TV news anchor, Lily Gruber, doing her thing, waiting to get an interview. I wanted to tell her how much I admired her. I just smiled and nodded a lot. In the meantime Valentina Vezzali had literally foiled her opponents and led her team to victory with a mix of furious action and romantic flair. Lily Gruber got in first but I was there too. 'I dedicate this gold medal to my mum who lives for her children,' declared Valentina. And there it was, even among elite athletes, it comes down to home and family. Later during their medal ceremony, Valentina and her teammates flung their victory bouquets into a crowd of adoring fans, in a typically dramatic Italian gesture.

In the weightlifting competition, I watched with a mix of incredulity and just a tinge of prudish disapproval as women lifted 150, 160 even 170 kilograms high above their heads, cheering them on to the pumping beat of *Love Shack* and the commentator's shouts of 'Good lift'!

Darling Harbour was a sea of stylish Europeans and so at any moment you could pretend you were somewhere fabulously continental having never even left home. Or you could just buy a pin.

After my last shift as a fencing vol', I managed to tiptoe through the tulip pots into Heineken House without a Dutch passport and party all night with lots of very tall people wearing orange and little flashing beer badges.

It was 16 glory days topped off by my very own ticker-tape parade!

FELICITY PONTONI, *Reporter*
HABERFIELD NSW

I was working as a paid worker on the South Gate bus region, as a bus coordinator and a pedestrian controller. We were to stop people crossing the road, due to traffic.

One afternoon, this husband and wife turned up and wanted to cross the road. Looking at the man, I was saying in the back of my head, 'I know you from somewhere but where?'

I told him he was unable to cross the road, because it was too dangerous. He was quite annoyed about this but his wife was quite nice about it. I put them on a shuttle bus to go to the entrance of the park.

After putting him and his wife on the bus, my boss, who was standing behind him the whole time, said to me, 'You didn't know who that was, did you?'

I replied, 'I knew the face but I couldn't put a name to it.'

'It was Steve Waugh,' he said, shocked as though I didn't know who he was.

'Of course,' I said.

After telling my family, I got ribbed a lot, because the rest of my family are cricket fans. Every time there is an Australian cricket match on, they always say, there's your mate.

DAVID HUGGINSON, *Traffic Control*
NEWCASTLE NSW

I set my alarm for 5 a.m. Didn't sleep a wink in case I missed it going off. I got up, showered, donned my uniform (boy, did I feel proud) and set off for Eastwood station. The train arrived on time and I got off at Strathfield to connect with the train for Olympic Park. That's where things turned bad.

When the train arrived I went to get on, but my leg fell down between the train and the platform. Luckily, I fell into the train and two young men helped me up. There was no blood on my trousers but by the time I got to Olympic Park my leg was extremely stiff and sore. Nothing was going to stop me doing my shift so I soldiered on to the Superdome. My supervisor took one look at the large bruise and I was made to sit down with an ice-pack on my leg, doing absolutely nothing. This was not what I had in mind for my first shift!

By lunchtime, shock had set in and I became dizzy, nauseous and almost passed out. A wheelchair was summoned and I was taken to first aid where I was examined and told I had to go home and rest. I was taken by wheelchair again (how embarrassing) right round the Superdome to the staff entrance and a nice volunteer driver took me door to door to my temporary home.

Next day it was doctors and x-rays. Fortunately no bones were broken but I was to rest with my leg up for several days, though I did mange to get back for five shifts. The bruise was something to behold – all the colours of the rainbow. In fact, as it changed colour I could have been a driver (purple), a security guard (green) and a Spectator Services volunteer (yellow). It was very pretty!

PAT NEIL, *Accreditation*
BERKELY VALE NSW

Volunteers were being asked for the Games, so myself and my husband (I am Dutch and my husband is Polish) said yes, we can do that. But then we realised we would be 77 and 73 years old and we thought they did not need old people. But then only a few months away from the Games, two of my younger sisters who were also volunteers with their husbands, kept telling me that yes, I could do it, they needed people like me. I am young at heart and a very active volunteer in various groups.

Well, then one day the letter came. I could collect my uniform and that was something. With my passport and papers I went off to Redfern. The feeling when I walked in the hall was yes, I am here, I will be a volunteer.

Then came the day: my very first day as a volunteer. My uniform on, out in the sunshine, I feel ten feet tall. My husband with the camera, click-click.

Off I went on the train to Homebush. It was exhilarating: people coming up to you, asking how and where to go and on my first day I did not know much myself. But I soon learnt.

My ten days were the biggest thing in my life and it is something that will stay with me forever. But there is one very important thing I have to say: without my husband it would not have been easy.

THEODORA WERLE, *Spectator Services*
SYDNEY NSW

My job was very satisfying. By assisting with bus navigation I could help guarantee that a bus full of people would be at their destination on time and smiling. My reward was witnessing the relief and satisfaction on the faces of the drivers and saying farewell to busloads of passengers.

Olympic bus drivers had it tough. You could appreciate the enormous pressure they underwent after spending time with them while they completed their routes. Many were school bus drivers from country towns. Sydney to them was an unknown, unpredictable area with unusually busy traffic conditions. Their buses were always brimming with people who were keen to reach their destinations on time and quick to show their displeasure if delayed. A driver who missed a turn or got lost would have difficulty getting back on track because of the size of the bus and the fact that their buses were not designed to travel in the back streets. Many were driving the buses that they drove in their home towns!

WALTER KORABELNIKOFF, *Navigator / Interpreter / Spectator Services*
SYDNEY NSW

Some staff members had warned me not to sit near boccia athletes in the dining hall as their poor muscle control often meant messy eating, but on this day I was so tired I didn't care. I sat down opposite some Argentinean boccia players with their personal carers. Ever since I began work with the Australian Paralympic Committee I had been very comfortable with different disabilities, however, for some reason I had let other staff members influence my thoughts of the boccia players and thus I tried not to watch these athletes eat. After a few minutes I began to realise I was being ridiculous and I looked up at the Argentinean team. I discovered that the personal carers were struggling to feed their athletes and food was going everywhere! However, instead of this being an embarrassment the carers and their two athletes were laughing hysterically and I too began to laugh! They saw me laughing and laughed even harder. These two young boccia players had the biggest and brightest smiles I've ever seen and they began waving at me. After much manoeuvring they drove their chin-directed electric wheelchairs over to me to say hello, which was quite a challenge seeing not only did they not speak English but they only speak by spelling words out with their feet on the base of their chairs.

To me, these young men not only encompassed the spirit of the Paralympic Games, but also were a perfect example of how even those with a severe disability can still participate in physical activity. I will never forget their shaky but warm hugs and their electric smiles.

NADIA BRANDON-BLACK, *Athlete Services*
BRISBANE QLD

Andrew is confined to a wheelchair as a result of being born with spina bifida. He became aware that volunteers were being sought for the Olympics and Paralympics, made an application and followed the normal processes of registration, interview, uniform given at roster orientation and formal training.

Andrew was placed with Spectator Services and given Stadium Australia as his location. His work centered around customer relations and helping people with directions.

Andrew was involved with the Olympics and Paralympics. He worked evening and night shift, and as with all volunteers was given a different daily task in a team which was coordinated by a supervisor.

Andrew's first experience was meeting with Juan Antonio

Samaranch who passed by his location. Juan put his hand on Andrew's shoulder and said, 'Keep up the good work. You boys and girls are doing a great job.'

We now go back a few months in Andrew's life. To the surprise of Andrew's family his father found a simple illness was diagnosed as a cancer problem and deterioration became rapid. Andrew's father died whilst he was working at the Olympics. He told his supervisor he would need some leave. The supervisor said, 'I'm sorry, come back when you feel ready.'

Andrew returned to the job two days later. That day Juan was on the phone to him and said, 'On behalf of SOCOG I want to pass on my condolences to yourself and your family.' Then followed calls from Kevan Gosper, Michael Knight, Sandy Hollway and Bob Carr. Andrew was further cheered up by the supervisor giving him a peck on the check and a hug. Andrew feels his total experience at both the Olympic and Paralympic Games and people's response to a great sadness in his life demonstrate the great bonding and spirit of kinship amongst all of the volunteers.

ANDREW ELLIS, *Spectator Services*
SYDNEY NSW

On Sunday 1 October 2000, the last day of the Olympic Games, I was fortunate to be working as a volunteer in the common Domain central area, outside the Aquatic Centre, where the men's marathon was to pass by after coming in through the South Gate on the way to the finish in the Stadium. It was a very cool day (not like the 30°C temperatures we had experienced on other days). The crowd lining both sides of the track became excited as the helicopters flew noisily above as the first runners came into sight. The contestants were cheered as they passed by and there were many flashes from cameras in the crowd as photographs were taken.

All this excitement went on for quite a while until the front runners had passed and the gap between contestants grew longer. Eventually a runner would come once in a while until the last few. It was during this time, after the crowd had dispersed, that a lone contestant (I cannot say runner for he was just walking at this stage) came along. The few people left to witness this were moved so much that they cheered and applauded him as he passed. Not only was he walking, but walking beside him was an Event volunteer (blue sleeve volunteer) who had taken off her jacket and given it to him to wear. It was a very moving moment that brought tears to your eyes, to think that this man had the courage to finish the event. I believe that what I witnessed was the true 'Olympic spirit'.

PATRICIA PATTERSON, *Spectator Services*
SYDNEY NSW

I was a volunteer at the Opening and Closing Ceremonies at the Superdome and to begin with I was assigned to the Letter A row to keep the athletes in their respective places. Amongst the As was the Argentinean group.The show was going on outside naturally and the athletes were waiting their turn to come out onto the arena for their ceremony; meantime we were kept busy by giving them food and drinks which they collected themselves in the concourse. I was standing alongside the Argentineans, which consisted of a large group of young spirited athletes. As time went by they got a bit bored and now and again burst out into songs, which I could not follow very well but the sound was cheerful. Apparently they were football songs, at times a bit rude. They sung they clapped and just kept themselves amused.

Over the loudspeakers came the news in English: 'Please note that toilet facilities are available along the concourse, but not outside in Stadium Australia.' I heard it a few times and then all of a sudden I realised that probably the athletes were not aware of the message, so I decided to ask them. I began in Spanish (I am Spanish from Spain), asking if they had listened to the announcement. Of course not they said ... ('*que va*') no way. Then I thought I better let them know what it was all about, but I realised to my horror that I could not translate the message easily, because I had not the exact translation. You see the word toilet is treated differently in different societies depending on the sensitivities. There are all sorts of euphemisms – some call it the bathroom (*baño*) others, wash basin (*levabo*), ladies (*señoras*), WC and so on, so it took me a little explanation which was rather embarrassing. However, I got the message across, as after a suitable interval the young fellows started to file towards the concourse and no doubt to the toilets.

ANTONIA HANNA, *Marshall*
NELSON BAY NSW

I found that the Italians would have won the gold medal for being the slowest team at the Olympics to have showers and get on the bus. Other teams seemed to finish training or a game, shower and be ready to leave 30 to 45 minutes later. But no, the Italians averaged an hour, some days even an hour and a half. It was worse when we had the bus drivers on tight schedules telling me to make them hurry up as they had to get back to the Village to drive another team somewhere.

I would tell the boys '*presto*' (hurry up), '*andiamo*' (let's go). Their response was, '*Con calma*, in Italy we do not rush.' Well my response to that was, 'You are no longer in Italy, get your butts on that bus as we have a schedule!' They just looked at me. I must say that after that they did try to be a little bit quicker, but it wasn't by much.

I will never forget the team walking out for their first game. Waiting in the manmade tunnel at the Dome the court announcer introduces the Italian team and the crowd responds with a huge roar. The boys had so much natural adrenaline pumping through their bodies you could feel it. As I stood there watching this team in amazement as they ran out onto the court, the team doctor takes my hand and leads me out with the team. I could have died.

ANDREA PETROCCO, *TLO for Italian Men's Basketball Team*
MELBOURNE VIC

I was totally surprised by how blasé I became about being around the stars of the show. During the rehearsals and the show, where we would talk to the stars telling them they are due on, when to go and start walking to their positions, I had the chance to talk to them and find out how excited yet nervous they were about performing in front of such a big crowd. About being an Australian performer, performing at the greatest entertainment show they will ever do in their lifetime, with other Aussies, and the amount of pride they had for the opportunity of a lifetime. It was meeting Nikki Webster that I realised this and Jimmy Barnes that pointed it out. But it was John Farnham, Olivia Newton John and Tina Arena who showed that emotion right in front of me, while watching the cauldron being lit. They were like kids in a lolly shop, eyes wide and happily talking about their experience with others that were around them. But you know the biggest thing that was hard for me to do with the assistant stage manager's position was not the endless, tiring rehearsals, the constant yelling to get people's attention, the frustration of repetition, but keeping it all a secret. It was fun for a while saying, 'I know something you don't know but I really cannot tell you what!' but as the show time came nearer and nearer, the more parts of the show I witnessed and learnt, I became aware of what I was saying and it just got harder and harder. I did it ... I did not tell a soul. After the ceremonies a huge sense of relief came over me as I didn't have to keep a secret anymore. My eyes were filled with tears, the sense of pride filling the body, the heart just opened up, and with the excitement that overcame me as that cauldron was being lit at the opening then extinguished at the closing, I realised that I had helped to make this all happen.

ANNETTE DINNING, *St Johns Ambulance / Assistant Stage Manager, Ceremonies*
SYDNEY NSW

I was privileged to work there as a volunteer and have quite a tale to tell! On my first day and much to my acute embarrassment, in the lunch room, for the very first time in my life I fainted. Within seconds I was assisted by qualified first-aid staff and subsequently taken by ambulance to Royal Prince Alfred Hospital. Again I had never before been a victim in an ambulance or taken to hospital. So, slightly recovering on the journey I was rather scared. One of the qualified UDAC members accompanied me and stayed until I was settled which was very comforting. After many tests I was able to ring my daughter and son-in-law and ask them to take me home.

They were highly amused to find me sitting up in bed attached to a drip and adhesive patches, guarding two huge carrier bags containing my uniform. The diagnosis of the registrar: old age! I am sure some of the volunteers who worked darned hard had more years than my 79. Fortunately I was able to return to UDAC and continue as a volunteer, which I thoroughly enjoyed and it was great fun.

JACKIE LANE, *Uniform Distribution*
PENRITH NSW

I should point out that I suffer from multiple sclerosis (MS) and I am limited in the distance which I can walk but fortunately I can still use my other faculties well. Therefore I felt that I would be able to perform any sedentary job, and that my disability would not interfere in any way with my ability to drive, to perform interviews or office duties. I should also pay tribute to the early volunteer driving staff who transported me between Central Station and Jones Street to allow me to fulfil my clerical duties.

Due to an exacerbation of my multiple sclerosis immediately prior to the Games, my neurologist suggested that I withdraw from my volunteer position for the Games. I suggested a compromise, which was agreed to both by my specialist and the Olympic rostering staff, whereby I was rostered to drive every second day. In addition, in the month prior to the Games I was involved in moving sedans and sprinter buses to and from various holding areas. During one of these moves my sprinter unfortunately had a minor collision with a car driven by a delightful Muslim lady which ended with hugs in a McDonald's parking area!

Some highlights of my Olympic and Paralympic experience are as follows:

When I drove three visitors from the shooting venue to Olympic Park, I managed to leave the toll passes in the boot of the car and I had to pull of the motorway. My passengers demonstrated to me that chivalry was not dead by getting out of the car and retrieving the passes.

I felt that the most wonderful experience I was privileged to have was driving the various officials, media and athletes from the Paralympic International Village. As I was needing to use a wheelchair myself to access the vehicle allocated to me by the end of the Paralympic Games, the reaction of Paralympians finding that a wheelchair was already occupying the boot space was always interesting.

It was interesting to observe people's reactions when they found that their rostered driver was using a very large walking aid to access the vehicle to which they were allocated. People were very helpful and at no time showed any unhappiness in being driven by a disabled person.

A swimmer from one of the smaller African countries was fascinated by the long stick which I was using. He was ambulatory, on a large metal stick which he used to propel himself along with. He tested my walking stick but decided he preferred his own.

Perhaps one of the most memorable experiences I had was not as a volunteer but being assisted to the shuttle bus at the end of the Opening Ceremony of the Paralympic Games by a volunteer who enthusiastically took me via a wheelchair to this area. He then informed me he was visually impaired and had just missed out by six-tenths of a second from representing Australia in athletics and was doing the next best thing, i.e. being a volunteer. The ride to the shuttle bus was hairy to say the least, but I hung in there and he felt happy to have been of value.

Another real highlight came when Ron and I joined in the volunteers' parade through the city. I was pushed in my wheelchair by Ron but fortunately other volunteers showed the true volunteer spirit by coming to Ron's assistance on the trek up the Hunter St Hill.

Overall the opportunity to be involved in the success of the Games is something which will not be forgotten. Our seven grandchildren have benefited by our involvement with the bits and pieces of memorabilia they have received and they had news for school 'Show and Tell' for quite some time after the Olympics. I found the whole experience magnificent and I will continue to dine out on my experience for quite some time to come.

EILEEN JAMES, *Driver*
SYDNEY NSW

'That guy is still smiling,' my team leader exclaimed, grinning as she walked up to me. 'What did you say to him?' she asked. I can't remember exactly what I said to the man, but I remember the moment and how rewarded I felt at having passed on my enthusiasm, not just directions, to someone.

My team and I were stationed in the common Domain on what we affectionately referred to as the 'dirty' side of the mag and bag. It was nearing the end of our shift and, after standing on my feet for hours, I was exhausted! The rush had passed and a few people were still arriving from the train to see the night events. I was standing in the middle of the ramp leading down to the north mag and bags. An Australian man approached me and I prepared myself to provide yet another lot of directions. Instead of asking for directions, the man took the time to stop and ask me if I was enjoying myself. Before I know it I was telling him all about my favourite time of day and about the amazing atmosphere this huge event had created.

The one specific thing I can remember telling him was how I loved Olympic Park at night. Night was definitely my favourite time. It cooled down and things became more relaxed. The solar powered light towers kicked in this amazing blue light along the side of the Stadium, and the lights in the trees also came on, twinkling through the leaves. The whole effect was extremely uplifting. Even though I was tired, trudging over the hill each night, I never once forgot to admire the view and the atmosphere at night.

On reflection I realise why it was one of my favourite moments at the Games. For two and a half weeks I spent many hours a day pointing people in the right direction, taking photos, and listening to their experiences, seeing how excited they were. This man took the time to ask me how I was enjoying myself and about my favourite moment so far. I didn't begrudge the millions of other people my time as I was prepared for it and it was my job, one that was going to involve sacrifices as well as providing the experience of a lifetime. But to have just one person interested in me and my role was more than I expected! So although I didn't get a photo of the moment, a gold medal wasn't involved and neither was an Olympian, it is my favourite memory and the one I think of most often. Whoever that man was, I want him to know that I appreciate him being so thoughtful, and I hope that he had a brilliant night that he will never forget, just like the memory he gave me.

TATIANA REGOS, *Spectator Services*
MELBOURNE VIC

Once they had all arrived it was quiet at the airport and they asked us if we would go help at the pedestrian crossing at Olympic Park … Seeing all the school children from kindergarten to university – unbelievable. They came down from Kempsey, Snowy Mountains, Merimbula, Parkes and further afield. All the little kindy-kids joined in pairs in long lines so they would not get lost. Nine hundred buses of school children per day, we were averaging. It was hard to find where the classes ended so we could stop them from crossing so we could let the traffic go. We had to extend our arms out to stop the people from crossing and I often had someone take me in their arms and waltz me around the footpath or give me bear hugs. All in good fun. Then we'd hear a toddler saying, 'Aussie, Aussie, Aussie', and a huge response of 'Oi, Oi, Oi!' It was great.

WARREN AND JUDITH MANUEL, *Load Zone Officer / Pedestrian Assistant*
SYDNEY NSW

I was asked by the chef de mission of Sweden if I would drive a bus with some of the Swedish equestrian team to Robert Sangster's Arrowfield Stud in the Upper Hunter Valley. One of the reasons for the tour was that a number of the horses from the Swedish equestrian team were closely related to the stud's thoroughbred sires.

It took three hours to get to the stud and after a tour we were served afternoon tea. The team wanted to know where all the kangaroos were; they thought they would see them all the way up from Sydney.

The stud manager took me aside and gave directions to go to the far end of the stud, which was very hilly. He said there was a large herd of kangaroos there and if we got there late afternoon we may see some.

I drove the bus to the area about 5 p.m. and coming round a bend on the side of a hill there were four kangaroos. Jumping out of the bus with their cameras the group charged up the hill to within 50 metres of the kangaroos. Then out of the trees came the rest of the herd with a number of females with little joeys in their pouch. There were about 25 kangaroos hopping around the hillside with the equestrians in pursuit, spending about an hour with them.

On the way back to the Village they all said the experience with the kangaroos would live with them forever.

In the following days in the Village, the sight of these equestrians hopping around the lawn telling team members of their experience, will live with me forever.

GORDON GRANT, *Driver*
KAREELA NSW

It went like this. Travel by bus each day from the 'Lindfield Hilton', the minus one-star Scout Hall with sardine like sleeping bags and no snoring protection, pretty tired from a restless night, tramp across the vast surrounds of the Stadium from the southern entrance (which really wasn't an entrance, because our highly suspicious bus was denied access) and wend your way like a group of Japanese tourists to the bowels of the carpark at the northern end of the Stadium.

Wait for the supervisor of the day, who was inevitably late dealing with matters of state and trying to juggle the logistics of staff and us. Some clever strategic planner had estimated the staff they would need and then multiplied by ten, which often meant more staff than visitors at a food stand. Admittedly, that was probably better than the other way around.

While waiting, attempt to grab a uniform when the supervisor arrived and invited you to line up for uniforms. There was always an air of panic as the much-needed XXL sized clothing diminished before your very eyes.

Without being rude about my colleagues, most of us were definitely not going to be mistaken for Olympic athletes so that the smaller sized clothing, more apt for the school children they had hired as paid staff, struggled to be fit for purpose.

This was decidedly humorous at times, and to see large men attempting to get the T-shirts over their more than ample physiques for quite some time would have brought tears to the eyes of the Three Stooges.

The allocation of staff was less than scientific, but somehow people seemed to peel off from the main group and take responsibility for a fries basket or beer tap as we marched like woodchucks through the Stadium.

I, myself, became an expert in cappuccino production in a short time, thanks to my daughter Emily, who was a 'pro' from previous waitressing jobs.

Apart from the productivity of the Rotarians (we are keeners, you know) one really interesting thing happened between the great multicultural public and the food handlers. Almost without exception, the school kids were lost (either in that inexplicable trance that afflicts young people) or in dealing with the variety of accents and funny people. The Rotary people were not. Being older and more experienced, they produced a 'duck in water' performance that engaged the foreign visitors and made the cappuccino or sausage roll mediums of communication, and symbols of inter-cultural understanding. It did my heart good.

As we bussed back after an eight-hour shift to the Hall of Horrors for get another night of what sounded like full-on saw-milling, my fatigue floated in a pool of pride and I finally appreciated what international goodwill and understanding really means.

ROWAN McCLEAN, *Food Outlet Assistant*
MELBOURNE VIC

I worked in the Dome for the first week of the Games in the Print Distribution room. As we only worked at half-time and at the end of the game, we all had lots of time on our hands. I'm not sure how it started, but I'm happy it did. The other PD room started to create things from stuff lying around. A few of us went down to have a look. They had made things related to the sport they worked with and also things from the Opening Ceremony. The two things that stick in my mind were the giant shuttlecock and the balloon with a garbage bag cut out to look like a shirt flying high above the room. That was Nikki Webster. Now this inspired me and my friend Joe.

So we took it upon ourselves to start a 'construction competition'. The first thing I made was the stage from the Opening Ceremony. I made it out of paper, cardboard and paddle-pop sticks we got from our 'new friend' who delivered food to the VIP area. Some of us stayed back many hours to get our creations ready for the judging day. The room was decorated with balloons, streamers and bits of cut-out newspapers stuck to the walls. It was the most colourful room on the whole site. We did it all when we weren't doing runs, but it got to the stage where everyone was enjoying it so much that we hated having to stop and do our 'real' job!

As time went on, people got more and more ideas for what to build. We used just about anything we could find. Even our drink containers from the train journey in. I would take home paddle-pop sticks to glue together for the train track that we made and hung from the ceiling with string.

By this stage, the room was looking the part with the full basketball court, backboards and even the floor markings. We had three offices and one of them was completely taken up with these creations. Finally, we added the cauldron to the stage by wrapping a print cylinder from the photocopier in paper. It really did look great.

Then we moved to the Superdome and me and my friend Joe decided to bring all our creations with us. We carried all the creations down Olympic Boulevard and people thought we were crazy. The 3-metre long paddle-pop train line got the most looks.

It was worth all the effort because we won Best Construction. I was nicknamed Construction Manager and I was very proud.

Never will I look at a cardboard box and not be reminded of the great times we had, sitting in a room watching the SOCOG live-feed while cutting and pasting.

DAVID SILLINCE, *Print Distribution*
TOONGABBIE NSW

It was pouring with rain and I had bronchitis and I had been appointed toilet monitor for the day. Dressed in my plastic poncho and plastic trousers I shifted the weight from one foot to another. Our team leader, a prison warder from the US who had volunteered at Atlanta, tried to keep our spirits up.

And then an elderly gentleman approached and said he wished to complain. It was after 11 a.m. and he wants to know why play had not commenced on Court 1. You could have floated ducks on the court. He had paid his money and he wanted to see the Williams sisters play. We explained that play would not commence until it had stopped raining and the court was dry. At this point it was still bucketing down. He insisted on completing a complaint form, huddled in the open telephone booth. We could hardly contain ourselves – we were awash and he expected play to commence!

Our team leader assured him she would pass on his complaint, which she did. What did he expect us to do – get on the phone to God? We smiled as he traipsed off through the deluge. Play finally commenced after 5 p.m.

INGRID RADFORD, *Spectator Services*
SYDNEY NSW

One story comes to mind – I was early one day and before I took up my duties as a Swiss timer at the Paralympics tennis. I was watching some athletes warm-up and got talking with a young pair from the Netherlands, Rubin Ammerlaan and Ricky Molier. They were doubles partners. Robin was so excited he had become a dad, for the first time, two days before leaving home to come to Australia and he was armed with a photo album and stories to show the event of the delivery of his son Danny. He said to me, 'My heart is in two places. I would love to be home with my wife and son and also I want to be here to represent my country and try to win a medal.' I was very taken in by Rubin. He was about the same age as my own son would have been, and he touched my heart with his friendliness and sincerity.

Some days later, I know exactly what Rubin meant as he and his partner Ricky Molier were playing our own Aussie doubles partners – David Hall and David Johnson for the gold medal – they did and they won so I said to him (Robin), I know how you feel with your heart in two places as I would have loved our Aussie pair to win the gold and yet I was pleased that the Netherlands' pair had won also. Robin and I swapped shirts – he loved our blue Aussie volunteers' shirts – and I will treasure it and the pin he gave me forever.

WENDY RILEY, *Swiss Timing*
SYDNEY NSW

I trained as a T3 driver to be depoted at Darling Harbour and I went to Sydney on several weekends to do my training. After the completion of my training I got the call to go to Sydney to get my uniform on 1 September. After spending a couple of days with my brother in Umina on the Central Coast and still no communication from SOCOG I rang to find out what was doing and to my surprise I was told my depot did not become operational till 15 September. So I asked to be given something to do because I was here for the duration. They then rostered me to the Indian team out at the Olympic Village for six days. On my completion of the six days I received a call on my mobile on my way home and I was asked if I would like to remain out at the Village. I said I quite enjoyed my time so far and I was told I could drive for Israel for the duration if I wished to remain there, to replace other drivers who asked to be reassigned. After finding the location of the compound I pressed the bell on the gate and noticed several cameras on me and when I was let through the gate my breath was momentarily taken away by two SWATS with flak jackets and the biggest machine guns I have ever seen and as I turned the corner heading to the office there was another one with another one.

As time went by I got to know some of the SWATS and the Mossad people in the compound. Everywhere I went with the athletes I had an armed escort in the minibus and an armed unmarked police car right behind me. Getting close to the end of the Olympics I was told, 'Quick, quick, take these two to 22 George Street, North Strathfield' (this was not on the training course). I said, 'Where the hell is George Street, North Strathfield?' Remembering I am from Melbourne Zev said, with a wide gesture of the hands, 'Down that way off Parramatta Road, take them there and you don't have to wait for them.'

So off we go and they have all their luggage with them. When I get to the car I look up the street directory then I discover they do not speak

English and stranger yet I have no police escort. So off we go and I find 22 George Street and I get an uneasy feeling that this is not right. It is a broken down weatherboard house with bars on the window. So I gesture to them to stay put while I check it out. I go up and ring the door bell and unknown to me the coach of the athlete team is right behind me. Just then an Asian girl opens the door and straight away the coach starts talking in Hebrew to the girl. She gives me a puzzled look and gestures for us all to come inside. By this time the young athlete is out of the car and I look inside and it has the look of a brothel (for a moment there I thought that perhaps they were supposed to come here but I said to myself, no I have got all their luggage in the car). So I do a great job. A kelpie cattle dog would be proud of me. I get them both back in the car; all the time the girl is pleading for us to come in. When we get inside the car the coach offers me his hand and I thought he wanted to shake my hand, but he had a phone number on it. So I ring it and a man answers in Hebrew so I said, 'I do not speak your language but I am outside 22 George Street. Where are you?' And he said, 'Not 22. Twenty-*three* George Street.'

When I get there he is waving to us from the first floor of an apartment block. After we unloaded the car I said to the two Israelis (which was translated by the bloke from the apartment), 'Are you sure you don't want to get back to 22 George Street for one hour?' They seemed to enjoy the joke very much and we shook hands and parted.

JIM PENROSE, *Driver*
COOLAROO VIC

EPISODE 2 – MISSION IMPOSSIBLE
SUBJECT: THE AMAZING ADVENTURES OF KEITHUS MAXIMUS
DATE: SUN, 24 SEPT 2000 09:37:58NZST

Hi Folks,
Just thought I would let you all know what I have been up to over here. After the last exciting episode where Joe Barnes and I got red carded and disqualified in a game against Australia there has been a lot of laughs and a lot of great volleyball (not by us).

Unfortunately we, the Kiwis, have found that although we have accreditation passes that allow us down to the field of play, we are not permitted to go onto the sand and if we hang around the stands watching the game we are quickly approached by the Spectator Services guards and told that we have to move on. We have also discovered that our uniforms that we have to wear as volunteers are very easily spotted from great distances so this made it even more impossible for us to hide somewhere and watch the games up close.

However, after being restricted to watching all the games on the back-of-house TVs and getting very frustrated at being so close but so far away, Joe and I decided to try a new tactic. We made our way through the first couple of checkpoints that we needed our passes for and then did a quick lap of the Stadium just checking out if there were any spare seats. It is apparently fine for us to walk through the Stadium as long as we don't stop and watch the game. Anyway, so we go through and had spotted a few spare seats in one area the looked like they would offer particularly good viewing. So with the speed of supermen we quickly removed our accreditation passes and volunteer shirts and as it was a very hot day the majority of the male members of the crowd were in singlets or topless so we confidently walked straight back past the guards and seated ourselves in the spare seats. This was perfect as we had a great view and no one could see our uniforms (cos we had taken them off) and our theory was that we could safely blend into the surrounding crowd. The game we had selected was a very feisty match between the hometown Australian No. 1 team and the USA No. 1 team. This was a very important match as the winner was guaranteed a spot in the next round.

As you can imagine, the Aussies had a heck of a lot of support and as it turned out we were seated the row behind a small but loud contingent of American supporters. We didn't think this was a problem until we realised that the American fans were quite prepared to try and out-yell the thousands of Aussies and to aid them with this they had brought their own plastic rubbish bins to bang on for more noise. This is where our little plan started to go sour because our attempt to blend in and quietly sit in the crowd only made us stand out more as we were the only crowd members in our area not yelling and stomping and making noise. Well this plus the fact that my theory when supporting sports is much like any other Kiwi I know in that 'I support any New Zealander ... and anyone that plays Australia' so there seemed only one thing to do. When in Rome and all that jazz, so we started to clap and cheer and stomp and yell and bang anything that we could get our hands on. Now we were blending like we have never blended before and having a great time doing so to boot. But just when we thought we could not stand out any more, the

MC did the unexpected and came up into the crowd. The MC is the guy whose job it is to hype up the crowd and he walks around with a microphone and generally just draws attention. We saw him coming and there was nothing that we could do about it. We couldn't leave; it was far too late for that. The MC started talking on the mike and waited until everyone in the Stadium could see where he was and then he gave our newfound American friends a brand new match volleyball for being such patriotic supporters. We could only laugh. Our original plan was to blend into the crowd and quietly watch some great volleyball but instead we unwillingly managed to make a spectacle of ourselves and not only got pointed out to the whole Stadium but also ended up on TV here too, thanks to our friendly MC. Luckily our manager admired our Kiwi ingenuity and wasn't worried about our exploits at all. I mean after all, we are volunteers. What are they gonna do? Dock our pay? Haha. Brilliant. Straight to plan B next time I think.

KEITH KINCAID, *Quality Control for Results*
CHRISTCHURCH NZ

" I remember working one day with a volunteer who was a great contributor.

I remarked, 'You don't look too well today.'

She replied, 'I'm part way through my sentence – I've got three months to live.'

I asked. 'Why are you here?'

And she said 'This is the best way to use up three weeks in the last three months of my life.'

A remarkable story. "

Gerry

I received many gifts whilst working at the Olympic Village. Working as a volunteer in one of the 22 resident centres scattered throughout the Village, it was a sure thing that each day I would receive some small token of appreciation from either an athlete, a coach or an official who resided in the Village. The stream of gifts was endless – bags, hats, badges – even a ticket to the Opening Ceremony.

However, there was one gift in particular that made me feel especially proud to have been a part of the Olympic experience. It came from a female athlete from Djibouti, a tiny country in north-eastern Africa. Djibouti had only four athletes competing, and being a relatively poor country, they had not brought much else with them to the Olympic Games. They didn't have multiple sets of tracksuits like most of the other athletes, nor did they have bags of pins to exchange with other pin traders or to give as presents to volunteers and other athletes.

On my last day in the Village however, this women gave me a gift that shone in comparison to even the brightest pin. She arrived at my resident centre with the Djibouti NOC, who explained to me in English that she had photocopied some postcards from Djibouti onto a big piece of paper so that I could see her home. She couldn't really speak any English so the Djibouti NOC told me about the places as she pointed them out. This was her gift to me – showing me her world in exchange for me showing her mine.

LAUREN KENNEALLY, *Athletes' Assistant*
ADELAIDE SA

Having been designated a T1 volunteer driver, I was gobsmacked when I was asked to be a driver for the Spanish Royal Family and in particular, Her Majesty Dona Sophia de Grecia y Hannover.

My nervousness dissipated upon my first meeting with the queen as she entered my vehicle along with her female protocol officer. Her Majesty promptly offered her hand, said hello and asked my name. 'Ahh, "Ramon" in Spanish – that will be easy to remember.' The plain-clothed policewoman beside me then laughingly mentioned I probably would have to put up with a lot of 'women's talk' en route to the Olympic Park.

Later in the week, as were leaving the Athletes' Village, the queen asked me; 'Ramon, don't you get tired waiting for me all the time?' To which I replied; 'No Your Majesty, it is indeed a privilege. Apart from helping my wife give birth to my three children this has been the second most interesting job I've had!' – to which she roared laughing.

Apart from the queen, the royal entourage consisted of the Crown Prince Felipe De Bourbon, Princess Elena and her husband Jaime de Marichalar and Princess Cristina. Also visiting was the queen's brother, H.R.M. King Constantin of Greece, who is presently in exile living in London.

On one occasion, the king was chatting to his sister as we drove out to Olympic Park: 'Sophie, you must come to see the athletes with me today, to hear the Aussies cheer. They don't just roar for their own, they roar for everybody!'

Another time, we were late leaving the tennis and the queen was to meet the king and the rest of her family at a harbourside restaurant. Her Majesty asked if we could go quickly so as not to be late. I politely explained that all volunteer drivers had been warned not to break the speed limit to which the queen jokingly asked the accompanying policewoman if she carried a blue light in her bag and if she could loan it to Ramon to put on the roof of the car?

Earlier during the visit, as we drove through the city, the queen mentioned that many people seemed to be talking to themselves as they walked along the streets. The protocol officer mentioned that they were actually talking on the their mobile phones to which the Queen again burst into laughter and said she hadn't realised there were so many personal phones in Australia.

On so many occasions Her Majesty was so gracious and displayed a delightful sense of humour. Her charm no doubt makes her a popular monarch and I know first hand that she thoroughly enjoyed her Sydney Olympic experience. For me, it was indeed a fascinating and highly memorable two weeks.

RAY G. LLOYD, *Driver*
SYDNEY NSW

I'd spent the morning driving three Kenyan team officials to Canberra where they had lunched with the Kenyan ambassador and seen some sights. On the return trip, Goulburn's Big Merino was an ideal driver reviver stop and naturally my three passengers climbed to the lookout at the top of the ram. While they were out of the car I bought three stubbies of Old Beer and placed them on the back seat of the car.

Once underway again they asked what was in the bag and I told them it was liquid refreshment for the journey but if they did not want it I would take it home as it was the beer I normally had at home.

While they were slow to finish the first traveller, they soon asked if we could make a further stop somewhere off the main highway to see a little of what they called outback Australia and purchase more liquid refreshments.

Wheeling off the highway we drove to Sutton Forest where we went into the local country pub with all of five locals present, including the publican.

That moment in time when we walked through the door was an experience none present would ever forget. Sutton Forest would never have imagined the Olympics coming to their little town but that is exactly what happened that day when three big Kenyans and a bloke in a volunteer's uniform walked into that pub.

The locals quizzed the Kenyan officials about the Games and their athletes and they answered all their questions and signed autographs for them.

With both parties enjoying the informality of the meeting we stayed almost an hour and as the publican had a special on large bottles of Old Beer we restocked to finish the trip.

Next day it was Olympics as usual, but I still smile to myself whenever I tell the story of the day I introduced the Kenyans to Old Beer, travellers, beasties and the pub at Sutton Forest.

ROBERT McLEAN, *Driver for Kenyan National Olympic Committee*
SYDNEY NSW

One of the 'challenging' jobs of being a Food Services assistant in the dining halls was to stand on the inside of the entrance door, and ensure none of the athletes, officials and their guests exited through the entrance door. (That's what the exit door is for obviously.) There was an electronic counter on the door that keeps a tally of the number of athletes and officials that were using the dining hall facilities and it would provide misleading statistics for SOCOG. There were plenty of signs both in English and French advising that there was 'no exit' through the entrance door.

On one particular day I was manning the entrance door, ensuring that appropriate exits occurred. Princess Anne came in and had lunch with the Great Britain team. I was doing the usual star spotting patrol while standing in my position and noticed Princess Anne collect her tray and place her own rubbish in the respective waste and recycling bins. I was thinking to myself, 'Wow! Even royalty throws their own rubbish away' and whilst in my daydream, I realised she was walking right up to the entrance door to exit. Now being the efficient little volunteer that I was, and remembering that we had previously been told to treat all athletes and officials the same, I pointed to the exit, and said, 'Excuse me Princess Anne, would you mind walking out through the exit door please.' With that she gave me a royal nod, and said, 'Of course dear, thank you very much.'

Following her exit, I then rushed around to the vollies close to me saying, 'I just told Princess Anne where to go! I just told Princess Anne where to go!'

When repeating this story to friends and family later on, all have remarked, 'I can't believe you called her Princess Anne and not Your Royal Highness', not one person actually criticising that I should have not bothered her and let her go through the entrance and have had more respect for the person that she is.

Brush with royalty continues ...

Following on from this Princess Anne debacle, about 40 minutes later the same day, I was in exactly the same 'responsible' spot, protecting the entrance door, and I spotted Prince Albert of Monaco having lunch with the Italian team. Following lunch, he gets up from the table, collects his tray, places his rubbish in the respective waste bins (common royalty sight by now) and then I notice he grabs a bottle of water from the fridge and places it in the pocket of his suit. He notices me watching him do this and comes up to me and says, 'You didn't see that did you.' I think to myself, 'As long as you go out the right door, you can put what you like in your pockets' and responded with, 'See what, Your Royal Highness?'

LINDA CAMPBELL, *Food Services Assistant*
BRISBANE QLD

At last, the day had arrived. I was to commence my volunteer duties at the Olympic Games. I arrived at Lidcombe station and ascertained the whereabouts of the bus that would take me to the Olympic Village. I needn't have worried as there were many people in the same boat as myself – unsure of their destination and job – all dressed in their Olympic uniform with the different colours to indicate their area of work, and proud as could be.

From the beginning, everyone was extremely friendly and excited about his or her part in this great Australian experience. The Village itself was another interesting situation. Meeting the other volunteers and paid staff, sizing each other up and being thrown into the 'job' was exhilarating and challenging. I was assigned to the information station in the main administration office of SOCOG and although I had attended a briefing session, the requirements of the 'job' were dazzling.

So to work. The Village was only about half full at the end of August when I started and everyone thought that it would be rather quiet and we would learn the 'job' slowly without any pressure. Oh, how wrong was that assumption!

Day one began with enquiries about every possible area of the Village. Questions such as 'How do I get from A to B?' to 'Where are the computers and fax machines?' and 'I'm hungry, what dining facilities are open?' to 'Can you provide me with an interpreter for Romanian or Cantonese or …?' The last question was asked in halting English and I was unable to help the person because of only speaking English. It was here that I decided how ignorant of other languages I was and my school French was nearly useless. But, slowly and surely, questions did get answered and mostly correctly, we hoped, as anxious faces relaxed and smiles appeared.

At the end of the first day, I felt that I would never be able to learn the ropes fast enough and went home feeling like a salmon swimming upstream when everyone else was travelling downstream. As I am a school teacher and usually in control of what is needed to be done, this was a perplexing feeling, tinged with anxiety. I wanted to be a part of this great Australian dream but wondered would I be able to give my best to all of these marvellous athletes from all over the world. However, I was consoled with the thought that tomorrow would present with many of the same questions and I would be of some use to the team.

What a shock was in store for me the next day. The questions were totally different to the day before and therefore answers had to be found for that day's arrivals from different countries. But, how exciting it was, if somewhat exhausting. Athletes that I had heard about or read about were suddenly standing in front of the counter, asking for help from the information team. No time for standing staring at our idols, just get on with the job and enjoy the experience. Later, it was fun to discuss with other team members, who we had seen, spoken to, travelled in the bus to the dining room with, stood next to in the queue for the meal etc. We were supposed to be volunteers with the right attitude to the famous, not to ask for autographs, but even mere mortal volunteers can be overcome with pride and interest.

As the Games drew closer, the impetus of the Village quickened to a fast and furious level. The Village filled up and it seemed that every skin colour on earth was representing their country and extremely proud to be at the Olympic Games. The flag ceremonies were formal but the presentations by the school children involved in those ceremonies was touching as primary school children sang, danced and wriggled through the welcoming ceremonies. At times, there wasn't a dry eye in the house as small children put so much effort into representing their country, Australia, in a welcome and their teachers beamed with pride. What a brilliant idea it was to include these children from all around the country.

The Opening Ceremony was absolutely marvellous and the feeling in the Village the day after, was one of joy, hope and happiness. Things began to get very serious from then on and athletes became more tense and concerned as their particular event loomed. It was very interesting to observe an athlete in the Village before their event and then afterwards. A win was great but participation was the focus and faces changed from a tenseness to a more relaxed attitude when competition was completed.

In the Village Square, athletes became just young people having fun. One day I observed Michael Klim and Ian Thorpe in the Village, acting like two teenage boys, sky-larking, laughing and teasing each other. It made me realise that most of the athletes were young and a tremendous amount of responsibility was resting on their shoulders. They had worked extremely hard to attain their position in a team and their country now asked them to perform at a top level and gain a medal if possible. What a dream! What a responsibility!

And so, the days of the Olympics moved on. The questions became more complex but slowly we did 'get a handle' on most of it. The atmosphere was fantastic; it was tiring but exhilarating, interesting and educational. Obscure countries were investigated, and for me a great learning curve took place.

LYNNE HALMARICK, *Information Station*
RUSSEL LEA NSW

Why was I, an ageing citizen, putting myself through this misery I thought as at 10 p.m. on a cold Sunday night in September I waited for my Olympic gentleman at Mascot. What did I know of a country in the far north of Europe? Surely Eskimos lived there? Would he speak English, my friends asked?

My experiences as an Olympic driver designated to drive for a senior Olympic official from Iceland began when to my surprise a very tall fair haired Viking was introduced as 'my man'. He spoke English fluently along with many other languages. Coming as he did from Iceland he had no concept of time or peak hour traffic so I sometimes had to go around the block a couple of times or park in the hotel car park and walk up the equivalent of five storeys to give him a call. Soon he'd come down with his happy smile and we'd be off. 'BarBra' he called me as he outlined his plan each day.

Ellert loved golf and I spent many happy hours parked at the golf course. My husband offered to take him to a 'real' golf course but when I saw how many strokes Ellert had on one hole I realised it was better left alone.

Each day was a wonderful and new experience. Where would we go today? Where would the bomb checks be? Who would I meet or see today? On one occasion we saw Henry Kissinger surrounded by bodyguards. He walked directly in front of the car. 'Don't run over him,' said Ellert. 'He is a very good man.'

My most embarrassing occurrence was when I lost my car, my beautiful blue Holden Commodore. We had gone to the ladies' soccer final at the Sydney Football Stadium. Faced with the prospect of spending all night alone in Moore Park car park and seeing another driver walking towards the Stadium I thought I'd follow. All went well until I reached the gate. One needed a pass to go inside and you had to leave the car key as security.

'Leave my car keys? Will they be here when I come back?'

'Oh we haven't lost any yet,' the officer said, so with great trepidation I made my way inside.

Dinner was delicious and not only that, there was a special viewing area where we could watch the soccer, which was very exciting going into extra time. About then I thought I'd better return to the car to await my call.

Found the gate, found the guard but couldn't find the keys. None of the keys seemed to match mine. Every key was turned out but no luck.

'Where are my keys?'

'I was really worried this would happen.'

'You'll have to help me.'

'What am I going to do?' So it went on.

Someone was sent to the car park to see if the car was still there. Tension was mounting as the roar of the crowd celebrating the end of the game became louder.

'May I have one more look at the keys please?' I said.

You guessed it. There were my keys in all their glory with an extra tag added when the relief driver had taken the car for service.

'Sorry,' I said, 'So sorry' as I slunk back to the car park and my beautiful Olympic car.

Relief surged through me as my guest told me of the exciting soccer match they had just seen. Thank goodness no one wanted to know what I had been doing all night.

BARBARA HAZELTINE, *Driver*
CASTLE HILL, NSW

The Olympic Games to me is the ultimate of excellence in sport. Striving to gain the selection in order to qualify for Olympic Games is a gigantic mountain which very few people will ever conquer. Once this hurdle is achieved then the next mountain looms – to prove to yourself that 'you have what it takes' to achieve ultimate success. Of course, there is only one gold, one silver, one bronze and very few athletes emerge as the 'victors'. I was fortunate enough to achieve a bronze medal in Tokyo in 1964 and the Olympic Games continues to draw me to this unique experience to witness the achievements of other young athletes.

Unfortunately, circumstances beyond my control prevented me from attending and being a part of the Olympic experience in Sydney 2000. So I decided in order to have some involvement with the Games, I would make application to be a volunteer in Melbourne at the soccer.

Interviews were arranged and I smiled when a young lady, the interviewer, asked me, 'What do you know of the Olympic Games? Can you tell me something significant about the Olympic Games?' I decided to be brief and not bore her with my 20-year career as an Olympic athlete, and responded with 'I have competed in three!' She quickly produced the appropriate form and I was in like Flynn.

A couple of briefing sessions, a uniform, a security pass (with snapshot – like a passport) and I was a fully-fledged volunteer set to take on the world of soccer fans. The majority of my fellow volunteers were interesting people from a variety of different backgrounds who were over the moon with Olympic Games fever. I did find it a little difficult to share their enthusiasm at first, as this to me was hardly the Olympic Games. However, I certainly got caught up in the appropriate mood after a very short period of time.

The sporting Mecca of Melbourne, the MCG, was a sight to behold and not only did I feel great pride in being a part of this once in a lifetime experience it brought back very vivid memories. As a young aspiring athlete, I travelled from country Victoria to view the likes of John Landy and Betty Cuthbert perform on the MCG in 1956. But I am getting off track.

Soccer was not a sport I had followed with interest over recent years, but the splendour of the occasions and the excitement associated with the Olympic Games, was certainly not lost on me. Adding to the excitement of the atmosphere, was the presence of the different nationalities from all over the world, many of them Australian citizens, parading, signing and dancing both outside and inside the MCG.

My responsibility as a volunteer was to provide directions to the visitors, and check tickets and security (no bottles, no pocket knives, no guns!). One person was ready to drop his pants because his keys were in a pocket in his jocks! I said it was okay, he could just go in! Most visitors were wonderful and very patient with the entry to the MCG being a little slower and more difficult than usual because of the tight security. Those that did protest were very impatient and vocal – I wanted to say to them, 'Remember Munich '72?' I was part of that tragedy and would never like to see the likes of that repeated.

I enjoyed many jovial moments both as a 'gate person' and around the meal tables with other volunteers. Friendships were formed and many have been ongoing with reunions already taking place.

One thing that brought back many of my Olympic memories was the parade of volunteers onto the MCG before the final soccer game. I remarked to others that you would think we were the athletes instead of just volunteers. The crowd cheered and clapped us as if we were the 'victors' and perhaps in our own small way we were.

JUDY POLLOCK, *Spectator Services*
Bronze Medallist in Athletics at Tokyo 1964
MELBOURNE VIC

I HAD THE TIME OF MY LIFE ...

'Mate, jawannabe in the Olympic team?' Australia's Number One advertising man Singo (John Singleton) drawled down the phone. 'There's no money, just a load of work, yawl be with a bunch of us looking after the media.' I said yes. I would have paid *him* to be part of the action! And thus began my voluntary role as assistant media director for the 2000 Australian Olympic Team.

Singo never made it, another mate, Alex Hamill, was my boss but you know what was strange? Everywhere I went I saw this little guy with bushy eyebrows. The night Andrew Gaze was named captain of the Australian Olympic Team, Andrew cuddled him! I said 'Andrew, let's get a picture with him!' Even Kim Beazley took a picture of Andrew and him. I'm at the tennis with Laurie Lawrence getting the crowd to cheer on that famous Yugoslavian tennis player, the lovely Jelena Dokic, and he's there again! Laurie and me had our picture taken with him again.

And then I'm out at the shooting to watch Michael Diamond try and win his second gold medal. I manage Michael. Have done for four years. Never seen him shoot. Thought I'd go along and help look after the media. Brocky's there.

We've all got our faces painted just like kids at a party. Michael wins gold. GOLD! The crowd erupts. Michael's mum runs to him past the security. The media are all over this amazing young man who's now won back-to-back gold medals.

Michael's coming over to me and I'm standing next to HIM. You know, the small guy with bushy eyebrows. I'm arm's length from Michael, he's in a daze, a zone – a twilight zone – a special zone only Olympic gold medallists get into during the hour after they've won. He hasn't seen HIM yet. So I point down at the little guy while jerking my head towards him hoping Michael will recognise who he is.

'Oh,' says Michael, 'er, er ...'

I don't think he's remembered the guy's name yet.

'Hello Prime Minister,' says Michael.

We had another picture.

It was an amazing time. First day of the Games I'm at the pool. It's the night Thorpy won his 400m gold medal, then backed up with the 4 x 100 boys to win another in the pool. I was there helping Ian Hanson arrange the drug tests, post event news conferences and get the swimmers back to the Village for a decent night's sleep before the next day's events.

The crowds have long gone. It's getting late. 10.30. Thorpy's had a rubdown then off to the news conference. I've gone off to commandeer a bus. Found a 42-seater just for Ian. Well Thorpy's BIG!

Now, I've got Michael Klim and Chris Fydler and it's 11.30. Only the cleaners are around. It's dark. I phone the team's HQ. Any transport? Quick as a flash there's Rob Thornton , the AOC director of logistics, out of bed and driving a minibus picking up Klimmy, Fydler and little ol' me from the back door of the now deserted Olympic pool. Gold medals in hand!

Back to the Village, it's quarter to midnight. 'Hungry, boys?' says I. Straight in to the dining room. Seats 5000-plus. Open 24 hours a day. They never close. Feed you anything your heart desires. I once ate five magnums at a single sitting and two bowls of apple crumble and custard. But don't tell my doctor!

So, there's Michael Klim, Chris Fydler and me eating supper in the Village at 11.45 when up comes a vision. It's Inge de Bruin. She joins us. Happiest girl in the world. She won a medal tonight too. Wants to go out and celebrate, have a glass of wine. H-A-P-P-Y Happy. I told her to wait till she finishes competing 'cos she needs to focus on her swimming. Lucky she took my advice 'cos she went on to win a few more medals! I went to bed happy that night, too.

Olympic Games in Sydney? Thanks Singo. Where do I send the cheque? I had the time of my life.

MAX MARKSON, *Assistant Media Director for Australian Olympic Team*
SYDNEY NSW

I count myself as an extremely lucky individual and credit a lot of my success in basketball to my longtime friendship with Australian Captain, Andrew Gaze. We were schoolmates in high school and have remained close friends ever since.

I won't forget the day I got home from work and my wife handed me an envelope from the organising committee of the Sydney 2000 Olympics. My first application was sent in 1996 and there had been hundreds of letters leading up to the Olympics. I always thought I may have been in with a chance to get a position as a basketball announcer, but you never get excited until it happens. I opened the letter and read that I had been accepted and was going to the Olympics.

Due to my close relationship with Andrew, I was one of many Australians that were hoping that he was chosen to carry the Australian flag in the Opening Ceremony. Andrew had told me that the ceremony was to take place in the foyer of the Superdome and that he thought he was choice to get it. I went over to the Superdome and was stopped by a number of security personnel and told that it was a private function and you needed a pass to get in. I tried to negotiate with the head of security but to no avail. My next effort was with a policeman, but that failed as well. I had to be content with seeing the announcement outside the glass doors. That didn't make it any less exciting and I can remember shouting, 'Yes! Yes! Yes!' and people around me must have thought me a little crazy.

Then came my lucky break. A photographer who I knew from Melbourne came out to say hi. He asked me why I wasn't inside and I said I didn't have a pass. He told me to wait a minute and he went in and got me a pass. Yes I was in.

I was feeling a little strange being it was a black tie affair and I had a track suit and runners on. That didn't bother me too much and I made my way though the crowd to congratulate my mate on getting the flag.

The first thing that Andrew said to me was, 'How the hell did you get in here?' I said 'Connections.' What a great moment for a great ambassador and a great bloke.

My fondest memory of the dedication of the volunteers was about the guy who worked at the rear exit to our hotel. He would sit at the bottom of the stairs with a view of absolutely nothing and check the passes of the patrons staying at the hotel. Every day I would enter and exit the hotel about ten times and there was my friend proudly sitting in his spot and excited to be part of the Olympics. Every day he was smiling and every day he was friendly and accommodating. To him I say well done and thank you for your contribution.

My most exciting moment came when I was chosen to be the announcer for the gold medal men's game. It may not seem like much to some people but after being involved in the sport for over 20 years and to be given this honour was the proudest sporting moment of my life.

I would like to finish by saying that all Australians should be proud of our achievements during the Olympics and it only reinforces that we are by far the best country in the world!

WAYNE PETERSON, *Basketball Announcer*
MELBOURNE VIC

I was privileged to be one of the 1000 dancers in the 'Love is in the Air' segment of the Olympics 2000 Closing Ceremony, and perhaps you will allow me to share with you some of my thoughts about the occasion. We had three strikes against us from the beginning:

- The music: we had to dance a samba with about 180 beats per minute. Being a competition dancer, I was used to dancing a samba at 120 beats per minute. Would my feet/hips/anything move fast enough?
- The surface: a sort of rubber matting laid on the running track to give the athletes non-slip traction, but rather difficult for dancers doing fast turns.
- The giant kewpie dolls: I do not know which idea came first: the 10-metre high dolls or the 1000 dancers, but whoever put these together missed the point of ballroom dancing. A lone dancer or even a group of dancers often need extra things to give their dance an energy lift: noisy shoes, exotic costumes, whatever. But ballroom and Latin American dancing are not just about dancing, they are about the relationship between two people. This is its extra thing. Ballroom dancing does not need 10-metre high dolls in principle, and in practice they were a disaster.

For about eight minutes, 1000 dancers appeared before a worldwide audience of billions. That averages to about a half a second of fame per dancer. I was rather lucky: I had about two seconds of world-wide coverage. But did my friends and relatives spread over three continents, waiting with bated breath to catch a glimpse of me, see me dancing? No. They saw me running witless to avoid being run over by a mountainous kewpie doll. The dolls scattered us like chaff in the wind, and when we did find a safe place to dance, the choregraphy had evaporated from our minds like the morning mist before the midday sun at Uluru.

The television directors loved it (the confusion), but luckily we were not dancing for them. We were dancing for the Olympic athletes, trying to give a little something back to them, as they had given to us their skill, endurance, and years of perseverance. And that worked. Only a metre in front of them we gave our eight minutes of passion and colour, and they revelled in it. The energy exchange between them, and us, and the volunteers alongside them, and the audience at our backs, made a crescendo of emotion that turned the eight minutes into a triangle of dream, fantasy, and reality. Never in my life have I experienced eight minutes like that.

The endless hanging around and the innumerable changes were a great pain, but were nothing. The eight minutes was the real thing.

DON HERBISON-EVANS, *Dancer*
SYDNEY NSW

Then on 20 September I was redeployed to the Tennis Centre starting at 7 a.m. Here the numerous volunteers were split into many smaller groups and taken to our work areas for various courts by a supervisor and then given our starting tasks. I had got into a group for court one and on a VIP entrance without knowing it. We were rotated during the day at various jobs.

I went through all the tasks – top security door, dungeon security, crowd directions and information outside the entrance to the Stadium and then on the inside, opening and closing the entrance door at the appropriate times. A ladies' match was on at the time so my fellow volunteer and myself had worked together for a short time. An official came up to us and informed us an important visitor was expected shortly for the next match, which was a men's game. I later found out the important visitor was Chelsea Clinton representing the American President, Bill Clinton.

The men had had their warm-up and the game was about to start. The ball was served and as instructed I promptly closed the door. The other volunteer working with me said Chelsea had just come into sight as I shut the door.

At the end of the first service I opened the small exit door at the side and allowed Chelsea and some security guards in and they stood at the side. I don't think Chelsea was upset at having the door closed on her but her security guards were probably not impressed. At the end of the first game an official escorted the party to their seats. I never saw Chelsea again as I was relieved from my position at 4 p.m. to complete my duties for the day. The whole experience from the games was tremendous but I think closing the door on Chelsea Clinton will be a talking point around my family for years to come.

ERNIE WHILES, *Accreditation*
SYDNEY NSW

The crowd control has been excellent with volunteers every few yards keeping things moving freely, always in a very cheerful manner, and keeping the masses (hundreds of thousands of them) going in the general way expected of them. The fact that the majority of the crowd are Australians and that we have been winning heaps of medals, (the most ever) has probably had quite a bit to do with it!

Trains, trains and more trains … although I have travelled by train all of my life, I don't think that I have been on and off quite so many trains as I have over the last month. I have been up and down so many railway steps, on and off so many platforms, that my legs were actually starting to ache from all of the climbing, which really surprised me, as having a two-storied house I did not expect this to be a problem.

Early mornings hurrying through the security guards set up outside the railway … prior to the games commencing only the workers, all racing to get to their jobs … place almost deserted, still dark, dawn light just starting to brighten up the area, currawongs calling ... no time at all this entire area will be filled with hundreds of thousands of people …

Morning commuter trains, normal workers trying to sleep, excited ticket holders with their families, everybody carrying backpacks, children laughing, babies crying, totally different atmosphere to what you would expect at this time of day… late night trains similar experience, trains arriving at station at 1 a.m. and people pouring off as if it is peak hour … a family left a small country town other side of Goulburn at 1 a.m. to be in time for morning athletic events …

One wet morning there is a peculiar smell in the office. I thought that it smelt like burning food, others thought electrical, a panic over the computers, switch them all off! … finally the source is found … one of the women drivers has put her socks in the microwave to dry! Unbelievable! She actually cooked them under 'baked potato'! … Sometimes you can't help wonder about the screening process used in selecting these people!

Late-night atmosphere particularly electric, beautiful balmy evenings, fairy lights in the trees, the huge solar panels lit up with blue lighting, the cauldron flame burning brightly, the most photographed single item in the whole place …

A trip into town after work to see all of the lights … the bridge is all lit up with the five Olympic Rings, looks terrific … Opera House has a display of coloured lighting alternating up and down its sails … the crowds are enormous but no trouble getting about … I don't go to Darling Harbour and miss the Laser Light Display, and also the boats all lit up, though I did see some around the quay ... two guys are abseiling down the side of one of the tall office blocks. They make shadow displays against the wall with the lighting playing on them, very clever …

Eventually the Games are over, one last morning I go to work … back home by now and catching the train from Wyee at 4.50 a.m. … arrive at Concord West and walk to SOP. Delightful early morning walk through bicentennial park … wish I could do it every day … takes 40 minutes to get to the office … never saw a soul except for a couple of security guards, very eerie, I have the entire huge complex all to myself … reassuring once I reach the office and find people … beginning to think that there was no one there at all!

So it is finally finished and Sydney honours all of the volunteers with a huge parade through the city … about 40,000 of us in all our colourful shirts, absolutely incredible scene … a marvellous high walking through the city with all of the crowds cheering us on … never been in a parade before … never likely to be again!… Bob Carr puts it all on for us and we have a big nosh up in the Domain, followed by a concert … a really great day … also picked up our new uniforms for the Paralympics … whatever am I going to do with all of these uniforms?!

PAMELA McGLINN, *Administration Assistant*
BUDGEWOI NSW

I had the honour and absolute pleasure of being invited to be attaché to the Central African Republic team. I'm fluent in French and they are a French-speaking country a bit bigger than New South Wales, located where the name says.

It was a fantastic experience. To be the local host of their three athletes and twice as many officials was a reminder of an important part of the Olympic philosophy. Their ability to participate in the Olympics is a big deal back home and keeps the spirit of sportsmanship alive in a very under-privileged country. It was great to be able to show them around Sydney, to help them with clothing and equipment and assist with a myriad of things a team needs so far from home.

The Olympic volunteers were a huge feature of the Games. There are so many great stories but a couple really stick out for me: I was at the sailing at Rushcutters Bay and running badly late to get to the Aquatic Centre at Homebush for the morning heats. Explaining my predicament to the volunteer Transport official I was told not to worry; they had a few cars and despite my lack of accreditation to have a car, they would get one for me. Grateful and relieved because I was really late by now, I hopped into the car and my spirits suddenly sank. My driver was a little lady who looked like she was heading for the bowling club. Val was old enough to be my mum but I need not have worried, she'd learned to drive tractors in the bush as a girl and drove supply trucks for the army during the Second World War. It took us exactly 31 minutes to go from Rushcutters Bay sailing to the Aquatic Centre, and that includes the security check at Homebush!

Attachés are bona fide members of the team. (Yes, my fourth Olympics! Three for Australia and one for the Central African Republic.) It was amazing for me to march in the Opening Ceremony after a break of 36 years since Tokyo. The Closing Ceremony was equally moving, but by then I was a wake-up to the system and realised that the two-hour assembly of the teams would be a bit of a dry experience. So I figured out that I could legally get to the VIP room in the Main Stadium with my attaché's accreditation, have some refreshment and get back to the team with time to spare. So I had a few cold ones with old mates and IOC luminaries before joining the athletes for that great mixed march-on that is such a feature since its inception in 1956.

Trouble was I had forgotten about my bladder. Can you believe there were more than 10,000 athletes and superstars on that field for over two hours without one loo? We were fenced in by huge kangaroos and other dazzling things going on during the ceremony and even the sub-stage under Kylie Minogue didn't have a loo. A volunteer noticed I was walking with funny crossed knees and said, 'C'mon, I'll take you through the security fence.' We went over the running track, past the dancing kangaroos and under the grandstand where there was a dark area with what seemed to be a few puddles left over from the Opening Ceremony water cascade. What a relief! What a Closing Ceremony!

Apart from ensuring my team was well looked after, my role as attaché had some fantastic side benefits. Attachés are allowed to sit with their teams and, if there's enough space, to sit with other teams. That's how I got to be poolside for the final of the 1500m freestyle. I took my seat early next to Don Talbot, my old (then young) coach. I was fearful of being kicked out to the VIP stand because the Central African Republic sure didn't have any finalists! About a half hour before the start I got the nod from the volunteer marshal that I could stay!

What an experience to be sitting with the Australian team, next to my coach, as Grant and Kieren battled it out in the pool, 40 years after my own victory in Rome. I felt like a teenager again. After the race I got my picture taken between Keiren and Grant and I can tell you there is no greater fan of these guys than me.

JOHN KONRADS, *Attaché to Central African Republic Team*
Australian Olympic Swimmer and Gold Medallist at Rome 1960
SYDNEY NSW

During the Olympics, I was a volunteer with Press Operations (photographic marshall) at the Sydney International Equestrian Centre, Horsley Park.

It was an incredible experience. I was at the side of the arena when Australia won gold in the teams three-day event. I lined up with other volunteers to hold Andrew Hoy's gold medal. Yes, it really was gold – 18 carat! I ran into Dawn Fraser in the toilet and Princess Anne in the practice arena. Most other volunteers had similar brushes with fame such as the one woman who quite literally ran into John Howard on the steps of the VIP area … and yes, according to this volunteer, he did say sorry.

Another volunteer, who was responsible for making sure people had accreditation to go into the stable area told a story about how he turned away this posh British woman because she didn't have the yellow band necessary for entering the stables … so Princess Anne walked the 500 metres or so back to the accreditation area to get a yellow band!

The most interesting story from my perspective as a volunteer is this:

It was the third day of the individual three-day event, the cross country leg. My job for the day was to trudge around the 7450m course and collect film and discs from the accredited Australian and international photographers.

The downside of this job was that I still had blisters from doing the same job during the teams event three days before. The upside was I would see some of the best eventing horses in the world jump the breathtakingly challenging course. The course comprised 30 sculptural jumps which had names like Funnel Web Shelter and Eureka Stockade to reflect Australian culture.

Every hour at a pre-arranged meeting place our volunteer minibus driver Rick would pick up the bags of film I and the volunteer I alternated with had collected.

Rick was an American but I couldn't detect an accent, even though he had only lived in Australia for two years. It was the second week of competition and by this time the eight volunteers in our group had got to know each other quite well.

I knew Rick was a vegetarian who spoke fluent Norwegian. He was a devoted family man who was worried about his daughter who was learning to drive and would panic and let go of the steering wheel in the middle of intersections.

He told me his wife had come to Australia when she was 18 months from New Zealand. They met in America and had been married for eight years. She loved hot chips with sweet chilli sauce. She was going to be at the cross country that day so I expected to meet her.

I had been walking the course for nearly an hour. I realised it was almost time to meet the bus for the first film delivery. I had been dawdling a little too slowly with so many magnificent horses to distract me. I had spent too long at the spectacular water jump (where spills are most likely) waiting to see Andrew Hoy jump his individual eventing horse, 'Swizzle In'.

I could see the bus already waiting so I picked up my pace. I was just about to cross the bridge when I saw something move in front of my foot. My legs turned to lead. It was a metre and a half long brown snake sunning itself in the uncommonly warm September sun. At the same time I saw New Zealand legend, Mark Todd on 'Eyespy 11' flying towards the bridge. Without thinking, I threw the yellow bag of film at the snake and ran in the opposite direction. The snake wriggled off into the river bed and off the track seconds before the horse came through.

My heart was still pumping more loudly than hoofs on bitumen when I reached the minibus. I had been so busy blurting to Rick about the snake that I had hardly noticed the woman sitting beside him. 'This is my wife, Lindy,' Rick said. The woman all in black, her hair tightly pulled into a bun turned around and smiled pleasantly. It was Lindy Chamberlain. Yes, *the* Lindy Chamberlain.

JULIA IRWIN, *Press Operations*
MELBOURNE VIC

One day I was asked to go to the Rushcutters Bay sailing venue and pick a man up to go to Homebush. I was given the instruction sheet which listed his name as Constantine Kin. When I got down to the venue I asked at each entrance to the sailing for a Mr Kin as I was told he needed the car urgently.

Eventually unable to find Mr Kin I went into the Cruising Yacht Club who let me use the phone, I rang up and politely asked if that was Mr Constantine Kin and I was told rather abruptly, 'You mean the King of Greece – King Constantin!'

Another day I was seconded by a protocol person for the Sultan of Brunei's brother's son. I had to drive the chef de mission to the airport where we met a Lady Ambassador for Brunei from Canberra.

The entourage arrived and a fleet of limos took everyone to Sydney. I was asked to follow and drove at breakneck speed to keep up with the other cars all breaking the speed limit. A truck followed with the prince's 55 pieces of luggage. During the afternoon we all assembled to go to Homebush. I stepped forwards and an arm shot out to restrain me as I had tried to step in front of the prince unknowingly.

As we drove up George Street in Sydney at one stage I was in another lane and my car got in front of the prince's whereupon the three gentlemen I was carrying all became hysterical and told me I could not get in front of the prince's car. The three gentlemen were the prince's doctor, one of the chief ministers of Brunei and another person who spent the whole trip on the phone arranging diplomatic passes to various cocktail parties.

I explained to these three august gentlemen that because of traffic conditions I had to go where I could but would endeavour to get behind the prince at the first opportunity. I did this and then kept right up close to the prince's car.

The entourage spent about an hour in the Olympic Village, spent being the operative word. When they all emerged the main driver was laden down with bags and bags of goodies. It had taken the sales person 35 minutes to process all the purchases through the visa machine.

On the way home we had to take Parramatta Road as an alternative route, which was hairy as I was supposed to keep up with the lead car at all times. I was pointing out places of interest on the way and making polite conversation. I pointed out Sydney Uni and there was no reply. I looked around and they were all fast asleep.

PAMELA MINSHALL, *Driver*
SYDNEY NSW

I was in London in 1993, when it was announced that Sydney would host the Olympic Games in 2001. Some friends from Sydney had made their way over to be at the announcement. Personally I didn't quite understand what all the fuss was about. I am a stereotypical Aussie sports lover, growing up glued to the TV during major international tournaments as well as following the local football and cricket. I have also completed in various sports growing up, most recently, women's State League indoor volleyball. Now seven years on, I can understand what all the fuss was about. It was an experience of a lifetime!

A friend had informed me about a volunteer that withdrew at the last minute. Next thing I knew I was the team liaison officer for the Korean women's volleyball team. The next few days were a whirlwind between rehearsals, meeting my supervisor and fellow volunteers and just trying to catch up on all the information and protocol that was involved. But no matter how hectic it was I felt like I was on 'cloud nine'.

As well as meeting all the people I was going to be working with and familiarising myself with my new duties, my first task was to meet the team. They had a training session organised and my job entailed making sure change rooms were clean, warm-up court was clear and all equipment necessary was at the ready. In my excitement and nervousness I think I got there an hour early! I was going to be responsible for a team competing at the Olympics – wow! I was curious to watch how they trained and prepared themselves. Finally their bus pulled up at the back where I was anxiously waiting to meet and greet them. With the aid of an interpreter, I introduced myself and guided them upstairs. One of my first thoughts was, 'They're not much taller than me, maybe there's hope for me yet.' I took care of their needs and just watched in awe as they trained. I was itching just to have a go, wanting to get an idea of what it would be like to train at that level. I don't expect I would have come close but would have loved a chance to embarrass myself anyway. Unfortunately language was a barrier. Their trainer spoke the best English, was very approachable and even cheeky at times. As the coach put the girls through their paces, you could sense the seriousness of it all and how focused they were, but picking his moments the trainer would say something and the girls would chuckle. Obviously I was oblivious to the joke but you got the feeling that even though the coach pulled them back into line quite quickly, that with all the demands of high level sport they were still having fun. Their session came to a close and as the bus drove off I thought: 'Time to buy a Korean phrase book.' (Easier said than done.)

My new pass allowed me access to the Athletes' Village, and I wasted no time in popping in for a visit. My friend and I had respective training sessions at Homebush. Both were cancelled, in fact we were made aware that the girls from Peru hadn't arrived in the country yet, which we thought a little strange, being about three days from competition. So we decided to go exploring. Homebush was now open to the public; people from near and far had come just to have a look. It was hard not to notice the international flavour as you walked along passing tourists, athletes and other international delegates. We got to a lookout point and managed to make out some flags hanging over balconies and stated the obvious: 'They're all there, the cream of the crop, the elite athletes of the world. Let's go meet them.' (That was a mean feat, as we headed in the general direction, by foot. It didn't look that far away. It was a fair hike, but worth it.)

We made our way through security. There was a sense of you can look but don't touch anything in case you break something! Technically our access was in case our teams needed our help at the Village. As we walked in we noticed a small welcoming ceremony being held. We stopped and realised it wasn't for us but thought it was a lovely gesture for the countries still arriving. Where to next? Map at the ready, we went in and out of administration buildings in an effort to find some information about the Peruvians. We walked around literally brushing shoulders with the athletes. My friend pointed out one or two she recognised. I just kept eyes wide open, senses alert again. That electric atmosphere, the bustle of a 'Village' full of Olympic athletes, it was awesome. We giggled like schoolgirls. I was also trying to track down a cousin who was the manager of the Israeli track and field team, but found that they were still training in Queensland. So we completed what we actually came to do but decided we weren't quite ready to leave yet. We kept walking around, looking and trying to recognise flags, smiling as we passed athletes, (I think that smile had been there since we walked in the door) we looked through windows and open doors as we walked around the accommodation areas. We finally tore ourselves away, this time hopping on a bus heading back to Homebush. We were in uniform and were approached by an American after some information. We obliged and then got chatting as you do! He introduced us to his 4-year-old son, mother and mother-in-law. We all got off the bus together and as we went our separate ways wished him good luck. Who was he? He was the husband of the female triathlete who two days later won gold. We were blown away. He had told us his wife was competing in the triathlon, and not being avid triathlon followers, had absolutely no idea who she was, only to find out two days later that she won. Beserk!

Finally, that one day Australia had been counting down to had arrived. I had a rehearsal in the morning. A small round-robin interstate volleyball tournament had been organised for us to use as practice. We went through the procedures and protocols involved in escorting the teams from the warm-up area to their respective area on court in the main arena. Being the final rehearsal, everything had to be perfect. While technical difficulties were being sorted out I got chatting to some of the Victorian boys, recognising a couple from my time playing State League. I was introduced to one or two that had competed for Australia and a couple who were reserves for the current team. There I was just talking and joking around with some of the finest indoor volleyballers in the country. I realised I wasn't a spectator here, I was going to get a real insight into the Olympics and its athletes. That I did, even more so than I could have ever imagined.

And then the Games began. My first day was dedicated to my volunteer duties. I went in early and had a look at how things were done for real. I also got my first taste of Olympic sport. After observing how things were done in the warm-up area, I headed into the main arena, sat in our allocated seats and waited. I just looked around, listening to the bustle of people getting into their seats and as the music began, the match was introduced and then teams were introduced individually. As they walked out in single file, the crowd became quite vocal and there was that atmosphere again – a chill ran up my spine. It was the Aussie girls up against Croatia. I felt truly spoilt – my first Olympic sporting experience and I was getting to see Australia compete. Unfortunately the girls couldn't match it with the Croatians and didn't start on a good note but it was only the first day.

Then before I knew it, it was my turn. I was excited and nervous too. I had to meet the girls as I had for their training session so up until I had to call them to line up for their walk to the main arena, everything was under control. During their warm-up I watched in awe and kept thinking, 'This was a team about to begin their plight towards Olympic Gold.' It blew me away, but not for long. I had to keep an eye on the clock to make sure they were on time to start this 'plight'. The head coach and assistant coach led, then the captain, followed by the rest of the team. The trainer and I held up the rear. This was interesting as their opponents lined up in the same formation right alongside. We were on our way. Single file went out the window as we reached the bottom of the stairs. Their calm surprised me. They seemed to be just chatting away as they made their way through the makeshift tunnel. As we arrived 'back stage', you heard the announcer entertaining the crowd. The captains went through the curtain for the coin toss, returned, then after collecting tracksuits into a basket I escorted the coaches and trainer around the back of the stands to the other side of the court. As I did this the teams and players entered the court as they were being introduced, similar to the start of a basketball game. Then it was my turn to go onto the playing area – mind you there was no grand introduction and no one cheered for me, but that's OK. I was hoping not to be noticed as I tried to dodge past television camera cables and wondering whether to pass in front or behind an officials' table. It all seemed quite daunting at the time but I made it through without falling flat on my face, so for that I was grateful. Then I went through all the things I was expected to do: checking drinks were at the correct temperature, towels were folded neatly, and making sure the interpreter wasn't far away. I then found my chair where I was to remain for the entire match, that being about six feet behind the coach/players' bench, best seat in the house as far as I was concerned. In a few short minutes the whistle blew for the start. I think I sat on the edge of my seat for the most part and admit I had trouble concentrating on the job at hand. I composed myself and during time-outs and substitutions I folded towels, resealed drinks and put jackets away. The match was great and quite close. I had no idea who was favourite. To my delight the Koreans started with a win, all be it in five sets. It was thoroughly entertaining. Before I knew it they made their way back to the change rooms and were boarding the bus to go back to the Village. I headed back up to complete my duties, which were to tidy up a bit and return keys. Then I was done and felt it went reasonably well, but I still needed a phrase book.

The competition was scheduled so that the men and women played on alternate days so I had every second day off. Surprisingly the Koreans had done very well defeating Germany and Peru, but unfortunately losing to Russia and Cuba. It was enough to get to the finals. Although language was still a problem (you wouldn't believe how hard it is to find a phrase book), we managed to communicate and got into a routine. Over the week I got used to what they needed and was able to anticipate when they needed it. They were fantastic and made my job very easy: they wouldn't let me carry anything and during a change of ends would bring the basket with them. I felt extremely lucky – not only were they friendly and polite but I got to witness some of the best volleyball I have ever seen. As a few others did at volleyball, I adopted myself out as a Korean supporter. I found myself trying to contain my frustration when they were down and hold back my joy at their triumphs. (Luckily we didn't play Australia!)

Their biggest test came in the first final against USA. It was so close and such an exciting match to watch. There was some controversial umpiring that went against the Koreans. They rose above it. It went down to the wire; match points were denied to both sides a few times. Neither team wanted to give in but unfortunately for the Koreans, after almost two hours they couldn't hold on any more. I really felt for them, they had given their all. I didn't know what to say to them in English after a game like that, let alone in Korean. Even if I could find something appropriate to say it would have taken me a week to say it (something as simple as 'hello' in Korean is some six syllables). The so-called good news was they had another two classification games ahead of them. The first was against China. You could tell the game versus USA had taken its toll. They put up a fight but you could see they were affected by the match they played only 12 hours earlier. Their Olympics ended on a losing note the next day against Croatia. After showering and changing they emerged smiling. They got together and presented me with gifts including a Korean top. They had earlier allowed me to have some photos with them and all signed their names in Korean on a mini volleyball. I had unfortunately lost my phrase book, so called in on my trusty interpreter. I was invited out for Korean barbecue lunch; I was not quite sure what I was in for. Before that, the girls congregated outside, as I approached they were being introduced to the president of the Korean Volleyball Federation and then I was beckoned to move forward and introduced. It was nice to be recognised, and I wish I still had that damn phrase book! I was informed that the girls were being praised for their efforts and understood that they had exceeded expectations.

On the last day of competition I went to watch the men's volleyball medal games, and to say farewell to some new friends (fellow volunteers) and in a way to say goodbye to Olympic volleyball. At the completion of the game, when the Stadium cleared we all congregated for a meeting. I had ducked out to pick up some more souvenirs, such as an Olympic volleyball and poster. I walked in half-way. We were being thanked for our efforts over not only the two weeks of the Olympics but for all the work done leading up to the event. The praise was appreciated even though I had no idea who this 'suit' was who was doing all the talking. As he finished I noticed the podiums near me, still intact. So I quickly got a friend nearby to take a snapshot of me standing on the gold medal podium. Wasn't sure if it was appropriate but all of a sudden I could see a number of people heading my way to get a cheap thrill of standing up there. I said my final goodbyes and thankyous and headed to the Village, not to eat, but to pick up tickets to the Closing Ceremony (I couldn't believe my luck). A friend joined me and we walked over to the Stadium. We were running late and when we presented our tickets at the gate, we were rejected and told to proceed to the Superdome. We turned to each other, very confused, and as we strolled over in that direction, inspected our tickets. They seemed like regular tickets with a seat number, but we noticed three interesting words printed on them: 'athletes' holding area'. Our realisation became reality as we were let inside. All of a sudden we were surrounded by Australian athletes. We looked at each other in absolute amazement with grins from ear to ear. We clutched at each other as we were being ushered outside, around the back. In a vain effort to find my cousin, we made our way through the sea of athletes, coming around to a tunnel that led us under the seating, straight onto the track. We could barely believe what we were doing: walking out with the athletes at the Closing Ceremony. It was the icing on the cake. I found my cousin and as he looked at me in shock I asked him, 'What kind of tickets did you get?' We laughed and I spent the next couple of hours getting a totally different perspective. When the formalities were over we danced around and partied with the athletes. We took a few snapshots. Inge de Bruin and Pieter van den Hoogenband were amongst the celebrities who didn't mind the intrusion of being photographed with a fan. It was as I said earlier, I wasn't a spectator. I felt I was part of the Olympics. (Hard not to when you end up in the middle of it the way we did.)

As I conclude I wonder whether this will be the end of my Olympic experience, I think not. Australia put on such a wonderful show, I haven't heard a bad word spoken about it. I feel thankful to the athletes and volunteers who made the Olympics what they were I had the time of my life and still am!

MICHELLE B, *TLO for Korea*
MELBOURNE VIC

A friend of mine (Michelle B.) from Melbourne came over to work in Sydney too. On the night of the Closing Ceremony she phoned me and told me that she got two tickets to the ceremony! I could not believe it! She asked me to join her. I was out of my mind – it was the greatest thing ever! I was so nervous. So we went to the Stadium and were able to walk in with the athletes. That was an amazing feeling – they were partying and singing and it was big! They were happy it was over and it was going to be a great night. We had our cameras with us and finally we were able to take photos of some of the athletes. They did not mind and were happy to do it. We got a photo with Pieter van den Hoogenband and Inge de Bruijn. It was really the best ending ever. I could not think of any better ending of my trip.

INGE SIEBEN, *Village Assistant*
AMSTERDAM HOLLAND

Originally, I was only planning to go to the Olympics for one week as a spectator. I am a widowed retiree, living in Melbourne, who eagerly took up the opportunity to buy tickets a year out from the Games, through the 'Mark Taylor' mail order. I managed to get a handful of single tickets to athletic sessions. Being a keen athlete as a girl, and having attended a couple of Olympic Athletic heats in 1956, it was emotionally very important to me to be part of the experience at the Olympic Stadium in 2000, in whatever small way I could.

In early September, as I prepared for my trip, I happened to see a story on the Channel Nine News about Olympic volunteers getting uniformed and trained. Suddenly, the desire to be more than a spectator took hold. I called my son, Paul, who was a coordinator for SOCOG Ticketing. By chance, there were a few last-minute places which came available among Ticketing's volunteers – and at the Aquatic Centre and Olympic Stadium of all places! Paul had never thought I would be interested in being the unpaid face of the sometimes thankless program of ticketing. Little did he know what I could handle. Raising five children and 45 years in the workforce, a few disgruntled spectators seemed like a pushover. I brought my flight forward, gave my tickets away as gifts and thus began a wonderful three weeks in Sydney.

I arrived Monday 11 September, moving into my son's Elizabeth Bay flat, nestled between the harbour and the wild world of Kings Cross. I instantly knew I was in Sydney and I had left the quiet suburbs of Melbourne far behind. Like a lot of Sydney locals and their guests at this time, we improvised by converting a two-bedroom flat into a three-bed flat and, on some days, if you include couches, as many as a five-bed flat. It was all part of the Olympic experience and it is amazing how adaptable we all became on our Olympic highs.

On Tuesday, I journeyed to Redfern and the colossal Uniform Distribution & Accreditation Centre, or UDAC as they called it – everything to do with SOCOG seemed to have an abbreviation. As I stood in the doorway, taking in the massive operation – the hundreds of staff, the kilometres of painted lines to follow, the signs of all shapes and sizes, pointing in all directions – I had my first moment of self-doubt. It looked like we were being fitted out for a war and I was wondering what a retiree from Melbourne was doing in the recruitment lines. Next thing I know, I am receiving my accreditation for both the Olympic Stadium and the Aquatic Centre, I am being measured, I am collecting my uniform, I am having it especially tailored to be a perfect fit, and finally I am being sent on my way home by the friendly staff. Suddenly, as I caught my breath, I thought maybe I could handle this after all.

My first rostered duty was Wednesday 13 September for the dress rehearsal of the Opening Ceremony. The Olympic Stadium is so enormous that, when there are seating problems, the box office is too far away for the ticketing staff to come to the rescue. To cope, Ticketing set up 'resolution desks' in the stands. These desks were to be my workplaces for the Games and the dress rehearsal was a great way to come up to speed quickly and learn on the job. I had a two-way radio, a mobile phone, a small number of spare tickets, some maps and (for the dress rehearsal) some ticketing professionals to show me the tricks of the trade. I was high up on Level 6 on what was to be the torch end of the Stadium. This became my place and routine for the athletic sessions to come. Dress rehearsal went very smoothly but I knew it would be a different story when the unhappy customers were not sitting in complimentary seats but $1,382 seats at the Official Opening Ceremony.

At the Opening Ceremony, my first tricky problem on my own with the public came with a wheelchair-bound lady and her husband presenting in front of my desk. Their tickets were for conventional seats but they now required a wheelchair position. Her husband had pushed her all the way up to the top of the never-ending circular ramp. Exhausted, they presented me with a letter which specifically said to go directly to the box office when you arrive at the Stadium (and not to enter the Stadium first!). Unfortunately, some of the few wheelchairs we still had up our sleeve had suddenly become camera positions at the last minute. I quickly got on the two-way radio and arranged a position on another

Hats off to you all … vollies gather for their daily briefing session. *(Photo courtesy of Alan Patching))*

Vollie, Vollie, Vollie, Oi Oi Oi! *(Photo courtesy of Alan Patching)*

If this is the White House, is this the President? *(Courtesy of Alan Patching)*

Host and hostess of 'Coles Cafeteria'in the Village: Ivan and Joan Moore, second and third from front right. *(Photo courtesy of Ivan Moore)* *See page 83.*

Lozza doing what he does best – stirring up a crowd! Here he is with some Village kitchen staff and is that a champion tennis player snuck in the back there? Full marks to the guy with the white gloves. *(Courtesy of Laurie Lawrence)* *See page10.*

Above: Joseph didn't realise it at the time, but the young woman from the Jordanian Horse Riding Team who posed with him in this photo is in fact Princess Haya of Jordan. Thank you Your Highness! *(Courtesy of Joseph Kalenderian)* *See page113.*

Left: Yumi reckons Luc Longley is the Aussie equivalent of her idol, Michael Jordan. She says 'I didn't realise how big he is until I saw this photo. I'm not a tall girl, but I'm no shorty at 5'6!' *(Courtesy of Yumi Pham-Vu)* *See page 45.*

Siobhan Paton's mum placed the gold medal that her daughter won that morning around the neck of a little boy passing by. Here he is with his mother who was as chuffed as he was. Mrs Paton said 'This is what Siobhan wants to do: work with disabled kids.' *(Courtesy of Barbara Firth)* *See page 123.*

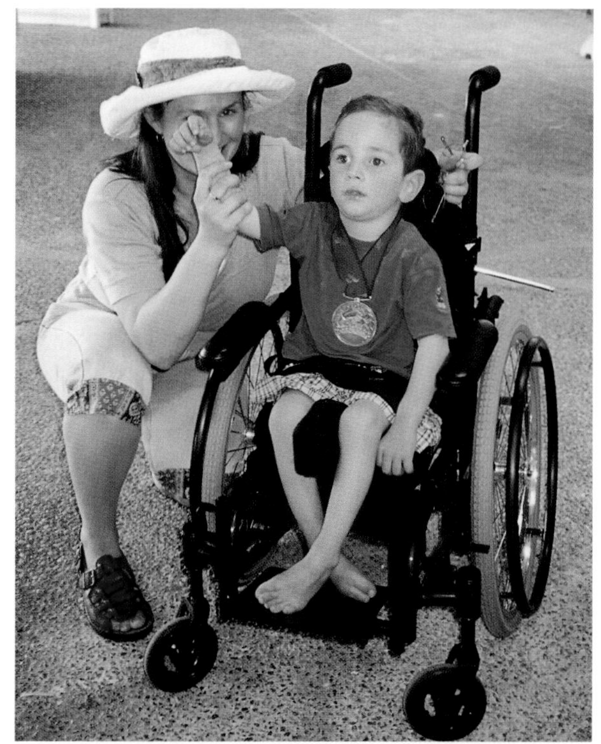

Smiling parking officers in Pram City. *(Photo courtesy of Alan Patching)*

Something to be proud of forever: the official accreditation card and the Certificate of Appreciation given to all volunteers for doing the hard yards.

level and (with the elevators out of use for security reasons), I had Spectator Services accompany the lady and her husband back the way they had come. As sympathetic as I was for their long walk, I felt I had tackled the problem and won. I was now ready for the challenges ahead.

As daunting as these problems were at first, I soon discovered that I was dealing with the same handful of problems over and over again and it was not long before I got into a rhythm at each session.

- No wheelchair spaces (needing to send people to other levels – and, sometimes, no access to lifts). Also, helping other people who had broken legs since purchasing their tickets needing easily accessible seats.
- Vertigo, vertigo and vertigo – the passport to a better seat. If I had a dollar for the number of times a maturing lady stood in front of my desk in hysterics, complaining about fear of heights from D price seats, while the concerned husband stood by her side insisting on a seat closer to the track, I would be a wealthy volunteer. I decided that there are a lot of good actors in the world.
- Stolen tickets – at least one lot per session: sometimes, people would buy tickets, report them stolen and then sell both lots to innocent people. Because it was the 'friendly Games', we almost never removed people but relocated as much as possible. Though the person behind such scams would sometimes find a new (and appropriate) second charge on their credit card after the Games.

I soon noticed that the number of complaints I had to deal with was somehow connected to how well Australia was doing. The better Australia was doing on the track and field, or in the pool, the quieter my desk. Another good reason to cheer on Australia.

I was lucky enough to work at the Aquatic Centre and Olympic Stadium for all the evenings' most exciting sessions. The Stadium had a wonderful staff dining room with a beautiful view of the track so I could eat a meal and watch the best events and share companionship with a wonderful group of fellow volunteers.

One day, I was standing on Kings Cross station and a homeless man walked back and forth in front of me. He eventually stopped right in front and said, 'I seen a lot of people dressed like that. Could you tell me what you are doing?' I replied that I was working as a volunteer at the Olympics. His reply – 'You are organising the Olympics!' He insisted on shaking my hand and walked down the platform telling anyone who would listen that I was the organiser of the Olympic Games. There is at least one person in the world who believes I organised the Olympics single-handed.

By Closing Ceremony, I felt like a ticketing wiz and was on top of problems in a flash. I confidently made my way around Sydney like it was my second home. I couldn't believe how far I had come from the day I nervously walked into the Uniform Centre, or the dress rehearsal when I was given a two-way radio for the first time in my life. It was amazing how the excitement, the camaraderie, the public support and my sense of my place in history lifted my confidence and brought out abilities I never knew I had.

Bring on the 2006 Commonwealth Games!

LORRAINE MURNANE, *Ticketing*
MELBOURNE VIC

Fortunately, we were able to secure luxury coach transport to move our volunteers between Sydney and Melbourne and also to the Olympic Stadium on workdays. However, the jewel in the crown was the accommodation. A large Scout Hall set in the leafy suburb of Lindfield was to become our home for the period of the Olympics. By Scout Hall standards, Lindfield is an excellent venue – large and with many rooms and a recently renovated and well-appointed kitchen. This 'four-star' accommodation was named 'The Lindfield Hilton' by the volunteers and will be fondly remembered for years to come by all who slept there and dined in the silver service 'Bill Oakley Restaurant'.

On Sunday 10 September 2000, Greg and Heather Matthews and Paul and Sue Fitz drove to Sydney to prepare the Lindfield Scout Hall for the arrival of the first group at the 'Lindfield Hilton' the following Tuesday evening. Their immediate reaction was that of the five-star rating of the accommodation, four and a half stars had got lost somewhere!

Firstly the whole Scout Hall was cleaned and vacuumed throughout. The main room was divided into two with one half being designated as the dining room and set up with 13 trestle tables. The other half was to accommodate 24 men together with the seven side rooms for the snorers in the pious hope that their isolation may allow others to enjoy a 'good night's sleep'. Two rooms used by the Venturers were allocated to the ladies. Arriving with the bus would be foam rubber mattresses and sleeping bags. Working on a presumption that the mattress width would be two feet, six inches and with the help of chalk, adequate space was available. This space became quite intimate when it was found that the mattresses were three inches.

Portable shower and toilet blocks were delivered and hooked up to the sewerage on the Monday. Paul assisted the driver in unloading the blocks in a very tight space. When completed, the driver, with shaved head and arms covered with tattoos, inquired as to what was going on. Paul explained that a group of Rotarians and their families and friends from Melbourne were coming in three groups to assist the Main Stadium caterers and were donating their earnings to charity. He stood for a moment then silently removed his leather gloves and extended his right hand to Paul with 'I would be proud if you would shake my hand!'

As time went on, the dulcet tones from our treasured chef made us wonder how Bill actually slept through his own snoring. Others were soon to experience this magnificent phenomenon. Bill, out of sheer exhaustion, or habit, or the need to rise early to prepare breakfast, was able to fall asleep almost the moment his head touched the pillow. By the time the third of our groups arrived Bill had been moved to sleep in a tent on the lawn outside the hall!

Our team worked in a variety of food and liquor buffets in the Main Stadium. We quickly became experts in cooking fish and chips, pizzas and hot dogs as well as serving that wonderful brew, Fosters. Also, as a bonus during the quieter work moments, we were able to view the Opening and Closing Ceremonies, Cathy Freeman's 400m final and other major events. It also provided us with the opportunity to explain to the young people working alongside of us what Rotary was all about and what we were trying to achieve from our involvement in the Olympics. We quickly gained their respect and often found ourselves providing guidance on day-to-day work matters.

The fellowship was overwhelming. A strong bond was built with other Rotary and Rotaract Clubs and long-term friendships were cemented, the latter resulting in new members to Rotary.

And now for some sidelights on the experience from Ann Ken:

In trying to write of some of the funny incidents I don't see anything funny about rising from a warm, comfy bed at 5 a.m. on a Friday morning to join another 40 or so people to travel on a bus to Sydney. It wasn't funny, but we had some fun. Everyone was required to introduce themselves using the microphone – there were long versions, short versions and some humorous stories. Introductions were essential because we had a number of Rotaracters and young non-member volunteers to assist us.

If sleeping on a mattress on the floor of a Scout Hall sounds like your idea of fun, we had that too. I also didn't realise that there were so many women out there who were able to snore at a noise level far exceeding some men I have known (I'm talking about father, brother and other relatives here). The snoring was funny, at first!

Our first shift on duty was funny too – that's because it took one of the young lads and myself about two hours to find our duty stall. We reckon by the time we had finished looking in numerous lifts, stairwell, fire exits and the like, we were probably ready for any emergency – we had such a good look around. Although come to think of it, we were still getting lost by the last day. Sometimes it was handy to get lost, you could always find a seat in the arena and watch the athletes. After all, wasn't that why we volunteered our services?

Working for 16- to 17-year-old 'bosses' was amusing at times. Very often they were full of instructions for us, but often with very little common sense. One young lady had me rotating pies from the top shelf of an oven to the next shelf and so on. Meanwhile pies were being sold from any section when things were really busy – I lost track and gave up on that job. It was easier to disappear to fill up the condiments bar, which was on the outside of the food outlet: one was able to have some fun, there, with the public who were all enjoying themselves.

On the way home our bus was expected to catch up with the third group of volunteers. We were hoping to meet for lunch and I was looking forward to this particularly because my fellow Rotarian/partner/lover, Graeme, was on the other bus. As close as we got was a phone call describing our positions on the highway, thus allowing us to wave to each other for a few seconds when the buses crossed paths. That was not funny, I was looking forward to a little kiss at least!

My friend Jenny and I were not too popular on the trip home because we were a little noisy, having too much of a giggle remembering the silly things we did as younger things. All the others had worn themselves out having such a good time (and working so hard), that they wanted to sleep all the way back to Melbourne. Well we were having fun!

And a poem from the Albert Park Club:

On behalf of the team from Albert Park Club,
We thank you for letting us share
A small part of history, we will never forget
The experience of just 'being there'

The memories we made we will treasure forever,
Some thrilled us and some horrified,
Like sleeping together with 31 men,
Making noises from all orifii.

A Rotary team is all chiefs and no braves,
As our bus driver learnt very fast,
Go this way, go that way, the poor guy had kittens,
Till we picked up the bedding at last!

Well the party's all over, it's all over Marcel!
But we're left with so many new friends
And we've added a page to the Rotary tale
A story we hope never ends.

NORTH BALWYN ROTARY OLYMPIC TEAM
MELBOURNE VIC

My Olympic volunteer experience was without the word of doubt the most wonderful experience in my lifetime.

When I decided to volunteer I was living in Sydney. Shortly after my husband and I moved to Palmers Island near Yamba. But having committed myself and wanting so much to be part of the Sydney 2000 Olympics it was full steam ahead. This meant travelling to Sydney and attending Granville TAFE for various modules. But it also gave me the chance to catch up with family and friends.

On completion of the 12 modules it was off to Redfern Distribution Centre to collect my uniform and accreditation. What a buzz!

In due course I was notified of my selection as driver to the secretary general of the IOC for Costa Rica. My first meeting with the secretary general and his wife at the Renaissance Hotel was polite and reserved but within two days I was greeted with a hug and kiss each morning and over the next two weeks a wonderful friendship and bond was formed with these delightful people who insisted I call them by their first names.

One day the secretary general had to attend an IOC meeting and he asked if I would take his wife out for the day. On asking if she would like to see a national park she was delighted at the suggestion. So we headed off for the Royal National Park. The dear lady was enthralled by the coastal scenery and bushland. As we continued on our journey it was as if on cue a flock of white cockatoos flew across in front and landed one metre from the road. The birds were so interested in feeding they seemed oblivious to us sitting in the car watching them. My companion had tears in her eyes at the spectacle of the beautiful birds. We also took in the hang gliders at Stanwell Park and lunched at a cliff top café selling homemade apple pie.

Toward the end of the Games all volunteers who had been associated with the Costa Rican entourage were invited to go sailing on Sydney Harbour as a thank you. No expense was spared with delicious food and wines to enjoy.

The sadness of saying farewell at Sydney Airport was lessened by the promise of keeping in touch which we have done with constant letters and cards. Friendships were also formed with fellow volunteers and as we marched as one through the streets of Sydney on our lap of honour I was bursting with pride at having played some part in the greatest Olympic Games ever.

JAN HUNT, *Driver*
YAMBA NSW

I started with SOCOG in the Ceremonies department in 1999. Part of the real joy of the job was working with the volunteers I met who were, without doubt, the success of the show.

Ceremonies required 12,000 performers on the field of play and 5000 backstage volunteers. In total there were near enough to 20,000 including the Closing Ceremony.

The 47,000 volunteers who were so highly praised, as well they might, did not actually include the ceremonies volunteers! Ceremonies volunteer numbers were drastically underestimated in the official SOCOG count!

That caused a big problem – it meant the majority of our volunteers had not been allocated any entitlements – travel, food, uniforms! Finally, after much negotiation with management, they were allocate Opening and Closing Ceremony T-shirts and pins, they were fed and were entitled to some travel. I can only say that they were a bunch of stalwarts.

Rehearsals were mostly held at a disused airfield at Quakers Hill, a long way out of central Sydney. In rain, freezing cold or searing heat, they turned up. They actually seemed to enjoy the carnival atmosphere which had developed after the colourful marquis and tents were erected. Sometimes the call was 7.30 a.m. and went on well after the sun had set. The volunteer performers had to wait for long periods of time, getting steps right or cues fine-tuned. The backstage volunteers were there to sew those superb costumes, measure all those 14,000 inside legs, waists, chests, etc., take endless roll calls to ensure that performers turned up for rehearsals, help performers with costumes, make-up; the list was endless. Once we got to rehearse at the Stadium, we had all become a well-run, confident 'close-knit' team.

Only two rehearsals were done in the Stadium before performing to a mere four billion television audience and 110,000 present in the Stadium. That night, everyone was very excited and I really didn't see many nerves – everything moved too fast for us to worry about worrying! My particular team, the cast assistants, were deployed all over SOP (Sydney Olympic Park) and also out at schools set up as bus hubs. Some helped with the horses and riders, most were at SIAC (Athletic Centre) an arena which adjoins the Stadium, others were across the precinct, making sure the cast moved efficiently from one place to another. Some helped with dressing artists, fixing hair and make-up. It is hard for people to realise the enormity of getting all those people in the right place, at the right time, in the right gear! The show really went without a hitch and it was mainly due to our volunteers. The days of the ceremonies were very long, stretching from 7.30 a.m. until well after midnight. I ran the volunteer tent at SIAC, where backstage crew could come and get a cuppa, ask questions, pick up a newsletter or just come and chat.

The night of the Opening Ceremony, very few volunteers (except the performers) saw any of the show. I was standing with volunteers at the volunteer tent and we could glimpse the North Stand through a gap between the South and East Stands. Then came the moment for us to see that wonderful flame rise up on its way to the top of the North Stand – I was one of the few who knew what was about to happen, having been in endless meetings discussing the cauldron! But nothing happened. All I could see was a great glow – but no sight of the ring of fire rising to its glorious heights! At the after-show party we heard what had actually happened. However, no one was told that night that only one minute's gas supply was left before it went out! How different the start of the Games would have been if we'd gone to black! But thanks to the heroes who got it moving and saved the day (or rather night) in a wet, dark cavern beneath the fiery focus of the entire world, the finale was as spectacular as had been meticulously planned.

After it was all over we marched in the volunteer parade, through the city streets carrying our ceremonies banner with pride. It was fantastic and for me it was the most emotional part of the whole Olympic experience. To be thanked so overwhelmingly by the city of Sydney was amazing.

This time was unique. I want to congratulate everyone who helped so willingly. We couldn't have done it without you. It will remain in my mind and heart forever.

Thank you.

GISELLA PAYNE, *Ceremonies Coordinator*
SYDNEY NSW

'Hurry Up And Wait' was the unofficial motto of my props crew for the Opening Ceremony. During the long days spent rehearsing, most of our time was spent waiting for rehearsals to start, waiting for cues and waiting to be told what's happening next.

TANIA KRAUS, *Props Assistant / Accreditation*
SYDNEY NSW

John Coates was the catalyst for me becoming a volunteer at the Sydney Olympics.

'Jon, how many Olympics have you been involved in now? Eight or nine?' asked John Coates. 'You'd make a great attaché ... lots of experience at the Games and good at problem solving!'

At the time I didn't give the suggestion much serious thought ... although it was nice of my friend to mention the possibility.

My name is Jon Donohue – I was selected as a swimmer to represent Australia at the 1956 Games in Melbourne. Indelible memories.

But none of my past could predict my Olympic journey in Sydney.

I picked up the phone. It was John Coates. 'You're in ... Uganda!'

'What ... Uganda?' I said

'Yeah, Uganda! Let me explain ... they only have a small team. Not too many hassles. They won't be asking for the world – just the basic involvement.'

I was interested even more when he said, 'You'll be able to really enjoy these Olympics.'

I agreed.

Major General Francis Nyangwesco was the man in charge of the Ugandan Olympic involvement. I first met the major general at Sydney's Regent Hotel, over a cup of coffee.

'How's it all going?' I asked.

'We have a bit of a problem. We don't have the money to pay for our tickets! The money is due to be paid at a meeting with SOCOG tomorrow.'

He looked a forlorn figure ... jaw almost on the coffee table. I thought, it can't be that big a problem ... they can't need too many seats.

'How many tickets?' I questioned.

'Twenty-seven thousand tickets!' was his reply.

It appeared, in a complex series of negotiations, the marketing rights to the total number of African nations had been sold to a company in Atlanta. The money would be used to pay for all the seats – each independent African nation's quota. Unfortunately, they had engaged the wrong company. Their promise of money never materialised. The company disappeared – bust. Shattered dreams appeared very much on the agenda.

A long story, but we found a solution. SOCOG was magnificent and very generous. The chef de mission, Francis, recaptured his smile and faith in humanity.

An unforgettable date is 2 August 2000. I had driven from Sydney along the scenic route – via the Great Ocean Road to Adelaide – to greet the tiny African nations touring party. They had been invited to Adelaide, for an Australian government funded training camp. Exhausted but excited, I waited to meet my team. I had gone to the trouble of organising three large luggage racks ... like the porters push at train stations. I guess I was expecting a substantial amount of luggage. Travelling teams always have excess baggage. After identifying the members, I was staggered at how light they were travelling. You could have packed the entire group's luggage into a Coles shopping trolley, with extra space to carry a slab of beer.

There were 15 athletes and four coaches – 19 in all.

Basically, they had only the clothes they wore on the plane. Another phone call to the major general confirmed they had no tracksuits or runners ... or money. Now it was time to pull in some favours ... 'Francis, no worries mate, I'll organise the gear!'

My wife, Pat, could see the girls chatting in a group together ... 'They have no knickers or bras!' The challenge began. We gave the girls $50 each to buy knickers and bras. Their only clothes were what they stood in. Fila supplied tracksuits and gear worth $115,000.

Margaret was the archer extraordinaire – but without a bow and arrow. She had big bright eyes and a sheepish smile. George was her coach ... and he was pretty sure she could borrow her equipment ... just like she did at home. A quick chat with the Archery Academy ... a lend wasn't on and that each bow of Olympic standard would set me back $10,500 ... much more sophisticated than Robin Hood and the one I use in my backyard. One conversation lead to another and with the help of Mike Latin at Optus and Channel 7 – they paid half each. Again, the spirit of generosity in this country was wonderful – so spontaneous. George wanted one too! Can you believe this.

Then we had Joe the breastroker – he arrived keen to compete but without any swimming costume or goggles. Being still a keen swimmer and surfer, I had my speedos and goggles in the boot of my car. At short notice Joe said, 'I'll take yours!'

Another competitor named Singal delivered the same yarn ... 'I have no gear at all!'

Now this is only the training camp we're talking about.

Next, I get another call from the major general telling me he can't make it to Australia for another couple of weeks. I'm now officially taking on the role of chef de mission for Uganda. I agree to be attaché, then I became a generous team manager – I barely know the group. But, day by day I get much closer ... especially to their needs.

As chef de mission, I meet every Thursday at 2 p.m. for strategic discussion – we have another difficulty. This time it is official Olympic accreditation. It seems four black athletes are not qualified to attend the Olympic Games ... but came to Australia as part of the one month's free training package. The oldest of the foursome is barely 18 ... they are still in Adelaide (15 athletes plus four coaches). I don't want to tell the kids they have to hop on a plane and go home – they think that they will be part of the Olympic Games. It shouldn't be done by phone and it's not my (the attaché's) real job ... so I'm back on the phone to Francis in Uganda. He says, 'You tell 'em!' I dug my heels in and spoke to Fred the swimming manager. In broken English, he told me he would undertake the task of telling each one individually ... and make the necessary travel arrangements. Phew ... I was pleased not to look into the eyes of four young spirited athletes only to break their hearts.

A matter of days before the Games begin there is a huge influx of international athletes at Sydney airport. Can you believe the first four members off the plane were the non-accredited ones ... aged 15, 17, 18 and 18. So young. Too late to turn back now. This could get ugly.

I spoke to Ben, the swim coach. 'Honestly,' he said, 'I just couldn't tell them. I was too embarrassed!' I bit my bottom lip ... so much I wanted to say, could have said. 'I'll take them to accreditation,' I did say. It became a long struggle, a test of patience past police and SOCOG security. I explained their awful predicament ... 'Been here a month, not good enough, but here they are anyway. Let's make it as pleasant as it can be.'

'While the others are accredited and see the photos and paperwork completed, could we please get these youngsters a lounge room with a television set. Away from the excitement of becoming acceptable to the Olympic Village for athletes.'

Basically, we have to get two boys and two girls out on the first available plane. They have no accreditation. It will take them 52 hours to return to Uganda. They have no money. They have no tickets. I have to attend opening ceremony practice with the official team. Once more I tell Fred, the swim manager, to tell them what has happened and why they will be going home.

In the meantime, I organised for my two assistants to grab a team car and to show the visitors Sydney. So off they go. Fifty dollars each in their hands, on a Sydney day trip. As one of the first teams to arrive on our shores, way back in August – these kids were photographed at Manly's

Ocean World, Bondi Beach, the Harbour Bridge and the Opera House. Amazingly, they would not be competing ... yet for a day, they would be stars.

Emirates came quickly to the party with free tickets. Customs were brilliant – absolutely no problems.

JON DONOHUE, *Attaché for Uganda*
Swimmer at 1956 Melbourne Games
SYDNEY NSW

I saw that volunteers were needed for the Games and as we (me and my wife Judy) are both retired I decided to ring up for an application form. Before I did, I asked Judy if she would like to volunteer also. As the answer was yes I therefore asked for two forms. When the forms arrived we discovered that they were extremely extensive.

'I'm not going to fill all that in,' was her reaction to the form. So I realised I could pick what I wanted to do. Darling Harbour was the easiest venue to reach so I turned to the page where the sports were listed. After a bit of thought I picked boxing and weightlifting as a second choice.

After a few months wait, in which I often thought I was not going to be needed, I received a phone call from a young lady who said she was from the boxing team and would I like to join them. It took me a nanosecond to reply in the affirmative. My wife didn't seem to show any interest. I received a letter containing details of going into the SOCOG building in town for a general meeting and interview. During the afternoon we were told that there was a shortage of volunteers so I asked could I bring my wife along. I thought maybe I could persuade her. I was also told during my interview that I was to be print supervisor which is a back-of-house job. I was quite excited about this although I would have preferred a field-of-play job.

When I arrived home I was going to ask Judy about changing her mind about volunteering, but before I could she said she had worked things out that she would be home all through the Games when I'd be out 'enjoying myself'. 'I'll volunteer, but only if I can work with you,' she said. Trying hard to keep a straight face I told her I would see what I could do. I'd already been told that she had to fill in the application form and send it straight to the boxing team, which I made sure she did immediately before any change of mind.

A week later Judy received a phone call to come into SOCOG for an interview and to bring me. So one Tuesday morning we presented ourselves and the four of us – us and Steve and Vanessa from the boxing team – had a meeting over a cup of tea in the canteen. As we had inherited a computer from our son, we had rudimentary computer skills. I was told I was there because my job was to be changed. Because we had these computer skills I was to sit at ringside and be the scoreboard interfacer and Judy was to sit a few seats away from me at ringside and be score validator which means she checks on her computer to see if the right boxer has been awarded the fight and what the scores were then, via headset, send the results out to the back-of-house computer operators for worldwide distribution.

Besides not knowing much about boxing, and also not being confident with computers (don't forget we're both 60 plus) Judy now started her worry period. This is the time when I made one of those 'funny' remarks which all husbands make but know we shouldn't. I said, 'There's only 75 sleepless nights to go before the start of the Games.' If only there was some way to retract words I would have been most thankful.

The hard work started now with several weekends spent in town at the IBM Centre learning our jobs and how to fit in with the other dozen or so in the boxing results team. Fortunately all the team – the volunteers and the IBM personnel – were easy to work with. The friendliness soon made all of us comfortable working together. These weekends, from 9 a.m. to 5 p.m. on both Saturdays and Sundays, were fairly intense so our roles could become second nature. It was during this time that I made another husband joke: 'If you make a mistake in the score,' I said, 'the whole world won't know for two minutes.' Why is it we only realise after saying these things that spouses don't have a sense of humour?

We discovered that amateur boxing, in spite of appearances, is a fairly safe sport. Heading a soccer ball often will probably do more damage to a player. Maybe that will explain the behaviour of some of your soccer playing friends.

We survived our training and the dress rehearsals at the Darling Harbour venues and feeling great in our new uniforms, which by the way were very comfortable, sat at ringside for the first bout on the first competition day. What an exciting day, made more so by the appearance of Muhammad Ali. The concentration for three and a half hour sessions left us drained but feeling great. At the debriefing session afterwards we compared notes and worked out where we could improve.

Unfortunately, the Games passed much too quickly. We met many famous boxers, saw good bouts, developed an appreciation for amateur boxing, which is nothing like professional boxing and enjoyed a remarkable few weeks. Yes, we survived. Judy sleeps soundly at night and there were no mistakes to be flashed around the world.

So now when our grandkids say, 'What did you do at the Olympics, Nanna?' Judy replies, with more than a hint of pride and achievement, 'I worked at ringside at the boxing!' I reckon she deserves a gold medal!

P.S. I think she wants to learn how to speak Greek just in case volunteers are needed in Athens.

RUSSELL REA, *Boxing Results*
SYDNEY NSW

There were many highlights during my 23 shifts at the Olympic and Paralympic Games as a Spectator Services host at Sydney Olympic Park. I watched the athletes march into the Stadium at both Games, stood on Kronos Hill as the F-111 lit its after-burner for the Closing Ceremony, met so many great people who also volunteered their time to make 'our' Games the best ever.

However, the moment that I still rate as the most magical is when a son and daughter of Ireland did their country proud. It was one of my last shifts and as I stood working in the Link Building information booth the finals of the boccia teams events (consisting of a male and female competitor) were being played in the pavilion next door.

The evenings were very quiet at the Paralympics. The school children had left and only the odd spectator wandered the park in between events. This allowed the hosts the opportunity to watch a number of sports during the night.

I had the chance this night to observe the final tense moments of the boccia team event between Ireland and Spain. Boccia is played by athletes with cerebral palsy. Some have limited movement in their limbs but still manage to play the game on their own. Others, though, have a severe disability which requires them to be assisted by an attendant who, with the use of a ramp for the ball to slide down, takes aim etc. for the athlete.

Ireland was behind with one end to go in the match but some well-placed shots allowed them to win the gold by a mere one point. This sent the place crazy with excitement as it was filled with family and friends of the athletes who flew to Australia all the way from Ireland.

It was great to feel the atmosphere of excitement, happiness and also disappointment. I was watching all this unfold from my vantage point near the athlete's exit to the arena. After the match had concluded the teams headed in my direction. The emotion was still overflowing. The Irish coach stood ready to greet his new champions. One of the victors, an athlete with an extreme disability, literally jumped out of his wheelchair into the arms of his coach. His attendant had tears flowing down his face and was hugging anyone in close proximity. The family then arrived and the tears of joy flowed freely.

This was all too much for me and I went out in sympathy, yes, I cried for the Irish. It was now my turn to man the info booth and this gave one of my fellow volunteers the chance to watch the medal ceremony.

I managed to compose myself, wiped the tears from my eyes and put on that happy smiling face the volunteers became famous for. Then the mother of one of the Irish gold medal winners came out of the pavilion, got her mobile phone directly in front of me and phoned the family in Ireland to pass on the great news. Again the tears flowed and I succumbed to the moment again as I searched for a tissue to dry our eyes.

This was my gold medal moment, being able to witness the joy and emotion that belongs to the Olympic and Paralympic Games.

GEOFF FERRIS, *Spectator Services*
BALGOWLAH NSW

While watching the volunteers march after the Games I noticed a few red shirts amongst the group. They were 'medical' – only a small number in the mass of people. It crossed my mind that most of those watching the Olympic and Paralympic Games had no idea of the complex medical coverage and activity going on behind the scenes. These Games had required the largest medical program of any sporting event and that program relied almost totally on volunteers. It was with this expectation that Dr Danny Stiel – the chief medical officer – a gastroenterologist with exceptional organising abilities, worked for almost nine years to ensure that our Olympic and Paralympic Games had the appropriate medical coverage. Patsy Trethowan from a nursing and public health background joined Danny in 1996 as the medical manager. It was Patsy who made the program work. I was lucky enough to be invited to join the team in 1997 to fill the role of deputy chief medical officer and head of athlete care.

The three of us worked with eight dedicated paid health professionals as the SOCOG staff to put in place the medical service. This small team recruited approximately 3500 volunteers, sent them optional rosters for their varied jobs, modified these rosters when they didn't suit and prayed those rostered would turn up on the day. They did turn up and they did a great job. They came from all over Australia, some taking leave, some leaving their jobs and some from Sydney trying to fit Games rosters on top of their usual workload. They came from all walks of life, from the newly graduated to professors and the elite in their fields. They worked in a fleeting structure with an unfamiliar hierarchy, often under significant stress, with the requirement for much thinking on their feet and adapting complex contingency plans to ensure smooth operations at the coalface.

Hats off to those with the less glamorous jobs. To the data entry operators and administrators who spent many days voluntarily at the SOCOG headquarters well away from any crowds, nightlife or the possibility of seeing an Olympic athlete or Paralympic athlete. They were there to contribute their bit to the Games, doing it with a smile and fulfilling an essential part of the program. To the night teams of the Village, the accident and emergency doctors, nurses and receptionists who worked night after night, occasionally receiving a very unwell official or athlete and not infrequently being woken to produce a condom when the pharmacy closed – clearly an emergency requirement!

Everyone who was involved in the Games has their stories and memories:

- The distress on the pharmacist's face who spotted the Olympic flame being tested a week prior to the Games at 2 a.m. and taking ten minutes to set-up tripod and camera only to see the flame disappear just as he was about to press the shutter.

- The pre-lighting of the flame which also caused the Swedish chef de mission some angst. Having arrived in the Village late from his long flight he went to bed, only to waken and see the flame burning. He became quite distraught in the belief he had slept for ten days and missed the Opening Ceremony.
- The training sports physician working closely with the Aboriginal women during the Opening Ceremony who has subsequently chosen to spend a big part of his elective year with the Aboriginal Medical Service in outback Australia.
- The hard-working dental surgeons who fitted one of the 154 sophisticated mouthguards emblazoned with the Olympic rings to an Olympic hockey player only to see that hockey player the next day take a ball flush in the mouth. Subsequent plastic surgery was required to the face but the teeth and maxilla were still intact. This made the work all worthwhile.
- The medical receptionist who wrote in to say she left her job as she had enjoyed the Olympic experience so much and had been treated so well that she realised her job was not for her and she was moving on to bigger and better things.
- The joy of the ophthalmic surgeon and optometrist who were consulting a patient during the Paralympics who for a significant number of years was technically blind and registered as such at the Paralympics. Within 20 minutes, and with appropriate lenses, the patient was able to read the second-bottom line on the eye chart. After his event he was handed his spectacles and through an interpreter it was indicated to him that his good fortune was tempered by the knowledge that he had competed in his last Paralympics.

It was the hope of the SOCOG staff that the volunteers would get out of the Games the things that had encouraged them to volunteer in the first place. From the tremendous feedback and many anecdotes arising from the event it would appear that, for most, the experience exceeded the expectation. The Games showed off Australians in their best light. Hopefully there will be many more events where this contributing spirit can again come to the fore, but this one will be hard to match.

DR KEN CRICHTON, *Deputy Chief Medical Officer and Head of Athlete Care*
SYDNEY NSW

People praise the Olympic volunteers. But as a Spectator Services host, one of the foot-soldiers with yellow collar and sleeve, I'd like to bat the compliments straight back to the opposite court.

I worked at the Sydney Entertainment Centre, which hosted the Olympics volleyball. My story is about small encounters with special people. Take those queuing to buy tickets outside the centre. Some stood for hours on end in the hot sun. 'We're OK, love,' they'd grin. Even the young woman in a wheelchair cheerfully refused help. 'I have water,' she said. 'I'm fine.'

One of those queuers gave me the nicest compliment I've ever had. After I had made a few weak jokes over the megaphone, he told me I should have been a stand-up comic. (And no, I don't think he was being sarcastic!)

I wasn't always so successful. I failed to help a tall good-looking Brazilian youth, here with a dance group, who had lost his mum. Nor could I assist a foreign visitor who wanted to buy 70 postcards at the centre to send home to friends.

Before each match session, ticket duty at the entry doors was fast and hectic. Check and rip, check and rip, chick and rep ... oops! Still they poured in. One morning a line of excited kids with painted flag faces filed through, the last and smallest little brother refusing to give up his ticket, no way, hadn't his dad told him to hang on to it?

Ushering inside the auditorium meant giving directions and a quick reshuffle when someone had sat in the wrong seat, this accomplished, generally, without complaint. When the game had started and everyone was tucked up neatly in their correct places, we had time to stand still and catch the action. One day, outsiders Australia beat Spain. Aussie Oi sounded very sweet. Should a volunteer show national bias? Under the circumstances, please excuse.

The Peruvians played a big match and lost it ... Nevertheless, their countrymen were heard to celebrate, and so they did, staging an impromptu concert at the top of the stairs. I asked a Peruvian woman, 'Do you always sing and dance like this?' She answered me proudly with a toss of long black hair. 'Of course. We are passionate people.'

On the final day Yugoslavia played Russia. Excitement and noise in the enclosed auditorium were intense, and peaked as Yugoslavia won. Later, when the spectators had gone, a lone athlete brought his gold medal back to the court and – each metre of his height a maiden's dream – posed patiently for photographs with (mostly female) volunteers.

Meet in Hyde Park for our big parade on the Thursday after the Games ended. We joked among ourselves that perhaps no spectators would turn up. But as we marched from the park into the street, we were met by a storm of cheers from ranks of friendly faces.

You beautiful people of Olympic Sydney – thanks!

WENDELL WATT, *Spectator Services*
SYDNEY NSW

While it has probably been said many times already, Sydney put on an incredible display of hospitality and should be very proud. As you would guess, I have attended several Olympic Games and always find that while the events and results tend to slip away it is the people involved that I remember. Your kindness and the extra effort you made to look after me are much appreciated and I will always remember them (Mounties are not used to being spoilt that way). You were as much a representative of your country as I was of mine and I think you were an exemplary ambassador, though you did keep driving on the wrong side of the road …

CST. DUNCAN POUND, *Canadian Mountie*
Son of Dick Pound, IOC Vice President
WHISTLER CANADA
(excerpt courtesy of volunteer **MAVIS BOOTH**)

During the Olympics John was on duty when a young Swiss diving competitor approached him and asked if he knew the name of the music being played on the PA system. He said sorry he didn't know. After the girl left, he thought that was not good enough and set about finding out. After asking several people, he found it was the music from *Forrest Gump*. Hours later he caught up with the girl and told her it was from *Forrest Gump*. She did not know what a 'Forrrest Goomp' was! John explained it was a popular movie a few years ago. She said it must have had a different name in Europe.

That night John told the story to his family. His eldest daughter Justine (out from England specially for the Games) told him he was a lousy old bastard, to go and buy it for the girl. So the next day John visited numerous record stores until he finally found it.

Then, of course, there was the problem of finding this girl again. After a lot of asking of the volunteers and no one had seen her, eventually one said, yes she'd seen her going into the change room. This lady volunteer went to the change room while John manned her post. Within a very short time, the volunteer was back with the girl in tow. When John gave her the CD she immediately threw her arms around him, through tears said she would tell her coach and boyfriend how kind he was etc. Then she presented John with an exclusive Swiss pin which he was thrilled with.

NOREEN MITCHELL *on behalf of her brother*
JOHN WARD, *Spectator Services*
HARRINGTON NSW

MAX TALKS TO PETER BROCK

“Brockie's the sort of person you spend a bit of time with and you feel he's made a difference to your outlook. This is a man who has raced cars when half a second could seal your fate permanently. He's fearless, intense, a man who's not afraid to say, 'Take a good hard look at yourself or you're going to lose this.' Olympic athletes respect that.”

Max

Max: In a snapshot, how did you get involved?

Peter: I'd run across Herb Elliot a few times, just at functions, and he said to me, 'Brockie, you sort of don't fit in with the usual mould of the racing-car type person.' He's a bit of a character so he knows that. He said, 'Would you like to come and have a bit of a chat with some of the workshops we've got going, just a few seminars here and there?' I said I'd love to. And from there it became a bit more serious where we actually had something called 'Attitude Seminars' and a number of people started going there including myself.

Max: So what was that – markers and butcher paper?

Peter: It was something like that. Anyway, I was a bit surprised that I had something to offer, not having been involved with the individual sports but being a sports enthusiast. (Of course I knew enough about it not to be a mug … well, that might be debatable for some of them.) And then he said, 'I'd like to offer you a job for the Olympics. I did this job over in Atlanta and I can't do it at the Sydney Olympics, I've got a more administrative role.' I said I'd love to.

Max: Great opportunity.

Peter: Yeah and I guess it's proof that in life you never know where it's going to lead you. You know, you've got this idea, you think, 'Sounds like a good thing, let's do it, let's have a red-hot go', then the next door opens and you have a go at that one and next thing you know the next one does. If you'd have said to me a year before the Olympics I'd get a job as a senior staff in the Olympic team, you'd go, 'Oh yeah.' It was just a fantastic experience.

Max: You were booked into athletics?

Peter: I had diving. I knew to be a good diver you had to make a splash. I mean that's the idea. The judges' score would go up; I was pretty good at that. I'd be sitting there sometimes and I actually started sounding like I knew what I was talking about. 'What do you think of that one?' and I'd say, 'Eight six I reckon' … I was dragging these words out, plucking them out of thin air. A lot of fun.

I had men's basketball which was great because you were dealing with some very senior professional athletes. Andrew Gaze, Shane Heale, those sort of guys – been there and back – and they'd also got used to working in an environment where the teams weren't necessarily a bonded team. They tended to bond after a few tournaments, after a few dramas. So here's a bunch of individuals, like a State of Origin team …

Max: Give me a typical day.

Peter: There was always someone somewhere wanting a talk, either over a meal or little cubbyhole of a room or at the warm-up track – I had passes that let me go anywhere. So you'd be wandering around the backblocks there and you'd find yourself with some of the elite athletes of the team – they were just human beings after all – and you were just hanging around chatting and you'd ask them if they need something, as simple as a five-minute shower or finding someone they want to speak to. So your role could be many and varied. I'd just say I'm here to do whatever you want, I'm here to ensure that you are able to achieve 100 per cent.

Max: So you must have seen some of these dreams come to fruition.

Peter: Sometimes they'd just do a personal best, and they'd be over the moon. And the press might ignore them, but I'd know the kid had done something extraordinary. I'd know that for Athens, this is going to make a huge difference.

You're in a privileged position because you know that maybe you've made some contribution. Occasionally they'd come up and say, 'Thank you. What you said made a lot of sense and today it just all came together.' And you walk away from that encounter thinking, 'That's pretty good …'

You asked me about a normal day. You get up just before six usually, get out for a swift shower, beat all these old buggers to the shower.

Max: You were in a little tight locker-room as well?

Peter: I had John Bertrand, Laurie Lawrence and Herb Elliot and there was a guy from security. It was senior staff. I'd get up, have a shower, do my exercises. I had to get them out of the way before the meeting would start. Herb would meet with Laurie, John and myself to plan out what we were going to do that day. We had to figure it out amongst ourselves and Herb pretty soon realised we knew what we were doing.

I initially went to some basketball games sitting on the sidelines with the team, like sitting on the bench. And I realised after a bit that I could be better for them whooping up the crowd. So I'd be out there doing a Laurie Lawrence. We had a ball getting the crowd going. You could see the results go up and down according to the mob.

The swimmers were a great group. Dawn Fraser rang me prior to the competition and asked me to speak to the men's and women's teams, give them a last-minute chat before they go into competition. Fantastic, I mean what a privilege. Here's Dawnie ringing me up and saying, 'Brockie, can you come down here, talk to the swimmers?'

So I had a chat firstly to the men's team, crowded into a tiny room. Then I spoke to the women's and they particularly wanted to talk about intimidation, which is something I knew a lot about. In motor-racing there's a bit of sledging done, but basically it's done in an overt manner where you've got cars being put places and facial expressions and little love-taps occasionally. So to remain focused on what you're doing despite these outside pressures is a skill you acquire. It does take some time. And they'd been copping all this Gary Hall Junior stuff – champion USA swimmer who made a bit of a show by saying he'd smash the Australian team like a guitar. I said to be honest with you, good on him. Let him get up there and play his guitar. My best advice to you when it comes to intimidation is don't get involved, take no notice of it, let them do their stuff. That's his stuff. Actually, it's interesting because Kieren Perkins came up a few days afterwards and said, 'Brockie, you actually nailed it. You're the first one who nailed it. People have been skirting around this for a while'.

All you've got to do is walk out there, you've got to set up on those blocks and you've got to dive in and swim like buggery.

You'd get to six or so events per day and certain warm-up sessions. Maybe an hour away from competing, so you'd talk to the private coach, chat to the athlete. As far as the athlete was concerned, if you were representing the hierarchy of the team, they want to know that even though they weren't expected to win gold, you were still there and you felt they were worthwhile supporting. I didn't necessarily pick on the people expected to win.

Max: How did you go with the names?

Peter: I did the blazer ceremony for the track and field and some of those athletes went on to create some sort of notoriety for themselves – Tatiana comes to mind. When they came up to get their blazer and I've read their names over the loudspeaker they'd walk up and whisper, 'It's really …'. Someone should have briefed me beforehand because they weren't exactly household names. Someone said to me, 'You murdered those names.' I did my best; I really apologise to those people. But over the weeks you get to know them.

Max: Food was a huge temptation apparently. It was a stunning cafeteria.

Peter: If you sat down with the girls from the hockey or the water polo they were more conscious of eating well than the men. They were more disciplined in all parts of their lives than the guys. Let's face it, on planet earth at this time, this is the epicentre of physical excellence. This is where it is – Sydney. In this bloody room. More people in here are aspiring to excellence as a concentrated effort than anywhere else that exists on earth at this moment.

Max: Good call.

Peter: A lot of them created problems for themselves by being stressed out. One interesting thing that's happened now is that psychologists are available for use after the event, the jump off the cliff. You could not blame the athletes for saying it's never going to get any better than this. My point is, that in life you challenge yourself and I'm a firm believer that the way you are is a result of the experiences you've had. At this point, you've challenged yourself to do something which is extraordinary. You've chosen to get yourself through that training machine to get yourself here and into the Olympics. Now, one part of you is saying, 'I don't really want to do this', another part of you is exhilarated, another part is saying, 'But what if I fail?' What all this is about is mental discipline. Stopping your mind running rampant and creating all sorts of unreasonable and unrealistic situations by reining your mind in. The moment you feel your mind doing this, stop. The moment you feel yourself getting into a huge emotional drama, stop. You've got to pat yourself on the back for challenging yourself. Not too many people do; they prefer to sit back and let life be very safe. You've chosen not to do this. You've got to know this is the fastest growth curve you could possibly put yourself through as individual character development. So pat yourself on the back. The only expectation you should ever have is that you must give it your best shot. You can't have regretful feelings if you've taken care of yourself beforehand because you've done everything that's humanly possible. You're not going to win every time you go out there. Sometimes it's someone else's turn. It's as simple as that.

Max: Looking back, were there top memorable images?

Peter: The basketball. We walked out of there singing. Some of those nights were magic. The team would come in and they'd see all their mates. It was electric.

Max: You were one of only a handful of people who knew the vulnerabilities and the strengths of the majority of them there, and then to watch it unfold in front of you. Where were you on the Cathy Freeman night?

Peter: I was with the athletes. We'd organised a barbecue ... we came back from the beach volleyball. We'd been doing stuff behind the scenes. I'd spent the day in the stands whipping up the crowd during that match. I ended up getting a lift back with the Lord Mayor of Sydney so I could be in time for the race.

And speaking of vulnerabilities: one night we had a talent quest at the Village. I remember I stood up there with Hayley Lewis, Gina Marooney and Ian Thorpe singing this song with John Williamson. None of us can sing. We were all just shocking.

Max: That's the stuff that you cherish forever.

PETER BROCK, *Athlete Liaison Officer*
MELBOURNE, VIC

As I sit here wondering where to begin, I recall the brilliant blue sky, the blimp, the music, the in-your-face smiles, endless happy 'Aussie Aussie Aussie!' ... And I think of my late father who attended the Melbourne Olympics. He always spoke of it with such passion, he said that you really had to experience the Olympics to understand the special feelings they give off.

My Olympic day began at 3.10 a.m. with a special Telstra Olympic wake-up call (that is, Ian Thorpe swimming for Australia, the crowd roaring in the background: 'Go Thorpie Go!). Take it from me, even at my age (63), the feet hit the floor with a burst of adrenaline, dressed, 20 minutes drive to Gosford Station all brightly decorated by colourful volunteers and big smiles. The 4.30 a.m. train delivered us in great numbers to wonderful Olympic Park.

As a volunteer it was one excitement after another. From the Opening Ceremony with the horses galloping on to *The Man from Snowy River* theme, to Cathy's race, to the volunteer's thank you parade – always surrounded by my family and my fellow Australians – it had to be heaven on earth.

Another of so many highs: picture Darling Harbour, the huge viewing screen, medal presentation, Australia's won gold, up goes the mighty flag, on comes the national anthem, up stands the enormous crowd and the singing echoes around the city. The pride and tears on happy faces – it was something else.

A writer I am not, but I had to try and get my message over. It was a thrill of a lifetime and shared by so many.

GLORIA COX *Spectator Services*
BATEAU BAY NSW

Part III

THE PARTY'S OVER

“So, what happens when it’s all over?

Two weeks after the Opening Ceremony, we’re in the Brown’s lounge room watching the biggest party unfold on the box – the Closing Ceremony. A different performance, but still engaging, and a true Sydney-style party. Proud is not the word to describe what we’d been through in the last two weeks.

In reality the Olympic Games, followed by the Paralympics, effectively stopped the nation. Australia didn’t merely stop, it hit the wall. The wheels of industry were parked kerbside. People who didn’t go were still obsessed by the Games – the mood was contagious. Televisions were powered up 24 hours a day like a permanent Internet connection, logged on to Olympic action. In shops from Fremantle to Rockhampton, the silver screens flickered away, and the roar of crowds filtered through curtained windows and onto the street.

I remember one evening about 6.30 p.m. my family and I visited a favourite pasta place in Malvern. The previous few nights Ian Thorpe and friends had torpedoed the pool breaking world records and winning a string of gold medals. Normally the last thing you want in a restaurant is the telly on, but the infection had spread and a portable television was perched above the pizza oven for all to see. Incredibly, it wasn’t turned on yet! Unanimous decision by the clientele. Set on. Just so we wouldn’t miss a race. Walking back to our car we noticed how many cafés and shops were illuminated by the blue tinge of TV land. My girls pointed out that everyone was watching the same show as us!

Yes, the country couldn’t do without being connected to Stadium Australia, the pool or the Velodrome. And what about Cathy mania? At 8.10 p.m., Monday 25 September 2000. Forget the Melbourne Cup, this was the race that truly stopped the nation. She was our favourite, our Cathy, one race from destiny. According to many vollies I’ve spoken to, the roar of the crowd was louder than anything they’d ever heard. It’s a wonder they didn’t hear it in Tasmania or on Cape York Peninsula. So many words have been written about that night, and so much has already been said, but you know the beaut thing about it? We all have our unique window into the event – the final of the women's 400 metres.

The spectators privileged to be in the stand, and the volunteers who were on duty, will never forget their closeness to that defining moment when Cathy, victorious, a spent force, collapsed on the tarmac – relived. She'd done what she had to do – win! 178.5 strides, decked out in a hooded body suit, aerodynamic and graceful – it took a lifetime and 49 unforgettable seconds for the prodigy from Mackay to become an Olympic gold medallist. She'd run faster than the best the world could muster. Destiny complete!

This was without doubt the most significant moment of competition in the XXVII Olympiad. Like millions of Aussies, I shared the moment at home, glued to the tireless television set. We opened a bottle of champagne – did you do something similar? – and tears of joy spilled over, ever so gently in the privacy of our lounge room.

And as if competion for 300 gold medals wasn't enough, we all stayed up for the graveyard shift, for a pair of never-say-die Aussies, Roy and H.G. Nelson. Their two hours of madcap verbal mayhem was a must-watch – it seemed that the whole world loved their point of view. Nothing was sacred – 'hello boys', 'battered sav' and 'wrong door' have ensured that gymnastics will never be the same again! And in between their fun and games, Roy and H. G. took time out to pay tribute to the enormous contribution made by the vollies, drawing attention to how much they'd added to the spirit of the Games.

So, day after day, night after night, for two weeks we were all sleep deprived but riding the wave of success that had swept the country. When it was all over, we were left with great memories, and they'll last forever. What was it like when it was all over for the vollies, Gerry?

Well, to be honest, for me it was a funny mixture of sadness that it was all over and a kind of relief. Lots of vollies went on to do the Paras, but I finished with the Closing Ceremony. I don't know that I could have kept going for much longer. Lots of us had stepped outside our normal lives for the two weeks, but we knew we had things piling up back at work. I think we were like mothers with sick kids – you don't know how you keep going day and night, but you just do. You had a job to do. However you look at it, it's something that we'll all remember for the rest of our lives.

Apart from anything else, we saw how Australians can rise to the occasion. Look at what a great job the NSW police did. They were friendly, willing to help, had creative solutions to problems, they were really professional. They behaved like helpful human beings, rather than law enforcers. And it was a great feeling for us, knowing that people trusted us because we were wearing the volunteers uniform. Visitors to the Games thought we could answer any question imaginable. And we did try to help. The volunteers were so well presented, too. Always neat and tidy. That was very good for our national image.

Now that it's over, you can see that the 2000 Olympic Games gave Australia an important place in world history. Sydney now has a starring role on the world stage and like many a good Broadway show it will run forever. The Homebush facilities have become the focal point of greater western Sydney. It has the Showgrounds, a range of magnificent sporting facilities, hotel accommodation, rail and water transport. Even light industrial and commercial industry is starting to be established in the area.

People continue to call me wanting to share a story, poem, song, life-changing experience. It was only in putting together this book that I've realised the enormous impact that volunteering had on so many people's lives. I have communicated with many volunteers, listened and read their stories and even a tough old guy like me has felt the lump in the throat and experienced watering of the eyes.

Max asked me the other day if I'd do it again. Yeah, of course I'd do it again. I'd throw my name in the hat and see what happens. I had a ball. ”

Max & Gerry

A year down the track, we're starting to especially miss our Wednesdays, when we used to go into town and work. We did that for six years leading up to the Games. We were so tired at the end of the Games that it was nice to have our ordinary lives back for a while. Now it's been a year I think the whole thing was like one of those trips you go on overseas: you enjoy the trip while you're there, but it starts to mean even more when you come back, and you go over things, and look at your photos, and talk about it. The Olympics have been a bit like that for Norm and me.

DOROTHY WILLIAMS, *Pioneer volunteer*
PROSPECT NSW

Question: Would I do it all again?
Answer: You bet I would, first in line.

WILLIAM COOPER, *Driver*
IPSWICH QLD

I saw a man training in a wheelchair along our road (a busy road). I thought he may be training for the Paralympics. I thought I could give him $50 for training. Then I saw the ad for Quilts 2000. I made my quilt and it sold almost straight away. In the meantime I was introduced to Ronald (the athlete) by our local paper. Later I found out that my quilt had been sold for $950 and Ronald himself had bought the quilt for his mother!

JANET SHEPHERD, *Quilter*
SYDNEY NSW

I met some famous Australians; they were all volunteers like me. They may not have been known by many, but famous all the same. They gave up their time just to be there. Worked long hours, up to 12 hours at a time, and the smiles never left their face. I have never worked so hard in my life, laughed so much and felt so close to the people I worked with, all within a two-week period.

MAUREEN McGOVERN, *Team Leader, Spectator Services*
WAUCHOPE NSW

When I remember the Sydney Olympics, I think ten out of ten, perfect, faultless, awesome, unbelievable, fabulous – and the hockey was good too! Running second to my experience of winning gold at the Sydney Olympics would be no mean feat in the scheme of things, and given my love for food and its abundance particularly, I was so impressed with the contributions of the volunteers that I put their gift up there with the dining hall experience – equal second in a very strong race and extremely high praise indeed! On every occasion that I saw an athlete or official needing something – anything at any time – there appeared a smiling, enthusiastic and most importantly, a helpful volunteer with a friendly face who was only too eager to assist.

They were everywhere, usually hunting in pairs, easily identifiable, friendly and positive. Nothing was too much trouble, too late or too hard. Peter Brock was a volunteer of a different kind (a liaison for Australian athletes) and he became well known amongst our team as a regular dining companion who was always good for a chat and an injection of energy. The bus drivers were happy, enthusiastic and most significantly good humoured. They were patient with athletes and visitors who spoke no English, and it was common to overhear foreign athletes (who did speak English) praising the organisation and professionalism of the team of volunteers as compared with their experiences at other Olympic Games. Enough to make an Aussie athlete proud!

For experience's sake the dining hall was a spectacle, not to mention a social arena, in itself. There was food as far as the eye could see, and seating for 15,000 at one time if required – maybe that was a myth but the possibility that it could be true made a big impression on me. It was the all-you-can-eat buffet of my dreams – literally because unfortunately our event continued for the duration of the Games and it wasn't until very late in the piece that we could indulge to our heart's content. It was a festival of fresh food in abundance, in any combination and at any time of day or night catering for all ethnic dietary requirements. Our first dining experience involved a supervised 'walk through' with one of the team dietitians who drew our attention to the information cards that accompanied all of the meals and snacks that were available detailing the fat, carbohydrate, protein and calorie content of all the food. As we had to weigh in every day (annoying), this information was useful as it would have been very easy to overeat and destroy all the hard work that had been done in this respect prior to our arrival in the Village. Hmmmm.

Not that I was preoccupied with the whole food thing (much), but it was interesting to watch what other athletes were eating while we weren't. In particular the athletes from poorer countries were so amazed by the plethora of food available that it was not uncommon for them to have three of four plates overflowing at one time, most commonly with the highest fat content that it was possible to create – Big Macs were very popular! Lamingtons were the snack of choice for our team with only two grams of fat in each … Needless to say, I haven't eaten one since. McDonalds was obviously a popular venue for us post-competition.

Eye candy of the human variety was an overwhelming drawcard for the dining hall and a welcome distraction from the considerable eating opportunities that were available. As a result, some athletes were fairly accused of spending an extraordinary amount of time 'hanging out' in the dining hall to satisfy more than their passion for food! The dining hall was a human zoo accommodating all body types – a good 'perv' not to mention a great dining experience in every sense thanks to the volunteers who managed, held security posts, checked bags, served food and generally ensured that the experience was sensational in every respect.

CLAIRE MITCHELL-TAVERNER, *Hockey player*
Australian Hockey Team Gold Medallist Sydney 2000
SYDNEY NSW

The Games so quickly came to an end. I wanted my last shift to last forever. I even begged to stay for the night shift.

CATERINA GIGLIO, *Spectator Services*
BANKSTOWN NSW

THE BEST OLYMPICS EVER

I drove everywhere in Olympic mode
They marked the lanes, streets and roads
Cars and buses had signs in view
Taking them to Homebush or the nearest venue
In Olympic talk that would be:
Drive to Regatta or the SOP
Go to Ryde to the WPV
Drop this off at the TOC
There the VTM may ask
'Has the SSM completed the task?'
I never knew, I just drove cars
Too many initials, too many stars
Some were grumpy, others said thanks
Most were nice as they climbed the ranks

A call was waiting in Westmead
I was the one to do the deed
In poncho, Commodore I went
Locals thought a hero'd been sent
They took some photos of the car
The uniform and the reluctant star
It was my moment of Olympic fame
Sadly no one asked my name
That was the driver's lot I guess
To give our all and very best
For little thanks and moments few
The Best Olympics we ever knew ...

SANDY MITCHELL, *Driver*
COOLUM BEACH QLD

I have been a volunteer since the 80s in India, Nepal, PNG, Pacific Islands and Pakistan for various Aid Organisations. I've experienced many dangerous situations and near escapes and seen much poverty, but I think the 2000 Olympics was a Lesson To The World.

JOHN HUGHES, *Spectator Services*
ADELAIDE SA

The whole experience is one that I will never forget. The pride rises whenever I see pictures of the Olympic flame. It was one thing that all volunteers claimed as their own.

TREVOR JORDAN, *Staff Support*
WEST WALLSEND NSW

In the Olympics, we saw all the players full of energy, competing in an enthusiastic spirit of a professional athlete. However, I felt a deep respect for the competitors in the Paralympics. They are not physically perfect like the professionals, but they are still fighting with their iron wills, training hard like the others. I really appreciate the people who invented the Paralympics. In the Olympics, the victory is divided between the top three athletes: gold, silver and bronze. However in the Paralympics every competitor deserved a medal. This is their victory against nature and life. The beautiful images of the participants in the Paralympics make us forget all of our labour and tiredness and we feel so happy about life. We have shared our happiness with the handicapped people.

I also had a great pride and honour. I feel proud for the Vietnamese community in Australia. We are Vietnamese with Australian citizenship and we will continue to contribute our best to the country we live in. This is to give in return what Australia has given to us over the last 30 years …

VAN INH LE, *Training Room Assistant*
SYDNEY NSW

I can't stop talking about the Olympic Games with my family and friends; it's not enough. If I had to do it all over again I would do it any time. I could be 80 years next time it might come back to Australia; I will still do it.

HELEN PLEDGER, *Uniform Distribution*
MELBOURNE VIC

By the time the Paralympics drew to a close, 'volunteermania' had definitely taken hold on the Sydney public. On the night of the Closing Ceremony I was constantly asked to sign little kids' T-shirts and tickets etc. I couldn't believe it. I must have signed 50 autographs between the Stadium and the railway station. This was mind-blowing. Perhaps it was my 15 minutes of fame that I've heard everyone gets sometime in their lives!

GARY WOMSLEY, *Spectator Services*
TOONGABBIE NSW

Highlights? Watching the *joie de vivre* of the athletes at the Opening and Closing Ceremonies. Seeing dedication and hard work pay off in results, usually another world record. Realising that people who are lucky enough to be 'whole' have nothing to complain about when you get right down to it. My absolute top experience was watching a disabled swimmer (who had only one leg and one arm) going like a threshing machine and winning his event. His smile, and the accolade of his peers, said it all for me and I was almost in tears with him.

JIM LITCHFIELD, *Venue Staffing*
ADELAIDE SA

I felt the Sydney Olympics implemented the philosophy of the original Games. They provided an atmosphere where problems were solved or not used to block activities. The 'opposition' party seemed to be on holidays and everyone appeared to be pulling in the same direction – at least from where I was stationed at the South Gate. We made life appear simple and it was sad to see the brakes and blockages being applied when the Games were over.

DAN BERGIN, *Spectator Services*
PYMBLE NSW

As the tumult of the extraordinarily successful Olympics and Paralympics dies, let's hope the spirit lives on.

The motto of the Paralympics says it all: 'Mind, body, spirit.'

It has been a record-breaking Games in every way, including the fact that Australia exceeded its Atlanta performance.

It has been a colourful time in the Village, where a wide variety of events has unfolded.

A seminal moment with a difference took place last Friday morning at the Australian team lounge. The look of intensity, if not agony, on the face of a young Paralympian as the seals were broken and he was handed his HSC examination paper was in sharp contrast to the cheerful faces of nearby medallists.

At the other end of the spectrum, the dance club has rocked and rolled to just about every kind of modern music, spearheaded by the Brazilian dance team somersaulting in their wheelchairs as they responded to the noisy beat.

I must be getting old as I was informed by one volunteer that the noise was relatively quiet to her young ears. To me, it sounded as if it was reverberating right through to Bronte, if not Boree Creek.

Then there was the sailor who managed to collapse a huge bin of cereal on to the floor, almost suffocating in a pile of Cornflakes. I guess this is one of the hazards of bulk supplies and big breakfast buffets.

Then there was drama during the welcoming ceremony for the Greek team when, after 100 renditions of correct national anthems, we had the wrong one. But good humour prevailed and a quick correction soon led to a full-on rendition of the magnificent Greek anthem.

The long convoys of wheelchairs being towed by vehicles in the Village were amazing, until the practice was stopped for safety reasons.

It's all over now and the big pack-up has started …

So let us hope we see the spirit of the Games kept alive.

TIM FISCHER, *Mayor of Paralympic Village*
Former Deputy Prime Minister
SYDNEY NSW

Both my wife and I were involved with the Olympic Closing Ceremony and at the conclusion of the proceedings we did not want to leave. We didn't want the night to end because we knew in the next few days it would be all over. As we slowly walked around the Olympic Stadium we could not help but notice an athlete pulling along a large shark fin (the shark fins on golf buggies used in the Greg Norman tribute). He looked lost and we asked him could we help. He told us he wanted to get back to the Athletes' Village. We were also heading to the Village so asked him to join us at it was difficult to give him directions from where we were, as a number of checkpoints had to be negotiated.

We could not help laughing to ourselves as we walked along with the athlete pulling this giant fin piled up with other Olympic memorabilia he had collected along the way. I asked him how he got the fin and he told us someone in the Vom (passageway under the Stadium) asked him for his German team shirt so he got the fin in return. Apparently it was someone with no authority to give the fin away as the Olympic memorabilia was being kept to auction off after the Games. As we walked and trundled along through the various checkpoints the security guards laughed and sent us on our way. By this time it was about 1 a.m. and we reached the closed road into the Village. As we made our way along the road there was shouting behind us and a large licorice-allsort shoe passed us, chased by numerous policemen on foot. The shoe suddenly stopped. He could see the road was blocked ahead; he got out of the shoe and ran off into the darkness.

The first policeman to arrive at the shoe came and stood with the shark fin and us and watched the pantomime. Oh, I wish we had had a movie camera to capture the fun and antics. It was just typical of the great atmosphere and fun of the night. Later in the Village when we asked the athlete from Germany how he was going to get the fin home, he replied his plans had changed, he had just heard from other athletes that if he took the fin to Darling Harbour he could get at least *two* shirts for it. He was last seen trying to manoeuvre the fin on the bus to Darling Harbour.

DENNIS OVERTON, *NOC Assistant*
WENTWORTHVILLE NSW

I've had a long history at the Olympics:
1956: Schoolboy
1960: Emergency, Water Polo Team
1964: Water Polo Team
1968: Water Polo Team – refused entry by Australian officials
1972: VC Water Polo Team
1992: Press at Barcelona
2000: Visitor at Sydney

I often think back to the Friendly Games of 1956 in my hometown of Melbourne. They provide the clearest memories of the fifties – a schoolboy at the time and, like most, madly into sport, the Games were Disneyland, Hollywood and the Tivoli all rolled into one big excitement machine.

Vladimr Kuts the Russian running machine, our whiz kids in the pool, the black and white TV pictures viewed through the shop window – all as clear as if it was 1996.

An even sharper image is the memory of getting into events, into the Olympic Village even into the change rooms at the new Olympic Pool without the hint of even a fake ID or Accreditation.

Who were these happy-go-lucky guards and ticket collectors?

Was this my first experience with volunteering?

Some were in armed service uniform – others in the dustcoats of the Melbourne Games Volunteer Brigade.

Whoever they were let me say thank you – albeit almost fifty years on!

Along with my schoolmate Keith Stackpole – who was to become the Vice Captain of our Australian Test Team, I got into any event of our choice – the MCG track and field, the pool for gold medal events.

Whatever!

And the ploy was always the same 'Mum's got our tickets insider mister' – 'In you go boys'. But I seem to recall more than one saying 'now come back for help if you can't find her'. These were volunteers – mid-fifties style – salt and pepper of the earth, so honest and caring, so vulnerable but just so pleased to be playing a role in the Olympics.

'It's in the genes' they say about the son or daughter of a star athlete who is showing some promise – it's hereditary. Well so it must be with volunteering! Those magnificent ambassadors in Sydney must have been related to those good folk from Melbourne.

But how things have changed.

There is a definitive line between volunteers and operators now – anything to do with the almighty dollar is handled by the pros – only the happiness, goodwill and enthusiasm is left to the volunteers.

Did I say 'only' – God forbid!

The honorary work provided by the volunteers and the great joy generated among the visitors by them was of immense value to the Games in all ways. They created happiness: happy people buy things; happy people tell their friends to come to Australia. Happy people stayed longer, spent more and enjoyed this country well in excess of budget.

Of course volunteers are at all Olympiads.

My first as an Olympian was Tokyo and the Japanese did a great job. The public, particularly the throngs of school kids were fantastic with their flag-waving, autograph-hunting and level of excitement but there was that touch of officialdom at entrance gates – bureaucracy won the day.

They may well have in Sydney but our volunteers were superstars.

The Japanese were pleasant, polite and helpful. It was much the same in Munich however the tragic shootings which marred the '72 Games make comparisons unfair.

I was in Barcelona in '92 and the Spaniards raised the hospitality bar to new heights.

'Sydney can't compete with this,' we in the Press Corp would say after one spectacular day followed another. But how wrong we were – Barcelona provides memories of great warmth and casual friendliness but Sydney did what none of us thought possible.

The volunteers of Australia at the Sydney Games to me were more impressive and had a greater and more positive effect on me than any of all of the Olympic venues.

It was the raw natural enjoyment of the role, the entertainer in them all fully blossoming and the almost invisible but very effective efficiency of the volunteers that rightly deserves the gratitude of a nation.

LEON WIEGARD, *President of the Olympians Club since 1997*
Triple Olympian, Water Polo, Tokyo 1964, Mexico City 1968 and Munich 1972
MELBOURNE VIC

WHO WILL EVER FORGET SYDNEY 2000?

I looked forward for so long to being able to welcome friends to our country after being the recipient of hospitality for many years. For two weeks the world's attention was to be focused on Australia and friends would be coming to me instead of me going to them. My basic plan was to be involved as much as possible so it was to be a Spectator Services host at the Main Stadium for morning track and field sessions, tickets to all evening sessions of track and field, and helping at the Olympic Reunion Centre during the first week of the Games …

A special highlight was befriending a 70-year-old female gymnast from the Yugoslav team in the 1948 Olympics, now living in New York. While in Sydney she was reunited with a brother she had not seen for 59 years. The family was split up during World War II: she ended up in the US and her two brothers in Australia. It was the thrill of her life. Another highlight was to welcome Irena Szewinska-Kirszenstein, track and field's greatest female athlete and now a Polish IOC member. We were travelling companions through the 1970s on the European competition calendar and have remained friends ever since.

Spectator Services duties resumed first morning of track and field and to see a full stadium, previously unheard of, was amazing. Ushering on the top level saw my major duty being to redirect people back down to lower levels after they had walked straight past level 2 and 3 where entrances were insufficiently signed. There were numerous instances of volunteers pushing wheelchairs all the way up the ramp, only to have to turn round and go back down. Teething problems!

After a marvellous week, all of a sudden Day 2 of Spectator Services turned sour. Already stories were beginning to surface about volunteers having problems with supervisors and it was my unfortunate experience to strike one who simply had no understanding of the job at hand and completely lacked communication skills. In summary, after being abused and threatened all day I did not return. I was fortunate to have a choice and was able to be rostered on at the Reunion Centre and had a wonderful time looking after fellow Olympians from all corners of the world. Unfortunately, the very next evening in the Stadium as a spectator, I witnessed the very same supervisor barring access to a personal friend of mine in the protocol area. This person has been a member of the Olympic Family for 40 years and spent every day in the area this supervisor claimed he was not accredited for. I apologised to him for her behaviour and he was gracious enough to shrug it off.

At the end of the Games it was fantastic to see the volunteers get the recognition they so rightly deserved. If only some of the supervisors could have learned from their volunteers. How did they get their positions in the first place?

I, like so many others, had waited with such expectation for Games time to come around, but after it was all over could not believe that in reality these expectations were exceeded in every aspect. To see the way so many people were able to be transported around Sydney in such an orderly fashion, to see the Main Stadium full for every session of competition, to wait for Cathy Freeman's race and to have the night turn out to be the greatest night of track and field ever, to renew so many friendships, the list could go on and on …

But above all, to see Sydney in party mode and be a sea of smiling faces for a fortnight will be the memory that remains longest. Well done Sydney.

GRAHAM CROUCH, *Spectator Services / Ticketing*
Sprinter at Montreal 1976
OCEAN GROVE VIC

When I was a little girl my Nan used to tell me stories of the 1956 Olympics when she, my mother and my uncle worked in the Members area. She told me how she sat on the seat vacated by Queen

Elizabeth II while it was still warm and the time when her friend Connie was running along excitedly telling everyone that the queen was coming and in the process nearly knocked over the queen herself! I was proud to be a volunteer in the 2000 Olympics, both as an Aussie and for my country's amazing achievement. It felt like my family had come the full circle.

KERRY ROSEVEAR, *Driver*
MELBOURNE VIC

Having bridged the two great Olympic Games in Australia – Melbourne 1956 as an Olympic athlete; in Sydney 2000 as an Olympic administrator – I went back to the Melbourne Official Report and also called on my memory about the subject of volunteers. Melbourne of course needed volunteers but the solution back then was to call on the Boy Scouts, the Girl Guides, St John Ambulance, the Air League and the Sea Scouts. As well, members of the Armed Forces were extensively deployed. So, contrary to the Sydney Games, the volunteers mostly came from established volunteer organisations and comprised mostly of young people.

We have to recall that compared with Sydney where 199 national teams took part there were 67 participants in Melbourne. In the case of Sydney almost 21,000 press and broadcaster accreditations were issued compared with less than 1000 for Melbourne. Security was not perceived as a major issue and the attendance by international and interstate visitors was very modest.

Even so, the volunteer effort, though moderate in numbers and younger in age, was highly commended in the Official Report of the XVI Olympiad of Melbourne 1956. Some of the duties listed read somewhat innocently and for example included: 'opening the door of the car of the Duke of Edinburgh when he arrived at various functions', 'assisting lost children taken by police to various points near arenas' and 'receiving and distributing results received from other venues'.

What however does stand out clearly in the Melbourne report is that Melbourne 1956 needed and gained huge value from their young volunteer force.

Nearly a half a century later, the Sydney Organising Committee (SOCOG) judged the need for 47,000 volunteers. The recruitment, training and allocation of this group of individuals was vital. The focus for the Armed Forces was on security as was the New South Wales Police and their commonwealth counterparts, who did a wonderful job in a most relaxed and friendly manner.

Within SOCOG we were conscious of the generosity of spirit of our volunteers who travelled from all parts of Australia at their own expense and found accommodation for a number of training sessions. At the time of the Games they worked long hours at all times of the day and night and rarely failed to report for their next duty. This pattern sustained through the Paralympics.

I had invaluable support from two excellent volunteer drivers, Marie and John. John in fact had been a fellow student back at Teachers College in Newcastle. Nothing was too much trouble for either and they knew their job well. Few would realise that many of us on SOCOG and the IOC worked a non-stop 18- to 20-hour schedule a day during the Games; my personal assistant Anne integral to such a schedule.

For me, the secrets of the success of the Sydney 2000 volunteers were those over 60 years – many even over 70 like my elder brother Peter – who rose at 4 a.m. daily to receive athletes and visitors at Sydney Airport. This mature-age group absorbed their training, stood by their jobs (some quite routine) demonstrated high morale, stimulated the younger and enthusiastic team members and used their common sense and wisdom with the unexpected.

- The careful selection process and training by SOCOG.
- The cultural cross-section of the team.

- Their willingness to go the extra distance in offering advice and assistance.
- Their friendliness and courtesy.
- Their team spirit.
- Their commitment to make the Sydney Games 'the best ever'.

The magic link between Melbourne '56 and Sydney 2000, for me, is the story of the volunteers. The Sydney 2000 volunteer force was the real face of our Olympic Games for our visitors and scored 'best ever' in their own right.

R. KEVAN GOSPER, *Vice President of the IOC, Vice President of SOCOG*
Silver Medallist, Athletics, Melbourne 1956
SYDNEY NSW

I read once that a country needs a tragedy of some kind to unite its people. How much better that a happy time could draw out such fellowship, enthusiasm, generosity, patience and good spirits, even when it rained or the temperatures soared.

ELIZABETH KEANE, *Accreditation Officer*
NERANG QLD

I was a yellow shirt in the south section of Spectator Services. I look back now and think, how did I do it? But I did and I will remember it for the rest of my life. I live at Wyong on the central coast and got up at 2 a.m. to get to the park at 5.30 a.m. for a 6 a.m. start every morning. It was still dark and I used to take a few minutes to go and stand under the flame and I can't explain how it made me feel that I was looking at the Olympics flame here in Australia. Wonderful. With a little bit of luck I will be in Athens in 2004 … I have already sent my volunteers form in!

RITA POTTEN, *Spectator Services*
TUGGERAH NSW

'Volunteer did not want any favours'

Four weeks ago Rita Potten, of Tuggerah, was in hospital.

Next week she will have a brain scan to see just how far her multiple sclerosis has advanced, but for the past two weeks she has put her condition from her mind to be a volunteer at the Olympic Games.

And no one at the Games knew, despite the fractured bone in her foot from a fall during a MS attack a month ago and despite the crushing exhaustion of 3 a.m. starts.

'I didn't put it on my application form and I didn't tell anyone about it because I didn't want to be treated any differently. I didn't want any special privileges,' an exhausted but proud Mrs Potten said after a final day that started at 3.30 a.m. on Sunday and finished at 1.30 a.m. on Monday.

Tomorrow she will march in Sydney in the thank you parade for Games volunteers.

'I think I'll be up the back. It will be more of a stroll than a march. But it will be wonderful.'

Mrs Potten was diagnosed with MS nearly 20 years ago, one week before her 40th birthday.

The diagnosis came after the mother of three teenagers suddenly and terrifyingly went blind over five days.

'Absolutely terrified I was. I just thought, what the hell's going on? I thought I had a brain tumour.'

Multiple sclerosis, a disease of the nervous system, produces lesions on the brain and spinal cord resulting in acute attacks and remissions.

Mrs Potten was totally blind for three weeks and partially blind for a year, was deaf for a period, paralysed and in a wheelchair for four years and is prone to falls because of nerve and muscle dysfunction.

Four weeks ago, after a week where 'I couldn't feel my feet very well', she fell, broke a bone and listened as doctors and physiotherapists said she would not be able to cope with 10 days on her feet as an Olympic Games volunteer.

'About a week before the Games I started to feel a bit better and I thought, I can do it. I had to buy bigger shoes because my feet swelled up but I knew I could do it.'

She was thrilled when Olympic great Betty Cuthbert, diagnosed with MS about the same time as Mrs Potten, was wheeled into Olympic Stadium with the torch at the opening ceremony.

'I thought, I know what you've been through. To enter the Stadium and hear the crowd, that for her would have been a highlight of her life. You don't get many highs when you're that far along with MS and for Betty Cuthbert, that was probably as good as gold.'

For 10 days Mrs Potten woke at 3 a.m., travelled to Homebush Bay by train for a 5.30 a.m. start, worked full days with few breaks and travelled home again to sleep and repeat the process again and again.

'I couldn't have done it without my family. My husband Bill did everything so I could sleep, my daughter-in-law Natalie looked after him, and my children and grandchildren rang and left messages on the answering machine saying how proud they were of me and how I could make it.

'They knew how important it was to me.'

She enjoyed the thrill of the Games, the happiness of the crowds, the laughter of the children and the unexpected brushes with celebrities.

'I gave lollies to children who wore their hats and sunscreen and when I looked up from one little boy there was Mark Taylor telling me I could give his son a lolly,' she said. 'I was helping a couple get on a bus and I asked them whether they'd had a good day, and they said, "We've just come to watch our daughter." I said, "Who's your daughter?" and they said "Susie O'Neill." She'd just won gold.'

(This article by Joanne McCarthy is reprinted with kind permission of the *Central Coast Express Advocate*.)

The thing that stands out to me in both the Olympics and the Paralympics is the terrific relationship the SES volunteers had with the police. (Thanks guys, we had a ball.) But most of all, I would like to say a big thanks to all the SES people: not only the road crew, but the ones that organised what group went where, the ones that bussed us around and the ones that kept us fed and watered. (Oh that beloved Franklin Springs Water – I hope I never see another bottle as long as I live.)

GRAHAM MITCHELL, *SES*
SOUTH SYDNEY NSW

The main legacy of the Games is all the new SES friends I have made. As the OVIP-A coordinator, I met SES volunteers from all over NSW – like Doris from Gosford, a 75-year-old lady who travelled down from the North Coast almost every day. I don't know what time she had to leave, but some of our starts were 3.30 a.m. Even after I sent her home very sick at the end of the Olympics, there she was back again for the

Paralympics with a note from her doctor just in case I didn't believe she was fit!

PAT JOHNSON, *SES coordinator*
SYDNEY NSW

I was not in a position to be a volunteer, but I would like to suggest a title: 'The Ring-ins'.

JIM LEARMONTH
SUNSHINE VIC

THE DAWNING OF NANCY
Up Collins Street we marched along
Amid the cheering crowd,
Following athletes tall and strong,
Feeling just a wee bit proud.
'Are you Dawn?' a small voice asked
'Were you at the Games?
'May I have your autograph
'Amongst other famous names?'
Since '56 I'd longed to be,
Part of Olympic fame,
Does it really matter much
That Dawn is not my name?

NANCY ROBERTSON, *MCG Information*
MELBOURNE VIC

As I stood outside the main arena an announcement was made over the loudspeaker thanking the volunteers. Wow, I thought … isn't that nice. But as I looked around in the midday sun I saw everyone was standing and clapping. It was overwhelming. I realised that through the volunteers, spectators from all across the globe had experienced Australian generosity and friendship. Through the volunteers, the spirit of Australia had been shared with the world.

LINDA SCHAFER, *Spectator Services*
MELBOURNE VIC

The Campbelltown SES was asked to provide a sausage sandwich stall on the day of the march. It was estimated they would need 5000 sausage sandwiches, but on the day over 8000 sausage sandwiches were served to the Olympic volunteers. People were running everywhere to butchers and shops to get more sausages and rolls.
PAT JOHNSON, *SES coordinator*
SYDNEY NSW

I marched in the parade in the city! I never imagined in my wildest dreams I would ever do this. I count myself privileged to have been an Olympic Games volunteer – especially as I will be 78 years old in March.
NORMA HOLT, *Information and Protocol*
SYDNEY NSW

Clad in my black Olympic News Service uniform, I looked like a member of the mafia compared to the other volunteers (at the parade) who were drenched with vibrant colours. We were united however by the white Akubra hats which were practical if not stylish!
MONIQUE SCHAFTER, *Olympic News Service*
MELBOURNE VIC

We walked for another ten minutes and I jokingly began to sign autographs. My brother and I laughed and laughed we were so amazed and happy. Mark (my brother) began giving high-fives and shaking people's hands. It went on and on and there were streamers and confetti coming from buildings. People were yelling and cheering. I cried and cried I was so touched. Placard after placard: 'Sydney says thanks'. The people were so beautiful. They opened their hearts; they were wonderful! Thousands of people, all different, just enjoying us and the moment. We passed parliament house and the politicians were all outside waving, cheering. I would never have dreamed in my life to be part of this …

Thanks Sydney, you were beautiful that day. The great things people say about you are all true!
PAUL SMITH, *VCC*
GOSFORD NSW

My most outstanding memory of the volunteers at the Games was when we finished our last race on the last night of competition. We had just won a bronze medal in the 4 x 100m medley relay, the first time in history for the S7 – S10 girls. We were ecstatic and glad we had come to the end of a very long meet. The volunteers were wonderful. Always a smiling face and there to lend a hand. I found this quite calming because of all the hype and nerves surrounding the competition.

After we received our medal, the Aussies ditched streamers everywhere. It was a sea of green and gold. We wrapped ourselves up in the streamers and marched off the pool-deck; the meet was over. As my teammates and I walked back through the corridors the music started pumping, songs that brought the memories back from the Opening Ceremony. *Great Southern Land, Down Under* ... of course we were hopping. Also getting into the groove were the volunteers at the pool. They were throwing streamers around, singing and dancing.

These people who had helped us and been there to support us for the whole two weeks needed a thank you. They had formed a line to face the crowd so they could show their thanks. Immediately I gathered up the girls and we ran along the length of the masses of volunteers to give them high-fives, hugs and have a chat. Many of them who we had seen and spoken to during the week were exhausted. They had worked so hard to make our Games the best.

The celebrations went on until all the public had left the pool. In fact, our whole team had left the pool. I really wanted to thank the volunteers. They worked tirelessly to make our lives easier on the biggest few days of our lives. Thank you!

PRIYA COOPER, *Captain of Australian Women's Paralympic Team*
Gold Medallist in Swimming at Barcelona, Atlanta and Sydney 2000
SYDNEY NSW

I taped the parade from the TV for my husband, Jochen, to see later as he was still sick in bed. Recently we got round to watching it and I discovered myself among the crowd. You can see me as long as you don't blink for too long!
PAULA FISCHER, *IBM Help Information*
SOUTH BAVARIA GERMANY

[To the tune of 'The Dublin Fusileers']
Melody by 'The Dubliners', Lyrics © Patrick Purcell October 2000

The call went out across the land, to fill the nation's need
An army vast was needed to help us do the deed,
To Sydney Town the Games had come, the world was coming here,
To help them all and give a hand,
The Sydney volunteers.

Chorus:
With a cheeky grin and a cheery wave, showing the way to go,
Happy smiles on every face, with never a hint of woe
Glory to Australia, now give three ringing cheers
A credit to the nation are
The Sydney volunteers.

They gathered here from far and near and trained to do their best,
The uniforms were glittering, but the smiles outshone the rest
The world watched on in wonder as the greatest Games came here,
As to the fore, need I say more
The Sydney volunteers.

Chorus

And when the Games were finally done, Juan Samaranch, he said:
'The Sydney Games are over, the flame will soon be dead,
But Sydney's Games were best ever and there's one reason clear –
The love and dedication of
The Sydney volunteers.'
PATRICK PURCELL, *Sailing Results*
LANE COVE NSW

I migrated to Australia in 1974 from South America but Sydney is my home.

Being a volunteer meant that I was able to give and take nothing back in return except wonderful memories. After such a rewarding experience, how wonderful it was for the people of Sydney to thank me and acknowledge my contribution to the Games by cheering all the volunteers on at the march through the city. Perhaps it was all the happy emotions or the sadness we felt for the end of the Games, but I didn't see a dry eye on the parade.

ESTHER RIVERO, *Airport Host / Spectator Services*
AUBURN NSW

After the Olympics had finished I took my clients to Bondi Beach so that they could enjoy the sand, sun and surf before going to Vaucluse for a farewell barbecue. Whilst at Bondi Beach, I was sitting on the sea wall at the northern end with another driver when Nick and Katherine Greiner came jogging past. Nick made a point of stopping to tie his shoelace and sarcastically commented, 'Where's all this hard work you volunteers are supposed to be doing?' To which the other driver promptly replied, 'Nick! You don't pay us enough money.' Katherine gave us the thumbs up and a smile for that comment.

JOHN CONDON, *Driver*
QUAKERS HILL NSW

After the premier, Bob Carr, gave his speech, he came down amongst the people and 'crowd surfed' over the people's heads. An American standing next to us couldn't believe his eyes. He exclaimed, 'Is that your premier?' We said yes and we were laughing with the crowd. 'We couldn't do that back home in the States – no way could we get within cooee of him,' he said. What a wonderful country we have. We are very proud Australians.

WARREN AND JUDITH MANUEL, *Load Zone Officer/Pedestrian Assistant*
SYDNEY NSW

It has been widely remarked that there was a cultural change in Sydney during the Games. People talked to each other. I know I did. I participated in innumerable conversations with strangers and not just those in volunteer uniforms. People talked to you on trains and on platforms. Practically everyone was somehow part of it whether as a volunteer, a spectator at one event or another, or just a Sydney resident. Everyone reckoned it was a wonderful success, and everyone seems to have enjoyed it. Typically, a woman I was sitting next to at a Paralympic swimming session admitted she had been critical of the Games beforehand, but now could not keep away: sceptic turned fan.

JEREMY STEELE, *NOC Assistant to Cameroon*
SYDNEY NSW

Nearly everyone agreed that the Sydney Olympics were probably the greatest ever held, and this was certainly the view of the President, Juan Antonio Samaranch. The facilities were outstanding, the organisation went like clockwork and the Games were notable for some truly outstanding performances, some of them by Australians such as Cathy Freeman and Ian Thorpe. But, to my mind, the one characteristic which distinguished the Sydney Olympic Games and gave them a very Australian flavour was the contribution made by the 47,000 volunteers. In their brightly coloured and easily recognised uniforms, they provided a friendly and very Australian presence with their unfailing courtesy, their good humour and their ability to provide answers to all manner of questions. Again and again people from overseas said to me that this was a feature they will always remember about that memorable sixteen days in Sydney in the year 2000.

THE HON. JOHN LANDY, *AC, MBE*
Bronze Medallist in Athletics Melbourne 1956
GOVERNOR OF VICTORIA

I was not at the Olympics as a volunteer but was touched by the Olympics in another way.

I live in Bendigo and I'm a taxi driver. One night just after the Olympics, I got a job at the local university. I picked them up and it was a man and his daughter with a Canadian accent. They said they had just come back from Sydney and were visiting their daughter in Bendigo who was an exchange student. I asked if they had been to the Olympics in Sydney and they said they had. The conversation continued and they said the highlight for them was the volunteers, how friendly they were and helpful.

This made me think how the volunteers touched everyone, not just people at or in the Olympics.

LAWRENCE MARTIN

BENDIGO VIC

My father represented South Africa in the African Games, not being able to compete in the Olympics because of his skin colour. Pyar hoped that perhaps one day, one of his boys could clinch the family sporting tradition in the Olympic Games here in Australia.

With obligation and without pressure he guided my greatest talent. As a junior, I represented Australia against New Zealand, Germany and Japan during separate international swimming invitations. One of the kids that came to watch me swim was Ian Thorpe. After years of swimming over 20,000 kilometres, I eventually became chronically fatigued and was forced to retire early. I then went on to play professional basketball after representing my country but developed chronic fatigue again. I guess it just wasn't my destiny.

After two generations of dedicating our lives towards making the Olympics and failing after coming so close broke my heart. My friends and family believe I must have been even more heartbroken having the job of escorting other athletes onto the podiums to receive their medals. My mother cried many times when she saw me on TV because after driving me to 11 sessions per week she knows that I should have been competing. I perceived my role as a privilege. I know what every single one of them went through, and as much as it breaks my heart not to compete, I feel so fortunate seeing the ecstatic exhilaration inside every locker room I walked into. I felt so majestic to lead out every convoy for the medal ceremonies because I understand what they were going through as an athlete myself. Their bliss gave me happiness because unlike most of the other volunteers, I really did understand exactly what they went through. I had to try so hard to hold the tears, I really don't know how I did it. This was the emotional pinnacle of my life.

It really is hard to believe after having completed my job as a volunteer. I got to experience over six events. I got to advise some of the most authoritative people in sport. I got to meet and work with many athletes and make new friendships. But most of all, I got the best job in the biggest event this country will host in decades to come and I am grateful.

ZAHIN SINGH, *Athlete Escort*
SYDNEY NSW

I am Nga Luu. I have been working at Arnotts about 15 years already. I took two weeks holidays for working as a volunteer at the Olympics. My position was giving out information and checking the tickets for the guests. I am very happy to work at the Olympic Games, even though I woke up early or stayed late or it was hot, cold or raining. I was exhilarated, because it was just the first time I'd met so many kinds of people. It made me very excited, interested – I had a great experience and made many friendships.

NGA LUU, *Spectator Services*
SYDNEY NSW

I come from Ardlethan NSW: a small country of 400 people and I live on a property growing mixed grain and sheep. My second son Stewart and his wife Gayle came home to help run the farm just before I lost my husband of nearly 40 years in January 1999. I guess I was a little lost and needed something to look forward to.

A friend, Michele Bentley, dragged me off to the Multiple District Convention of Lions International in Brisbane, May 1999, and it was there we found out that volunteers were needed so Michele convinced me to fill out the application. About six months went by and I heard nothing so I promptly forgot about it until I was at a wedding and happened to sit opposite Susie Thomas from Olympic Recruitment. The subject came up and I said they didn't seem to want me but to my surprise I had two phone calls early the next week. I am so pleased I didn't miss out.

I worked in Spectator Services and couldn't wait to get to work every day. Just the atmosphere of being part of the greatest show on earth was enough to keep you going and the exercise was great. I lost half a stone so that was an extra bonus.

The bus drivers were great. On one particular evening I was the only passenger on the trip to my daughter's home in Frenchs Forest. When we arrived at my bus stop, the driver said you're not going into that car park on your own at this time of night. I said it was okay, but he said he would wait until my headlights came on. It was a great feeling to know someone cared.

The people we met on the bus trips to and from work were all interested in what we were doing, where we came from and what made us offer our services. Everybody spoke to anybody like we were all one big happy family. I would like to think Sydney would stay that way forever.

The lollies we were given to hand out were a great tool to keep little feet moving. One mum told me it was magic when I was able to get her small daughter on her feet after she sat down and refused to move. I also carried around my neck a bottle of bubbles and would make them float around at times, much to the enjoyment of the young and not-so-young. I was really moved when a small boy came up to me, shook my hand and congratulated me on the great job the volunteers were doing.

I also worked at the Paralympics' shooting events. That is an experience I will never forget and I don't think I will ever complain about little things ever again. The spirit and commitment to their sport was inspirational and innovative.

Since I came home I have been invited to speak at the school and the local Red Cross and that was great. I spoke for nearly two hours and they were still asking questions. Those that could not be part of the event wanted to soak up as much of it as possible from someone who had actually been there. I was amazed how they were all caught up in my enthusiasm.

I am also a member of the Lions Club of Ardlethan and will be on the District Cabinet in the coming Lions Year. I hold the positions of Secretary Treasurer and am kept pretty busy with that as well as working a couple of days a week at the local garage and I do all the bookwork for the farm. There are many local organisations in our small town and they seem to cover most of the charities known to Man. At some time or other over the last 40 years I have probably worked for all of them. That's what happens in small towns – people pitch in and do what has to be done.

JUDY DAY, *Spectator Services*
ARDLETHAN NSW

To be in Sydney during the Olympic Games and to feel the spirit and excitement generated by such an event was an amazing experience. To have played a part in the success of the Games, and to have represented Australia in the eyes of the world whilst sharing in the spirit of friendship and goodwill was, no doubt, the most enriching experience of my life.

FRITH HATFIELD, *Spectator Services*
TOWNSVILLE QLD

I'm now suffering post-Olympics depression and am off to see my psychiatrist.

ROSS WYLDE-BROWNE, *Sailing Results*
CANBERRA ACT

Due to the nature of our role as Spectator Services hosts, we were always on duty whilst wearing our uniforms. Spectators would often approach us during our break period and, I found that on occasions, these periods could be even busier than when we were officially on duty. Furthermore, I became so used to working as a Spectator Services host that on the occasions that I was at Olympic Park as a spectator I found myself preparing to answer queries from other spectators before I realised I was not in uniform. That took a bit of getting used to. The thing I miss most about my role, now that the Olympic Games are over, is being of assistance to spectators who have queries.

HEATH HATFIELD, *Spectator Services*
TOWNSVILLE QLD

I remember being in the Superdome café with about 100 other volunteers, watching Cathy Freeman win her 400m gold medal on the TV – and being just 400 metres away from her – and wishing I was there …
I remember the spectator who gave me the Sunday paper liftout of over 47,000 volunteer names. She asked me my name and said, 'Thank you' …

I remember running into people I know. Fancy that: millions of visitors and I ran into two families that I knew …

I remember my aching feet that just went numb after a few days. I remember going up and down the stairs and my knees not wanting to bend anymore. Thank goodness for those lifts …

I remember wearing my shirt to the office one day and being asked to make coffee and directions to get from A to B …

I remember going to the Sydney Swans match in April 2001 with my uniform on and being asked at the bus stop which stop to get. I remember sitting in my seat and a fellow spectator came up to me and asked me where she should be sitting (must have been those yellow sleeves). It was my pleasure to be of service …

I remember it as the best time of my life.

ROS STEVENS, *Spectator Services*
INGLEBURN NSW

The following day on the way home to Perth still in our uniforms, John (my son) said he didn't even mind if the plane went down, he had had the best time ever!

BRONWYN HARMSEN, *Spectator Services*
PERTH WA

A fellow volunteer who manned the Venue Communications Centre (VCC) and I were chatting one day and we discovered that we were both in the same sailing club and had our own sailing boats only two boats apart on the hard stand at our club and we'd never met before. Back at the club a month or two after the Games I saw him and called out jokingly as if I was calling him through the VCC. Someone's head popped up from another boat and yelled, 'Were you there too?!'

RICHARD MURRAY, *Spectator Services*
SYDNEY NSW

I heard another story of one of the volunteers – a senior citizen and a battler – who just wanted to contribute. He made his way to Sydney from one of our country towns in Victoria and volunteered as a driver. He was appointed as the driver for the President of Zambia (I think it was), starting his duties about a week before the Games. He was with the president all through and apparently the relationship was friendly. Some time after the Games the man received a letter and tickets for a return trip to Zambia, all expenses paid.

LINDSAY GAZE, *former coach of the Australian Basketball Team*
Multi-Olympian Basketballer
MELBOURNE VIC

Friendly, enthusiastic and patriotic are words I feel epitomised the awesome spirit of our biggest and most successful team at the Sydney Olympics: the massive group of volunteers who helped to make the Games a spectacular memory.

As an athlete, arriving at venues and moving around the Olympic sites was a joy thanks to the fabulous work of our volunteers who were always on hand with a welcoming smile.

Moreover, the volunteer program surpassed all global expectations, so much so, that I believe it should be the template/benchmark for future Olympic Games.

It was extraordinary.

KIEREN PERKINS, OAM, *Swimmer*
Gold Medallist at Barcelona and Atlanta, Silver Medallist at Sydney 2000
MELBOURNE VIC

There was such a pride from my full cast. An incredible feeling of oneness and connectedness, the power of which still resides in me now … It was interesting to meet up with cast members from time to time after in the streets of Sydney. They would come up to me and say, Remember me? I was Sturt Desert Pea number 69 or Snow Gum number 34.

PETER WILSON, *Segment Director of 'Nature' at the Opening Ceremony*
CANBERRA ACT

On one particular day during the Olympics our supervisor told us there was a lady from Salt Lake City, the site of the upcoming Winter Olympics in 2002, who would like to speak to a couple of the volunteers about their experiences. My friend Annette and I both happened to be available and so we had a chat to Jenny from Salt Lake City. We spoke about our experiences and Jenny even took a bit of a video. Afterwards, we didn't give the matter another thought.

Imagine my surprise when one day after the Paralympics, I checked my emails and there was one from Jenny inviting Annette and me over to Utah for two weeks in February 2001 for their volunteer kickoff events. Talk about being in the right place at the right time … we just couldn't believe it; this sort of thing only ever happened to other people!

We had a marvellous time. We had to do four presentations at different venues with over 2500 in the audience each time. Mitt Romney (the Michael Knight of their organising committee) was the host at each show along with a celebrity host, the one for the last show being Marie Osmond. We came on stage to *Down Under* in our Olympic uniforms waving our Aussie flags. Then we spoke with the hosts for a few minutes about our experiences. We even did the Aussie chant at the last two shows. The Americans are desperately trying to think of something to equal 'Aussie, Aussie, Aussie, Oi, Oi, Oi!'

GWEN GRIEVES, *Venue Staffing*
SYDNEY NSW

This experience led me to reassess my career path. After the Games, I gave up my executive assistant job with a big government corporation and I am now (at the age of 54) studying full-time to obtain accreditation in translating and interpreting which would ultimately allow me to work with French-speaking migrants and businesses.

NICOLE BANNISTER, *Information Assistant*
WOLLSTONECRAFT NSW

Day Sixteen (The Carnival Is Over)

The carnival is over friends – the party lights are fading,
The athletes of the universe have finished their parading
With just a tinge of sadness, now the world is going home,
And so I come to writing this – one final, simple poem.
Sixteen days of memories, now where does one begin?
I'm sure it must be sparked by what my heart has felt within,
As Australians, we will reminisce the night that got us started,
When a kid they tagged 'Thorpedo' took the water, lion-hearted.
With his relay team; they rocked our lives – they raised the country's roof,
Had the wait been worth the glory? Here existed certain proof.
It rated on the Richter Scale, this cavalcade of noise,
From then, all ears were ringing with the 'Aussie's and the 'Oi's
Yet the colour of the medals didn't make us so hysteric,
The day I realised this was when we cheered a lad named Eric.
You see, for swimming pools, his land of birth was not the most renowned,
And let's approach this honestly, he very nearly drowned.
But courage is a mighty thing – it stared him in the face.
And Eric Moussembini was the winner of his race.
We dare not go much further in the context of achieving
What this man accomplished? Well, it goes beyond believing.
The oar of Steven Redgrave in its fifth Olympics straight,
Win its fifth Olympic gold – now there's a true Olympic great.
While we welcome little Leisel – just a 15-year-old kid
We say goodbye to Susie and give thanks for what she did.
From the headache tablet scandal, and the bogong months that flew,
To the Wagga Wagga jeweller who snapped up Maurice's show.
The Hackett/Perkins showdown, and the changing of the guard,
The smile of every volunteer who worked so very hard.
There was triumph, there was tragedy – they always live together,
There was rain and there was wind, but it was mostly perfect weather.
What will be the highlight that your soul will hold forever?
From the twenty-seventh athlete's Games – the best Olympics ever.
In the memories of many, there'll be one without a doubt,
A magic that personified what sport is all about.
Expectation marked her quest, determination powered,
Inspiration, sweet success, then jubilation showered.

It really did unite us in a unique sort of way
In the interest of a common dream, we somehow owned this day
We were up enough already, now our hearts were even higher,
So we finish where we started – Cathy Freeman and her fire
The flame has been extinguished, but its glow will always pride us,
The warmth it gave for sixteen days will always burn inside us.
Now we look towards the future where we'll meet again in Greece
The carnival is over friends, now go, but go in peace.
RUPERT MCCALL, *Sports Nut and Poet*
BRISBANE QLD

All in all we had a great time and would do it again but not necessarily *tomorrow.*
NEIL, PATRICIA AND LUKE CLUNES, *Dining Room and Baggage Assistance*
MORAYFIELD QLD

I'm trying to find an experience that competes with the bond felt there. Maybe we never will and the only thing we hold on to is the photos, the pins collected, the uniform still hanging in the wardrobe, those blasted bum-bags and the memories. Maybe that's enough.
NICHOLE CAMPBELL, *Protocol Attendant*
BRISBANE QLD

We've got one of the best lots of memorabilia you can imagine, and we've finally displayed it all in a room in our house. It's full of total memories. We've got framed posters, with our special Merit Certificate from Samaranch himself having pride of place on the big wall. Only a few people got those, and you had to be nominated by three different areas of SOCOG to be eligible. We've got badges we received for volunteer hours put in: you got them for 100, 200, 300, 500, 750 and 1000 hours and so on. We've got every edition of *The Sydney Spirit.* And we're having a special glass case built for the torches. An American offered $10,000 for my torch because of its significance, but it's worth more to me to have it. Norm's got his from the Paras, and a medal he received from the 1956 Olympics. We go into that room now the Games are over, and we just remember how great it all was.

Soon we'll be off to the Davis Cup as volunteers – we can pick and choose what events we do now.

DOROTHY WILLIAMS, *Pioneer volunteer*
PROSPECT NSW

From the time they said they were having the Olympic Games in Sydney, Tom was on the phone every day to see if he was selected and to get tickets for certain events. He was in Sydney for just on five weeks working at the Games and taking part in the Volunteers parade. The experience was one of the highlights of his life. He was very proud to represent Western Australia and when he came back he was always wearing his uniform with pride and acknowledgement that he was doing his bit for Australia.

Tom died suddenly at home of a heart attack on Wednesday, 17 January 2001, at the youthful age of 44. He left a wife Suzanne and three children: Thomas (21), Aaron (18) and Karina (16).

He was buried in his Olympic uniform.

THE BIRD FAMILY *on behalf of*
TOM BIRD, *Spectator Services*
MANDURAH WA

The Olympic Games for me was my dream come true. As a little girl I always wanted to sing and dance and act, and I got to do all of this in front of the biggest audience ever; I was able to perform at the beginning and again at the end of the 'best Games' in history.

Not only was I able to perform at the Opening and Closing Ceremonies, but the whole Olympic experience gave me the opportunity to meet so many different and wonderful people. I believe everyone involved in these Games have become friends through this experience because we have a special bond.

I especially remember the many volunteers who dedicated so many hours to the Olympics, from the drivers who picked me up, to the backstage people who looked after me. I've even met the lady who sewed some of my Closing Ceremony dress – she actually lives quite close to me. Of course, many volunteers worked not just during the actual Games, but for many weeks or months before.

The thing I remember most about the volunteers is that they were always smiling.

Like many I believe these Games showed people all around the world what a fantastic country Australia is, and how lucky we are to live here.

I think that it's the spirit of all volunteers, and not just those who were Olympic volunteers, that is part of what makes Australia the great place it is. The spirit of people who see that something needs doing, and just get in and do it, all to make the world a little better and a little brighter for everyone.

Follow your dreams.

NIKKI WEBSTER, *Star performer in the Opening and Closing Ceremonies*
SYDNEY NSW

Australians love their sport and will cheer and encourage anyone or any team, particularly if they are the underdog. That's the way we are. It did not matter what event you went to, even at the more obscure sports the support was always there. Many athletes said the support was what pushed them over the line. They loved it.

Would I do it all again? In a heartbeat.

MAUREEN TREVANION, *Loss Investigator*
CANBERRA ACT

A YEAR DOWN THE TRACK

"What happens now? It's a year since the Olympic Games and we may never see them in Australia again in my lifetime. Every person involved, including the billions who were merely spectators, had a unique experience. All the memories are stored away in our neck-top computers – that one and a half kilograms of blob housed between our ears. How have these memories impacted on us as individuals and as a nation?

I know that many athletes have had a tough time coming to terms with post competition blues. At least they have access to sports psychologists to soften their landing – not so the vollies.

'I really, really miss the Games, you know!' confided more than one volunteer. A common hangover, I suspect, and who could blame those heroes for feeling this way?

The volunteers were the real heroes of our Games. They didn't run, jump, swim or cycle their way to fame. They didn't receive gold medals for their performance, but they were our national heroes nonetheless. Instantly recognisable in their distinctive uniforms, they won gold over and over again for their unwavering helpfulness and friendliness, for the power of their smiles. They won gold for their importance in the overall success of the Games.

The way Australia is perceived overseas is now so much better because of the marathon run by more than 60,000 ordinary Australians who gave up their time to make a difference. Travel overseas post-Games and it's not unusual to have someone say, 'You're from Australia? You guys sure did a great job with the Olympics – good on ya!' And of course we unashamedly accept the credit for what we (Ric Birch, the athletes, the vollies, the architects, administrators, creative directors and so on) helped to create: an unforgettable spirit of collaboration.

We live in a world dominated by information technology, yet our remarkable vollies confirmed that when it comes to the crunch, it's the people that matter. The volunteers confirmed that it's our ability to communicate with one another that counts most. Marry to this enormous enthusiasm, the ability to 'get on with it', a laconic sense of humour and the mischief that dwells in almost all of us Aussies, and you have the mortar that held all the building blocks together.

Aussies have the ability to rise to the occasion, and then to be able to relax and have a genuinely good time. That's the ideal the vollies lived up to – and for that we are indebted to them forever.

Lots of vollies have stood up and talked about their experiences at various functions. Scrapbooks and photo albums and showcases of memorabilia have taken on the dimension of family heirlooms – never to be sold. Journals have been kept and embellished with memories. We hope this book will be added to your collection of stories and tributes, and that it's a way of cherishing other people's memories as well as your own.

For many, Athens and 2004 beckons. 'How fast can I learn Greek?' is a common question. Others have discovered the spirit of volunteering and continue to offer their services in lots of different and creative ways, some at other sporting events like the Davis Cup. The volunteers are proof of the life lesson that we gain so much more by giving.

At the ticker-tape parade held in their honour, we witnessed a massive mobile jigsaw of volunteers. We saw their spirit, energy, generosity, and unbridled spontaneous happiness. Bus drivers, farmers, accountants, pensioners, secretaries, teachers, builders, caterers, doctors – the vollies came together from all walks of life. This book has been an amazing insight into how that jigsaw was pieced together to create what Juan Antonio Samaranch described as simply the most dedicated and wonderful volunteers ever.

Thank you one and all for your efforts and your stories. ”

Max & Gerry

ACKNOWLEDGEMENTS

First, an enormous thank you to everyone who suggested a name, story, phone number, address, email or fax number. Your contacts have been an invaluable contribution to the book. Collecting the stories was just like asking for assistance at the Games: we were met with only helpfulness and goodwill.

Without the support of TAFE NSW, this project would have been a non-starter. First there was Janet Chester who led me to Janet Stewart, Director of Marketing and Business. She in turn authorised the great TAFE effort driven by Ricki Blackwell with help from Ruth Rodriquez and Peter Holden. The TAFE NSW mail out in the early days got a great response and was a good start to our pile of stories. Thank you for your cooperation.

Thanks also to the people who helped organise the day when Max and I met hundreds of volunteers at the Sydney Swans first 2001 match, especially to Deb Thompson and Shane Harmon. Thanks to Mark Lollback for helping me hand out all those fliers.

Thanks to Tim Fischer who kindly gave us his Paralympic Village diary to use and to my old mate Lindsay Gaze who offered every encouragement and some great contacts.

The book would not have been completed without the resources of Exportise Pty Ltd, export advisors and consultants, and the application of Carolyn Cliffe, typist extraordinaire.

And last but not least, my wife, Helen, who put up with me during the double whammy of my volunteering experience when I was coming and going at all hours, and then the extra hours put in to getting this book on the road. She also organised a special photo-shoot with me and the kids at Hurlstone Park Childcare Centre where she is the Director. This wonderful experience opened my eyes to the joy the 2000 Olympics brought to the children of Sydney.

Here's my Honour Roll for services above and beyond the call of duty:

Bev Bennett (Quilts)
Dr Ken Crichton
Lynette Gregory
Pat Johnson (SES)
Melissa Kimmerly (SOCOG)
John Maclurkin
Dr Louise Mazzarolli
Philip Mitchell-Taverner
Bill Oliver
Andrea Petrocco

Gerry

Special thanks go to IOC Vice-President Kevan Gosper, both for his personal contribution to the book and for approaching Juan Antonio Samaranch to pen the foreword. Thanks to Sandy Hollway for offering to help us – SOCOG was very fortunate to have someone of your calibre at the forefront.

To Herb Elliot, Laurie Lawrence, Peter Brock and John Bertrand: thanks for sharing unique insights into your support roles without betraying the trust of the athletes. To John Landy, the man who brought sportsmanship, integrity and character to the track and who is now the distinguished Governor of Victoria, your words of celebration mean a lot to all volunteers.

To Alan Patching, former Stadium Australia CEO and Project Director, thanks for letting us use your fantastic photos. They really capture the significant moments, and show how important the volunteers were in the big scheme of things. I wish we had room for all of them. To Tony Rafty, a man who has distorted thousands of famous heads in order to capture their essence, thanks for allowing us to reproduce some of them here. For once it wasn't my nose, teeth and mo being tampered with!

To Andrew Gaze who has represented Australia at five Olympics, thank you for allowing us to use your thoughts and photograph. To Nikki Webster, thanks for coming through with your tribute while you were studying for exams and producing your first album. We appreciate your thoughts.

To Raelene Boyle, we'll never forget the part you played in the Opening Ceremony or your enormous contribution to track and field. Raelene, you are a truly wonderful lady. Many thanks and keep well. And to all the other Olympians, past and present, who feature in this book, your Olympic spirit lives on in these pages. Thank you for your contributions.

Allen & Unwin once more have been positive and superb to work with. The team–and I do emphasise team–was always willing to go the extra yard in order to produce a better result. The look, feel and sound of this collection is a credit to their preoccupation with excellence. A huge thank you to Sue Hines, Andrea McNamara, Jennifer Castles and Rebecca Perovic.

And finally, extra special thanks to my wife Kerry who has been an integral part in the creation of this book: a sounding board of unique honesty and patience. Her love has allowed the book to grow without anxiety and tension. This has been a natural birth … a beautiful child: on time, wonderful to hold and to look at! A book to cherish.

Max

For the first time in Olympic history, one training organisation had sole responsibility for training the employees, contractors and volunteers for both the Sydney Olympic and Paralympic Games. TAFE NSW – the largest training provider in the southern hemisphere – was this organisation, delivering more than one million hours of training to a 'Gamesforce' of 110,000 people.

Many commentators have attributed the smooth running and friendly nature of the Sydney Games to the efficiency, dedication and warmth of the more than 50,000 volunteers – trained by TAFE NSW. Coming together from right across Australia, the volunteers were a revelation and made Australia proud. To effectively train so many people for so many tasks, a three-tiered training framework was implemented: orientation, venue-specific training and job-specific training.

Senior Management of the Sydney Organising Committee for the Olympic Games (SOCOG) was also trained to ensure their skills were fine-tuned to best respond to the unique challenges of the Games.

TAFE NSW was active from boardrooms to buses. Because it was crucial that the transportation infrastructure of Sydney would cope with the challenges posed by the Olympics, more than 18,000 volunteers and paid Transport Services staff were trained on behalf of the Olympic Roads and Transport Authority. 'Village English' – classes in practical Australian English run inside the Olympic Village for Olympic athletes and officials were devised, planned and conducted. Village English provided participants with a constructive way to use their 'down time'.

Hundreds of businesses peripheral to the Games completed Customer Relations 2000 workshops to ensure they were up to speed on the best ways to serve customers, including those with disabilities and those from different cultural backgrounds. Customer Relations 2000 was offered by TAFE PLUS (the commercial arm of TAFE NSW).

TAFE NSW is proud to have contributed to the success of, and goodwill generated by, the Sydney 2000 Olympic and Paralympic Games and relished the challenge of conducting the biggest training exercise of its kind ever undertaken in Australia, and continues to design and offer flexible and responsive training to suit all needs.

VOLUNTEERS HONOUR ROLL

This list is reproduced with the permission of *The Daily Telegraph*, Sydney.

Please let us know if you were a volunteer at the Sydney Olympic or Paralympic Games and your name is not on this list, or if you would prefer to be removed from the list, and we will adjust future editions. Send your request in writing to The Volunteers, Allen & Unwin, 406 Albert Street, East Melbourne VIC 3002.

A

AADIL Naseem, AANENSEN Rhonda, AARONSON Michael, AASTAP Arild, ABADIA SAAVEDRA, Osman, ABAID Sulaiman, ABAS Emir, ABAUL Lypso, ABBAS Abdulfattah, ABBAS Danny, ABBAS Emma, ABBATE Adam, ABBENHUYS Deborah, ABBEY Martin, ABBOTSFORD-SMITH Andrew, ABBOTT Alfred, ABBOTT Ann, ABBOTT Catherine, ABBOTT Kim, ABBOTT David, ABBOTT Latifa, ABBOTT Lauren, ABBOTT Marcus, ABBOTT Peter, ABBOTT Sue, ABBOUD Elias, ABDEI-MALEK Ave, ABDEL-AHAD John, ABDEL-MALAK Rizk, ABDEL-MALEK Ange, ABDEL-MALEK Ave, ABDELMALEK Adly, ABDI Nadia, ABDI Rasmid, ABDINI Jim, ABDIPRANOTO Andrea, ABDUL RAZER Ahmar, ABDUL-MASSIH Melissa, ABDULAHAD Paul, ABDULHAK Senka, ABDULLA Issam, ABDULLAH Abdul, ABDULLAH Brian, ABDULLAH Ishak, ABE Nami, ABEDNEGO Sunny, ABEL Jan, ABEL Pat, ABELA Michelle, ABELA Rosemary, ABELAS Haralabos, ABELAS Markos, ABELITIS Lesley, ABELSOHN Lesley, ABENDANO Jhing, ABERCROMBIE Scott, ABERNETHY Wendy, ABESKA Christine, ABEY Louise, ABEYASINGHE Rani, ABEYNAIKE Anthony, ABHILASH Atish, ABHILASH Neeru, ABHILASH Nirmala, ABHILASH Shammi, ABIASSAF Assaf, ABID Freda, ABIHANNA Cheryl, ABIKHAIR Tracey, ABINENO Albert, ABITBOL Chantal, ABOU ALI Ali, ABOU-CHEDID Dolly, ABOU-GHAIDA Naouaf, ABOUDEHN Robert, ABOUMELAYA Sam, ABOUTANIOS Souraya, ABRAHALL Hela, ABRAHAM Asha, ABRAHAM Lee, ABRAHAM Mary, ABRAHAMIAN Arsine, ABRAHAMS Col, ABRAHAMS David, ABRAHAMS Emma, ABRAHAMS Glenys, ABRAHAMS Kim, ABRAHAMS Ray, ABRAHAMSON Gaby, ABRAMS Merv, ABRAMS Robyn, ABREA Mary, ABU ISSA Ashraf, ACCARDO Joe, ACHEAMPONG Barbara, ACHERNDONG Emmanuel, ACHILLES Jon, ACHMAD Suhandi, ACHURCH Barry, ACIAR Cesar, ACKERMAN John, ACKERMAN Mary, ACKERMAN Max, ACKERS Kelly, ACKLAND Roxanne, ACKMAN Bernadette, ACKMAN Greg, ACKRILL Jo-Anne, ACKROYD Beryl, ACKROYD Bill, ACOSTA Rodrigo, ACOTT John, ACREMAN Darrin, ACTON Ben, ACTON Ian, ACTON John, ACTON Josh, ACWORTH Claire, ACWORTH Melissa, ADA Gokhan, ADA Melissa, ADAIKALASWAMY Gasper, ADAIR Mark, ADAM Bob, ADAM Caroline, ADAM Catherine, ADAM Jen, ADAM Jennifer, ADAM Jocelyn, ADAM Peter, ADAM Graham, ADAMS Alanna, ADAMS Barry, ADAMS Barbara, ADAMS Brad, ADAMS Bruce, ADAMS Carol, ADAMS Charlotte, ADAMS Chris, ADAMS Christopher, ADAMS David, ADAMS Debbie, ADAMS Dorothy, ADAMS Esma, ADAMS Fiona, ADAMS Geoff, ADAMS Gordon, ADAMS Heather, ADAMS Jeanette, ADAMS Jenny, ADAMS Jennifer, ADAMS Jennifer, ADAMS Jesse, ADAMS Judy, ADAMS Kathy, ADAMS Kaylene, ADAMS Kristy, ADAMS Krisha, ADAMS Lindsay, ADAMS Lorraine, ADAMS Luke, ADAMS Margaret, ADAMS Marcia, ADAMS Margaret, ADAMS Matthew, ADAMS Grant, ADAMS Michael, ADAMS Rachel, ADAMS Richard, ADAMS Ron, ADAMS Sam, ADAMS Yvonne, ADAMSON John, ADAMSON Mark, ADAMSON Matt, ADAMSON Olga, ADAN Mugabe, ADASI Belinda, ADCOCK Desmond, ADCOCK John, ADDANKI Samuel, ADDICOTT Dean, ADDIS Liz, ADDIS Matt, ADDISON Lyn, ADDISON Andrew, ADDISON Gayle, ADDISON Jim, ADDISON Jan, ADDISON Linda, ADDISON-JONES Jenniie, ADDISON-WEISS Barbara, ADDLEY Michelle, ADE Steph, ADECER Lou, ADEGBULUGBE Orobola, ADEM Trevor, ADEMA Kyle, ADETUNMBI Taiwo, ADHIKARI Deependra, ADIB Wadad, ADINATA Glen, ADIO Musibau, ADKIN Roger, ADKINS Alison, ADKINS George, ADKINS Robyn, ADLDINGER Herbert, ADLER Joan, ADLER Mayan, ADLER Warren, ADLOUNI Bill, ADOLPHE Lindsay, ADOLPHE Marie, ADORNI Alexandra, ADORNI Max, ADRA Dib, **ADRIAANSEN Tony**, ADRIAANSEN Peter, ADRIAN Garcia, ADSETT Arthur, ADVIENTO Mayrose, AEBI Andrew, AEBI Fritz, AEBI Tracy, AFA Manu, AFARIDAN Pash, AFATZANIS Katina, AFFOLTER Erika, AFZAL Ali, AGAHARI Ian, AGAPIOU Christine, AGAR Nihal, AGASSI Matthew, AGATE Col, AGATI Anna, AGATYN Martin, AGBAYANI Danilo, AGBAYANI Renee, AGBULOS Bob, AGCAOILI Salee, AGER Alfred, AGER Bruce, AGG Luke, AGGETT Susanne, AGGIO-WARMAN Ursula, AGHARI Don, AGIUS Mary, AGIUS Mark, AGLAND Chris, AGNELLO Danny, AGNELLO Lou, AGNELLO Rosanna, AGNEW Alana, AGNEW Cameron, AGNEW Karen, AGNEW Nat, AGOO Renato, AGOSTINO Vince, AGRAWAL Rakesh, AGRAWAL Ravi, AGRIESTI Larry, AGUEGNEHU Aberra, AGUIAR Helen, AGUILA Nap, AGUILAR Cecilia, AGUILAR Chay, AGUILAR Oscar, AGUILAR PJ, AGUILERA Karen, AGUILERA Maria, AGUIRRE Gabbie, AGUS Kate, AGUSTINA Kat, AGUSTINA Tina, AGYEMANG Paul, AH KAU Doris, AH MATT Helen, AH TA Vai, AHAMER Silvia, AHAMNOS George, AHEARN Wayne, AHEARN Yvonne, AHERN John, AHERN John, AHERN Kirsty, AHERN Michael, AHLING Tom, AHMAD Munir, AHMAD Sakinah, AHMADIAN Rooz, AHMADZADA Mir, AHMED Adnan, AHMED Ashraf, AHMED Tutul, AHMED Ahmed, AHMED Kamal, AHMED Kazi, AHMED Mohammed, AHMED Naushad, AHMED Salu, AHMED Syed, AHMED Toshi, AHN Young-Sik, AHSAN Mizan, AI Chuanyi, AIELLO Dianna, AIELLO Melissa, AIKEN Mike, AILWOOD Peter, AING Sophy, AING Sophearom, AINIS Stuart, AINSWORTH Benia, AINSWORTH Brett, AINSWORTH Bronwyn, AINSWORTH Sally, AINSWORTH Zina, AIONO Rudi, AIR Sue, AIRAKSINEN Katja, AIRD Nick, AIRES Francis, AISH Andrew, AITCHISON Brett, AITCHISON Lorna, AITKEN Adam, AITKEN Beth, AITKEN Colin, AITKEN Liz, AITKEN Ken, AITKEN Maggie, AITKEN Pamela, AITKEN Scott, AITKENHEAD Gary, AJAMI Kathy, AJANOVIC Jo, AJAYAPRANA Mataji, AJAYI Eric, AJIZ Kaiser, AKARI Ammar, AKAUOLA John, AKAUOLA Luke, AKEHURST Arthur, AKELE Maurice, AKEROYD Margot, AKGUL Filiz, AKHURST Bill, AKIN Mert, AKIYAMA Naoko, AKKOC Sam, AKTAN Su, AL JAYASHI Hussein, AL-JELOO Nahren, AL-MELHAM Carlos, AL-NAJJAR Faez, AL-NAJJAR Mahmoud, ALAGICH Joe, ALAGNA Christina, ALAGNA Chris, ALAGNA David, ALAM Alam, ALAM Md., ALAM Michael, ALAM Mohammad, ALARCON Andres, ALARCON Eggy, ALARCON Patricia, ALARCON Paul, ALASHHAB Maysoon, ALATINI Tonga, ALBANESE Carmine, ALBANESE John, ALBANESE Noah, ALBANESE Teresa, ALBANO Agatha, ALBERG Franziska, ALBERGA Frank, ALBERT Joe, ALBERTO Rodolfo, ALBRECHT Sandra, ALBRECHT Helmi, ALBURO Oscar, ALBURY Alicia, ALBURY Brendan, ALBURY Maria, ALCARRAZ Teobaldo, ALCHIN John, ALCOCK Cliff, ALCOCK Ted, ALCOCK Lyn, ALCOCK Terence, ALCORN Brian, ALCORN Bronwyn, ALCORN Derek, ALCORN Mary, ALDEN Margaret, ALDER Christine, ALDER Errol, ALDERDEN Rebecca, ALDERTON Elizabeth, ALDERTON Joanne, ALDHAM Andrew, ALDIN Eric, ALDRED Jessica, ALDRED John, ALDRED Matthew, ALDRED Phil, ALDRICH Kirsten, ALDRICH Rosemary, ALDRIDGE Brenda, ALDRIDGE Daniel, ALEKNA Janet, ALEKNA Paull, ALEMBAKIS Vasili, ALESSI John, ALEXAKIS Peter, ALEXANDER Carl, ALEXANDER Catherine, ALEXANDER Con, ALEXANDER Des, ALEXANDER Faye, ALEXANDER Fran, ALEXANDER George, ALEXANDER Jacinta, ALEXANDER Jim, ALEXANDER Jane, ALEXANDER Jessamy, ALEXANDER Jodie, ALEXANDER Kevin, ALEXANDER Lisa, ALEXANDER Mark, ALEXANDER Maria, ALEXANDER Nerida, ALEXANDER Norma, ALEXANDER Philip, ALEXANDER Rhonda, ALEXANDER Robert, ALEXANDER Robert, ALEXANDER Bob, ALEXANDER Robyne, ALEXANDER Ron, ALEXANDER Royce, ALEXANDER Shantha, ALEXANDER Stephen, ALEXANDER Tania, ALEXANDER Joe, ALEXANDERSON Peter, ALEXANDRATOS Harry, ALEXANDRINO Dulce, ALEXANDROU Donna, ALEXANDROU Evan, ALEXANDROVA Elitza, ALFONSO Fonz, ALFORD Alister, ALFORD Colleen, ALFORD John, ALFORD Raymond, ALGE Brigitte, ALGER Belinda, ALGIE Robert, ALHAFITH Jamil, ALI Adan, ALI Ali, ALI Hasim, ALI Hydar, ALI Leyakat, ALI Lukie, ALI Michael, ALI Sajjad, ALI Mir, ALI Mohshin, ALI Ronnie, ALI Rishad, ALI Rishad, ALI Sacayo, ALI Safder, ALI Shak, ALI Sharon, ALIAGA Shirley, ALIBERTI Marianna, ALIBHAI Arva, ALIBHAI Rashida, ALIFERIS Eva, ALIM Azlina, ALIVERTI Shirley, ALKHUB Mohammed, ALKUINO Lynn, ALLA Marianne, ALLAN Andria, ALLAN Barbara, ALLAN Danielle, ALLAN Deanne, ALLAN Ingrid, ALLAN Janys, ALLAN Jihn, ALLAN Joanne, ALLAN Joan, ALLAN John, ALLAN Katherine, ALLAN Mark, ALLAN Mark, ALLAN Nicholas, ALLAN Paulette, ALLAN Penny, ALLAN Rick, ALLAN Rob, ALLAN Robyn, ALLAN Robyn, ALLAN Scott, ALLAN Shirley, ALLAN-VOETS Genevieve, ALLARDICE Chris, ALLBUTT Haydn, ALLCROFT Richard,

ALLDRITT Liz, ALLDRITT Stuart, ALLEMANO Ivana, ALLEN Alisha, ALLEN Barney, ALLEN Beryl, ALLEN Bernadette, ALLEN Bev, ALLEN Cathy, ALLEN Dave, ALLEN Dave, ALLEN Don, ALLEN Doreen, ALLEN Eddie, ALLEN Libby, ALLEN Fiona, ALLEN Helen, ALLEN Hugh, ALLEN James, ALLEN James, ALLEN Jane, ALLEN Jase, ALLEN John, ALLEN John, ALLEN Joy, ALLEN Judith, ALLEN Julie, ALLEN Karin, ALLEN Kelly, ALLEN Kenneth, ALLEN Kerry, ALLEN Kevin, ALLEN Nisha, ALLEN Maureen, ALLEN Melissa, ALLEN Mike, ALLEN Michael, ALLEN Peter, ALLEN Ray, ALLEN Robyn, ALLEN R bert, ALLEN Stephanie, ALLEN Vivienne, ALLEN Warwick, ALLEN Wayne, ALLENBY Rhonda, ALLENDE Lucy, ALLEY Suzanne, ALLIE Sedick, ALLINGHAM Haydn, ALLISON Tony, ALLISON Debbie, ALLISON Heather, ALLISON Kay, ALLISON Phillippa, ALLISON Rosemary, ALLISON Shane, ALLISTON Pat, ALLITT Ann, ALLMAN Collette, ALLMAN Peter, ALLMAN Thelma, ALLOM Nicole, ALLOTT Carly, ALLOUCHE Renee, ALLPASS Joan, ALLSOP Allan, ALLSOPP Nicole, ALLSOPP Rebecca, ALLURI Kiran, ALLY Mustafa, ALLYBOKUS Shah, ALM Gillian, ALMAIDE Betty, ALMALIKI Ghassan, ALMASI Sussie, ALMEIDA Andres, ALMEIDA Fatima, ALMEIDA Lynette, ALMEIDA Peter, ALMENDRADES Isabel, ALMENDRALA Sesil, ALMOAIL Moha, ALMOHTY Rita, ALODA Murphy, ALONO Bianca, ALONSO Albert, ALP Michael, ALPASLAN Abdul, ALPE Justine, ALPERSTEIN Diane, ALPS Catarina, ALSALAMI Mohammed, ALSTON Barbara, ALSTON Don, ALTARAS Andrei, ALTARAS Michel, ALTAS Victoria, ALTE Vigdis, ALTER Dan, ALTMANN Elisa, ALTMANN Leanne, ALTOUVAS Margarita, ALTSTADT Peter, ALTWASSER Colette, ALURY Henry, ALVARES Sarah, ALVAREZ Asun, ALVAREZ Cynthia, ALVAREZ Hugo, ALVAREZ Jasmin, ALVAREZ Joe, ALVAREZ Jose, ALVAREZ Joseph, ALVARO Angela, ALVARO Joe, ALVERGNE Celine, ALVES Susana, ALVOS Jane, ALWAY Kellie, ALWINE Heather, ALWISHEWA Jayantha, ALY Muhammad, ALYOUSEF Nedal, AMANO Yukie, AMARANATH Rakitha, AMARANATH Thinushka, AMBANELLI Rene, AMBER Amber, AMBROSE Ann, AMBROSE Lim, AMBROSE Toni, AMBROSE JR Peter, AMELIDOU Penelope, AMER Ros, AMES Caasie, AMES Jill, AMESBURY Christopher, AMESBURY Wendy, AMESTOY Gladys, AMESTOY Miguel, AMEY Margaret, AMIN Kiran, AMIOTT Carole, AMIRAFSHAR Iraj, AMITUANAI Teresa, AMJADI Shahriar, AMMANN Denis, AMMANN Doris, AMMIT Margo, AMOAHENE Benjamin, AMODIO Tony, AMORES Hannah, AMORES Lucita, AMORES Lucinda, AMOS Annette, AMOS Jill, AMOS Larry, AMOS Max, AMPS Carol, AMR Dia, AMREIN Sergio, AMVRAZIS Elizabeth, AMY Neville, AN Kevin, AN Se Jin, AN Jin, ANABALON Douglas, ANAGNOSTOPOULOS Maria, ANANIN Katya, ANASTASIADIS Agnes, ANASTASSIADIS Angela, ANASTASSIOU Louis, ANCANS Brigita, ANCHEL Igor, ANCICH Mary, ANDA Elizabeth, ANDA Loreto, ANDAN Abdulkarim, ANDERIESZ Myles, ANDERSEN Anne, ANDERSEN Annette, ANDERSEN Doug, ANDERSEN Jason, ANDERSEN Michael, ANDERSEN Paul, ANDERSEN Phil, ANDERSEN Sean, ANDERSEN Thomas, ANDERSEN-WARD John, ANDERSON Amanda, ANDERSON Amanda, ANDERSON Annie, ANDERSON Tony, ANDERSON Barbara, ANDERSON Jock, ANDERSON Brian, ANDERSON Bruce, ANDERSON Cameron, ANDERSON Carol, ANDERSON Carol, ANDERSON Carolyn, ANDERSON Chris, ANDERSON Col, **ANDERSON Corryn**, ANDERSON Craig, ANDERSON Damien, ANDERSON David, ANDERSON David, ANDERSON David, ANDERSON Diana, ANDERSON Donald, ANDERSON Ted, ANDERSON Elizabeth, ANDERSON Erin, ANDERSON Eve, ANDERSON Gilda, ANDERSON Gladys, ANDERSON Glenn, ANDERSON Glenn, ANDERSON Graeme, ANDERSON Heather, ANDERSON Heidi, ANDERSON Helen, ANDERSON Jock, ANDERSON James, ANDERSON Jan, ANDERSON Nell, ANDERSON Jayne, ANDERSON Jeanette, ANDERSON Jenny, ANDERSON Jenny, ANDERSON Jo, ANDERSON Joanne, ANDERSON John, ANDERSON Jack, ANDERSON John, ANDERSON John, ANDERSON Katie, ANDERSON Keith, ANDERSON Kerry, ANDERSON Kerry, ANDERSON Laura, ANDERSON Leanne, ANDERSON Lee, ANDERSON Liam, ANDERSON Linda, ANDERSON Lynette, ANDERSON Lyn, ANDERSON Maralyn, ANDERSON Margaret, ANDERSON Mary, ANDERSON Peggy, ANDERSON Mike, ANDERSON Michael, ANDERSON Mike, ANDERSON Moira, ANDERSON Murray, ANDERSON Narelle, ANDERSON Nigel, ANDERSON Pat, ANDERSON Trish, ANDERSON Peter, ANDERSON Gay, ANDERSON Rob, ANDERSON Bob, ANDERSON Bob, ANDERSON Shirley, ANDERSON Simon, ANDERSON Simon, ANDERSON Stuart, ANDERSON Stuart, ANDERSON Sue, ANDERSON Sue, ANDERSON Susan, ANDERSON Theresa, ANDERSON Tim, ANDERSON Tim, ANDERSON Valerie, ANDERSON Warwick, ANDISON Ewen, ANDO Akiko, ANDRADE Omar, ANDREA Lily, ANDREACCHIO Denise, ANDREACCHIO Pina, ANDREASEN Harek, ANDREASSEN Kari, ANDREATINI Deanna, ANDREATTA June, ANDREAZZA Mary, ANDREEVA Iskra, ANDREOTTA Pietro, ANDRES CHUN Marilyn, ANDREW Brad, ANDREW Ian, ANDREW Jo, ANDREW John, ANDREW John, ANDREW Lilian, ANDREW Marg, ANDREW Michelle, ANDREW Patty, ANDREWARTHA Nikki, ANDREWS Alan, ANDREWS Catherine, ANDREWS Darren, ANDREWS Donna, ANDREWS Geoff, ANDREWS Jan, ANDREWS Jenny, ANDREWS Kate, ANDREWS Kathy, ANDREWS Kaye, ANDREWS Kelly, ANDREWS Mark, ANDREWS Megan, ANDREWS Mel, ANDREWS Paul, ANDREWS Peter, ANDREWS Reanzi, ANDREWS Richard, ANDREWS Buddha, ANDREWS Scott, ANDREWS Stephanie, ANDREWS Stephen, ANDREWS Sue, ANDREWS Tim, ANDREWS Eve, ANDRICH Olga, ANDRIKONIS Craig, ANDRIOLO Kerrie, ANDRION Ruby, ANDRIOTIS Paul, ANDROSZCZUK Leon, ANDRUSZKO Diana, ANDRZEJAK Peter, ANDRZEJEWSKI Bob, ANE Nathalie, ANEKAWIJAYA Theresa, ANG Allan, ANG Angelina, ANG Rachel, ANG Konrad, ANG Richard, ANG Susan, ANG Tee, ANGEL Lesley, ANGELAKOS Peter, ANGELICAS Gina, ANGELIS John, ANGELL Jack, ANGELL Prue, ANGELO Richard, ANGELOS Simone, **ANGELOS Adreana**, ANGELOSANTE Don, ANGELUCCI Claudia, ANGKING Mark, ANGLAND Kylie, ANGLEM David, ANGOVE Nev, ANGUS Barbara, ANGUS Colin, ANGUS Don, ANGUS Jennifer, ANGUS Lorna, ANGUS Steph, ANGUS Stuart, ANIN Raya, ANKERS Kathleen, ANN Mulcahy, ANNAND Juliette, ANNE Rosalind, ANNEA George, ANNELLS Desley, ANNEN Hubert, ANNENKOVA Irina, ANNESLEY Brett, ANNETT Paul, ANNETT Robyn, ANNETTS Mark, ANNING Kim, ANNING Kristy, ANNING Maryanne, ANNIS-BROWN Julie, ANOIT Wars, ANSCOMBE Ray, ANSELL David, ANSELL John, ANSELL Russell, ANSELL Warren, ANSEN Colleen, ANSONS Jessie, ANSTEE Pamela, ANSTIS Annette, ANSTIS Hec, ANTAKI Sid, ANTAKY Sid, ANTHONISZ Jake, ANTHONY Ben, ANTHONY Chang, ANTHONY Kevin, ANTHONY Laurel, ANTHONY Marina-Portia, ANTHONY Mike, ANTHONY Natale, ANTHONY Ray, ANTHRAK Vivianne, ANTILL Harley, ANTILL Peter, ANTON Paul, ANTONAKOS Angela, ANTONIO Ata, ANTONIOLLI John, ANTONIOLLI Phillip, ANTONY Scott, ANTONY Veronica, ANTOSZ Christine, ANTURKAR Narendra, ANTWAN Maria, ANTYPAS George, ANTZOULATOS Constantinos, ANUM Emman, ANUWATUDOM Tom, ANWIN Jo, AOUAD Tony, AOUAD Wendy, AOUAR Fay, AOUS Yacine, APELIS Ivars, APIATA Gael, APIATA Harriete, APOLONY Ron, APON Magda, APONTE Christina, APOTSIS Maria, APPADOO Marco, APPELBEE Caroline, APPELDOORN Brain, APPELHOF Arnold, APPELT Doreen, APPELT Jannie, APPLEBY Belinda, APPLEBY Dave, APPLEBY Don, APPLEBY Ian, APPLENEE Caroline, APPLETON Matthew, APPLEYARD Tony, APPLIN Sarah, APPODURAI Thana, APPS Cecily, APPS Julie, APPS Michael, APPS Peter, APRIL Welch, APSITIS Michelle, APTE Kathryn, APTER Paul, APTHORPE Linda, APTHORPE Michael, APTHORPE Paul, APULU Esther, AQUIHON Theresa, AQUILINA Peter, AQUILINA Tyson, AQUINO Fabian, AQUINO Marta, ARAKAWA Koji, ARANHA Praveen, ARAPETA Klngi, ARATANI Naoko, ARAUJO DOS SANTOS Karla, ARAVANOPULES Aquiles, ARAVENA Andre, ARBER Trish, ARBLASTER Tim, ARCHANGELE Gabriel, ARCHER David, ARCHER Derek, ARCHER Elaine, ARCHER Gary, ARCHER Marion, ARCHER Nikki, ARCHER Douglas, ARCHER Sian, ARCHIBALD Andrew, ARCHIBALD Cheryl, ARCHIBALD Joseph, ARCHIBALD Sharon, ARCHINAL Thea, ARCIDIACONO Lara, ARDILL Matthew, ARDRIAN Deni, ARELLANO Lupe, ARENA

Melissa, ARGALL John, ARGENT Christine, ARGENTO Faye, ARGIRELLIS Costa, ARGUE Steve, ARGY Re, ARGYROUS George, ARIAS Jose, ARIAS Maria, ARIEF Iwan, ARIEF Stephanus, ARIFI Al, ARIFIN Mathevani, ARIKA Ida, ARIMA Satoshi, ARIMADO Gloria, ARIMADO Harley, ARION LASSEN CORDEIRO Marcello, ARKHIPOV Konstantin, ARKINSTALL Renee, ARKINSTALL-STOLLER Meldi, ARKLEY Joe, ARKOUDIS Catherine, ARKOUDIS Koula, ARLEGUI Luis, ARLEGUI Patrick, ARLEGUI Patricio, ARLENGHI Karen, ARLETT Jayne, ARMAN Odile, ARMARI Jina, ARMENIS Elena, ARMITAGE Andy, ARMITAGE Liz, ARMITAGE Katrina, ARMITAGE Rosie, ARMITAGE Steven, ARMITSTEAD Chris, ARMOUR Isobel, ARMOUTOCLOU Helen, ARMS Paul, ARMSTRONG Alicia, ARMSTRONG Charlotte, ARMSTRONG Claire, ARMSTRONG Colin, ARMSTRONG Daniel, ARMSTRONG David, ARMSTRONG Esperanza, ARMSTRONG Frank, ARMSTRONG Graham, ARMSTRONG Heather, ARMSTRONG Hollie, ARMSTRONG Jimmy, ARMSTRONG Jeff, ARMSTRONG Jessie, ARMSTRONG Jill, ARMSTRONG Jo, ARMSTRONG John, ARMSTRONG John, ARMSTRONG Julie, ARMSTRONG Juliet, ARMSTRONG Kathy, ARMSTRONG Kaylene, ARMSTRONG Kelly, ARMSTRONG Ken, ARMSTRONG Leah, ARMSTRONG Lee, ARMSTRONG Lynn, ARMSTRONG Lyndal, ARMSTRONG Nicki, ARMSTRONG Noel, ARMSTRONG Noel, ARMSTRONG Paul, A MSTRONG Phil, ARMSTRONG Bob, ARMSTRONG Robyn, ARMSTRONG Suzanne, ARMSTRONG Valentine, ARMSTRONG Warwick, ARMSTRONG Yvette, ARMSTRONG-SMITH Nicholas, ARNAUD Frances, ARNAUTOVICH Mile, ARNDELL Ashlee, ARNEIL Miriam, ARNEMAN William, ARNOLD Christopher, ARNOLD David, ARNOLD Dieter, ARNOLD Gil, ARNOLD Ian, ARNOLD Karen, ARNOLD Kim, ARNOLD Llyn, ARNOLD Rob, ARNOLD Sonya, ARNOLD Susan, ARNOLD Vanessa, ARNOTT Alison, ARNOTT Alistair, ARNOTT Graeme, ARNOTT James, ARNOTT Jeremy, ARNOTT John, ARNOTT Sharon, ARNOTT Susie, AROMIN Lourdes, ARON Rachel, ARONEY Fran, ARORA Anju, ARORA Santosh, AROSENIUS Fia, AROUSI Nathan, AROYAN Natalie, ARRATOON Merridee, ARREGIN Alba, ARRUA Hannibal, ARSIWALLA Zoheir, ARTHUR Cass, ARTHUR Cathie, ARTHUR Celeste, ARTHUR John, ARTHUR Mark, ARTHUR Michael, ARTHUR Pauline, ARTHUR Richard, ARTHUR Warren, ARTIN George, ARTINIAN Arthur, ARTLETT Tim, ARUDA CAMPOS Mauricio, ARUDPRAGASAM Shiv, ARULANANDAM Anton, ARUMUGAM Nagaruban, ARUMUGAM Sivanesan, ARUMUGIAM Thayalini, ARUNDAVARAJA Rajan, ARUNDEL Lloyd, ARUNTHAVANATHAN Sutharsan, ARUS Mohamed, ARVANITIS Diva, ARYA Narendra, ARYAL Ujjwal, ASADULLAH Pia, ASAHINA Nobby, ASAMOAH Benjamin, ASANO Aki, ASANO Terumi, ASARIS Solveiga, ASCHNER Susan, ASCIAK Tony, ASCIAK Nick, ASCROFT David, ASERIOS Cris, ASGAR Riza, ASH Liz, ASHBURN Rob, ASHBURN Susan, ASHBY Eric, ASHBY Lindsay, ASHBY Rob, ASHBY Ron, ASHCROFT Amy, ASHCROFT Dale, ASHCROFT Fay, ASHCROFT Wayne, ASHDOWN Mark, ASHE Deanna, ASHE Paul, ASHENDEN Judy, ASHFORD Jan, ASHFORD Roger, ASHHURST-EMERY Robbie, ASHLEY Dane, ASHLEY Michelle, ASHLEY Noeline, ASHMAN Christine, ASHMAN Debbie, ASHMORE Diane, ASHPOLE Helen, ASHPOLE Roy, ASHTON Boyd, ASHTON Ted, ASHTON Rick, ASHTON Louise, ASHTON Margaret, ASHTON Meredith, ASHTON Michelle, ASHTON Lance, ASHWELL Barbara, ASHWIN Simon, ASHWORTH David, ASHWORTH Graham, ASHWORTH Yvette, ASIM Muhammad, ASKELL Maree, ASKER Sally, ASKEW Sean, ASKEW Stephanie, ASKINS Gordon, ASLANIAN Sonia, ASMUSSEN Kate, ASOKUMAR Sigan, ASPIN Martin, ASPINALL Ken, ASPREY Elvire, ASQUITH Peter, ASSAF Henry, ASSANTE Jessica, ASSEGAFF Syafiq, ASSENHEIM James, ASSHETON John, ASSOUD Hanadi, ASSOUM Henry, ASTALOSH Julie, ASTALOSH Tom, ASTBURY Jason, ASTILL Carolyn, ASTILL Dennis, ASTILL John, ASTILL Nikki, ASTILL Paul, ASTLE Barry, ASTLE Stephanie, ASTON James, ASTON Mary, ASTRELLA Grant, ASTRELLA Ronnie, ASTRUC Philippe, ASUIT Elmer, ASUNCION Vivienne, ATAIA Ash, ATALLA John, ATALLAH Adel, ATCLIFFE Ben, ATHA Mavis, ATHA Peter, ATHAIDE Virginia, ATHANASATOS Leo, ATHANASOPOULOS Sophie, ATHANASOPOULOS Yianni, ATHARI Athari, ATHERTON Marilyn, ATHERTON Peta, ATHIS George, ATILA Elizabeth, ATININGRUM Gita, ATKIN David, ATKIN John, ATKIN Joy, ATKINS Alec, ATKINS Bernie, ATKINS Beth, ATKINS Brett, ATKINS Cliff, ATKINS Gayle, ATKINS Jill, ATKINS Judi, ATKINS Leanne, ATKINS Maureen, ATKINS Nicole, ATKINS Marshall, ATKINS Suzy, ATKINS Vikki, ATKINSON Andrea, ATKINSON Deb, ATKINSON Deborah, ATKINSON Greg, ATKINSON Lorraine, ATKINSON Luwei, ATKINSON Mark, ATKINSON Meredith, ATKINSON Michael, ATKINSON Paul, ATKINSON Beckie, ATKINSON Sallyanne, ATKINSON Sandra, ATKINSON Sue, ATKINSON Bim, ATMADJA Melfie, ATPUTHARAJAH James, ATTANA Charlie, ATTAR Sam, ATTARD Anthony, ATTARD Bernie, ATTARD Chantal, ATTARD Manny, ATTARD Emmanuel, ATTARD Erin, ATTARD George, ATTARD Jodie, ATTARD Joe, ATTARD Joseph, ATTARD Manuel, ATTARD Nina, ATTARD Philip, ATTARD Ranee, ATTARD Rebecca, ATTARD Yvonne, ATTENBOROUGH Crystal, ATTENBOROUGH John, ATTENBOROUGH Stanley, ATTERIDGE Melanie, ATTERTON Betty, ATTERTON EMARA Gloria, ATTEWELL Fay, ATTIA Carmen, ATTO Emil, ATTRIDGE Duncan, ATTUELL Keith, ATTUELL Mary, ATTUQUAYEFIO Mary, ATTWOOD Larry, ATTWOOD Sybil, ATWAL Rajinder, ATWELL Beatrice, ATWELL Kirsten, ATWOOD Erinore, ATWOOD Roy, ATZEMIS Helen, AU Albert, AU Albert, AU Alex, AU Christopher, AU Grace, AU Stanley, AU Tony, AU Wendy, AU Wendy, AU YEUNG Chun, AU-YEUNG Franky, AU-YEUNG Helen, AUCHTERLONIE Don, AUCHTERLONIE Mary, AUCHTERLONIE Warren, AUDAS Kate, AUDEN Teresita, AUDIBERT Oliver, AUDSLEY Kim, AUE Gilbert, AUELUA Khalid, AUERBACH Marsden, AUFFRET Loic, AUGOLOUPIS Steven, AUGUSTSON Kerry, AUHL Cheryl, AULD Jenny, AULD David, AULD Emma, AULD Peter, AULETTA Nadia, AULSEBROOK Gordon, AULSEBROOK Lani, AUMEERALLY Rasnad, AUNG Shwe, AURAHA Fred, AURISCH Gregory, AURISCH Nicole, AUSBURN Ann, AUSSEL John, AUST David, AUSTEN Karli, AUSTEN Kim, AUSTEN Phil, AUSTEN Trevor, AUSTERA Yvonne, AUSTIC Bob, AUSTIN Alan, AUSTIN Alison, AUSTIN Andrew, AUSTIN Tony, AUSTIN David, AUSTIN Gill, AUSTIN Grant, AUSTIN Graham, AUSTIN Ian, AUSTIN Janet, AUSTIN Jo, AUSTIN Kaizer, AUSTIN Bill, AUSTIN Michele, AUSTIN Neville, AUSTIN Noni, AUSTIN Pat, AUSTIN Rob, AUSTIN Ron, AUSTIN Ruth, AUSTIN Sarah, AUSTIN Tania, AUSTIN Trevor, AUSTIN Bruce, AUSTIN-GLEN Aaron, AUSTINE Fred, AUZINS Olafs, AVAKIAN Shant, AVALOS Teresa, AVALOS Xiomara, AVELING Chantelle, AVELING Meredith, AVERIS Neil, AVERY Anthony, AVERY Col, AVERY Garry, AVERY Ian, AVERY Jill, AVERY Keith, AVERY Louise, AVERY Rhiannon, AVERY Wayne, AVGERINOS Eva, AVGOLOUPIS Smarov, AVI-GUR Joshua, AVIET Ashley, AVIET Derrick, AVILA Joaquin, AVINS Shelagh, AVIS Diane, AVIS Ted, AVIS John, AVIS Karen, AVIS Nola, AVIS Ron, AVISON Gary, AVISON Annie, AVTAROVSKI Trene, AW Sean, AW Ric, AWAD Antoinette, AWAD Chris, AWADALLA Peter, AWAMLI Sam, AXFORD Kimberley, AXISA Frank, AYAD Nancy, AYDIN Seval, AYERS Monika, AYGUN Firat, AYLING Rob, AYLMER John, AYLMER Kate, AYLOTT John, AYLOTT Bill, AYLWIN Louise, AYNSLEY Belinda, AYNSLEY-COOKE Elizabeth, AYOUB Antoine, AYOUB George, AYOUB Joseph, AYOUB Sandra, AYRE Jim, AYRE Kellie, AYRE Mark, AYRE Suzanne, AYRES Carolyn, AYRES Cheryl, AYSHFORD Matt, AYZIN Oleg, AZAMI Masa, AZAR Domit, AZCONA MENACHO Zully, AZER Andrew, AZHAR Ozzie, AZOURY John, AZZI Elissar, AZZOPARDI Jeff, AZZOPARDI Karen.

B

BAAK-BUS Maryke, BAARD Paul, BAB Aziz, BABA Akiko, BABA Chris, BABA Erika, BABB Dick, BABBAGE Cris, BABBAGE Scott, BABBINGTON Kim, BABIC Ivan, BABILONIA Susano, BABINCZKY Steve, BABINGTON Camilla, BABINGTON-LEES Venetia, BACA FLOR Juan, BACALES Pat, BACIC Alex, BACIC Craig, BACIC Norma, BACK Rob, BACKERS Leo, BACKHOUSE Dan, BACKHOUSE Greg, BACKHOUSE Jackie, BACKHOUSE Kerry, BACKHOUSE Mark, BACKHOUSE Warren, BACKHUS Garry, BACKHUS Tarran, BACOLOD Agnes, BACON Carolyn, BACON Mark, BACON Margaret, BACON-ROWE Rae, BACSAFRA Michele, BADAMI Sushila, BADANI BALOOCH Farooq, BADARAU Alexandra, BADAWI Albert, BADBY David,

BADDEPUDI Ram, BADDER Avril, BADER Charbel, BADGER Annette, BADGER Barry, BADGER Bob, BADIA Mary, BADMAN Janine, BADMAN Roger, BADMAN David, BADOVINAC Milena, BADVE Rupa, BAE Dandy, BAE Esabelle, BAE Annie, BAE Min-Ho, BAECKER Hans-o, BAEHNK Lee, BAEK Jason, BAENSCH Sue, BAER Jacki, BAETZ Bradley, BAGADZINSKI Alex, BAGALA Teresa, BAGAN Sheelagh, BAGARIC Deanna, BAGAYATKAR Sanjiv, BAGGALEY Betty, BAGGE Alan, BAGGS Ken, BAGGS Nyoli, BAGGS Tammy, BAGHERI Edmund, BAGLEY Helen, BAGNAIL Arthur, BAGNALL Vanda, BAGNAT Linda, BAGNATI Tiago, BAGSHAW Ainslie, BAGSHAW John, BAGTAS Mary, BAGTAS Ramon, BAGUS Jun, BAGUST Les, BAHAMONDEZ Cindy, BAHEER Assad, BAHRAMI Bahram, BAI Victor, BAI Mitchell, BAIKIE Jean, BAILEY Aaron, BAILEY April, BAILEY Cameron, BAILEY Carrie, BAILEY Catherine, BAILEY Clare, BAILEY David, BAILEY Fiona, BAILEY Graham, BAILEY Harvey, BAILEY Helen, BAILEY Jason, BAILEY John, BAILEY John, BAILEY Jon, BAILEY Kath, BAILEY Lisa-Maree, BAILEY Lyn, BAILEY Margaret, BAILEY Pat, BAILEY Philip, BAILEY Raymond, BAILEY Robyn, BAILEY Ron, BAILEY Sarah, BAILEY Stephen, BAILEY Vicki, BAILEY John, BAILLACHE David, BAILLIE Ben, BAILLIE Dianna, BAILLIE Malcolm, BAILLIE Noelle, BAILLIE Patricia, BAILLIE Scott, BAILLO-JONES Nelly, BAILLY Nicholas, BAILYE Kylie, BAIN Anne, BAIN Ted, BAIN Jenny, BAIN Ken, BAIN Simon, BAIN Sue, BAIN-DONOHUE Suzanne, BAINBRIDGE Amy, BAINBRIDGE Barry, BAINES Denver, BAINES Kylie, BAINI William, BAINS Harpal, BAINS Shalinder, BAIRD Anne, BAIRD Brian, BAIRD Carol, BAIRD David, BAIRD John, BAIRD John, BAIRD Jon, BAIRD Bob, BAIRD Vicki, BAIRD Wilma, BAIRSTOW Karen, BAISE Gary, BAJADA Noel, BAJADA Simon, BAJUSZ Liz, BAJWA Navreet, BAKAS Amelia, BAKER Alison, BAKER Anthony, BAKER Tony, BAKER Ben, BAKER Beverley, BAKER Brenda, BAKER Brian, BAKER Brian, BAKER Caleb, BAKER Carolyn, BAKER Carole, BAKER Catherine, BAKER Chris, BAKER Christine, BAKER Christine, BAKER Claire, BAKER Claire, BAKER Tony, BAKER Colin, BAKER Dean, BAKER Derek, BAKER Donna, BAKER Doug, BAKER Earle, BAKER Beth, BAKER Emily, BAKER Gary, BAKER Gary, BAKER Gina, BAKER Graham, **BAKER Grant**, BAKER Greg, BAKER Heather, BAKER Heidi, BAKER Helen, BAKER Jacqueline, BAKER James, BAKER Jill, BAKER John, BAKER John, BAKER Josie, BAKER Julie, BAKER Julie, BAKER Julia, BAKER Karin, BAKER Kathy, BAKER Keith, BAKER Ken, BAKER Ken, BAKER Kevin, BAKER Kim, BAKER Kris, BAKER Lauren, BAKER Lee, BAKER Lorraine, BAKER Lyn, BAKER Marea, BAKER Margaret, BAKER Mark, BAKER Margaret, BAKER Mick, BAKER Myrtle, BAKER Natasha, BAKER Nick, BAKER Pat, BAKER Pat, BAKER Peter, BAKER Peter, BAKER Raymond, BAKER Richard, BAKER Bob, BAKER John, BAKER Sally, BAKER Saskia, BAKER Sita, BAKER Sorrel, BAKER Stu, BAKER Susan, BAKER Troy, BAKER Vince, BAKER-DEKKER Suzanne, BAKER-PARIENTE Chantal, BAKIJA Dusan, BAKIJA Ivana, BAKOPANOS Stephen, BAKUNOWICZ David, BAKUS Jan, BAL Vinay, BALAAM Matthew, BALABA Dammi, BALAGTAS Bernie, BALAGTAS Evelyn, BALAKRISHNAN Kris, BALAKRISHNAN Kris, BALAKUMAR Bala, BALASINGHAM Nish, BALASINGHAM Judita, BALASUBRAMANIAN Gay, BALASUBRAMANIAN Lakshmi, BALAVU Kali, BALBI Wendi, BALBI Donald, BALCH Randall, BALCOMBE Peter, BALDACCHINO Desiree, BALDACCHINO George, BALDACCHINO Gillian, BALDACCHINO Joseph, BALDACCHINO Pierre, BALDIN Silvano, BALDING Rachel, BALDING Ray, BALDISSERA Kerry, BALDOCK Karen, BALDOCK Monica, BALDOCK Wendy, BALDONADO Rolmar, BALDRY Kerry, BALDWIN Bronwyn, BALDWIN Joel, BALDWIN Peter, BALDWIN Phil, BALDWIN Rhys, BALDWIN Richard, BALDWIN Simon, BALDWIN Therese, BALDYGA Melinda, BALE Judith, BALE Kristine, BALE Francoise, BALE Patricia, BALEH Hacene, BALENDRA Dharshika, BALENDRAN Ganesh, BALENDRAN Balen, BALENZUELA Graham, BALES John, BALGUNAN Nad, BALI Bali, BALI Bali, BALILA Ray, BALIOZIAN Archbishop, BALKEMA John, BALKEN John, BALL Angus, BALL Chris, BALL David, BALL Greg, BALL Joy, BALL Leanne, BALL Lindsay, BALL Melinda, BALL Mike, BALL Nick, BALL Patricia, BALL Rhonda, BALL Bob, BALL Roy, BALL Tetsuko, BALL Tim, BALL Warwick, BALL Wendy, BALLANGARRY Jenny, BALLANGARRY Vera, BALLANTYNE Dean, BALLANTYNE Don, BALLANTYNE Melissa, BALLARD Bruce, BALLARD Liz, BALLARD Harry, BALLARD Howard, BALLARD David, BALLIN Fred, BALLIU Jeannette, BALMACEDA Ryan, BALMAIN Col, BALMAIN Greg, BALOGH Julie, BALOGH Tibor, BALSAMO Roberto, BALTHASAR Jane, BALTUSSEN Chris, BALUYOT Myra, BALZAN Pamela, BALZER Fiona, BALZOLA Gary, BAMBURY Maur, BAMFORD Andrew, BAMFORD David, BAMFORD Joanne, BAMFORD Lyn, BAMFORD Melanie, BAMFORD Stephen, BAN Martha, BANAAG Ariston, BANBURY Andrea, BANCO Lucia, BANCO Margarita, BANCROFT Jenny, BANDELA Prakash, BANDIAN Ramon, BANERJEE Debbie, BANEZ Paulo, BANFIELD Brian, BANFIELD John, BANG Bang, BANH William, BANHALMI Rosalie, BANHAM Margaret, BANHAM Melanie, BANHAM Neil, BANIK Daniel, BANISTER James, BANKOWSKI Marcela, BANKS Tony, BANKS Caroline, BANKS Carol, BANKS Cory, BANKS David, BANKS Jim, BANKS Kristen, BANKS Margaret, BANKS Norman, BANKS Bob, BANKS Sally, BANKS Sally, BANKS Sharon, BANKS Sue, BANKS Susan, BANNER Richard, BANNERMAN John, BANNERMAN Reg, BANNING Brenda, BANNING Wendy, BANNINK Troysie, BANNISTER Lisa, **BANNISTER Nicole**, BANNON Brian, BANNON Liam, BANNURA Sol, BANOS GALVEZ Annabella, BANSAL Riddhi, BANSAL Sunny, BANTING Jane, BANWAIT Amardeep, BANYAI Andrew, BAO Qlong, BAO Tianxiao, BARAC Dragica, BARAHONA Lissette, BARAJAS CALLES Lilian, BARAKAT Lewi, BARAMILI Nicholas, BARAN Askin, BARANCEWICZ Belinda, BARANETS Galina, BARANKO Stephanie, BARASSO Muriel, BARBAGALLO Melina, BARBAGALLO Tina, BARBARA Natalia, BARBARICH Marko, BARBARO Domenic, BARBARO Domina, BARBATO Elizabeth, BARBE Ghislaine, BARBER Brett, BARBER Christie, BARBER Donna, BARBER Don, BARBER Elizabeth, BARBER Betsy, BARBER Graeame, BARBER Jeremy, BARBER Kathy, BARBER Margaret, BARBER Nicole, BARBER Paul, BARBER Peter, BARBER Ray, BARBIE Rose-Marie, BARBIERI Alice, BARBOSA Alessandro, BARBOUR Tim, BARCELON Mon, BARCHET Marlies, BARCHIA Idris, BARCHIESI Matteo, BARCK Eric, BARCLAY Cathie, BARCLAY Dane, BARCLAY David, BARCLAY Luke, BARCLAY Bob, BARCLAY Sophie, BARCLAY Veronica, BARCLAY Bernard, BARDA Daniel, BARDEN Melissa, BARDENWERPER JR Tom, BARDOS Elizabeth, BARDOSSY Anibal, BARDSLEY Nikki, BARFORD Carole, BARFORD Julie, BARFORD Bob, BARGES Nerida, BARHAM Norman, BARICH Barra, BARIOL Nino, BARKAS Dianne, BARKER Tony, BARKER Astrid, BARKER Brendon, BARKER Carole, BARKER Cathy, BARKER Christine, BARKER David, BARKER Michael, BARKER Dennis, BARKER Gail, BARKER Geoff, BARKER Gordon, BARKER Jason, BARKER Jeremy, BARKER John, BARKER Karina, BARKER Katie, BARKER George, BARKER Margaret, BARKER Ray, BARKER Mary, BARKER Nikki, BARKER Paul, BARKER Rod, BARKER Sandy, BARKER Steve, BARKER Sue, BARKER Terri, BARKER Bill, BARKHAM Andrew, BARKHAM Tracy, BARKLA Les, BARKLAY David, BARKS Bob, BARLETTA Sam, BARLING Tim, BARLOW Tony, BARLOW James, BARLOW John, BARLOW Judy, BARLOW Kerri-Ann, BARLOW Kerry, BARLOW Margaret, BARLOW Peter, BARLOW Ray, BARLOW Robyn, BARLOW Ross, BARLOW Stephen, BARLOW Sue, BARLOW Warren, BARLOW Wayne, BARNA Katherine, BARNABO Gary, BARNACHEA Neil, BARNARD Ian, BARNARD Jan, BARNARD Jay, BARNARD Kimba, BARNARD Peter, BARNAUD Stephanie, BARNEA Anat, BARNEKOW Patrick, BARNERSOI Dieter, BARNES Alan, BARNES Albert, BARNES Andrew, BARNES Andrew, BARNES Andy, BARNES Angela, BARNES Anne, BARNES Anna, BARNES Barbara, BARNES Catherine, BARNES Cheyne, BARNES Chris, BARNES Chris, BARNES Chris, BARNES Clare, BARNES David, BARNES David, BARNES Don, BARNES Fenella, BARNES Frank, BARNES Greg, BARNES Gregory, BARNES Helen, BARNES James, BARNES Jenny, BARNES Jessica, BARNES Jo, BARNES John, BARNES Joe, BARNES Judi, BARNES Judy, BARNES Kurt, BARNES Barnes, BARNES Linda, BARNES Lisa, BARNES Lynley, BARNES Maree, BARNES Margaret, BARNES Marilyn, BARNES Michael, BARNES Patrick,

BARNES Paul, BARNES Peter, BARNES Phil, BARNES Richard, BARNES Robert, BARNES Robert, BARNES Rochelle, BARNES Ron, BARNES Rosie, BARNES Roy, BARNES Samantha, BARNES Steve, BARNES Susan, BARNES Tiff, BARNES Tim, BARNES Ronni, BARNES Vicky, BARNETSON Jane, BARNETT Beatrice, BARNETT Ben, BARNETT Dave, BARNETT Eileen, BARNETT Grant, BARNETT Jack, BARNETT Karen, BARNETT Neil, BARNETT Nick, BARNETT Owen, BARNETT Steve, BARNETT John, BARNEWALL Carmel, BARNHOORN Simone, BARNIER Karen, BARNIER Neville, BARNIER Ray, BARNIER Bill, BARNOY Michelle, BARNSLEY Kay, BARNSLEY Raelene, BARNWELL Carmen, BARON Cherie, BARONE Anthony, BARPALIAS Steven, BARR Andrea, BARR Cathryn, BARR Erin, BARR Gerri, BARR Don, BARR Jane, BARR Katherine, BARR Mary, BARR Margaret, BARR Simon, BARR Stewart, BARR Wendy, BARR-DAVID Judy, BARR-DAVID Martin, BARRACLOUGH Karen, BARRACLOUGH Kay, BARRATT Henry, BARRATT Jeff, BARRATT Mark, BARRATT Sandra, BARRAZA Nancy, BARRECA Crystal, BARRECA Marlene, BARRELL Chantelle, BARRENECHEA Liz, BARRERA Lidia, BARRET Erwan, BARRETT Amelia, BARRETT Barb, BARRETT Chris, BARRETT Di, BARRETT Doug, BARRETT Elizabeth, BARRETT Liz, BARRETT Jason, BARRETT John, BARRETT Lanna, BARRETT Miranda, BARRETT Pat, BARRETT Crash, BARRETT Peter, BARRETT Jack, BARREY Simon, BARRIE Helen, BARRIE Jim, BARRIE Lance, BARRIE Shane, BARRIE Sue, BARRIE Trevor, BARRIENTOS Maritza, BARRINGTON Michael, BARRINGTON Phil, BARRIO Pablo, BARRIOS Gaby, BARROETA Maria, BARRON Ann, BARRON Brian, BARRON Christopher, BARRON Dahni, BARRON Dinah, BARRON Donna, BARRON John, BARRON Karen, BARRON Leonie, BARRON Linda, BARRON Lorraine, BARRON Lorraine, BARRON Margaret, BARRON Marcus, BARRON Natalie, BARRON Pamela, BARRON Peter, BARRON Robin, BARRON Rob, BARROW Andrew, BARROW Brian, BARROW Faye, BARROW Norm, BARROWCLIFF Mark, BARROWS Louis, BARRY Alison, BARRY David, BARRY Fiona, BARRY Gayle, BARRY Ian, BARRY Johnnie, BARRY Margaret, BARRY Marianne, BARRY Maureen, BARRY Michelle, BARRY Michelle, BARRY Patrick, BARRY Phillipa, BARRY Shawn, BARRY Simon, BARRY Suzanne, BARRY Thomas, BARRY Tim, BARRY Wilkinson, BARRY Zach, BARSANTI Frank, BARSBY Helena, BARSI Kevin, BARTA Robert, BARTELS Daniel, BARTELS Geoff, BARTELS Peter, BARTER Jim, BARTHO Don, BARTHO Catherine, BARTHOLOMEW Kimberly, BARTHOLOMEW Margaret, BARTKIEWICZ Sara, BARTL Benjamin, BARTLE Carole, BARTLETT Alan, BARTLETT Alex, BARTLETT Angela, BARTLETT Tony, BARTLETT Colin, BARTLETT Coralee, BARTLETT Daniel, BARTLETT Derek, BARTLETT Emma, BARTLETT Gordon, BARTLETT Ian, BARTLETT Jenny, BARTLETT Ken, BARTLETT Mayet, BARTLETT Mike, BARTLETT Nikki, BARTLETT Pete, BARTLETT Raymond, BARTLETT Richard, BARTLETT Robert, BARTLETT Roy, BARTLETT Sandi, BARTLETT Sylvia, BARTLETT Paul, BARTLEY Melissa, BARTLEY Pauline, BARTOK Michael, BARTOLD Simon, BARTOLO Jessica, BARTOLO John, BARTOLOVIC Yvonne, BARTON Andrew, BARTON Belinda, BARTON Bruce, BARTON Carley, BARTON Col, BARTON Colin, BARTON Des, BARTON Doreen, BARTON Gayle, BARTON Paul, BARTON Peter, BARTON Ro, BARTON Sharon, BARTON Shane, BARTON Suzanne, BARTON Val, BARTOS Bev, BARTRAM Chris, BARTRAM Lucinda, BARTRUM Jane, BARTY Brooke, BARTY John, BARWICK Matthew, BARWICK Sami, BARZANJI Diyar, BASARILI Fatos, BASEGGIO Mery, BASELL Jane, BASFORD Lee, BASHA Alyce, BASHA Belinda, BASHA Pamela, BASHA Tanya, BASHA Zia, BASHAN Zev, BASHAR Jahirul, BASHARAT Haris, BASIL John, BASILE Susan, BASILE Vito, BASKETT Rachael, BASNAYAKE Ashani, BASNET Sagar, BASS Rebecca, BASSAL Alan, BASSER Geoffrey, BASSETT Keith, BASSI Hardip, BASSI Kuldip, BASSI Paolo, BASSUTTI Pablo, BASSUTTI Pablo, BASTA Christina, BASTIAMPILLAI Ramani, BASTIAN Katharina, BASTIANON Sharon, BASTON Pat, BASTON Mandy, BASTON Joyce, BATALLA Mel, BATALLER Walter, BATAN Pascal, BATCHELER Peter, BATCHELOR Margaret, BATCHELOR Tracey, BATE Amy, BATE John, BATE Lauren, BATE Peter, BATE Vanessa, BATEMAN Alan, BATEMAN Sam, BATEMAN Greg, BATEMAN Judith, BATEMAN Kath, BATEMAN Mark, BATEMAN Mark, BATEMAN Matt, BATEMAN Ray, BATEMAN Sylvia, BATEMAN-PAUL Heath, BATES Alan, BATES Anne, BATES Barbara, BATES Barry, BATES Elpis, BATES Glenn, BATES Jan, BATES Jenny, BATES Joel, BATES Michelle, BATES Mitchell, BATES Natalie, BATES Richie, BATES Bob, BATES Rob, BATES Rosemary, BATES Sally, BATES Suzy, BATES Trevor, BATES Trista, BATESON Carol, BATESON Don, BATESON Lorraine, BATEUP Brad, BATEUP Chris, BATEY Cathy, BATEY Derek, BATEY Pauline, BATEY Sam, BATH Chris, BATH Christopher, BATH Denise, BATH Jenny, BATHE Gai, BATHERSBY Dominic, BATHERSBY Doug, BATHERSBY Nina, BATHGATE Angus, BATISTA DA COSTA BROOKS Mirileia, BATISTIC Patricia, BATKIN Nadia, BATKIN Shane, BATKOVIC Marica, BATLEY John, BATLEY Michael, BATLEY Ruth, BATSIKAS Kon, BATSON John, BATSON Judy, BATSON Paul, BATT Charmaine, BATT Jessica, BATTEN Sue, BATTEN Tanya, BATTERSBY Karen, BATTERSBY Kerry, BATTERSBY Kristen, BATTISHILL Janice, BATTISSON Ben, BATTLE Joanne, BATTLEY David, BATTLEY Veronica, BATTOCCHIO Robert, BATTUNG Jeffrey, BATTY Alice, BATTY Craig, BATTY Jack, BATTY Janice, BATTY Julia, BATTYE Sally, BAU Lisa, BAUER Detlef, BAUER Leo, BAUER Matt, BAUER Samara, BAUER Sigi, BAUER Steven, BAUKH Simon, BAUKNECHT Audrey, BAULCH Tony, BAULCH Crosbie, BAULCH Jan, BAUM Alison, BAUMANN Mark, BAUMGARMTNER Bruce, BAUTISTA Wendy, BAWI Jamal, BAXENDALE Chrissy, BAXENDELL Dirk, BAXTER David, BAXTER David, BAXTER Denise, BAXTER Emma, BAXTER Fay, BAXTER Glenn, BAXTER Gregory, BAXTER Jim, BAXTER John, BAXTER Ken, BAXTER Lynette, BAXTER Rose, BAXTER Scott, BAXTER Sharon, BAYAN Maria, BAYLASY Hong, BAYLES Bob, BAYLEY Clive, BAYLEY David, BAYLIS Karen, BAYLIS Nardia, BAYLISS Keith, BAYLISS Peter, BAYLISS Sue, BAYLY Moya, BAYLY Paul, BAYNE Joyce, BAYNES Allan, BAYNES Glenys, BAYNIE Therese, BAYRANTE Jose, BAYSARI Tania, BAZ Alex, BAZ Carolyn, BAZAN Lucian, BAZOUNI Teresa, BAZZI Ibrahim, BEACH Rhonda, BEACHAM Ann, BEACHAM Peter, BEACHLEY Rex, BEACHLEY Sally, BEACROFT Craig, BEACROFT David, BEADMAN-GREEN Pauline, BEADSWORTH Sam, BEALE Geraldine, BEALE John, BEALE Jules, BEALE Mary, BEALE Paul, BEALE Philip, BEALE Bill, BEALES Chris, BEALES Paul, BEAMAN Beverly, BEAMISH Straun, BEAMS Mike, BEAN Andrew, BEAN Yvonne, BEARD Carmen, BEARD Gwynneth, BEARD Helen, BEARD Joanne, BEARD Jodi-Ann, BEARD Marion, BEARD Max, BEARD Bob, BEARD Rod, BEARDSLEE Margaret, BEARDSLEE Robert, BEARZOT Sue, BEASHEL Paul, BEASLEY Kerri, BEASLEY Stephen, BEASLY Emma, BEASLY Lydia, BEAT Trish, BEATH Rob, BEATO Eloise, BEATON Debbie, BEATON Jim, BEATON Sharon, BEATON Wendy, **BEATSON Graham**, BEATSON Rosalie, BEATTIE Carol, BEATTIE David, BEATTIE Beattie, BEATTIE Jane, BEATTIE Peg, BEATTIE Norm, BEATTIE Ronald, BEATTIE Scott, BEATTON John, BEATTON June, BEATTS Frances, BEATTY Robyn, BEATTY Wal, BEAUCHAMP Arnold, BEAUCHAMP Diane, BEAUCHAMP Glen, BEAUDOIN Sylvie, BEAUMONT Barry, BEAUMONT Carolyn, BEAUMONT Damien, BEAUMONT Judith, BEAUMONT Melissa, BEAUMONT Steve, BEAVAN Miriam, BEAVAN Terry, BEAVEN Amanda, BEAVER David, BEAVER Irena, BEAVER John, BEAVER Sally, BEAZLEY Arch, BEAZLEY Ian, BEAZLEY Kate, BEAZLEY Pauline, BEAZLEY Richard, BEAZLEY Robert, BEBBINGTON Jan, BEBY Jean, BECCARIS Debbie, BECEJSKI Erik, BECEJSKI Marko, BECERRA Angelica, BECHARA Joseph, BECHLER Klara, BECHLER Norman, BECK Adrian, BECK Anita, BECK Freya, BECK Hilary, BECK Jan, BECK Jess, BECK Sue, BECKER Fred, BECKER Joan, BECKERS Ernestine, BECKETT Jan, BECKETT Jean, BECKETT John, BECKETT Mick, BECKETT Pete, BECKETT Sue, BECKHOUSE Helen, BECKHOUSE Ross, BECKINSALE Rosemary, BECKMAN Amy, BECKMANN Ralph, BECKWITH Lynn, BECKWITH Rob, BECKWITH Shirani, BECQUET John, BECROFT Greg, BECROFT Sarah-Jane, BEDDIE Kaylene, BEDDOW Tammy, BEDELOVSKI Lile, BEDER Debbie, BEDFORD Dennis, BEDFORD Jackie, BEDFORD Jill, BEDFORD June, BEDFORD Katherine, BEDI Kulbir, BEDI Ran, BEDROSSIAN Shavarsh, BEDWANI Jack, BEDWELL Dorothy,

BEDWELL Kathryn, BEDWELL Bob, BEDWELL Walter, BEECH Brett, BEECH Emely, BEECH Paul, BEECHAM Rowena, BEECHER Gai, BEECROFT John, BEEFORTH David, BEEHAG Ted, BEEHAG Mary, BEEKME ER Betty, BEELAERTS Selina, BEER Anne, BEER Jock, BEER Gary, BEER Geoffrey, BEER Doryl, BEER Kaye, BEER Paul, BEERS Galen, BEERTSEN Cavell, BEERWORTH Kate, BEESLEY John, BEETON Warren, BEEVOR Stan, BEGA Joe, BEGBIE Matthew, BEGBIE Patrick, BEGER Anthony, BEGG Charles, BEGG Angela, BEGG Jennie, BEGG Jenny, BEGG John, BEGG Leanne, BEGG Michael, BEGG Stewart, BEGGS Bob, BEGLEY Francis, BEGNELL Jamie, BEGOVIC Anica, BEGUE-YOLDI Isra, BEGUIN Michel, BEH Debbie, BEHAGG Neville, BEHAN David, BEHAN Janette, BEHAN Kerry, BEHDJET Altan, BEHR Janet, BEHRENS David, BEHRENS Johannes, BEHRINGER Denise, BEISHUIZEN Karen, BEJCZI Les, BEKELE Assefa, BEKENS Joseph, BEKINK Rachel, BEKIS Trent, BEKKER Carmen, BEKOS Anna, BELANI Michael, BELAPURKAR Vijay, BELBIN Phil, BELCHEFF Daniella, BELCHEFF-MIRCESKI Belcheff, BELCHER Bill, BELEC Richard, BELEGRIS Jim, BELEL Belel, BELEN-BALITACTAC Sonia, BELFIELD Patricia, BELFORD Barry, BELGROVE Tracee, BELL Alison, BELL Anna, BELL Barry, BELL Cameron, BELL Caroline, BELL David, BELL Debbie, BELL Denis, BELL Desna, BELL Dione, BELL Fred, BELL Gavin, BELL George, BELL Graham, BELL Graham, BELL Harry, BELL Ian, BELL Jan, BELL Jane, BELL Jane, BELL Jean, BELL Jenni, BELL Jeremy, BELL Jill, BELL Joan, BELL Jack, BELL John, BELL Gerald, BELL John, BELL John, BELL Kaylene, BELL Ken, BELL Leah, BELL Leonie, BELL Lou, BELL Lyn, BELL Marrion, BELL Margaret, BELL Margaret, BELL Maureen, BELL Natalie, BELL Peter, BELL Peter, BELL Peter, BELL Phil, BELL Dinga, BELL Rhonda, BELL Richard, BELL Robin, BELL Robin, BELL Roberta, BELL Jeff, BELL Bob, BELL Rosie, BELL Ross, BELL Sharon, BELL Sue, BELL Tamara, BELL Terry, BELL Tristan, BELL Vanessa, BELL Veronica, BELLAMY Andy, BELLAMY Andrew, BELLAMY Ann, BELLAMY Frank, BELLAMY Phil, BELLAMY Shane, BELLAMY Wendy, BELLANTONI Narelle, BELLCHAMBERS Grenville, BELLEAR-MAYERS Tamara, BELLENGER Benoit, BELLERO Vicki, BELLETTE Allisa, BELLETTE Keith, BELLEW Patricia, BELLEZA Luis, BELLI Sabina, BELLING Erica, BELLINGER Caroline, BELLOFIORE Sebastian, BELLON Ronnie, BELMAR Erika, BELME Maria, BELONOGOFF Larissa, BELOT Michael, BELSHAW John, BELSKY Stan, BELTON Tony, BEN-SEFER Ellen, BENAD Sandra, BENAROOS John, BENAZZI Al, BENCKE Angus, BENCKE James, BENCKE Joanna, BENDALL Ken, BENDALL Kirk, BENDEICH Stephen, BENDER Heather, BENDER Rich, BENDLE Kaye, BENECKE Keith, BENEDEK Ily, BENEDETTO Sandona, BENGALI Banoo, BENHAM Christine, BENHAM Ray, BENHAM Bill, BENHIAM Robert, BENIC Sarah, BENINATI Valerie, BENITEZ Gerry, BENITEZ Rossbee, BENIVENTO Gino, BENJAMIN Asher, BENJAMIN Christopher, BENJAMIN Crystal, BENJAMIN Esther, BENJAMIN Gerry, BENJAMIN Matthew, BENJAMIN Pamela, BENJAMIN Richard, BENJAMIN Roger, BENKENDORFF Peter, BENKOVIC Adam, BENN Kris, BENN Lyn, BENNEIT Beth, BENNER Christine, BENNETT Adam, BENNETT Alan, BENNETT Alan, BENNETT Allison, BENNETT Allan, BENNETT Andrew, BENNETT Andrew, BENNETT Anna, BENNETT Barbara, BENNETT Bev, BENNETT Brian, BENNETT Brian, BENNETT Brian, BENNETT Bryce, BENNETT Carolyn, BENNETT Kitty, BENNETT Chris, BENNETT Christopher, BENNETT David, BENNETT Diane, BENNETT Don, BENNETT Doris, BENNETT Ted, BENNETT Emma, BENNETT Gary, BENNETT George, BENNETT Harvey, BENNETT Helen, BENNETT Ian, BENNETT Janet, BENNETT Jan, BENNETT John, BENNETT John, BENNETT Julia, BENNETT Julie, BENNETT June, BENNETT Kane, BENNETT Katherine, BENNETT Laurie, BENNETT Leanne, BENNETT Lynda, BENNETT Marian, BENNETT Marie, BENNETT Mardi, BENNETT Marilyn, BENNETT Michelle, BENNETT Neil, BENNETT Peter, BENNETT Robert, BENNETT Ryan, BENNETT Sarah, BENNETT Sian, BENNETT Tania, BENNETT Peter, BENNETT Bill, BENNETTS Debbie, BENNETTS Gordon, BENNETTS John, BENNETTS Lesley, BENNETTS Sam, BENNIE Alex, BENNIE Marc, BENNIER Leon, BENNINGTON Ray, BENNISON Chris, BENOIT Alphonse, BENOIT Chris, BENOIT Steve, BENSAIDI Halim, BENSLEY Heather, BENSLEY Keith, BENSLEY Scott, BENSLEY Sue, BENSO Mario, BENSON Al, BENSON Buffy, BENSON Glen, BENSON Ian, BENSON Judy, BENSON Kim, BENSON Leonie, BENSON Lesley, BENSON Liz, BENSON Jane, BENSON Meagen, BENSON Mefanwy, BENSON Paul, BENSON Bob, BENSON Shane, BENSTEAD June, BENSTEAD Lionel, BENSTOCK Simon, BENT Janne, BENT Kylie, BENT Ray, BENTALL Ian, BENTANCOR Elbio, BENTHAM Harry, BENTICK-OWENS Pia, BENTLEY Adrian, BENTLEY Alison, BENTLEY Peter, BENTLEY John, BENTLEY Julia, BENTLEY Kim, BENTLEY Leanne, BENTLEY Lee, BENTLEY Lesley, BENTLEY Lorraine, BENTLEY Michele, BENTLEY Natalie, BENTLEY Omar, BENTLEY Sylvia, **BENTLEY-JOHNSTON Sue**, BENTON Sharon, BENTON Bill, BENYON Peter, BENYON Phillip, BENZ Anna, BENZ Christiane, BERAKHI Abraham, BERASAIN Christina, BERBARI Roger, BERBOTTO Angelo, BERDU Vivian, BERE Fred, BERENICE Glenn, BERENSON Pamiela, BERENTSON Peter, BERESFORD Don, BERESFORD Elizabeth, BERESFORD Garry, BERESFORD John, BERESFORD June, BERG Don, BERG Harry, BERG Kathleen, BERG Bob, BERG Sarah, BERG Seppo, BERG Therese, BERGAGNIN Kim, BERGAN Jim, BERGAN Monica, BERGAN Paul, BERGAN Sean, BERGE Torill, BERGELIN Terry, BERGER Helena, BERGER Ken, BERGER Nicole, BERGERSEN Suzanne, BERGHOFER Lynn, **BERGIN Daniel**, BERGIN David, BERGIN Mel, BERGLUND Catherine, BERGLUND Erik, BERGLUND Monica, BERGMAN Robert, BERK Adam, BERKE William, BERKELEY David, BERKELEY Margaret, BERKHOUT Yvonne, BERKOVITS Rita, BERLANGA Lita, BERLINGERI Dante, BERMAN Andrew, BERMAN Graeme, BERMAN Tim, BERNARD Peter, BERNARDI Rita, BERNARDINO Lelith, BERNARDO Mervy, BERNARDO Stephen, BERNASCONI Alison, BERNASCONI Paul, BERNAYS Renee, BERNDT Roland, BERNE Christine, BERNE Nadine, BERNHARD Cheryl, BERNIER Christine, BERNIER Yves, BERNSTEIN Bettina, BERNTSEN Mandy, BERNTSSON Sofia, BERRA Loreley, BERRELL Deb, BERRELL Don, BERRIDGE Michelle, BERRIMAN Ann, BERRIMAN Belinda, BERRIMAN Bronwyn, BERRIMAN Duncan, BERRY Alex, BERRY Andrew, BERRY Celia, BERRY Colin, BERRY David, BERRY David, BERRY Geoff, BERRY George, BERRY Greg, BERRY Jayne, BERRY Kelly, BERRY Maria, BERRY Maureen, BERRY Michael, BERRY Mike, BERRY Suzanne, BERRY Glenn, BERTA Zoltan, BERTENS Elisa, BERTHOLD Michele, BERTHOLD Rachel, BERTHON Linda, BERTI Ben, BERTINAT Maria-Teresa, BERTINETTI Monique, BERTOLISSIO Linda, BERTOLLA Max, BERTOLOTTI Battista, BERTON Andre, BERTONI Fay, **BERTRAM John**, BERTRAM Kylie, BESANCON Janet, BESOMO Margaret, BEST Catherine, BEST Chris, BEST Geraldine, BEST Nathan, BEST Noel, BEST Paul, BEST Bob, BEST Ross, BEST Sarah, BEST Val, BEST Victor, BEST Victor, BEST Wendy, BESTER Chris, BESTER Damian, BETANCUR Andres, BETANZOS ALONSO Pilar, BETAR Chris, BETBEDER-MATIBET Liz, BETHELL Debbie, BETHWAITE Carolyn, BETHWAITE Mark, BETTINGTON Angela, BETTINGTON Susan, BETTINI Toni, BETTS Ken, BETTS Margaret, BETTY Andrew, BETTY Betty, BEUDEKER Bryan, BEVAN Betty, BEVERIDGE Cathy, BEVERIDGE Geoff, BEVERIDGE Neil, BEVERLEY Mark, BEVILACQUA Nestore, BEVIN Edith, BEVIS Ron, BEVITT Joseph, BEYDOUN Chebibe, BEYERS Jenny, BEYERS Stephen, BEYNON Cec, BEZZINA Jessica, BEZZINA Maria, BHAGANI Sixten, BHALLA Rob, BHAMJI Faizal, BHANDARI Bikash, BHANDARI Wishu, BHARADWAJ Vijay, BHARDWAJ Vidya, BHARGAVA Sudhir, BHARGAVA Suman, BHAT Shashi, BHATHAL Dave, BHATIA Bill, BHATNAGAR Rachana, BHATNAGAR Ritika, BHATT Dipak, BHATT Pranav, BHATTACHARJEE Sumita, BHATTACHARVEE Sulata, BHATTARAI Bal, BHOIR Manvendra, BHOLE Neela, BHOLE Salil, BHUTADA Kamal, BI Ellen, BIADY John, BIALOWAS Marisa, BIANCO Theresa, BIBBY Roger, BIBI Khizra, BIBILE Cuda, BICANIC Bill, BICEVSKI Mile, BICHEL Tricia, BICKELL Marion, BICKERSTAFF Paul, BICKERTON Bruce, BICKFORD Denise, BICKFORD Ted, BICKNELL Linda, BICSAK Shannon, BIDDLE Denise, BIDDLE Greg, BIDDLE Helen, BIDDLE Sonja, BIDDLECOMBE Mary, BIDEGAIN Maiana, BIDENCOPE Judy, BIDENCOPE Peter, BIDNER Sunny, BIDOT Laurent, BIDZOVSKI Louie, BIDZOVSKI Sonja, BIEGA Stan, BIELSTEIN Becky, BIERMANN Matthew, BIESKE Judy, BIETOLA Maria, BIFFIN Neville, BIGATTON Danny, BIGGIN

Christina, BIGGS Bek, BIGHAM Don, BIGNALL Melanie, BIGNELL Beryl, BIGNELL Chris, BIGNOLD Ginetta, BIGSWORTH Kerrie, BIHARI Les, BIKI Karen, BILAL Mohammad, BILBOE Rachel, BILEANSCHI Alexandru, BILGIN Ayse, BILICH Bill, BILLAH Masum, BILLETT Pam, BILLIARDS Cathy, BILLIARDS Joanne, BILLIARDS Bob, BILLING Estelle, BILLING Kylie, BILLING Pamela, BILLING Ross, BILLINGS Heather, BILLINGTON Malcolm, BILLINGTON Wilf, BILLS Don, BILLS Katrina, BILLSBOROUGH Kevin, BILNEY Linda, BILOUS Jennifer, BILTON Geoffrey, BINCH Wayne, BINDA Louise, BINDLEY Kristin, BINDRA Manraj, BINDRA Preeti, BINFIELD Milvia, BINGHAM Jill, BINGHAM Julieanne, BINGHAM Lisa, BINGHAM Myles, BINIAHAN Romeo, BINIKOU Eleftheria, BINKINS Cath, BINNIE Kirsten, BINNS Jennifer, BINNS Kathryn, BINNS Nigel, BIONDI Lyn, BIORDI Mauro, BIR Helen, BIRCH Arthur, BIRCH Dianne, BIRCH John, BIRCH June, BIRCH Peter, BIRCH Richard, BIRCHALL Edward, BIRCHALL Gary, BIRCHELL Ray, BIRCKEL Jenny, BIRD Ann, BIRD Tony, BIRD Cari, BIRD David, BIRD Gerry, BIRD Kristen, BIRD Maria, **BIRD Tom**, BIRD Tom, BIRDIE Mithra, BIRDSALL Keith, BIRDSALL Mark, BIRDSALL Robert, BIRELLO Adriana, BIRGES Shahnaz, BIRKETT Geoffrey, BIRKS Greg, BIRMINGHAM Kathleen, BIRNEY Yuko, BIRO George, BIRRELL Andrew, BIRRELL Scott, BIRSE Sharon, BIRSS George, BIRSS Marge, BIRTLES Elaine, BIRTLES Jenny, BIRTLES Terry, BISANDER Jill, BISBY Roger, BISCHOF Robert, BISH Adelle, BISHELL Karen, BISHOP Alan, BISHOP Andrew, BISHOP Bernice, BISHOP Brad, BISHOP Delwyn, BISHOP Dinie, BISHOP Fiona, BISHOP Geoff, BISHOP Jim, BISHOP Jeffrey, BISHOP Jenny, BISHOP Judd, BISHOP Kevin, BISHOP Michael, BISHOP Pauline, BISHOP Peter, BISHOP Rachael, BISHOP Robin, BISHOP Robyn, BISHOP Stephen, BISHOP Trevor, BISHWOKARMA Nabin, BISNETTE Linda, BISS Edwige, BISSAKER Elizabeth, BISSAKER Jim, BISSELING Claire, BISSET Leanne, BISSETT Karen, BISTA Jivan, BISTA Jwala, BISWAS Santanu, BITABARA Lynn, BITABARA Rene, BITAR Linda, BITHELL Jack, BITTAR Jenni, BITTLE Michelle, BITTMANN Cheryl, BIZ Fran, BIZIMOVSKA Violeta, BIZUNEH Tafese, BJELANOVIC Maree, BJORKLUND Linda, BLACK Alison, BLACK Belinda, BLACK Colin, BLACK Debbie, BLACK Narelle, BLACK Grant, BLACK Gwen, BLACK Ian, BLACK Jim, BLACK James, BLACK John, BLACK Jo, BLACK Judy, BLACK Lara, BLACK Mark, BLACK Peggy, BLACK Nathan, BLACK Olga, BLACK Paul, BLACK Peter, BLACK Richard, BLACK Sarah, BLACK-ALLEN Caitlin, BLACKALL Peggy, BLACKALL Bob, BLACKBOURNE Ali, BLACKBURN Allan, BLACKBURN Darren, BLACKBURN Gabrielle, BLACKBURN John, BLACKBURN Judy, BLACKBURN June, BLACKBURN Lisa, BLACKBURN Terry, BLACKBURNE Maureen, BLACKBURNE John, BLACKBURNE Joan, BLACKBURNE Terry, BLACKER Mike, BLACKETT Graeme, BLACKETT Kevin, BLACKETT Richard, BLACKFORD Andrew, BLACKFORD Kathryn, BLACKFORD Sue, BLACKHALL Amanda, BLACKLEY Tanya, BLACKMAN Glen, BLACKMAN Heather, BLACKMAN Lynne, BLACKMAN Margaret, BLACKMAN Bob, BLACKMAN Susan, BLACKMORE Derek, BLACKMORE James, BLACKMORE Jim, BLACKMORE Julie, BLACKMORE Luke, BLACKMORE Robert, BLACKMORE-TUFFY Mal, BLACKSHAW Brewster, BLACKSHAW Daniel, BLACKSHAW Rod, BLACKSHAW Sonia, BLACKSHAW Sylvia, BLACKSTONE Audrey, BLACKWELL Debra, BLACKWOOD Anne, BLACKWOOD Cathie, BLADEN Helen, BLADES Isabel, BLAETTLER George, BLAIN James, BLAIN Marg, BLAIR Frank, BLAIR Barbara, BLAIR Darren, BLAIR Davina, BLAIR Gordon, BLAIR Sally, BLAIR Sandra, BLAIR Stacey, BLAKE Allan, BLAKE Brad, BLAKE Carmel, BLAKE Carmel, BLAKE Colin, BLAKE Faith, BLAKE Helen, BLAKE Jeff, BLAKE Judith, BLAKE Keith, BLAKE Kieran, BLAKE Marie, BLAKE Naomi, BLAKE Nick, BLAKE Nicole, BLAKE Peter, BLAKE Rodney, BLAKE Rona, BLAKE Sam, BLAKE Shirley-Anne, BLAKE Simon, BLAKELEY Craig, BLAKELY Joy, BLAKELY Ron, BLAKELY Stacey, BLAKEMORE Kath, BLAKER Charlie, BLAKERS Liam, BLAKEWAY Mary, BLAKEY Alan, BLAKEY Lorraine, BLAKSTON Kerry, BLANCARTE Jose, BLANCH Jenny, BLANCH Nerida, BLANCHARD Edna, BLANCHARD Gary, BLANCHARD Jeremy, BLANCHARD Karen, BLANCHARD Terry, BLANCHFIELD John, BLANCO Fred, BLAND Mal, BLAND Marion, BLAND Margaret, BLAND Peter, BLAND Simon, BLANDA Andrew, BLANDA Eva, BLANDIN DE CHALAIN Vicki, BLANDIN DE CHALAIN Marilys, BLANDINO Lucia, BLANK Ken, BLANK Margaret, BLANKS Veronica, BLANSJAAR Rasa, BLANZAN Bert, BLASDALL Scott, BLASS Heinz, BLASSE Andre, BLASZCZYK Wally, BLAXLAND Peter, BLAYDEN Melissa, BLAYMIRES John, BLAZEK Katerina, BLAZELY Shane, BLAZEWICZ Monika, BLAZIC Zoran, BLAZLEY Sharni, BLAZQUEZ James, BLEASDALE Darryl, BLEASDALE Jenny, BLEDHILL Keith, BLEICHER Kerrin, BLEIKER Vivianne, BLENCOWE Craig, BLENCOWE Ian, BLENCOWE Jacinta, BLENCOWE Jean, BLENCOWE Margaret, BLENMAN Donna, BLENMAN Ken, BLEVINS Victoria, BLICK Daniel, BLIGHT Leonie, BLIGHT Lois, BLINMAN Gordon, BLINMAN Prunella, BLINMAN Victor, BLISS Peter, BLISS Phyl, BLISS Suzanne, BLISSETT Lynda, BLISSETT Tony, BLOCH Leif, BLOCH Maggie, BLOCH Sandra, BLOEM Kristie, BLOGG Meg, BLOM Lyndal, BLOM Peter, BLOMELEY Neville, BLOMFIELD Lyn, BLOMFIELD Peter, BLONDELL James, BLONDELL Josefin, BLONDELL Karin, BLOOD Jessica, BLOOM David, BLOOM Judy, BLOOM Julie, BLOOM Marlene, BLOOM Philip, BLOOMFIELD Alan, BLOOMFIELD Alan, BLOOMFIELD Gayle, BLOOMFIELD Mike, BLOOMFIELD Margaret, BLOOMFIELD Paul, BLOOR Nicholas, BLOTT Col, BLOUNT Alan, BLOW Linda, BLUE Ann, BLUE Kate, BLUETT Sarah, BLUHDORN Frances, BLUMENFELD Walter, BLUMENTHAL Lorin, BLUMER Jane, BLUNDELL Cecilia, BLUNDELL James, BLUNDELL Peter, BLUNDELL Vicki, BLUNDEN Peter, BLUNT Irene, BLUNT Phill, BLUNT Wendy, BLYDE Sally, BLYTH Emily, BLYTH Garry, BLYTH Julie, BLYTH Lynda, BLYTH Nat, BLYTHE Josh, BLYTHE Liza, BO Tony, BOACHIE Steven, BOADEN Darren, BOAG Steph, BOALER Hazel, BOARD Anthony, BOARD Meg, BOARD Robin, BOARD Yasmin, BOASE Graham, BOATE Alan, BOBBERT Eva, BOBBIN Gordon, BOBBIN Maureen, BOBEK Regi, BOBETH Mary, BOBROWSKI Alice, BOCHENEK Henrietta, BOCK Andrew, BOCK Ellie, BOCK Lynn, BOCK Martin, BOCKOS Costa, BOCTOR Mina, BOCXE Lisa, BODAK Mark, BODART Christine, BODDY Helen, BODEL Jacqui, BODEN Neil, BODIE Airlie, BODIE Donald, BODMAN Sue, BODNAR Andrew, BODONYI Garry, BODSWORTH Jim, BODY Julia, BODY Bill, BODYCOTE Vanessa, BOEHM Christie, BOEHM Monika, BOEHM Sandy, BOEHM Tim, BOEKESTEIN-HAY Mary, BOERS Meg, BOERS Susanne, **BOERSEN Sarah**, BOERSMA Derek, BOES Nick, BOESENBERG Pam, BOETEL Christian, BOETTCHER Jenny, BOEY Sandra, BOFINGER Debbie, BOFINGER-WEBER Tonja, BOGAERTS Gloria, BOGDANOVSKI Elves, BOGENHUBER Max, BOGGITT Pat, BOGGS Sandra, BOGHOSSIAN Houri, BOGLARI Boldi, BOGLARI-DAVYKOZA Oksana, BOGLE Kaye, BOGTOUR Romani, BOHAN Alanna, BOHDAN Vladimir, BOHLSEN Beryl, BOHNOVA Bibiana, BOHR Alexandra, BOIDIN Rebecca, BOIKOV Marina, BOJANAC Tania, BOJE Angela, BOJE Garry, BOJE Harry, BOK Kwan, BOKIL Rupali, BOKOR David, BOLAND Alex, BOLAND Angela, BOLAND Daniel, BOLAND Frank, BOLAND Helen, BOLAND Father, BOLAND Julie, BOLAND Kate, BOLAND Ken, BOLAND Ruth, BOLAND Sarah, BOLAND Thomas, BOLDISTON Brad, BOLDISTON Maurice, BOLEHALA Glenn, BOLER Graeme, BOLER Jeff, BOLGOFF Michel, BOLIN Melissa, BOLITHO Alan, BOLITHO Ben, BOLITHO Glenda, BOLITHO Michael, BOLITHO Paul, BOLLINGER Adam, BOLLINGER Heather, BOLLOM Cheryl, BOLMAT Anna, BOLOMEY Luisa, BOLSOVER Patricia, BOLT Lynette, BOLT Mindy, BOLTIN Phillip, BOLTON Adam, BOLTON Ainsley, BOLTON Ann, BOLTON Debbie, BOLTON Elizabeth, BOLTON Kristine, BOLTON Nikki, BOLTON Shane, BOLTON Shirley, BOLTON Sue, BOLTON Wayne, BOLZAN Gianna, BOMAN Brigid, BOMBALA Helen, BOMZON Lionel, BONACCORSO Tony, BONATTI Daniel, BONATTI Daniel, BONAVENTURA Mark, BONAVIA Margaret, BONAZINGA Maria, BOND Tony, BOND Anthony, BOND David, BOND Geoff, BOND Graham, BOND Ian, BOND James, BOND Joe, BOND John, BOND Kenneth, BOND Judith, BOND Ken, BOND Ken, BOND Martene, BOND Bondy, BOND Marg, BOND Matthew, BOND Monique, BOND Nick, BOND Rob, BOND Robert, BOND Steve, BOND Suze, BOND Warren, BONDARENKO Tara, BONDINI Jeanette, BONE Alison, BONE Ian, BONE Paul, BONE Robyn, BONELLO Julie, BONHAM David, BONHAM Ron, BONHAM Vera,

BONIFACIO Leah, BONIFACIO Deryk, BONNEL Michel, BONNER Anne, BONNER Dennis, BONNER Elizabeth, BONNER Fran, BONNER Mike, BONNER Sid, BONNESS Sonja, BONNEY Lesley, BONNEY Maureen, BONNEY-MILLETT Jenny, BONNICI Rita, BONNIE James, BONNITCHA Jacqui, BONNITCHA Jonathan, BONNY Louise, BONOMI Beverley, BONOMI Michelle, BONOMINI Cherrel, BONSER Frank, BONSER Janette, BONTIKOULIS Alex, BONTOFT Ray, BONVENTI John, BONZI FACHINI GOMES Julia, BOOCOCK Judy, BOOCOCK Justin, BOOK Lorna, BOOKER Carolyn, BOOKER Greg, BOOKER Ray, BOOLE Grace, BOOLE John, BOOLE Kevin, BOON Jan, BOON Michele, BOON Ron, BOON Tamara, BOON William, BOONEN Bert, BOORMAN Andrew, BOORMAN Daniel, BOORMAN Debbie, BOORMAN June, BOORMAN Norwood, BOOTH Annelise, BOOTH Benjamin, BOOTH Brian, BOOTH Colin, BOOTH Colin, BOOTH Dallas, BOOTH Diane, BOOTH Ernie, BOOTH Frank, BOOTH Gillian, BOOTH Henry, BOOTH John, BOOTH Karen, BOOTH Lauren, BOOTH Lynne, BOOTH Lynne, BOOTH Marcel, **BOOTH Mavis**, BOOTH Nicola, BOOTH Nikki, BOOTH Rach, BOOTH Robert, BOOTH Robert, BOOTH Rosemary, BOOTH Sue, BOOTH Susan, BOOTH Suzette, BOOTH Tim, BOOTH Vicky, BOOTHEY Michelle, BOOTHMAN Alice, BOOTHMAN Eric, BOOTHROYD Rowland, BOOTS Harvey, BORCHERT Lydia, BORCHERT Lydia, BORDEOS Debbie, BORDEOS Dorothy, BORECKI Enilda, BOREHAM Jim, BOREHAM Jim, BOREHAM Julie, BOREHAM Leila, BOREHAM Pat, BOREHAM Richelle, BORG Angelo, BORG Carmen, BORG Emanuel, BORG John, BORG John, BORG Karen, BORG Lindsay, BORG Lorraine, BORG Lou, BORG Sam, BORG Shamere, BORG Shane, BORG Stephen, BORG Victor, BORGER Gillian, BORGER Jeanette, BORGIA Tony, BORHAM Allan, BORKUMAH Hope, BORLAND Iain, BOROS-DJEVI Tom, BORRER Emile, BORRIE Stuart, BORROW Aaron, BORTER Andrea, BORTHWICK John, BORTHWICK William, BORTOLOTTO Louise, BORWICK Adam, BOS Thea, BOS Mark, BOS Sarah, BOSANAC Denise, BOSANQUET Stephen, BOSCH Lindsay, BOSCOTT Elizabeth, BOSE Sandhya, BOSE Tusher, BOSELEY Julie-Anne, BOSEVSKI Peter, BOSHIER Marlene, BOSHOFF Donovan, BOSHOFF Eric, BOSI Peter, BOSIRE Sooze, BOSISTO Ada, BOSLEY Daniel, BOSNICH Pauline, BOSNJAK Vic, BOSNJAKOVIC Jasmina, BOSSHARD Pascal, BOSSON Cliff, BOSTOCK Byron, BOSTOCK Liz, BOSTOCK Jim, BOSTON Nathalie, BOSWELL Frederick, BOSWORTH Rebecca, BOSZE Franko, BOT Stephen, BOTEK Premysl, BOTHAM Sue, BOTT Julian, BOTTA Joe, BOTTLE Catherine, BOTTOM Arthur, BOTTOM Barbara, BOTTOM Karen, BOTTRELL Jenny, BOTTRELL Noel, BOU-ABDOU Joseph, BOUCHAFAA Khaled, BOUCHER Bobbi, BOUCHER Chadd, BOUCHER David, BOUCHER Melissa, BOUCHER Michael, BOUCHET-VIRATTE Solene, BOUCHET-VIRETTE Max, BOUGHEY Gwen, BOUGHTON Tony, BOUGHTON-DENT Joe, BOUHASSOUNE Aicha, BOULANOVITCH Sasha, BOULLOSA Sonia, BOULTON Barry, BOULTON Dave, BOULTON John, BOULTON Nigel, BOULTON Toni, BOUN Theany, BOUNDY Kaylene, BOUNGNASENG Davone, BOUNTINOS Andrea, BOUQUET Anthony, BOUREZ Martial, BOURGEOIS Genevieve, BOURK Harry, BOURKE Allison, BOURKE Darryl, BOURKE John, BOURKE June, BOURKE Kathleen, BOURKE Kelly, BOURKE Ken, BOURKE Mary, BOURKE Maureen, BOURKE Patrick, BOURKE Robert, BOURKE Ron, BOURKE Sarah, BOURKE Sheree, BOURKE Stephen, BOURKE Stephen, BOURKE Sue, BOURNE Dave, BOURNE Julia, BOURNE Margaret, BOURNE Matt, BOURNELIS Mario, BOURRIGAN Marc, BOUSTANI Nada, BOUSTRED Niell, BOUT Anita, **BOUTAGY John**, BOUTROS George, BOUTROS Jamie, BOUTROS Sam, BOVARD Geoff, BOWD Colin, BOWDEN Andrew, BOWDEN Tony, BOWDEN Tony, BOWDEN Col, BOWDEN Elizabeth, BOWDEN Garry, BOWDEN Ian, BOWDEN Ken, BOWDEN Ken, BOWDEN Mary, BOWDEN Paul, BOWDEN Ray, BOWDEN Renee, BOWDEN Robyn, BOWDEN Rosemarie, BOWDEN Ventry, BOWDEN Virginia, BOWDITCH Glynne, BOWDITCH Shane, BOWDITCH Tahlia, BOWDLER Emily, BOWE Martin, BOWE Rylie, BOWELL Jeremy, BOWEN Angela, BOWEN Ann, BOWEN Brian, BOWEN Carole, BOWEN Fraser, BOWEN Giles, BOWEN John, BOWEN Kevin, BOWEN Natalie, BOWEN Nathan, BOWEN Tyson, BOWER Ashley, BOWER Frank, BOWER Gen, BOWER Jill, BOWER Kathryn, BOWER Mick, BOWER Bob, BOWER Verity, BOWER Walter, BOWERMAN Melissa, BOWERS Charles, BOWERS Elaine, BOWERS John, BOWERS John, BOWERS Peter, BOWERS Sydney, BOWES Andrew, BOWES John, BOWIE Christine, BOWIE John, BOWKER Margaret, BOWKER Robert, BOWLER Keith, BOWLES Amanda, BOWLES Godfrey, BOWLES Jennie, BOWLES Keith, BOWLES Regina, BOWLES Vic, BOWLING Lee, BOWMAN Carole, BOWMAN Debbie, BOWMAN Kevin, BOWMAN Margaret, BOWMAN Matt, BOWMAN Bob, BOWMAN Trish, BOWMAN Ronnie, BOWMAN Warren, **BOWN Don**, BOWN Neil, BOWSHER Jacqueline, BOWYER Brad, BOWYER Colin, BOWYER John, BOX Greg, BOX Jim, BOX Julie, BOX Noel, BOX Tony, BOXALL Paddy, BOXSELL Garry, BOXX Jacob, BOYAGES Stella, BOYAKOVSKY Serge, BOYCE Alan, BOYCE Caroline, BOYCE Jane, BOYCE Pauline, BOYCE Peter, BOYCE William, BOYD Barbara, BOYD Bev, BOYD Carmen, BOYD Dan, BOYD Graeme, BOYD Jamie, BOYD Jason, BOYD Jeanette, BOYD Joel, BOYD John, BOYD Kendra, BOYD Roy, BOYD Luke, BOYD Margaret, BOYD Marcia, BOYD Noelle, BOYD Noel, BOYD Paula, BOYD Peter, BOYD Stephen, BOYD Warren, BOYER Jo, BOYES Barbara, BOYES Bill, BOYKETT David, BOYLE Andrew, BOYLE Beverley, BOYLE Debbie, BOYLE Diane, BOYLE Di, BOYLE Greg, BOYLE John, BOYLE John, BOYLE Kathryn, BOYLE Ken, BOYLE Maureen, BOYLE Richard, BOYLE Bob, BOYLE Shaun, BOYLEY Max, BOYNTON Karen, BOYS Allan, BOYS Kristen, BOYS Bob, BOYTON Diane, BOZIC Annie, BOZIKIS Denise, BOZINOVSKA Anelia, BOZINOVSKI Bobby, BOZZETTO Toni, BRAAKHUIS Simone, BRAAMSKAMP Aj, BRAAT Tom, BRABAZON Ian, BRABENEC Mary, BRABENEC Sophie, BRABHAM Debbie, BRABHAM Wendy, BRACEFIELD Emma, BRACEFIELD Robyn, BRACEY Elizabeth, BRACHER Uelp, BRACKEN Andrew, BRACKEN Daisy, BRACKENREG Jennifer, BRACKS Renee, BRADBERRY Diana, BRADBERY Juan, BRADBURN Clive, BRADBURN Jenine, BRADBURY Sue, BRADD Bradd, BRADDEN Joe, BRADDICK Jackie, BRADDY Justin, BRADEY Kathy, BRADFIELD Christine, BRADFIELD Janelle, BRADFORD Craig, BRADFORD Daphne, BRADFORD Dennis, BRADFORD Jonathan, BRADFORD Ken, **BRADFORD Kylie**, BRADFORD Maxwell, BRADFORD Sandra, BRADFORD Thomas, BRADLEY Andrew, BRADLEY Barbara, BRADLEY Cliff, BRADLEY David, BRADLEY David, BRADLEY Derek, BRADLEY Eric, BRADLEY Heather, BRADLEY Josie, BRADLEY Kathleen, BRADLEY Ken, BRADLEY Kerrie, BRADLEY Latisha, BRADLEY Michael, BRADLEY Rachael, BRADLEY Rheola, BRADLEY Sami, BRADLEY Sandy, BRADMORE Phil, BRADSHAW Andrew, BRADSHAW Carla, BRADSHAW Doug, BRADSHAW Eva, BRADSHAW John, BRADSHAW Johnny, BRADSHAW Kristen, BRADSHAW Peter, BRADSTREET Lucy, BRADWELL Harriet, BRADWELL Pat, BRADY Barry, BRADY Cheryl, BRADY Christopher, BRADY Darren, BRADY Howard, BRADY Isabella, BRADY Jeaninne, BRADY Marita, BRADY Matt, BRADY Meredith, BRADY Michelle, BRADY Joan, BRADY Trish, BRADY Peter, BRADY Robyn, BRADY Roger, BRADY Sarah, BRAGG Kerry, BRAGIAS Harry, BRAHAM Roger, BRAID Christopher, BRAID Simon, BRAIDWOOD David, BRAIDWOOD Meryl, BRAIN Audrey, BRAIN Cliff, BRAIN Doug, BRAIN George, BRAIN Jan, BRAITHWAITE Jean, BRAITHWAITE Pamela, BRAKELL Monica, BRAMBERGER Kym, BRAMLEY Jane, BRAMMALL Aimee, BRAMMER Jennifer, BRAMWELL Gavin, BRAMWELL Sarah, BRAN Audrey, BRANAGH Melissa, BRANCATISANO Amy, BRANCATO Giacomo, BRANCH Brennan, BRANCOLINO Maria, BRAND Bev, BRAND Brian, BRAND Beth, BRAND Robyn, BRAND Stuart, BRANDL John, BRANDLI Marco, BRANDON Fay, BRANDON John, BRANDON Josie, BRANDON Judy, BRANDON Kate, BRANDON Mark, BRANDON Shelley, **BRANDON-BLACK Nadia**, BRANDT Cornelius, BRANDT Dasha, BRANDT Nan, BRANDT Per, BRANIA Aj, BRANIFF Samantha, BRANN Sue, BRANNAN John, BRANNIGAN Gail, BRANSDON Tony, BRANSDON Jo, BRANT Yvonne, BRANTHWAITE Bruce, BRASH Warren, BRASSEL Jon, BRASSIL Cecilia, BRASSIL Tom, BRATANIEC Stan, BRATTON Wayne, BRAUER Margaret, BRAUN Brigitte, BRAUN Cheryl, BRAUN Gus, BRAUN Peter, BRAUNSTEIN Paula, BRAUNTHAL Simon, BRAY Anita, BRAY Diane, BRAY Jane, BRAY

Kathleen, BRAY Kerry, BRAY Pam, BRAY Peter, BRAY Sarah, BRAYBON Bev, BRAYBON Lindsay, BRAYBON Glenn, BRAYLEY Dorothy, BRAYNE Paula, BRAZIER Joanna, BRAZIL Cathy, BRCIC Diana, BREADEN Phil, BREADMAN Craig, BREAR Christine, BREARS Sarah, BRECHT Robert, BRECKENRIDGE Brian, BRECKENRIDGE Dean, BRECKENRIDGE John, BRECKENRIDGE Mikel, BRECKENRIDGE Susanne, BREDEN Jamie, BREDEN Meredith, BREE Patricia, BREED Bernie, BREEN Christopher, BREEN Jim, BREEN Maresa, BREEN Richard, BREEN Tery, BREENE James, BREESE Janice, BREESE Ross, BREEZE Grant, BREEZE Naomi, BREHENY Ben, BREIDAHL William, BREITNER Tony, BREJSEK Dennis, BREMER Rudi, BREMNER Kyla, BREMNER Susan, BRENNAN Alice, BRENNAN Annmaree, BRENNAN Anne-Marie, BRENNAN Brien, BRENNAN Dan, BRENNAN Dawn, BRENNAN Gary, BRENNAN Harry, BRENNAN Jeannette, BRENNAN Kevin, BRENNAN Kevin, BRENNAN Lachlan, BRENNAN Lisa, BRENNAN Lyn, BRENNAN Noelene, BRENNAN Trish, BRENNAN Trish, BRENNAN Paul, BRENNAN Peter, BRENNAN Peter, BRENNAN Ray, BRENNAN Rick, BRENNAN Rod, BRENNAN Ron, BRENNAN Yvonne, BRENNAN-KUSS Jo, BRENNEN Fay, BRENNER Karen, BRENT Eleanor, BRENT Michael, BRENTNALL Pamela, BRERETON Andrew, BRERETON Evan, BRERETON George, BRERETON Megan, BRERETON Nicky, BRESLIN Maureen, BRESNAHAN Brian, BRESSINGTON Mark, BRESSLER Warren, BRETNALL Heather, BRETT Cassandra, BRETT Jim, BRETT John, BRETT Kay, BRETT Marianne, BRETT Patricia, BRETT Philip, BRETT Rebecca, BRETT YOUNG Donald, BRETTELL Robyn, BRETTIG Kendall, BREUER Louise, BREUNISSEN Marc, BREW Cynthia, BREW Mary, BREW Robbie, BREWER Rob, BREWER Bill, BREWIN Karen, BREWIS Terry, BREWSTER Alan, BREWSTER Robert, BREWSTER Sarah, BRIAN Nikkola, BRIAN Russell, BRIANT Louise, BRIARS Philip, BRIBOSIA Michel, BRICK Stan, BRIDEAU Bill, BRIDEOAKE Roma, BRIDGE Christine, BRIDGE Jacque, BRIDGE Peter, BRIDGE Rob, BRIDGE Warwick, BRIDGEMENT Kaye, BRIDGES Andrew, BRIDGES Tim, BRIDGETT Lisa, BRIDGETT Victor, BRIDGMAN Caerleoon, BRIDGWOOD Wade, BRIEGER Tracey, BRIEN Bernadette, BRIEN John, BRIEN Mike, BRIERLEY Harry, BRIERLEY Len, BRIERLEY Shirley, BRIERS Elaine, BRIESE Hilary, BRIFFA Dagmar, BRIFFA Mary, BRIGDEN Doris, BRIGDEN Robyn, BRIGGS David, BRIGGS Denis, BRIGGS Derick, BRIGGS Donna, BRIGGS Dot, BRIGGS Elizabeth, BRIGGS Garry, BRIGGS Jim, BRIGGS Jason, BRIGGS Kelly, BRIGGS Margaret, BRIGGS Mick, BRIGGS Raymond, BRIGGS Bob, BRIGGS Stephanie, BRIGGS Sue, BRIGHT Ashok, BRIGHT Elaine, BRIGHT George, BRIGHT Jackie, BRIGHT Judi, BRIGHT John, BRIGHT Matt, BRIGHT Michael, BRIGHT Pete, BRIGHT Reavi, BRIGHT Sue, BRIGHTON Susan, BRIGSTOCK John, BRILL Deborah, BRILL Lauris, BRILL Nicola, BRILMAN John, BRIMBLE Marcelle, BRIMBLECOMBE Peter, BRINCAT-COTTON Carmen, BRINDELL Joyce, BRINDLE Charlie, BRINDLE Geoff, BRINER Anne, BRINGANS Kristin, BRINK Anne, BRINK Marsha, BRINKMAN Allan, BRINKWORTH Ryan, BRINLEY Kaye, BRINLEY Paul, BRIODY Jane, BRIODY Kerryn, BRIODY Kim, BRIOT Allan, BRIQUE Stephen, BRISBANE Jenny, BRISBY Louise, BRISCOE John, BRISCOE Innes, BRISCOE Olive, BRISCOE Peter, BRISCOE Richard, BRISSETT Joanne, BRISTOW Ernie, BRISTOW Jane, BRISTOW Kim, BRISTOW Lorna, BRISTOW Rhonda, BRISTOW Trevor, BRITNELL Don, BRITNELL Janet, BRITO Tamara, BRITON Jan, BRITOS John, BRITT Peter, BRITTAIN Michael, BRITTAIN Sue, BRITTEN Ian, BRITTO Andrew, BRITTO Andre, BRITTON Donna, BRITTON Nicole, BRITTON Peter, BRNCATO Lina, BROAD Benjamin, BROAD Daniel, BROAD Joan, BROAD Kel, BROAD Nicolla, BROAD Richard, BROADBENT Barbara, BROADBENT Sonia, BROADHEAD Ben, BROADHEAD Jane, BROADHEAD Jenni, BROADHEAD Ken, BROADHURST Norm, BROADHURST Steve, BROADLEY Julie, BROADLEY Kim, BROADSTOCK Jake, BROCK Faye, BROCK John, BROCK Michelle, **BROCK Peter**, BROCK-MARTIN Pau , BROCKINGTON Pete, BROCKLEY Paul, BRODIE Joan, BRODIE John, BRODIE Meg, BROE Fiona, BROE John, BROGAN Kay, BROGAN Trish, BROGAN Ross, BROGDEN Veronica, BROMELL Cheryl, BROMELL David, BROMFIELD Erin, BROMFIELD Geoff, BROMFIELD Joshua, BROMHAM Steve, BROMLEY Alicia, BROMLEY Janice, BROMLEY Leanne, BROMLEY Ruth, BROMPTON Steve, BROMWICH Harvey, BROMWICH Lorraine, BRONOTTE Jane, BRONSON Kevin, BRONTE Rebecca, BRONZINO JR Joesph, BROOK Diane, BROOK Jeremy, BROOK Michelle, BROOK Philip, BROOKE Colin, BROOKE Libby, BROOKE Lauren, BROOKE Lauren, BROOKE Lyn, BROOKE Matt, BROOKER Cathie, BROOKER Dolores, BROOKER Pauline, BROOKER Raymond, BROOKER Tanya, BROOKES Alan, BROOKES Camilla, BROOKES Carol, BROOKES David, BROOKES Dylan, BROOKES Liz, BROOKES Matt, BROOKES Skye, BROOKFIELD Glen, BROOKS Carolyn, BROOKS Damon, BROOKS David, BROOKS Janelle, BROOKS Jess, BROOKS John, BROOKS John, BROOKS Kathy, BROOKS Kevin, BROOKS Lesley, BROOKS Anne, BROOKS Louise, BROOKS Michael, BROOKS Norm, BROOKS Ondria, BROOKS Peter, BROOKS Clive, BROOKS Reg, BROOKS Rod, BROOKS Tracie, BROOKS Victoria, BROOKTON Edward, BROOME Jason, BROOME June, BROOMFIELD Roslyn, BROOMHALL Helen, BROOMHALL Rick, BROOMHEAD June, **BROPHY Denis**, BROPHY Marj, BROSCHOFSKY Tony, BROSCHOFSKY Linda, BROSOLO Jon, BROSSARD Violaine, BROTHERSTON Christine, BROTHERSTON Natalie, BROTHERSTON Robert, BROTHERTON Joan, BROUGHAM Lee, BROUGHAM Matt, BROUGHTON Garry, BROUGHTON Jeanette, BROUGHTON Sharee, BROUN Jan, BROUWER Peter, BROWN Adam, BROWN Alan, BROWN Al, BROWN Alan, BROWN Abbey, BROWN Alex, BROWN Alison, BROWN Angus, BROWN Annette, BROWN Anne, BROWN Annette, BROWN Ann, BROWN Annette, BROWN Tony, BROWN Antonia, BROWN Beatrice, BROWN Brenda, BROWN Caleb, BROWN Cameron, BROWN Caroline, BROWN Carolyn, BROWN Cathy, BROWN Charles, BROWN Charmain, BROWN Christine, BROWN Christopher, BROWN Clarinda, BROWN Cleve, BROWN Colleen, BROWN Colin, BROWN Damien, BROWN Darrell, BROWN David, BROWN David, BROWN David, BROWN David, BROWN Dave, BROWN David, BROWN David, BROWN Debbie, BROWN Deborah, BROWN Dianne, BROWN Donna, BROWN Donna, BROWN Duncan, BROWN Dwayne, BROWN Ted, BROWN Eileen, BROWN Liz, BROWN Eric, BROWN Laurie, BROWN Fiona, BROWN Fiona, BROWN Ross, BROWN Frederick, BROWN Garry, BROWN Garry, BROWN Garry, BROWN Gary, BROWN Gary, BROWN George, BROWN George, BROWN George, BROWN Geoffrey, BROWN Geraldine, BROWN Martin, BROWN Graham, BROWN Graham, BROWN Graeme, BROWN Graham, BROWN Graham, BROWN Greg, BROWN Gregory, BROWN Harry, BROWN Hazel, BROWN Heather, BROWN Heather, BROWN Hilary, BROWN Ian, BROWN Ian, BROWN Isabel, BROWN James, BROWN Jim, BROWN Jan, BROWN Jane, BROWN Jason, BROWN Jeff, BROWN Jeff, BROWN Jennifer, BROWN Jen, BROWN Jennifer, BROWN Jess, BROWN Jill, BROWN Joan, BROWN Joel, BROWN John, BROWN John, BROWN John, BROWN John, BROWN Joseph, BROWN Joe, BROWN Joy, BROWN Julieen, BROWN Julie, BROWN Julie, BROWN Justin, BROWN Katie, BROWN Kate, BROWN Kathleen, BROWN Louise, BROWN Keith, BROWN Kellie, BROWN Ken, BROWN Kerry, BROWN Kim, BROWN Kim, BROWN Kym, BROWN Laraine, BROWN Laura-Lee, **BROWN Laurette**, BROWN Laura, BROWN Lawrie, BROWN Lesley, BROWN Lexie, BROWN Lisa, BROWN Lisa-Joy, BROWN Lorraine, BROWN Lyndsay, BROWN Lyn, BROWN Malcolm, BROWN Malcolm, BROWN Mary, BROWN Margaret, BROWN Mark, BROWN Mary, BROWN Marilyn, BROWN Mark, BROWN Margaret, BROWN Matthew, BROWN Maureen, BROWN Maxine, BROWN Max, BROWN Merady, BROWN Merv, BROWN Michael, BROWN Michael, BROWN Michele, BROWN Michelle, BROWN Nan, BROWN Nathaniel, BROWN Nick, BROWN Nicola, BROWN Noeline, BROWN Noel, BROWN Pam, BROWN Pamela, BROWN Pat, BROWN Patrick, BROWN Pat, BROWN Pat, BROWN Keith, BROWN Paul, BROWN Pauline, BROWN Paul, BROWN Peter, BROWN Peter, BROWN Peter, BROWN Andy, BROWN Philip, BROWN Philip, BROWN Quentin, BROWN Ray, BROWN Ray, BROWN Becky, BROWN Rebecca, BROWN Richard, BROWN Richard, BROWN Robert, BROWN Robyn, BROWN Robert, BROWN Rona, BROWN Ron, BROWN Russell, BROWN Russell, BROWN Sam, BROWN Sam,

BROWN Sandie, BROWN Saxby, BROWN Sean, BROWN Sheena, BROWN Shirley, BROWN Sonya, BROWN Sophie, BROWN Stephanie, BROWN Steve, BROWN Steven, BROWN Steve, BROWN Stuart, BROWN Stuart, BROWN Sue, BROWN Sue, BROWN Suzanne, BROWN Syd, BROWN Terry, BROWN Terry, BROWN Trevor, BROWN Val, BROWN Vee, **BROWN Verena**, BROWN Vicki, BROWN Victoria, BROWN Vivienne, BROWNE Annette, BROWNE Chris, BROWNE Dave, BROWNE David, BROWNE Delmar, BROWNE Des, BROWNE Belle, BROWNE Emily, BROWNE Geoff, BROWNE Hayley, BROWNE Ian, BROWNE Isabel, BROWNE Ken, BROWNE Margaret, BROWNE Phillip, BROWNE Ray, BROWNE Bob, BROWNE Samantha, BROWNE Sarah, BROWNE Shirls, BROWNE Sue, BROWNE Tom, BROWNE Vic, BROWNER Katherine, BROWNIE Nancye, BROWNING Catherine, BROWNING Fiona, BROWNING Melinda, BROWNING Rick, BROWNING Simon, BROWNING Bill, BROWNJOHN Sue, BROWNLEE Dewi, BROWNLIE Joshua, BROWNSCOMBE Jeff, BRUCE Angela, BRUCE Angela, BRUCE Anita, BRUCE Ben, BRUCE Brian, BRUCE Carol, BRUCE Christine, BRUCE Daniel, BRUCE Donna, BRUCE Beth, BRUCE Elise, BRUCE George, BRUCE Grant, BRUCE Brucie, BRUCE Ian, BRUCE Karlie, BRUCE Kerry, BRUCE Kevin, BRUCE Kirsten, BRUCE Leona, BRUCE Mark, BRUCE Maureen, BRUCE Robert, BRUCE Rosalind, BRUCE Stan, BRUCE Tom, BRUCE Vivienne, BRUCH Susan, BRUCKDORFER Suzy, BRUDER Mandy, BRUENISHOLZ Eva, BRUGGEMANN Richard, BRUGGY Elsie, BRUGGY Lyndon, BRUHN Jenny, BRUHN Kelly, BRUIN Tessa, BRUININK John, BRUINSMA Pat, BRULLO Tina, BRUMMELL Bernie, BRUMMELS Doug, BRUNDRETT Gwen, BRUNELLO Damian, BRUNETTA Nardi, BRUNKER Debra, BRUNNER Jasmine, BRUNO Giuseppe, BRUNSKILL Katie, BRUNT Nicola, BRUNTON Mary, BRUNTON Sheila, BRUNTON Tim, BRUTON Lisa, BRUTON Peggy, BRUZGULIS Maris, BRUZSA Les, BRYAN Lesley, BRYAN Lynelle, BRYANT Tony, BRYANT Barbara, BRYANT Bronwen, BRYANT Christine, BRYANT Diane, BRYANT Dorothy, BRYANT Frankie, BRYANT Graeme, BRYANT Jane, BRYANT Jenny, BRYANT Joseph, BRYANT Ken, BRYANT Leila, BRYANT Margaret, BRYANT Grace, BRYANT Nick, BRYANT Nicole, BRYANT Angus, BRYANT Bob, BRYANT Sharon, BRYANT Steve, BRYANT Susan, BRYCE Alison, BRYCE Dale, BRYCE Gary, BRYCE Grace, BRYCE Shelley, BRYCE Richard, BRYCE Robyn, BRYCE Sharyn, BRYDSON Tom, BRYEN Keith, BRYEN Michael, BRYEN Steve, BRYNNER Catherine, BRYSON Julie, BRYSON Katie, BRYSON Zoe, BUBIC Andy, BUBICIC Ron, BUCCIARELLI Gianna, BUCH Niket, BUCHAL Melanie, BUCHAN Jim, BUCHAN Patti, BUCHANAN Ally, BUCHANAN David, BUCHANAN Liz, BUCHANAN Gary, BUCHANAN Gordon, BUCHANAN Grace, BUCHANAN Hugh, BUCHANAN Kate, BUCHANAN Louise, BUCHANAN Lyn, BUCHANAN Lynne, BUCHANAN Malcolm, BUCHANAN Meg, BUCHANAN Bob, BUCHANAN Shaun, BUCHANEN Sam, BUCHHOLZ Bernie, BUCHMANN Paula, BUCHNER Kate, BUCHOLTZ Fred, BUCHOLZ Karen, BUCHTA Richard, BUCINSKAS Algis, BUCK Elisabeth, BUCK Glenda, BUCK Malcolm, BUCKINGHAM Katie, BUCKLAND Barbara, BUCKLAND John, BUCKLAND Kenneth, BUCKLAND Tanya, BUCKLAND Thomas, BUCKLE Ian, BUCKLE Melissa, BUCKLE Richard, BUCKLEY Anne, BUCKLEY Ben, BUCKLEY Karen, BUCKLEY Mike, BUCKLEY Paul, BUCKLEY Rachel, BUCKLEY Rob, BUCKLEY Shaunagh, BUCKLEY Siobhan, BUCKLEY Sue, BUCKLEY Terry, BUCKLEY Terry, BUCKMAN Ken, BUCKMAN Stan, BUCKMASTER Cathy, BUCKMASTER Kevin, BUCKNELL Sarah, BUCKROYD Adam, BUCTON Jill, BUCTON Keith, BUCZAK Shirley, BUDAI June, BUDD Cheryl, BUDD Ron, BUDD Yvonne, BUDDE Roi, BUDDE Lana, BUDDEE Andrew, BUDDEN Pat, BUDDEN Peter, BUDGE Gareth, BUDGE Lindsay, BUDGE Nadine, BUDGE Robert, BUDI SANTOSO Yeni, BUDIMAN Miranda, BUDIN Leo, BUDIN Norm, BUDINSKI Fernanda, BUDLONG David, BUESNEL-MAY Glenn, BUFFETT Stuart, BUFTON Elise, BUGAR Monika, BUGARIN Robin, BUGDEN Paquita, BUGENI Doris, BUGG Dorothy, BUGG Kevin, **BUGGY Mary**, BUGLEDICH Margaret, BUHAGIAR Nathan, BUHAGIAR Zoe, BUHLER Brian, BUI Thi, BUI Bui, BUI Kim, BUKAN Parvaneh, BUKSH Barbara, BULAN Anita, BULDERSON Danielle, BULFONI David, BULGER Pat, BULGIN Kylie, BULK Patricia, BULKA Paul, BULL Alan, BULL Cheryl, BULL Colin, BULL David, BULL Devon, BULL Liz, BULL Glenn, BULL Helen, BULL Ian, BULL Jackie, BULL McQuinn, BULL Marg, BULL Melissa, BULL Neale, BULL Nigel, BULL Sarah, BULL Yolande, BULLEN Albert, BULLEN Margot, BULLEN Megs, BULLINGHAM Shirley, BULLIVANT Joan, BULLIVANT Ronald, BULLMORE Sue, BULLOCK Chris, BULLOCK Jean, BULLOCK Kathy, BULLOCK Steve, BULLUSS enevieve, BULLUSS John, BULMER Craig, BULMER Janelle, BULTITUDE Jim, BULU Reg, BUMB Jan, BUN Heng, BUN Mara, BUNBURY Christina, BUNBURY Bob, BUNCEL John, BUNCLE Adrian, BUNKER Alison, BUNKER Emma-Jayne, BUNNY Regan, BUNT Barb, BUNT Cathy, BUNT Ken, BUNT Lis, BUNTING Emily, BUNTING Meg, BUONOCORE Salvatore, BURCH Tania, BURCHETT Kerry, BURCHMORE Noel, BURCKHARDT Kristy, BURDEN Sybil, BURDEN Thomas, BURDETT Bill, BURDETT Kathy, BURDON Kerrie, BURDON Pauline, BURDON Sharon, BURFITT Peter, BURFORD Christopher, BURGDORF Catherine, BURGE-LOPEZ Peter, BURGESS Chris, BURGESS Diane, BURGESS Ian, BURGESS Jacky, BURGESS Jenny, BURGESS Jim, BURGESS Joanne, BURGESS Joel, BURGESS John, BURGESS Laurie, BURGESS Lee, BURGESS Lucinda, BURGESS Matt, BURGESS Mel, BURGESS Pam, BURGESS Patty, BURGESS Paul, BURGESS Peter, BURGESS Rachael, BURGESS John, BURGESS Scott, BURGESS Sharon, BURGESS Stuart, BURGESS Warren, BURGHARD Mary, BURGMAN Martin, BURGOS Lisa, BURGOYNE Annette, BURJI Surinder, BURKE Andy, BURKE Anne, BURKE Barbara, BURKE Barbara, BURKE Barry, BURKE Brandon, BURKE Brenda, BURKE Dawn, BURKE Frank, BURKE Gary, BURKE Ken, BURKE Pat, BURKE Raina, BURKE Roger, BURKE Rosemary, BURKE Ros, BURKE Shirley, BURKE Steve, BURKE Tania, BURKE Terry, BURKE Tim, BURKE Warren, BURKE Wayne, BURKETT Helen, BURKETT Kevin, BURKETT Trevor, BURKEVICS Bren, BURKHART John, BURKITT Wendy, BURLE Sergio, BURLEIGH Lilia, BURLEIGH Rachel, BURLEY Gloria, BURLEY Leonie, BURLEY Ngaire, BURLEY-JONES Michele, BURMAN Alan, BURMAN Allison, BURMAN Liz, BURMAN Gabi, BURN Alastair, BURN Mehau-Pa, BURNE Andrew, BURNE Col, BURNE Craig, BURNE Scott, BURNEIKIS Algis, BURNELL Bob, BURNELL Tom, BURNES Col, BURNES Kim, BURNESS Di, BURNET Ian, BURNETT Gemma, BURNETT Neville, BURNETT Bob, BURNETT Suzie, BURNETT Tracey, BURNHEIM John, BURNISTON Alan, BURNS Andrew, BURNS Barbara, BURNS Carmen, BURNS Debbie, BURNS Erin, BURNS Greg, BURNS Jamie, BURNS Jane, BURNS Janet, BURNS Judy, BURNS Katie, BURNS Kay, BURNS Kay, BURNS Kelvin, BURNS Kerrie, BURNS Kevin, BURNS Lee, BURNS Linda, BURNS Mitchell, BURNS Natalie, BURNS Pamela, BURNS Peter, BURNS Racheal, BURNS Rick, BURNS Dick, BURNS Robert, BURNS Rod, BURNS Roman, BURNS Shaun, BURNS Sharon, BURNS Sheldon, BURNS Shirley, BURNS Tennille, BURNS Vanessa, BURNS Wesley, BUROKAS Bill, BURR Daniel, BURR Dianna, BURR Gordon, BURRAGE Sandy, BURRELL John, BURRETT Roslyn, BURRIDGE Esther, BURRIDGE Raynee, BURRIDGE Bill, BURRILL Kirsty, BURRIS Bill, BURRISS Scott, BURROUGH Sue, BURROUGHS John, BURROW Alison, BURROW Barrie, BURROW Greggory, BURROWES Darryl, BURROWS David, BURROWS Liz, BURROWS Peter, BURSILL David, BURSON Peter, BURSTON Susan, BURT Andrew, BURT Celia, BURT Daniel, BURT David, BURT Greg, BURT Jenny, BURT John, BURT Mal, BURT Margaret, BURT Diana, BURT Pauline, BURT Raymond, BURT Tracey, BURTENSHAW Barbara, BURTON Alec, BURTON Barbara, BURTON Bruce, BURTON Elissa, BURTON Evelyn, BURTON Graham, BURTON James, BURTON Joyce, BURTON Julie, BURTON Karen, BURTON Karen, BURTON Kelly, BURTON Kim, BURTON Lucy, BURTON Lynelle, BURTON Marjorie, BURTON Marie, BURTON Marilyn, BURTON Margie, BURTON Monica, BURTON Philippa, BURTON Rachael, BURTON Sam, BURTON Steven, BURVILL Marlene, BURVILLE Mary, BURWOOD Mark, BURZACOTT Gary, BUSA Tina, BUSE Doreen, BUSH Andrew, BUSH Annette, BUSH Carolyn, BUSH Carol, BUSH Darren, BUSH Dudley, BUSH Elaine, BUSH Jan, BUSH Jane, BUSH Joan, BUSH John, BUSH Julie, BUSH Keith, BUSH Keith, BUSH Melissa, BUSH Natalie, BUSH Nerolle, BUSH

Olga, BUSH Paul, BUSH Toni, BUSHBY Donald, BUSHBY Les, BUSHBY Margaret, BUSHBY Mary, BUSHBY Norma, BUSHBY Rhonda, BUSHBY Bob, BUSHBY Sue, BUSHELL Dean, BUSHELL Mick, BUSPAKES Kitt, BUSSE Janice, BUSSEY Graeme, BUSSEY Anne, BUSTAMANTE David, BUSTAMANTE Gerardo, BUSTELO Raul, BUSUTTIL Christine, BUSUTTIL John, BUSUTTIL Michelle, BUTCHATSKY Virginia, BUTCHER Anthony, BUTCHER Belinda, BUTCHER Chris, BUTCHER Edward, BUTCHER Ian, BUTCHER Ian, BUTCHER Jim, BUTCHER Jonathan, BUTCHER Tina, BUTCHER Katheryn, BUTCHER Ken, BUTCHER Kylie, BUTCHER Lucinda, BUTCHER Nerida, BUTCHER Fay, BUTCHER Rachel, BUTERA Gina, BUTERA John, BUTLER Amanda, BUTLER Angela, BUTLER Tony, BUTLER Cade, BUTLER Chantelle, BUTLER Chris, BUTLER Barry, BUTLER Glenda, BUTLER Graeme, BUTLER Graham, BUTLER Graham, BUTLER Helen, BUTLER Helen, BUTLER Hugh, BUTLER Linda, BUTLER Lynn, BUTLER Margaret, BUTLER Megan, BUTLER Michael, BUTLER Noel, BUTLER Nola, BUTLER Peter, BUTLER Dick, BUTLER Rowan, BUTLER Russell, BUTLER Sally, BUTLER Scott, BUTLER Steve, BUTLER Sue, BUTLER Tim, BUTLER Trevor, BUTLER Warren, BUTLER BROWN Claire, BUTT Barrie, BUTT Craig, BUTT Gail, BUTT Kate, BUTT Margaret, BUTT Sophie, BUTTENSHAW Maxwell, BUTTENSHAW Bob, BUTTERFIELD Stacey, BUTTERWORTH Cheryl, BUTTERWORTH Greg, BUTTERWORTH Lybia, BUTTERWORTH-BOORD Natalie, BUTTIGIEG Annette, BUTTIGIEG Joe, BUTTIGIEG Karen, BUTTIGIEG Norm, BUTTINI Raffaella, BUTTINI Sandro, BUTTON Cheryl, BUTTON Colin, BUTTON Melinda, BUTTRISS Bryan, BUTTRISS Luke, BUTTSWORTH Joel, BUTTSWORTH Sandra, BUTZ Michael, BUUTS Sarah, BUVINIC Helen, BUX Lily, BUXTON Alan, BUXTON Dennis, BUXTON John, BUZZA Stuart, BUZZOLINI Mascia, BYE Sandie, BYERLEY Patricia, BYERS Lal, BYERS Di, BYKA Vijay, BYLES Noel, BYLOS Winsome, BYLOS Maisie, BYRNE Angela, BYRNE Belinda, BYRNE Bernie, BYRNE Brenda, BYRNE Brian, **BYRNE Caroline**, BYRNE Dave, BYRNE Frank, BYRNE Garry, BYRNE Graham, BYRNE Grant, BYRNE Joan, BYRNE John, BYRNE Kevin, BYRNE Kris, BYRNE Lisa, BYRNE Marianne, BYRNE Maureen, BYRNE Michael, BYRNE Padraic, BYRNE Pat, BYRNE Peter, BYRNE Ros, BYRNE Terry, BYRNE Tim, BYRNE Tommy, BYRNES Les, BYRNES Carley, BYRNES Damian, BYRNES Dorothy, BYRNES Eric, BYRNES Glenn, BYRNES Rick, BYRNES Shona, BYRNES Tim, BYRNES Bill, BYRON Denis, BYRON Karen, BYRON Narelle, BYRON Joyce, BYSTRICIAN Jiri, BYTHEWAY Jenna, BYTNEROWICZ Chris, BYUN Young-Joo, BYWATER Richard, BYWATER Wendy.

C

CABALLERO Alison, CABEZAS Patricia, CABLE Clint, CABOT Sarah, CABOT Steve, CABRERA Beth, CABRERA Humberto, CABRERA Maurice, CABRERA Bob, CABRERA Tom, CABUTE Riza, CACERES Daniel, CACHIA Cecile, CACHIA Jenny, CACHIA Phillip, CADD John, CADD Lynn, CADD Jean, CADDEN Louise, CADDY Amanda, CADEN Des, CADGE Angele, CADICK Alex, CADICK Kay, CADMAN Ralph, CADORNIGARA Plutarch, CADWALLADER Belinda, CADWALLADER Georgie, CADWALLADER Meredith, CADY Jackie, CAELLI Joan, CAESAR Clare, CAESAR Daniel, CAESAR Paul, CAESAR Joyce, CAESAR Kathryn, CAESAR-THWAYTES Richard, CAFE Claire, CAFE Dennis, CAFE Ken, CAFISO David, CAGEAO Santos, CAGER Lisa, CAGLIERO Antony, CAGLIOSTRO Vince, CAHILL Adrian, CAHILL Brian, CAHILL Chris, CAHILL Frederick, CAHILL Gillian, CAHILL Heather, CAHILL Karen, CAHILL Lauren, CAHILL Lynsell, CAHILL Maureen, CAHILL Merri, CAHILL Michelle, CAHILL Peter, **CAHOON Bradley**, CAIA Tony, CAIN Barry, CAIN Colin, CAIN Gabrielle, CAIN Mandy, CAIN Marc, CAIN Matthew, CAIN Michelle, CAIN Neill, CAIN Steve, CAINE John, CAINE Peter, CAINES Emma, CAINS Kathryn, CAINS Virginia, CAIRN-DUFF Doreen, CAIRN-DUFF Ron, CAIRNCROSS Nathan, CAIRNCROSS Claudette, CAIRNCROSS Melanie, CAIRNDUFF Chris, CAIRNEY Sarah, CAIRNS Andrew, CAIRNS Angela, CAIRNS Douglas, CAIRNS Jan, CAIRNS Jo, CAIRNS Peter, CAIRNS Rau, CAJES Remy, CAKEBREAD Peter, CALA Michael, CALABRESE Tino, CALABRESI Linda, CALABRIA Peter, CALABRO Isabella, CALABRO Romina, CALANDRA Sam, CALANGI Khristine, CALANGI Marie, CALANGI Maximino, CALANGI Shiela, CALARA Alvard, CALCOTT Sharon, CALDAREVIC Maria, CALDART Francesca, CALDBECK-MOORE Thea, CALDECOTT Keith, CALDER Gregory, CALDER Matthew, CALDER Maureen, CALDER Paul, CALDER Phillippa, CALDER Stephanie, CALDERAZZO Adey, CALDERON Patricia, CALDERON Bob, CALDERSMITH Brian, CALDERWOOD Butch, CALDWELL Bruce, CALDWELL Elaine, CALDWELL Grant, CALDWELL Jackie, CALDWELL Bundle, CALDWELL Margaret, CALDWELL Robert, CALDWELL Steve, CALDWELL Tania, CALDWELL Zeta, CALDWELL PETERSON Ben, CALE Sandi, CALLAGHAN Betty, CALLAGHAN Carla, CALLAGHAN Glen, CALLAGHAN Clarke, CALLAGHAN Denise, CALLAGHAN Gary, CALLAGHAN Ivan, CALLAGHAN Josh, CALLAGHAN Joy, CALLAGHAN Kerry, CALLAGHAN Lindsey-Anne, CALLAGHAN Martin, CALLAGHAN Michael, CALLAGHAN Pam, CALLAGHAN Paul, CALLAGHAN Peter, CALLAGHAN Reay, CALLAGHAN Rob, CALLAGHAN Roger, CALLAGHER Jo-Ann, CALLAHAN Denise, CALLANAN Mary, CALLANDER Wendy, CALLAWAY Mark, CALLEJA Andrea, CALLEJA Maria, CALLEJA Victor, CALLEN David, CALLEN Phil, CALLENDER Jean, CALLIER Lukas, CALLIER Trisha, CALLIGAS Maria, CALLINAN Robert, CALLINGHAM Geoff, CALLINGHAM Margaret, CALLISTER Kimi, CALLOW Darren, CALLUY John, CALMAN Susan, CALTABIANO Santo, CALUGAY Chris, CALVERT Elaine, CALVERT Josie, CALVERT Lorelle, CALVETE Manola, CALVI Jeanette, CALVO Di, CAMA James, CAMAC Anne, CAMALIG Villiesa, CAMARA Jocelyn, CAMARENA Katie, CAMARSH Kay, CAMBAGE Ruth, CAMDEN Jodie, CAMDEN Lorraine, CAMDEN Philip, CAMENZULI James, CAMENZULI Patricia, CAMER Reg, CAMERELLI Umberto, CAMERON Alan, CAMERON Alix, CAMERON Allan, CAMERON Ann, CAMERON Tony, CAMERON Barbara, CAMERON Berry, CAMERON Bruce, CAMERON Chris, CAMERON Clare, CAMERON Barry, CAMERON Donald, CAMERON Fergus, CAMERON Geoff, CAMERON Gordon, CAMERON Graeme, CAMERON Hayley, CAMERON Heather, CAMERON Holly, CAMERON Ian, CAMERON Chris, CAMERON James, CAMERON Jo, CAMERON Alex, CAMERON Kathleen, CAMERON Kerith, CAMERON Lindy, CAMERON Marlene, CAMERON Merryl, CAMERON Pam, CAMERON Pat, CAMERON Paul, CAMERON Robert, CAMERON Robyn, CAMERON Ron, CAMERON Simon, CAMERON Steve, CAMERON Sue, CAMERON Terry, CAMERON Virginia, CAMERON Wendy, CAMERON-JOHNS Tony, CAMERON-LEE Heike, CAMILLERI Tony, CAMILLERI Christine, CAMILLERI Frank, CAMILLERI John, CAMILLERI Louise, CAMILLERI Mark, CAMILLERI Mick, CAMILLERI Michelle, CAMILLERI Paul, CAMILLERI Yvonne, CAMINITI Danni, CAMMACK Marcus, CAMPBELL Russell, CAMPBELL Allyson, CAMPBELL Barbara, CAMPBELL Bruce, CAMPBELL Chris, CAMPBELL Colin, CAMPBELL Colin, CAMPBELL Danielle, CAMPBELL Daniel, CAMPBELL Darryl, CAMPBELL David, CAMPBELL David, CAMPBELL Deion, CAMPBELL Denzil, CAMPBELL Elizabeth, CAMPBELL Fleur, CAMPBELL Gabe, CAMPBELL Gail, CAMPBELL Graham, CAMPBELL Hannah, CAMPBELL Heather, CAMPBELL Helen, CAMPBELL Helen, CAMPBELL Ian, CAMPBELL Ian, CAMPBELL Irene, CAMPBELL Ron, CAMPBELL Jess, CAMPBELL Jillian, CAMPBELL Joe, CAMPBELL Judy, CAMPBELL Julie, CAMPBELL Katy, CAMPBELL Keiko, CAMPBELL Kerrie, CAMPBELL Kevin, CAMPBELL Kirsten, CAMPBELL Leanne, **CAMPBELL Linda**, CAMPBELL Louise, CAMPBELL Luke, CAMPBELL Maria, CAMPBELL Maureen, CAMPBELL Mel, CAMPBELL Melanie, CAMPBELL Nats, CAMPBELL Neil, **CAMPBELL Nichole**, CAMPBELL Rose, CAMPBELL Pauline, CAMPBELL Peter, CAMPBELL Peter, CAMPBELL Pete, CAMPBELL Rach, CAMPBELL Robert, CAMPBELL Robert, CAMPBELL Rodney, CAMPBELL Ross, CAMPBELL Sandy, CAMPBELL Sarah, CAMPBELL Sarah, CAMPBELL Sharon, CAMPBELL Shirleyann, CAMPBELL Stephen, CAMPBELL Sue, CAMPBELL Toni, CAMPBELL Viki, CAMPBELL Wanda, CAMPBELL Wayne, CAMPBELL Wendy, CAMPBELL William, CAMPBELL Bill, CAMPBELL-BUTLER Anthony, CAMPBELL-PATTERSON Robbie, CAMPESE Wakako, CAMPEY Don, CAMPION Fay, CAMPION Joanne, CAMPION Margaret, CAMPION Peter, CAMPISI Laura, CAMPOS

Juan, CAMPOS Milly, CAMPOS GONZALEZ Marcos, CAMPTON Ann, CAMPTON Don, CAMPTON Maria, CAN Ulker, CANALESE Joseph, CANARD Marion, CANAS Canas, CANAVAN June, CANDILORO Bruna, CANDILORO Sam, CANDILORO Steve, CANDIOTTI Ruben, CANDLER Renee, CANDLER Rick, CANDRA Swandi, CANDRICK Ted, CANDY Pauline, CANE Steven, CANGIAMILA Rob, CANHAM Elissia, CANHAM Linda, CANHAM Terry, CANNAVO Maureen, CANNING Greg, CANNING Nikki, CANNON Anita, CANNON Christine, CANNON Gill, CANNON Lyndy, CANNON Paul, CANO Felipe, CANOQUENA Costa, CANSDELL Fran, CANSFIELD-SMITH Christine, CANSFIELD-SMITH Tim, CANSICK Stuart, CANTALI Maria, CANTARELLA Christine, CANTON Annette, CANTOR Barry, CANTURI Angelina, CANTWELL KC, CANTWELL Roger, CANTWELL Vicki, CANU Jan, CANUTE Ina, CANUTE Peter, CANVIN Thomas, CAO Catherine, CAO Jane, CAO Li, CAO Shao, CAO Weifeng, CAON Suzan, CAPALDI Aldo, CAPANNA Dionne, CAPDOR Christine, CAPE Sophie, CAPEL Bmitry, CAPEL Jay, CAPEWELL Claire, CAPEWELL Max, CAPIZZI Mark, CAPIZZI Matt, CAPLAN Sophie, CAPOBIANCO Susan, **CAPON Rob**, CAPORN Adam, CAPORN Lorraine, CAPOVILLA Marisa, CAPOZZI COMIS Maria, CAPPELLETTO Walter, CAPPELLI Dianne, CAPPELLIN Sergio, CAPPER Evelyn, CAPPS Judith, CAPSANIS Tessa, CAPSIS George, CAPUYAN Jhosie, CAR Julie, CARABALLO Luis, CARAPELLOTTI Anna, CARAVAN Jean-pierre, CARAVELLO Dominic, CARAVIAS Tony, CARBINE Glenda, CARBONE Carol, CARBONE Domenico, CARBONE Mario, CARBONE Vic, CARBONI Adriana, CARBUTT Kel, CARD Jayde, CARDEN Melanie, CARDENAS Eduardo, CARDENAS Lilia, CARDENAS Sebastian, CARDIA CUNHA Shana, CARDON Yohann, CARDWELL Frances, CARDWELL Josh, CARDWELL Norm, CAREW Mark, CAREW Rob, CAREW Russell, CAREY Cherilyn, CAREY Dee, CAREY Judy, CAREY Kerrelyn, CAREY Max, CAREY Louise, CAREY Maria, CAREY Margaret, CAREY Narelle, CAREY Penny, CAREY Steve, CAREY Susan, CAREY Tracey, CAREY Val, CAREY Veronica, CAREY Bill, CAREY FINCH Simon, CARGILL Jenni, CARGILL Kirsty, CARILLO Kevin, CARINO Ed, CARLE Amanda, CARLE Lesley-Anne, CARLESS Laura, CARLEY Geoff, CARLILE Jacqui, CARLILL Christopher, CARLISLE Alan, CARLISLE-GRAHAM Joy, CARLISLE-JONES Su, CARLOS Lili, CARLOSS Noel, CARLOW Marilyn, CARLSEN Lesley, CARLSON Nartira, CARLTON Christine, CARLUCCI Anthony, CARLYLE Alan, CARLYON David, CARLYON Kim, CARLYON Kim, CARMALT Alan, CARMAN Frank, CARMICHAEL James, CARMICHAEL Josh, CARMICHAEL Thomas, CARMODY Annabelle, CARMODY John, CARMONT Carole, CARNEGIE John, CARNEIRO Maria, CARNEY Amber, CARNEY Eric, CARNEY Graham, CARNEY Ian, CARNEY Warren, CARNUCCIO Joe, CARNUCCIO Michael, CARO David, CAROZZI Piers, CARPENTER Amy, CARPENTER Darrell, CARPENTER Dionne, CARPENTER Liz, CARPENTER Steve, CARPENTER Bruce, CARPINO Vincent, CARR Tony, CARR April, CARR Ashley, CARR Brenda, CARR Danielle, CARR David, CARR Elizabeth, CARR Gary, CARR Gardie, CARR Helen, CARR Jennifer, CARR John, CARR John, CARR Justin, CARR Linda, CARR Linda, CARR Marcia, CARR Matt, CARR Naomi, CARR Nick, CARR Nicole, CARR Nicrel, CARR Nigel, CARR Paul, CARR Peter, CARR Sophie, CARR Steven, CARR Terry, CARR Wendy, CARR-BROWN Chris, CARRAFA David, CARRANZA Carla, CARRANZA Malou, CARRASCO Andrew, CARRASCO Miguel, CARRATT Hayley, CARRENO Paul, CARRETO Emilo, CARRETO Frieda, CARRETO Patricia, CARREY Jim, CARRICK Alicia, CARRICK Beverly, CARRICK Max, CARRICK Myles, CARRICK Cindy, CARRINGTON Michelle, CARRINGTON Micheal, CARRINGTON Tracey, CARRION Nancy, CARRITT Rebecca, CARROLL Brian, CARROLL Celia, CARROLL Tina, CARROLL Elizabeth, CARROLL Elizabeth, CARROLL Fiona, CARROLL Greg, CARROLL John, CARROLL Juliet, CARROLL Logan, CARROLL Louise, CARROLL Mary, CARROLL Mark, CARROLL Monica, CARROLL Nathan, CARROLL Niall, CARROLL Owen, CARROLL Richard, CARROLL Bob, CARROLL Rory, CARROLL Sean, CARROLL Steve, CARROLL Sue, CARROLL Jak, CARROLL Tim, CARRON Caroline, CARRUTHERS Anne, CARRUTHERS Annette, CARRUTHERS Auriol, CARRUTHERS Brett, CARSE Stuart, CARSON Di, CARSON Irene, CARSON Allison, CARSON Jo, CARSON Joanne, CARSON Marie, CARSON Maureen, CARSON Noel, CARSON Tom, CARSON Vic, CARSTENS Jean-Paul, CARTEAU Elisabeth, CARTER Andrew, CARTER Anna, CARTER Babs, CARTER Benjamin, CARTER Carol, CARTER Cec, CARTER Cheryl, CARTER Chikako, CARTER Chris, CARTER Cliff, CARTER Colleen, CARTER Deidre, CARTER Don, CARTER Fiona, CARTER Jean, CARTER John, CARTER Katriona, CARTER Kaye, CARTER Keith, CARTER Kym, CARTER Lauren, CARTER Leanne, CARTER Lee, CARTER Len, CARTER Lew, CARTER Lyn, CARTER Joy, CARTER Meg, CARTER Mencia, CARTER Nicki, CARTER Olivia, CARTER Jill, CARTER Paul, CARTER Peter, CARTER Philip, CARTER Ray, CARTER Rhys, CARTER Stacey, CARTER Steven, CARTER Verna, CARTER Warren, CARTER Wayne, CARTER Bill, CARTIANU Ted, CARTLAND Emma, CARTWRIGHT Anthony, CARTWRIGHT Fiona, CARTWRIGHT Jeff, CARTWRIGHT Kaye, CARTWRIGHT Margaret, CARTWRIGHT Pauline, CARTWRIGHT Sandra, CARUANA Anthony, CARUANA Josie, CARUSO Antony, CARUSO Carol, CARUSO Carla, CARUSO Vince, CARUZI John, CARVAJAL Raquel, CARVALLO Melissa, CARVER Robert, CARVETH Sally, CARWANA Tanya, CARY Megan, CARY Becci, CARY Warwick, CASACELI Loretta, CASADIO Cinzia, CASAGRANDE Zaccaria, CASAMENTO Sonia, CASAS Oscar, CASAS Tony, CASAURANG Emmanuelle, CASBURN Phillip, CASCAIS Maria, CASCUN-VALENCIC Sarah, CASEY Anne-Nicole, CASEY David, CASEY Jim, CASEY Judy, CASEY Majella, CASEY Mary, CASEY Matthew, CASEY Monica, CASEY Nance, CASEY Peter, CASEY Sarah, CASH Graham, CASHEL William, CASHION Mark, CASHMAN Anita, CASHMAN Coral, CASHMAN Garry, CASHMAN Mike, CASHMAN Ralph, CASIDSID Nette, CASIDSID JR Jun, CASKA John, CASNICO Leonardo, CASPERSON Jennifer, CASS Brian, CASS Julie, CASS Shelley, CASS-DUNBAR Randy, CASSANO Leny, CASSAR Edgar, CASSAR Joe, CASSAR Trish, CASSAR Stephen, CASSEL Julie, CASSEL Lola, CASSELL Barbara, CASSELL Brad, CASSELL John, CASSELL Sarah, CASSELL Stewart, CASSELLS Brigid, CASSELLS Heather, CASSELLS Michele, CASSEMATIS George, CASSETTARI Stephen, CASSIAN Angie, CASSIDY Alec, CASSIDY Belinda, CASSIDY Col, CASSIDY Jenny, CASSIDY Katrina, CASSIDY Kathryn, CASSIDY Mark, CASSIDY Nerolli, CASSIDY Peter, CASSIDY Rachel, CASSIDY Sally, CASSIDY Wes, CASSIDY Zoe, CASSIMATIS John, CASSIMATIS Mark, CASSIMATIS Sophie, CASSIMATY Anthony, CASSIMATY Chrissie, CASSIMATY Syd, CASSIS Antoine, CASTANEDA Christian, CASTANEDA Hazel, CASTANEDA Oscar, CASTANEROS Aida, CASTANHA Guilherme, CASTELL-BROWN TC, CASTELLETTO Alida, CASTELLINO Daryl, CASTGIR Abc, CASTILE Paula, CASTILLO Ben, CASTILLO Erwin, CASTILLO Francis, CASTINE Chris, CASTINE Kate, CASTINE Richard, CASTLE Andy, CASTLE Belinda, CASTLE Belinda, CASTLE Jenny, CASTLE Karina, CASTLE Keith, CASTLE Les, CASTLE Linda, CASTLE Maureen, CASTLE Peter, CASTLE Phillip, CASTLEHOUSE Christine, CASTLEHOW Heather, CASTLETON Graeme, CASTLEY Susan, CASTRISOS Jean, CASTRISOS Roz, CASTRO Edith, CASTRO Ed, CASTRO Hugo, CASTRO Cecilia, CASTRO Mario, CASTRO Nazare, CASTRO Nikki, CASTRO-MARTINEZ Adriana, CASWELL Elaine, CASWELL Sheena, CATALANO Daniela, CATALANO Vera, CATALLO Edwin, CATANIA Michael, CATANZARITI Dominic, CATCHLOVE Eliza, CATCHPOOLE Vic, CATEAU Cecile, CATEN Beryl, CATER Daniel, CATER Elaine, CATES Andrew, CATES Bronwyn, CATHCART Vivienne, CATHERALL Jade, CATHERIN Dominic, CATHERINE Marilyn, CATO Damian, CATO Kenneth, CATON Doris, CATON Yvonne, CATORALL Belinda, CATT Adrian, CATT Allan, CATT Steve, CATTANACH Jan, CATTARINUZZI Luisa, CATTELL Matthew, CATTO Denis, CATTUZZO Tania, CAUCHI Alfred, CAUDULLO Helen, CAULFIELD Greg, CAUNT Steven, CAUNT Trevor, CAUSBY Penny, CAUSER Marjorie, CAUSER Noel, CAUSON Kathryn, CAUSON Max, CAUST Elmo, CAV Nicky, CAVACO Adelaide, CAVALLARO Rosa, **CAVANAGH Hatsue**, CAVANAGH John, CAVANAGH John, CAVANAGH Michelle, CAVANAGH Pamela, CAVANAGH Sarah, CAVANAGH Tim, CAVANAGH Wendy, CAVANAUGH David, CAVE Val, CAVELL Adrienne, CAVELL Carole, CAVENAGH Libby, CAWLEY Sue, CAWOOD

Geoff, CAWOOD Gregory, CAWSEY Shellee, CAWTE Ian, CAWTE Michelle, CAWTHORN Daryl, CAYZER Tory, CAZALET-SMITH Fiona, CAZAR Erick, CAZENAVE Selvi, CECCATO Jen, CECCHIN Anna-Marie, CECHANSKI Janet, CECINS Janis, CEDENO Andres, CELEA Daniella, CELIC Heather, CELIO Dom, CELLEDONI Louise, CELLONA Julieta, CEMALI Ozdem, CEN Zhi, CENCIGH Reno, CENDANA Suding, CENIT Cenit, CENIUK Margaret, CENTOFANTI Claude, CERDA-PAVIA Elizabeth, CEREZO Mari-Mar, CERNA Carlos, CERNA Deb, CERNOT Ugo, CEROLI Rosanna, CERONE Mark, CERONE-DAWBNEY Linda, CERVETTO Bill, CESAR Mario, CESARO Serge, CESNIK Peter, CETIN Akin, CETINICH George, CEWE-OEHMAN Karin, CHA Andrew, CHA Sang-Dae, CHAALAN Rhoda, CHABREL Desmond, CHAD Kate, CHAD Paul, CHADBOURNE Ed, CHADD Tim, CHADHA Chand, CHADHA Rita, CHADWICK David, CHADWICK Gwenda, CHADWICK Warren, CHAE Sunny, CHAE Ji-Eun, CHAFFER Ray, CHAFFEY Wayne, CHAFFEY Brooke, CHAFFEY Peter, CHAFFEY Rex, CHAGGAR Ajitpal, CHAHINE Aida, CHAHINE Sid, CHAI Huiting, CHAI Imelda, CHAI Sharon, CHAIB Nordine, CHAITOW Jonathan, CHAKRABORTY Sumalya, CHAKRAVARTY Subhangi, CHALK Joan, CHALKE Emma, CHALKER Dawn, CHALLINOR Lynne, CHALLITA Gina, CHALMERS Bruce, C ALMERS Dale, CHALMERS Emma, CHALMERS-POTTER Toni, CHAM Douglas, CHAM Vivian, CHAMBERLAIN Catherine, CHAMBERLAIN David, CHAMBERLAIN Deb, CHAMBERLAIN Garry, CHAMBERLAIN Helen, CHAMBERLAIN James, CHAMBERLAIN Lloyd, CHAMBERLAIN Paul, CHAMBERLAIN Rex, CHAMBERLIN James, CHAMBERS Lyn, CHAMBERS Chris, CHAMBERS Jill, CHAMBERS Joyce, CHAMBERS Julie, CHAMBERS Ann, CHAMBERS Maureen, CHAMBERS Olivia, CHAMBERS Pat, CHAMBERS Chambers, CHAMBERS Susan, CHAMBERS Timothy, CHAMI Khalil, CHAMI Nadia, CHAMPION Belinda, CHAMPION Beryl, CHAMPION Debbie, CHAMPION Ernie, CHAMPION Russ, CHAMPION Kerry, CHAMPION Wilma, CHAMRONG Thirak, CHAN Alan, CHAN Alan, CHAN Albert, CHAN Alex, CHAN Alice, CHAN Amanda, CHAN Amy, CHAN Andrew, CHAN Angela, CHAN Angela, CHAN Anita, CHAN Annette, CHAN Betty, CHAN Brian, CHAN Cecilia, CHAN Charles, CHAN Edward, CHAN Simon, CHAN Connie, CHAN David, CHAN Dennis, CHAN Dominic, CHAN Donald, CHAN Douglas, CHAN Edwin, CHAN Elsie, CHAN Francis, CHAN Gary, CHAN George, CHAN Greta, CHAN Hannah, CHAN Hei, CHAN Helen, CHAN Helen, CHAN Helen, CHAN Herika, CHAN Lammy, CHAN Natalie, CHAN Hong, CHAN How, CHAN Howard, CHAN Howard, CHAN Irene, CHAN Jackson, CHAN Jackson, CHAN Jodie, CHAN Joel, CHAN John, CHAN Karen, CHAN Karen, CHAN Kelvin, CHAN Karen, CHAN Kenneth, CHAN Hoe, CHAN Kim, CHAN Eric, CHAN Leanne, CHAN Karen, CHAN Lita, CHAN Lulu, CHAN Lynnette, CHAN Mabel, CHAN Mannie, CHAN Mark, CHAN Mark, CHAN Marco, CHAN Maria, CHAN Mayin, CHAN Michael, CHAN Michael, CHAN Betty, CHAN Olivia, CHAN David, CHAN Pat, CHAN Patricia, CHAN Patsy, CHAN Paul, CHAN Peter, CHAN Peter, CHAN Philip, CHAN Ping, CHAN Pui, CHAN Vicky, CHAN Rachel, CHAN Ricci, CHAN Sharon, CHAN Amy, CHAN Charles, CHAN Siu, CHAN Stephanie, CHAN Susan, CHAN Sylvia, CHAN Celine, CHAN Janet, CHAN Brian, CHAN David, CHAN Tom, CHAN Chan, CHAN Jackie, CHAN Toby, CHAN Trinity, CHAN Dairie, CHAN Tsz, CHAN Vivian, CHAN W.Liwanna, CHAN Dany, CHAN Wai, CHAN Chris, CHAN Wan, CHAN Wendy, CHAN Iris, CHAN Simon, CHAN Yat, CHAN Yat, CHAN Carmen, CHAN YAI CHING Sandra, CHANDALLY Sharon, CHANDLER Allan, CHANDLER Carol, CHANDLER David, CHANDLER Dave, CHANDLER Greig, CHANDLER James, CHANDLER Jenny, CHANDLER Pippa, CHANDLER Richard, CHANDLER Shaun, CHANDLER Thelma, CHANDRA Alex, CHANDRA Alzira, CHANDRA Amit, CHANDRA Julie, CHANDRA Marcellus, CHANDRA Merlin, CHANDRA Seema, CHANDRA Tjan, CHANDRA Vishal, CHANDRACHUDAN Neeraja, CHANDRAN David, CHANDRASEKARAN Chandra, CHANDRASENA Nirmal, CHANEKON Tiffany, CHANEY Aaron, CHANEY John, CHANEY Margie, CHANEY Rosemary, CHANG Chang-Hee, CHANG Chia, CHANG Douglas, CHANG Esther, CHANG Evonne, CHANG Gilman, CHANG Grace, CHANG Howie, CHANG Hyangsook, CHANG Colin, CHANG Linda, CHANG May, CHANG Sam, CHANG Sang-Won, CHANG Taylor, CHANG Teresa, CHANG Tshung, CHANG Wan, CHANG Wei, CHANG Joy, CHANG Young, CHANG Jessica, CHANG Yuling, CHANG CHIN LUAN Steven, CHANGTOO Pranee, CHANNELL Glenn, CHANNELL Sandra, CHANNELLS Darryl, CHANNELLS Michelle, CHANNELLS Rita, CHANNON Michelle, CHANNON Therese, CHANSAMOOTH Anfernee, CHANT Samantha, CHANT Vanessa, CHAO Eileen, CHAOVALIT Patamanont, CHAPERON Danique, CHAPLIN Denise, CHAPLIN Mike, CHAPLIN Robyn, CHAPLIN Vicky, CHAPMAN Alan, CHAPMAN Brian, CHAPMAN Annette, CHAPMAN Barbara, CHAPMAN Brian, CHAPMAN Catherine, CHAPMAN Catherine, CHAPMAN Christine, CHAPMAN Dorothea, CHAPMAN Elizabeth, CHAPMAN Ernie, CHAPMAN Betty, CHAPMAN Francis, CHAPMAN Gary, CHAPMAN Geoff, CHAPMAN Georgie, CHAPMAN Graeme, CHAPMAN Graeme, CHAPMAN Graham, CHAPMAN Grant, CHAPMAN Halina, CHAPMAN Derek, CHAPMAN Ian, CHAPMAN Jodie, CHAPMAN John, CHAPMAN Karen, CHAPMAN Kate, CHAPMAN Kathleen, CHAPMAN Lyn, CHAPMAN Maureen, CHAPMAN Bob, CHAPMAN Sophie, CHAPMAN Sue, **CHAPMAN Tracy**, CHAPMAN Tracey, CHAPMAN Troy, CHAPMAN Yvette, CHAPPELL David, **CHAPPELL Therese**, CHAPPIUS Pauline, CHAPPLE Allan, CHAPPLE Mandy, CHAPPLE Annelie, CHAPPLE Colin, CHAPPLE Daniel, CHAPPLE Geoff, CHAPPLE Jean, CHAPPLE Neale, CHAPPLE Reginald, CHAPPLE Scott, CHAPPLE Shelley, CHAPPLE Sid, CHARALAMBOU Sonia, CHARALAMBOUS Anne, CHARBINE Hisham, CHARD Donna, CHARD Jenny, CHARD Margaret, CHARETTE Jason, CHARGE Betty, CHARGE Jo, CHARGE Lynne, CHARGE Neil, CHARGE Vanessa, CHARILAOU Harry, CHARILAOU Helen, CHARITY Faith, CHARKAWI Fay, CHARKER Elaine, CHARLES Brit, CHARLES Emma, CHARLES Rob, CHARLES Wayne, CHARLSTON-PEARCE Sharon, CHARLTON Alan, CHARLTON Alicen, CHARLTON Angus, CHARLTON Ewan, CHARLTON Marian, CHARLTON Lucy, CHARLTON Murray, CHARLTON Robert, CHARLTON Sarah, CHARLTON Sue, CHARLTON Tom, CHARLTON Warren, CHARLWOOD Geoffrey, CHARPENTIER Sophie, CHARRETT David, CHARTER Ron, CHASE Colin, CHASE Col, CHASE Heather, CHASE Lillian, CHASE Bob, CHASELING Margaret, CHASLE Aimee, CHASTON Jenny, CHATFIELD Tony, CHATKAEW Natalie, CHATWIN Yvonne, CHAU Charles, CHAU Kinh, CHAU Raymond, CHAU Yennie, CHAUDHRI D, CHAUDHRY Aamir, CHAUDHRY Asim, CHAUDHRY Afif, CHAUDHRY Rajah, CHAUDHRY Sumrah, CHAUHAN Arun, CHAUHAN Bhagwat, CHAV Ta, CHAVEZ Barbara, CHAVEZ Eliana, CHAVEZ Gueza, CHAVEZ Carolina, CHAWLA Priya, CHAWSHIN Amelda, CHE Sze, CHEA Bun, CHEA Ty, CHEADLE Eleanor, CHEADLE Kevin, CHEADLE Sally, CHEAH Joe, CHEAH June, CHEAH Kuan, CHEAH Stephen, CHEALES Barry, CHEALS Hazel, CHEAM Joyce, CHEAN Raymond, CHECKER Michelle, CHEE Andrew, CHEE Charmaine, CHEE Herb, CHEE Wilfred, CHEESEMAN Matt, CHEESMAN Gary, CHEESMAN Pamela, CHEETHAM Brett, CHEETHAM Dennis, CHEETHAM Helen, CHEETHAM Kylie, CHEETHAM Marjorie, CHEETHAM Penny, CHEETHAM Tom, CHEETI Nanda, CHEGWIDDEN Grahame, CHEGWIDDEN Neil, CHEKROUN Majid, CHELBERG George, CHELLAMUTHU Ben, CHELLAPPAH Selva, CHELTON Rene, CHELVANAYAGAM Chelva, CHEMLER Ron, CHEN Albert, CHEN Alice, CHEN Allan, CHEN Andy, CHEN Annie, CHEN Anthea, CHEN Bert, CHEN Carmen, CHEN Catherine, CHEN Eddy, CHEN Charles, CHEN Chang-Kai, CHEN Chee, CHEN Chun, CHEN Fang, CHEN Fiona, CHEN Joan, CHEN Hua, CHEN Irene, CHEN Jack, CHEN Jane, CHEN Chen, CHEN Jennifer, CHEN Jian, CHEN Lily, CHEN Justin, CHEN Joy, CHEN Juan, CHEN Justin, CHEN Kevin, CHEN Maverick, CHEN Kuo, CHEN Lei, CHEN Joe, CHEN Lily, CHEN Michael, CHEN LingYun, CHEN Lorraine, CHEN Mary, CHEN Mian, CHEN Peggy, CHEN Peter, CHEN Radeth, CHEN Robert, CHEN Sally, CHEN Sandy, CHEN Sen, CHEN Shang-Yih, CHEN Shi, CHEN Tina, CHEN Titi, CHEN Victor, CHEN Wenwu, CHEN Wei, CHEN Wei-xiang, CHEN Wei-Xiang, CHEN Wei, CHEN Wei, CHEN Wu-Sheng, CHEN William, CHEN May, CHEN Xue, CHEN Eli, CHEN YU, CHEN Kathy, CHEN Master,

CHEN Zao-Wei, CHEN David, CHEN Jan, CHEN Zhong, CHEN Zhong, CHENERY Mark, CHENEY Debby, CHENEY Gail, CHENG Bessy, CHENG Carol, CHENG Cheryl, CHENG Curtis, CHENG David, CHENG Derek, CHENG Eddy, CHENG Eva, CHENG Hiu, CHENG Jason, CHENG Jennifer, CHENG Joanne, CHENG Joseph, CHENG Judy, CHENG Katrina, CHENG Kevin, CHENG Kenny, CHENG Kwan, CHENG Mandy, CHENG Micheal, CHENG Nancy, CHENG Neil, CHENG Olivia, CHENG Rick, CHENG Ronny, CHENG Proson, CHENG Siu, CHENG Sue, CHENG Terence, CHENG Timothy, CHENG Wendy, CHENG Wilson, CHENG May, CHENG Ya-Wen, CHENG Tammy, CHENG Yvonne, CHENH Lyly, CHENOWETH Lawrie, CHEONG Anthony, CHEONG David, CHEQUER Ron, CHEREDNICHENKO Natasha, CHERIAN Sunny, CHERNENKO Yuri, CHERROUK Nesrine, CHERRY Ceridwen, CHERRY Monica, CHERRY Robyn, CHERTOK Eugene, CHERVONSKY Sonya, CHESSELL Adam, CHESSELL Bruce, CHESTER Kevin, CHESTER Margaret, CHESTER Robyn, CHESTER Rob, CHESTER Steve, CHESTER-MASTER Robert, CHESTERKING Carolina, CHESTERTON Valerie, CHETTLE Brian, CHETTY Kribbs, CHETTY Naven, CHETTY Rajen, CHEUK Christine, CHEUNG Ada, CHEUNG Adrian, CHEUNG Adrian, CHEUNG Alda, CHEUNG Alice, CHEUNG Anthony, CHEUNG Arlene, CHEUNG Catherine, CHEUNG Cody, CHEUNG Doreen, CHEUNG Eddy, CHEUNG Eddie, CHEUNG Flora, CHEUNG Kylie, CHEUNG Gerald, CHEUNG Gwinny, CHEUNG Hans, CHEUNG Helena, CHEUNG Helen, CHEUNG Alvin, CHEUNG Jackie, CHEUNG Jacqueline, CHEUNG Ka, CHEUNG Ka, CHEUNG Ki, CHEUNG Anne, CHEUNG Linda, CHEUNG Louisa, CHEUNG Marie, CHEUNG Michael, CHEUNG Nathan, CHEUNG Ozona, CHEUNG Ricky, CHEUNG Queenie, CHEUNG Angela, CHEUNG Vivian, CHEUNG William, CHEUNG Wendy, CHEVASSUS Patrick, CHEVIS John, CHEW Alicia, CHEW Anna, CHEW Antony, CHEW Ching, CHEW David, CHEW Gail, CHEW John, CHEW Korin, CHEW Lisa, CHEW Nicole, CHEW Rae, CHEW Richard, CHEW Roselyn, CHEW Bobby, CHHAI Sokkien, CHHAN Bryan, CHI Candy, CHI Marianne, CHI Tony, CHIA Irmgard, CHIA Karen, CHIA Renee, CHIA Cheryl, CHIALVO Nicky, CHIAM Ying, CHIANESE Joe, CHIARELLI Kaylene, CHIAZZARO-BALIERO Veronica, CHIBA Clara, CHIBA Deepa, CHIBA Meera, CHIBA Teresa, CHICK Amanda, CHICK Chloe, CHICK Bill, CHICK Winnie, CHICKONOSKI Tom, CHIDEL Dean, CHIDZEY Maria-Elena, CHIE Michelle, CHIEN Amanda, CHIEN YIN Angela, CHIENG Chieng, CHIEU Tuyen, CHIHA Anthony, CHIK Bena, CHILBY Debbie, CHILCOTT Karen, CHILCOTT Kerry, CHILCOTT Michael, CHILD Dane, CHILD Sylvia, CHILDS Judy, CHILDS Kerrie, CHILDS Lea, CHILDS Margaret, CHILDS Maurice, CHILTON John, CHILTON Michael, CHILVERS Doug, CHIN Sharine, CHIN Irene, CHIN Jade, CHIN Li-Anne, CHIN Robyn, CHIN Sze, CHIN Jin, CHINCA Mark, CHING Arthur, CHING Gary, CHING K, CHING Alan, CHINN Lois, CHINNOCK Adele, CHIODA Adriana, CHIODA Joe, CHIOU Andrew, CHIOU Ling, CHIPCHASE Lyn, CHIPIZUBOV Nicholas, CHIPLIN Olivia, CHIPMAN Carrie, CHIPMAN Warwick, CHIRGWIN Janet, CHIRGWIN Reg, CHIRGWIN Shirley, CHIRKOFF Robyn, CHIROKOV Alex, CHISHOLM Alison, CHISHOLM Heather, CHISHOLM-BREEN Caroline, CHISNALL Bruce, CHISWICK Dennis, CHITNIS Amit, CHITTICK Robert, CHITTY Carol, CHIU Antonia, CHIU Anthony, CHIU Billy, CHIU Francis, CHIU Jone, CHIU Julie, CHIU Kitty, CHIU Lawrence, CHIU Lily, CHIU Richard, CHIU Sylvia, CHIU Tor, CHIU Wing, CHIU-CHONG David, CHIVAS Brett, CHIVAS Ralph, CHIVELL Bec, CHIVERS Carol, CHIVERS Col, CHIVERS Jan, CHIVERS Jenny, CHIVERS Ric, CHIVILO Jenny, CHNG Chang, CHNG Lilian, CHO Anna, CHO Coliza, CHO Deborah, CHO Doah, CHO Hyeon, CHO Katherine, CHO Sujin, CHO Cecilia, CHO Joshua, CHO Yong, CHOAT Sarah, CHOCHULA Olga, CHOE Julia, CHOI Angela, CHOI Anna, CHOI Arnold, CHOI Bo-Mun, CHOI Eun, CHOI Sunny, CHOI Vada, CHOI Patrick, CHOI Jaewon, CHOI Jason, CHOI Jin, CHOI Jinny, CHOI Jung, CHOI Kyunghee, CHOI Midge, CHOI Marinda, CHOI Anne, CHOI Ronson, CHOI Sam, CHOI Darvi, CHOI Yoon-Hee, CHOI Yoonhee, CHOI Yunhee, CHOK Jimmy, CHOLAKYAN Arda, CHOLEWKA Kate, CHOLIPSKI Margaret, CHOLSH Alex, CHONG Alan, CHONG Chris, CHONG Ernest, CHONG Karl, CHONG Karen, CHONG Moon, CHONG Rachel, CHONG Soo, CHONG Terry, CHONG Wati, CHONG Yik-Yen, CHONG Yvonne, CHOO David, CHOO Eric, CHOO Min-Ha, CHOO Chris, CHOO Young, CHOONG Jeremy, CHOPRA Kaka, CHOPRA Rohit, CHORFADI Rebecca, CHOROBSKI Marek, CHORREZ Lissette, CHOUBENITCHEV Nikolai, CHOUCAIR Amin, CHOUEIRI Mansour, CHOUKRALLAH-KAZEMI Hadi, CHOW Austin, CHOW Barbara, CHOW Bonnie, CHOW Connie, CHOW Esther, CHOW Henrietta, CHOW Jackson, CHOW Anna, CHOW Kanny, CHOW Marcus, CHOW Mary, CHOW Michael, CHOW Ngai, CHOW Queenie, CHOW Stephen, CHOW Tony, CHOW Rudolph, CHOW Yvonne, CHOWDHURY Abu, CHOWDHURY Amit, CHOWDHURY Atiq, CHOWDHURY Fariha, CHOWDHURY Georgina, CHOWDHURY Jessie, CHOWDHURY Tawfiq, CHOY Jono, CHOY Jonathan, CHOY Shuen, CHOY Charles, CHRISINIS Stacey, CHRISP Vanessa, CHRISTENAS Gail, CHRISTENSEN Brett, CHRISTENSEN Garry, CHRISTENSEN Shannon, CHRISTENSEN Margaret, CHRISTENSEN Paul, CHRISTENSEN Per, CHRISTENSEN Robin, CHRISTER John, CHRISTIAN Anita, CHRISTIAN Jan, CHRISTIAN Neville, CHRISTIAN Terry, CHRISTIE Sandy, CHRISTIE Anne, CHRISTIE Charmian, CHRISTIE Craig, CHRISTIE Doreen, CHRISTIE Jan, CHRISTIE John, CHRISTIE John, CHRISTIE John, CHRISTIE Marea, CHRISTIE Myrell, CHRISTIE Robert, CHRISTIE Susie, CHRISTIE Trevor, CHRISTINE Jhony, CHRISTINE Rulia, CHRISTLO Peter, CHRISTMAS Tamara, CHRISTMASS Brett, CHRISTOFF Kathryn, CHRISTOFF Lucille, CHRISTOFIDES Peter, CHRISTOFIDES Sue, CHRISTOPHER Jim, CHRISTOPHER Lucy, CHRISTOPHER Nesbitt, CHRISTOPHER CHELLIAH Shanmugam, CHRISTOPHERS Andrew, CHRISTOPHERSON Jamie, CHRISTOPHORATOS Alexandra, CHRISTOPHOROU Stavros, CHRISTY-SELL Lisa, CHROMIAK Fiona, CHRONOPOULOS Greg, CHRYSANTHOU Gloria, CHRYSTAL David, CHRYSTAL Greg, CHU Allen, CHU Alvina, CHU Amy, CHU Lisa, CHU Chan, CHU Desmond, CHU Edward, CHU Edwin, CHU George, CHU Ginia, CHU Betty, CHU I-Wen, CHU Jenny, CHU Kenneth, CHU Lilian, CHU Cecilia, CHU Angel, CHU Simson, CHU Stephanie, CHU David, CHU Tammie, CHU Tony, CHU Vonne, CHU Yvonne, CHUA Ivan, CHUA Nicki, CHUA Terry, CHUA Winnie, CHUA Yew-Wee, CHUAH Chin, CHUANG Christine, CHUBAK Helen, CHUBB John, CHUCK Jo, CHUDLEIGH Anna, CHUEN Shawn, CHUGG Chris, CHUI Alice, CHUI Anita, CHUI Jeffrey, CHUI Jason, CHULANIMALA Abeysirinarayana, CHULIO Anna, CHUN Gordon, CHUNG Angela, CHUNG Anne, CHUNG Bernard, CHUNG Cheng, CHUNG Chris, CHUNG Christina, CHUNG Cindy, CHUNG Coni, CHUNG Dale, CHUNG Dexter, CHUNG Eugenia, CHUNG Giang, CHUNG Ilah, CHUNG Irene, CHUNG Ka, CHUNG Kevin, CHUNG Chung, CHUNG Kenneth, CHUNG Richard, CHUNG Louise, CHUNG Martin, CHUNG Melanie, CHUNG Michael, CHUNG Dr, CHUNG Rex, CHUNG Samuel, CHUNG Seung, CHUNG Melissa, CHUNG Sim, CHUNG Sook, CHUNG Stanley, CHUNG Steven, CHUNG Sammy, CHUNG Chung, CHUNG Grand, CHUNG Terry, CHUNG Tessa, CHUNG Vicky, CHUNG Wendy, CHUONG David, CHUPRINA Alexander, CHURCH Al, CHURCH David, CHURCH Frank, CHURCH Jeremy, CHURCH Sharon, CHURCHES Michael, CHURCHILL John, CHURCHILL Pete, CHUTIMA Prasunnakarn, CHYDZINSKI Agata, CHYLA Tracey, CIANCI Lucy, CIANCI Nina, CIANCIO Maria, CIANTAR Cheryl, CIANTAR Joe, CIARCIELLO Angela, CIARCIELLO Saverio, CIAVOLA Joe, CICCO Pina, CICCO Lucy, CICCOLO Francesco, CID Natalia, CIDADE Cristina, CIELOS Emma, CIESIELSKI Jozef, CIFRANIC George, CIFTCIOGLU Sezgin, CILESIO Cecelia, CIMINO John, CIMINO Max, CIMINO Tania, CINCOTTA Keith, CINEL Michelle, CINELLI Frances, CINELLI George, CINI Anthony, CINI Suzanne, CINQUE Peter, CIOCCARELLI Lesley, CIPRIOTTO Maximillian, CIRCOSTA Tony, CIRILLO Gus, CIRILLO Bruno, CIRILLO Lena, CISTERNINO Helen, CISTULLI Vincent, CITROEN Lou, CIVITI Anna, CKLAMOVSKI Tania, CLAASSENS Ron, CLAESSEN Jerome, CLAGUE Babs, CLANCY Joan, CLANCY Kevin, CLANCY Leigh, CLANCY Mark, CLANCY Melissa, CLANCY Bob, CLANCY Sophia, CLANCY Stephen, CLANCY-LOWE Martyn, CLAPHAM Nathan, CLARE Aileen, CLARE Tony, CLARE John, CLARE Kim, CLARE Lisa, CLARE Ronnie, CLARE-ADAMS Sandy, CLARIDGE Glenda, CLARINGBOLD Megan, CLARK Alan, CLARK Alan, CLARK Allun, CLARK Andrew, CLARK Andrew, CLARK Tony, CLARK Tony, CLARK Bertha, CLARK Brendan, CLARK Bruce, CLARK Cheryl, CLARK

Cherry, CLARK Damian, CLARK David, CLARK Dave, CLARK Deborah, CLARK Denise, CLARK Dianne, CLARK Domenica, CLARK Don, CLARK Faye, CLARK Geoff, CLARK George, CLARK Gordon, CLARK Helen, CLARK Ian, CLARK John, CLARK Josh, CLARK Judi, CLARK Kathryn, CLARK Kel, CLARK Ken, CLARK Ken, CLARK Keryn, CLARK Kylie, CLARK Leanne, CLARK Len, CLARK Lorraine, CLARK Martin, CLARK Matthew, CLARK Merrilee, CLARK Meredith, CLARK Nadine, CLARK Nancy, CLARK Nat, CLARK Nick, CLARK Norm, CLARK Tricia, CLARK Joan, CLARK Rachel, CLARK Rachel, CLARK Ralph, CLARK Ralph, CLARK Rhonda, CLARK Ricky, CLARK Robyn, CLARK Boo, CLARK Rosemary, CLARK Rowen, CLARK Sara, CLARK Sheree, CLARK Sidney, CLARK Tania, CLARK Tracey, CLARK Veralea, CLARK Walter, CLARK Wendy, CLARK Glenda, CLARK-DUFF Belinda, CLARK-DUFF Lyn, CLARKE Adam, CLARKE Amber, CLARKE Amy, CLARKE Andrew, CLARKE Andrew, CLARKE Andrew, CLARKE Annette, CLARKE Anne, CLARKE Belinda, CLARKE Beverley, CLARKE Brett, CLARKE Bruce, CLARKE Carmen, CLARKE Cecilia, CLARKE Christina, CLARKE Christopher, CLARKE Corina, CLARKE Dave, CLARKE Debbi, CLARKE Deryck, CLARKE Dian, CLARKE Eleanor, CLARKE Emmi, CLARKE Geoff, CLARKE Jill, CLARKE Graham, CLARKE Greg, CLARKE Harry, CLARKE Helen, CLARKE Ian, CLARKE Irene, CLARKE James, CLARKE Jan, CLARKE Jenny, CLARKE John, CLARKE John, CLARKE John, CLARKE Joan, CLARKE Joyce, CLARKE Judy, CLARKE Kat, CLARKE Kathryn, CLARKE Kellie, CLARKE Kerry, CLARKE Lachlan, CLARKE Lesley, CLARKE Linda, CLARKE Lisa, CLARKE Lois, CLARKE Louise, CLARKE Luke, CLARKE Lyneene, CLARKE Lyn, CLARKE Margaret, CLARKE Maurie, CLARKE Maureen, CLARKE Mervyn, CLARKE Murray, CLARKE Nola, CLARKE Pat, CLARKE Paul, CLARKE Paul, CLARKE Peter, CLARKE Rick, CLARKE Bob, CLARKE Bob, CLARKE Sandy, CLARKE Shirley, CLARKE Sidney, CLARKE Stephen, CLARKE Sue, CLARKE Taylor, CLARKE Tony, CLARKE Trevor, CLARKE Trisha, CLARKE William, CLARKE William, CLARKSON Haze, CLARKSON Rebecca, CLARKSON Steve, CLARKSON Toni, CLARKSTONE Jo, CLATWORTHY Frank, CLAUSCEN Darren, CLAUSEN Christine, CLAUSEN Errol, CLAV JO Milagros, CLAVIN Robyn, CLAXTON Mark, CLAY Allen, CLAY Cammaron, CLAY Judy, CLAY Shelley, CLAYBOURN Joanne, CLAYDON David, CLAYFIELD Joy, CLAYSON Greg, CLAYTON Adrian, CLAYTON Adrian, CLAYTON Dale, CLAYTON Dana, CLAYTON Bob, CLAYTON Julie, CLAYTON Kevin, CLAYTON Margarita, CLAYTON Margaret, CLAYTON Neil, CLAYTON Pauline, CLAYTON Paula, CLAYTON Sue, CLAYTON Wendy, CLEAR Deirdre, CLEAR Judy, CLEARSON Carolyn, CLEARY Andrew, CLEARY Graham, CLEARY Mark, CLEARY Micheal, CLEARY Nathan, CLEARY Phillip, CLEARY Rick, CLEASBY Carol, CLEASBY Paul, CLEAVER Lloyd, CLEAVER Matthew, CLEAVER Stan, CLEERE Michael, CLELAND Bob, CLEMENS Heather, CLEMENS Laura, CLEMENS Neville, CLEMENT Annette, CLEMENT Joan, CLEMENT Junette, CLEMENTS Belinda, CLEMENTS Darill, CLEMENTS John, CLEMENTS Kenneth, CLEMENTS Lucille, CLEMENTS Richard, CLEMENTS Ross, CLEMENTS Sharon, CLEMENTS Thomas, CLEMMENSEN Vini, CLEMONES Clem, CLEMONES Linda, CLENDINNING Ken, CLERKE Lynne, CLERKIN Tina, CLEUR Hazel, CLEVELAND Richard, CLEVERLEY Shellstar, CLIFF Glenys, CLIFF Janet, CLIFF Margaret, CLIFFE Kevin, CLIFFORD Charlene, CLIFFORD Graeme, CLIFFORD Jill, CLIFFORD Leisa, CLIFFORD Mark, CLIFFORD Maureen, CLIFFORD Neil, CLIFFORD Paul, CLIFFORD Sandra, CLIFT Grahame, CLIFT Jennifer, CLIFTON Diana, **CLIFTON Fairlie**, CLIFTON Michael, CLIFTON Morgan, CLIFTON Philip, CLIFTON Sue, CLIMIE Bec, CLIMSTEIN Mike, CLINCH Carol, CLINCH Deirdre, CLINCH Donna, CLINCH Milton, CLINCH Bill, CLINTON Camille, CLIPSHAM Beth, CLIPSHAM Matthew, CLISBY Liz, CLISSOLD Jonathan, CLISSOLD Neil, CLOCK Michael, CLODE Cam, CLOHESY Aaron, CLONARIS Michael, CLONDA Carin, CLOPADOFSKY Alejandro, CLOSE Dave, CLOSE Jade, CLOSE Peter, CLOSE Rhonda, CLOSE Ruth, CLOSE Zoie, CLOTHIER Kris, CLOTHIER Paul, CLOUGHER Margaret, CLOUGHESSY Monica, CLOUT Penni, CLOUTIER Caroline, CLOWES Lorraine, CLOWRY John, CLOWRY Margaret, CLOWRY Phil, CLOWRY Val, CLUBB Judith, CLUCAS John, CLUCAS Phill, CLUGSTON Caroline, CLUGSTON Helen, CLUNE Kath, CLUNE Louise, CLUNE Stephen, **CLUNES Luke, CLUNES Neil, CLUNES Patricia**, CLUNN Darren, CLUSS Troy, COAD Ron, COADY Carol, COATES Alison, COATES Barry, COATES Carne, COATES Kim, COATES Melanie, COATES Pam, COATES Priscilla, COATES Dick, COATES Richard, COATES Vicki, COBB Margaret, COBBLE Sylvia, COBCROFT Anne, COBCROFT Bronwyn, COBCROFT Ian, COBLEY Peter, COBRADOR Marivic, COBURN Emma, COCCA Martin, COCCA Melanie, COCCHINI Kristy, COCCO Giordana, COCHRANE Barbara, COCHRANE Che, COCHRANE Darrell, COCHRANE Lindsay, COCHRANE Melissa-Sue, COCHRANE Nathan, COCHRANE Reg, COCHRANE Sharon, COCHRANE Thomas, COCHRANE Wendy, COCK Laurie, COCKAYNE Kate, COCKBILL John, COCKBURN John, COCKBURN Judy, COCKBURN Mercia, COCKERILL Trevor, COCKING Danielle, COCKRAM Corinne, COCKREM Brian, COCKS Alan, COCKS Daryl, COCKS Gill, COCKS Graeme, COCKS Jean, COCKS John, COCKS Lee-Ann, COCKS Dennis, COCKS Bob, COCKS Robyn, COCKSHELL John, CODD Beck, CODLING Russ, COE Bruce, COE Margaret, COE Noreen, COELHO Andressa, COELHO Kelly, COELHO Manuel, COEN Wolfgang, COFFEN Franca, COFFEY Tony, COFFEY Dee, COFFEY Jim, COFFEY Rosita, COFFEY Simon, COFFILL Peter, COFFMAN Dave, COGDON Gwen, COGDON Terry, COGGAN Louise, COGGAN Meaghan, COGHLIN Tina, COGZELL Linda, COHEN Brian, COHEN Clare, COHEN David, COHEN David, COHEN Debbie, COHEN Libby, COHEN Gordon, COHEN Harvey, COHEN Ingrid, COHEN Jack, COHEN Larry, COHEN Robert, COHEN Tony, COHN Bernie, COHN Pam, COKAYNE Jane, COKER Ellen, COKER Geoff, COKER Jennifer, COKER Julian, COLACO Glenn, COLACO Ian, COLAGIURI Vincent, COLAGROSSI Matthew, COLAHAN Ellen, COLAK Kadir, COLBERT Stephanie, COLBORNE-VEEL Catherine, COLBRAN Jim, COLBRAN Suzi, COLCLOUGH Beck, COLCOTT Wayne, COLE Alan, COLE Amanda, COLE Bryan, COLE Carole, COLE Christine, COLE Denise, COLE Dee, COLE Liz, COLE Frank, COLE Helena, COLE Ila, COLE Jeff, COLE Karen, COLE Ken, COLE Laurie, COLE Laurie, COLE Lex, COLE Lorna, COLE Lynne, COLE Lynette, COLE Mandi, COLE Marie, COLE Maureen, COLE Moira, COLE Roger, COLE Ross, COLE Rowena, COLE Sue, COLE Sue, COLE T, COLE Victoria, COLE Wayne, COLEBORN Louise, COLEBORN Terry, Warrick, COLEBY Caroline, COLEFAX Ruth, COLEMAN Andrew, COLEMAN Angela, COLEMAN Christine, COLEMAN Chris, COLEMAN Cindy, COLEMAN Liz, COLEMAN Ewen, COLEMAN Henry, COLEMAN Jess, COLEMAN John, COLEMAN Judy, COLEMAN Julia, COLEMAN Kathryn, COLEMAN Ken, COLEMAN Laura, COLEMAN Lauren, COLEMAN Laurie, **COLEMAN Nat**, COLEMAN Nikki, COLEMAN Patrick, COLEMAN Peter, COLEMAN Peter, COLEMAN Raylee, COLEMAN Rosemary, COLEMAN Stuart, COLEMAN Vicki, COLEMAN Viv, COLEMAN Wilma, COLENSO Jenny, COLES Jane, COLES Jo, COLES Ken, COLES Steve, COLETTI Elena, COLEY Martin, COLGAN Kathy, COLIGADO Alan, COLINA ROJAS Pedro, COLJA Jo, COLL Peter, COLLAOETTI Pancho, COLLARD Annita, COLLARD Linda, COLLATON Narelle, COLLESS Heather, COLLETT Jodie, COLLETT Michelle, COLLETTE Dave, COLLETTE Katherine, COLLEY Alex, COLLEY Dembo, COLLEY Kerry, COLLEY Rhianne, COLLEY Terence, COLLIE Ken, COLLIER Christopher, COLLIER Diane, COLLIER Kathleen, COLLIER Lyn, COLLINA Matthew, COLLINGE Emma, COLLINGS Ian, COLLINGS Ross, COLLINGWOOD Carla, C OLLINS Amanda, COLLINS Tony, COLLINS Barbara, COLLINS Christopher, COLLINS Colleen, COLLINS David, COLLINS Deidre, COLLINS Desiree, COLLINS Frank, COLLINS Gail, COLLINS Gary, COLLINS Garry, COLLINS Graeme, COLLINS Graeme, COLLINS Helen, COLLINS Helen, COLLINS Jackie, COLLINS James, COLLINS Janelle, COLLINS Jennifer, COLLINS Jenny, COLLINS Jenner, COLLINS Jillian, COLLINS John, COLLINS Julie, COLLINS Karen, COLLINS Kathryn, COLLINS Kathryn, COLLINS Leigh, COLLINS Les, COLLINS Linette, COLLINS Lola, COLLINS Madeleine, COLLINS Mags, COLLINS Tainia, COLLINS Mark, COLLINS Mark, COLLINS Marg, COLLINS Mick, COLLINS Michelle, COLLINS Natalie, COLLINS Nick, COLLINS Nicole, COLLINS Paul, COLLINS Peter, COLLINS Rebecca, COLLINS Richard, COLLINS Sally, COLLINS Stephanie, COLLINS Terry, COLLINS Terrence, COLLINSON David, COLLIS Kath, COLLIS Peter, COLLIS Peter, COLLIS

Stephie, COLLISON Brian, COLLISON Kate, COLLISON Frank, COLLISON Mary, COLLISS Warren, COLLITS Brendon, COLLIVER Ed, COLLYER Gayle, COLLYER Jill, COLLYER Michael, COLLYER Ray, COLMAN Melissa, COLMAN Robyn, COLMER Vanessa, COLOUHOUN Dave, COLQUHOUN Catherine, COLQUHOUN Colin, COLQUHOUN Steve, COLQUHOUN Timothy, COLSTON Emily, COLUCCIO Frank, COLVILLE Doug, COLVILLE Judith, COLWELL Mark, COLWELL Sam, COLYER Alison, COMAN Ben, COMANIUK Deborah, COMARMOND Daniel, COMARMOND Jason, COMARMOND Julieanne, COMARMOND Kristie, COMARMOND Margaret, COMBE Faye, COMBEN Allan, COMBER Denis, COMBER Lyn, COMBES Andrew, COMERFORD Tara, COMERTPAY Bilal, COMERTPAY Emrah, COMERTPAY Meltem, COMERY Anne, COMINO George, COMINO Ros, COMISH Viv, COMITO Sarah, COMMERFORD Peter, COMMINS Tony, COMNINOS Patrick, COMOR Mick, COMPTON Cathie, COMPTON Kevin, COMPTON Mark, COMPTON Michael, COMYNS Colin, CON FOO Pamela, CONALTY John, CONATY Jack, CONCEIGAO Francisco, CONCHE David, CONDEN Graham, CONDEN Jennifer, CONDIE Richard, CONDON Alan, CONDON Allison, CONDON Brian, CONDON Daniel, CONDON Daniel, CONDON Debbie, CONDON Fred, CONDON Graham, CONDON Jan, **CONDON John**, CONDON Kathryn, CONDON Kelly, CONDON Leona, CONDON Lynette, CONDON Nikkie, CONDON Bob, CONDON Ron, CONDON Sarah, CONDON Thomas, CONEY Suzanne, CONGDON Karina, CONGDON Mim, CONIGLIO Kris, CONLAN Brad, CONLAN Patrick, CONLEY Bev, CONLEY Caroline, CONLEY Gail, CONLON Julie, CONLON Melanie, CONN Bruce, CONNAH Paul, CONNAH Thomas, CONNANE Kathy, CONNANE Peter, CONNAUGHTON Seamus, CONNEELY Maggie, CONNELL Adele, CONNELL Daryl, CONNELL David, CONNELL Lizzie, CONNELL Frances, CONNELL Julie, CONNELL Matt, CONNELL Paul, CONNELL Peter, CONNELL Rita, CONNELL Bob, CONNELL Sean, CONNELL Susie, CONNELLY Kristy, CONNELLY Marcel, CONNELLY Michelle, CONNELLY Michael, CONNELLY Ruth, CONNELLY Vicki, CONNERY Joan, CONNOLLY April, CONNOLLY Cheryl, CONNOLLY Geoff, CONNOLLY Lorraine, CONNOLLY Maryann, CONNOLLY John, CONNOLLY Stephen, CONNOLLY Vivien, CONNOR Beth, CONNOR Bruce, CONNOR Gayle, CONNOR Graham, CONNOR Joy, CONNOR Kerryn, CONNOR Kevin, CONNOR Lynette, CONNOR Michael, CONNOR Pam, CONNOR Phillip, CONNOR Steve, CONNOR Stewart, CONNOR Stuart, CONNORS Ivan, CONNORS Margot, CONOLLY Judy, CONOLLY Peter, CONOMOS Antonia, CONOMOS Ari, CONQUIT Damien, CONQUIT Rosemary, CONRAD Kathleen, CONRAN Peter, CONROY Anne-Marie, CONROY Christopher, CONROY Greg, **CONSAUL Sheila**, CONSIDINE Andrew, CONSIDINE Liz, CONSIDINE Mary, CONSORTI Jana, CONSTABLE Renee, CONSTANDINOU Christakis, CONSTANTIN George, CONSTANTINI Marcello, CONSTANTINIDOU Anna, CONSTANTINOU Bill, CONTARDO Flor, CONTRACTOR Pashmina, CONTRERAS Melania, CONVERY Alan, CONVEY Cathy, CONVEY Thomas, CONWAY Alison, CONWAY Charito, CONWAY Libby, CONWAY James, CONWAY Mrs, CONWAY Sanchita, CONWAY-POWLES Ian, CONWELL Ross, CONYBEARE Leith, COOGAN Gerard, COOK Alex, COOK Alex, COOK Tony, COOK Beryl, COOK Bryan, COOK Christina, COOK Cynthia, COOK Denise, COOK Denise, COOK Dominic, COOK Noel, COOK Joe, COOK Emily, COOK EEric, COOK Gary, COOK Geoff, COOK Gregory, COOK Grigor, COOK Ian, COOK Ian, COOK Jackie, COOK Jean, COOK Jean, COOK Joanne, COOK Kelvin, COOK Larry, COOK Leanne, COOK Leisa, COOK Lois, COOK Lynne, COOK Marion, COOK Melissa, COOK Mick, COOK Muriel, COOK Darryl, COOK Patricia, COOK Peter, COOK Rob, COOK Rosie, COOK Steve, COOK Stephanie, COOK Stephanie, COOK Stephen, COOK Theresa, COOK Vanessa, COOK Bruce, COOK Wayne, COOK Wendy, COOK Bill, COOKE Anton, COOKE Ed, COOKE Heidi, COOKE Liam, COOKE Nicki, COOKE Paul, COOKE Robert, COOKE Robert, COOKE Rowan, COOKE Sandra, COOKE Simeon, COOKMAN James, COOKMAN Karen, COOKSLEY Barbara, COOKSLEY Grahame, COOKSLEY Ken, COOKSON Peter, COOLEY Sophie, COOLICAN Myles, COOLING Lee, COOLING Michelle, COOMBE Lisa, COOMBE Mark, COOMBE Richard, COOMBER Jane, COOMBES Calvin, COOMBES Jason, COOMBES Kristyn, COOMBES Lesley, COOMBES Pat, COOMBS Bruce, COOMBS Heather, COOMBS Leanne, COOMBS Leonard, COOMBS Malcolm, COOMBS Rebekah, COOMBS Bob, COOMBS Selena, COON Kim, COON Ruby, COONAN Pat, COONEY Jeanette, COONEY Judith, COONEY Kim, COONEY Nicole, COONEY Rosa, COONEY Steve, COOPER Adam, COOPER Gus, COOPER Adrian, COOPER Alan, COOPER Andrew, COOPER Anabelle, COOPER Ashley, COOPER Barry, COOPER Boyd, COOPER Brenton, COOPER Brian, COOPER Brian, COOPER Brooke, COOPER Bronwyn, COOPER Carol, COOPER Carole, COOPER David, COOPER Erin, **COOPER Bill**, COOPER Harry, COOPER Ian Thomas, COOPER Ian Francis, COOPER Irene, COOPER Irene, COOPER Janine, COOPER Jan, COOPER Jan, COOPER Jenny, COOPER Jennifer, COOPER Jillian, COOPER Jodi, COOPER Judy, COOPER Justin, COOPER Karen, COOPER Karon, COOPER Kim, COOPER Lauren, COOPER Leanne, COOPER Leanne, COOPER Lena, COOPER Lyndell, COOPER Mal, COOPER Merrilyn, COOPER Mike, COOPER Michelle, COOPER Neneth, COOPER Neville, COOPER Norman, COOPER Pat, COOPER Pat, COOPER Patricia, COOPER Pauline, COOPER Peter, COOPER Rachel, COOPER Rachel, COOPER Rita, COOPER Bob, COOPER Robert, COOPER Roy, COOPER Sheila, COOPER Shirley, COOPER Stephanie, COOPER Steve, COOPER Steve, COOPER Susi, COOPER Victoria, COOPER Bill, COOPER Bill, COOPERPAYTEN Jill, COOPER-POULTNEY Elaine, COOPER-SMITH Lanny, COORAY Ione, COOREY Anthony, COOREY Norma, COOREY Stephen, COOTE Alison, COOTE Annalise, COOTE Lillian, COO TE Emma, COOTE Joe, COOTE Bob, COOTE Sam, COOTEE Chantal, **COOTES Cwen**, COOTES Hayston, COOTES Melinda, COOTS Colleen, COPAS Chris, COPE Sue, COPELAND Alan, COPELAND Grace, COPELAND Julia, COPELAND Peter, COPELAND Philip, COPELLO Beatriz, COPINI Allah, COPINI Liz, COPLAND Melissa, COPLEY Caroline, COPLEY Esty, COPLEY Jennifer, COPLEY Julie, COPP Chris, COPPARD Debbie, COPPING Jennifer, COPPING Les, COPPING Neville, COPPOLA Sue, COPSEY Nathan, CORAL Edgar, CORBAN Sandra, CORBEN Alan, CORBEN Rita, CORBETT Christy, CORBETT Doug, CORBETT Emily, CORBETT Shirley, CORBIN Roger, CORBIN Stephen, CORBISHLEY Glyn, CORBY John, CORBY Les, CORBY Maggie, CORBY Sydney, CORCORAN Alex, CORCORAN Brendan, CORCORAN John, CORCORAN Peter, CORCORAN Sharon, CORCORAN Stephen, CORDEN Daniel, CORDNER HUNT Kammy, CORDOULIS Samantha, CORDWELL Keffed, CORE Darryl, COREY John, CORFIELD Greg, CORFIELD Robyn, CORFIELD Roslyn, CORIO Susan, CORK Steve, CORKE Derran, CORKILL Gary, CORKILL Andrew, CORKILL Narelle, CORKIN Basil, CORLESS David, CORLETT Kerli, CORLETTE Deanne, CORLEVICH Aldo, CORMACK Leanne, CORMACK Peter, CORMANN Mathias, CORMIE Lola, CORMIE Jill, CORMIO James, CORNE Nicki, CORNELIUS Jason, CORNELL Tony, CORNELL Leonie, CORNELLY Matthew, CORNER Greg, CORNER Linda, CORNER Mamari, CORNER Margot, CORNER Stewart, CORNEY Peter, CORNFORD Gillian, CORNFORD John, CORNISH Jim, CORNISH Jewels, CORNISH Marion, **CORNISH Pam**, CORNISH Reg, CORNISH Rhonda-Lea, CORNISH Robyn, CORNISH Sally, CORNISH Sarah, CORNISH Stephen, CORNWELL Alf, CORNWELL Betty, CORNWELL Helen, CORNWELL Phil, CORONA Marcela, CORONA-MONGE Marilia, CORONEOS Aliki, CORP Andrew, CORP Anthony, CORPUS Cris, CORPUS Cridanta, CORPUZ Maria, CORPUZ Robert, CORR Lance, CORREA Eduardo, CORREIA Dany, CORREIA Joseph, CORRENTE Giuseppe, CORRIE Heather, CORRIGAN Brian, CORRIGAN Lisa, CORRIGAN Neville, CORRY Jane, CORRY John, CORSETTI Joe, CORSO Ben, CORSO Sharon, CORTES Cristian, CORTES Angela, CORTESE Mary, CORTEZ Veronica, CORTIS Paul, COSENTINI Vince, COSGRIFF Rohan, COSGROVE David, COSGROVE Kate, COSGROVE Peter, COSGROVE Sharon, COSLOVICH Deborah, COSSARI Sam, COSSART Geoff, COSSART Heather, COSSELL Phil, COSSETTINI David, COSSOR Chris, COSTA Tony, COSTA Anula, COSTA Mario, COSTA Marcela, COSTA Robert, COSTANDI Nabill, COSTANZO Cozi, COSTANZO Rosa, COSTECALDE Jerone, COSTELLO Ted, COSTELLO Grant, COSTELLO James, COSTELLO John, COSTELLO Michael, COSTELLO Nicole, COSTELLO Pat, COSTELLO Paul, COSTELLO Rachael, COSTELLO Susan,

COSTELLOE Michelle, COSTER Natalie, COSTI Zev, COSTIGAN Cathy, COSTIN Faith, COSTIN Nunny, COSTIN Rhonda, COSTIN Rod, COTEN Ned, COTMAN Hugh, COTTEE Geoff, COTTER Dell, COTTER Jenny, COTTER Jane, COTTER Isabel, COTTER Paul, COTTERILL Col, COTTERILL Hayley, COTTERILL Ursula, COTTI Jo, COTTIER Darren, COTTLE Des, COTTLE Margaret, COTTLE Nance, COTTON David, COTTON Haley, COTTRELL Benjamin, COTTRELL Jeff, COTTRELL Susan, COUCH Sara, COUGHLAN Craig, COUGHLAN Dianne, COUGHLAN Jonathan, COUGHLAN Sally, COUGHLIN Loretta, COUGHRAN Jason, COUGHRAN Ross, COULIN Ryan, COULL Christine, COULL Michael, COULON Chantal, COULON Daniel, COULSON Susan, COULSON Suzanne, COULSTON Graeme, COULTON Allan, COUNTER Chris, COUNTER Val, COUPE Lyn, COUPER Diana, COUPER Garry, COURAULT Helene, COURI Jim, COURT Helen, COURTENAY Marney, COURTENAY Victoria, COURTNEY Diane, COURTNEY Gary, COURTNEY Howard, COURTNEY Grant, COURTNEY Norma, COURTNEY Tehya, COURTS Don, COUSINS John, COUSINS John, COUSINS Phil, COUSINS Rosemary, COUSINS Tony, COUSLEY Eric, COUTLIS Cathy, COUTSONICAS Antigone, COUTTS Annette, COUTTS Gillian, COUTTS Dawn, COUTTS Jason, COUTTS Jesse, COUTTS Joan, COUTTS Sandra, COUTTS-SMITH Tony, COUVRET Paul, COUZENS Gillian, COVENTRY James, COVILL Debbie, COVILL Noel, COVILLE Charles, COWAN Donald, COWAN Jo, COWAN Ian, COWAN John, COWAN Len, COWAN Mark, COWARD Dena, COWARD Kitty, COWARD Wayne, COWARD Wayne, COWE Val, COWELL Tony, COWELL Darren, COWELL Dennis, COWELL Kirsty, COWELL Neville, COWELL Bob, COWELL Susan, COWEN Marty, COWGILL Lauren, COWGILL Melissa, COWIE Elizabeth, COWIE John, COWIE Julie, COWIE Bill, COWIN John, COWLE Alison, COWLEY Roger, COWLEY Katie, COWLEY Kaye, COWLEY Vickie, COWLING Kirralee, COWLING Meredith, COWLING Peter, COWLING Phill, COWLISHAW Del, COX Andrea, COX Ange, COX Belinda, COX Cristine, COX Danielle, COX Dani, COX Dave, COX David, COX Deborah, COX Don, COX Elaine, COX Felicity, COX Fiona, COX Gary, COX Glen, COX Glenys, **COX Gloria**, COX Gordon, COX Graham, COX Greg, COX Ian, **COX Jane**, COX Janice, COX Jo-Anne, COX John, COX Katherine, COX Keith, COX Lenice, COX Lorriane, COX Michelle, COX Narelle, COX Nichola, COX Pat, COX Penelope, COX Peter, COX Rachelle, COX Robert, COX Robin, COX Roger, COX Ross, COX Tamara, COX Trina, COX Winsome, COXON Glen, COXON-ELLIS Di, COXSEDGE Brett, COY Bryan, COY Val, COYLE Di, COYLE Ron, COYLE Shirley, COZADINOS Alison, COZADINOS Michelle, CRABB Jeffrey, CRABB Steve, CRABTREE Dave, CRABTREE Scott, CRACK Lynette, CRACKNELL Gary, CRACKNELL Helen, CRACKNELL Veronica, CRADDOCK Daniel, CRADDOCK Kathy, CRADDOCK Suzanne, CRAFT Mick, CRAGG Tracey, CRAGO Bruce, CRAIG Dianne, CRAIG Graeme, CRAIG Greg, CRAIG Jack, CRAIG Judith, CRAIG Kay, CRAIG Lyn, CRAIG Phillip, CRAIG Richard, CRAIG Sue, CRAIG Sue, CRAIG Warren, CRAIGIE Jane, CRAIK John, CRAIN Pam, CRAIN Rosemary, CRAM Jason, CRAME Jeremy, CRAMER Harry, CRAMER Johann, CRAMER Peter, CRAMMOND Sarah, CRAMPTON Keith, CRAMPTON Michael, CRAMPTON Sharyn, CRANCH Bob, CRANCH Tracey, CRANDELL Wayne, CRANE Adam, CRANE Chris, CRANE Fiona, CRANE Gabrielle, CRANE Heather, CRANE Hellen, CRANE Karen, CRANE Mary, CRANFIELD Dallas, CRANKSHAW Karl, CRANKSHAW Sue, CRANLEY Gina, CRANNEY Brooke, CRANNEY John, CRANNIS Cindie, CRANSON Angela, CRANSTON Ashley, CRANSWICK Hugh, CRANSWICK Sarah, CRAPP Robyn, CRAS Melanie, CRAWFORD Alan, CRAWFORD Barbara, CRAWFORD Barry, CRAWFORD David, CRAWFORD David, CRAWFORD Derek, CRAWFORD Emma, CRAWFORD Erin, CRAWFORD Gerald, CRAWFORD Gordon, CRAWFORD Jenny, CRAWFORD Jennifer, CRAWFORD Joanne, CRAWFORD John, CRAWFORD Megan, CRAWFORD Michael, CRAWFORD Natasha, CRAWFORD Grace, CRAWFORD Peter, CRAWFORD Peter, CRAWFORD Rachel, CRAWFORD Sally, CRAWFORD Scott, CRAWFORD Tom, CRAWFORD Tim, CRAWHALL Graham, CRAWLEY Anne, CRAWLEY Kelly, CRAWLEY Neil, CRAWLEY Terry, CRAWSHAW Peter, CRAYGE Peggy, CRAYSON Peter, CREAGH Sunanda, CREAL Jennifer, CREAMER Debbie, CREAMER Gordon, CREANE Sarah, CREARY Ronald, CREASER Helen, CREE Jeff, CREECE Virginia, CREED Emma, CREED Fiona, CREED Fiona, CREEK Mark, CREES Kerry, CREGAN Noleen, CREGAN Trish, CREHAN Ellen, CREHAN Noel, CREIGHTON Heather, CREIGHTON Justin, CREIGHTON Kay, CREIGHTON Bill, CRELLIN Norm, CRELLIN Ann, **CREMEN Neal**, CREMER Leon, CREMER Rowena, CRENN Marine, CRESCINI Girard, CRESWICK Margaret, CRESWICK Robert, CRETAN Penny, CREUTZBERG Regina, CREW Troy, CREWS Brian, CRIBB Terry, CRICHTON Jenny, CRICHTON Robert, CRICHTON Vikki, CRICK Elizabeth, CRICK Kaz, CRIDLAND Gai, CRIDLAND Ken, CRILLY Julia, CRIPPS Lynn, CRIPPS Roger, CRISAFI Vince, CRISOSTOMO Ervaija, CRISP Barry, CRISP Bradley, CRISP Darrin, CRISPIN Darren, CRISPIN John, CRISPIN Vicki, CRISPO George, CRISTOFOLETTI Claudine, CRITCHELL Maureen, CRITCHLEY Anthony, CRITCHLEY Critch, CRITCHLEY Ian, CRITCHLEY Jennifer, CRITCHLEY Jeremy, CRITCHLEY John, CRITCHLEY Lara, CRITCHLEY Sam, CRITOPH Stephen, CRITTENDEN Debbie, CRITTENDEN Jenny, CRITTENDEN Sue, CROAKER Susan, CROATTO Norma, CROCE Rob, CROCKER Tony, CROCKER Claire, CROCKER Jennifer, CROCKER Maree, CROCKER Phil, CROCKFORD Carina, CROFOS Keith, CROFT Christine, CROFT Glenn, CROFT Kerrie, CROFT Leah, CROFT Maia, CROFT Nathan, CROFT Jean, CROFTON Alison, CROGAN Samantha, CROKE Margaret, CROKE Matthew, CROKER Kath, CROKER Kevin, CROKER Manda, CROKER Margaret, CROKER Margaret, CROKER Mark, CROKER Sally, CROLL John, CROMBIE Andrew, CROMPTON Gary, CROMPTON Marion, CRONAN Beajey, CRONAN Kaye, CRONAN Bill, CRONIN Brooke, CRONIN Gail, CRONIN Janette, CRONIN Kate, **CRONIN Philip**, CRONIN Tony, CRONIN Ursula, CROOK Alisha, CROOK Barbara, CROOK Helen, CROOK John, CROOK Val, CROOKEY Sharon, CROOKS Iris, CROOKS Nicole, CROOT Don, CROOT Nicole, CROPPER Katrina, CROPPER Tom, CROSBIE Jason, CROSBY Lyn, CRO BY Jo, CROSBY Piet, CROSBY Tony, CROSDALE Lorna, CROSKY Sean, CROSLAND Jane, CROSS Alan, CROSS Ally, CROSS Andrew, CROSS Barry, CROSS Belinda, CROSS Brian, CROSS Caryn, CROSS Clayton, CROSS David, CROSS Dorothy, CROSS Enid, CROSS Gillian, CROSS Harley, CROSS Jaymie, CROSS Joan, CROSS Danny, CROSS Kathleen, CROSS Maree, **CROSS Mark**, CROSS Marjorie, CROSS Mervyn, CROSS Marie, CROSS Nathan, CROSS Nina, CROSS Steve, CROSS Terry, CROSS Tom, CROSS Tom, CROSSEN Tom, CROSSFIELD Kylie, CROSSIN Melinda, CROSSING Georgie, CROSSING Lisle, CROSSLAND Nellie, CROSSLEY Ketty, CROSSLEY Lee, CROSSLEY Michael, CROSSLEY Rob, CROSSMAN Anne, CROSSMAN Bevan, CROSSAN Jane, CROSSMAN Jenny, CROSSMAN Ken, CROSSON Jean, CROSSWHITE Ian, CROSTHWAITE Alison, CROSTHWAITE Geoff, CROTEAU Lyne, CROTHERS William, CROTT Frank, **CROUCH Graham**, CROUCH Nonie, CROUCHEN Shaz, CROUCHER Benjamin, CROUCHER Geraldine, CROUCHER Tom, CROUCHER Vickie, CROUCHLEY John, CROUCHMAN Joyce, CROUCHMAN Ken, CROW Adrian, CROW Lester, CROW Marcus, CROW Sandra, CROWDER Jo, CROWDER Peter, CROWE Cassandra, CROWE David, CROWE John, CROWE Matt, CROWE Nicole, CROWE Noeleen, CROWE Patrick, CROWE Sandra, CROWE Scott, CROWE Steve, CROWE Susan, CROWE Tracey, CROWELL Kay, CROWHURST Roger, CROWIE Kevin, CROWLEY Dennis, CROWLEY Geoff, CROWLEY Jenny, CROWLEY Moya, CROWLEY Noel, CROWLEY Sally, CROWLEY Ursula, CROWLEY Vicki, CROWN Brendon, CROWTHER Di, CROWTHER Iain, CROWTHER Joanne, CROWTHER Paula, CROWTHER Steve, CROXFORD David, CROXON Annisa, CRUICKSHANK Adam, CRUICKSHANK David, CRUICKSHANK Matthew, CRUICKSHANK Raymond, CRUICKSHANK Shirley, CRUIKSHANK Carol, CRUMP Lesley, CRUNDWELL Don, CRUSE Barrie, CRUSE Mark, CRUZ Angelo, CRUZ Leonides, CRUZ Onna, CRUZ Rodrigo, CRUZ Vicky, CSARDASKYRIACOU Kate, CSESZKO-MUNN Hannie, CSONKA John, CSONT Zoe, CSUBA Eileen, CTIBOR Jiri, CTIBOROVA Katerina, CUADROS GARROT Romulo, CUARESMA Andrea, CUARESMA Jennifer, CUARESMA Renan, CUARESMA Rhona, CUBITT Barbara, CUBITT Geoffrey, CUBITT Ian, CUBITT Judy,

CUBITT Terri, CUBITT Vaughan, CUBOS Jowell, CUCA Nikola, CUELL Murray, CUENCA Leanne, CUI Don, CUI John, CULBERT Danny, CULBERT Jodi, CULBERT Valda, CULEY Mary, CULFF Ian, CULHANE Peter, CULHANE Sarah, CULHANE Terry, CULIG Helene, CULKIN Neal, CULKIN Kay, CULKOFF Sandy, CULL Sophia, CULLEN Aileen, CULLEN Alan, CULLEN Chris, CULLEN Daelyn, CULLEN Greg, CULLEN Helen, CULLEN John, CULLEN John, CULLEN Kay, CULLEN Lynda, CULLEN Margaret, CULLEN Nancye, CULLEN Rob, CULLEN Roy, CULLEN Ross, CULLEN Cooper, CULLEN Wayne, CULLINANE Jacqui, CULLIVER Patricia, CULSHAW Beverley, CUMBERBATCH Olivia, CUMEN Yusuf, CUMING Michael, CUMMERFORD Ian, CUMMERFORD Margaret, CUMMING Daniel, CUMMING Lauren, CUMMING Lyn, CUMMING Mark, CUMMING Maria, CUMMINGS Connie, CUMMINGS Julie, CUMMINGS Nick, CUMMINGS Tennille, CUMMINGS Travis, CUMMINS David, CUMMINS Denise, CUMMINS Elizabeth, CUMMINS George, CUMMINS Richard, CUMMINS Royce, CUMNER Linda, CUNANAN Antonio, CUNANAN Romana, CUNDELL Barny, CUNEO Marilyn, CUNEO Paul, CUNHA Carlos, CUNHA Shana, CUNINGHAME Pat, CUNLIFFE Alison, CUNLIFFE Colin, CUNNEEN Erin, CUNNEEN Trish, CUNNINGHAM George, CUNNINGHAM Andy, CUNNINGHAM Anna, CUNNINGHAM Bernadette, CUNNINGHAM Catherine, CUNNINGHAM Corey, CUNNINGHAM David, CUNNINGHAM Diane, CUNNINGHAM Douglas, CUNNINGHAM Liz, CUNNINGHAM Jan, CUNNINGHAM John, CUNNINGHAM Julie, CUNNINGHAM Kerrie, **CUNNINGHAM Mary**, CUNNINGHAM Megan, CUNNINGHAM Neil, CUNNINGHAM Pat, CUNNINGHAM Peter, CUNNINGHAM Bob, CUNNINGHAM Robyn, CUNNINGHAM Ross, CUNNINGHAM Ross, CUNNINGHAM Shari, CUNNINGHAM Shirley, CUNNINGHAM Shona, CUNNINGHAM Sue, CUNNINGHAM Wilma, CUNNINGTON Anna, CUPIT Cathy, CUPITT Amie, CUPITT Brett, CUPITT Ursula, CURBY Merlene, CURBY Terry, CURD Diane, CURD Philip, CURDIE John, CURDIE Morton, CURKO Dajana, CURLEY Chris, CURLEY David, CURLEY Jen, CURLEY Mike, CURNOCK David, CURNOW Geoffrey, CURNOW John, CURNOW Linda, CURNOW Melville, CURNOW Vern, CURNOW Yvonne, CURRALL Carly, CURRALL Doug, CURRAN Debbie, CURRAN Edwina, CURRAN Eunice, CURRAN Haydee, CURRAN Jeremy, CURRAN Buzz, CURRAN Timothy, CURRELL Ebony, CURREY Tracey, CURRIE Alice, CURRIE Blair, CURRIE Chris, CURRIE Elvira, CURRINCKX Jill, CURRY Carina, CURRY Joanne, CURRY Maree, CURRY Michael, CURRY-HYDE Henry, CURRYHYDE Jo, CURTAYNE Tony, CURTIN Austin, CURTIN Chris, CURTIN David, CURTIN James, CURTIN Jennie, CURTIN John, CURTIN Mike, CURTIN Patrick, CURTIN Richard, CURTIN Rob, CURTIN Bob, CURTIN Tim, CURTIS Bob, CURTIS Andrew, CURTIS Annette, CURTIS Brad, CURTIS Cameron, CURTIS Ian, CURTIS James, CURTIS Jan, CURTIS Jack, CURTIS Ken, CURTIS Lisa, CURTIS Mark, CURTIS Trish, CURTIS Stephen, CURTIS Susan, CURTISS Fran, CURWEN Peter, CURZON Adrian, CUSACK Danielle, CUSACK Ivan, CUSACK Jacqui, CUSACK Jim, CUSACK Wendy, CUSCHIERI Anna, CUSCHIERI Julian, CUSCHIERI Louise, CUSH Sarah, CUSTANCE Nancy, CUSTANCE Jim, CUSTANCE William, CUTAJAR Edward, CUTAJAR Ray, CUTHBERT Jodie, CUTHBERT Lloyd, CUTHBERT Pam, CUTHBERT Vanessa, CUTHILL Maureen, CUTLER Andrew, CUTLER Jenny, CUTLER Kris, CUTLER Maureen, CUTLER Ros, CUTMORE Matthew, CUTRONI Tony, CUTTLE Terry, CUTTRISS Louise, CUTULI Lynette, CUY Mary, CUYA Liliana, CUZENS Kaye, CUZNER Cheryl, CUZNER Martin, CVIJETIC Vera, CVORO Nenad, CYMBALAK Eva, CZARNECKI Eddie, CZERKIES David, CZERWONKA Joanna, CZORNIJ Claire.

D

D'ABRERA Cheryl, D'ALESSANDRI Marie, D'ALESSANDRO Mark, D'ALESSANDRO Sonia, D'ANGELO Marcella, D'ANTONIO Brooke, D'ANTONIO Debbie, D'ANTONIO Trent, D'ARCHY James, D'ARCHY Jannifer, D'ARCY Barbara, D'ARCY Brendan, D'ARCY Emma, D'ARCY Jordan, D'ARCY Melinda, D'CRUZ Anthony, D'CRUZ Greer, D'CRUZ Marie, D'CRUZ Roheela, D'ESTE John, D'MONTE Shaun, D'MORAIS Frederic, D'MORAIS Sonali, D'OMBRAIN Kim, D'ONOFRIO Joe, D'SILVA Elaine, D'SILVA John, D'SILVA Yvan, D'SOUZA Annemarie, D'SOUZA Debbie, D'SOUZA Elaine, D'SOUZA Irene, D'SOUZA Miriam, D'SOUZA Nicole, D'SOUZA Nigel, D'SYLVA Tyson, D'VAS Mary, DA COSTA QUAGLIO Leila, DA CRUZ Melville, DA LAPA-SOARES Maria, DA LAPA-SOARES Reg, DA ROCHA NETTO Milton, DA SILVA Amanda, DA SILVA Eduardo, DA SILVA Willie, DA SILVA Jackie, DA SILVA Jose, DA SILVA Marcio, DA SILVA Vanessa, DAAWOD Kardonia, DABELSTEIN Brenda, DABIT Jane, DABLAN Nazha, DABLAN Youssef, DACHS Jan, DACHS Paul, DACICH Natalie, DACRE Allan, DADAK Christine, DADSWELL Peter, DAGELET James, DAGG Diana, DAGG Ken, DAGG Kevin, DAGGETT Maud, DAGHER Joseph, DAGHERO Paula, DAGLISH Bruce, DAHER Billy, DAHER Elizabeth, DAHER Abiz, DAHL Bree, DAHL Megan, DAHLEN Helen, DAHLITZ Patti, DAHROUG Muhammad, DAI Alison, DAI Xiaohong, DAIGLE Janine, DAIN Alison, DAINTER Les, DAINTER Susie, DAIZLI Hajja, DAL SANTO Matt, DALAL Dilkhush, DALBY Sharon, DALE Andrew, DALE Angela, DALE Beverley, DALE Cheryl, DALE Desma, DALE Gavin, DALE Gemma, DALE Geoff, DALE Jeffrey, DALE Kate, DALE Katrina, DALE Kylie, DALE Lewis, DALE Nick, DALE Riva, DALE Robert, DALE Roger, DALEY Christa, DALEY Damien, DALEY John, DALEY Maurice, DALEY Michael, DALEY Fil, DALEY Bill, DALI Joseph, DALKIN Sarah, DALL Keith, DALLA-POZZA Elizabeth, DALLAM Rebecca, DALLAS Kevin, DALLEY Barbara, DALLI Gwen, DALLI Gwendoline, DALLI Joseph, DALLINGER Lorraine, DALLY Ann, DALPRA Michele, DALRYMPLE Michelle, DALRYMPLE Bill, DALTON Brian, DALTON Carl, DALTON Chris, DALTON Danny, DALTON Dianne, DALTON Elly, DALTON Isis, DALTON Jack, DALTON Joy, DALTON Karen, DALTON Mike, DALTON Norman, DALTON Richard, DALTON Robyn, DALTON Seamus, DALTON Vernon, DALWOOD Margaret, DALY Alison, DALY Andrew, DALY Ben, DALY Dru, DALY Greg, DALY James, DALY Janine, DALY Karen, DALY Lawrie, DALY Lorraine, DALY Martin, DALY Patrick, DALY Peter, DALY Richard, DALY Terence, DALY Yvonne, DALZELL Allan, DALZIEL Dominique, DALZIELL Penny, DAM Thuy, DAMBMAN Carl, DAMEN John, DAMIANOU David, DAMJANOVIC Marisa, DAMM Jenny, DAMMEREL Zelva, DAMODARAN Omprakash, DAMON Pam, DAMOULARIS Anthony, DAMPNEY James, DANAHER Rebecca, DANARO Joe, DANCIS Mike, DANCIS Rudi, DANCKWERTS Annette, DANCKWERTS Chris, DANE Allison, DANECEK Dan, DANES Evelyn, DANES Keith, DANG Binh, DANG Jen, DANG Lyly, DANG Ngoc, DANG Quang, DANG Phuong, DANG Sanh, DANG Triet, DANI Alex, DANI Ibrahim, DANI Linda, DANIEL Alison, DANIEL Andrew, DANIEL Catherine, DANIEL Don, DANIEL Heather, DANIEL Phil, DANIEL Bob, DANIEL Sandra, DANIEL Shelley, DANIEL Tracey, DANIELE Dominic, DANIELLI Arnold, DANIELS Chris, DANIELS Fred, DANIELS Greg, DANIELS Karen, DANIELS Kez, DANIELS Melissa, DANIELS Mike, DANIELS Toni, DANKOVA Eliska, DANKS Katherine, DANN Aynsleigh, DANN Linda, DANN Sandra, DANN Teri, DANO Michal, DANON Stephen, DANSIE Adam, DANUATMODJO Junita, DANYLUK Harley, DAO Diep, DAOUD Fay, DARAS Leon, DARAS Marissa, DARBON Garry, DARBY Allen, DARBY Allan, DARBY Bernice, DARBY Chris, DARCY Carla, DARCY Darren, DARCY Matthew, DARE Jenny, DARE John, DARE Lesley, DARGAN Yuri, DARIN Rex, DARIO Danni, DARK Graeme, DARLEY Ariel, DARLING Mark, DARLING Robin, DARLINGTON Mike, DARLINGTON Sarah, DARMADJI Handoko, DARMAWAN Krish, DARMAWATY Amalia, DARMENIA MaryRose, DARNELL Jenny, DAROCZY Judit, DARR Joan, DARRAGH Carolyn, DARRELL Lisa, DARROCH Ann, DARROCH Susan, DARROUGH Neila, DART Andrea, DARTNELL Don, DARTNELL Phil, DARTNELL Rosemary, DARTNELL Trevor, DARVEY Jennifer, DARVODELSKY Anne, DARYANANI Nina, DAS Krishna, DAS GUPTI Goutam, DASCO Grace, DASH Annika, DASH Jan, DASH John, DASHWOOD Jennifer, DASHWOOD Maxine, DASHWOOD Steve, DASILVA Tony, DASKEY Joan, DASKEY John, DASS Satish, DASZKIEWICZ Tamara, DATE Ken, DATKO George, DATTA Raj, DATTANI Bala, DATUIN Florida, DAUBAGNA Vincent, DAUBNEY Melissa, DAUJOTIS Ray, DAUK Stephen, DAUM Jim, DAVAA Muggie, DAVE Kiran, DAVE Dave, DAVEN Tom, DAVENEY Roslyn, DAVENPORT Ben, DAVENPORT Denise, DAVENPORT Jan, DAVENPORT Lynda, DAVENPORT Sue, DAVER Mithi, DAVERIADAMS Louisa, DAVEY Allie, DAVEY Glenn, DAVEY Gustin, DAVEY Katrina, DAVEY Leon, DAVEY Marg, DAVEY Nicolette, DAVEY

Rob, DAVEY Roly, DAVEY-STARR Josephine, DAVID Benjamin, DAVID Garfield, DAVID Glenn, DAVID Gwen, DAVID Jerry, DAVID Kelli, DAVID Marla, DAVID Paul, DAVID Raquelle, DAVID Stefan, DAVID Tim, DAVIDS Eva, DAVIDS Johanna, DAVIDS Ralph, **DAVIDSON Alan**, DAVIDSON Ann, DAVIDSON Anna, DAVIDSON Brady, DAVIDSON Christian, DAVIDSON Edwin, DAVIDSON Geoff, DAVIDSON Graham, DAVIDSON Janet, DAVIDSON Jenny, DAVIDSON Jenny, **DAVIDSON Julie**, DAVIDSON Katrina, DAVIDSON Lisa, DAVIDSON Louise, DAVIDSON Lyn, DAVIDSON Melissa, DAVIDSON Michael, DAVIDSON Michelle, DAVIDSON Moira, DAVIDSON Nathan, DAVIDSON Norita, DAVIDSON Paul, DAVIDSON Renae, DAVIDSON Robert, DAVIDSON Bob, DAVIDSON Ross, DAVIDSON Shirley, DAVIDSSON Chatarina, DAVIE Campbell, DAVIES Ann, DAVIES Ann, DAVIES Beryl, DAVIES Beryl, DAVIES Brian, DAVIES Caliene, DAVIES Chris, **DAVIES Cleveland**, DAVIES Clifford, DAVIES Beth, DAVIES Frank, DAVIES Gary, DAVIES Geoff, DAVIES Geoff, DAVIES Gerry, DAVIES Glynne, DAVIES Graham, DAVIES Graeme, DAVIES Greg, DAVIES Greg, DAVIES Gunda, DAVIES James, DAVIES Janet, DAVIES Jenni, DAVIES John, DAVIES John, DAVIES John, DAVIES Jojo, DAVIES Judy, DAVIES Justine, DAVIES Keith, DAVIES Kerry, DAVIES Lachlan, DAVIES Margaret, DAVIES Mark, DAVIES Marie-Anne, DAVIES Margaret, DAVIES Martin, DAVIES Matthew, DAVIES Megan, DAVIES Merv, DAVIES Michael, DAVIES Neil, DAVIES Patricia, DAVIES Paul, DAVIES Peter, DAVIES Peter, DAVIES Ken, DAVIES Rob, DAVIES Robyn, DAVIES Ron, DAVIES Ros, DAVIES Sandra, DAVIES Sohayla, DAVIES Sonia, DAVIES Stacey, DAVIES Sue, DAVIES Taffy, DAVIES Therese, DAVIES Tom, DAVIES Vince, DAVIES-SCOURFIELD Charles, DAVIESSMITH Graham, DAVILA Edward, DAVIN Jean, DAVINI Damian, DAVINI Gloria, DAVINO Joe, DAVIS Adele, DAVIS Ali, DAVIS Allan, DAVIS Andrew, DAVIS Ange, DAVIS Angela, DAVIS Tony, DAVIS Avril, DAVIS Beryl, DAVIS Bev, DAVIS Brett, DAVIS Bruce, DAVIS Kate, DAVIS Charbel, DAVIS Chad, DAVIS Cherie, DAVIS Chris, DAVIS Colleen, DAVIS Colin, DAVIS Cyril, DAVIS David, DAVIS Dawn, DAVIS Desmond, DAVIS Dianne, DAVIS Doreen, DAVIS Ted, DAVIS Eileen, DAVIS Erin, DAVIS Eunice, DAVIS Ewen, DAVIS Francine, DAVIS Gail, DAVIS Gail, DAVIS Gary, DAVIS Grant, DAVIS Graham, DAVIS Greyd'n, DAVIS Gwyn, DAVIS Helen, DAVIS Ian, DAVIS Ilona, DAVIS Jacquelene, DAVIS Jackie, DAVIS Jim, DAVIS Jan, DAVIS Jane, DAVIS Jenny, DAVIS Jodie, DAVIS Tim, DAVIS Jack, DAVIS Jonathan, DAVIS Julie, DAVIS Karen, DAVIS Kelli, DAVIS Ken, DAVIS Kevin, DAVIS Kevyn, DAVIS Kyle, DAVIS Linda, DAVIS Lucy, DAVIS Lynne, DAVIS Mardi, DAVIS Matt, DAVIS Melisa, DAVIS Mike, DAVIS Miles, DAVIS Neville, DAVIS Noel, DAVIS Pam, DAVIS Pat, DAVIS Paul, DAVIS Penny, DAVIS Peter, DAVIS Pete, DAVIS Peter, DAVIS John, DAVIS Peter, **DAVIS Phyllis**, DAVIS Phyl, DAVIS Beck, DAVIS Robin, DAVIS Barry, DAVIS Ron, DAVIS Ron, DAVIS Sally, DAVIS Sharon, DAVIS Sharon, DAVIS Stan, DAVIS Stephen, DAVIS Sue, DAVIS Tana, DAVIS Tracie, DAVIS LEE Judith, DAVIS-SMITH Michael, DAVISON Harry, DAVISON Davo, DAVISON Lyndall, DAVISON Paul, DAVISON Paul, DAVISON Philippa, DAVOREN Brad, DAVY Brett, DAVY Caroline, DAVY Ruth, DAVY Bill, DAWE Simon, DAWES Andrew, DAWES Annette, DAWES Denise, DAWES Jemma, DAWES Loren, DAWES Richard, DAWES Samantha, DAWES Scott, DAWES Wendy, DAWKINS Beth, DAWKINS Ray, DAWLINGS John, DAWOOD Faris, DAWS Aaron, DAWS Janet, DAWS Jemina, DAWS Kate, DAWS Kyle, DAWS Tim, DAWSON Andrew, DAWSON Andrew, DAWSON Annette, DAWSON Tony, DAWSON Barrie, **DAWSON Barry**, DAWSON Campbell, DAWSON Catherine, DAWSON Cate, DAWSON Christopher, DAWSON Diane, DAWSON Dorothy, DAWSON Ellis, DAWSON Eric, DAWSON Fay, DAWSON Glen, DAWSON Harold, DAWSON Jess, DAWSON John, DAWSON John, DAWSON Julieanne, DAWSON Ka on, DAWSON Keith, DAWSON Kim, DAWSON Lara, DAWSON Lucas, DAWSON Marg, DAWSON Michelle, DAWSON Mike, DAWSON Naomi, DAWSON Pam, DAWSON Peter, DAWSON Sue, DAWSON Terry, DAWSON Dawso, DAWSON Trent, DAY Briohny, DAY Carol, DAY Dave, DAY David, DAY Donald, DAY Bob, DAY Georgia, DAY Gweneth, DAY Howard, DAY Judy, DAY Ken, DAY Kevin, DAY Lyn, DAY Matt, DAY Mike, DAY Michelle, DAY Mike, DAY Michele, DAY Mitch, DAY Peter, DAY Peter, DAY Robert, DAY Roy, DAY Ruth, DAY Warren, DAYA Pranita, DAYKIN Liz, DE ALMEIDA NETO Bill, DE ALVIA Mary, DE ANGELIS Ben, DE ANGELIS Giovanna, DE ANGELIS Maria, DE ANTONIO Jorge, DE BAIZE Sharon, DE BEER Estelle, DE BELLE Bernadette, DE BELLIS Dianne, DE BEUS Robert, DE BOER Robert, DE BONDE Kim, DE BORTOLI Guy, DE BOUTER Ann, DE BRINCAT Jae, DE BROGLIO Anne, DE BRUYN Jean, DE BRUYN Stephen, DE CARVALHO Celise, DE CHESNE Louise, DE COSTA Ronald, DE COUET Claudia, DE CRUZ William, DE FIGUEIREDO ESTEVES Claudia, DE GINESTET Alexandra, DE GIORGIO Adam, DE GLANVILLE Janelle, DE GRAAF Lyn, DE GRAAF Simon, DE GRATIE Ellen, DE GROOT Johanna, DE GROOT Stephen, DE GUZMAN Divina, DE GUZMAN Rina, DE HIGHDEN Michelle, DE HOMMEL Chantal, DE JAGER Nona, DE JAGER Sharon, DE JESUS Lorna, DE JONG Arno, DE JONG Darren, DE JONG Fiona, DE JONG Trish, DE JONG Winsome, DE JONGH Mara, DE JONGH Lisa, DE JONGH Robert, DE KAUWE Vevil, DE KEIZER Els, DE KONING Glen, DE KONING Hester, DE LA CRUZ German, DE LA CRUZ Maria, DE LA GARDE Jan, DE LA GARDE Tom, DE LA MOTTE Mick, DE LA PIEDRA Raul, DE LA TORRE Chantelle, DE LA TORRE Pablo, DE LAINE Bridget, DE LAINE Fleur, DE LAMOTTE Julie, DE LANEY Joyce, DE LANG Carl, DE LEEDE Tony, DE LEON Gus, DE LEON Jose, DE LEON Marlon, DE LORENZO-CROWE Carmelina, DE LOW Dorothy, DE LUCA Marisa, DE LUCA Terence, DE LUNA Mary, DE LUNA Paul, DE MAIN Ami, DE MANINCOR George, DE MARCHI Tania, DE MARCO Kate, DE MELO Luiz, DE MORTON Brendan, DE MUNITIZ Arthur, DE NICOLA Lili, DE OLIVIERA Samuel, DE PAULA Maria, DE PIETRO Laura, DE POORTERE Roger, DE RAVIN Beverley, DE REZENDE Ineke, DE RIDDER Henrietta, DE RONDE Metse, DE RONDE Natalie, DE ROOIJ Klaasje, DE ROOY Nick, DE ROSA David, DE ROSE De, DE ROZA KNIGHT Tara, DE RUITER Richard, DE SAIN Antoinette, DE SILVA Ami, DE SILVA Damika, DE SILVA Satigo, DE SILVEIRA Lawrence, DE SIMONE Maria, DE SOUZA Jim, DE SOUZA Jeverley, DE SOUZA Samantha, DE SOYSA Ravi, DE SOYSA Shanta, DE SZELL Kalman, DE TARLE Ning, DE TROY-LAW Odile, DE VARGAS TABERA Cristina, DE VEGA Ben, DE VERA Emma, DE VILLA Marichu, DE VILLA Nicanor, DE VILLIERS Richard, DE VOS Milroy, DE VRIES Anita, DE VRIES Peter, DE VRIES Bill, DE WAARD Ann-Maree, DE WIJN Kaye, DE WIT Catherine, DE WIT Jonathan, DE ZILVA Alan, DE ZYLVA Rachael, DE-FINA David, DE-FINA Marina, DE-FINA Mish, DE-LA-WARR David, DEACON Allan, DEACON Amy Leigh, DEACON Brenda, DEACON Christine, DEADMAN Thomas, DEADY Patricia, DEAKES Scott, DEALL Julie, DEAN Barry, DEAN Brendan, DEAN Clifford, DEAN Denis, DEAN Dorothy, DEAN Esther, DEAN Faith, DEAN Gary, DEAN Geoff, DEAN Helen, DEAN Jason, DEAN Jeanette, DEAN Jodie, DEAN Julie, DEAN Luke, DEAN Mark, DEAN Mark, DEAN Michelle, DEAN Oliver, DEAN Pam, DEAN Peter, DEAN Richard, DEAN Rob, DEAN Ross, DEANE Ricki, DEANE John, DEANE Maggie, DEANE Paul, DEANE Peter, DEANE Rebecca, DEANE Robyn, DEANS Ann, DEANS Cecil, DEANS John, DEANS Kylie, DEANS Peter, DEANS Sylvia, DEAR Dolores, DEAR Ian, DEAR Sally, DEARE Steven, DEARING Des, DEARING Diane, DEARING Heather, DEARING Howard, DEARING Jason, DEARING John, DEARING Kirrily, DEARING Bob, DEARING Wayne, DEARLOVE Kevin, DEARLOVE Paul, DEAS Ryan, DEAS Theresa, DEAVES William, DEAYTON Julie, DEB Pradip, DEBARTOLO Bianca, DEBEBE Sifrashwork, DEBECK Denise, DEBELLE Guy, DEBEVEC Helena, DEBNAM Craig, DEBNAM Fred, DEBNAM Max, DEBNAM Patricia, DEBNAN Graham, DEBNER Rebekka, DEBONO Margaret, DEBONO Mathew, DEBONO Mitchell, DEBRINCAT Joe, DEBRINCAT Maureen, DEBS Carol, DECARIE Joan, DECARLO Alfred, DECEAN Emma, DECHAUFEPIE Nadine, DECHNICZ Alex, DECHNICZ Helen, DECHNICZ Tay, DECK Wilf, DECKER Lesley, DECKER Tom, DECLERCK Alexandra, DEDICH Nicholas, DEDMAN Andrew, DEDONA Eddie, DEE Brett, DEED Marj, DEED Ray, DEEGAN Liz, DEEGAN Luke, DEEGAN Michael, DEEHAN Moira, DEEHAN Pete, DEEKS Nick, DEER Chris, DEER Helene, DEER Bruce, DEER Tim, DEFINA Defina, DEGELING Kellie, DEGENHARDT Scott, DEGENNARO Michael, DEGOTARDI Jon, DEGUARA Kelly, DEHOON Adrian, DEIGHTON

Rebekah, DEITZ Stuart, **DEJONG Anthony**, DEKALB Denise, DEKIE Peter, DEKKER Geraldine, DEKKER Judy, DEKKER Anneleen, DEKKER Richard, DEL CASTILLO Fernando, DEL CID CABRERA Elton, DEL FIERRO Eugene, DEL MUNDO Nadh, DEL PINO LOPEZ Leslie, DEL RIEGO Frank, DELA TORRE Ecuardo, DELAFORCE Glenda, DELAFORCE Jason, DELAFORCE Noel, DELAHAY Pascal, DELAMONT Mongo, DELAMOTTE John, DELANDER Steven, DELANEY Tony, DELANEY Mike, DELANEY Edwin, DELANEY Harry, DELANEY Jenni, DELANEY John, DELANEY Kerrie, DELANEY Merrilyn, DELANEY Michiko, DELANEY Peter, DELANEY Ron, DELANEY Ron, DELANEY Shirley, DELANEY Sylvia, DELANEY Vicki, DELANG Sue, DELANGEN Jeannette, DELANY Beryl, DELAROCHE SOUVESTRE Louis, DELATOUR Chris, DELAVERE Penny, DELESCLUSE Camille, DELGADO Carina, DELGADO Robert, DELGADO Isabel, DELIC Edina, DELIC Emir, DELINO Rachel, DELISEO Peter, DELL Les, DELLA CA Ryan, DELLA CASA Vin, DELLA TORRE Gianni, DELLA TORRE Jenny, DELLA-CAMERA Eddie, DELLAFOSSE Cynthia, DELLE COSTE Fiona, DELLE COSTE Lisa, DELLE COSTE Dino, DELLER Ann, DELLER Bob, DELLING Lorna, DELLOCOSTE Dino, DELLOW Michelle, DELMAN Adrian, DELMAS Melanie, DELMEGE Garry, DELMONT Ronald, DELPHIN Rachel, DELPLACE-SMITH Annie, DELPRATT Dave, DELSUPEXHE Vincent, DELUCA Christine, DELVES Bill, DEMAJO Pierre, DEMARIA Ernesto, DEMASI June, DEMEIO Stephen, DEMERAL Neil, DEMERTJIS Manuel, DEMETRI Eddie, DEMETRIOS Andrew, DEMICOLI Fred, DEMIR Dogan, DEMIRALP Nihal, DEMIRIS Katrina, DEMKIW Robert, DEMMER Hugh, DEMORAIS Dario, DEMOS Candy, DEMOSTHENOUS Adriana, DEMPSEY Margaret, DEMPSEY Mike, DEMPSEY Patricia, DEMPSTER Arthur, DEN ENGELSMAN Pamela, DEN OTTER Bianka, DEN OTTER Hans, DENCH Charlie, DENDA Kayo, DENDOUNE Nadir, DENE Sean, DENENBERG Steve, DENENBERG Sue, DENES Andrew, DENEV Dencho, DENG Bao, DENG Peter, DENG Roland, DENG Christine, DENG Joey, **DENGATE Amanda**, DENGATE Rachael, DENHAM Tony, DENHAM Nathan, DENHAM Nathalie, DENING Barry, DENING Katryna, DENIS Denis, DENISON Phillip, DENISON Troy, DENKEL Matt, DENLEY Lucy, DENMAN Geoff, DENNETT Amanda, DENNETT Ben, DENNEY Greg, DENNIEN Graham, DENNING Elaine, DENNIS Col, DENNIS David, DENNIS Debbie, DENNIS Ivan, DENNIS James, DENNIS Kristy, DENNIS Les, DENNIS Lisa, DENNIS Maxine, DENNIS Megan, DENNIS Murray, DENNIS Trish, DENNIS Rebecca, DENNIS Sandra, DENNIS Stephen, DENNIS Val, DENNIS William, DENNISON Sandra, DENNISS Cherylee, DENNISS Liz, DENNY Dick, DENT Garry, DENT Kevin, DENT Nicholas, DENT Nikki, DENT Sean, DENTON Angela, DENTON Craig, DENTON Peter, DENZONGPA Sonam, DEO Siddharth, DEPESTEL-OLIVERA Lieve, DEPIAZZI Jill, DEPIAZZI Julie, DEPOMA Nesta, DEREUVER Romina, DERHAM Grant, DERICHS Hartmut, DERKSEN Lucy, DERKSEN Ted, DERKYI George, DERKYI Sophia, DERMAWAN Hendry, DERNEE Geoff, DERRICK John, DERRICK Keiren, DERRICK Rosalie, DERRICOTT Davina, DERRICOURT Frances, DERRIN Jack, DERWIN Tony, DERZEKOS Jim, DESAI Biren, DESAI Farhaana, DESAI Raksha, DESAI Yamini, DESAILLY Annette, DESANTIS Catherine, DESCHAUER Natalie, DESFOSSES Joseph, DESKOSKI Olivia, DESMARCHELIER Judy, DESMARCHELIER Paul, DESMOND Belinda, DESMOND Keith, DESMOND Barney, DESOUKEY Mick, DESOUZA Douglas, DESOUZA Sharon, DESOUZA Wycliff, DESPEA Tracey, DESPOTOVIC Dragica, DESRUMAUX Flo, DESSAIX Brenda, DESTON Debbie, DETHAN Martine, DETONI Zvonko, DETTINO Carmen, DEUTSCH Jorge, DEUTSCH Linda, DEVAI Ivan, DEVAI Judy, DEVAI Robert, DEVENDRA Arun, DEVENE Nivette, DEVENNY Mark, DEVER Amanda, DEVER Nerida, DEVER Paul, DEVEREAUX Bill, DEVESON Lance, DEVI Anjila, DEVINE Carol, DEVINE Frances, DEVINE James, DEVINE Ken, DEVINE Lara, DEVINE Ron, DEVINE Stephen, DEVINE Bill, DEVINS Karina, DEVITT Phil, DEVJAK Giovanni, DEVLIN Robert, DEVLIN Fiona, DEVLIN Greg, DEVLIN Jan, DEVLIN Michael, DEVLIN Yvonne, DEVON Steve, DEVOS Anthony, DEVOY Raymond, DEVRIMOL Tayfun, DEWAN alit, DEWAR Paul, DEWAR Richard, DEWAR Sharon, DEWAR Ulla, DEWDNEY John, DEWDNEY Micheline, DEWEY Elaine, DEWHURST Rob, DEWHURST Reg, DEWHURST Solveig, DEWHURST Steven, DEWS Arthur, DEY Dipangshu, DEZARNAULDS Camille, DHAKAL Pradip, DHANJAL Pardip, DHARMADI Paulina, DHARMAWAN Herbert, DHEURLE Colette, DHILLON Jasjit, DHILLON Tek, DHINGRA Janakdeep, DHINGRA Richa, DHOSI Kate, DHULIPALA Srikanth, DHURJATI Kiran, DI BARTOLOMEO Jennifer, DI BENEDETTO Luigi, **DI CERTO Matilda**, DI DONATO Andrew, DI DONATO Lina, DI GENUA Francesco, DI GIOVANNI Rita, DI LEO Jessica, DI MARCO Katrina, DI MAURO Aliscia, DI MEZZA Sonia, DI PAOLA Ina, DI PIETRO Gaby, DI SALVIA Lauren, DI STEFANO Giulio, DIAB Samir, DIACCI Peter, DIACONO Jose, DIAMANTES Marika, DIAMOND Chris, DIAMOND David, DIAMOND Ian, DIAMOND John, DIAMOND Peter, DIAMOND Toula, DIAS Muditha, DIAS Eslyn, DIAS Ruwanie, DIAS Shenan, DIAS Trina, DIAW Fatima, DIAZ Ali, DIAZ Arturo, DIAZ Arthur, DIAZ Empera, DIAZ Lalio, DIAZ Ferdie, DIAZ Grisel, DIAZ Marisa, DIAZ Odilio, DIAZ Patricia, DIAZ Perfecto, DIB Ghania, DIB Robert, DIBBIN Jenny, DIBBLEE Anne-Marie, DIBDIN Myyung, DIBDIN Yung, DIBLEY Kenneth, DIBLEY Leonie, DIBOWSKI Anna, DICHIERA Jennifer, DICK Gary, DICK Bruce, DICK Ken, DICK Kris, DICK Luisa, DICK Stephen, DICKENS Maureen, DICKENS Ros, DICKENSON Rachel, DICKER Julie, DICKERSON Rita, DICKERSON Rob, DICKERSON Sandy, DICKESON Corie, DICKESON Kev, DICKIE John, DICKIE Peter, DICKIE Rachel, DICKIN Barbara, DICKIN Hannah, DICKINS Harold, DICKINS Paul, DICKINSON Ashleigh, DICKINSON Hayley, DICKINSON Susan, DICKSON Alan, DICKSON Bruce, DICKSON Chris, DICKSON Gavin, DICKSON Jen, DICKSON Ken, DICKSON Kim, DICKSON Margaret, DICKSON Pam, DICKSON Pat, DICKSON Richard, DICKSON Bob, **DICKSON Robert**, DICKSON Robert, DICKSON Sharyn, DICKSON Sharon, DICKSON Tamara, DICKSON Tim, DICKWELLA Sanjeena, DIEBERT Ben, DIEBERT Carlie, DIEBOLD Roger, DIEDERICKS Anne, DIEDRICH Patrick, DIEMAR Vicki, DIEP Chau, DIEPEVEEN Dirk, DIERIKX Bob, DIERKES Bill, DIETERLE Oliver, DIFFEN Joe, DIFFIN Peter, DIFFLEY Eila, DIFFORD Justine, DIFUNTORUM Kim, DIGAL Claudette, DIGBY Andrew, DIGBY John, DIGBY Kelvin, DIGGINS Brett, DIGGINS Lester, DIGGINS Paula, DIGGINS Sue, DIGIGLIO Tania, DIGNAM Russell, DIGNAN Fiona, DIGNAN Raymond, DIJKSTRA Dirk, DIKKENBERG Jo, DILETTI Carl, DILGER Louise, DILLA Edsil, DILLER John, DILLEY Sandra, DILLON Don, DILLON Laurie, DILLON Michael, DILLON Stan, DILLON Wendy, DILLOW Grace, DILWORTH Erica, DILWORTH Geoff, DILWORTH Jan, DILWORTH Penny, DIMCIC Simone, DIMECH Andrew, DIMECH Lawrence, DIMENT Philip, DIMENT Tim, DIMICHIEL Ann-Marie, DIMICHIEL Lorraine, DIMITRAKOPOULOS Peter, DIMITRIADIS Margaret, DIMITROPOULOS Con, DIMITROPOULOS Jim, DIMMICK Rob, DIMOND Tara, DIMOPOULOS Katina, DIMOS John, DIMOSKA Marina, DINAMARCA Teresita, DINESEN NEERGAARD Allen, DING Jun, DING Victor, DING Yen-Ping, DINGCONG Joanne, DINGLE Georgina, DINGLE Marlene, DINGWALL Gordon, DINGWALL Rose-Marie, DINH Hong, DINH Khanh, DINH Cuong, DINH Binh, DINHAM Ian, DINNEEN Robyn, DINNELL Belinda, DINNELL Stephanie, DINNEN Naomi, DINNIE Keiran, **DINNING Annette**, DINNING James, DINNING John, DINOIA Jesse, DIOMIS Con, DIONIO Abby, DIONISIO Antonio, DIONNE Patrice, DIPOLD Von, DISABATINO Megan, DISAURO Sandra, DISBERY Clive, DISHER Jim, DISIBIO Kathryn, DISOUZA Nelson, DISSANAYAKE Reggie, DISSANAYAKE Rohan, DISTEFANO Lee, DITCHBURN Grame, DITTON Junelle, DITTRICK Cheryl, DITTY Sam, DIU Gina, DIURNOCANNAVO Maria, DIVE Janette, DIVE Jean, DIVER Wendy, DIWAKAR Shaon, DIX Margaret, DIXEN Mark, DIXEN Tom, DIXON Bert, DIXON Andrew, DIXON Angus, DIXON Don, DIXON Graham, DIXON Cecil, DIXON Jo, DIXON Jo, DIXON Joy, DIXON Karan, DIXON Kay, DIXON Mike, DIXON Paul, DIXON Richard, DIXON Richard, DIXON Rob, DIXON Rohan, DIXON Steve, DIXON Terrence, DIXON Wendy, DIXON HUGHES David, DIZICK Betty, DIZON Babes, DIZON Manny, DJEMAL Enver, DJI Fie, DJOKOVIC Bossa, DJONGKAH Cissillia, DJUKIC Dushan, DJUKOVIC Ana, DJURACIC Daniel, DJURIC Aleksandar, DJURICIN Roger, DJURICIN Roger, DO Harry, DO Hun, DO Jenny, DO Khang, DOAE Costica, DOAN Joseph, DOBBIE Daniel, DOBBIN George, DOBBINS Heather, DOBELL Ken, DOBELL Rod, DOBELL-BROWN Andrew, DOBESON Richard, DOBLE Paul, DOBRIC Romel, DOBRINSKI Leon, DOBSON Frank, DOBSON Gab, DOBSON

Hannah, DOBSON Linda, DOBSON Richard, DOCHERTY Diane, DOCHERTY Josette, DOCK Cindy, DOCKER Kerry, DOCKING Carolyn, DOCKSEY Judy, DOCKTER Patty, DODD Ann, DODD Barry, DODD Cheryl, DODD Gary, DODD John, DODD Julie, DODD Kylie, DODD Marilyn, DODD Ryan, DODD Bruce, DODD Olive, DODDS Belinda, DODDS Beryl, DODDS Cliff, DODDS Jan, DODDS Linda, DODDS Marco, DODDS Patsy, DODDS William, DODS Gwen, DODSWORTH Sean, DOECKE John, DOECKE Rebecca, DOEHRING Eunice, DOEL Jeanne, DOEL Justin, DOENAU John, DOERR Katie, DOFTER Terry, DOGAN Ender, DOGGETT Clare, DOGGETT Douglass, DOHERTY Alan, DOHERTY Anita, DOHERTY Bernice, DOHERTY Jan, DOHERTY Edna, DOHERTY Kate, DOHERTY Kevin, DOHERTY Kim, DOHERTY Matt, DOHERTY Pauline, DOHERTY Rebecca, DOHERTY Shirley, DOHLVIK Helena, DOI Yukari, DOIG Ruth, DOKULIL Elizabeth, DOKUMCU Cihan, DOLAN Cherie, DOLHEGUY Kellie, DOLINIS John, DOLL Justin, DOLLISSON Kate, DOLOSWALA Indrani, DOMAGALA Renae, DOMARS Malcolm, DOMAZAR Harry, DOMENICI John, DOMENY Lisa, DOMESHOK Rita, DOMINEY Maggie, DOMINGUEZ Tony, DOMINGUEZ Junior, DOMINGUEZ Cecille, DOMINISH Clyde, DOMLIJA Drago, DOMONKOS Noemi, DON Grahame, DONA Noel, DONACHIE Josephine, DONAGHY Bill, DONAHOO Paul, DONALD Clare, DONALD Geoff, DONALD Guy, DONALD John, DONALD Sancha, DONALDSON Cameron, DONALDSON Christine, DONALDSON Helen, DONALDSON Robert, DONALDSON Roger, DONALDSON Shireen, DONAT Jimmy, DONATI Betsy, DONATINI Luke, DONATO Damian, DONAYRE Andrew, DONE Charlie, DONEGAN Vicki, DONELAN Phil, DONELLY Elizabeth, DONEMAN Jane, DONEVSKA Lin, DONEY Dhuruwal, DONG Jessie, DONG Qing, DONG Mary, DON GES Sharon, DONKIN Belinda, DONKIN Jean, DONKIN Steve, DONKIN Stuart, DONLAN Steve, DONLEVY Rosemary, DONLEY Tony, DONLEY Irene, DONLON Lorry, DONNAN Rick, DONNELLAN Sally, DONNELLAN Cheryl, DONNELLAN Elizabeth, DONNELLAN John, DONNELLEY Graham, DONNELLY Brett, DONNELLY David, DONNELLY Elizabeth, DONNELLY Elizabeth, DONNELLY Gill, DONNELLY Graham, DONNELLY Jane, DONNELLY Jeff, DONNELLY John, DONNELLY John, DONNELLY Kathy, DONNELLY Margaret, DONNELLY Margaret, DONNELLY Paul, DONNELLY Peter, DONOGHUE Brendan, DONOGHUE Judith, DONOGHUE Keith, DONOGHUE Matthew, **DONOHOE JD**, DONOHUE Alanna, DONOHUE Carole, DONOHUE Ivor, DONOHUE Lisa, DONOHUE Patrick, DONOHUE Pat, DONOHUE Patrick, DONOHUE Paul, DONOHUE Thomas, DONOSO Benny, DONOSO Caroline, DONOVAN Brad, DONOVAN Catherine, DONOVAN Geoff, DONOVAN Jim, DONOVAN Jo, DONOVAN John, DONOVAN Lynnette, DONOVAN Morrie, DONOVAN Peter, DONOVAN Philip, DONOVAN Steve, DONOVAN Sue, DONOVAN Susan, DONOVAN Terry, DONOVAN TD, DONSKY Van, DONSWORTH Beverley, DONSWORTH Roger, DOO Daniel, DOO Geoff, DOODIE Tony, DOOHAN Andrew, DOOHAN Daniel, DOOHAN Stephanie, DOOLAN Alessandra, DOOLAN Amie, DOOLAN Graham, DOOLAN Kay, DOOLAN Shirley, DOOLEY Damian, DOOLEY Geoff, DOOLEY Janice, DOOLEY Jenny, DOOLEY John, DOOLEY Keith, DOOLEY Learne, DOOLEY Lorelle, DOOLEY Robert, DOOLEY Steve, DOPPER Terry, DOPSON Bridget, DOPSON Maurie, DORAHY Andrew, DORAHY Carly, DORAHY Jenny, DORAIRAJAN Sathish, DORAN Barbara, DORAN Chris, DORAN Jim, DORAN Beck, DORBON Barbara, DORIAN Jane, DORIGO Toni, DORING David, DORKHAM Zak, DORLING Kate, DORLING Val, DORMAN Ian, DORMAN Jim, DORMAN Pam, DORMER Damian, DORN Joan, DORNEY Brett, DOROSHENKO Anya, DORREEN Ann DORREEN Marcus, DORRELL Janine, DORRELL Ryan, DORRIAN Deborah, DORRIAN Louise, DORRICOTT Agnes, DORRICOTT Jason, DORRICOTT Jodie, DORRINGTON Cameron, DORRINGTON John, DOS REMEDIOS Michael, DOS SANTOS Carlos, DOSEN Tony, DOSEN Sarah, DOSSETT Byron, DOSSETTO Robert, DOUANGBOUPHA Phavanna, DOUANGBOUPHA Vannida, DOUBE Peter, DOUBKO Lara, DOUBLE John, DOUEIHI Sarkis, DOUGHAN Brian, DOUGHAN Carmen, DOUGHENEY Kylee, DOUGHERTY Kerrie, DOUGHERTY Robert, DOUGHTY Beatrice, DOUGHTY Frank, DOUGLAS Alison, DOUGLAS Amber, DOUGLAS Brenton, DOUGLAS Carl, DOUGLAS Faye, DOUGLAS Grace, DOUGLAS Graham, DOUGLAS Helen, DOUGLAS Jim, DOUGLAS James, DOUGLAS James, DOUGLAS Jan, DOUGLAS Jennifer, DOUGLAS John, DOUGLAS John, DOUGLAS Joy, DOUGLAS Kerry, DOUGLAS Kim, DOUGLAS Leigh, DOUGLAS Margot, DOUGLAS Margaret, DOUGLAS Phill, DOUGLAS Richard, DOUGLAS Sarah, DOUGLAS Stephen, DOUGLAS Wayne, DOUGLASANDERSON Sharon, DOUGLASS Annette, DOUGLASS Belinda, DOUGLASS June, DOUGLASS Margaret, DOUGLASS Sharon, DOUMBOS Jan, DOUROUDIS Peter, DOUST Graham, DOUST Jim, DOUST Sharon, DOUST Wendy, DOVE Jenny, DOVELLOS Manuel, DOVER Bernice, DOVER Wal, DOW Allen, DOW Arthur, DOW David, DOW Julie, DOWD Grace, DOWD Kellie, DOWD Maree, DOWDS Tara, DOWELL Sharon, DOWER Helen, DOWERAH Utpal, DOWIE Bill, DOWLING Aaron, DOWLING Annette, DOWLING Brendan, DOWLING Jenny, DOWLING Pat, DOWN Grahame, DOWN Steph, DOWNER June, DOWNER Leigh, DOWNES Alan, DOWNES Andrew, DOWNES Brenda, DOWNES Judith, DOWNES Pat, DOWNES Rhonda, DOWNES Yvonne, DOWNEY James, DOWNHAM Jan, DOWNIE Bert, DOWNIE Bronwyn, DOWNIE Carole, DOWNIE Chris, DOWNIE David, DOWNIE Loretta, DOWNIE Nate, DOWNIE Pat, DOWNIE Peter, DOWNIE Rob, DOWNIE Wayne, DOWNING Amanda, DOWNING Harry, DOWNING Jenny, DOWNING Liam, DOWNING Michelle, DOWNMAN Mike, DOWNS Nikki, DOWNS Peter, DOWNS Trevor, DOWRICK Brennon, DOWSETT John, DOWSETT Michael, DOWSON Alan, DOWTON Gabe, DOYLE Anne, DOYLE Chris, DOYLE Clare, DOYLE Grant, DOYLE Doyley, DOYLE Jim, DOYLE Janet, DOYLE Jeff, DOYLE Jenny, DOYLE John, DOYLE Judith, DOYLE Karen, DOYLE Kevin, DOYLE Kevin, DOYLE Ky, DOYLE Laurel, DOYLE Lensey, DOYLE Lorraine, DOYLE Lorraine, DOYLE Mark, DOYLE Matthew, DOYLE Michael, DOYLE Monica, DOYLE Peter, DOYLE Peter, DOYLE Prue, DOYLE Richard, DOYLE Rod, DOYLE Ronald, DOYLE Shaun, DOYLE Stephen, DOYLE Sue, DOYLE Teena, DOYLE Tim, DOYLE Justin, DRABKINA Galina, DRACA Angie, DRACOPOULOS Maria, DRADY Michelle, DRAGE Sarah, DRAGOI Doina, DRAGOI George, DRAIN David, DRAKE Ben, DRAKE Loretta, DRAKE Philip, DRAKE Rose, DRAKOS Constantine, DRAKOS George, DRAKOS Nick, DRAPER Adelle, DRAPER Betty, DRAPER Bruce, DRAPER Bryan, DRAPER Colleen, DRAPER Gordon, DRAPER Jason, DRAPER Phil, DRAPER Roslyn, DRAPER Stewart, DRAUNIKAU Eleni, DRAYER Janny, DRAYER Wim, DRAYTON Charles, DRAYTON Frank, DRAYTON Francis, DRAYTON Ken, DRAYTON Rodney, DREDGE Rohan, DREGHORN Alex, DRENNAN David, DRENNAN Jocelyn, DRENTH Harm, DRESNER Philippa, DRESSLER Eric, DRESSLER Hermann, DREVES Robert, DREW Karen, DREW Larni, DREW Lucy, DREW Michelle, DREW Noel, DREW Norma, DREWE Ben, DREWE Mal, DREWE Philip, DREWE Vicki, DREWETT Jennifer, DREWNIANKA Gull, DREWNIANKA Klaus, DREYER Kimberlee, DRIEBERG Lilliane, DRIES Brenda, DRIESEN Tim, DRIESSEN John, DRIESSEN Paul, DRIGUEZ Henry, DRING Paul, DRISCOLE Diane, DRISCOLL Al, DRISCOLL Greg, DRISCOLL Phil, DRISCOLL Timothy, DRISCOLL Wayne, DRISSLER Andrea, DRITSAKIS Sylvia, DRIVER Beverley, DRIVER Helen, DRIVER Kristy, DROMEY Tashen, DRORY-WIENSTOCK Ami, DROSSOS Bill, DROULIAS Angelique, DRUCE Lynne, DRUCE Rod, DRUERY Robyn, DRUITT Margaret, DRUITT Murry, DRUMMEY Peter, DRUMMOND Annette, DRUMMOND David, DRUMMOND Fiona, DRUMMOND Janine, DRUMMOND Jason, DRUMMOND Julie, DRUMMOND Mary, DRUMMOND Margaret, DRUMMOND Natasha, DRUMMOND Rebecca, DRUMMOND Sandra, DRURY Amanda, DRURY Craig, DRURY David, DRURY Rob, DRURY Jenny, DRURY Jill, DRURY Merv, DRURY Paul, DRURY Trevor, DRYBURGH George, DRYBURGH Linden, DRYDEN Nigel, DRYDEN Pat, **DRYDEN Phil**, DRYER Gloria, DRYNAN Ron, DRYSDALE Katie, DRYZA Jo, DU Lucky, DU Ling, DU Lmh, DU Helen, DU MOULIN Phillip, DUALSKY Marcotibor, DUANE Carol, DUARTE Anita, DUARTE Milca, DUBOIS Scott, DUBOIS Tim, DUBOSE DJ, DUBOSQ Ming-Celine, DUBROJA Irena, DUBYK Alla, DUCE Robin, DUCK Geoff, DUCK Jennifer, DUCK Judith, DUCK Michael, DUCKEK Herman, DUCKETT Madeline, DUCKITT Yvonne, DUCKWORTH John, DUCKWORTH Megan, DUDEK Matthew, DUDLEY Tony, DUDLEY Bret, DUDLEY John, DUENSER Heinz,

DUFF Christine, DUFF Chris, DUFF Frank, DUFF Margaret, DUFF John, DUFFELL Tony, DUFFELL Helen, DUFFELL Matthew, DUFFELL Roy, DUFFEY Chris, DUFFEY Kevin, DUFFIELD Christine, DUFFIN Maureen, DUFFUS Margaret, DUFFY Betty, DUFFY Brennden, DUFFY Darralyn, DUFFY Ted, DUFFY J, DUFFY John, DUFFY Judith, DUFFY Juliet, DUFFY Marie, DUFFY Margaret, DUFFY Michelle, DUFFY Peter, DUFFY Gerard, DUFFY Ron, DUFFY Lynne, DUFFY Shannon, DUFFY Tom, DUFFY Bill, DUFTY Liz, DUFTY Myreen, DUFTY Rae, DUGAN David, DUGAN Matthew, DUGANOV Sasha, DUGGAN Anthony, DUGGAN Christine, DUGGAN Geoff, DUGGAN Jane, DUGGAN Jeannette, DUGGAN Jenny, DUGGAN Marg, DUGGAN Michael, DUGGAN Neil, DUGGAN Pat, DUGGAN Roger, DUGMORE Maureen, DUGUID Ray, DUKE Carole, DUKE Lorna, DUKER Ethel, DUKES Darren/Dukesy, DUKES Val, DUKIC Dorde, DULEY Stefan, DULLER George, DULSON Peter, DUM Jimmy, DUMA Andrew, DUMA Mary, DUMARESQ Marg, DUMITRACHE Dan, DUMONT Jacques, DUMONT Pauline, DUMPER Stan, DUNATOV Marie, DUNBAR Brian, DUNBAR Di, DUNBAR Ian, DUNBAR John, DUNBAR Marian, DUNBAR Nola, DUNBAR-KASZONYI Barbara, DUNBAR-POOLE Colin, DUNBAR-POOLE Joanna, DUNCAN Amanda, DUNCAN Ann, DUNCAN Anne, DUNCAN Barbara, DUNCAN Belinda, DUNCAN Bernadette, DUNCAN Cathy, DUNCAN Garry, DUNCAN Glen, DUNCAN Gwen, DUNCAN Sam, DUNCAN Matthew, DUNCAN Bob, DUNCAN Ronda, DUNCAN Shellee, DUNCAN Sonja, DUNCOMBE Glen, DUNCOMBE Kel, **DUNCUM Norma**, DUNDAS Viv, DUNDON Vanessa, DUNDOVIC David, DUNFORD Brian, DUNFORD Cindy, DUNFORD Lu, DUNFORD Pauline, DUNGARWALLA Rubiya, DUNGARWALLA Shamoon, DUNHAM Andrew, DUNHAM Colin, DUNHAM Pauline, DUNIAM Shona, DUNK Andrew, DUNK Jill, DUNK Leanne, DUNK Bob, DUNKERLEY Kathryn, DUNKERLEY Owen, DUNKLEY David, DUNLOP Al, DUNLOP Jennie, DUNLOP Peter, DUNLOP Bob, DUNMORE Laurel, DUNN Andrew, DUNN Barb, DUNN Ben, DUNN Brian, DUNN Bruce, DUNN Catherine, DUNN Williams, DUNN David, DUNN Edwina, DUNN Faye, DUNN Geoff, DUNN Irene, DUNN Dick, DUNN Janice, DUNN Josh, DUNN Joy, DUNN Julie, DUNN Julie, DUNN Karen, DUNN Linda, DUNN Mandy, DUNN Marie, DUNN Margaret, DUNN Melissa, DUNN Nathan, DUNN Noel, DUNN Philip, DUNN Priscilla, DUNN Rachel, DUNN Bec, DUNN Ron, DUNN Russell, DUNN Steve, DUNN Terry, DUNNACHIE Sandy, DUNNE Geoff, DUNNE Noreen, DUNNE Robert, DUNNE Sue, DUNNE Bill, DUNNER Veronica, DUNNING Jeff, DUNSDON Mark, DUNSTAN Barbara, DUNSTAN Denise, DUNSTAN Michael, DUNSTAN Wally, DUNSTER Frank, DUONG Helen, DUONG Hoang, DUONG Julianna, DUONG Tu, DUONG Tu, DUPILLE Bruce, DUPLOCK Shirley, DUPLOCK William, DURAN Rich, DURANTE Lou, DURAS Peter, DURBIDGE Carmel, DURHAM Gillian, DURIC Nina, DURICIC Michael, DURIE Ben, DURIE Donald, DURIE Doug, DURKOWYAK Carol, DURLING Pippa, DUROCHER Katheryn, DUROCHUR Steve, DURRANS Sarah, DURRANT Aliso n, DURRANT Ted, DURRANT Megan, DURRANT Sue, DURSTON Bev, DURSUN Anne, DURSUN Dilek, DURSUN Tanner, DURYEA Adam, DUSELIS Alide, DUSHEIKO Dana, DUSTIN Bonnie, DUSTING Alan, DUTCH Martin, DUTHIE Alison, DUTHIE Heather, DUTHIE James, DUTTA Arup, DUTTON Elanor, DUTTON Dudgeon, DUTTON Richard, DUYVESTYN Mike, DUYVESTYN Renee, DWIGHT Rita, DWYER Barry, DWYER Brian, DWYER Carolyn, DWYER Diana, DWYER Dominic, DWYER Ellen, DWYER Evelyn, DWYER Michael, DWYER Jan, DWYER Janet, DWYER Jillian, DWYER Lyn, DWYER Mary, DWYER Michael, DWYER Owen, DWYER Rey, DWYER Robert, DWYER Roselee, DWYER Steve, DWYER Timothy, DWYER Bill, DWYERTOMASIC Ruth, DYAL Kewal, DYBALL Allan, DYBALL Andrew, DYBALL Jeff, DYBALL Robyn, DYBALL Robert, DYBALL Warwick, DYCE Donnita, DYCE Peter, DYE Amanda, DYE Andrew, DYE Brian, DYER Clifford, DYER Dennis, DYER Jim, DYER Karen, DYER Luke, DYER Shanny, DYER Shelley-Ann, DYER Tricia, DYER Valerie, DYET Keith, DYET Sharon, DYKE Carol, DYKE Shane, DYKSTRA Kathryn, DYKSTRA Rob, DYMOCK Georgina, DYONG Meviz, DYSON Greg, DYSON Lee, DYSON Wendy, DYTMAN Andrew, DZAKULA Diana, DZARIR Joshua, DZUBUR Dinka.

E

EACOTT Allan, EACOTT Beryl, EADEHILDER Russell, EADIE George, EADIE Kieran, EADON Chris, EAGER John, EAGER Robin, EAGLES Beryl, EAGLES Chris, EAGLES Mick, EAGLES Pam, EAGLESTON Jenny, EAGLETON Chris, EAGLETON Di, EAGLETON Liz, EAGLETON Hazel, EAKIN Matthew, EAKINS Norm, EALES Rosemary, EAMES Shane, EAMES Nick, EAMES Samantha, EAMMANO Varinya, EANG Chentra, EARDLEY Betsy, EARDLEY Giff, EARDLEY Gifford, EARIXSON Rob, EARL Aileen, EARL Felicity, EARL Brian, EARL Rhonda, EARL Tarnya, EARLE Sandy, EARLEY Jaimie, EARLEY Trisha, EARLS Bill, EARLY Olga, EARNSHAW Jodie, EARP Judy, EASDOWN Tony, EASEY Bevan, EASON David, EAST Alan, EAST David, EAST Neryl, EAST Robert, EAST Vic, EASTERBROOK Jim, EASTGATE Anne, EASTGATE Kathryn, EASTHAM Janine, EASTHAM Matt, EASTLEY Helen, EASTLEY Ian, EASTMAN Kate, EASTMAN Peter, EASTON Anne, EASTWOOD Eamon, EASTWOOD John, EASTWOOD Kelly, EASTWOOD Krythia, EASTWOOD Margaret, EATELL Glenn, EATHER Col, EATHORNE Belinda, EATON Carolyn, EATON Crispian, EATON David, EATON Keith, EATON Norma, EATON John, EATON Susan, EBBOTT John, EBEJER Miriam, EBEL Judy, EBEL Peter, EBERLE Betty, EBERLE Maxwell, EBERT Brad, EBERT Cathy, EBERT Valerie, EBINA Satoru, EBNER John, EBNER Judy, EBRAHIM Jonathan, EBRILL John, EBSTEIN Claire, EBY-HODGSON Sara, ECCLES Felicia, ECCLES Karena, ECCLESTON Kay, ECCLESTON Louise, ECCLESTON Michael, ECCLESTON Steven, ECHEVERRI Carlos, ECKERMANN Nicole, ECKFORD Melissa, ECKLEY Margaret, ECO Erikar, ECO Wilma, ECONOMOS Nick, EDAVELLI Goutham, EDDIE Aimee, EDDIE Cathy, EDDIE David, EDDINGTON Blake, EDDY Barry, EDDY Brian, EDDY Carolyn, EDELMAN Bruce, EDEN Kevin, EDENTON Julie, EDER Margaret, EDGAR Bruce, EDGAR Graham, EDGAR Malcolm, EDGAR Mark, EDGAR Sandi, EDGE Ken, EDGE Sally, EDGELL Linden, EDGERTON James, EDGERTON Laurel, EDGTTON Natalie, EDISON Kate, EDLUND Lucy, EDMISTON David, EDMONDS Brian, EDMONDS Diana, EDMONDS Joshua, EDMONDS Judith, EDMONDS Tracey, EDMONDSON David, EDMONDSON Michelle, EDMUNDS Maureen, EDMUNDS Nome, EDMUNDS Peter, EDNEY Barbara, EDNEY Dean, EDSALL Val, EDSON Barry, EDWARD CHARLES Ted, EDWARD PILLAI Nathalie, EDWARDS Alf, EDWARDS Allan, EDWARDS Allan, EDWARDS Amanda, EDWARDS Amy, EDWARDS Ann, EDWARDS Barbara, EDWARDS Barbara, EDWARDS Barry, EDWARDS Ben, EDWARDS Benjamin, EDWARDS Beryl, EDWARDS Bev, EDWARDS Brian, EDWARDS Brian, EDWARDS Bruce, EDWARDS Bruce, EDWARDS Carol, EDWARDS Caroline, EDWARDS Craig, EDWARDS Daniel, EDWARDS David, EDWARDS Deborah, EDWARDS Denise, EDWARDS Derek, EDWARDS Dianne, EDWARDS Doug, EDWARDS Dylan, EDWARDS Elizabeth, EDWARDS Erana, EDWARDS Frank, EDWARDS Glen, EDWARDS John, EDWARDS Ian, EDWARDS Jacqueline, EDWARDS Jan, EDWARDS Janet, EDWARDS Jeanette, EDWARDS Joanne, EDWARDS Jodie, EDWARDS John, EDWARDS John, EDWARDS Julie, EDWARDS Karen, EDWARDS Kathryn, EDWARDS Keith, EDWARDS Kelly, EDWARDS Lauren, EDWARDS Liana, EDWARDS Maiya, EDWARDS Malcolm, EDWARDS Mark, EDWARDS Marie, EDWARDS Mark, EDWARDS Mark, EDWARDS Margaret, EDWARDS Marylou, EDWARDS Mere, EDWARDS Michelle, EDWARDS Michael, EDWARDS Natasha, EDWARDS Glenn, EDWARDS Jo, EDWARDS Sherry, EDWARDS Pat, EDWARDS Paul, EDWARDS Penny, EDWARDS Polly, EDWARDS Ray, EDWARDS Robyn, EDWARDS Bob, EDWARDS Robert, EDWARDS Bob, EDWARDS Sarah, EDWARDS Sarah, EDWARDS Sarah, EDWARDS Scott, EDWARDS Simone, EDWARDS Steve, EDWARDS Steve, EDWARDS Sue, EDWARDS Sue, EDWARDS Suzi, EDWARDS Suzanna, EDWARDS Tammie, EDWARDS Taryn, EDWARDS Tony, EDWARDS Vicki, EDWARDS Bill, EDWARDS Bill, EDWINSMITH Olivia, EDWORTHY Nadine, EDWORTHY Robyn, EE Derrick, EFFENEY Cathy, EFFENY Benjamin, EFSTATHIOU Helen, EFSTATHIOU Helen, EFSTATHIOU Kim, EGAN Brian, EGAN Coralie, EGAN Daphne, EGAN Eddie, EGAN Eileen, EGAN Gerard, EGAN Gordon, EGAN Jim, EGAN Joe, EGAN Kenneth, EGAN Ken, EGAN

Lynne, EGAN Michael, EGAN Kevin, EGAN Robert, EGAN Sandra, EGELTON Jane, EGERSZEGI Charles, EGGAR Kate, EGGAR Tim, EGGELTON Chad, EGGER John, EGGERS Simone, EGGINS Bill, EGGINS Steve, EGGLESTON Boyd, EGGLESTON Damian, EGGLESTON John, EGGLETON Crystal, EGGLETON Daphne, EGGLETON Elise, EGGLETON Lia, EGGLETON Michael, EGGLETON Steve, EGGLETON Susan, EGTBERTS Pam, EHMSEN Alicia, EHN Mary, EHRENBERG Fred, EHRICH Michelle, EHRLICH Les, EHVART Inga, EIBL Mark, EICHMANN Isla, EICHMANN Trevor, EICHORN Ivan, EICKHOFF Philip, EID Elie, EID Lima, EIDSVIK Erik, EIME Kenny, EIPPER James, EISEN Paul, EISENHAUER Peter, EISENHUTH Joan, EISZELE Chris, EJZENBAUM Naomi, EKANAYAKE Kay, EKERMAWI Sam, EKERT Margaret, EKSTEIN Robert, EKTOROS Helen, EL BADAOUI Kamel, EL GAWLY Ash, EL GINDI Nadia, EL GINDI William, EL HAKIM Norman, EL HELOV Mary, EL KHEIR Omar, EL ZEIN Zahi, EL-AHMAD Mimi, EL-HASCHIMI Karim, EL-ISSA Monte, EL-KOTOB Fred, EL-MOSELHI Sarah, EL-SAIDY Aboul, ELACHY Josephine, ELAHI Elahi, ELAM Lara, ELAOG Arian, ELBISSER Jean, ELBOURNE Ben, ELD Michael, ELDAHABY Sylvia, ELDER Den, ELDER Neil, ELDER Margaret, ELDER Melody, ELDER Norma, ELDER Lindy, ELDER Sue, ELDERSHAW Brett, ELDERSHAW Ian, ELDRIDGE Barbara, ELDRIDGE Dianna, ELDRIDGE Kim, ELDRIDGE Lisa, ELDRIDGE Mark, ELDRIDGE Matthew, ELDRIDGE Melanie, ELDRIDGE Paul, ELDRIDGE Rae, ELEY Kevin, ELFORD Bronwyn, ELFVERSON Julie, ELFVERSON Wayne, ELGAFI Barbara, ELGAMAL Adib, ELGAWLY Gillian, ELGUETA Yennifer, ELHAGE Abdul, ELHILALY Taj, ELIA Steve, ELIAS Anne, ELIAS Brad, ELIAS George, ELIAS Lorraine, ELIAS Paul, ELIAS Suzy, ELINA Bo, ELISSAVETTCHENKO Ivan, ELIZABETH Aileen, ELIZES Jose, ELKENHANS Margaret, ELKHATIB Ahmed, ELKINGTON Judith, ELKINGTON Norma, ELKINGTON Wayne, ELKUSCH Joseph, ELLEDGE Arthur, ELLEM Diana, ELLEM Pamela, ELLERY Brooke, ELLERY John, ELLETT Maxwell, ELLICOTT Gemma, ELLICOTT Jane, ELLICOTT Loretta, ELLIKER Barry, ELLIOT Adam, ELLIOT Charles, ELLIOT Sylvia, ELLIOTT Barry, ELLIOTT Brad, ELLIOTT David, ELLIOTT Don, ELLIOTT Doug, ELLIOTT Duncan, ELLIOTT Gloria, ELLIOTT Howard, ELLIOTT Iain, ELLIOTT John, ELLIOTT Kieran, ELLIOTT Louise, ELLIOTT Lyn, ELLIOTT Lynn, ELLIOTT Lynne, ELLIOTT Marie, ELLIOTT Bob, ELLIOTT Stephen, ELLIOTT Susan, ELLIOTT Theresa, ELLIOTT Virginia, ELLIOTT Frank, **ELLIS Andrew**, ELLIS Angela, ELLIS Bev, ELLIS Bronwyn, ELLIS Cecily, ELLIS Bob, ELLIS Colvin, ELLIS Daryl, ELLIS David, ELLIS Denny, ELLIS Emma, ELLIS James, ELLIS Jeanette, ELLIS Joanne, ELLIS John William, ELLIS John Charles, ELLIS Kim, ELLIS Mal, ELLIS Margaret, ELLIS Margaret, ELLIS Mike, ELLIS Pattyann, ELLIS Pat, ELLIS Philip, ELLIS Philip, ELLIS Ralph, ELLIS Robyn, ELLIS Rodney, ELLIS Ronnie, ELLIS Sarah, ELLIS Sharon, ELLIS Sonia, ELLIS Tristan, ELLIS Virginia, ELLIS Roy, ELLIS Yvonne, ELLISON Colin, ELLISON Lyn, ELLISON Paul, ELLISON Ruth, ELLJOTT David, ELLSTON Julie, ELMASRI Ronda, ELMORE James, ELMSLIE Barbara, ELMSLIE Peter, ELPHICK Gillian, ELPHICK Karen, ELPHINSTON Maureen, ELPHINSTON Nicole, ELPHINSTONE Diane, ELSA Antonio, ELSAWI Yasmin, ELSEY Melanie, ELSLEY Mark, ELSON Pam, ELSTON Brooke, ELSTON Bryan, ELSUKHEN Jacques, ELSWORTH Cathie, ELUKA Anil, ELUKA John, ELUWAWALAGE Damayanthie, ELVIN Carole, ELVINS Vicki, ELVY Dawn, ELVY Jamie, ELWAKKAD Gasser, ELWARD Jackie, ELWELL Janette, ELWELL Bob, ELWIN Peter, ELWING Roslyn, ELY Kaz, EMBELTON Richard, EMBURY Rob, EMERSON Bev, EMERSON Charmaine, EMERSON Darren, EMERSON Denise, EMERSON Graeme, EMERSON Natacha, EMERSON Pam, EMERSON Robyn, EMERSON Steve, EMERTON Gillian, EMERTON Lorraine, EMERY Edward, EMERY Glenda, EMERY John, EMERY Bobbie, EMES Tanya, EMMERICK Jelena, EMMERICK Richard, EMMERICK Tim, EMMERSON Eileen, EMMERSON Ian, EMMERSON Jean, EMMERSON Jill, EMMERSON Sheila, EMMETT Katy, ENARES Nas, ENASIO Jacob, ENASIO Margaret, ENC David, ENCISO Lilia, ENDICOTT-DAVIES Ivor, ENDICOTT-DAVIES Morgan, ENDRESEN Kjersti, ENEGD Mbark, ENG Daniel, ENGEL Dorothy, ENGEL Helmut, ENGEL Kevin, ENGEL Elizabeth, ENGELANDER Jacqui, ENGELANDER Nikki, ENGELBRECHT Lionel, ENGELBRECHT Bill, ENGELE Matthew, ENGELHARDT Annett, ENGELSMAN Guy, ENGEMANN Nadia, ENGERT Amanda, ENGERT Grahame, ENGERT Vicki, ENGLAND Kim, ENGLAND Kris, ENGLAND Philip, ENGLAND Rohan, ENGLE Snowy, ENGLER Darryl, ENGLERT Michelle, ENGLEZOS Kalle, ENGLISH Jenny, ENGLISH Judith, ENGLISH Peter, ENGSTROM Annelie, ENGUTAN Hazel, ENIS Jeannette, ENKE Roy, ENNO Karen, ENOCH James, ENOCK Barbara, ENOCK David, ENRIGHT Chris, ENRIQUEZ Erica, ENRIQUEZ Ray, ENSBY Cherilyn, ENSOR Anna, ENTHALER Gunther, ENTWISTLE Sarah, ENUS Anton, EOM Hyum, EORDOGH Barbara, ERBACHER Ron, ERBS Cassy, ERDMANIS Margaret, ERFULAT Murat, ERICHSEN Grete, ERICHSEN Steve, ERICKSON Darren, ERICKSON Diane, ERICKSON Jeff, ERICKSON Mark, ERICSSON Butti, ERIKSSON Camilla, ERIKSSON Bengt, ERIKSSON Fredrik, ERIKSSON Linda, ERIKSSON LAIDAN Sofie, ERKOVSKI Bobby, ERLICH Danny, ERNST Bjoern, ERRINGTON Greg, ERTOK Oz, ERVASTI Lisa, ERVIN Patricia, ERVIN Wayne, ERVINE Danielle, ERWIN Pam, ERWOOD Jon, ESAU Ronald, ESAU Valerie, ESCALON Margarita, ESCALON MENJIVAR Ricardo, ESCARTIN Maggie, ESCHLER Nola, ESCOBAR Marcia, ESCOBAR Steve, ESCOFFIER Blandine, ESCOFFIER May-Lin, ESCREZA Philipp, ESCUDERO Mariluz, ESCUETA Jovie, ESHO Stephen, ESLAVA Victoria, ESLER Melissa, ESLICK Robert, ESMAILI Gisia, ESMUNDO Rafael, ESPARON John, ESPARZA PEREZ Manuel, ESPEDIDO Bjorn, ESPEJO Jay, ESPEJO VERGARA Pablo, ESPIDOL SANTOS Marian, ESPINOZA Wendy, ESPINOZA Willie, ESPOSITO Steven, ESSENSTAM Gary, ESSEY Jerome, ESTALILLA Gerry, ESTALL Meg, ESTANILLO John, ESTANISLAO Oscar, ESTBERGS Elizabeth, ESTCOURT Lucy, ESTCOURT Peter, ESTEBAN Mercedes, ESTENS Fran, ESTEVENS Jaime, ESTIGOY Elmer, ESTORES Divinia, ESTREICH Janelle, ESTRELLA Alfredo, ESTRELLA Tim, ETHERIDGE Emily, ETHERIDGE Karen, ETHERIDGE Kate, ETHERIDGE Meredith, ETHERIDGE Stephen, ETHERINGTON Terrence, ETHERINGTON SMITH Mike, ETIENZA Nelflor, ETIKS Vama, ETRI Harry, ETRI Khaled, ETRI Zyad, ETTERIDGE Jan, ETTRIDGE Tony, EURELL Shannon, EURIPIDOU Tess, EUSTACE Karherine, EVA Helen, EVANGELISTA Albert, EVANGELISTA Alberto, EVANGELISTA Mary, EVANGELISTA Robert, EVANGELISTA Rodel, EVANS Alex, EVANS Amanda, EVANS Angie, EVANS Angela, EVANS Anne, EVANS Bronwen, EVANS Bruce, EVANS Bryony, EVANS Carolyn, EVANS Ceinwen, EVANS Danny, EVANS David, EVANS Dave, EVANS Doug, EVANS Drew, EVANS Elaine, EVANS Ellen, EVANS Emyr, EVANS Frank, EVANS Garnet, EVANS George, EVANS Geoff, EVANS Gillian, EVANS Graham, EVANS Tonissoo, EVANS Helen, EVANS Helen, EVANS Helen, EVANS Helen, EVANS Emy, EVANS Irene, EVANS Jim, EVANS Jean, EVANS Jeff, EVANS Jenny, EVANS Joan, EVANS Joan, EVANS Joe, EVANS Joseph, EVANS Julian, EVANS Justin, EVANS Kathleen, EVANS Kathryn, EVANS Ken, EVANS Ken, EVANS Kenny, EVANS Kerrie, EVANS Lauren, EVANS Lawrie, EVANS Leanne, EVANS Lesley, EVANS Lesley, EVANS Linden, EVANS Lyndsey, EVANS Mark, EVANS MaryEllen, EVANS Margaret, EVANS Margaret, EVANS Matthew, EVANS Gary, EVANS Michael, EVANS Mitzi, EVANS Mitchell, EVANS Neil, EVANS Pauline, EVANS Paul, EVANS Peter, EVANS Pete, EVANS Rachel, EVANS Rhys, EVANS Richard, EVANS Richard, EVANS Roberta, EVANS Robert, EVANS Ron, EVANS Robin, EVANS Roy, EVANS Roy, EVANS Sarah, EVANS Sharon, EVANS Sheridan, EVANS Stephen, EVANS Steven, EVANS Susan, EVANS Travis, EVANS Troy, EVANS Warren, EVANSON Nicholas, EVEILLE Edward, EVELEIGH Francis, EVELY Coral, EVENDEN Don, EVENDEN Ellen, EVENDEN Jenny, EVENDEN Phill, EVERETT Aron, EVERETT Cliff, EVERETT Ed, EVERETT Iain, EVERETT Juliet, EVERETT Pat, EVERILL Paul, EVERILL Rochelle, EVERINGHAM Ian, EVERINGHAM Judith, EVERINGHAM Laura, EVERINGHAM Martha, EVERINGHAM Ginny, EVERS Greg, EVERS Gregg, EVERT Paul, EVERTON Brad, EVERTON Mark, EVESSON Gemma, EVESSON Michael, EVIAN David, EWAN Amelia, EWELL III Robert, EWENS Wilf, EW ER Lisa, EWIN Brian, EWIN Gemma, EWING Graham, EWING Ian, EWINGS Darren, EWORHO Christopher, EXCELL Andrew, EXCELL Kelly, EXNER Evan, EXNER Kate, EXPOSITO Jose, EXPOSITO Santi, EXTON Sheila, EYERS Anthony, EYERS Kathleen-Kathy, EYERS Rachel, EYLES Christine, EYNON

Ken, EYNON Marianne, EYNSTONE Therese, EYVAZ Ish, EZEKIEL Joe, EZEKIEL Shelley, EZZY Josie, EZZY Simone.

F

F Ivor, FABBRO-STOTT Mia, FABER Margaret, FABER Richard, FABER Robyn, FABIAN Belinda, FABIAN Lawrence, FABILLAR Cathy, FABINY Bob, FABRE Laure, FABRE Sebastien, FABRIS MOREIRA Daniela, FACCHINA John, FACCHINI Angelo, FACER Mary, FACER Vic, FACEY Steve, FADAEI Ali, FADDY Steven, FAEEH Milad, FAEHRMANN Joanne, FAGAN Anne, FAGAN Katie, FAGAN Kylie, FAGAN Tom, FAGGELLA Adrian, FAHEY Brian, FAHEY Fred, FAHEY Nola, FAHLE Trasy, FAHMY Sara, FAHNDRICH Marco, FAHY Brad, FAI Marty, FAICHNEY Andrew, FAINT Rod, FAIR Ken, FAIRBAIRN Dave, FAIRBAIRN Jason, FAIRBAIRN Jo, FAIRBAIRN Marie, FAIRBAIRN Monica, FAIRBROTHER Alan, FAIRBROTHER Aussie, FAIRBROTHER Jill, FAIRE Shoshana, FAIRFAX Jean, FAIRFULL Jo, FAIRHALL Marie, FAIRHALL Murial, FAIRHURST Nigel, FAIRHURST Sylvia, FAIRJONES Amanda, FAIRLIE Alicia, FAIRLIE Shane, FAIRLIE-CUNINGHAME Georgie, FAIRS Syd, FAIRWEATHER Scott, FAITHFULL Tony, FAITHFULL Melanie, FAIZ Hosai, FAIZ Parwin, FAJARDO Renato, FAKES Sue, FAKHOURI Nassir, FAKHRI Iqbal, FAKHRI Munezzah, FAKHRI Zak, FAKTHONG Krit, FALCONER Carol, FALCONER Gwenda, FALCONER Ian, FALCONER Jennifer, FALCONER Jill, FALCONER Ken, FALCONER Jane, FALCONER Max, FALIEROS Christina, FALK Inge, FALK Jo, **FALK Peter**, FALKENHAGEN Shaun, FALLA Baden, FALLA Joanne, FALLA Salome, FALLON Chris, FALLON Frederick, FALLON John, FALLON Max, FALLON Patricia, FALLON Warren, FALLOON Graham, FALLS Jan, FALLSHAW Daniel, FALTAS Lucy, FALUSI Les, FALUSI Marj, FALUSI Sarika, FALVEY Leah, FALVEY Lynette, FALVO Giosefina, FALZON Joe, FALZON Bill, FAMERON Giancarlo, FAN Eddie, FAN John, FAN Kevin, FAN Kit, FAN You, FAN Frank, FANDERLINDEN Craig, FANDRICH Heidi, FANG Anita, FANG Yanna, FANGIDAE Feri, FANNING Bernadette, FANSHU John, FANTL Nikki, FANTO Matthew, FARAH Alison, FARAH Chantelle, FARAM Amy, FARAONE Frances, FARCICH Tony, FARDELL Greg, FARDELL Kate, FARDELL Kevin, FARDELL Margaret, FARES Eva, FARFAN Christian, FARGEAT Lyonel, FARHAND Jay, FARHAT Hussein, FARINA Frank, FARINA Louise, FARKAS Michael, FARLAND Catherine, FARLEIGH Martine, FARLEY Erin, FARLEY Lisa, FARLEY Mel, FARLEY Bob, FARLOW John, FARLOW Lorraine, FARMAKIDIS Bill, FARMER Hugh, FARMER Joanne, FARMER Loli, FARMER Nic, FARMER Ruth, FARMSON Engan, FARNCOMB Bill, FARNES Corrine, FARNWORTH Tina, FAROUQUE Salma, FARQUHAR Kim, FARQUHAR Jim, FARQUHAR Jennifer, FARQUHARSON Brett, FARQUHARSON Lesley, FARQUHARSON James, FARQUHARSON Miffy, FARQUHARSON Terry, FARR Barbara, FARR Brett, FARR Colin, FARR Marilyn, FARR Matthew, FARR Richard, FARR Rod, FARR Ron, FARRALL Robin, FARRAR Cameron, FARRAR Dennis, FARRAR Geoff, FARRAR Graeme, FARRAR Lister, FARRAR Martin, FARRELL Angela, FARRELL Barbara, FARRELL Brian, FARRELL Hendley, FARRELL Madeleine, FARRELL Marg, FARRELL Martin, FARRELL Tom, FARRELLY Dennis, FARRELLY John, FARRELLY Stephen, FARRINGTON Gina, FARRINGTON Pat, FARRIS Lorna, FARRONATO Jenny, FARROW Hamish, FARROW Ron, FARRUGIA Bree, FARRUGIA Elvira, FARRUGIA Laurie, FARRUGIA Grace, FARRUGIA Judith, FARRUGIA Karyn, FARRUGIA Louis, FARRUGIA Mary, FARRUGIA Rita, FARRY Pascale, FARRY Peter, FARTHING Hayley, FARTHING Kim, FASAN Rebecca, FASCIOLI Virginia, FASLIOLI Alex, FASULO Maria, FATAI TAULEPA Eti, FATCHEN Julie, FATNA Yahiaoui, FATONE Gabbi, FATUROS Gordon, FAULDS John, FAULKNER Elizabeth, FAULKNER Ian, FAULKNER Noel, FAULKNER Rebecca, FAULKS Christie, FAULKS Harry, FAULKS Jane, FAULL Robert, FAUSER Jane, FAVARO Sandy, FAVELL Mark, FAVORITO Ben, FAVOT Michelle, FAVRETTO Esther, FAWCETT Brook, FAWCETT Doug, FAWCETT Shirley, FAWKE Tracy, FAWKNER Joanna, FAWKNER Laurie, FAWKNER Tom, FAWL Terry, FAWZI Fawzi, FAY Carolyn, FAY Rob, FAYE Liz, FAYE Maryelle, FAZEL Waise, FAZIO Frank, **FAZIO Wendy**, FAZZARI Angelina, FEAIN Cathy, FEATHER Ann, FEATHER Scott, FEATHERSTON Jodi, FEATHERSTONE John, FEATHERSTONE-LITTLE Debra, FEBEY Connie, FEBRUARY Cheryl, FECHNER Julie, FEDELE Diego, FEDELI Peta, FEDER Catherine, FEDERICI Fabio, FEDOR Ivan, FEDOROVITCH Ludmila, FEEBREY Aline, FEEBREY Michelle, FEENEY Carmel, FEENEY Johanna, FEENEY Michelle, FEENSTRA Frances, FEHON Peter, FEHON Terry, FEIGELSON Maya, FEIGELSON Sam, FEIRER Mair, FEIRSON Jean, FEIZAKS Peter, FELDHAKE Nippy, FELDMAN Jonathan, FELDMAN Nathan, FELEDY Denis, FELET Alba, FELICE Tanya, FELIPE Elsie, FELIPE Marbeen, FELIX Karine, FELIX Magda, FELIX Milre, FELKER Jared, FELLAS Katrina, FELLI Romain, FELLOWS Susan, FELMINGHAM Carole, FELSCH Michael, FELSCH Sue, FELSTET Anne, FELTHAM Kathryn, FELTON Cedric, FELTON Graham, FELTON Ian, FELTON Sally, FEMIA Luke, FENASSE Renee, FENECH Tony, FENECH Anthony, FENECH Jeff, FENECH Jo, FENECH John, FENECH John, FENECH Kate, FENECH Raylene, FENECH Steve, FENECH Sue, FENECK Wayne, FENELON Mary, FENG Gewei, FENG Feng, FENG Jian, FENG Jim, FENG Lily, FENG Lucy, FENG Mary, FENG Yin, FENG MING Tou, FENLON Olivia, FENN John, FENN Neville, FENN Rachelle, FENN Vanessa, FENNELL Denise, FENNELL Mary, FENNELL Peter, FENNER Robin, FENTON Aragorn, FENTON Colin, FENTON Gwen, FENTON Karen, FENTON Robyn, FENTON Fred, FENWICK Clare, FENWICK Laura, FENWICK Bob, FEORE Anita, FERELLA Maria, FERELLA Santina, FERGUS Sue, FERGUSON Andrew, FERGUSON Ann, FERGUSON Anthony, FERGUSON Christina, FERGUSON Claire, FERGUSON Don, FERGUSON Kieth, FERGUSON Keith, FERGUSON Geoff, FERGUSON Glenys, FERGUSON Grant, FERGUSON Helen, FERGUSON Ian, FERGUSON Jim, FERGUSON Jillian, FERGUSON John, FERGUSON John, FERGUSON Julie, FERGUSON Kathy, FERGUSON Katherine, FERGUSON Louis, FERGUSON Luba, FERGUSON Mark, FERGUSON Rob, FERGUSON Shaw, FERGUSON Roy, FERGUSON Gus, FERGUSON Sam, FERGUSON Scott, FERGUSON Bill, FERGUSSON Jenny, FERGUSSON Terry, FERHAT Yasmina, FERLAS Harry, FERNANCE John, FERNANDES Adelino, FERNANDES Gavin, FERNANDES Josie, FERNANDES Lalita, FERNANDES Rush, FERNANDEZ Benjamin, FERNANDEZ Brendan, FERNANDEZ Cheryl, FERNANDEZ Clement, FERNANDEZ Doug, FERNANDEZ Javier, FERNANDEZ Javier, FERNANDEZ Oscar, FERNANDEZ Ramon, FERNANDEZ Sabrina, FERNANDEZ Dee, FERNANDEZ Stewart, FERNANDEZ Thomas, FERNANDEZ RIOS Alicia, FERNANDO Douglas, FERNANDO Manoj, FERNANDO Marguerita, FERNANDO Mike, FERNANDO Nihara, FERNANDO Rohan, FERNANDO Srimal, FERNANDO Kushan, FERNIE Caroline, FERNIE David, FERNIE Judy, FERNIE Paul, FERNLEY Michelle, FERNS Judith, FERNS Michael, FEROS Crisy, FERRAN Steve, FERRANDA John, FERRARA Helen, FERRARI Grace, FERRAZ Marina, FERREIRA Allan, FERREIRA Ana, FERREIRA Elisabeth, FERREIRA Myrna, FERREIRA Tami, FERREIRA CORDOBA Juan, FERRER Nicole, FERRER Santiago, FERRERS Tony, FERRES Graham, FERRES Susan, FERRETT Bruce, FERRIER Kate, FERRIER Bill, FERRINGTON Kay, FERRIS Brian, FERRIS Liz, **FERRIS Geoff**, FERRIS Joe, FERRIS Mark, FERRIS Ann, FERRIS Natalie, FERRIS Robert, FERRO Mariebel, FERRY Evelyn, FERSTER Evelyn, FETTELL Joanne, FEWINGS Barbara, FEWKES Cedric, FEWSON Teri, FEYER Pat, FEYZENY Samantha, FIAY Martin, FICHO Carlos, FICK Rod, FICKEL Anni, FICKEL Bob, FIEDLER Manfred, FIEDLER Tony, FIEL Pedro, FIELD Amber, FIELD Barb, FIELD Brian, FIELD Dawn, FIELD Elizabeth, FIELD Gordon, FIELD Gordon, FIELD Jan, FIELD Jayne, FIELD Kate, FIELD Mari, FIELD Paul, FIELD Morgann, FIELD Murray, FIELD Ron, FIELD Russell, FIELD Sarah, FIELD Wayde, FIELDER Edward, FIELDER Katrina, FIELDER Martin, FIELDER Prue, FIELDING Andrew, FIELDING Kath, FIELDING Barry, FIELDING Carly, FIELDING Dianne, FIELDING Julie, FIELDING Kevin, FIELDING Noreen, FIELDING Roslyn, FIELDING Sheila, FIELDS Janice, FIENI Fabrizio, FIFE Joyan, FIGGIS Helen, FIGUERAS PASTELLS Anna, FIGUEREDO Washington, FIGUEROA Eric, FIGUEROA Mauricio, FIHLEBON Celeste, FIKKERS Johanna, FIKKERS Bill, FILATOFF Helen, FILDES Graham, FILDES John, FILES Andrew, FILEVSKAIA Natalia, FILIPCZYK Rebecca, FILIPETTO Sam, FILIPPIN Maree, FILLA Eva, FILLA-DWEHUS Anja, FILLERY Janette, FILLERY Yvonne, FILMER Tracy, FILOCAMO John, FILSELL Jennifer, FILSELL Kerrie, FILTNESS Fiona,

FILTNESS Ronald, FINANCE Barbara, FINARDI Grace, FINCH Anne, FINCH Darren, FINCH John, FINCH Micky, FINCH Simon, FINDLATER Ron, FINDLAY Ian, FINDLAY Jane, FINDLAY Jill, FINDLAY Robyn, FINDLEY Bill, FINGER Fiona, FINGLAND Annika, FINIANOS Joseph, FINIGAN Cathryn, FINK Paul, FINKEL Sheldon, FINKELSTEIN Rebecca, FINLAY Audra, FINLAY Bob, FINLAY David, FINLAY Gary, FINLAY Jade, FINLAY Jennie, FINLAY John, FINLAY Lorraine, FINLAY Mollie, FINLAY Shane, FINLAYSON Cristie, FINLAYSON Helen, FINLAYSON Neil, FINLAYSON Sue, FINN Caley, FINNANE Hugh, **FINNEGAN Dianne**, FINNEMORE Ciay, FINNERAN Peter, FINNEY Cathy, FINNEY Debbie, FINNEY Bill, FINNIE Jon, FINNIGAN David, FINSTERWALD Monika, FINUCANE Joe, FINUCCI Danny, FIORANI Franco, FIORE Katrina, FIORE Mark, FIORENZA Grace, FIORETTO Paul, FIQUET Cecilia, FIRIGOU Georgia, FIRKIN Graham, FIRKIN Pheona, FIRKINS Chris, FIRMAN Wayne, FIRMAN Judy, FIRMAN Stan, FIRST Alex, FIRTH Anna, **FIRTH Barbara**, FIRTH David, FIRTH Dianne, FIRTH Don, FISCHER Belinda, FISCHER Caroline, FISCHER Edel, FISCHER Evica, FISCHER Ilana, FISCHER Jim, FISCHER Joe, FISCHER Loraine, FISCHER Michael, FISCHER Michael, **FISCHER Paula**, FISCHER Stephen, FISCHETTI Marie, FISH George, FISHBURN Robert, FISHER Ali, FISHER Jean, FISHER Brian, FISHER Carmel, FISHER Col, FISHER Colin, FISHER Craig, FISHER David, FISHER Debra, FISHER Jan, FISHER Gavin, FISHER Glenn, FISHER Ilona, FISHER Jacinta, FISHER Jackie, FISHER Karen, FISHER Kylie, FISHER Lauraine, FISHER Mark, FISHER Margaret, FISHER Nev, FISHER Noela, FISHER Pam, FISHER Paul, FISHER Peter, FISHER Peter, FISHER Rachel, FISHER Rebecca, FISHER Richard, FISHER Bob, FISHER Rosa, FISHER Thelma, FISHER Vicki, FISHER Terry, FISHLOCK Aaron, FISHLOCK Natalie, FISHLOCK Paul, FISHWICK Harry, FISK Allan, FISK Anthony, FISSCHER Jill, FITCH Debbie, FITCH Garry, FITT Judith, FITTLER Jim, FITTOCK Vanessa, FITTOLANI Adrian, FITTOLANI Paul, FITTOLANI Rachel, FITTON Colin, FITZCLARENCE Dixie, FITZGERALD Aimee, FITZGERALD Anneke, FITZGERALD Brian, FITZGERALD Kate, FITZGERALD Celine, FITZGERALD Darren, FITZGERALD Dennis, FITZGERALD Elizabeth, FITZGERALD Helen, FITZGERALD Helen, FITZGERALD Holly, FITZGERALD Ian, FITZGERALD Ivan, FITZGERALD Jim, FITZGERALD Janice, FITZGERALD Jeff, FITZGERALD Jennie, FITZGERALD Jenny, FITZGERALD Kate, FITZGERALD Kay, FITZGERALD Jack, FITZGERALD Lesa, FITZGERALD Marcelle, FITZGERALD Margaret, FITZGERALD Michelle, FITZGERALD Mike, FITZGERALD Mike, FITZGERALD Trish, FITZGERALD Peter, FITZGERALD Peter, FITZGERALD Peter, FITZGERALD Robert, FITZGERALD Shani, FITZGERALD Suzy, FITZGERALD Sue, FITZGERALD Terry, FITZGIBBON Barry, FITZGIBBON Elvis, FITZGIBBON Liam, FITZGIBBON Mavis, FITZHARRIS Craig, FITZHARRIS Lloyd, FITZPATRICK Margot, FITZPATRICK Carolyn, FITZPATRICK Bill, FITZPATRICK Janet, FITZPATRICK Jenny, FITZPATRICK John, FITZPATRICK John, FITZPATRICK Kathy, FITZPATRICK Leonard, FITZPATRICK Pat, FITZPATRICK Paul, FITZPATRICK Prue, FITZPATRICK Robin, FITZPATRICK Ruth, FITZPATRICK Sue, FITZPATRICK Tracey, FITZPATRICK Wayne, FITZROY Stuart, FITZSIMMONS Jill, FITZSIMMONS Jo, FITZSIMMONS Justin, FITZSIMMONS Kerry, FITZSIMON James, FITZSIMONS Chantal, FITZSIMONS Deb, FITZSIMONS John, FIU Ema, FIXTER Kellie, FJELLSTAD Christina, FLACK Donald, FLACK Keith, FLACK Paul, FLACK Peter, FLAHIVE Sharron, FLAKELAR David, FLAKELAR Nina, FLAKEMORE Katrina, FLAMBAS Ody, FLAMINI Katia, FLANAGAN Annette, FLANAGAN Don, FLANAGAN Eileen, FLANAGAN George, FLANAGAN Margaret, FLANAGAN Mark, FLANAGAN Michael, FLANAGAN Milton, FLANAGAN Noel, FLANAGAN Val, FLANNERY Gerry, FLANNERY Isabella, FLANNERY Karen, FLANNERY Margaret, FLANNERY Melissa, FLANNERY Sean, FLATMAN Durn, FLATT Dave, FLAVELL Ryan, FLAVELLE Chris, FLAXMAN John, FLECHA Wilma, FLEET Mary, FLEET Paul, FLEETON Kenneth, FLEGG Carolyn, FLEITH Natalie, FLEMING Allan, FLEMING Benjamin, FLEMING Christina, FLEMING Dan, FLEMING Betty, FLEMING Elly, FLEMING Greg, FLEMING Howard, FLEMING Janine, FLEMING Joe, FLEMING Lola, FLEMING Sharon, FLEMING Stacey, FLEMING Stephanie, FLEMING Stephen, FLEMING Tallaesen, FLEMING Tim, FLEMING Tracy, FLEMMING Coral, FLEMMING David, FLEMMING Paul, FLEMMING Michael, FLEMMING Natasha, FLEMMING Priscilla, FLESSNER Fiona, FLETCHER Alison, FLETCHER Amanda, FLETCHER Barbara, FLETCHER Beryl, FLETCHER Cassy, FLETCHER Cay, FLETCHER Fletch, FLETCHER Diana, FLETCHER Dorothy, FLETCHER Graeme, FLETCHER Hugh, FLETCHER Ian, FLETCHER Ian, FLETCHER Jane, FLETCHER Justin, FLETCHER Kenneth, FLETCHER Kevin, FLETCHER Lynda, FLETCHER Mike, FLETCHER Patrick, FLETCHER Peter, FLETCHER Philip, FLETCHER Rachel, FLETCHER Rebecca, FLETCHER Rod, FLETCHER Paul, FLETCHER Shaun, FLETCHER Simon, FLETCHER Stewart, FLETCHER Tracey, FLETCHER Fletch, FLETCHER Wayne, FLETT Rosemary, FLETT Sue, FLICK Bruce, FLIGHT Peter, FLINT Alan, FLINT Carol, FLINT Gail, FLINT Jan, FLINT Rhonda, FLINT Bob, FLISSINGER Dianne, FLOOD Allan, FLOOD Brendon, FLOOD Douglas, FLOOD Geoff, FLOOD Jenny, FLOOD John, FLOOD Shirley, FLORENCE Mark, FLORES Eduardo, FLORES Mercedes, FLORESTINO Agatha, FLORIO John, FLORY Helen, FLORY Lucas, FLOVIE Pierre, FLOWER David, FLOWERS Ashleigh, FLOWERS Brock, FLOYD Rossco, FLUIN Joseph, FLUX-BALIN Marianne, FLYNN Adam, FLYNN Alan, FLYNN Bill, FLYNN Brian, FLYNN Chris, FLYNN Don, FLYNN Gregory, FLYNN Heather, FLYNN Joanne, FLYNN Joanne, FLYNN John, FLYNN Julie, FLYNN Lee, FLYNN Patrick, FLYNN Tricia, FLYNN Rita, FLYNN Shane, FLYNN-MORO Pat, FOCHESATO Terri, FOCKS John, FODA Richard, FODA Sandy, FOEKEN John, FOGARTY Belinda, FOGARTY Daniel, FOGARTY Dianne, FOGARTY Eva, FOGARTY John, FOGARTY Louise, FOGARTY Nuala, FOGARTY Rhonda, FOGARTY Richard, FOGARTY Fog, FOGERTY Amy, FOGERTY Brian, FOGGITT Peter, FOGLIANI Simon, FOGWELL Linda, FOK Bernard, FOK Heidi, FOK Siu, FOKES Allan, FOKES Shannon, FOLAUHOLA Lynda, FOLDEN Peter, FOLESI Glynis, FOLETTA Victoria, FOLEY Bert, FOLEY Barry, FOLEY Brendan, FOLEY Denis, FOLEY Des, FOLEY Gareth, FOLEY Jessica, FOLEY Kylie, FOLEY Mal, FOLEY Mark, FOLEY Rita, FOLEY Sheila, **FOLEY Vera**, FOLEY Vicki, FOLEY Wayne, FOLHA Ivy, FOLINO-GALLO Tina, FOLKARD Berri, FOLKARD Roscoe, FOLLETT Wendy, FOLMER Tina, FOLPP Mick, FOLTA Christine, FOLTA Sharley, FOLWELL Katie, FOLWELL Melissa, FONDAUMIERE Della, FONG Alan, FONG Bess, FONG Canny, FONG Chi, FONG Edward, FONG Jacinta, FONG Jacinta, FONG Jeng, FONG Jessie, FONG Anita, FONG Maurice, FONG Monica, FONG Roman, FONG Sally, FONG Tsz, FONG KEE Lionel, FONMOA Saverina, FONSECA Elizabeth, FONTAINE Patricia, FONTANA Jan, FONTANA Nick, FONTANA Vivienne, FONUA Salote, FOO Tony, FOO Yong, FOO Colin, FOO Jo-Ann, FOO Justine, FOO Keng, FOO Kim, FOO Sharon, FOOKS Henry, FOOKS Marilyn, FOORD Maree, FOOTE Andrew, FOOTE Kerry, FOOTE Norm, FOOTE Robin, FOOTT James, FOOTT Julie, FOOTT Sarah, FORAN Gary, FORBEF-BIRAM Margaret, FORBES Drury, FORBES Geraint, FORBES Jan, FORBES Linda, FORBES Peter, FORBES Bob, FORBES Shane, FORBES Tamara, FORBES Terry, FORCK Diana, FORCK Jill, FORD Alex, FORD Allen, FORD Allison, FORD Amanda, FORD Angela, FORD Roy, FORD Brian, FORD Daniel, FORD Doug, FORD Elaine, FORD Glenn, FORD Joanne, FORD Judy, FORD Karen, FORD Karen, FORD Kevin, FORD Kevin, FORD Kylie, FORD Matt, FORD Matthew, FORD Melissa, FORD Melissa, FORD Michael, FORD Michelle, FORD Michael, FORD Natalie, FORD Olivia, FORD Peter, FORD Rachel, FORD Robyn, FORD Ruth, FORD Simon, FORD Stephanie, FORD Susan, FORD Suzy, FORD Terry, FORDCONROY Elizabeth, FORDE Betty, FORDE Ryn, FOREMAN Lauren, FORESHEW Tony, FORESHEW Chris, FORESHEW James, FORESTIERI Marc, FORGAN Di, FORGE Trevor, FORK Lina, FORLIANO Dolly, FORLI NO Gerry, FORMAN Oscar, FORMBY Liz, FORMENTON Themis, FORMOSA George, FORMOSA Kim, FORNALSKI George, FORNASARI Nives, FORNASIER Tony, FOROUZANDEH Sam, FORREST James, FORREST Ken, FORREST Mark, FORREST Michael, FORREST Robert, FORREST Shawn, FORREST Suzanne, FORRESTER Christine, FORRESTER Janet, FORRESTER Maree, FORSDIKE Matt, FORSHAW Marianne, FORSON Robert, FORSSTROM Malin, FORST Tanya, FORSTER Allen, FORSTER Colin, FORSTER Gareth, FORSTER Ian, FORSTER Lesley, FORSTER

Lesley, FORSTER Natalie, FORSTER Noel, FORSTER Peter, FORSTER Ray, FORSTER Ross, FORSYTH Alan, FORSYTH Chris, FORSYTH Ed, FORSYTH Elizabeth, FORSYTH Elizabeth, FORSYTH Elizabeth, FORSYTH Graham, FORSYTH Kate, FORSYTH Tania, FORSYTH Wendy, FORSYTHE Ralph, FORT Graeme, FORTALEZA Ricardo, FORTE Madalena, FORTEY Carol, FORTH Brian, FORTI Jessica, FORTUNE Bernard, FORWOOD Janine, FOSCA Flavia, FOSCA Maria, FOSS Sue, FOSSEY Joy, FOSTER Ade, FOSTER Biddy, FOSTER Tony, FOSTER Barry, FOSTER Christine, FOSTER Deborah, FOSTER Denis, FOSTER Emma, FOSTER Gabby, FOSTER Grahame, FOSTER Graham, FOSTER Greg, FOSTER Janina, FOSTER Karen, FOSTER Lara, FOSTER Lorraine, FOSTER Marie, FOSTER Ria, FOSTER Mark, FOSTER Merryl, FOSTER Nat, FOSTER Neil, FOSTER Neina, FOSTER Penny, FOSTER Peter, FOSTER Peter, FOSTER Ray, FOSTER Rebekah, FOSTER Tony, FOSTER Tom, FOSTER Vicki, FOSTER Gerry, FOSTERKITTRELL Janelle, FOSTON Jenny, FOTHERINGHAM Carol, FOTI Caterina, FOTOPOULOS Joy, FOTOPOULOS Voula, FOUDA Ibrahim, FOULDS Robyn, FOUNTAIN Marian, FOUNTAS Nick, FOUQUERAY Annick, FOWLER David, FOWLER Diana, FOWLER Dimity, FOWLER Elaine, FOWLER Geraldine, FOWLER Gina, FOWLER Jim, FOWLER Janet, FOWLER Jessica, FOWLER Bryan, FOWLER John, FOWLER Mary, FOWLER Nikki, FOWLER Ross, FOWLER Ruth, FOWLER Sheree, FOWLIE Ian, FOX Alex, FOX Allison, FOX Brad, FOX Esmirna, FOX Heather, FOX Foxy, FOX Inara, FOX Isabel, FOX Jacqui, FOX Lucas, FOX Lyndon, FOX Margaret, FOX Margaret, FOX Michael, FOX Michael, FOX Pat, FOX Penelope, FOX Richard, FOX Ron, FOX Shirley, FOX Shirley, FOX Valerie, FOXHILL Denise, FOXHILL Simon, FOXLEY Leanne, FOXTON Rebecca, FOXTON Viv, FOYE Gail, FOYSTER Chris, FOZZARD Jane, FRADEL Min, FRAGOUDAKIS Kon, FRAKES Kerrie-Anne, FRAME Dawne, FRAME Leah, FRAME Peter, FRAME Ron, FRAME Sharon, FRAMPTON Debi, FRAMPTON Peta, FRANCESCHINI John, FRANCESCHINI Luciano, FRANCIS Allan, FRANCIS Brad, FRANCIS Charles, FRANCIS Colin, FRANCIS Craig, FRANCIS David, FRANCIS Debbie, FRANCIS Denise, FRANCIS Doug, FRANCIS Dwayne, FRANCIS Felicity, FRANCIS Helen, FRANCIS Jennifer, FRANCIS Jenny, FRANCIS Julie, FRANCIS Keith, FRANCIS Martin, FRANCIS Marietta, FRANCIS Mary-Jane, FRANCIS Max, FRANCIS Mel, FRANCIS Milly, FRANCIS Ron, FRANCIS Shannon, FRANCIS Stella, FRANCIS Stephen, FRANCISCO Gil, FRANCISCO Ricky, FRANCKE Justine, FRANCKE Simone, FRANCO Dominic, FRANCO Maurice, FRANCO Robert, FRANCOLI Gloria, FRANGAKIS Penelope, FRANGELLI Jess, FRANGULIS Spiros, FRANJESEVIC Ivan, FRANK Erica, FRANK James, FRANK Klaus, FRANK Yvonne, FRANKEWILLIAMS Marg, FRANKHAM Corrina, FRANKLAND Kathie, FRANKLIN Andrew, FRANKLIN Cheryl, FRANKLIN David, FRANKLIN Eitan, FRANKLIN Liz, FRANKLIN Ken, FRANKLIN Lorraine, FRANKLIN Mark, FRANKLIN Michael, FRANKLIN Richard, FRANKLIN Simone, FRANKLIN Stacey, FRANKLIN Bill, FRANKS Colleen, FRANKS Glenn, FRANKS Jim, FRANKS Matthew, FRANKS Valerie, FRANKS Warwick, FRANKUM Jane, FRANSEN John, FRANSEN Leo, FRANSEN Lesley, FRANSEN Margaret, FRANTZIS Effie, FRANULOVICH Perry, FRANZ Godfrey, FRANZ Ryan, FRANZE Vince, FRAPICCINI Jan, FRARE Joe, FRASER Ali, FRASER Alisa, FRASER Andrew, FRASER Ben, FRASER Carmen, FRASER Carolyn, FRASER Kate, FRASER Cathy, FRASER Clair, FRASER David, FRASER Doug, FRASER Gillian, FRASER Helen, FRASER Jim, FRASER Jeremy, FRASER Joanne, FRASER Kathy, FRASER Katrina, FRASER Kelly, FRASER Mary, FRASER Megan, FRASER Meryll, FRASER Samantha, FRASER Sandra, FRASER Tammie, FRATER Colin, FRATRIC Monika, FRAVNFELTER Anna, FRAWLEY Josephine, FRAZER Daiva, FRAZER George, FRAZER Larry, FREAK Donna, FREAME Helen, FREAN Isobel, FREDE David, FREDERIC RENE ROBERT Frederic, FREDERICKS Ben, FREDERIKSEN Nick, FREE Les, FREEBURY Suzie, FREEDMAN Jamie, FREEDMAN Marc, FREEMAN Anna, FREEMAN Anthony, FREEMAN Bethany, FREEMAN Carolyn, FREEMAN Elissa, FREEMAN Kay, FREEMAN George, FREEMAN James, FREEMAN Jean, FREEMAN Jenny, FREEMAN John, FREEMAN Kala, FREEMAN Keiren, FREEMAN Lauren, FREEMAN Marj, FREEMAN Martine, FREEMAN Marnee, FREEMAN Mike, FREEMAN Michelle, FREEMAN Naomi, FREEMAN Nicci, FREEMAN Nigel, FREEMAN Noel, FREEMAN Peter, FREEMAN Philip, FREEMAN Robert, FREEMAN Ryoko, FREEMAN Samantha, FREEMAN Sandy, FREEMAN Sonja, FREEMAN Sparra, FREEMAN Suellen, FREEMAN Wally, FREER Anne, FREER Brett, FREER Ryan, FREGON Elizabeth, FREITAS NANTES Mario, FREMLIN Irene, FRENCH David, FRENCH Glenn, FRENCH Jason, FRENCH French, FRENCH John, FRENCH Michelle, FRENCH Robbie, FRENCH Roger, FRENCH Roger, FRENCH Scott, FRENCH Stephen, FRENCH Thomas, FRENCH Tim, FRENKEL Sarah, FRESHWATER Jennine, FRESHWATER Sharyn, FRESHWATER Terry, FRETER Jenny, FRETWELL Lisa, FRETWELL Marrianne, FRETWELL Ray, FREUDENSTEIN Shelby, FREW Allan, FREW Archie, FREW Lynn, FREWEN Brent, FREY Belinda, FRIBORG George, FRICHOT Carolyn, FRICKER Anthony, FRICKER Brooke, FRIDON Paikan, FRIED Diego, FRIEDMAN Anita, FRIEDMAN Carol, FRIEDMAN Jeff, FRIEDMAN Zev, FRIEDMANN Frank, FRIEDMANN John, FRIEL Annabelle, FRIEND Barry, FRIEND Coral, FRIEND Kevin, FRIEND Phil, FRIES Milan, FRIES Robert, FRIES Vanessa, FRIPP John, FRITCHLEY Robert, FRITH Allison, FRITH David, FRITH Ian, FRITH John, FRITH Paul, FRITH Suzie, FRITH Will, FRITZ Julian, FRITZ Mark, FRITZ Bob, FRIZELL Sonya, FRIZELLE David, FRODSHAM Hayley, FROEHLING Kurt, FROHREICH Amanda, FROMBERG Barbara, FROMSON Darren, FRONDA C hris, FRONDOSO Albert, FRONEMAN Malcolm, FROST Andrew, FROST Anthony, FROST Danielle, FROST David, FROST Geoff, FROST Greg, FROST James, FROST Kerryanne, FROST Marie, FROST Michael, FROST Petrina, FROST Robin, FROST Sarah, FROST Simon, FROST Stuart, FROST Stuart, FROST Sylvia, FROST Vadim, FROW Joan, FRUHWALD Ange, FRULLANI Greg, FRUMAR Lisa, FRY Albert, FRY Chris, FRY Doug, FRY John, FRY Rebecca, FRY Shirley, FRYAR Jon, FRYDRYCH Connie, FRYER Allan, FRYER Ben, FRYER Jay, FRYER John, FRYER Judy, FRYER Katie, FRYER Kerrie, FRYER Kerry, FRYER Neil, FRYIRS Timothy, FU Anita, FU Jay, FU Eric, FU Wei, FU Stanley,FUCCILLI Francesca, FUCCILLI Luciana, FUCHS Rolf, FUCHS Ulli, FUENTEFRIA Priscilla, FUENTES Beatriz, FUENTES Erick, FUENTES David, FUENTES Igor, FUENTES Mildred, FUENTES SALAS Maria, FUENTES-FERNANDEZ Lucia, FUERST Charles, FUGE Bob, FUGLBJERG Vibeke, FUJIMAKI Yuki, FUJINAMI Takako, FUJINOBU Seiko, FUJITA Atsuko, FUJITA Eri, FUKUSHIMA Eri, FULCHER Jan, FULCHER Rik, FULHAM Margaret, FULHAM Michael, FULL Norman, FULLAGAR John, FULLBROOK Lauraine, FULLER Adam, FULLER Bruce, FULLER Carolyn, FULLER Chris, FULLER Diane, FULLER Ern, FULLER Frank, FULLER Grant, FULLER Hilary, FULLER Karon, FULLER Trina, FULLER Melody, FULLER Michael, FULLER Neil, FULLER Pat, FULLER Shayne, FULLER Stacey, FULLER Stuart, FULLER Tim, FULLERTON Cheryl, FULLERTON Liz, FULLERTON Tricia, FULLICK Mark, FULLOON Tarnie, FULTON Joan, FULTON Sharon, FUNG Amy, FUNG Angelina, FUNG Grace, FUNG Henry, FUNG Paul, FUNG Vicky, FUNG Mary, FUNG Nancy, FUNG Natalie, FUNG Rex, FUNG Rhonda, FUNG Samson, FUNKE Jeremy, FUNNELL Gwen, FUNNELL Jill, FUNNELL Kylie, FUNNELL Paul, FUNSTON Kim, FUOTI Giovanna, FURFARO Theodora, FURIA Lucio, FURLONG Maree, FURNELL Eddie, FURNEY Jen, FURNEY Marie, FURNEY Bill, FURNISS Cheridan, FURSDON Alison, FURSE-ROBERTS Emily, FURSLAND Anita, FURSMAN Louise, FURUYA Hiroshi, FURUYA Yoshiko, FURZE Bree, FURZE Elaine, FURZE Midori, FURZER Grant, FUSEDALE Warren, FUSER Yvette, FUSINATO Bree, FUTCHER Paul, FUTRYK Jason, FUTTER Andrew, FUTYMEAD Joe, FUZES Peter, FYFE Judy, FYLES Natasha.

G

GAAL Bela, GAAL Bela, GAAL Zsuzsanna, GABBEY Adam, GABBRIELLI Felicity, GABELA Catherine, GABIN Mervyn, **GABRIEL Delmar**, GABRIEL Faye, GABRIEL Fouad, GABRIEL Gerard, GABRIEL Iarere, GABRIEL Maria, GABRIEL Mel, GABRIEL Michael, GABRIEL Paul, GABRIELLI Josie, GACESA Jasmina, GACITUA Eduardo, GACOIN Marie, GACUMA Napoleon, GAD Tom, GADALETA Joan, GADD Felicity, GADD Shirl, GADDES Kevin, GADDES Lyn, GADDI Marciano, GADE Elaine, GADE Les, GADEY Reddy, GADSBY Allan, GADSBY Kate, GADSBY Paula, GADSDEN Aneta,

GAFFNEY Tony, GAFFNEY Carolyn, GAFFNEY John, GAFFNEY Judy, GAFFNEY Mary, GAFFNEY Meaghan, GAFFNEY Paul, GAFFNEY Peter, GAFFNEY Wal, GAGAN Robert, GAGE Paul, GAGEN Ray, GAGER Loraine, GAGNON Dean, GAGNON Steven, GAGNUSS Arthur, GAHA Alan, GAHA Lewis, GAHA Sharon, GAHRMANN Tina, GAILEY Sarah, GAISFORD Edna, GAISFORD Keith, GAJDA Kim, GAL Diane, GALACE Joseph, GALAEN Leif, GALAFASSI Susan, GALANG Agnes, GALANTAI Bill, GALATI Tony, GALAVODAS Natasha, GALAZ Jose, GALBRAITH Denise, GALBRAITH Graham, GALDIES Mariana, GALE Bryson, GALE Chris, GALE Col, GALE Kerry, GALE Lisa, GALE Lucinda, GALE Margaret, GALE Max, GALE Pamela, GALE Peter, GALE Phil, GALE Ron, GALE Tavaa, GALE Yvonne, GALEA Eddie, GALEA Lisa, GALEA Melanie, GALEA Michael, GALEA Michael, GALEA Pia, GALEA Sam, GALIC Mick, GALICEK John, GALIEL Nadia, GALIEL Tofick, GALIMBERTI Gianfranca, GALIN Alexandra, GALIPEAU James, GALISTAN Ronald, GALL Greg, GALL Harriet, GALLAGHER Andrew, GALLAGHER Ann, GALLAGHER Barbara, GALLAGHER Cherie, GALLAGHER Cathryn, GALLAGHER Colette, GALLAGHER Denise, GALLAGHER Emma, GALLAGHER Jeannie, GALLAGHER Jenni, GALLAGHER John, GALLAGHER Marie, GALLAGHER Meaghan, GALLAGHER Melinda, GALLAGHER Mick, GALLAGHER Michael, GALLAGHER Michelle, GALLAGHER Johnston, GALLAGHER Paul, GALLAGHER Paul, GALLAGHER Raymond, GALLAGHER Richard, GALLAGHER Ron, GALLAGHER Sarah, GALLAHER Mark, GALLARD Paul, GALLASCH Rosita, GALLATY Geoff, GALLATY Geoff, GALLE Cameron, GALLE Peter, GALLERY Diane, GALLERY Ian, GALLERY Nick, GALLES Angie, GALLIMORE Jeff, GALLIROPOULOU Vassiliki, GALLO Adam, GALLO Deena, GALLO Gabriella, GALLON Max, GALLOWAY Howard, GALPERN Igor, GALPERN Julie, GALPERN Tania, GALTON Willy, GALVES Alberto, GALVIN Celine, GALVIN Graham, GALVIN Jeff, GALVIN Bill, GALWEY Robyn, GAMAL Muhammad, GAMBARO Josephine, GAMBETTA Danielle, GAMBETTA Jo, GAMBIAN Karen, GAMBLE Carla, GAMBLE Daniel, GAMBLE David, GAMBLE Gretchen, GAMBLE Kris, GAMBLE Rod, GAMBLE Ron, GAMBLE Zoi, GAMBOA Fernando, GAMBOTTO Leandro, GAMIT Laurice, GAMMIE Nicky, GAMVROS Laura, GAMWELL Ruth, GAN Adele, GAN Mei, GAN Thian, GAN Thomas, GAN Aaron, GANA Claudia, GANA Ervin, GANASAN Jaya, GANDAWINATA Linda, GANDER Gloria, GANDERTON Conway, GANE Tony, GANE Chris, GANE Steve, GANESHARATNAM Ganesh, GANESHARATNAM Suresh, GANGEMI Patricia, GANGEMI Pizzolo, GANIBE Helen, GANKO Marta, GANNAWAY Alannah, GANNON Anne, GANNOULIS Nick, GANT Dean, GANTA Rajesh, GAO Jane, GAO Wei, GAO York, GAO Tom, GAPPS Danny, GARA Marie-France, GARAI Fred, GARAI Paul, GARAN Symon, GARATE Carlos, GARATSHUN John, GARATY John, GARAY VALVERDE Betto, GARBE Johanna, GARBUTT David, GARCIA Angel, GARCIA Jennifer, GARCIA Julio, GARCIA Laura, GARCIA Paulene, GARCIA Tlaloc, GARD Pat, GARDA Rolf, GARDAM Jody, GARDEM Ben, GARDEM Robyn, GARDENER Roger, GARDINER Brenda, GARDINER Cathy, GARDINER Christine, GARDINER Darren, GARDINER Deborah, GARDINER Denise, GARDINER Gerry, GARDINER Jason, GARDINER Jo, GARDINER Linda, GARDINER Liz, GARDINER Lyndall, GARDINER Mandy, GARDINER Peter, GARDINER Reg, GARDINER Stephen, GARDNER Anita, GARDNER Ann, GARDNER Betty, **GARDNER Dave**, GARDNER Ian, GARDNER Isabel, GARDNER Janis, GARDNER Joan, GARDNER Jody, GARDNER John, GARDNER Julie, GARDNER Kevin, GARDNER Kim, GARDNER Krichelle, GARDNER Linda, GARDNER Maggie, GARDNER Margaret, GARDNER Marguerite, GARDNER Bruce, GARDNER Paul, GARDNER Reginald, GARDNER Victoria, GARDNIR Flo, GARDOS Vanessa, GARDOZ George, GARDUNO Natalia, GARGANO Isabella, GARGETT Phillip, GARGISO Giovanna, GARGOULAKIS George, GARLAND Ann, GARLAND Nick, GARLAND Steve, GARLICK Allan, GARLICK Jan, GARLICK Lynn, GARLICK Paul, GARLING Cath, GARMAN Callista, GARMENT Justine, GARNER Barry, GARNER Betony, GARNER Jim, GARNER John, GARNETT Graham, GARNETT Graham, GARNETT Michelle, GARNETT Sue, GARNEV Ilia, GARNHAM Andrew, GARNHAM Barbara, GARNSEY Coral, GAROT George, GARRARD Deanne, GARRARD Meredith, GARRARD Peter, GARRARD Peter, GARRASH Keith, GARREAU Aurelien, GARRETT Mitch, GARRETT Rod, GARRICK Gervais, GARRICK Mark, GARRICK Roger, GARRISON Blake, GARRITY Leonard, GARRY Irwin, GARRY RAYMOND Gent, GARSIA Irma, GARSKE Arthur, GARSUTA Artie, GARSZTKA David, GARTH Janelle, GARTH Karen, GARTH Katherine, GARTH Leanne, GARTNER Cornelia, GARTNER Michal, GARTSIDE Patricia, GARUFO Maria, GARUTI Kerry, GARVEN Fae, GARVEY Brian, GARVEY Claire, GARVEY Helen, GARVEY John, GARVEY Michael, GARVEY Tim, GARVIN Phil, GARVRILOVIC Ken, GARWOOD Linda, GARZA Marina, GASILIAUSKAS Peter, GASILIAUSKAS Robyn, GASKELL David, GASKIN Lee, GASMIER Sue, GASON Paul, GASPARI Robyn, GASPARI Roberto, GASPARINI Katharine, GASSON Bridget, GASSON Jim, GASTALDELLO Secondo, GATELY Anita, GATELY Lil, GATELY Shannyn, GATELY Suzette, GATENO Jenny, GATERELL Lori, GATES Brian, GATES Chris, GATES Felicity, GATES George, GATES Graham, GATES John, GATES Bill, GATLAND Jo, GATLEY Reg, GATLEY Ron, GATRELL Alec, GATT Del, GATT Joanne, GATT Lawrence, GATT Nina, GATTAS Alison, GATTAS Berenice, GATTAS Berenice, GATTAS Ray, GATTI Pina, GAUCI Ben, GAUCI Henry, GAUCI Jenny, GAUCI Matt, GAUCI Nancy, GAUCI Tim, GAUCI Tracey, GAUDIOSI Andy, GAUGHAN Jo, GAUGHAN John, GAUL Jeanette, GAUL Matt, GAULD Cassandra, GAUNT Theo, GAUS Katharina, GAUT Karen, GAUTA Sonia, GAUTAM Abhishek, GAVAGHAN Brian, GAVATHAS Bill, GAVESTON Rob, GAVIGLIO Olive, GAVIN Barry, GAVIN Brian, GAVIN Bruce, GAVIN Dawn, GAVIN Graeme, GAVIN Madelene, GAVIO Guido, **GAVRANICH Michelle**, GAVRILOVIC Dean, GAVRILOVIC Kristina, GAVRILOVIC Stefan, GAWN Charmane, GAWNE Wendy, GAWTHORNE Keith, GAWTHROP Martin, GAY Albert, GAY Bert, GAY Kate, GAY Doug, GAY Gregory, GAY Gwen, GAY John, GAY Kate, GAY Kelly, GAY Laura, GAY Margaret, GAY Matt, GAY Pat, GAY Bob, GAY Ron, GAY Susan, GAYDON Suzanne, GAYFORD Jon, GAYLARD Melanie, GAYNOR Al, GAYNOR Luke, GAYNOR Milt, GAZAL Heidi, GAZDARICA Sylvia, GAZE Jillian, GAZIVODA Matt, GAZO Jean, GAZZARD Edward, GAZZARD Kate, GAZZOLA Iole, GE Mei, GEACH Leann, GEAGEA Big, GEAKE Maurice, GEANELLOS Charles, GEAR Barbara, GEAR Elaine, GEAR Margaret, GEAR Ron, GEARY Alex, GEARY Claire, GEARY Jane, GEARY Rod, GEARY Susanne, GEASON Geoffrey, GEASON Leanne, GEASON Monica, GEBHARD Hans, GEBHART Tony, GEBRAN Therese, GEBREIGZIABHEK Berhane, GEBREMARIAM Lily, GEDDES Annabelle, GEDDES Margery, GEDGE George, GEDLING Aaron, GEE John, GEE Joy, GEE Nathan, GEEKIE Ted, GEERCKENS Wendy, GEERKENS Kevin, GEEVES Brad, GEGENHUBER Sonia, GEGGIE Judi, GEGGIE Ruth, GEHRER Alex, GEHRIG Kyle, GEHRUNG Ewald, GEIA Jeremy, GEIER Renate, GEIGER Edwina, GEIST Francois, GEISZLER Chris, GELBER Kath, GELLARD Lindy, GELLER Robert, GELLERT Erika, GELLERT Jason, GELONESE Bruno, GEMELL Andrea, GEMELL Susan, GEMMELL Cherie, GEMMELL Gavin, GEMMELL Graeme, GEMMELL Lola, GEMMELL-SMITH Katie, GENCIANA Roquita, GENDY Joe, GENECARD Pierre, GENESINI Angela, GENGE Cheryl, GENGE Louise, GENN Darlene, GENOVESE Mel, GENOVESE Gabriella, GENRICH Tracey, GENT Gordon, GENT Lesley, GENT Norm, GENT Ray, GENTLE Mark, GENTLE Sharon, GENTLE Tim, GEOGHEGAN Chris, GEOGHEGAN Peter, GEOGHEGAN Rachael, GEOGHEGAN Bill, GEORGALAS Maria, GEORGARIS Marilyn, GEORGAS Toni, GEORGAS Silvio, GEORGE Brad, GEORGE Caraline, GEORGE Deb, GEORGE Diane, GEORGE Edmund, GEORGE Elizabeth, GEORGE Gabbie, GEORGE Jasmin, GEORGE Jill, GEORGE John, GEORGE Kathy, GEORGE Keren, GEORGE Leanne, GEORGE Malcolm, GEORGE Margaret, GEORGE Matthew, GEORGE Mike, GEORGE Pat, GEORGE Phil, GEORGE Raph, GEORGE Robert, GEORGE Bob, GEORGE Ron, GEORGE Roy, GEORGE Sabina, GEORGE Sally, GEORGE Sandi, GEORGE Shirley, GEORGE Stacey, GEORGE Valerie, GEORGE Wal, GEORGE Zane, GEORGESON Steph, GEORGIADIS George, GEORGIOU Chrissy, GEPPERT Judith, GERACITANO Tony, GERADA Charles, GERADA Godwin, GERADA Marie, GERAGHTY E len, GERAGHTY Faye, GERAGHTY Francette, GERAGHTY Terry, GERANTONIS Paul, GERBER Robyn, GERBI

Valter, GERGES Maria, GERGES Mina, GERHART Frieda, GERHAT Jill, GERKE Rhiana, GERLACH Maxwell, GERMAIN Ray, GERMAN Victor, GERMANN Joe, GERMANOS George, GERMEAU David, GERMIAN Selah, GERRARD Brett, GERRIE Dave, GERRING John, GERRISH Jennifer, GERRISH Sandy, GERRITZEN David, GERRY Beverly, GERSBACH Ben, GERSBACH Helen, GERSHKOVICH Joseph, GERSTELING Reginald, **GERSTL Heinz**, GERSTL Yvonne, GERTENAAR Lois, GERUASONI Carlos, GERVASONI Carlos, GERVASONI Gloria, GESCH Jason, GESCKE Dieter, GETHINGS Cyril, GETTS Sandra, GEUDER Lyndie, GEWARGIS Joseph, GEYER Kevin, GEYTENBEEK Jenny, GHADIRIAN Roya, GHALI Emad, GHALI Fiby, GHAMA Jason, GHAN-HLINKA Nenita, GHANEM Robert, GHANI Daniel, GHANI Sandra, GHANI Shareen, GHARIBIAN Liz, GHASSEMI Kourosh, GHATTAS Julie, GHAZAL Merela, GHAZIKIAN Harry, GHELANI Indu, GHILOTTI Adrian, GHIMIRE Sumesh, GHORI Mohammed, GHORRA Amanda, GHOSH Ratna, GHOSN John, GHOSSAIN Clare, GHULIANI Jot, GIACOMIN Greg, GIACOMO Andrew, GIAMBOI Tony, GIAMBOI Mary, GIANNAKAKI Eleni, GIANNAKIS Katrina, GIANNIS Stephanie, GIANNONE Matthew, GIANOLLA Denice, GIANOTTO Elizabeth, GIARDIUI Anna, GIATRAS Anna, GIBB Betty, GIBB Fiona, GIBB Joan, GIBB Joseph, GIBB Xiaoming, GIBBENS Wendy, GIBBESON Ian, GIBBINS Daphne, GIBBONS David, GIBBONS Eric, GIBBONS Jacqui, GIBBONS Margaret, GIBBONS Steven, GIBBONS Sue, GIBBS Andrew, GIBBS Tony, GIBBS Craig, GIBBS Beth, GIBBS Jan, GIBBS Jon, GIBBS Kerry, GIBBS Libby, GIBBS Margaret, GIBBS Nathan, GIBBS Neil, GIBBS Sally, GIBBS Steven, GIBBS Warner, GIBBS Bruce, GIBLETT Ben, GIBLETT Lynda, GIBLIN Belinda, GIBLIN Diane, GIBLIN Fiona, GIBLIN Lesley, GIBLIN Sandy, GIBSON Allan, GIBSON Allan, GIBSON Allan, GIBSON Andrew, GIBSON Anne, GIBSON Ann, GIBSON Tony, GIBSON Tony, GIBSON Carol, GIBSON Katy, GIBSON Col, GIBSON David, GIBSON Dean, GIBSON Debbie, GIBSON Elizabeth, GIBSON Liz, GIBSON Frances, GIBSON Heather, GIBSON Jan, GIBSON Jan, GIBSON Janet, GIBSON Kathy, GIBSON Kathy, GIBSON Keryl, GIBSON Kingsley, GIBSON Leonard, GIBSON Louise, GIBSON Lucy, GIBSON Marilen, GIBSON Melissa, GIBSON Penny, GIBSON Ray, GIBSON Rhonda, GIBSON Rosemary, GIBSON Sue, GIBSON Suzie, GIBSON Victoria, GIBSON Wayne, GIBSON Wenda, GIBSON Bill, GIDLEY Sarah, GIDLEY-BAIRD Gavin, GIEBELER Ivanka, GIEMZA Dominik, GIESE Bernd, GIFFIN Rod, GIFFORD John, GIFFORD Chris, GIFFORD Ted, GIFFORD Judy, GIFFORD Rebecca, GIFFORD Robert, GIFFORD Shannon, GIGG Tom, **GIGLIO Caterina**, GIGLIO Roberto, GIL Georgina, GILBERT Amanda, GILBERT Andrew, GILBERT Andrew, GILBERT Chris, GILBERT Darren, GILBERT Dave, GILBERT Graeme, GILBERT Helen, GILBERT Margaret, GILBERT Julie, GILBERT Kelly, GILBERT Kerry, GILBERT Mark, GILBERT Simon, GILBERT Maresce, GILBERT Matt, GILBERT Sabine, GILBERT Sue, GILBERTH Keith, GILBERTSON Erik, GILCHRIST Mary, GILCHRIST Rhonda, GILDART Maureen, GILDER Helen, GILDER Jenny, GILDERDALE Adrian, GILDINA Elena, GILDINA Luda, GILDING Rie, GILDING Sandra, GILES Barry, GILES Barb, GILES Ingrid, GILES Jim, GILES Jill, GILES Judy, GILES Kim, GILES Lyn, GILES Marcus, GILES Marie, GILES Renee, GILES Robert, GILES Sandra, GILES Tim, GILFILLAN Justin, GILFORD Ian, GILHAM Kylie, GILHOOLY Jim, GILHUUS Martin, GILIADOV Stanislav, GILKES Ainsley, GILL Alan, **GILL Bob**, GILL David, GILL Delma, GILL Elizabeth, GILL Gagandeep, GILL Genevieve, GILL Herdip, GILL Izumi, GILL Jaswin, GILL Leneice, GILL Lynette, GILL Matthew, GILL Matthew, GILL Meredith, GILL Moira, GILL Rasvinder, GILL Richard, GILL Robyn, GILL Rose, GILL Sam, GILL Sarah, GILL Val, GILLAM Garry, GILLAM Roma, GILLAN Alison, GILLARD Beryl, GILLARD Phillip, GILLEN Ashley, GILLESPIE Alison, GILLESPIE Gail, GILLESPIE Kylie, GILLESPIE Maureen, GILLESPIE Patrick, GILLESPIE Patrick, GILLESPIE Bob, GILLETT Jacki, GILLETT John, GILLETT Shirley, GILLIAN Philomena, GILLIBRAND Michelle, GILLIES Alex, GILLIES Angie, GILLIES Linda, GILLIES Karen, GILLIES Kim, GILLIGAN Ian, GILLIGAN Jim, GILLIGAN Julia, GILLIGAN Suzanne, GILLILAND Bob, GILLINGS Nick, GILLINGS Susanna, GILLIS Lesley, GILLIS Peter, GILLIVER-SMITH Michelle, GILLMER Blake, GILLOTT Sharon, GILLROY Ted, GILLS Sandie, GILMORE Alison, GILMORE Paul, GILMORE Roy, GILMOUR Benjamin, GILMOUR Brian, GILMOUR Ian, GILMOUR Janelle, GILMOUR Mathew, GILMOUR Pam, GILOVITZ Rosaleen, GILROY Denise, GILSHENEN Joanne, GILVEAR Fran, GIM Susie, GIMBERT Judy, GIMBERT Traci, GIN Catherine, GIN Li, GINDI Wendy, GINGRAS Christian, GINIS Di, GINN Simon, GINN Steve, GINNANE Lisa, GINNS Harry, GINROINI Bernardo, GINTOWT Pat, GINTY David, GIORGAS Nicki, GIORGINI Antony, GIORIA Jo, GIOSKOS Gina, GIOTIS Chrisanthi, GIOVANELLI PRIOR Beverley, GIRAMONJO Joseph, GIRARDI Don, GIRAUD Pascal, GIRAUD-KINLEY Catherine, GIRGIS Eddie, GIRI Rama, GIRONDA Sam, GIROUX Sandra, GIRVAN Chris, GIRVAN Girvo, GIRVAN June, GISBORNE Matthew, GISBORNE Sue, GISSING Jeffrey, GITTINS Sandy, GITTINS Andrew, GITTINS Graham, GITTINS Janine, GITTOES Denise, GIUDICE Maureen, GIUFFRE Dave, GIUFFRE John, GIUSTRA Adriana, GIUTTARI Joe, GIV Fredrika, GIV MASIHI Mary, GIVAN Jim, GIVANANDAM Nirmala, GIVORSHNER Isaac, GIZZO Pasquale, GLACKEN Phoebe, GLADMAN Rachael-Anne, GLADSTONE Sue, GLAEBATSAS Glennis, GLAGOVS Audrey, GLANVILLE David, GLANVILLE Mark, GLANVILLE Matthew, GLARE Michael, GLAROS Emmanuel, GLASER Paul, GLASGOW Norma, GLASS Jean, GLASS Lynn, GLASS Michael, GLASS Warren, GLASS Bill, GLASSON Angus, GLASSON Morris, GLASSON Sylvia, GLASSON Wendy, GLAVAN Nada, GLAVES Marie, GLAVES Phil, GLAVINIC Zoran, GLAW Harry, GLAZEBROOK John, GLAZEBROOK Peter, GLAZER Diana, GLEAVE Fay, GLEAVE Gayanne, GLEAVE Mark, GLEDHILL Dawn, GLEDHILL Paul, GLEDHILL Tim, GLEDHILL Bill, GLEESON Anthony, GLEESON Carina, GLEESON Cherie, GLEESON Christopher, GLEESON Daniel, GLEESON Dean, GLEESON Elizabeth, GLEESON Georgia, **GLEESON Gerry**, GLEESON Iris, GLEESON John, GLEESON Katie, GLEESON Linda, GLEESON Mandy, GLEESON Margaret, GLEESON Mick, GLEESON Michael, GLEESON Pat, GLEESON Pat, GLEESON Pat, GLEESON Tricia, GLEESON Shiuaun, GLEESON Tom, GLEN Mary, GLENDENNING Joan, GLENNAN Robin, GLENNAN Troy, GLENNIE Shirley, GLEREAN David, GLIENER Shaina, GLIGIC Dusan, GLOCK Pam, GLOSS Peter, GLOSSOP Sarah, GLOVER Ali, GLOVER Alison, GLOVER Cara, GLOVER Elyse, GLOVER Grant, GLOVER Jane, GLOVER Kevin, GLOVER Lorraine, GLOVER Melissa, GLOVER Paul, GLOVER Rich, GLOVER Robyn, GLOVER Robyne, GLOWACKA Ursula, GLUGA Doina, GLUGA Elvis, GLUGA Ion, GLUSESKI Toni, GLUYAS Andy, GLYDE Raymond, GLYNN Ann, GLYNN Wal, GNANAKUMARAN Krishnaverny, GNIEL Karin, GO Anna, GO Ben, GO Richard, GOADBY Matthew, GOARD Marion, GOATHER Jerry, GOBBE Chris, GOBBE Maria, GOBERT Diane, GOBERT Terry, GOCK David, GOCK Helen, GOCK Victor, GOCKEL Regina, GODAU Karl, GODBOLT Paul, GODBY Christine, GODBY Ian, GODBY Leanne, GODDARD Christopher, GODDARD Jason, GODDARD John, GODDARD Karen, GODDARD Keith, GODDARD Nadine, GODDARD Pam, GODDARD Peter, GODDARD Tanya, GODDE Greg, GODEC Michael, GODENZI Marco, GODFREY Art, GODFREY David, GODFREY Ed, GODFREY John, GODFREY Julie, GODFREY Kenneth, GODFREY Kim, GODFREY Margaret, GODFREY Norma, GODFREY Robert, GODFREY Rosina, GODFREY Sandra, GODFREY Shirley, GODFREY Wayne, GODINET Mila, GODKIN Estelle, GODKIN Gavin, GODKIN Maureen, GODKIN Sean, GODL John, GODOY Fil, GODSELL Brian, GODSON Lyn, GODWARD Georgia, **GODWELL Maria**, GODWIN Joanne, GODWIN Stewart, GOEDDE Elizabeth, GOEL Ashish, GOERL Harry, GOERNITZ Sonja, GOFF Russell, GOGGIN Myfanwy, GOH Damien, GOH James, GOH Jeff, GOH Kiah, GOH Sherene, GOJAK Denis, GOJNICH Natasha, GOLAFSHAN Ben, GOLAMUNNABI Mohamed, GOLD Jeremy, GOLD Kenneth, GOLD Michael, GOLD Shane, GOLD Steven, GOLD Warren, GOLDBERG Lionel, GOLDBERG Ross, GOLDEN Chris, GOLDEN Elizabeth, GOLDEN Paul, GOLDEN Tony, GOLDFINCH Mary, GOLDIE Dawn, GOLDIE Marjorie, GOLDIE Pam, GOLDIE Wendy, GOLDING Barry, GOLDING John, GOLDING Mary, GOLDING Steve, GOLDMAN Fran, GOLDMAN Ilga, GOLDMAN Julie-Ann, GOLDMAN Peter, GOLDMAN Robyn, GOLDMAN Zell, GOLDRICK Helen, GOLDRICK Lisa, GOLDSBRO David, GOLDSBRO Luke, GOLDSBURY David, GOLDSMITH John, GOLDSMITH Judy, GOLDSMITH Sarah, GOLDSMITH Sid, GOLDSTAT Joshua, GOLDSTEIN Dina, GOLDSTEIN Jason,

GOLDSTEIN Jenny, GOLDSTEIN Ya , GOLDSTIVER Nathan, GOLDSWORTHY Larraine, GOLDSWORTHY Rebecca, GOLDTHORP Michele, GOLEBIEWSKI Mark, GOLIGHTLY Trevor, GOLLAKOTA Rama, GOLLAN Marian, GOLLEDGE Brian, GOLOD Maria, GOMERSKI Rolf, GOMES Kerry, GOMEZ Aukje, GOMEZ Ivan, GOMEZ Jaime, GOMEZ Randy, GOMEZ Yolande, GOMIERATO Valli, GOMM Val, GOMOLA Mike, GONCALVES Neville, GONCALVES ANJOS Armenio, GONG Gillian, GONINON Cheryl, GONINON Philip, GONSALVES Cheryle, GONZAGA Anna, GONZAGA Sabiniana, GONZALES Abby, GONZALES Diego, GONZALES Frank, GONZALES Pilar, GONZALES Roel, GONZALEZ Alicia, GONZALEZ Amanda, GONZALEZ Francisco, GONZALEZ Gladys, GONZALEZ Glenda, GONZALEZ Greg, GONZALEZ Beatriz, GONZALEZ Joe, GONZALEZ Juan, GONZALEZ Richard, GONZALEZ Roland, GONZALEZ AGUDO Cristina, GONZALEZ-MANQUEL Francisco, GONZO Lizzy, GOOCH Deb, GOOCH Fred, GOOCH Kerry, GOOD Alison, GOOD Libby, GOOD Gina, GOOD Naomi, GOODACRE Elliott, GOODALL Gary, GOODALL Joanne, GOODALL Noel, GOODALL Pauline, GOODALL Pauline, GOODALL Suzanne, GOODE Barry, GOODE Gail, GOODE Kevin, GOODE Sharnielle, GOODEAR Maurice, GOODEAR Ray, GOODEN Adrian, GOODES Sasha, GOODHEW Kenneth, GOODHEW Tenny, GOODHIND Brian, GOODING Karlee, GOODING Mark, **GOODING Marion**, GOODLEY Penelope, GOODLIFFE David, GOODMAN Carmel, GOODMAN Bill, GOODMAN Juliet, GOODMAN Madeline, GOODMAN Wayne, GOODMAN-JONES Robyn, GOODRIDGE Rebecca, GOODROPE Amy, GOODSELL Christopher, GOODSELL Megan, GOODSELL Val, GOODSTONE Nicholas, GOODWIN Adrian, GOODWIN Brett, GOODWIN Colleen, GOODWIN Dave, GOODWIN Dianne, GOODWIN Harry, GOODWIN Janine, GOODWIN Jeffrey, GOODWIN Barry, GOODWIN Tony, GOODWIN John, GOODWIN Karen, GOODWIN Kim, GOODWIN Luke, GOODWIN Nadene, GOODWIN Heather, GOODWIN Phyl, GOODWIN Robert, GOODWORTH Jill, GOODYEAR Michelle, GOOIKER Hans, GOOLD Bill, GOOLEY Geoffrey, GOOLEY James, GOOLEY Patricia, GOON Tracie, GOONESEKERA Sharmini, GOONEY Les, GOOREVICH Leo, GOOSAKOFF David, GOOT Josh, GOPALAKRISHNAN Anueja, GOPEZ Cheryl, GORDON Ashley, GORDON Barbara, GORDON Carol, GORDON Catherine, GORDON Cindy, GORDON Eddie, GORDON Helen, GORDON Jenny, GORDON Jenny, GORDON John, GORDON John, GORDON Julie, GORDON Justin, GORDON Kate, GORDON Kathy, GORDON Kay, GORDON Keith, GORDON Kerry, GORDON Leanne, GORDON Les, GORDON Les, GORDON Lindsay, GORDON Marie, GORDON Peter, GORDON Rebecca, GORDON Richard, GORDON Steve, GORDON Sue, GORE Chris, GORE Jenny, GORE Sid, GOREJONES Lydia, GORFINKEL Lauren, GORGIEVSKA Mel, GORGIOUS Anwar, GORHAM Brett, GORHAM Brenda, GORHAM Margaret, GORING-SIEBERT Kiril, GORKOFF Tonya, GORMAN Andrew, GORMAN Breff, GORMAN Brooke, GORMAN Carissa, GORMAN Jeff, GORMAN Lyall, GORMAN Lyn, GORMAN Maureen, GORMAN Peter, GORMAN Rebecca, GORMAN Ronald, GORMAN Shirley, GORMAN-PLANT David, GORNALL-THODE Heloise, GORNALL-THODE Julian, GOROSTIZA Fernando, GORRICK Carolyn, GORRICK Gill, GORRIE Jeff, GORRIE Julia, GORRIE Shirley, GORRING Chris, GORRING Jo, GORSKI Ian, GORTAN Bruno, GORTLEY Michael, GORTON Cindy, GORTON Emma, GORTON Jenny, GORTON Judith, GORTON Robin, GOSANO Thomas, GOSBELL Nerida, GOSBELL Vanessa, GOSBY Rick, GOSLING Christine, GOSLING David, GOSLING Francis, GOSLING Marjorie, GOSLING Paul, GOSLING Samantha, GOSLING Sarah, GOSPER Craig, GOSPER Peter, GOSPO Paul, GOSPODARCZYK Kerry, GOSS Sonja, GOSS Tiffany, GOSSAGE Glenda, GOSSIP Naomi, GOSSLAND Niall, GOSSLING Maureen, GOSWELL Glenys, GOSWELL John, GOSWELL Goswell, GOTH Natascha, GOTO Arashu, GOTO Eri, GOTSIS Nick, GOTTING Bernie, GOTTING Bruce, GOTTS Kevin, GOTTSCHLING Peter, GOUDGE Christina, GOUGH John, GOUGH Joszefina, GOUGH Les, GOUGH Lyn, GOUGH Michael, GOUGH Richard, GOULD Tony, GOULD Cheryl, GOULD Chris, GOULD Danielle, GOULD Jennie, GOULD Jack, GOULD Lauren, GOULD Lea, GOULD Len, GOULD Maureen, GOULD Michelle, GOULD Mick, GOULD Pat, GOULD Perry, GOULD Peter, GOUMAND Sylvain, GOUMAS Effe, GOUNAGIAS Athanasios, GOUNTARAS Maria, GOURBEILLE Pierre, GOURGOURAS Vas, GOURLAY Jenny, GOURLAY Jeremy, GOURLEY Myrtle, GOURLIE Kris, GOURVIL Gil, GOUTZIOS George, GOUVEIA Silvana, GOVER Peter, GOVERNO Edgar, GOVERNOR Patricia, GOVEY Catherine, GOVINDA RAJ Pavin, GOVINDRAM Ranee, GOW Eileen, GOW Leanne, GOW Lucy, GOWSMITH Gordon, GOWANS Kim, GOWENLOCK Kenneth, GOWER Alex, GOWER Carol, **GOWER Iris**, GOWER Yasuko, GOWERS Kathie, GOWING Jill, GOWING Robert, GOWING Wendy, GOWLAND Ryan, GOWLETT Darryl, GOWMAN Doreen, GOWMAN John, GOYAL Arjun, GOYMER Margaret, GOYMER Ray, GRABOWSKI Adam, GRABOWSKI Alice, GRACAN Isabel, GRACE Celia, GRACEY Jacki, GRACEY Jennifer, GRACIA Lina, GRACIA Rebecca, GRACIE Denis, GRACIE Peter, GRACIE Rebecca, GRACIE Sandra, GRACZYNSKI Joanna, GRADY Liz, GRADY Kate, GRADY Linda, GRADY Mark, GRADY Robyn, GRADY Sam, GRAEFLING Jason, GRAETZ Sarah, GRAF Hans, GRAF Steve, GRAFF Jodi, GRAFITTI Luciano, GRAFITTI Jeanette, GRAGEDA Sisy, GRAHAM Alan, GRAHAM Alan, GRAHAM Allan, GRAHAM Anne, GRAHAM Anne, GRAHAM Anne, GRAHAM Tony, GRAHAM Belinda, GRAHAM Brenda, GRAHAM Brian, GRAHAM Brian, GRAHAM Cas, GRAHAM Carol, GRAHAM Carl, GRAHAM Catherine, GRAHAM Christie, GRAHAM Clare, GRAHAM Daniel, GRAHAM Darren, GRAHAM Darren, GRAHAM David, GRAHAM Dave, GRAHAM David, GRAHAM Debbie, GRAHAM Dennis, GRAHAM Diane, GRAHAM Dougal, GRAHAM Edmund, GRAHAM Eric, GRAHAM Sian, GRAHAM Greg, GRAHAM Jodie, GRAHAM Jodie, GRAHAM John, GRAHAM John, GRAHAM Kath, GRAHAM Ken, GRAHAM Mal, GRAHAM Sue, GRAHAM Mary, GRAHAM Margaret, GRAHAM Mark, GRAHAM Matthew, GRAHAM Maureen, GRAHAM Mel, GRAHAM Michelle, GRAHAM Nicole, GRAHAM Pam, GRAHAM Patti, GRAHAM Paul, GRAHAM Peter, GRAHAM Peter, GRAHAM Philip, GRAHAM Rita, GRAHAM Ross, GRAHAM Roger, GRAHAM Penny, GRAHAM Chic, GRAHAM Sara, GRAHAM Sarah, GRAHAM Sherelle, GRAHAM Sue, GRAHAM Tamara, GRAHAM TG, GRAHAM Bill, GRAHAM-NYE Jason, GRAHAM-SMITH Denzil, GRAHAME Belinda, GRAHAME Helena, GRAINGER Graham, GRAINGER Maurice, GRALTON Rachel, GRANATA John, GRANC Andrew, GRAND Margaret, GRANDE Mary, GRANDE ROMERO Vanessa, GRANEY Barbara, GRANEY David, GRANFIELD Matthew, GRANGER Freda, GRANGER Mark, GRANNON Geoff, GRANT Allan, GRANT Andrew, GRANT Andrew, GRANT Andrew, GRANT Belinda, GRANT Bradley, GRANT Brian, GRANT Carlee, GRANT Denise, GRANT Diana, GRANT Doreen, GRANT Eddy, GRANT Fiona, GRANT Gerry, **GRANT Gordon**, GRANT Graham, **GRANT Joan**, GRANT Jodie, GRANT Joe, GRANT Judy, GRANT Julie, GRANT June, GRANT Kate, GRANT Keith, GRANT Keith, GRANT Kimm, GRANT Lee, GRANT Linda, GRANT Marjorie, GRANT Mark, GRANT Maurice, GRANT Murray, GRANT Nick, GRANT Penny, **GRANT Bob**, GRANT Robert, GRANT Sandra, GRANT Varelle, GRANTTAYLOR Penny, GRANTER Don, GRANTHAM Diana, GRANTHAM Matt, GRANTHAM Una, GRASER Carlo, GRASON Ian, GRASS Sam, GRASSI Carmen, GRASSI Fernando, GRASSO Gerry, GRASSO Lidia, GRASSO Bob, GRATSOUNAS Nick, GRATTAN Christine, GRATTAN-SMITH Tony, GRATTON Leezab, GRATWICK-SARLL Sabine, GRAU Juliet, GRAVARE Magnus, GRAVES Arthur, GRAVES Bernard, GRAVES Doris, GRAVES Gregory, GRAVES Ian, GRAVES Karen, GRAY Adrian, GRAY Ann, GRAY Arthur, GRAY Barbara, GRAY Bev, GRAY Brian, GRAY Christine, GRAY David, GRAY Dean, GRAY Donna, GRAY Doug, GRAY Earl, GRAY Elena, GRAY Elizabeth, GRAY Emily, GRAY Frederick, GRAY Ian, GRAY Janelle, GRAY Janet, GRAY Janet, GRAY Jenne, GRAY Jenny, GRAY Joanna, GRAY Jonti, GRAY Jon, GRAY Kate, GRAY Kat, GRAY Kelli, GRAY Kim, GRAY Linda, GRAY Liv, GRAY Mark, GRAY Margaret, GRAY Maz, GRAY Margaret, GRAY Maxine, GRAY Max, GRAY Maxwell, GRAY Michael, GRAY Nathan, GRAY Nev, GRAY Nicole, GRAY Pamela, GRAY Pat, GRAY Peter, GRAY Phil, GRAY Rebecca, GRAY Ron, GRAY Simon, GRAY Susan, GRAY Terry, GRAY Tom, GRAY Tim, GRAY Walter, GRAY Wendy, GRAY Bill, GRAYBILL Bill, GRAYDEN Mark, GREACEN Sandra, GREALY Giovanna, GREANEY Clayton,

GREANEY Olivia, GREAVES Bette, GREAVES Betty, GREAVES Densill, GREAVES Geoff, GREAVES Jennifer, GREAVES Peter, GREBER-RAINER Ian, GREBERT Mal, GRECH Arthur, GRECH Deborah, GRECH Paul, GRECH Stephanie, GRECL Christine, GREEF Chris, GREEF Daniel, GREELISH Jeanette, GREELISH Jessica, GREEN Adam, GREEN Alaine, GREEN Brian, GREEN Catherine, GREEN Clinton, GREEN Daniel, GREEN Roger, GREEN David, GREEN Dennis, GREEN Dennis, GREEN Don, GREEN Eileen, GREEN Ernest, GREEN Gail, GREEN Gary, GREEN Geoff, GREEN Graham, GREEN Greg, GREEN Helen, GREEN Helen, GREEN Helga, GREEN Henry, GREEN Ian, GREEN Jackie, GREEN Jim, REEN Jane, GREEN Jean, GREEN Jennie, GREEN Heath, GREEN John, GREEN Kelly, GREEN Kevin, GREEN Kim, GREEN Lesley, GREEN Lorna, GREEN Louise, GREEN Lindsay, GREEN Mary, GREEN Margaret, GREEN Marie, GREEN Nola, GREEN Jean, GREEN Pam, GREEN Paul, GREEN Penny, GREEN Rebecca, GREEN Richard, GREEN Rod, GREEN Ron, GREEN Rozanne, GREEN Sheila, GREEN Shirl, GREEN Susan, GREEN Tania, GREEN Terry, GREEN Terry, GREEN Tim, GREEN Tracey, GREEN Tracey, GREEN Tracey, GREEN Troy, GREEN Sr, GREEN Valerie, GREEN Vicky, GREEN Wayne, GREENBERG Connie, GREENE Coleen, GREENE Jill, GREENE John, GREENE Justine, GREENFIELD Betty, GREENHALGH Kelly, GREENHALGH Maureen, GREENHAM Katie, GREENING Denise, GREENISH Brenda, GREENISH Tim, GREENLEES Vincent, GREENSLADE Callina, GREENSLADE Janis, GREENSMITH Bob, GREENTREE Betty, GREENUP Phillip, GREENWAY Chris, GREENWAY Diane, GREENWAY Terry, GREENWOOD Claire, GREENWOOD Daniel, GREENWOOD Dot, GREENWOOD Dorothy, GREENWOOD Ted, GREENWOOD Geoff, GREENWOOD Jarrod, GREENWOOD Keith, GREENWOOD Lynn, GREENWOOD Mike, GREENWOOD Robert, GREENWOOD Ros, GREENYER Daniel, GREER Ailsa, GREER Bob, GREGAN Marguerite, GREGG John, GREGG Matthew, GREGG Michael, GREGORY Akiko, GREGORY Alex, GREGORY Tony, GREGORY Neva, GREGORY Christopher, GREGORY Debbie, GREGORY Doug, GREGORY Gregory, GREGORY Jared, GREGORY Jill, GREGORY Jodie, GREGORY Kate, **GREGORY Lynette**, GREGORY Michael, GREGORY Neil, GREGORY Fae, GREGORY Richard, GREGORY Trevor, GREGORY Warwick, GREGSON Allan, GREGSON Margaret, GREGSON Rachel, GREGSON Terrie, GREIG Alex, GREIG Ben, GREIG Col, GREIG Deidre, GREIG Alex, GREIG Kendra, GREIG Mary, GREIG Natalie, GREIG Ros, GREIGE Steve, GREINER Kirsten, GREIVE Peta, GRENDA Tim, GRENDALL Nicki, GRENENGER Joy, GRENOT Dominic, GRESTE Edgars, GREUTER Chris, GREVETT Douglas, GREWAL Amardeep, GREWAL Harri, GREWAL Jaz, GREY Dave, GREY Doug, GREY Frank, GREY Kathleen, GREY Margaret, GREY Pauline, **GRIBBLE Denise**, GRIBBLE Frank, GRICE Jeanette, GRIEBE Connie, GRIEN Jacob, GRIEN Larissa, GRIEN Lee, GRIEN Peter, GRIERSON George, GRIERSON Rae, GRIERSON Sandie, GRIESEMER Bernard, GRIEVE Barbara, GRIEVE Hamish, GRIEVE Stu, **GRIEVES Gwen**, GRIEVES Kevin, GRIFFEN Bob, GRIFFIN Amy, GRIFFIN Chris, GRIFFIN Edwina, GRIFFIN Elaine, GRIFFIN Frederick, GRIFFIN Hays, GRIFFIN John, GRIFFIN Kaydn, GRIFFIN Kelly, GRIFFIN Ken, GRIFFIN Kenneth, GRIFFIN Marie, GRIFFIN Mary, GRIFFIN Mick, GRIFFIN Peter, GRIFFIN Mick, GRIFFIN Shane, GRIFFIN Shoshanna, GRIFFIN Ross, GRIFFITH Alan, GRIFFITH Delwyn, GRIFFITH Eve, GRIFFITH Glen, GRIFFITH Elizabeth, GRIFFITH Ross, GRIFFITHS Alan, GRIFFITHS Alan, GRIFFITHS Brett, GRIFFITHS Brendan, GRIFFITHS Christine, GRIFFITHS Deanna, GRIFFITHS Elaine, GRIFFITHS Ian, GRIFFITHS Janet, GRIFFITHS Jason, GRIFFITHS John, GRIFFITHS John, GRIFFITHS Josh, GRIFFITHS Justin, GRIFFITHS Gordon, GRIFFITHS Kerry, GRIFFITHS Lisa, GRIFFITHS Louisa, GRIFFITHS Lucy, GRIFFITHS Mary, GRIFFITHS Margaret, GRIFFITHS Matthew, GRIFFITHS Matthew, GRIFFITHS Michael, GRIFFITHS Nigel, GRIFFITHS Trish, GRIFFITHS Pennie, **GRIFFITHS Rebecca**, GRIFFITHS Robyn, GRIFFITHS Rona, GRIFFITHS Rosalyn, GRIFFITHS Steve, GRIFFITHS Sue, GRIFFITHS Thomas, GRIGG Adam, GRIGG Helen, GRIGG Merv, GRIGGS Paul, GRIGGS Randall, GRIGGS Bill, GRIGOR Steve, GRIGORA Pauline, GRIGORIAN Sassoon, GRIGUOL Ivan, GRILK Stephen, GRILL Andrew, GRILLIOT Richard, GRILLIS Father, GRILLS Gail, GRILLS Maggie, GRIMA Connie, GRIMA Hollie, GRIMA Jane, GRIMA Marian, GRIMBLE Sally, GRIME Julie, GRIMES Staf, GRIMLEY Bruce, GRIMMOND Jenni, GRIMMOND John, GRIMSHAW Beverley, GRIMSHAW Errol, GRIMSHAW Howard, GRIMSHAW Patricia, GRIMSHAW Scott, GRIMSON Lorraine, GRIMSON Bob, GRIMSTON Ralph, GRIMWADE Lisa, GRIMWOOD Lauren, GRIMWOOD Sue, GRINDROD Gail, GRINTER Kate, GRIPPO Catherine, GRISARD Jo, GRISON Nolwenn, GRISS David, GRISSELL Mark, GRITTEN Juliette, GRNESKI Tome, GROB Barry, GRODEN Anna, GROENEWEGEN Els, GROGAN Peter, GROLL Ross, GROLMAN Syd, GRONOW Matt, GRONOWSKI Sue, GROOM Lyndal, GROOM Sandra, GROOM Sharon, GROOMS Beverly, GROPPENBACHER Deidra, GROPPENBACHER Greg, GROS Katrin, GROSAS Alf, GROSE Gilly, GROSE Gillian, GROSE Ian, GROSE Louis, GROSE Ron, GROSS Louise, GROSS Magda, GROSS Maree, GROSSBECHLER Franz, GROSSE Peter, GROSSER Naomi, GROSSI Daniel, GROSSMAN David, GROSVENOR Monique, GROTH Brett, GROTH Coral, GROTH Joan, GROTHEN Peter, GROTTO George, GROUBE Tony, GROUBE Joyce, GROUNDS Phillip, GROUNDWATER Peter, GROVE Andrew, GROVE Laurie, GROVE Peter, GROVE Sandra, GROVENOR Laurie, GROVER Shashi, GROVES Tyne, GROVES Bianca, GROVES Christopher, GROVES Karen, GROVES Nadine, GROVES John, GROVES Sacha, GROZDAN Zrinski, GRUBB Richard, GRUBMIER Steve, GRUCA Margie, GRUEL Niki, GRUGGEN Wendy, GRUIA Carolin, GRUJIC Todor, GRULICH Gary, GRULICH Larry, GRUMMITT Chris, GRUNDEL Simon, GRUNDEMAN Lauren, GRUNDEMAN Olivia, GRUNDEMAN Shannon, GRUNDY Alan, GRUSOVIN Paul, GRUSZKA Monica, GRZEGOLEC Lena, GRZIC Peter, GRZIC Warren, GU Arthur, GU Jiawei, GU Junjian, GU Pan, GU Peter, GU Jessie, GUADALQUIVER Arturo, GUAJARDO Luis, GUAN Lynn, GUANA-JARRIN Christian, GUANA-JARRIN Estephan, GUANCO Teza, GUARALDO Mariana, GUARDIANI Rosa, GUARESCHI Maria, GUARROCHENA Lesley, **GUARROCHENA Ray**, GUBB Ann, GUBBAY Lily, GUBBAY-JENKIN Lois, GUBERINIC Bobby, GUBIANI Josie, GUDELJ Zak, GUDGE Andrew, GUDMANN Colleen, GUDMANN Leigh, GUEBELI Marc, GUEORGUIEVA Raadi, GUERIN Sydney, GUERNIER John, GUERRA Maria, GUERRA Rolando, GUERRERA Lee, GUERRERA Maria, GUERRERA Michael, GUERRINI Robert, GUERRY Annette, GUERTNER Daniel, GUEST Daryl, GUEST Graeme, GUEST Justyne, GUEST Lisa, GUEST Nicholas, GUEST Pat, GUEST Peter, GUEST Simon, GUEVARA Lou, GUGGER Eda, GUIA Dave, GUIFFRE Vin, GUILBERT Marc, GUILDFORD Karen, GUILFOYLE Darren, GUILLEMIN Gilles, GUILLEMOT Lisa, GUILLET Clementine, GUILLOCHON Nela, GUINDY Ezzat, GUINEA Ana, GUINEY Kate, GUINEY Neil, GUINTO Manuel, GUIRGUIS Aida, GUIRGUIS Lili, GUIRGUIS Sam, GULCZYNSKI Kate, GULLAPALLI Murthy, GULLETT Lucy, GULLI Joe, GULLIFORD Helen, GULLINE Marina, GULLIVER Alan, GULLO Sam, GULLOTTI Helena, GULPERS Hubert, GULSOY Tamer, GULUMIAN Shahik, GUMBLETON Lynne, GUMPOLD Michael, GUNARATNA Niro, GUNASEKARA Upananda, GUNASENA Supun, GUNASINGAM Sinthu, GUNASINGHAM Gune, GUNASINGHE Lance, GUNATILAKA Doreen, GUNATILAKA Justin, GUNAWAN Hendri, GUNAWAN PUTRA Andreas, GUNAWARDENA Erandi, GUNERATNE Romesh, GUNN Don, GUNN Grahame, GUNN Jasmine, GUNN Margaret, GUNN Rebecca, GUNNING Belinda, GUNNING Clayton, GUNNING Mirtha, GUNNING Paul, GUNNING Paul, GUNTHORP Ian, GUNTHORPE Dudley, GUO Min, GUO Nancy, GUO Pan, GUPPY Jessica, GUPPY Peter, GUPTA Aruna, GUPTA Mayank, GUPTA Mini, GUPTA Pawan, GUPTA Praveen, GUPTA Punita, GUPTA Sushil, GURCHENKO Nicholas, GURD Helen, GUREVICH Alex, GURNEY Barbara, GURTALA Pandji, GURTMAN Liz, GURUNG BJ, GURUNG Dipan, GURUNG Gobin, GURUNG Roshan, GURUNG Tika, GUSBETH Alison, GUSBETH Michael, GUSEVSKA Amanda, GUSKE Peter, GUSTAFSON Kay, GUTHERSON Heather, GUTHREY David, GUTHRIE Brian, GUTHRIE Carolyn, GUTHRIE Jacinta, GUTHRIE Judy, GUTHRIE Robert, GUTIERREZ Claire, GUTIERREZ Ivan, GUTIERREZ Ricardo, GUTIERREZ ZENTENO Sandra, GUTSCHE Anton, GUTTA Sameer, GUTTRIDGE Adrienne, GUY Angela, GUY Catherine, GUY Nicola, GUY Rod, GUYER Lyn, GUYER Robert, GUYER Warren, GUZMAN Al, GUZMAN HELLADO

Monica, GWAK Jason, GWILYM Jack, GYAKYI Gordon, **GYECSEK Lisa**, GYLER Michelle, GYRN Liz.

H

HA Alan, HA Andrew, HA David, HA Davin, HA Dominic, HA Eric, HA Jean, HA Robert, HA Toan, HA Vicky, HAACK Danielle, HAACK Joe, HAAG Matthieu, HAAGE Margaret, HAARMANN Claudia, HAARSMA Nicole, HABAK Marien, HABAK Warren, HABAN Gratzian, HABASHY Angela, HABER Angela, HABER Jean, HABER Rog, HABERBUSCH Bennett, HABERBUSCH Kim, HABERMANN Cath, HABERMANN Tina, HABERMANN Vince, HABERMEHL Tonia, HABHEGGER Heidi, HABIB Sadih, HABIB Syed, HACK Anthony, HACK Michael, HACKELTON John, HACKET Kristina, HACKETT Claire, HACKETT Jacqueline, HACKETT Reece, HACKING Harold, HACKING Kate, HACKNEY Christy, HACREROA Hami, HADAWAY Tim, HADDAD Damen, HADDAD Jazz, HADDAD Joseph, HADDAD MarieTherese, HADDAD Michael, HADDAD Ray, HADDADI Mohamed, HADDOCK Candace, HADDOCK Nora, HADDOCK Warren, HADDON Daphne, HADDON Don, HADDON Fay, HADDON John, HADDON Trevor, HADDOW Helen, HADDRICK Lyn, HADDRICK Lorraine, HADDRICK Ron, HADDRILL Simon, HADEE Vicky, HADFIELD Kerry, HADFIELD Lynette, HADFIELD Pauline, HADIFE Abraham, HADIWANA Indriani, HADLEY Roy, HADLEY Anthony, HADLEY Bernadette, HADLEY Bruce, HADLEY Carmel, HADLEY June, HADLEY Kathy, HADLEY Rob, HADLEY Ros, HADODO Rebecka, HAEGELE Katty, HAEHNLE Jann, HAEREROA Hemi, HAERTSCH Carol, HAEUSLER Hilary, HAFESJEE Rumana, HAFESJEE Sohail, HAFFNER Joseph, HAGA Ervin, HAGE Colleen, HAGEMAN Jill, HAGENAARS Jessie, HAGENBRUCH Debbie, HAGENSON Deirdre, HAGERI Hugo, HAGIWARA Brooke, HAGON Tony, HAGON Clare, HAGUE Jonathan, HAHN Kevin, HAIDARI Narges, HAIG Barbara, HAIG James, HAIGAZIAN Addis, HAIGH Doug, HAIGH Douglas, HAIGH Elaine, HAIGH Lauren, HAIGH Margaret, HAILE Ron, HAILES Darren, HAIM Eleanor, HAIN John, HAINES Babette, HAINES Cat, HAINES Faye, HAINES Lana, HAINES Robyn, HAINES Rochelle, HAINES Tristan, HAIR Birgit, HAIR Brad, HAIR James, HAIRA Craig, HAIRE Di, HAIRE Len, HAJDU Erica, HAJI-HASHI Sadia, HAJJE Anthony, HAJNAL John, HAKELS Bob, HAKIM Lokman, HALASZ Elisabeth, HALASZ Paul, HALBESMA Janine, HALBWIRTH Elena, HALCROW Jean, HALDANE Sarah, HALDANE Sarah, HALDEMAN Barry, HALDERMAN Barry, HALE Charissa, HALE David, HALE Natalie, HALE Trish, HALE Sarah, HALES David, HALES Narelle, HALES Pennie, HALEY Stephen, HALFAR Adela, HALIM Budi, HALIM Cheryl, HALIM Christina, HALIM Edy, HALIM Henry, HALIM Herlina, HALIM Indry, HALIM Jai, HALIM Rusly, HALIMAN Mira, HALIR Peter, HALKETT Cathy, HALL Adam, HALL Alexander, HALL Alison, HALL Charlotte, HALL Barry, HALL Barbara, HALL Bethan, HALL Brian, HALL Brian, HALL Jeanette, HALL Cate, HALL Don, HALL Doug, HALL Ted, HALL Gary, HALL Grant, HALL Heather, HALL Fay, HALL Jarrod, HALL Jeanette, HALL Jenny, HALL Jewell, HALL John, HALL John, HALL Julia, HALL Katrina, HALL Kay, HALL Kerrie, HALL Lennox, HALL Malcolm, HALL Mary, HALL Mavis, HALL Maxine, HALL Melissa, HALL Michael, HALL Nathan, HALL Trish, HALL Tricia, HALL Robin, HALL Ron, HALL Ross, HALL Steven, HALL Suellen, HALL Sun, HALL Tracey, HALL Ulrich, HALL-CAVANAGH Lynne, HALLAJ Dominique, HALLAK Aylee, HALLAM Craig, HALLAM Daryl, HALLAM Elaine, HALLAM Narelle, HALLAM Marie, HALLAWI Alen, HALLEEN Catherine, HALLETT Don, HALLETT Margo, HALLETT Richard, HALLETT Ruth, HALLEY Craig, HALLEY Nell, HALLIBURTON Ian, HALLIBURTON Norman, HALLIDAY Amanda, HALLIDAY Amber, HALLIDAY Bianca, HALLIDAY Glen, HALLIDAY Dawn, HALLIDAY Janet, HALLIDAY Penny, HALLIDAY Brock, HALLIDAY Sam, HALLIGAN Mal, HALLING Lianne, HALLING Marlene, HALLIT Annette, HALLMANN Geoff, HALLS Charmaine, HALLS Helen, HALLUR Arun, HALMAN Dianne, HALMAN Johannes, **HALMARCK Lynne**, HALMU Sorana, HALMY Roslyn, HALPIN Angela, HALPIN Carl, HALPIN Joanne, HALPIN Lorraine, HALSE Simone, HALSTEAD Ted, HALSTEAD Rene, HALSTEAD John, HALSTEAD Sarah, HALTER Tilly, HALTON Gerard, HALVARI Mona, HALVERSON Karen, HAM David, HAMAKHAN David, HAMAL Catherine, HAMAMA Ayman, HAMAN George, HAMANO Naoko, HAMASAKI Shinji, HAMATSU Tomomi, HAMBLIN Kate, HAMEISTER Paul, HAMELEERS Anna, HAMER Chris, HAMER Gai, HAMER James, HAMER Ruth, HAMERNIK Richard, **HAMEY Kathleen**, HAMEY Val, HAMIDI Othmane, HAMIEH Louise, HAMILTON Braden, HAMILTON Brian, HAMILTON Carol, HAMILTON Christina, HAMILTON Colin, HAMILTON David, HAMILTON Des, HAMILTON Elroy, HAMILTON Frank, HAMILTON Gail, HAMILTON Harvey, HAMILTON Ian, HAMILTON Jacqui, HAMILTON Jacinta, HAMILTON Jacqui, HAMILTON Jann, HAMILTON Joanne, HAMILTON John, HAMILTON John, HAMILTON Julia, HAMILTON Karen, HAMILTON Ken, HAMILTON Kerryn, HAMILTON Kim, HAMILTON Laurie, HAMILTON Lyn, HAMILTON Mardi, HAMILTON Marcia, HAMILTON Margaret, HAMILTON Mark, HAMILTON Marnie, HAMILTON Margaret, HAMILTON Margaret, HAMILTON Melissa, HAMILTON Melanie, HAMILTON Melissa, HAMILTON Michaela, HAMILTON Neil, HAMILTON Steve, HAMILTON Stephen, HAMILTON Su-Anne, HAMILTON Thomas, HAMILTON Trevor, HAMILTON Vanessa, HAMILTON-SMITH Roanna, HAMMANN Matt, HAMMENT Tara, HAMMERMAN Lee, HAMMILL Amber, HAMMILL Clare, HAMMON Anthea, HAMMOND Andrew, HAMMOND Belinda, HAMMOND Chere, HAMMOND Gerard, HAMMOND Jan, HAMMOND Jean, HAMMOND John, HAMMOND Joyce, HAMMOND Kerrie, HAMMOND Leigh, HAMMOND Marjorie, HAMMOND Paul, HAMMOND Paul, HAMMOND Peter, HAMMOND Richard, HAMMOND Robin, HAMMON D Roy, HAMMOND Sam, HAMMOND Steve, HAMMOND Tanya, HAMMOND Wayne, HAMMOND PARKER Stephen, HAMMONDS Shelley, HAMO Talasiu, HAMON Joyce, HAMPSON Gerry, HAMPSON Noelene, HAMPSON Paul, HAMPTON Allan, HAMPTON Laurie, HAMPTON Mark, HAMPTON Matt, HAMPTON-TAYLOR Marcia, HAMSHAW Les, HAMSITZIS Maria, HAMSITZIS Vicki, HAN Chong, HAN Davy, HAN Mabel, HAN Elizabeth, HAN Gene, HAN Henley, HAN Jaepil, HAN John, HAN Jung, HAN Paul, HAN Pam, HAN Shelley, HAN Sebastian, HAN Thomas, HAN Theresa, HAN Yuna, HANBIDGE Helen, HANCOCK Allana, HANCOCK Amy, HANCOCK Bruce, HANCOCK Cathy, HANCOCK Dot, HANCOCK Erica, HANCOCK George, HANCOCK Jon, HANCOCK Ken, HANCOCK Kim, HANCOCK Lorraine, HANCOCK Michael, HANCOCK Michelle, HANCOCK Mike, HANCOCK Ray, HANCOCK Ray, HANCOCK Sharyn, HANCOCK Simon, HANCOCK Stephen, HANCOCK Tim, HANCOCK Trevor, HANCOCK Warrick, HANCOCK Bill, HANCOX George, HAND Geoff, HAND Robyn, HAND Suzanne, HANDAJA Eddy, HANDCOCK Darrel, HANDEL Bob, HANDKE Anne-Marie, HANDLEY Claire, HANDLEY Colin, HANDLEY Eric, HANDLEY Honn y, HANDLEY Marilyn, HANDOYO Chris, HANDS Allen, HANDS Jarrah, HANDS Kerri-Anne, HANDS Phil, HANDSAKER Anne-Maree, HANEMAN John, HANG James, HANGHOFER Sylvia, HANIMYAN Robert, HANISCH Claudia, HANJA Nazima, HANKIN Andrew, HANKINSON Amy, HANKINSON Robert, HANKINSON Roger, HANKS Emma, HANLAN Judy, HANLEY Brian, HANLEY Fay, HANLEY Jim, HANLEY Manfred, HANLEY Maree, HANLEY Megan, HANLEY Mick, HANLEY Paul, HANLEY Thelma, HANLON Adam, HANLON Judi, HANLON Penny, HANLY Mal, HANLY Paul, HANN Vicki, HANNA Adele, HANNA Amal, **HANNA Antonia**, HANNA Anthony, HANNA Bernadette, HANNA Caroline, HANNA Chrystal, HANNA David, HANNA Jason, HANNA Jim, HANNA Mauri, HANNA Michael, HANNA Morris, HANNA Nazar, HANNA Sam, HANNAFORD Brian, HANNAFORD Lee, HANNAFORD Natalie, HANNAFORD Sandra, HANNAH Jacqui, HANNAH Jenny, HANNAH Joyce, HANNAH Ross, HANNAH Sue, HANNAM Pam, HANNAN Alana, HANNAN Dawn, HANNAN Georgia, HANNAN Kaye, HANNAN Pam, HANNAY Sue, HANNELL Grahame, HANNELLY Lis, HANNELLY Mike, HANNEMANN Peter, HANNIGAN Chris, HANNON Ally, HANNON Georgie, HANNON Lynette, HANNS Bradley, HANRAHAN Bryan, HANRAHAN John, HANRAHAN Mick, HANRATTY Michael, HANSCHE Sanora, HANSCOMBE John, HANSEN Brian, HANSEN Chris, HANSEN Damien, HANSEN Daphne, HANSEN David, HANSEN Emma, HANSEN Freddy, HANSEN Gary, HANSEN Ian, HANSEN Irene, HANSEN Jesper, HANSEN Judy,

HANSEN Karl, HANSEN Kerry, HANSEN Kevin, HANSEN Kim, HANSEN Konrad, HANSEN Ian, HANSEN Michelle, HANSEN Mogens, HANSEN Nathalie, HANSEN Trish, HANSEN Penelope, HANSEN Peter, HANSEN Russel, HANSEN Ryan, HANSEN Stephen, HANSFORD Aaron, HANSFORD Max, HANSHAW Margo, HANSIMIKALI Evan, HANSING Jilly, HANSON Alex, HANSON Allan, HANSON Andrea, HANSON Tony, HANSON Cheryl, **HANSON Clare**, HANSON Ebbe, HANSON Jo, HANSON Ruth, HANSON Paula, HANSON Paul, HANSON Bob, HANSON Stephen, HANSON Tom, HANSON-BENEY Kathi, HANSRA Amandeep, HANSRA Kamaljeet, HANTOS Cathryn, HANTOS Vince, HANTSCHL Gerhard, HANZAKI Fumiko, HANZAR Carol, HAO Lucy, HAPI Tai, HAPWELL Lynette, HAQUE Md.naimul, HAR James, HAR Jeffrey, HAR Rita, HARA Chieko, HARA Sachie, HARAKAKOS Dennis, HARALABIDIS John, HARALAMBAKIS Bill, HARAN Francis, HARB Layla, HARB Mike, HARB Ramia, HARBECK Nick, HARBER Mark, HARBISON Elizabeth, HARBISON Emily, HARBISON Sandra, HARBISON Bill, HARCH Cathy, HARCOMBE Ingrid, HARCOURT Andrew, HARDAKER Allan, HARDAKER Heather, HARDAKER Junko, HARDCASTLE Barbara, HARDCASTLE David, HARDER Barbara, HARDER Kevan, HARDES Andrew, HARDES Wendy, HARDGRAVES Glyn, HARDGROVE John, HARDIDGE Emily, HARDIE Geraldine, HARDIE Ian, HARDIE Layne, HARDING Annie, HARDING Bert, HARDING Col, HARDING Elaine, HARDING Heather, HARDING Kay, HARDING Kerry, HARDING Lauretta, HARDING Leonie, HARDING Margaret, HARDING Mary-Ann, **HARDING Muriel**, HARDING Pam, HARDING Paula, HARDING Peter, HARDING Rebecca, HARDING Robert, HARDING Rod, HARDING Ron, HARDING Troy, HARDINGE Maxine, HARDINGHAM Vince, HARDJANTO Andra, HARDJOWIJONO Senopati, HARDMAN Brian, HARDMAN Lesley, HARDWICK Clare, HARDWICK Colleen, HARDWICK Keith, HARDWICK Mark, HARDWICK Pat, HARDY Allison, HARDY Tony, HARDY Bruce, HARDY Carla, HARDY Deb, HARDY Geoffrey, HARDY Jane, HARDY Joann, HARDY Marian, HARDY Mark, HARDY Pam, HARDY Peter, HARDY Bob, HARDY Roger, HARDY Sarah, HARDY Shauna, HARDY Steve, HARDY Steve, HARDY Terry, HAREN Marg, HARFIELD Tony, HARGRAVE John, HARGRAVE Robyn, HARGRAVES Maggie, HARGREAVES John, HARGREAVES Narelle, HARGREAVES Neill, HARI Hari, HARIPRASED JOSHI Barry, HARIYANTO Ernest, HARJANTO Ignatius, HARKIN Bob, HARKINS Bruce, HARKINS Michael, HARKNESS Bruce, HARKNESS Ian, HARKNESS Jade, HARKNESS Joanne, HARKNESS Yvonne, HARLAND Amy, HARLAND Joanne, HARLAND Kim, HARLAND Pat, HARLAND Bob, HARLE Fay, HARLEY Alf, HARLEY Anne, HARLEY Neil, HARLEY Sylvia, HARM Chris, HARMAN Alex, HARMAN Matt, HARMAN Nigel, HARMER Beryl, HARMER Maria, HARMER Paul, HARMER Sue, HARMON Alisia, **HARMSEN Bronwyn**, HARMSEN John, HARMSEN Victor, HARNETT Gill, HARNWELL Warwick, HAROUCHE Cathy, HARPER Anita, HARPER Bruce, HARPER Bernard, HARPER Donald, HARPER Gai, HARPER Helen, HARPER Lorraine, HARPER Michael, HARPER Bob, HARPER Simone, HARPLEY Ian, HARPLEY-CARR Aaron, HARRADINE Chris, HARRICKS Robby, HARRICKS Tania, HARRIDEN Kim, HARRIDGE Dawne, HARRIES Bernie, HARRIGAN Dennis, HARRIGAN Peggy, HARRIGAN Robin, HARRIMAN Lynn, HARRINGTON David, HARRINGTON Andrew, HARRINGTON Cary, HARRINGTON Denese, HARRINGTON Joan, HARRINGTON John, HARRINGTON Kelly, HARRINGTON Lynn, HARRINGTON Margaret, HARRINGTON Mick, HARRINGTON Patricia, HARRINGTON Trish, HARRINGTON Peter, HARRINGTON Reg, HARRIOTT Celia, HARRIOTT Leonie, HARRIOTT Vince, HARRIS Adam, HARRIS Adam, HARRIS Vic, HARRIS Alison, HARRIS Mandy, HARRIS Barry, HARRIS Bruce, HARRIS Carole, HARRIS Carol, HARRIS Carl, HARRIS Caroline, HARRIS Caroline, HARRIS Chris, HARRIS Chris, HARRIS Christopher, HARRIS Danielle, HARRIS David, HARRIS Del, HARRIS Denise, HARRIS Donna, HARRIS Elaine, HARRIS Emma, HARRIS Graham, HARRIS Helen, HARRIS Helen, HARRIS Harry, HARRIS Ian, HARRIS Jan, HARRIS Jan, HARRIS Janine, HARRIS Joel, HARRIS John, HARRIS John, HARRIS John, HARRIS John, HARRIS John, HARRIS Judy, HARRIS Karen, HARRIS Kasey, HARRIS Kaye, HARRIS Kerry, HARRIS Kim, HARRIS Kirsty, HARRIS Lauren, HARRIS Len, HARRIS Lilly, HARRIS Lillian, HARRIS Margret, HARRIS Mardi, HARRIS Mat, HARRIS Neil, HARRIS Nick, HARRIS Noel, HARRIS Paul, HARRIS Paul, HARRIS Phillip, HARRIS Reginald, HARRIS Richard, HARRIS Bob, HARRIS Ross, HARRIS Rosie, HARRIS Sam, HARRIS Sandra, HARRIS Scott, HARRIS Shane, HARRIS Shirley, HARRIS Sian, HARRIS Stephanie, HARRIS Stefan, HARRIS Susie, HARRIS Susie, HARRIS Susan, HARRIS Tom, HARRIS Tom, HARRIS Toni, HARRIS Trent, **HARRIS Vic**, HARRIS Wade, HARRISON Alasdair, HARRISON Anne, HARRISON Arthur, HARRISON Brian, HARRISON Ann, HARRISON Christine, HARRISON Dan, HARRISON Harro, HARRISON Elizabeth, HARRISON Faye, HARRISON Gemma, HARRISON Grahame, HARRISON Gregory, HARRISON Ian, HARRISON Jan, HARRISON Jane, HARRISON Jenna, HARRISON Jo, HARRISON Jo, HARRISON John, HARRISON John, HARRISON John, HARRISON Kathy, HARRISON Kaye, HARRISON Kenny, HARRISON Kylie, HARRISON Len, HARRISON Eve, HARRISON Louise, HARRISON Lynette, HARRISON Mark, HARRISON Marcia, HARRISON Matt, HARRISON Patricia, HARRISON Paul, HARRISON Rhondda, HARRISON Bob, HARRISON Robert, HARRISON Robert, HARRISON Robert, HARRISON Russell, HARRISON Sally, HARRISON Scott, HARRISON Sonia, HARRISON Steve, HARRISON Susan, HARRISON Val, HARRISON Veronica, HARRISS Phil, HARROLD Rob, HARROLD Suzanne, HARROP Elise, HARROULD Edwin, HARROWELL Miranda, HARROWER Lyn, HARSAS Phillip, HART Adrian, HART Amanda, HART Ann, HART Boris, HART Ben, HART Bruce, HART Christine, HART Christina, HART Clive, HART David, HART Diana, HART Dorin, HART Gerard, HART Graham, HART Greg, HART Ian, HART Jessica, HART John, HART Julie, HART Katie, HART Ken, HART Lionel, HART Lyn, HART Mary, HART Merredith, HART Monica, HART Nathan, HART Norma, HART Rob, HART Rose, HART Stephen, HART Sue, HART Sue, HART Susan, HART Val, HARTANTO Hartanto, HARTATI Vera, HARTATI Yen, HARTE Kylie, HARTER Jacques, HARTIGAN Julie, HARTIGAN Julie, HARTLEY Brett, HARTLEY Clare, HARTLEY Dale, HARTLEY Helen, HARTLEY John, HARTLEY J on, HARTLEY Kay, HARTLEY Lisa, HARTLEY Sally, HARTLEY Suzie, HARTMAN Hank, HARTNESS Tony, HARTNEY Leia, HARTOG Nathalie, HARTOG Olivier, HARTOG Sebastien, HARTONO Diana, HARTSHORN Brett, HARTSHORN Grant, HARTZ Cynthia, HARUN-RASHID Mohammad, HARVEY Anne, HARVEY Arnold, HARVEY Barrie, HARVEY Ben, HARVEY Cheryl, HARVEY Clinton, HARVEY David, HARVEY Denise, HARVEY Erika, HARVEY Francis, HARVEY Glen, HARVEY Glenda, HARVEY John, HARVEY Helen, HARVEY Ian, HARVEY Jenny, HARVEY Joan, HARVEY John, HARVEY John, HARVEY Karen, HARVEY Kate, HARVEY Ken, HARVEY Kevin, HARVEY Lisa, HARVEY Louise, HARVEY Lynette, HARVEY Marilyn, HARVEY Michael, HARVEY Paul, HARVEY Penny, HARVEY Raylee, HARVEY Richard, HARVEY Russell, HARVEY Russell, HARVEY Ryan, HARVEY Samantha, HARVEY Sarah, HARVEY Scott, HARVEY Sharon, HARVEY Terry, HARVISON Barbara, HARVY Karina, HARWICK Jack, HARWIN Don, HARWIN Evelyn, HARWOOD Abby, HARWOOD Cameron, HARWOOD Georgie, HARWOOD Jennifer, HARWOOD Kerrie, HARWOOD Sandra, HARWOOD Troy, HASCHYNSKI Ivan, HASELL Lucy, HASHEMI-NEZHAD Sanaz, HASHIM Nehash, HASHISH Mahmoud, HASHIZUME Yuka, HASIBAR Michelle, HASIC Sam, HASKARD Carolyn, HASKETT Lisa, HASKINS Brady, HASKINS Harmony, HASLAM Brian, HASLAM Melissa, HASSALL Alan, HASSALL Geoff, HASSALL Geoffrey, HASSAM Emma, HASSAN Hassan, HASSAN Teresa, HASSELL Amy, HASSELL Ron, HASSELL Tom, HASSELMAN Glen, HASSETT Erica, HASSETT Irene, **HASSETT Patt**, HASSO Claudia, HASSO Nibbe, HASSONA Sally, HASTIE Rachael, HASTIE Sarah, HASTIE Will, HASTINGS Adam, HASTINGS Barbara, HASTINGS Scott, HASWELL Adele, HASWELL Janet, HATCH Julia, HATCH Norman, HATCHER Bindi, HATCHER Chloe, HATCHER Jean, HATCHER Judi, HATCHER Rodney, HATCHER Sally, HATCHER Sam, HATCHER Sue, HATCHMAN Jeffrey, **HATFIELD Frith**, HATFIELD Geoff, **HATFIELD Heath**, HATFIELD Hilary, HATFIELD Jim, HATHAWAY Ron, HATTANGADI Anuj,

HATTERSLEY Kelly, HATTERSLEY Will, HATTLEY Jenny, HATTOM Alice, HATTON Beryl, HATTON Debbie, HATTON John, HATTON Mick, HATTON Serena, HATTON Ursula, HATTORI Lei, HATZSY Virginia, HAUGAARD Morten, HAUGH Margaret, HAULTAIN-GALL Matthew, HAUNG Tina, HAUSCHILD Marcelo, HAUSOUL Johan, HAUTU Kate, HAVAS Eva, HAVELKA John, HAVERFIELD Karlie, HAVRANCIKOVA Janka, HAVRON Kerry, HAWES Caroline, HAWES Geoff, HAWES Jane, HAWES Patricia, HAWGOOD Gareth, HAWKE Criag, HAWKE Debbie, HAWKE Trixie, HAWKE Bill, HAWKEN Annette, HAWKEN Kathleen, HAWKEN Matthew, HAWKER Michael, HAWKES Bert, HAWKES Barbara, HAWKES Roger, HAWKEY Peter, HAWKEY Terry, HAWKINS Allisson, HAWKINS Annette, HAWKINS Barry, HAWKINS Eric, HAWKINS Ian, HAWKINS Ja, HAWKINS Jacqui, HAWKINS Jim, HAWKINS Jean, HAWKINS Jeff, HAWKINS Jeff, HAWKINS Jeff, HAWKINS Joel, HAWKINS John, HAWKINS Joseph, HAWKIN Kathy, HAWKINS Mary, HAWKINS Melanie, HAWKINS Meryl, HAWKINS Noel, HAWKINS Steve, HAWKINS Tom, HAWKINS Trevor, HAWKINS Bill, HAWKINS Carol, HAWKRIDGE Cheryl, HAWKS Lynette, HAWKSHAW Ian, HAWKSHAW Jayne, HAWKSHAW Kate, HAWLEY Arthur, HAWLEY Sam, HAWORTH Erik, HAWSON Lesley, HAWSON Michael, HAWTHORNE Amy, HAWTHORNE Daryl, HAWTHORNE Steve, HAWTIN Paula, HAY Andrew, HAY Gerry, HAY Joan, HAY Jace, HAY Margaret, HAY Paulette, HAY Wendy, HAY Wilma, HAYASAKA Kaz, HAYASAKA Michie, HAYASHI Hiroko, HAYASHIDA Maako, HAYASHIDA Mickey, HAYCRAFT John, HAYDAR Joe, HAYDEN Kathy, HAYDEN Kirsty, HAYDEN Peter, HAYDEN Shena, HAYDON Phillipa, HAYDON Rachel, HAYDON Ron, HAYES Tony, HAYES Tony, HAYES Ashley, HAYES Ashlee, HAYES Briony, HAYES Caroline, HAYES Cathy, HAYES Cheryl, HAYES David, HAYES David, HAYES Dominic, HAYES Ewan, HAYES Gerald, HAYES Glenis, HAYES Jacky, HAYES Jan, HAYES Justin, HAYES Ken, HAYES Kesni, HAYES Kylie, HAYES Les, HAYES LD, HAYES Linda, HAYES Lindsay, HAYES Mike, HAYES Pauline, HAYES Paul, HAYES Phil, HAYES Rob, HAYES Robyn, HAYES Suellyn, HAYES Susan, HAYES Sue, HAYES Tom, HAYES Bill, HAYESST CLAIR Malela, HAYGARTH Anita, HAYLES Jacqui, HAYLLAR Richard, HAYLOCK Robert, HAYMAN Anthony, HAYMAN James, HAYMAN David, HAYMAN Eric, HAYMAN Keith, HAYMAN Roger, HAYMAN Sarah, HAYNE Elaine, HAYNE Glynis, HAYNE Sarah, HAYNES David, HAYNES Greg, HAYNES Julie, HAYNES Lara, HAYNES Lyn, HAYNES Marielou, HAYNES Michael, HAYNES Patrick, HAYNES Pat, HAYNES Peter, HAYNES Peter, HAYNES Raymond, HAYNES Susan, HAYNES Tim, HAYNES Virginia, HAYNES-GORDON Bev, HAYS Lucy, HAYTER George, HAYTER Karen, HAYTER Ross, HAYWARD John, HAYWARD Tina, HAYWARD Peter, HAYWARD Pip, HAYWARD Philip, HAYWARD Bill, HAYWOOD Cheryl, HAYWOOD Deirdre, HAYWOOD Joan, HAYWOOD Kaaren, HAYWOOD Lindsay, HAZEL Keith, HAZELL Anthony, HAZELL Daryll, HAZELL Don, HAZELL James, HAZELL Jodie, HAZELL Lee, HAZELL Lyn, HAZELL Mike, HAZELL Pat, HAZELL Yvonne, HAZELMAN Martin, **HAZELTINE Barbara**, HAZELTON John, HAZELTON Scott, HAZELTON Ronnie, HAZELWOOD Rebecca, HAZLEWOOD Keith, HE Gavin, HE Ansen, HE Marian, HE Qi, HE Ying, HEAD Helen, HEAD John, HEAD Nigel, HEAD Terry, HEAD Victoria, HEAD Virginia, HEAH Richard, HEAL Helen, HEAL Jenny, HEALEY Angela, HEALEY Colin, HEALEY Dereck, HEALEY Renee, HEALION Pat, HEALY David, HEALY Fenton, HEALY Jo, HEALY Joan, HEALY John, HEALY Jon, HEALY Luci, HEALY Matthew, HEALY Sue, HEANE Barbara, HEANEY Eileen, HEANEY Irene, HEANEY Ron, HEANEY Sharon, HEAP Don, HEAP Karen, HEAP Neville, HEAP Bob, HEARD Denis, HEARD Gregory, HEARD John, HEARD Mal, HEARD Steve, HEARES Delores, HEARN Frances, HEARN Rowan, HEARN Warren, HEARNE Sue, HEARSCH Darryl, HEASLIP Bill, HEASMAN Jenny, HEAT Alex, HEATH Andrew, HEATH Diane, HEATH Dot, HEATH Gary, HEATH Jacinta, HEATH Kirstie, HEATH Les, HEATH Michael, HEATH Stuart, HEATH Wendy, HEATHCOTE Carly, HEATHCOTE Greg, HEATHCOTE Joan, HEATHCOTE John, HEATHCOTE Marion, HEATHCOTE Peter, HEATHER Chris, HEATHER Cozette, HEATHER Jim, HEATHWOOD Annette, HEATHWOOD Mary, HEAVENS Kerri, HEAZLE Terry, HEAZLEWOOD Ange, HEAZLE WOOD Terry, HEBDEN David, HEBERLE Milanna, HECKENDORF Gordon, HECTOR Cath, HECTOR Liz, HEDDEMA John, HEDGE Carolyn, HEDGER Alan, HEDGER Malcolm, HEDGER Norm, HEDGER Simon, HEDGES Amy, HEDGES Carol, HEDGES Dennis, HEDGES Rachel, HEDGES Simon, HEDGES Sue, HEDLEY Barry, HEDLEY Lyn, HEDLEY Steven, HEDWAN Joe, HEELEY Peter, HEELIS Jim, HEEREN Martha, HEFFERNAN Beryl, HEFFERNAN Ted, HEFFERNAN Emma, HEFFERNAN Matthew, HEFFERNAN Matthew, HEFFERNAN Patricia, HEFFERNAN Paul, HEFFERNAN Wayne, HEGARTY Marc, HEGARTY Vanessa, HEGGARTY Scott, HEGGELUND Bianca, HEGNER Glen, HEGNER Rosemary, HEHIR Tara, HEID Dieter, HEIDE Petra, HEIDELBACH Lisa, HEIDKE Lorraine, HEIDRICHAS Andrea, HEIL Coralie, HEILBUTH Luke, HEILER Ron, HEINE Adam, HEINE Wendy, HEINKE Robyn, HEINRICH Mark, HEINS Henk, HEINZ Briana, HEIRICH Dario, HEITMAN Anglea, HELDON Stuart, HELLEMAN Michael, HELLEN Matina, HELLENPACH Elizabeth, HELLER Dominic, HELLER Lauren, HELLESSEY Paul, HELLIAR John, HELLINGS Belinda, HELLINGS Jasmine, HELLINGS Robyn, HELLWIG Jason, HELLWIG Karen, HELLYER Wayne, HELMAN Gillian, HELMERS Craig, HELMERS John, HELMRICH Tessie, HELMS Peter, HELSON Jennifer, HELSON Warren, HELY Carl, HELY Janelle, HELY Margaret, HEMBLING Doris, HEMING Margaret, HEMINGWAY Anita, HEMINGWAY Soren, HEMMERLE Aaron, HEMMERLE Max, HEMMERSBACH Sarah, HEMPHILL Craig, HEMPHILL Danielle, HEMPHILL Reen, HEMPHILL Kerry, HEMPHILL Rebecca, HEMPSTEAD Craig, HEMS Denise, HEMSWORTH Graham, HENAO Orlando, HENAWAY Mark, HENAWAY Toni-Maree, HENCH Vandy, HENDEL Sophia, HENDERSON Ann, HENDERSON Ann, HENDERSON Antony, HENDERSON Chris, HENDERSON Col, HENDERSON David, HENDERSON Dean, **HENDERSON Fiona**, HENDERSON Geoff, HENDERSON George, HENDERSON Ian, HENDERSON Jan, HENDERSON Jeanette, HENDERSON Jennifer, HENDERSON Jo, HENDERSON Hendo, HENDERSON John, HENDERSON Judith, HENDERSON Keathea, HENDERSON Lachlan, HENDERSON Lloyd, HENDERSON Matthew, HENDERSON Monique, HENDERSON Narelle, HENDERSON Ray, HENDERSON Grant, HENDERSON Ruth, HENDERSON Sid, HENDERSON Steven, HENDERSON Steve, HENDERSON Teresa, HENDERSON Tom, HENDERSON Tracey, HENDRICKS Asma, HENDRICKSON Kym, HENDRIKS Rolf, HENDRIKSE Mieke, HENDRY Bernie, HENDRY Chris, HENDRY Barbara, HENDRY Janine, HENDRY Murray, HENDRY Michelle, HENDRY Siale, HENDRYX Andy, HENG Giles, HENG Sinath, HENKENSIEFKEN Claus, HENLEY Araxie, HENLEY Kim, HENLEY Linda, HENLEY Bob, HENLEY Roger, HENLEY-BOESTEN Jos, HENMAN Beverly, HENMAN Paul, HENNEKAM Paul, HENNES Lois, HENNESS Keith, HENNESS Margaret, HENNESSEY Julie, HENNESSY Briana, HENNESSY Cyril, HENNESSY Desley, HENNESSY Jack, HENNESSY Jim, HENNESSY Jane, HENNESSY Jill, HENNESSY John, HENNESSY Kath, HENNESSY Kym, HENNESSY Michael, HENNESSY Michael, HENNESSY Pamela, HENNESSY Sean, HENNESSY Sharonne, HENNI Mo, HENNING Caroline, HENNING Keith, HENNING Oskar, HENNING Roger, HENNINGS Simon, HENNOCK Lesley, HENRICKS David, HENRICUS Allan, HENRISSON Ashley, HENRY Adrian, HENRY Alison, HENRY Debbie, HENRY Debbie, HENRY Denise, HENRY Elise, HENRY Florgina, HENRY Fran, HENRY Karen, HENRY Kim, HENRY Leathica, HENRY Neil, HENRY Neville, HENRY Norah, HENRY Ray, HENRY Rhonda, HENRY Robyn, HENRY Robert, HENRY Sue, HENRY Terry, HENRY Tom, HENRY Thomas, HENRY Bill, HENSBY Larry, HENSCHKE Christopher, HENSCHKE Rebecca, HENSHALL Beryl, HENSLER Kerrielea, HENSLEY Judy, HENSLEY Morgan, HENSLEY Nichole, HENSON Colin, HENSON Josh, HENSON Linley, HENSTOCK Jennifer, HENSTOCK Michelle, HENSTOCK Terry, HENTSCHKE Manfred, HENTY Robert, HENTZSCHEL Debbie, HENWOOD Janet, HENZEN Johan, HEO Yun-Ho, HEPBURN Jenny, HEPBURN John, HEPBURN Kirstie, HEPPER John, HEPPERLIN Sue, HEPWORTH Crissy, HEPWORTH Bess, HERAGHTY Lorraine, HERBEN Frans, HERBENER Wolf, HERBERT Tony, HERBERT Gerry, HERBERT Glennis, HERBERT Helen, HERBERT Helene, HERBERT Malcolm, HERBERT Rosemary, HERBERT Stephanie, HERBERT Glenn,

HERBERT Yvette, HERBERTSON Jenny, HERBERTSON Lisa, HERBERTSON Robert, HERBIG Nicole, **HERBISON-EVANS Don**, HERBORN Daniel, HERCOK Tony, HERD Robert, HERDE Angie, HERDMAN Micheal, HERETIS John, HERFORD Rosemarie, HERFT Lorensz, HERIOT Robert, HERISSON George, HERKENRATH Lisa, HERKESS Alexander, HERLIHEN Nanette, HERLIHY Nicholas, HERMENS Rich, HERMEZ John, HERMILI Lisa, HERMIZ Eva, HERN Matt, HERN Peter, HERN Rob, HERNANDEZ Bert, HERNANDEZ Luis, HERNANDEZ Manny, HERNANDEZ Mary, HERNANDEZ Michael, HERNANDEZ Pedro, HERNANDEZ ZAPOT Forencio, HERNANDO Tony, HERNOWIBOWO Budi, HERRERA Renato, HERRERA AROSEMENA Daniel, HERREROS Bill, HERRETT Leanne, HERRICK April, HERRIDGE Hayley, HERRIDGE James, HERRIMAN Leanne, HERRING John, HERRING Marc, HERRING Sandy, HERRIOT Rosie, HERRMANN Jan, HERRON Lisa, HERRON Sam, HERRUWIBOWO Irvan, HERSANT Warren, HERSCH Lisa, HERZIG Rys, HERZOG Peter, HESOM Brian, HESPE Ted, HESS Margurite, HESS Michelle, HESS Shirley, HESS Sue-Anne, HESSE Griet, HESSE Kate, HESSION Lindy, HETERICK Nerida, HETHERINGTON Diana, HETHERINGTON Jan, HETHERINGTON Julie, HETHERINGTON Kelly, HETHERINGTON Len, HETHERINGTON Brian, HETHERINGTON Sharon, HETHERINGTON Simone, HETHORN June, HETTIARACHCHIGE Buddika, HEUBERGER Susanne, HEUCHAN Alison, HEUFEL Vince, HEUVEL Bianca, HEWATT Les, HEWAWASAM Aruna, HEWESTON Amy, HEWETT Tony, HEWETT David, HEWETT David, HEWETT Kettie, HEWETT Lois, HEWETT Maree, HEWETT Marie, HEWETT Mary, HEWETT Matthew, HEWETT Tom, HEWITT Cathy, HEWITT Eleanor, HEWITT Ian, HEWITT Jane, HEWITT Louise, HEWITT Maree, HEWITT Meredith, HEWITT Michael, HEWITT Roger, HEWITT Sharon, HEWITT Virginnia, HEWLETT Brian, HEWSON Kev, HEWTON David, HEXTALL Vicky, HEXTELL David, HEY Kati, HEY-CUNNINGHAM Barbara, HEYDON Kathy, HEYER Rob, HEYES Judith, HEYMAN Joanne, HEYS Lauragh, HEYWOOD Annette, HEYWOOD Denis, HEYWOOD Narelle, HEYWOOD Narelle, HEYWOOD Sophie, HIAM Marc, HIBBARD Ronald, HIBBERD Pam, HIBBERSON Paul, HIBBERSON Teri, HIBBERT Glenn, HIBBERT Laurence, HIBBERT Zoe, HIBBETT Fiona, HIBBLE Bill, HIBBLE Len, HICK Adrienne, HICKEY Andrew, HICKEY Daryl, HICKEY Denise, HICKEY Greg, HICKEY John, HICKEY Krystyne, HICKEY Peter, HICKLING Helen, HICKMAN Arvind, HICKMAN David, HICKMOTT Luke, HICKS Aldous, HICKS Amanda, HICKS Drew, HICKS Colin, HICKS Danny, HICKS Dennis, HICKS Glenda, HICKS Janie, HICKS Merrin, HICKS Peter, HICKS Shirley, HICKS Wendy, HICKSON Peter, HICKSON Stan, HIDAKA Satoru, HIDALGO Monica, HIDALGO Vivian, HIDAYAT Henry, HIDAYAT Irene, HIDAYATNO Nella, HIDE Carolyn, HIDE Helen, HIDE Neil, HIDES Billette, HIE Tcheng-Ling, HIEBLER Peter, HIELMAN Paul, HIELMAN Ronda, HIENG Steve, HIEP Ria, HIGGIN Rod, HIGGINS Barry, HIGGINS Barry, HIGGINS Chris, HIGGINS Dave, HIGGINS Edith, HIGGINS Frances, HIGGINS Frank, HIGGINS Gail, HIGGINS Rex, HIGGINS Graham, HIGGINS Guy, HIGGINS Gwen, HIGGINS John, HIGGINS Karen, HIGGINS Kath, HIGGINS Lyn, HIGGINS Matthew, HIGGINS Maureen, HIGGINS Naomi, HIGGINS Natalie, HIGGINS Sophie, HIGGINS Steve, HIGGINS Vincent, HIGGINS Vince, HIGGS Amanda, HIGGS Anna, HIGGS Duncan, HIGH Bert, HIGHAM Ailsa, HIGHAM Nicole, HIGHFIELD Maura, HIGHLANDS Lynda, HIGHMAN Ruth, HIGHMOOR Joanne, HIGINBOTHAM Brian, HIGNETT Ron, HIGSON Jean, HIGUCHI Naoko, HII Aurysia, HIJWEL Samih, HIKITA Tsuyoshi, HILAIRE Nathan, HILDEBRANDT Mark, HILDER Matt, HILDER Murray, HILDING Eva, HILDITCH Amanda, HILDITCH Michells, HILI Albert, HILI Gail, HILI Mario, HILL Alex, HILL Alexandra, HILL Alison, HILL Alison, HILL Barbara, HILL Bruce, HILL Carol, HILL Caron, HILL Casey, HILL Cathy, HILL Catherine, HILL Catherine, HILL Christine, HILL Dave, HILL David, HILL Dennis, HILL Doug, HILL Erin, HILL Eunice, HILL Fred, HILL Gary, HILL Geoff, HILL Gloria, HILL Gordon, HILL Graham, HILL Jacquie, HILL Jarrod, HILL Jarrod, HILL Jason, HILL Joan, HILL Jodi, HILL John, HILL Jonathon, HILL Justin, HILL Kaarina, HILL Ken, HILL Kevin, HILL Kurt, HILL Laura, HILL Linda, HILL Lisa, HILL Malcolm, HILL Marie, HILL Mary, HILL Mary, HILL Matthew, HILL Maurie, HILL Michael, HILL Morna, HILL Nick, HILL Nick, HILL Pat, HILL Penny, HILL Penelope, HILL Rach, HILL Rebecca, HILL Renea, HILL Rikki, HILL John, HILL Ron, HILL Sasha, HILL Scott, HILL Sharon, HILL Sharon, HILL Shannon, HILL Sigi, HILL Simon, HILL Simone, HILL Steve, HILL Steve, HILL Su, HILL Susan, HILL Tania, HILL Tui, HILL Tori, HILL Bill, HILL JR Elmer, HILLARD Belinda, HILLARD Helen, HILLE Sarah, HILLEARY Bill, HILLER Emma, HILLER Jenny, HILLER John, HILLER Sue, HILLERY Terry, HILLIARD Debby, HILLIARD Mark, HILLIARD Pam, HILLIER Andrew, HILLIER Cecil, HILLIER Clare, HILLIER Frances, HILLIER Katherine, HILLIER Stephen, HILLIG Volker, HILLMAN Andrew, HILLMAN Tony, HILLS Bronwyn, HILLS Lyn, HILLS Nicholas, HILLS Sally, HILLSDON Dianne, HILLY Diana, HILLYARD Gai, HILLYARD Grant, HILLYER Rosemary, HILTERBRAND David, HILTERBRAND Jenny, HILTON Tony, HILTON Brenda, HILTON Brian, HILTON Gai, HILTON John, HILTON Kristie, HILTON Pam, HILTON Doug, HIMMELHOCH Marg, HINCAPIE Cata, HINCE Bob, HINCH Brett, HINCHCLIFFE Alan, HINCHCLIFFE John, HINCHCLIFFE Wayne, HINCHCLIFFE Xanthe, HINCHLEY Niel, HIND Frank, HIND Graham, HIND Michael, HINDE Derek, HINDER Tony, HINDES Eric, HINDLE Connie, HINDLE Heather, HINDLE Sarah, HINDLE Stanley, HINDMARCH Arthur, HINDMARSH Phillip, HINDMARSH Sandy, HINDS Al, HINDS Russell, HINDS Stuart, HINDSON Rob, HINE Geoff, HINES Dennis, HINES Joan, HINES John, HINES Robert, HING Alfred, HING Jessie, HING Mi, HINGAIA Jean, HINGERTY Matt, HINGSTON Jenny, HINGSTON Trevor, HINGSTROM Niels, HINKINS John, HINKINS Lorraine, HINKLEY Judy, HINKLEY Peta, HINKS Don, HINKS John, HINKS Jordie, HINSBY Ann, HINSCHEN Dot, HINTON Cliff, HINTON Colin, HINTON Des, HINTON John, HINTON Mark, HINTON Neil, HINTON-BAYRE Anton, HINWOOD Ione, HINWOOD Valerie, HINZ Lynda, HIPOLITO Bienvenido, HIPSLEY Kate, HIRA Hutokshi, HIRA Rakhshandeh, HIRA Rumi, HIRANI Kanti, HIRAO Miki, HIRATA Kentaro, HIRATA Masami, HIRD Kate, HIRD Ken, HIRD Margaret, HIRD Melissa, HIROMOTO Miyuki, HIRONS Ann, HIRONS Michael, HIRRSCHOFF Tom, HIRSCH Frank, HIRSCH Sandra, HIRSOVESCU Dan, HIRST Bruce, HIRST Julie, HIRST Kerri, HIRST Lyn, HIRST Noela, HIRST Rachel, HIRST Sue, HIRT John, HIRUMA Eisuke, HIRUN-US Nui, HISHINNMA Kenta, HISHON Claire, HISSEY Ian, HISTED Joe, HITCHCOCK Denise, HITCHCOCK Geoff, HITCHCOCK Katie, HITCHCOCK Trina, HITCHELL Lynnette, HITCHELL Walter, HITCHEN Barb, HITCHEN Len, HITCHEN Tom, HITCHINER Karen, HLAING Mu, HLEDIK Peter, HLEDIK Susanne, HO Anne, HO Beatrice, HO Betty, HO Charles, HO Tony, HO Cynthia, HO Liz, HO Elizabeth, HO Esther, HO Eugene, HO Hsin-Wei, HO Joanne, HO Joseph, HO Louisa, HO Gigi, HO Kristie, HO Lai, HO Linh, HO Lok, HO Lucas, HO Tennifer, HO My, HO P K, HO Paul, HO Sabrina, HO Inoka, HO Stephen, HO Teresa, HO Bao, HO Vivian, HO Dixon, HO Wai, HO Wan, HO Wendy, HO Ying, HO Jade, HO-SHON Michael, HOAD Liz, HOADLEY David, HOANG Andrew, HOANG Joseph, HOANG Leo, HOANG Long, HOANG Makisa, HOANG Tam, HOANG Thu, HOANG Vinh, HOANG Vu, HOARAU Cheryl, HOARAU James, HOARE Andrew, HOARE Barry, HOARE Dawn, HOARE Rod, HOARE Steve, HOARE Tim, HOARE Tim, HOBART Cathy, HOBART Bob, HOBBINS Patrick, HOBBINS Daina, HOBBS Cassy, HOBBS Jenny, HOBBS Kim, HOBBS Leonie, HOBBS Randall, HOBBS Robyn, HOBBS Robert, HOBBS Ron, HOBBS Sarah, HOBDEN Daniel, HOBSON David, HOCH Mandy, HOCKEY Daniel, HOCKEY Julie, HOCKEY Michael, HOCKEY Graeme, HOCKEY Stephen, HOCKING Barry, HOCKING Barry, HOCKING Fiona, HOCKING Ian, HOCKING Julie, HOCKING Kathleen, HOCKING Jill, HOCKING Mark, HOCKING Narelle, HOCKING Ron, HOCKING Sarah, HOCKINGS Frank, HOCKINGS Tristan, HOCKLEY Alana, HOCKLEY John, HOCKLEY Robert, HOCTOR Stephen, HODDA Danielle, HODDA Elaine, HODDER Bob, HODDER Shaun, HODGE Avril, HODGE Carol, HODGE Chelsea, HODGE Dinah, HODGE Gordon, HODGE Greg, HODGE Jack, HODGE John, HODGE John, HODGE Linda, HODGE Margaret, HODGE Matt, HODGE Megan, HODGE Ros, HODGEKISS Pam, HODGEKISS Neal, HODGEKISS Ros, HODGEKISS Sandra, HODGEKISS Sandra, HODGES Andrew, HODGES Ben, HODGES Jenni, HODGES Karen, HODGES Les, HODGES Matt, HODGES Melanie, HODGES Patricia, HODGES Pete, HODGES Peter, HODGES Robin, HODGES

Bruce, HODGES Shayne, HODGES Tim, HODGES Tracey, HODGES Wendy, HODGESS Robyn, HODGETT Michael, HODGETTS Carol, HODGETTS Dallas, HODGETTS Danya, HODGETTS Graham, HODGETTS Lisa, HODGINS Maree, HODGKINSON Leigh, HODGKINSON Trevor, HODGSON Mandy, HODGSON Brian, HODGSON Dave, HODGSON Dennis, HODGSON Elisabeth, HODGSON Gill, HODGSON Jennifer, HODGSON Judith, HODGSON Marion, HODGSON Nick, HODGSON Paul, HODGSON Peter, HODGSON Phil, HODGSON Robyn, HODGSON Vicki, HODGSON Vicki, HODGSON William, HODIS Emma, HODSON Tom, HOEFNAGELS Barbara, HOEHN Renee, HOELZER Karl, HOENER Dirk, HOENIG Daniel, HOEVE Maarten-Jan, HOFER Patrick, HOFF Frank, HOFFMAN Dave, HOFFMAN Hans, HOFFMAN Jenny, HOFFMAN Marlene, HOFFMANN Beate, HOFFMANN Corinne, HOFFMANN Erich, HOFFMANN Graeme, HOFFMANN Judith, HOFFMANN Sharon, HOFMAN Damian, HOFMANN Stefan, HOFR Lubomir, HOFSTETTER Kon, HOGAN Anthony, HOGAN Dannielle, HOGAN Doug, HOGAN Joanne, HOGAN Kimball, HOGAN Lynnie, HOGAN Mark, HOGAN Mary, HOGAN Mary, HOGAN Robyn, HOGAN Vikki, HOGAN Wendy, HOGARTH Caroline, HOGARTH David, HOGARTH John, HOGARTH Joy, HOGARTH Kevin, HOGARTH Tricia, HOGARTH Shannon, HOGARTH Bill, HOGARTH Yvonne, HOGBEN Lisa, HOGG Allan, HOGG Charmain, HOGG Eileen, HOGG Judy, HOGG Malcolm, HOGG Hoggy, HOGG Robyn, HOGG Simon, HOGGAN Veronica, HOGGARTH Tracy, HOGHTON Suzie, HOINVILLE Krystle, HOJEL Carrol, HOJEL John, HOKIN Robert, HOKIN Rodney, HOLANI Annette, HOLANI Tevita, HOLBROOK Eileen, HOLCROFT Anna, HOLCROFT Roger, HOLCZER Peter, HOLDAWAY Nerida, HOLDEN Bev, HOLDEN Elaine, HOLDEN John, HOLDEN Greg, HOLDEN Hugh, HOLDEN Rhiannon, HOLDEN Wendy, HOLDER Del, HOLDER Ron, HOLDERNESS Sara, HOLDING Julie, HOLDING Nick, HOLDING Raylene, HOLDSWORTH Jeff, HOLDSWORTH Paul, HOLDSWORTH Brian, HOLDWAY Kate, HOLE Barry, HOLE Jason, HOLE Maria, HOLENSTEIN Lenore, HOLGATE Carol, HOLGATE David, HOLGATE James, HOLGATE Peter, HOLGATE Rob, HOLIAN Kevin, HOLICKY Gus, HOLLAI Gus, HOLLAND Anthony, HOLLAND Arthur, HOLLAND Chas, HOLLAND Rob, HOLLAND David, HOLLAND Frank, HOLLAND Gloria, HOLLAND Jane, HOLLAND Janice, HOLLAND John, HOLLAND Karron, HOLLAND Keith, HOLLAND Lisa, HOLLAND Lorraine, HOLLAND Maree, HOLLAND Michael, HOLLAND Milunka, HOLLAND Natalie, HOLLAND Nick, HOLLAND Nicole, HOLLAND Pat, HOLLAND Pat, HOLLAND Rae, HOLLAND Ramon, HOLLAND Ray, HOLLAND Bob, HOLLAND Robyn, HOLLAND Shez, HOLLAND Tracey, HOLLAND Tracy, HOLLANDS Loretta, HOLLANDS Margi, HOLLANDS Rachel, HOLLE Keith, HOLLE Klaus, HOLLEY Christine, HOLLEY Gillian, HOLLEY Helen, HOLLEY Peter, HOLLIDAY Brochelle, HOLLIDAY Kate, HOLLINGBERY Peter, HOLLINGS Win, HOLLINGSWORTH David, HOLLINGWORTH Mick, HOLLINGWORTH Sandy, HOLLINS Kevin, HOLLINS Wayne, HOLLIS Jo, HOLLIS John, HOLLIS Rodney, HOLLIS Susanne, HOLLIS Nikki, HOLLISTER Kerrie-Ann, HOLLITT Brett, HOLLOW Sally, HOLLOWAY Alison, HOLLOWAY Alison, HOLLOWAY Anne, HOLLOWAY David, HOLLOWAY David, HOLLOWAY Jill, HOLLOWAY Joe, HOLLOWAY Tanya, HOLLOWELL Joy, HOLLWECK Peter, HOLLY John, HOLLYWOOD Taliesen, HOLM Alec, HOLM Barbara, HOLM Lea, HOLM Mark, HOLMAN Brian, HOLMAN Justin, HOLMBERG Anita, HOLMES Andrew, HOLMES Barbara, HOLMES Barry, HOLMES Brenden, HOLMES Charles, HOLMES Christine, HOLMES Ted, HOLMES Elaine, HOLMES Fiona, HOLMES Gregory, HOLMES Helen, HOLMES Jacob, HOLMES John, HOLMES Julie, HOLMES Julia, HOLMES Kate, HOLMES Lisa, HOLMES Maxwell, HOLMES Trish, HOLMES Pat, HOLMES Reg, HOLMES Ruth, HOLMES Susanne, HOLMES Susan, HOLMES Toni, HOLMES Victoria, HOLMQUEST Naomi, HOLMWOOD Justin, HOLOBRODSKYJ Yurij, HOLST John, HOLT Andrew, HOLT Christine, HOLT Helen, HOLT Jason, HOLT Joanna, **HOLT Norma**, HOLT Wendy, HOLT Bill, HOLTOM Wendy, HOLYLAND Mary, HOLZ Bruce, HOLZ Raylene, HOLZER Sonja, HOLZMAN Benji, HOMEMING Jess, HOMER Caroline, HOMEWOOD Jennifer, HOMOLA Fladia, HOMOLA Stefan, HOMPART Dalila, HOMSI Khalil, HON Karen, HON Paulina, HON Tony, HONAN Greg, HONCIKOVA Petra, HONDA Giselle, HONDA Koji, HONDA Rhonda, HONER Gladys, HONEY George, HONEY Ray, HONEYBROOK Brett, HONEYBROOK Kay, HONEYSETT Mark, HONEYSETT Peter, HONEYWELL Ken, HONG Linda, HONG Kam, HONG Nari, HONG Robert, HONG Sunny, HONG Sun, HONG Sun, HONG Jocelynn, HONG Sze, HONG Swan, HONG Young, HONG Yu, HONGPRAPHAWONG Salin, HONOS Dimitri, HOOD Carol, HOOD Debra, HOOD Ian, HOOD James, HOOD Jane, HOOD John, HOOD Joy, HOOD Marion, HOOD Mike, HOOD Simon, HOOD William, HOOGHUIS Tineke, HOOGSTAD Stuart, HOOGSTRATEN Dianne, HOOI Roger, HOOI Shan, HOOK Chris, HOOK Kelli, HOOK Lisa, HOOK Trinity, HOOKE Alana, HOOKE Alex, HOOKE Hamish, HOOKHAM Rhonda, HOOKINS Tim, HOOKWAY Vanessa, HOOPER Allen, HOOPER Craig, HOOPER Gloria, HOOPER Jason, HOOPER Kathy, HOOPER Peter, HOOPER Ron, HOOPER Sue, HOOSON Michele, HOOTON Jessica, **HOOTON Bob**, HOPA Tom, HOPE Emma, HOPE Jane, HOPE Maureen, HOPE Ronald, HOPES Lisa, HOPEWELL Grace, HOPGOOD Donna, HOPGOOD Warren, HOPKINS Alan, HOPKINS Carrie-Anne, HOPKINS Gladys, HOPKINS Janette, HOPKINS Jenny, HOPKINS Kelly, HOPKINS Leoni, HOPKINS Maria, HOPKINS Mel, HOPKINS Bob, HOPKINS Russ, HOPLEY Clare, HOPLEY Frances, HOPLEY Morgan, HOPLEY Paul, HOPMAN Henry, HOPMAN Winston, HOPPENBROUWER Frank, HOPPER David, HOPPER Diana, HOPPER Karen, HOPPER Stephanie, HOPPITT Jean, HOPPITT Russell, HOPSON Carmen, HOPSON Theodore, HOPTON Steven, HOPWOOD Nichele, HOQ Monzu, HOQUE Enamul, HOR Sandip, HORA Dun, HORA Priscilla, HORA Wendy, HORADAM Kerry, HORAM Pam, HORAM Peter, HORAN Lisa, HORDER Bill, HORDERN Rowena, HORE John, HORE Pauline, HORIUCHI Hiromi, HORLEY Sandra, HORL CK Ross, HORMANN Cheryl, HORN Daryl, HORN David, HORN Eileen, HORN Eric, HORN Leesa, HORN Lesley, HORN Stephanie, HORNBROOK Sue, HORNBY Hornblower, HORNBY Karynne, HORNE Alison, HORNE Anne, HORNE Barry, HORNE Graham, HORNE Karen, HORNE Kelly, HORNE Mary, HORNE Naomi, HORNE Nathan, HORNE Shelly, HORNE Steve, HORNEMAN Tony, HORNEMAN Marilyn, HORNEMAN Merryn, HORNER Glenn, HORNER Zac, HORNER Ralph, HORNIAK Peter, HORNIBROOK Beverly, HORNIGOLD Carl, HORNIMAN Neta, HOROZAKIS Tass, HORROCKS Anne, HORSBURGH Abbey, HORSBURGH Mandy, HORSBURGH Michelle, HORSEY Toni, HORSFALL Alan, HORSFALL Bill, HORSFIELD Jamie, HORSFIELD Sue, HORSLEY Neil, HORSLEY Thelma, HORTENSE John, HORTON Alan, HORTON Bassma, HORTON Bernie, HORTON Bronwyn, HORTON Chad, HORTON Kathy, HORTON Kristy, HORTON Nicci, HORTON Tracy, HORVAT Sam, HORVATH Dianna, HORVATH Josef, HORVATH Michal, HORVATH Ray, HORWOOD Gary, HORWOOD Peter, HORWOOD Stewart, HOSA Bronwyn, HOSCHKE Petrea, HOSFORD Pat, HOSHIZAWA Miwa, HOSIE Andrew, HOSIE Col, HOSKIN Abigail, HOSKIN Julianne, HOSKING Ray, HOSKING Tracey, HOSKINS Barb, HOSKINS Melanie, HOSNI Les, HOSOKI Ralph, HOSSAIN Ana, HOSSAIN Akash, HOSSAIN Capal, HOSSAIN Samia, HOSSEINI Zahra, HOTHAM Ken, HOTORAN George, HOTSON Donald, HOTTELMANN Ellen, HOU Holly, HOU Yi, HOU Julie, HOUGH Andrew, HOUGHTON Dianne, HOUGHTON Jackie, HOUGHTON Keith, HOUGHTON Lyn, HOUGHTON Phillip, HOUHOULIS Sandra, HOULDSWORTH Karen, HOULT Licinda, HOULTON Ronald, HOURIGAN Ted, HOURIGAN Tony, HOURIGAN Veronica, HOURIHAN Fleur, HOURMOZI Monica, HOUSEIN Jef, HOUSEIN Joyce, HOUSEMAN Jennie, HOUSTON Donald, HOUSTON Jason, HOUSTON Ryan, HOUSTON Scott, HOVENDEN Ian, HOVSEPIAN Silvana, HOW Ai, HOWARD Adam, HOWARD Alba, HOWARD Alistair, HOWARD Beryl, HOWARD Beryl, HOWARD Bertie, HOWARD Bree, HOWARD Brian, HOWARD Brian, HOWARD Carmel, HOWARD Chris, HOWARD Davi, HOWARD Elizabeth, HOWARD Gary, HOWARD Glennis, HOWARD Graham, HOWARD Helen, HOWARD Jim, HOWARD John, HOWARD John, HOWARD Joe, HOWARD Joyce, HOWARD Julie, HOWARD Julian, HOWARD Karn, HOWARD Ken, HOWARD Kylie, HOWARD Les, HOWARD Marcia, HOWARD Marg, HOWARD Martin, HOWARD Matt, HOWARD Oswald, HOWARD Pam, HOWARD Rachael, HOWARD Rachel, HOWARD Sarah, HOWARD Sian, HOWARD Steve, HOWARD Warren, HOWARD William,

HOWARD Yolanda, HOWARTH Dean, HOWARTH James, HOWARTH Steve, HOWDEN Anthony, HOWDEN Keith, HOWDEN Bob, HOWDEN Bill, HOWE Tony, HOWE Beverley, HOWE Frank, HOWE Geoff, HOWE Ian, HOWE James, HOWE Jill, HOWE John, HOWE Judy, HOWE Kayleen, HOWE Lucy, HOWE Maija, HOWE Susan, HOWELL Dawn, HOWELL Kate, HOWELL Jacinda, HOWELL Buzz, HOWELL Lawrence, HOWELL Lesley, HOWELL Madeline, HOWELL Peter, HOWELL Slade, HOWELL Susanne, HOWELLS Lee, HOWELLS Rosemary, HOWES Aiko, HOWES Chris, HOWES Jenny, HOWES Joel, HOWES Jon, HOWES Teresa, HOWES Mort, HOWES Rube, HOWETT Jessie, HOWETT Jessie, HOWEY Andrew, HOWIE Colleen, HOWIE Douglas, HOWIE Ros, HOWISOW Holly, HOWITT Chris, HOWITT Dianne, HOWITT Jodie, HOWLAND Denzil, HOWLAND John, HOWLAND Robb, HOWLE Lynette, HOWLETT Laura, HOWLETT Hutchings, HOWLETT Melinda, HOWLETT Vern, HOWLETT Warren, HOWS John, HOWSE Charles, HOY Tony, HOY Charmaine, HOY Elizabeth, HOY Karen, HOY Les, HOY Margaret, HOY Rob, HOY Sandy, HOY Yvonne, HOYER Dorothy, HOYET Frederique, HOYLE Kylie, HOZACK Heather, HRABE Nicolle, HRAST Peter, HRBAC Michael, HRISTOFSKI Frida, HRISTOFSKI Kathy, HRONOPOULOS Theo, HRONOPOULOS Bill, HRUBAN Mikki, HRUBAN Lilly, HRUZ Josef, HRVOJ Cheryl, HRYCYK Mathew, HSIEH Mike, HSIEH Bill, HSU Brian, HSU Jean, HSU Josephine, HSU Wei-Chun, HU Ben, HU Tom, HU Maggie, HU Vivian, HU Elly, HUA Erica, HUA Jenna, HUA Phuong, HUA Stephen, HUA Tailan, HUANG Alan, HUANG Amy, HUANG Andrew, HUANG Anna, HUANG Annie, HUANG Chai-Yi, HUANG Anita, HUANG Andy, HUANG Garry, HUANG Jimmy, HUANG Helen, HUANG Janice, HUANG Jack, HUANG Josephine, HUANG Kaining, HUANG Philip, HUANG Ren, HUANG Eileen, HUANG Tony, HUANG Linda, HUANG Wenwei, HUANG Yi, HUANG Yuffrey, HUARD Geoff, HUBATA Jana, HUBBARD Frank, HUBBARD Graeme, HUBBARD Jacqueline, HUBBARD Jan, HUBBARD Kevin, HUBBARD Robert, HUBER Peter, HUBERT Stephan, HUBINGER Julieanne, HUCKEL Wendy, HUCKER Carol, HUCKERBY Sandra, HUCKLE Clare, HUDA Meraj, HUDGSON Jacqui, HUDSON Adam, HUDSON Brett, HUDSON Brian, HUDSON Eric, HUDSON Erica, HUDSON Gary, HUDSON Geoff, HUDSON Graeme, HUDSON Helen, HUDSON Jayne, HUDSON Jean, HUDSON John, HUDSON Kerry, **HUDSON Kevin**, HUDSON Louise, HUDSON Lyndall, HUDSON Matt, HUDSON Phil, HUDSON Sue, HUDSON Terry, HUDSON Xina, HUDSPITH Joan, HUDSWELL Ray, HUENERMUND Bruno, HUETT Berwin, HUFF Belinda, HUFF Jeff, HUFTON Rita, HUGEN Sid, HUGG Karen, HUGGARD Kathryn, **HUGGINSON David**, HUGH Therese, HUGHES Alan, HUGHES Alison, HUGHES Allen, HUGHES Anthony, HUGHES Brian, HUGHES Craig, HUGHES Dallas, HUGHES Diann, HUGHES Dusty, HUGHES Liz, HUGHES Emma, HUGHES Erin, HUGHES Frank, HUGHES Geoff, HUGHES Geoff, HUGHES Gerry, HUGHES Gerard, HUGHES Gilbert, HUGHES Howard, HUGHES Jean, HUGHES Jennifer, HUGHES Joan, **HUGHES John**, HUGHES John, HUGHES Karin, HUGHES Katherine, HUGHES Kent, HUGHES Kerry, HUGHES Kylie, HUGHES Lister, HUGHES Mary, HUGHES Matt, HUGHES Melinda, HUGHES Merle, HUGHES Mick, HUGHES Trish, HUGHES Pat, HUGHES Peter, HUGHES Pete, HUGHES Peter, HUGHES Malcolm, HUGHES Rod, HUGHES Ronald, HUGHES Roz, HUGHES Roseanne, HUGHES Ruth, HUGHES Sam, HUGHES Samantha, HUGHES Sandy, HUGHES Sim, HUGHES Simon, HUGHES Stephen, HUGHES Tom, HUGHES Tom, HUGHES Thomas, HUGHES Vicki, HUGHES Vivienne, HUGHES Bill, HUGHES Bill, HUGHSON Sally, HUGILL Dianne, HUGMAN Malcolm, HUGUENIN Kerry, HUGUENIN Leesa, HUGUENIN Lynn, HUI Emily, HUI Eric, HUI Felix, HUI Gina, HUI Henry, HUI Mandy, HUI Sandra, HUI Terence, HUI Wai, HUKINS Lynley, HULL Chris, HULL David, HULL Diane, HULL Jim, HULL Ken, HULL Margaret, HULL Mitch, HULLICK Ken, HULLS Enid, HULME Adrian, HULME Ben, HULME Joyce, HULSKAMP Elka, HULSKAMP Irene, HULSKAMP Nick, HULSON-CALVERT Jude, HUMA Roderick, HUMAR Leo, HUMBERSTONE Richard, HUMBERT Laura, HUMBLE Brett, HUME Andrew, HUME Charles, HUME Ken, HUME Leanne, HUME Nick, HUME Steve, HUMPHREY Barbara, HUMPHREY Don, HUMPHREY Janette, HUMPHREY Jan, HUMPHREY Sally, HUMPHREY Louise, HUMPHREY Lyndell, HUMPHREY Paula, HUMPHREY Paul, HUMPHREY Sy, HUMPHREY Jordan, HUMPHREYS David, HUMPHREYS Graham, HUMPHREYS Jim, HUMPHREYS John, HUMPHREYS Jonathan, HUMPHREYS Lynne, HUMPHREYS Robin, HUMPHREYS Roy, HUMPHREYS Sue, HUMPHREYS Vicki, HUMPHRIES Amber, HUMPHRIES Carla, HUMPHRIES Mimi, HUMPHRIES Gen, HUMPHRIES Jane, HUMPHRIES John, HUMPHRIES Linda, HUMPHRIES Naomi, HUMPHRIES Rebecca, HUMPHRIES Robert, HUMPHRYS Graham, HUMPHRYS Kirsty, HUNG Elmer, HUNG Jacqueline, HUNG Janet, HUNOLD Donna, HUNT Alicia, HUNT Andrew, HUNT Anthony, HUNT Barry, HUNT Becky, HUNT Cassandra, HUNT Chris, HUNT Colette, HUNT Danielle, HUNT Gary, HUNT Faye, HUNT Graeme, HUNT Graham, HUNT Don, HUNT Jamie, HUNT Jane, **HUNT Jan**, HUNT Jessica, HUNT Joel, HUNT Lance, HUNT Claire, HUNT Margaret, HUNT Nelson, HUNT Robyn, HUNT Ron, HUNT Sally, HUNT Shane, HUNT Suwannee, HUNT Wayne, HUNT Yvonne, HUNTER Chris, HUNTER Chris, HUNTER Di, HUNTER Libby, HUNTER Erin, HUNTER Geoff, HUNTER Geoff, HUNTER Gill, HUNTER Graham, HUNTER Heather, HUNTER Olwyn, HUNTER John, HUNTER John, HUNTER Karen, HUNTER Kerry, HUNTER Kevin, HUNTER Kim, HUNTER Lisa, HUNTER Lidy, HUNTER Madeline, HUNTER Marie-Therese, HUNTER Neal, HUNTER Nick, HUNTER Paul, HUNTER Phil, HUNTER Bob, HUNTER Shelley, HUNTER Tracy, HUNTER Vilma, HUNTER Bill, HUNTINGTON Chris, HUNTINGTON Ron, HUNTLEY Geoff, HUNTLEY Judith, HUNTLEY Milena, HUNTRISS Debra, HUNTSMAN Leone, HUNTSMAN Bob, HUNYADI Luke, HUR Joon-Ho, HUR Young, HURD Margaret, HURFORD Christine, HURFORD Richard, HURL Steven, HURLEY Alan, HURLEY Christina, HURLEY Elisabeth, HURLEY Helen, HURLEY John, HURLEY Mark, HURLEY Mags, HURLEY Michael, HURLEY Paul, HURLEY Ron, HURLEY Sue, HURLSTONE Alfred, HURN Kaye, HURNDELL Sue, HURREN Phil, HURRY Tony, HURST Angela, HURST Graeme, HURST Jack, HURST Marilyn, HURST Phil, HURST Sam, HURTADO Maria, HURWITZ Mark, HURWOOD Lyn, HUSADA Darius, HUSEBY Miriam, HUSEYIN Ece, HUSKEN Fred, HUSSAIN Ahmad, HUSSAIN Hussain, HUSSAIN Sultan, HUSSAIN Zafirul, HUSSEINI Dima, HUSSELL Jason, HUSSEN Mohammad, HUSSON Thomas, HUSTON une, HUSZCZO Helen, HUTABARAT Ester, HUTABARAT Jasper, HUTAPEA Anthony, HUTCH Kylie, HUTCHESON Leanne, HUTCHINGS Ann, HUTCHINGS Carol, HUTCHINGS Faye, HUTCHINS Allan, HUTCHINS Christopher, HUTCHINS Geoff, HUTCHINS Meg, HUTCHINS Shaun, HUTCHINS Therese, HUTCHINSON Allan, HUTCHINSON Andrew, HUTCHINSON Angela, HUTCHINSON Annette, HUTCHINSON Bruce, HUTCHINSON Daniel, HUTCHINSON Danielle, HUTCHINSON Denise, HUTCHINSON Dora, HUTCHINSON Duane, HUTCHINSON Emma, HUTCHINSON Gillian, HUTCHINSON John, HUTCHINSON Kathy, HUTCHINSON Louise, HUTCHINSON Paul, HUTCHINSON Phill, HUTCHINSON Ruth, HUTCHINSON Susan, HUTCHINSON Trevor, HUTCHINSON Val, HUTCHINSON Wendy, HUTCHISON Bethany, HUTCHISON Courtney, HUTCHISON David, HUTCHISON Gordon, HUTCHISON John, HUTCHISON Noela, HUTCHISON Paul, HUTCHISON Robert, HUTT Alex, HUTT Leesa, HUTTLY Mary, HUTTON Andy, HUTTON Brendan, HUTTON Edna, HUTTON John, HUTTON Morrie, HUTTON Tim, HUTTON Tony, HUXLEY Liz, HUXLEY Marnie, HUXLEY Melissa, HUXLEY Monette, HUXLEY-BRIAND Marc, HUXSTEP Steve, HUYNH Cam, HUYNH Chinh, HUYNH Cafa, HUYNH Hanh, HUYNH Vinh, HUYNH Jeff, HUYNH Julia, HUYNH Lilan, HUYNH Michael, HUYNH Natalie, HUYNH Perri, HUYNH Phi, HUYNH Serina, HUYNH Tan, HUYNH Thuan, HUYNH Van, HUYNH Van, HUYNH Vinh, HUYNH Will, HUYNH William, HUZIJ Greg, HUZZEY Lynda, HVAAL Ida, HWAN Austin, HWANG Chul, HWANG Gyu, HWANG James, HWANG Kevin, HWANG Ki-Hoo, HWANG Michael, HWANG Sj, HWANG Jenny, HYATT Sue, HYDE Bruce, HYDE Gregory, HYDE Lorne, HYDE Nicholas, HYDE Peter, HYDE Philippa, HYDE Robyn, HYDE Robert, HYETT Bev, HYETT David, HYETT Margaret, HYETT Mel, HYKER Alison, HYLAND David, HYLAND Melinda, HYLES Katie, HYLLAND Aase, HYMAN Lynette, HYNARD Adele, HYNDMAN Reg, HYNDS Alan, HYNE Jennifer, HYNES John, HYPATIDIS Paul, HYSLOP Mark, HYSLOP Ray, HYUN Ian, HYUN Jung.

I

I RAJAH Kannon, I-RAJAH Mugunthan, IACCARINO Clara, IACONO Stefano, IAFIGLIOLA Luis, IANITTO Sandra, IANNAZZO Rob, IANNUNZIO Antonia, IASTREBOVA Val, IBANEZ Antonio, IBARBURU Cris, IBARBURU Ruth, IBBETT Janine, IBBOTSON Ann, IBBOTSON Peggy, IBELS Vicky, IBRAHIM Abdi, IBRAHIM Adel, IBRAHIM Ameer, IBRAHIM Amin, IBRAHIM Ash, IBRAHIM Charbel, IBRAHIM Danny, IBRAHIM Emily, IBRAHIM Farhan, IBRAHIM Farida, IBRAHIM Jimmy, IBRAHIM Meissa, ICHIGUCHI Yuka, ICKERINGILL Norm, IDSTEIN Julie, IEONG Carey, IFFLAND Mary, IGNACZ Phillipa, IGNATYCHEVA Svetlana, IHEANACHO Grace, IHTNAREVICH Suad, IIDA Hiro, IIJIMA Risako, IISMAA Siiri, IISMAA Tiina, IKEDA Chishin, IKOSIDEKOS George, ILAGAN Fel, ILAO Jerald, ILBERY Jaki, ILIC Dan, ILIC Glen, ILIC Jenny, ILIEVSKI Chris, ILIEVSKI Viki, ILIJASEVIC Srecko, ILIOPOULOS Pauline, ILKOVSKI Alex, ILLIDGE Prue, ILLY Garland, ILOTT Dan, ILTER Jennifer, IM Ae, IM Nari, IMAI Yuko, IMANI Leyli, IMBER Shirley, IMHOF Gav, IMISON Dianne, IMMONEN Erja, IMMONEN Hendrik, IMMONEN Karl, IMMONEN Susan, IMRE John, INABINET Dale, INALL Neil, INALL Tim, INALL Tracy, INCHBOLD Benita, INCZE Zsolt, INDOLOS Christina, INDRAKANTI Sarath, INGERSON Phyl, INGHAM Annette, INGHAM Don, INGHAM Betty, INGHAM Jan, INGHAM Roy, INGHAM Susan, INGHAM Tom, INGLEFINGER Megan, INGLES George, INGLIS Andrew, INGLIS Angela, INGLIS Bazza, INGLIS Helen, INGLIS Madeline, INGLIS Wesley, INGRAM Alison, INGRAM Anthony, INGRAM Brian, INGRAM David, INGRAM Dixie, INGRAM Geoff, INGRAM Geoffrey, INGRAM June, INGRAM Kellie, INGRAM Laurie, INGRAM Matt, INGRAM Maureen, INGRAM Max, INGRAM Peter, INGRAM Richelle, INGRAM Tony, INGS Bronwyn, INGS Keely, INGS Mathew, INGS Natalie, INGS Sue, INGS Vanessa, **INH LE Van**, INKSTER Joyce, INMAN David, INMAN Jenny, INMAN Sarah, INNERST Bonnie, INNES Alwyn, INNES Bruce, INNES John, INNES Mal, INNES Sandra, INOKAI Niki, INOUE Chisato, INOUE Manami, INOUE Hiro, INSKIP Faye, INSON Jeremy, INTHAVONG Khaek, INWOOD Paul, IOAKIM Niki, IOANNOU Joanne, IP Ada, IP May, IP Carrie, IP Vera, IPKENDANZ Peter, IPPINDO Anthony, IPPOLITI Eda, IPPOLITO Louis, IRANI Nazneen, IRANI Shiraz, IRANI Vispi, IRAWAN Catherine, IREDALE Connie, IREDALE Gypsy, IRELAND Adrian, IRELAND Anita, IRELAND Colin, IRELAND Gabby, IRELAND John, IRELAND John, IRELAND Kate, IRELAND Louise, IRELAND Mark, IRELAND Toni, IRIBARNE Gabriel, IRISH Anne, IRISH Jo, IRONS Terry, IRONSIDE Charles, IRONSIDE Sarah, IRVIN Denny, IRVIN Kusuma, IRVIN Spencer, IRVINE Carol, IRVINE Duncan, IRVINE Robert, IRVINE BROWN Jenny, IRVINE-BROWN Greg, IRVING Jenny, IRVING Mat, IRVING Bill, IRWIN Belinda, IRWIN Brad, IRWIN Garry, IRWIN Russell, IRWIN Joy, **IRWIN Julia**, IRWIN Rebecca, IRWIN Shannon, IRWIN Vanessa, ISAAC Brigid, ISAAC Brian, ISAAC Rosemary, ISAACS Daniel, ISAACS David, ISAACS Lynette, ISAACS Robyn, ISAACSON David, ISAACSON Mark, ISAIAS Costa, ISAKSEN Kevin, ISAKSEN Knut, ISBERG Robyn, ISBERG Bjorn, ISEDALE Grant, ISEDALE Marney, ISENBERG Nicole, ISER David, ISER Jeannine, ISER Silviu, ISHERWOOD Amanda, ISHIBASHI Takuma, ISHIBASHI Yusuke, ISHIDA Keiko, ISHIGURO Sachiko, ISHIHARA Tatsuya, ISHII Hajime, ISHIZU Masako, ISHIZUKA Daisuke, ISIDORI Linda, ISKANDAR Hassan, ISKANDAR Irma, ISKANDAR Ramzi, ISKENDERIAN Sylvia, ISKOV Kenn, ISKOV Leonie, ISKRA Marko, ISLAM Seemab, ISLAM Shariful, ISLAM Md., ISLAM Nazrul, ISLES Jessica, ISLES Steve, ISLIP David, ISLIP Lucinda, ISLIP Thelma, ISMAIL Zimba, ISMAIL Khalid, ISMAIL Shaira, ISON John, ISRAEL Maria, ISRAEL Nicolas, ISRAELSKI Peter, ISSA Andrew, ISSA Sana, ISSANCHON Gary, ISTED Louise, ITANI Samia, ITEN Moses, ITO Akiko, ITO Fumiko, ITO Haru, ITO Reiko, ITO Sachiko, ITO Yoshie, ITURRIETA Katia, ITZSTEIN Sue, IULIANO Anne, IUS Luisa, IUTCOVICH Mara, IVAKOV Alexander, IVANOV Anthony, IVANOV Liliana, IVANOV Vlad, IVANOVA Irina, IVANOVSKI George, IVERS Gerry, IVERS Rebecca, IVERSEN Karina, IVES John, IVEY Rockey, IVIMEY Harry, IVIN Kevin, IVIN Bill, IVINS Roberta, IVINSON Jason, IVORY Kimberley, IWAN Lisa, IWASAKI Ryoko, IYER Ram, IYNGKARAN Kuna, IZARD Beverley, IZCI Gunay, IZMAILOVA Mansoura, IZZET Ali, IZZO Joanne.

J

JAAFAR Abdul, JABBOUR Lorraine, JABOUR Valerie, JABRO Maria, JACENKO Anna, JACIMOSKA Olivera, JACINTO Lola, JACK Chris, JACK Ross, JACK Steven, JACKA Kate, JACKA Larry, JACKA Tracey, JACKETT Brian, JACKMAN David, JACKMAN Margaret, JACKMAN Bill, JACKSON Alan, JACKSON Alan, JACKSON Albert, JACKSON Mandy, JACKSON Amy, JACKSON Angela, JACKSON Anita, JACKSON Tony, JACKSON Barbara, JACKSON Barry, JACKSON Betty, JACKSON Brian, JACKSON Brian, JACKSON Bryan, JACKSON Clare, JACKSON David, JACKSON Denis, JACKSON Dianne, JACKSON Don, JACKSON Ellie, JACKSON Erin, JACKSON Margaret, JACKSON Frank, JACKSON Gabrielle, JACKSON Jacko, JACKSON Greg, JACKSON Greg, JACKSON Gwen, JACKSON Helen, JACKSON Ian, JACKSON Jim, JACKSON Jennifer, JACKSON Jo, JACKSON John, JACKSON Judy, JACKSON Karen, JACKSON Kendy, JACKSON Leanne, JACKSON Leigh, JACKSON Leonie, JACKSON Lionel, JACKSON Lisa, JACKSON Margaret, JACKSON Anne, JACKSON Margaret, JACKSON Marie, JACKSON Megan, JACKSON Melissa, JACKSON Merv, JACKSON Mike, JACKSON Peter, JACKSON Peter, JACKSON Peter, JACKSON Bec, JACKSON Reid, JACKSON Richard, JACKSON Robyn, JACKSON Bob, JACKSON Ron, JACKSON Rosemary, JACKSON Ross, JACKSON Sandra, JACKSON Selwyn, JACKSON Sharon, JACKSON Sheilah, JACKSON Stephen, JACKSON Stewart, JACKSON Stuart, JACKSON Stuart, JACKSON Sue, JACKSON Terry, JACKSON Terry, JACKSON Terrence, JACKSON Tom, JACKSON-CARROLL Casper, JACKSON-CARROLL Courtney, JACKSON-SMALE Alistair, JACOB Amy, JACOB Mark, JACOB Nabill, JACOB Ross, JACOB Zeena, JACOBI Kate, JACOBS Anne, JACOBS Barry, JACOBS Terry, JACOBS Eliza, JACOBS Jake, JACOBS Ivan, JACOBS Janice, JACOBS John, JACOBS Margot, JACOBS Margaret, JACOBS Margot, JACOBS Michelle, JACOBS Stephen, JACOBS Wayne, JACOBSEN Clive, JACOBSON John, JACOBSON Charlie, JACOBSON Linette, JACOBSON Therese, JACOMB Brendan, JACQUES Celina, JADID Ammar, JADRAN Ahmad, JADRAN Ahmad, JADUN Omar, JAEGGI John, JAENSCH Sue, JAESCHKE Sadie, JAFFAR Hydi, JAFFREY Noni, JAGANATH Ivy, JAGASIA Uday, JAGELMAN Ian, JAGGER Alisha, JAGGER Jenny, JAGICIC Tony, JAGIELLO Anna, JAGLA Judy, JAGPAL Manpreet, JAGUSCH Ilsa, JAHSHAN Sandra, JAIN Dave, JAIN Megha, JAINPHAW Zau, JAIYAWONG Lani, JAJA Michael, JAKAS Con, JAKIMOVSKI Tracey, JAKSA Julia, JAKU James, JALIL Humaira, JAMDAGNI Rishi, JAMES Alanna, JAMES Alex, JAMES Allan, JAMES Amity, JAMES Armstrong, JAMES Arthur, JAMES Aven, JAMES Bruce, JAMES Carmen, JAMES Chad, JAMES Clinton, JAMES Darren, JAMES David, JAMES Gary, JAMES Glenys, JAMES Greta, JAMES Ian, JAMES Irene, JAMES Janice, JAMES Jenni, JAMES Jewel, JAMES Jocelyn, JAMES Karen, JAMES Katrina, JAMES Katrina, JAMES Keith, JAMES Leanne, JAMES Lisa, JAMES Lorraine, JAMES Lynnette, JAMES Mary, JAMES Melissa, JAMES Mike, JAMES Neryl, JAMES Nikki, JAMES Nick, JAMES Trish, JAMES Paddy, JAMES Paul, JAMES Peter, JAMES Peter, JAMES Ray, JAMES Phillip, JAMES Reg, JAMES Robyn, JAMES Robyn, JAMES Ron, JAMES Roz, JAMES Russell, JAMES Saul, JAMES Shero, JAMES Tonner, JAMES Victor, JAMES Warren, JAMESON Jason, JAMIESON Al, JAMIESON Barb, JAMIESON Don, JAMIESON Libby, JAMIESON Maree, JAMIESON Mike, JAMIESON Ray, JAMIESON RebeccaJane, JAMIESON Warren, JAMIESON Rick, JAMIN Rick, JAMSEK Alois, JAMSHIDI Fariborz, JANCETIC Steven, JANDA Patrick, JANES Peter, JANES Dianne, JANETZ Frank, JANEVSKI Chris, JANG John, JANG K B, JANG Stephen, JANICSKA Tony, JANIK Gabrielle, JANKALNS Eric, JANKOVIC Barb, JANKOWSKI George, JANKS Ellis, JANMAAT Jan, JANMAAT David, JANORN Charikan, JANOWSKI Joe, JANSE DE JONGE Xanne, JANSEN Daniel, JANSEN Diane, JANSEN Gwendoline, JANSEN Ian, JANSEN Janna, JANSEN Julie, JANSEN Luke, JANSEN Celonia, JANSEN Melinda, JANSEN Richard, JANSON Ken, JANSONS Robyn, JANSSEN Gerrit, JANSSEN Kath, JANSSENS Judy, JANSSON Tony, JANSZ Elaine, JANTO Rudy, JANVRIN Chantal, JAP Budi, JAP Ie, JAPAL Bryony, JAPANIDZE Mikheil, JAPPIE Riefqah,

JAQ UE Jaime, JAQUES Candice, JAQUES Nicki, JARAS Mary, JARDINE Jo, JARDINE Rosealeen, JARDINE ESQUIRE Jards, JARMAN Carl, JARMAN Clare, JARMAN Denise, JARMAN Don, JARMAN Joan, JARMAN Len, JARRATT Gwennie, JARRATT Ian, JARRETT Tony, JARRETT Colin, JARRETT Dawn, JARRETT Ed, JARRETT Jim, JARRETT John, JARRETT Miriam, JARRETT Neville, JARRETT Pat, JARRETT Tracey, JARRETT Trevor, JARVIE James, JARVIE Sue, JARVIS Anne, JARVIS Jean, JARVIS Kylie, JARVIS Margaret, JARVIS Neville, JARVIS Norm, JARVIS Raylene, JARVIS Rhia, JARVIS Rodney, JARVIS Joyce, JARZIN Dan, JASER Sami, JASIAK Nell, JASIM Mohamed, JASKOLSKI Anna, JASKOLSKI Matthew, JASNY Yvette, JASPRIZZA Brian, JASPRIZZA Robyn, JASTRZEBSKA Sandra, JAUCO Vic, JAUHARI Hari, JAUNCEY Sarah, JAUNCEY Sarah, JAVIER Eniong, JAVIER Jhun, JAVOS Virginie, JAY Geoff, JAY Graeme, JAYADEV Sheila, JAYAMAHA Jay, JAYARAJAN Earnest, JAYARATNAM Jaya, JAYARATNAM Sivahangai, JAYARETNAM Devarajan, JAYASEKARA Titus, JAYASEKERA Roger, JAYASINGHE Kamal, JAYASINGHE Rohan, JAYASUNDARA Nadeen, JAYASUNDERA Nilanthi, JAYATILAKA Jayya, JAYATILAKE Patrick, JAYEWARDENE Winodh, JAYONA Manny, JAZBEC Melita, JEAMBAR Pierre, JEAN Lisa, JEANES Dave, JEANS PJ, JEBAMONEY Nim, JECKELL Pam, JEDRZEJCZYK Chris, JEFFCOTT Pat, JEFFELS Melinda, JEFFERIES Diana, JEFFERS Rose, JEFFERSON Alanna, JEFFERSON Nyle, JEFFERY Dawn, JEFFERY Liz, JEFFERY Melinda, JEFFERY Peter, JEFFERY Phil, JEFFERY Warren, JEFFERY Yvonne, JEFFERYS Jennifer, JEFFREE Jenny, JEFFREE Ken, JEFFREE Ray, JEFFREE Raymond, JEFFREE Wayne, JEFFRESS Ray, JEFFREY Andy, JEFFREY Jay, JEFFREY Peter, JEFFRIES Robyn, JEFFRIES Robert, JEFFS Graham, JEFTIC Ljubisa, JEGATHESAN Jeiram, JEK Darwin, JELACA Mile, JELANY Annisa, JEMMESON Margaret, JEN Scott, JENICEK Alena, JENKIN Cara, JENKIN Maurice, JENKINS Aida, JENKINS Alan, JENKINS Alan, JENKINS Tony, JENKINS Cameron, JENKINS Cathryn, JENKINS David, JENKINS Vanessa, JENKINS Emily, JENKINS Emma, JENKINS Graham, JENKINS Helen, JENKINS John, JENKINS John, JENKINS Karen, JENKINS Madeleine, JENKINS Melanie, JENKINS Naomi, JENKINS Peter, JENKINS Jessie, JENKINS Rhona, JENKINS Bob, JENKINS Ronda, JENKINS Sally, JENKINS Simon, JENKINS Sue, JENKINSON Beverley, JENKYNS Peter, JENNAR Scott, JENNER Gerry, JENNER Raymond, JENNER Bec, JENNIFER BELL Emma, JENNINGS Amy, JENNINGS Helen, JENNINGS Ian, JENNINGS Jacqui, JENNINGS Maureen, JENNINGS Sue, JENSEN Brian, JENSEN Heike, JENSEN Helle, JENSEN Janet, JENSEN Ove, JENSEN Peter, JENSEN Raymond, JENSEN Shirley, JENSEN Wendy, JENSON Cathy, JEONG Erik, JEONG Minhee, JEONG Yong, JEPSON Paul, JERATH Naina, JEREMY Angela, JEREMY John, JERKOVIC Paula, JERMYN Andrew, JERMYN Peter, JERVIS Bianca, JERVIS Beth, JESSE Kathy, JESSENBY Sarah, JESSEP Debra, JESSON LJ, JESSOP Suzanne, JESSUP Elizabeth, JESSWEIN John, JESUS Michael, JESUS Rosa, JESUSSEK Stephanie, JEUNG Kim, JEW Loretta, JEX Bob, JEYARAJAH Niro, JEYASEELAN Anne, JEYENDREN Jey, JEZEWSKI Deborah, JEZO Ivan, JHAVERI Suha, JI Susan, JI Elizabeth, JI Christine, JIANG Lan, JIANG Lele, JIANG Minghai, JIANG Ming, JIANG Runqing, JIANG Shao, JIANG Susan, JIANG David, JIANG Ying, JIANG Yuan, JIAO Charlie, JIAO Chuan, JILG Karl, JIMENEZ Fernando, JIMENEZ John, JIMENEZ DIAZ Adrana, JIN Feng, JIN Jane, JIN Jia, JIN Li, JIN Li, JIN Lim, JIN Yi, JIN Yin, JIN YoungHuon, JIN David, JIN Simon, JIN Lyn, JINANARONG Suksan, JINDIA Poonam, JIVAN Mayuri, JO Su, JOACHIM Aubrey, JOACHIM Nelum, JOANNES Mandy, JOB Ashley, JOBBINS Di, JOBBINS Stephen, JOBLING Ian, JOBLING Ralph, JOBSON Greg, JOBSON Melissa, JOBSON Bob, JOCE Donna, JODEIKIN Bianca, JODZIO Craig, JOFFE Lynn, JOGIA Jainesh, JOHANSEN Jermund, JOHANSEN Keith, JOHANSEN Margaret, JOHANSEN Natasha, JOHANSSON Bryan, JOHANSSON Julie, JOHANSSON Karina, JOHANSSON Per, JOHN Bruce, JOHN Annie, JOHN Jacob, JOHN Thomas, JOHN EDWIN Clarke, JOHN WILLIAM John, JOHNBECK Birte, JOHNS Katie, JOHNS Lorae, JOHNS Mark, JOHNS Phil, JOHNS Rebecca, JOHNSON Alex, JOHNSON Andrew, JOHNSON Ann, JOHNSON Barry, JOHNSON Belinda, JOHNSON Bernard, JOHNSON Beverley, JOHNSON Brian, JOHNSON Brian, JOHNSON Charlotte, JOHNSON Cherie, JOHNSON Johnson, JOHNSON Colleen, JOHNSON Col, JOHNSON Craig, JOHNSON Cynthia, JOHNSON Dan, JOHNSON David, JOHNSON Russell, JOHNSON David, JOHNSON David, JOHNSON David, JOHNSON Dean, JOHNSON Debbie, JOHNSON Delcia, JOHNSON Dennis, JOHNSON Denise, JOHNSON Dianne, JOHNSON Doug, JOHNSON Drew, JOHNSON Chapman, JOHNSON Edwina, JOHNSON Edwina, JOHNSON Ross, JOHNSON Eric, JOHNSON Eric, JOHNSON Fay, JOHNSON Felicity, JOHNSON Fiona, JOHNSON Ross, JOHNSON Jed, JOHNSON Glen, JOHNSON Grace, JOHNSON Greg, JOHNSON Helen, JOHNSON Ian, JOHNSON Janet, JOHNSON Jeffrey, JOHNSON John, JOHNSON Joy, JOHNSON Joy, JOHNSON Judy, JOHNSON Julie, JOHNSON Julie, JOHNSON Kaz, JOHNSON Karen, JOHNSON Keith, JOHNSON Kelvin, JOHNSON Kerry, JOHNSON Kirk, JOHNSON Laura, JOHNSON Lesley, JOHNSON Lesley, JOHNSON Lorraine, JOHNSON Marj, JOHNSON MaryCaroline, JOHNSON Melinda, JOHNSON Mickey, JOHNSON Murray, JOHNSON Nicholas, JOHNSON Norma, **JOHNSON Pat**, JOHNSON Pat, JOHNSON Pat, JOHNSON Tricia, JOHNSON Patricia, JOHNSON Paul, JOHNSON Paul, JOHNSON Pete, JOHNSON Peter, JOHNSON Philip, JOHNSON Phil, JOHNSON Ralph, JOHNSON Rita, JOHNSON Robyn, JOHNSON Robert, JOHNSON Ronald, JOHNSON Rosemary, JOHNSON Ross, JOHNSON Sarah, JOHNSON Sharlane, JOHNSON Sue, JOHNSON Suzanne, JOHNSON Sylvia, JOHNSON Terry, JOHNSON Thomas, JOHNSON Bill, JOHNSON William, JOHNSTON Alistair, JOHNSTON Amanda, JOHNSTON Anne, JOHNSTON Brad, JOHNSTON Brian, JOHNSTON BJ, JOHNSTON Carol, JOHNSTON Carolyn, JOHNSTON Chris, JOHNSTON Denise, JOHNSTON Denis, JOHNSTON Dianne, JOHNSTON Donna, JOHNSTON Dorn, JOHNSTON Eddie, JOHNSTON Eileen, JOHNSTON Elaine, JOHNSTON Gary, JOHNSTON Grant, JOHNSTON Grant, JOHNSTON Heather, JOHNSTON Heather, JOHNSTON Helen, JOHNSTON Henry, JOHNSTON Jim, JOHNSTON Jeremy, JOHNSTON Krystal, JOHNSTON Joyce, JOHNSTON Malcolm, JOHNSTON Mandy, JOHNSTON Margaret, JOHNSTON Mike, JOHNSTON Nicole, JOHNSTON Patsie, JOHNSTON Polly, JOHNSTON Brett, JOHNSTON Peter, JOHNSTON Rachael, JOHNSTON Ray, JOHNSTON Rhoda, JOHNSTON Bob, JOHNSTON Robert, JOHNSTON Sandra, JOHNSTON Sarah, JOHNSTON Shirley, JOHNSTON Steve, JOHNSTON Susan, JOHNSTON Suzanne, JOHNSTON Val, JOHNSTON Bill, JOHNSTON Yvette, JOHNSTON-KNOCK Gail, JOHNSTONE Wally, JOHNSTONE Bruce, JOHNSTONE Bruce, JOHNSTONE Coby, JOHNSTONE Donna, JOHNSTONE Glenda, JOHNSTONE Hamish, JOHNSTONE Harley, JOHNSTONE Julia, JOHNSTONE Karl, JOHNSTONE Noel, JOHNSTONE Peita, JOKSOVIC Mira, JOLICOEUR Sylvio, JOLLIFFE Claire, JOLLIFFE Fran, JOLLIFFE Kristy, JOLLIFFE Trish, JOLLIFFE Sarah, JOLLIFFE Sharon, JOLY Jean, JOMAA Howaida, JON EDWARD Jon, JONAS Anne-Marie, JONAS Ivan, JONAS Peter, JONES Aaron, JONES Adele, JONES Alan, JONES Alan, JONES Alan, JONES Brian, JONES Alexandria, JONES Alison, JONES Alison, JONES Allan, JONES Andrea, JONES Anita, JONES Ann, JONES Arnold, JONES Gus, JONES Barbara, JONES Barbara, JONES Basil, JONES Bernie, JONES Breckon, JONES Brett, JONES Brian, JONES Bronwyn, JONES Bruce, JONES Carmen, JONES CJ, JONES Caroline, JONES Caroline, JONES Cheryl, JONES Christopher, JONES Colin, JONES Coleen, JONES Colleen, JONES Craig, JONES Daniel, JONES Daniel, JONES Daphne, JONES Dave, JONES David, JONES David, JONES Deborah, JONES Desiree, JONES Desiree, JONES Di, JONES Don, JONES Donald, JONES Doreen, JONES Les, JONES Liz, JONES Elizabeth, JONES Elmo, JONES Emily, JONES Ernest, JONES Evelyne, JONES Ross, JONES Gail, JONES Garry, JONES Gary, JONES Gloria, JONES Graham, JONES Greg, JONES Gregory, JONES Gwyn, JONES Hayley, JONES Isobel, JONES Jim, JONES Jenny, JONES Jenny, JONES Jenny, JONES Jessica, JONES Joan, JONES Joelle, JONES Jo, JONES Josephine, JONES Joy, JONES Judy, JONES Judy, JONES Julia, JONES Julie,

JONES Julian, JONES JJ, JONES Karen, JONES Karen, JONES Karine, JONES Kathy, JONES Kate, JONES Katherine, JONES Katherine, JONES Kath, JONES Kaye, JONES Keith, JONES Kerry, JONES Kim, JONES Kim, JONES Kirsten, JONES Kyle, JONES Kym, JONES Lachlan, JONES Laura, JONES Leanne, JONES Dudley, JONES Leo, JONES Les, JONES Les, JONES Lindy, JONES Lucy, JONES Luned, JONES Mark, JONES Margaret, JONES Mark, JONES Marion, JONES Margaret, JONES Marnie, JONE Mat, JONES Matthew, JONES Maureen, JONES Max, JONES Meaghan, JONES Meinir, JONES Mel, JONES Merv, JONES Meryl, JONES Michael, JONES Michael, JONES Roy, JONES Mick, JONES Michelle, JONES Michael, JONES Michael, JONES Nerelle, JONES Neville, JONES Nicolas, JONES Nick, JONES Neat, JONES Owen, JONES Pat, JONES Pat, JONES Paul, JONES Paul, JONES Paula, JONES Paul, JONES Peter, JONES Peter, JONES Peter, JONES Phil, JONES Rachel, JONES Rachel, JONES Raymond, JONES Raymond, JONES Rebecca, JONES Spike, JONES Rhonda, JONES Richard, JONES Rob, JONES Robert, JONES Bob, JONES Rob, JONES Robert, JONES Felix, JONES Roger, JONES Roger, JONES Ron, JONES Ron, JONES Ron, JONES Ronald, JONES Rosemary, JONES Rosslyn, JONES Ross, JONES Ross, JONES Roy, JONES Sandra, JONES Sandra, JONES Sandy, JONES Sarah, JONES Sarah, JONES Scott, JONES Shane, JONES Shayne, JONES Sonia, JONES Steve, JONES Steve, JONES Steven, JONES Steve, JONES Steven, JONES Steven, JONES Steven, JONES Stephen, JONES Stuart, JONES Stuart, JONES Suzanne, JONES Richard, JONES Tracey, JONES Trefor, JONES Trevor, JONES Val, JONES Vaughan, JONES Virginia, JONES Viviane, JONES Ron, JONES Wesley, JONES Yvonne, JONES-PRICHARD Suzanne, JONESRAPAEA Shelley, JONES-YOB Joy, JONES-YOB Robert, JONG GUN Kim, JONGEBLOED Christine, JONGEBLOED Mark, JONJEV Slavica, JONKIND Margaret, JONNABHATLA Praveen, JONQUIERES David, JOO Chung, JOO Doo, JOO Yo, JOORAWON Komal, JOORSHARI Masood, JOOS Mislav, JOPSON Jill, JORDAN Alan, JORDAN Cathy, JORDAN Christopher, JORDAN Dennis, JORDAN Ted, JORDAN Francesca, **JORDAN John**, JORDAN Katrina, JORDAN Phillip, JORDAN Ray, JORDAN Robert, JORDAN Rosalyn, JORDAN Sandra, **JORDAN Trevor**, JORGENSEN Anne, JORGENSEN Christine, JORGENSEN Julie, JORIS Sophie, JORQUERA Miguel, JORSSEN Kurt, JOSCELYNE Adam, JOSCELYNE David, JOSCELYNE Robyn, JOSE Wal, JOSELIN Jeannie, JOSEPH Angela, JOSEPH David, JOSEPH Edmond, JOSEPH Glenna, JOSEPH Helen, JOSEPH Jennifer, JOSEPH Lyn, JOSEPH Lyn, JOSEPH Marie, JOSEPH Reginald, JOSEPH Roy, JOSEPH Shobha, JOSEPH Talia, JOSEPH Therese, JOSEPHS Jane, JOSHI Chintan, JOSHI Deepak, JOSHI Dharmesh, JOSHI Gaurav, JOSHI Kish, JOSHI Mihirkumar, JOSHI Milind, JOSHI Pooja, JOSHI Raj, JOSHI Bonnie, JOSHI Shree, JOSHI Van, JOSHUA Fiona, JOSLIN Addie, JOSLIN Meredith, JOSLYN-NEILL Anthony, JOUBERT Henry, JOUDO Len, JOVANOVIC Nikola, JOVANOVIC Jim, JOVANOVICH Rachel, JOVCEVSKA Bilyana, JOVE Gloria, JOVEVSKI Heather, JOWETT Andrew, JOWETT Maureen, JOWSEY Horrie, JOY Lawrence, JOY Yvonne, JOYAN Rauf, JOYCE Coral, JOYCE Dani, JOYCE Elizabeth, JOYCE Greg, JOYCE Jennie, JOYCE Kaye, JOYCE Kevin, JOYCE Ray, JOYCE Renee, JOYCE Rhonnie, JOYCE Shellie, JOYES Jenifer, JOYES John, JOYNES Des, JOYNES Isobel, JOYNSON Kathleen, JOZELICH Natalie, JU Jamie, JU Seoungmi, JU Gloria, JUDD Amanda, JUDD Betty, JUDD John, JUDD Raewyn, JUDD Warren, JUDDERY Mark, JUDE Lucy, JUDGE Tony, JUDGE Lorraine, JUDGE Katie, JUDGE Bob, JUDGES Chris, JUKES Marilyn, JUKKOLA Katja, JUKKOLA Martti, JULIAN Beulah, JULIEN Dale, JULIUS Kate, JULIUS Sharne, JUN Helena, JUN Susannah, JUNES Denise, JUNG Chris, JUNG Eck, JUNG Jung-i, JUNG Ji, JUNG Jin, JUNG Kelly, JUNG Mary, JUNG Mi, JUNG Ryck, JUNG Sung, JUNG WonKyung, JUNG Won-Mi, JUNKER Urs, JUNOD Eliane, JUNOR Kevin, JUNOR Rachael, JUPP Amanda, JUPP Stephanie, JURE Navin, JURIC Ante, JURISIC Tony, JUROSS Lena, JUROTTE Frank, JURYGA Kasia, JURYS Vida, JUSTICE Dawn, JUSTICE Dorothy, JUSUF Cleony, JUTOT Sandy, JVANCICH Terry.

K

KAADI Basil, KAAN Dan, KAASIK Anni, KABAN Roman, KABIRSCHKE Michael, KABLE Barry, KABLE Beverley, KABLE Jenny, KABLE Roy, KACEW Lizzie, KACHKA Michal, KACZKA Sue, KACZMAREK Kristof, KACZOR Tom, KADAR Peter, KADDOUR Mick, KADER Sam, KADIRAGAMU Nithiya, KADIRAGAMU Sittampalam, KADJAHLO Martin, KADOTA Miwako, KADWA Becky, KAEHLER Damian, KAEHNE Joan, KAFKA Smaranda, KAHI-MIANJI Ali, KAHLER Kirsten, KAHLER Yvonne, KAHN Esther, KAHN Max, KAHN Vic, KAIKATI Chris, KAIL Tom, KAILO Ture, KAINE Rory, KAIO Debra, KAIROUZ Mirna, KAISER Angie, KAIUI Moeau, KAJONPEERAKUP Pop, KAKAROUBAS Fotis, KAKO Yousif, KAKUDA Yuki, KALACHE Lina, KALANTZI Tina, KALAS Leo, KALEDA Irena, KALEEL Shoky, **KALENDERIAN Joseph**, KALEY Mathew, KALINER Staci, KALINOWSKI Delys, KALISH Larry, KALITHRAKAS Helen, KALLENBERGER Niki, KALMAN Imre, KALOGEROPOULOS Jenny, KALORAN Harry, KALOTY Harpal, KALPAGE Kamani, KALRA Tilak, KALTENBACHER Beryl, KALVA Ramanakalva, KAMADA Yuko, KAMAL Amanjit, KAMALACHANDRAN Merhala, KAMARA Moses, KAMARAS Helen, KAMBOURIS Jamie, KAMEI Sayuri, KAMENJAS Ilija, KAMENZIN Otto, KAMERMAN Ian, KAMIKURA Jun, KAMINENI Sai, KAMINIC Juso, KAMINSKI Lou, KAMINSKI Sandra, KAMMEL Rod, KAMMERMANN Eva, KAMP Gerard, KAMP Shannan, KAMPER Joyce, KAN Edmund, KAN Cathy, KAN Michael, KAN Patrick, KAN Stephen, KANAAN Edward, KANAGANAYAGA SINGAM Angie, KANARIS Tina, KANCILIJA Mirosav, KANCILIJA Uros, KANDA Megumi, KANDIL Sayed, KANE Donna, KANE Frank, KANE Judith, KANE Justine, KANE Lorraine, KANE Ray, KANE David, KANEKO Kaza, KANEKO Takemasa, KANELLOS Terry, KANESH Natasha, KANEVSKY Mark, KANG Albel, KANG David, KANG Hung, KANG Jenny, KANG Julia, KANG Ken, KANG Olivia, KANG Sylvia, KANG Youme, KANGATHARAN Bharathi, KANIEL Natalie, KANITKAR Ajay, KANITKAR Anjali, KANITKAR Mohan, KANIZAY Jane, KANJ Mohamad, KANNAN Mani, KANNANGARA Siri, KANNARD Nicholas, KANSAKAR Elina, KAO Eddie, KAPETAS Paul, KAPLAN Natalie, KAPLANIS Chris, KAPNISTI Tina, KAPOSVARAC Dejah, KAPPERT Gerrit, KAPULONG Zaldy, KAPUSTIN Victor, KARA Kevin, KARABATSOS Steve, KARABAY Ace, KARABETSOS Andrew, KARAFILIS Diane, KARAGOZOGLU Naz, KARAHLIS Nick, KARAITIANA Bill, KARAKAYA Tomy, KARAKOTCHIAN Mary, KARAN Kusla, KARANOVIC Dijana, KARAOGLU Kaan, KARAOLIS Helen, KARATASOS Mary, KARDACHI Beverley, KARGER Peter, KARGOTICH Steve, KARHU Pia, KARIDIS Nicolas, KARIM Rez, KARIM Riaz, KARIM Sargon, KARKALA SYEB Liyak, KARKKAINEN Michael, KARKOUKLI Vicken, KARLBURGER Cosima, KARLSEN Margrethe, KARNADI Ronny, KARNCHANAKUL Kittipan, KARNER Linda, KARNUPS Imants, KARP Dani, KARPEL Olga, KARPIN Geoffrey, KARPIN Sonja, KARRI Alicia, KARSKENS Bill, KARUNAKARAN Haran, KARUNAKARAN Karu, KARUNAMBAL CHELLANIUTHU Saravana, KARUNANANDAGE Wimal, KARUNANANDE Ruwan, KARUNANAYAKE Sasanka, KARUNATHILAKE Priyanga, KARUNATHILAKE Nilanga, KARUNATILAKE Navodi, KARUNAWEERA Kalpani, KARVELIS Nicholas, KARYDIS Annette, KASEPUU Elda, KASEPUU Ulo, KASERMAN Len, KASHEM Jony, KASMARIK Kathryn, KASMAS Con, KASPER Alessandra, KASPRZAK Lucy, KASSAS Moses, KASSOUF Vicki, KASTANIAS Atha, KASTANIAS Emmanuel, KASTANIAS Steven, KASTANIAS Steven, KASTEEL Henk, KASTEL Mendel, KATAOKA Sachiko, KATAOKA Saori, KATEHOS Nick, KATEJULASRIROJ Pornthip, KATEN Cathy, KATER Jess, KATER Vicky, KATO Akiko, KATO Kumi, KATO Masako, KATONA Tom, KATRIB Ned, KATS Alex, KATSIKIS Vicki, KATSINAS Bianca, KATSURAYAMA Tomoko, KATZ Francis, KATZ Roman, KAU Jiann, KAU Jiann, KAUFMAN Allan, KAUFMAN Jan, KAUFMAN Janice, KAUFMAN John, KAUFONONGA Opiesi, KAULMANN Elke, KAUR Davinder, KAUR Kalwant, KAURIJOKI Jo, KAUTER Allan, KAVANAGH Bert, KAVANAGH Claire, KAVANAGH David, KAVANAGH Gary, KAVANAGH Linda, KAVANAGH Michael, KAVANAGH Michael, KAVANAGH Paulette, KAVARATZIS Demi, KAVARATZIS Maria, KAVARATZIS Poppi, KAVAZOS Rob, KAVCIC Vilma, KAVIERIS Theo, KAWABATA Junko,

KAWABE Mayu, KAWAGUCHI Toshi, KAWAKAMI Kotoko, KAWECKI Monika, KAY Cheryl, KAY Geoff, KAY Jen, KAY Jenny, KAY Jenny, KAY John, KAY Les, KAY Maria, KAY Nicole, KAY Ros, KAYAIAN Areen, KAYE Denise, KAYE Elaine, KAYE Emma, KAYE MariaTheresa, KAZACOS George, KAZAN Christina, KAZANTZOPOULOS George, KAZI Tas, KAZINS Markus, KAZZI Charbel, KAZZI Vic, KCESHNEV Valery, **KE Jenny**, KE Anthony, KEADY Jenny, KEALEY Mitchell, KEAM Adam, KEAN Kath, KEAN Phillip, KEAN Vincent, KEANE Anthony, KEANE Damian, **KEANE Elisabeth**, KEANE Jeff, KEANE Trisha, KEANE Rob, KEANEY Frank, KEANEY Bryan, KEAR Maureen, KEARL Colin, KEARNEY Alison, KEARNEY Bernie, KEARNEY Elizabeth, KEARNEY Peter, KEARNEY Bec, KEARNEY Richard, KEARNY-KIBBLE Mathilde, KEARY Will, KEAST Alan, KEAST Grahame, KEAST Jeremy, KEATES Coralie, KEATING Gary, KEATING Lisa, KEATING Rebecca, KEATING Terri, KEATING Bill, KEAY Annette, KEAYES Len, KEBEDE Solomon, KEBSCH Margaret, KECSKESOVA Iveta, KEEBLE Kay, KEEBLE Marge, KEEBLE Peter, KEECH Ian, KEECH Wendy, KEEDLE Amy, KEEGAN John, KEEGAN Julie, KEEGAN Kathleen, KEEGAN Lorraine, KEEGAN Pat, KEEGAN Richard, KEELER Kerry, KEELEY Graeme, KEELTY Gavin, KEEN Alan, KEEN Tony, KEEN Ken, KEEN Kenneth, KEEN Lorraine, KEEN Raymond, KEEN Siobhan, KEENA Chris, KEENA Gaenor, KEENA Harry, KEENAN Damian, KEENAN Grainne, KEENAN Ken, KEENE Rosemary, KEENIHAN Tamara, KEEP Christine, KEEPIN Jocette, KEET Jake, KEETLEY Dion, KEEVERS Jan, KEFALLINOS Diane, KEFFORD Mike, KEG Brian, KEHOE Emily, KEHOE Linda, KEHOE Phil, KEHRIS Spyros, KEIGHLEY Marion, KEIL Sophie, KEILEY Stephen, KEILTY Lorraine, KEIR Lucy, KEIR Pip, KEIRLE Alan, **KEITH Ian**, KEITH June, KELAITA Valmai, KELDER Yvette, KELEHER John, KELEMEN Suzanne, KELEN George, KELL Lizzy, KELL Mick, KELL Pam, KELL Ron, KELL Sally, KELLAR Randy, KELLEHER Arthur, KELLER Tony, KELLER Franziska, KELLER Jann, KELLER Natasha, KELLER Paul, KELLER Robyn, KELLERMAN Bernard, KELLERMANN Bruce, KELLERMANN Bill, KELLERT Deborah, KELLERT John, KELLERT Maree, KELLERT Matthew, KELLERT Richard, KELLET Bob, KELLETT Brad, KELLETT David, KELLETT Joan, KELLETT John, KELLETT Harry, KELLEY Erin, KELLEY Paul, KELLEY Stanley, KELLO Christene, KELLOWAY Hayley, KELLS Barb, KELLS Christine, KELLS June, KELLS Ric, KELLY Andrew, KELLY Anthony, KELLY Ned, KELLY Breda, KELLY Brian, KELLY Christopher, KELLY Coral, KELLY Dale, KELLY Dawn, KELLY Debbie, KELLY Dianne, KELLY Dot, KELLY Emma, KELLY Felicity, KELLY Gail, KELLY Geoff, KELLY Glenys, KELLY Glen, KELLY Greg, KELLY Les, KELLY Data, KELLY Kay, KELLY Jenny, KELLY Jenise, KELLY Jenny, KELLY John, KELLY John, KELLY John, KELLY Jo, KELLY Judy, KELLY June, KELLY Justin, KELLY Katie, KELLY Katrina, KELLY Paul, KELLY Laura, KELLY Linda, KELLY Lis, KELLY Margaret, KELLY Marc, KELLY Marg, KELLY Martin, KELLY Meghan, KELLY Melissa, KELLY Pam, KELLY Patsy, KELLY Trish, KELLY Peter, KELLY Pete, KELLY Phil, KELLY Phillip, KELLY Rebecca, KELLY Renae, KELLY Richard, KELLY Ron, KELLY Rosanne, KELLY Ruth, KELLY Sasha, KELLY Scott, KELLY Scott, KELLY Shea, KELLY Sophie, KELLY Terry, KELLY Tim, KELLY Troy, KELLY Troy, KELLY Val, KELLY Violet, KELLY Warren, KELLY Wendy, KELLY Bill, KELLY William, KELLY CAROL Kearney, KELLY-RINGROSE Amber, KELMAN Ken, KELMAN Sarah, KELSEY Des, KELSO Julie, KELSO Tricia, KELTON Dave, KELTON Joanna, KELTON Warren, KELTY Adam, KEMBER Nicky, KEMENT Suleyman, KEMER Jen nie, KEMER Zaven, KEMISTER Melanie, KEMM Tony, KEMM Kate, KEMM Shelagh, KEMP Alison, KEMP Carolyn, KEMP Christine, KEMP Christine, KEMP David, KEMP Des, KEMP Lannie, KEMP Garry, KEMP Graeme, KEMP Greg, KEMP Heather, KEMP Helene, KEMP John, KEMP Kylie, KEMP Lexie, KEMP Margaret, KEMP Paul, KEMP Peter, KEMP Rebekkah, KEMP Ron, KEMP Shaun, KEMP Sue, KEMP Travis, KEMPKENS Martyn, KEMPPAINEN Pia, KEMPTON-BARNES Stacy, KEMSLEY Heather, KENAGHAN Glenyse, KENAH Lorraine, KENAH Vanessa, KENCH Margaret, KENCH Susan, KENDAL Kristine, KENDALL Ann, KENDALL Craig, KENDALL Glen, KENDALL Mike, KENDALL Noel, KENDALL Paul, KENDALL BAKER Jackie, KENDELL David, KENDERES Richard, KENDRICK Rachel, KENEALLY Jane, KENNA Chris, KENNA Robyn, KENNA Therese, KENNARD Jill, KENNARD Sian, KENNAUGH Bob, KENNAWAY Tara, **KENNEALLY Lauren**, KENNEDY Adrian, KENNEDY Alex, KENNEDY Allan, KENNEDY Audrey, KENNEDY Brendon, KENNEDY Bruce, KENNEDY Col, KENNEDY Craig, KENNEDY Debbie, KENNEDY Dee, KENNEDY Dimity, KENNEDY Elizabeth, KENNEDY Gerry, KENNEDY Harry, KENNEDY Jamie, KENNEDY Jim, KENNEDY Jan, KENNEDY Jenny, KENNEDY Jennifer, KENNEDY John, KENNEDY John, KENNEDY John, KENNEDY Jonine, KENNEDY Linda, KENNEDY Louise, KENNEDY Margaret, KENNEDY Maree, KENNEDY Michael, KENNEDY Michelle, KENNEDY Michelle, KENNEDY Michael, KENNEDY Mick, KENNEDY Paul, KENNEDY Peter, KENNEDY Peter, KENNEDY Raph, KENNEDY Rohan, KENNEDY Sandra, KENNEDY Shirley, KENNEDY Steve, KENNEDY Sue, KENNEDY Tom, KENNEDY Virginia, KENNEDYDAVIDSON Leanne, KENNELLY David, KENNELLY Joe, KENNELLY Robert, KENNER Daniel, KENNETT Norm, KENNETT Peter, KENNETT Ross, KENNEWELL David, KENNING Jeannot, KENNINGTON Don, KENNINGTON Donald, KENNY Bernie, KENNY Carolyn, KENNY Catherine, KENNY Craig, KENNY Dale, KENNY Dave, KENNY Franceen, KENNY Rosemary, KENNY Lisa, KENNY Louise, KENNY Michael, KENNY Michelle, **KENNY Nola**, KENNY Penelope, KENNY Russ, KENNY Sheila, KENNY Steven, KENOS Angg, KENSELL Barbara, KENSEY Christine, KENT Chris, KENT Adam, KENT Adrian, KENT Anne, KENT Caroline, KENT Christian, KENT Hannah, KENT Heather, KENT Jodie, KENT John, KENT John, KENT John, KENT Judith, KENT Mick, KENT Peter, KENT Rachel, KENT Siobhan, KENT FORD William, KENT-JONES Simon, KENTISH Alexi, KENTWELL Ted, KENWARD Gail, KENWARD Sharron, KENWORTH Jody, KENWORTHY Steven, KENYON Peter, KEOGH Brett, KEOGH Debbie, KEOGH Simon, KEOGH Sue, KEOGH Verity, KEOGH-DAVIES Sharyn, KEOWN Bruce, KEOWN John, KEOWN Teresa, KEPERT Sarah, KEPPEL Anna, KEPPIE Patricia, KERA Francis, KERBY John, KERBY Thomas, KEREMA Helju, KERIN Michael, KERLEY Jennie, KERNEY Kenneth, KERNOHAN Jayne, KERR Allen, KERR Amanda, KERR Andrew, KERR Lindy, KERR David, KERR David, KERR Doris, KERR Duncan, KERR Geoff, KERR Geoff, KERR Guy, KERR Jan, KERR Keith, KERR Kevin, KERR Penny, KERR Rebecca, KERR Rhonda, KERR Roger, KERR Sandra, KERR Scott, KERR Sue, KERRIDGE Susan, KERRIGAN Bernadette, KERRUISH Grahame, KERRY Sarah, KERSHAW Alan, KERSHAW Garry, KERSHAW Roger, KERSHAW Sharne, KERSLAKE Ellen, KERSTEN Amie, KERSTEN Bob, KERSUN Mary, KESHAVA Ajay, KESHAVA Kesh, KESHVANI Nisar, KESIC Bessy, KESKI-NUMMI Irene, KESKULA August, KESSELL Allan, KESTER Dora, KESTER Jennifer, KESTER Karen, KETELAAR Sharon, KETHESPARAN Ranjan, KETTLE Sam, KETTLER Michel, KETTNER Rosalie, KEUNG Debbie, KEUTCHA TCHOUHAN Stephane, KEY Josephine, KEYS Andy, KEYS Celeste, KEYS Chas, KEYS Chris, KEYS Dawn, KEYS Janice, KEYS Matt, KEYS Ron, KEYS Ross, KEYS Sandra, KEYS Tricia, KEYS Wayne, KEYTE Robert, KEYWORTH Andrew, KEZOVSKI Linda, KEZOVSKI Bob, KHAIRANI Khairani, KHALAF Awad, KHALAJABADI Negin, KHALID Ahmad, KHALIFEH Alyce, KHALIL Mak, KHAMBATTA Jamsheed, KHAMIS Heba, KHAMMARATH Pino, KHAMMARATH Tony, KHAN Aamir, KHAN Abdul, KHAN Ahad, KHAN Ahmed, KHAN Khan, KHAN Arif, KHAN Intaj, KHAN Kawsar, KHAN Mahmad, KHAN Masud, KHAN Shanedul, KHAN Misbah, KHAN Naeem, KHAN Nasim, KHAN Riffat, KHAN Rishad, KHAN Safeeya, KHAN Saleem, KHAN Sobia, KHAN Shezi, KHAN Shakeel, KHAN Sonia, KHAN Winston, KHANAL Satish, KHANDELWAL Aarti, KHANDHAR Avani, KHANI Zara, KHARE Peter, KHARMAN Danny, KHARROUBI Fathi, KHARTU Allecia, KHATRI Man, KHATRI Nina, KHAW Alan, KHAZHINER Greg, KHAZMA HAMMOUD Mary, KHEIR Lina, KHIN AUNG Simon, KHINE Mi, KHIO Siew, KHIO Suemin, KHNOUF Joseph, KHO Hyoun, KHODR Ahmad, KHONG Hue, KHONG Linda, KHONG Susan, KHOO Kim, KHOPKAR Charu, KHOR Connie, KHOR Swee, KHOSHABEH Sara, KHOSHBAKHT Hilda, KHOSLA Anu, KHOUDAIR Peter, KHOUREY Luke, KHOUREY Matt, KHOURY Andre, KHOURY Anthony, KHOURY Carolina, KHOURY Danny, KHOURY Johnny, KHOURY Joe, KHOURY Lynette, KHOURY Michelle, KHOURY Nabil, KHOURY Rose, KHOURY Sheryl, KHOURY Tania, KHOUWANDI Anton, KHUMAN Nimarta, KHUN Eva, KHUNAVUTH Tom, KHUONG

Manh, KHURSHED Farhad, KHY Samnang, KI Joseph, KIANG Michael, KIAT Hosen, KIBBLER Alan, KIBEL Martyn, KICKBUSH Kal, KIDD Adrian, KIDD Barbara, KIDD Brad, KIDD Kris, KIDD Michael, KIDD Sally, KIDD Sandra, KIDD Simon, KIDDELL Julie, KIDSON Trevor, KIEFER Lorna, KIEHNE Geoff, KIELSHOLM Mette, KIELY Daniel, KIELY Jeff, KIELY Jessica, KIELY Martin, KIEM Michael, KIERATH Tom, KIERNAN Bernie, KIERNAN Lyn, KIERNAN Tyrone, KIFF Annette, KIJPANONT Wattanakorn, KIKUCHI Kaoru, KIKUCHI Ryoko, KIKUCHI Shogo, KILAZOGLOU James, KILBORN Marion, KILBURN Kristine, KILBURN-WATT Elisabeth, KILBURNWATT Naomi, KILBY Allan, KILBY Louise, KILBY Jan, KILBY Margaret, KILBY Rob, KILDEY Amy, KILDEY Tony, KILGOUR Robert, KILICOGLU Cemil, KILKEARY John, KILLA Vipal, KILLEEN Jenny, KILLEEN Paul, KILLEY Tony, KILLIAN Paul, KILLWORTH Barbara, KILMARTIN Darren, KILMARTIN Melissa, KILMETIEVA Larissa, KILNER Flora, KILPATRICK Don, KILPATRICK Donald, KILPATRICK Max, KILSBY Kevin, KIM Ae, KIM Agnes, KIM Anne, KIM Bo, KIM Bomin, KIM Bub-Lae, KIM Byung, KIM Charlie, KIM Kim, KIM Gemma, KIM David, KIM Daniel, KIM David, KIM Dong, KIM Eddy, KIM Eun, KIM Eun, KIM Eun, KIM Grace, KIM Helena, KIM Mark, KIM Hong, KIM Hyeyoung, KIM Jackie, KIM Helen, KIM Hyo-Soon, KIM Hyun-Jin, KIM Margaret, KIM Sally, KIM Eunice, KIM James, KIM Jahyi, KIM Jane, KIM Fresh, KIM Jenny, KIM Kim, KIM Joon, KIM Ji, KIM Christy, KIM June, KIM Jason, KIM Ji-Hyun, KIM Peekay, KIM Lucy, KIM Jin, KIM Jake, KIM Kiki, KIM Jung, KIM Anastasia, KIM Kim, KIM Antonio, KIM Kyung, KIM Kyung-Soon, KIM Leo, KIM Leo, KIM Linda, KIM Marshall, KIM Michelle, KIM Min, KIM Min, KIM Miyoun, KIM Marion, KIM MooYoun, KIM Moon, KIM Melanie, KIM Nicky, KIM Nicole, KIM Ok-Soon, KIM Paul, KIM Peter, KIM Robin, KIM SangMoon, KIM Sangmin, KIM Sarah, KIM Sherry, KIM Seuk-Young, KIM Seung, KIM Seul-a, KIM Sarah, KIM Sue, KIM Rosa, KIM Cecilia, KIM Soon-Jung, KIM Soo-Jin, KIM Sook, KIM Soo, KIM Stephen, KIM Su-mi, KIM Susan, KIM Stella, KIM Tae, KIM Yeong, KIM Yeon, KIM Yong-Soo, KIM Young-Hee, KIM Young, KIM-SING Terry, KIMBALL Chris, KIMBER Joel, KIMBER Lyle, KIMBLE Garry, KIMBLE Jean, KIME Colleen, KIME Kerry, KIMMINS Tania, KIMPEL Stephen, KIMURA Michiko, **KINCAID Keith**, KINCH Gene, KINCHINGTON Michael, KINDER Paul, KINDYNIS Kerry, KING Alan, KING Alex, KING Alicia, KING Alwyn, KING Amanda, KING Amy, KING Angela, KING Ango, KING Ann, KING Anton, KING Barry, KING Bernie, KING Briohny, KING Bronwyn, KING Carmel, KING Cheryl, KING Clive, KING David, KING David, KING Deb, KING Donald, KING Eileen, KING Betty, KING Elizabeth, KING Erin, KING Geoffrey, KING Graeme, KING Greg, KING Heidi, KING Helen, KING Jacki, KING James, KING Jason, KING John Christopher, KING John William, KING John Maxwell, KING Joseph, KING Judy, KING Karen, KING Kathleen, KING Keith, KING Kristian, KING Lee, KING Leonard, KING Lindsay, KING Lynn, KING Lynne, KING Jonathan, KING Maria, KING Mike, KING Myrle, KING Narelle, KING Olwyn, KING Pamela, KING Peter, KING Rebecca, KING Rei, KING Robin, KING Robert, KING Bob, KING Sally, KING Sereena, KING Simon, KING Tanya, KING Tom, KING Tiina, KING Wilhelmina, KING William, KINGCOTT Marie, KINGCOTT Neville, KINGHAM Catherine, KINGHAM David, KINGHAM John, KINGHAM Stan, KINGHORN Bruce, KINGKAEWCHAROENCHAI Panthip, **KINGSFORD SMITH Ian**, KINGSFORDSMITH Tony, KINGSHOTT Lawrence, KINGSLAND Alice, KINGSTON Hilda, KINGSTON Janet, KINGSTON Judith, KINGSTON Karen, KINGSTON Kerry, KINGSTON Orlaith, KINGSTON Rhondda, KINGSTON Terry, INGSTON Warwick, KINGSTON Wendy, KINHANE Paul, KINKADE Justine, KINNA Adrienne, KINNA Peter, KINNAIRD Ian, KINNAIRD Mick, KINNE Marie, KINNEAR David, KINSELA John, KINSER Jody, KINSER Theresa, KINSKI Xavier, KINSKY Anne, KINZETT Nic, KIPPAX Victoria, KIPPAYA Fundikira, KIRAGU Tamara, KIRBY Carol, KIRBY Catherine, KIRBY Judy, KIRBY Kevin, KIRBY Ray, KIRBY Robert, KIRBY Susan, KIRCHNER Dieter, KIRIEVSKY Anatoly, KIRIEVSKY Peter, KIRIYAMA Kaori, KIRK Joan, KIRK John, KIRK Bill, KIRKALDY Glenn, KIRKALDY Sharon, KIRKBRIDE Ben, KIRKBY Barbara, KIRKBY Brian, KIRKBY Warren, KIRKBY Katrina, KIRKBY Michael, KIRKER Barry, KIRKHAM Anthony, KIRKHAM Denise, KIRKHAM Ian, KIRKHAM Lee, KIRKHAM Margaret, KIRKHAM Pamela, KIRKLAND Les, KIRKLEY James, KIRKMAN Bruce, KIRKMAN Christine, KIRKMAN Glenn, KIRKOUDIS Evlin, KIRKPATRICK Glenyis, KIRKPATRICK Lee, KIRKPATRICK Mary, KIRKPATRICK Margherita, KIRKPATRICK Meredith, KIRKWOOD Belinda, KIRKWOOD Dean, KIRKWOOD Lauren, KIRKWOOD Sandra, KIRPICHNIKOV Annette, KIRSHNER Nick, KIRSNER James, KIRSTEN Inge, KIRTLEY Bill, KIRTON Laurel, KIRWAN Holly, KIRWAN Sara, KIRWIN Sandra, KISE Yumiko, KISH Alicia, KISLITSA Paul, KISS Cathy, KISS Kristina, KISS Istvan, KISS Zoltan, KISSELL James, KISSUN Rowena, KITA Masanori, KITAGAKI Mikiko, KITALA Regina, KITAMURA Francis, KITAMURA Natsuko/Nats, KITCHEN Margaret, KITCHER Frank, KITCHIN Alison, KITCHING Stuart, KITJAPIPAT Aries, KITO Ryosuke, KITSON Robert, KITTERINGHAM Carole, KITTO Alison, KITTO Fay, KIZI Con, KJELLBERG Johanna, KJOERLAUG Asle, KJOLLER Heather, KLAF Igor, KLAGES Sarina, KLAIBER Sarah, KLAR Lili, KLAR Hans, KLARE-SCHULZ Mara, KLARENAAR Melinda, KLARENAAR Paul, KLARICH David, KLASS Hilda, KLAUS Otto, KLAUSEN Clem, KLAVINS Felikss, KLCOVAUSKY Jakob, KLEEMEYER Marlene, KLEES Deidre, KLEIBERG Alex, KLEIN Leo, KLEIN Marcus, KLEIN Neville, KLEIN Noel, KLEINIG Danny, KLEIST Peter, KLEORES Paul, KLEPETKO John, KLICIN Colin, KLIMCZAK Olga, KLIMKO Cheryl, KLIMKO Lydia, KLINDWORTH Brian, KLINE Colin, KLINEBERG David, KLINGE Gerd, KLINGER Michelle, KLINGLER Lilian, KLOCZKO Simeon, KLOMP Fleurette, KLOMP Karen, KLOMP Lee, KLONIS Edward, KLOVSTAD John, KLUG Georgie, KLUJIN Kerry, KMENT Milan, KMET Andy, KMET Mick, KNAPP Conrad, KNAPP Michelle, KNEALE Peter, KNEBL Patricia, KNEEBONE Phil, KNEEBONE Scott, KNEEN John, KNEIDER Morgan, KNEIPP Laurie, KNELL Sharon, KNELLER Eric, KNELLS Jorg, KNEVITT Andrew, KNEZEVIC Antonia, KNIBB Ann, KNICK Kelly, KNIFE Tony, KNIGHT Andrea, KNIGHT Anne, KNIGHT Ben, KNIGHT Corrie, KNIGHT Mrs, KNIGHT Chris, KNIGHT Dara, KNIGHT Eden, KNIGHT Geoff, KNIGHT Jeffery, KNIGHT Jocelyn, KNIGHT John, KNIGHT Laurie, KNIGHT Malcolm, KNIGHT Margie, KNIGHT Pearl, KNIGHT Peter, KNIGHT Peter, KNIGHT Ray, KNIGHT Rosemaree, KNIGHT Steve, KNIGHT Stephen, KNIGHT Steve, KNIGHT Suzanne, KNIGHTS Carolyn, KNIGHTS Gerry, KNIGHTS Heather, KNIGHTS Julie, KNIGHTS Terry, KNIGHTS Tracy, KNOCK Knocky, KNOL Vicky, KNORR Heidi, KNOTT Clive, KNOTT Judy, KNOTT Julie, KNOTTS Paul, KNOWLES Craig, KNOWLES Damien, KNOWLES Daryll, KNOWLES Diane, KNOWLES Frank, KNOWLES Geoff, KNOWLES Hermione, KNOWLES Kevin, KNOWLES Mentie, KNOWLES Paul, KNOWLES Phoebe, KNOWLES Roberta, KNOWLES Robert, KNOWLES Rolly, KNOWLES Virginia, KNOX Andrew, KNOX Des, KNOX Fi, KNOX Grahame, KNOX Gwen, KNOX Hamish, KNOX Kai, KNOX Karen, KNOX Keith, KNOX Ken, KNOX Lucy, KNOX Nett, KNOX Sarah, KNOX Stephen, KNOX Jeff, KNOX Will, KNOX Bill, KNUDSEN Ellen, KNUDSEN Gitte, KNUDSEN Hazel, KO Alan, KO Alan, KO Alice, KO Joanne, KO Edward, KO Haengmoon, KO Judy, KO Irene, KO Jung, KO Kwang, KO Dora, KO Young, KOAY Kevin, KOBAYASHI Chie, KOBAYASHI Masato, KOBAYASHI Mayumi, KOBAYASHI Yoshi, KOBAYASHI Yoshie, KOBEISSI Wafa, KOBLAR Branko, KOBLAR Helen, KOBLER Terry, KOBORI Kana, KOBZAR Eugenia, KOBZAR Viatcheslav, KOCH Ann, KOCH Lili, KOCH Veronica, KOCH Clare, KOCH Renata, KOCISZEWSKI Katrina, KOCKEN Madeleine, KOCSIS Andrew, KOEFOED Holger, KOEHLER Steve, KOELLNER Grahame, KOELLNER Mel, KOEN Rachel, KOEN Sarah, KOENIG Arno, KOENIG Wally, KOENIG ZUMAETA Cesar, KOENIGSEDER Ziggy, KOETTIG Chris, KOFOD Charina, KOGLIN Kristy, KOGUS Aviva, KOH Ben, KOH Leonard, KOH Jet, KOH Jonathan, KOH Tang, KOH Teo, KOHLER Jacquie, KOHLER Ladislaus, KOHLER Leanne, KOHLHAGEN Shoko, KOHN Catherine, **KOHN Judy**, KOIKE Yuko, KOIMTSIDIS Anna, KOIRALA Era, KOIZUMI Mihoko, KOK Amy, KOK Thomas, KOK Edsard, KOK Erwin, KOK Fah, KOK Ramona, KOK Jim, KOKAVEC Wally, KOKINIDIS Christina, KOKKE Ange, KOKKORIS Angela, KOLAR Christie, KOLAR MaryAnn, KOLARIK Jenny, KOLAROVA Angela, KOLDING Annegrete, KOLESAR Juraj, KOLEV Bob, KOLEVA Iliana, KOLEVSKI Igor, KOLKMANN Jeffrey, KOLLBERG Bjorn, KOLODZIEJ Brett, KOLODZIEJ Kerrie, KOLODZIEJ Natalie, KOLODZIEJ Richard, KOLOKITAS Helen,

KOLOSKI Lana, KOMAKIS Desi, KOMAR Thomas, KOMATSU Ai, KOMINATOS Angela, KOMONIEWSKI Leonard, KOMOREK Ron, KONAKCI Kerem, KONAKCI Mine, KONDAGARI Manjula, KONDANGI VEERA RAGHAVAN LN, KONDO Kimie, KONEMANN Beck, KONETSCHKA Henry, KONG Frank, KONG Lisa, KONG Louis, KONG Melody, KONG Yant, KONG Tina, KONG Winnie, KONIECZNY Pawel, KONIK Peter, KONIK Val, KONING Hans, KONING Kaye, KONNECKE Arthur, KONNECKE Les, KONNECKE Peter, KONNECKE Sue, KONNYVONG Para, KONNYVONG Tats, KONOPACKI Jessica, KONOPKA Belinda, **KONRADS John**, KONSTANTINOV Orfey, KONSTANTOPOULOS John, KONTELLIS Marianne, KONTOS Georgia, KONZA Ellen, KOO Kin, KOO Marian, KOO Terence, KOON Alice, KOONIN Justin, KOOP Sarah, KOOPER Hil, KOPACZ George, KOPECEK Dasha, KOPETZ Peter, KOPP Darrin, KOPP Jim, KOPPENBERG Elsenoor, KOPPMAN Anthony, KOPPMAN Joseph, KOPPMAN Phillip, KOPTI Norma, KORABELNIKOFF Val, **KORABELNIKOFF Walter**, KORBER John, KORCZYNSKI Ewa, KOREIS Voyen, KORENEFF Ingrid, KORENT Hilda, KOREVAAR Jack, KORHONEN Heikki, KORHONEN Ben, KORI Tomohiko, KORIAKOVA Oksana, KORNBERG Charlie, KORNFELD Frank, KORNHABER Liz, KORNIE Frank, KOROTKI Nina, KORRAS Kaliopi, KORSANOS Effie, KORSCHENKO Louisa, KORSMAN Vanessa, KORT Gina, KORTHS Gunnar, KOSA Peter, KOSAC Angela, KOSARAJU Aravind, KOSASIH Hendra, KOSASIH Shirley, KOSCHARSKY Andrew, KOSH Barrett, KOSH Elaine, KOSHELEVA Julia, KOSHKARIAN Nerses, KOSINAR Martin, KOSKELAINEN Trudi, KOSKY Marg, KOSKY Marcel, KOSMALA James, KOSMAN Donnah, KOSPARTOV Nikolas, KOSSERIS Alana, KOSTADINOVA-SHISHKOV Tina, KOSTALAS Rachel, KOSTELLIS Petros, KOSTEN John, KOSTENKO Alex, KOSTER Judith, KOSTER Louise, KOSTER Natalie, KOSTIAINEN Raimo, KOTAKA Shunya, KOTEFF Narelle, KOTEK Jen, KOTEL Danny, KOTEVSKA Svetlana, KOTEVSKI Petre, KOTHANDARAMAN Ramani, KOTLAR Isabella, KOTOWSKI John, KOTRALA Suman, KOTSIKAS Mark, KOTSIOPOULOS Poppy, KOTSOMITIS Patricia, KOTWAL Sharad, KOTYCHEVA Irina, KOTZ Deborah, KOTZE Nerina, KOTZE Tracy, KOUFOS Anne, KOUKIDES Sophie, KOUNALAKI Eleni, KOUREAS Myra, KOUTNIK Howard, KOUTOULLAS Kellie, KOUTSOUBOS Connie, KOUTTS Ann, KOUTTS Georgia, KOUVATAS Cynthia, KOUVELAS John, KOVAC Emina, KOVAC Maria, KOVAC Steve, KOVACEVIC Kathee, KOVACEVIC Katarina, KOVACIC Natasha, KOVACICEK John, KOVACS Andy, KOVACS Barbara, KOVACS George, KOVACS George, KOVACS Kriszta, KOVACS Michael, KOVACS Susan, KOVALEVSKY Larry, KOVALOFF Barbara, KOVALOFF Gemma, KOWALENKO Leonie, KOWALUK Shelley, KOZAITIS Pk, KOZAK Vita, KOZIWODA Shane, KOZLOWSKI Zaneta, KOZNIECZNY Pawel, KRAAL Marlene, KRAAL JP Malcolm, KRADENIAN Anita, KRAFT Gunter, KRAGH Kel, KRAJ-KRAJEWSKI Maya, KRAJEWSKI Lukas, KRALJEVIC Dominik, KRAMEL Peter, KRAMER Tom, KRAMER-MAIER Jacqueline, KRANEN Judy, KRANENBURG Alex, KRANENBURG Carol, KRANENBURG Tanya, KRASS Janette, KRASSOI Maryanne, KRASSOVSKAIA Natalia, KRASSOVSKY Mick, KRASTEV Mario, KRASTEV Gina, KRATIUK Adam, KRATS Josephine, KRATTLI Simon, KRAUCE Jim, KRAUS Dan, KRAUS Eugene, **KRAUS Tania**, KRAUSE Christoph, KRAUSE Lauren, KRAUSE Martin, KRAUSMANN Annette, KRAUTMAN Ingrid, KREISMANIS Mara, KREMER Meg, KREMER Jennifer, KREMLIDIS Peter, KREMP Chris, KRESKAY Craig, KRESTOVSKY Lana, KRETCHMANN Lynda, KRETI Steven, KRETSCHMER Claudia, KRIAUZA Algis, KRIEDEMAN Pat, KRIEGER Kraig, KRIKETOS Dianne, KRIKETOS Voula, KRIKORIAN Vatche, KRIPALANI Akshay, KRISENTHAL Leah, KRISENTHAL Vicki, KRISHNA Rani, KRISHNA Cynthia, KRISHNA Kumar, KRISHNA Venu, KRISHNADAS Mahesh, KRISHNARAJAH Thambi, KRISNA YANTI Nadya, KRISNANDANI O tovana, KRISTAKOVA Zuz, KRISTALY Melinda, KRISTIAN Frank, KRISTIAN Margaret, KRISTIANTO Kris, KRIVANEK Darius, KRIZANOVIC Steve, KRLEVSKI Vesna, KROCHMALIK Annette, KROENHERT Greg, KROGH Trish, KROLKE Sonia, KROLL-SIMMUL Tiiu, KRONBERG Anastazia, KRONEMBERG Dwight, KROP Maryke, KROP Nancy, KROPF Oliver, KROSLAKOVA Katarina, KRSTICEVIC Mike, KRSTIN Nada, KRUBALLY Makka, KRUCKEMEYER Thomas, KRUG Silke, KRUGER Erika, KRUGER Hazel, KRUGER Joanne, KRUIJER Emma, KRUMINS Andrew, KRUNICH Rosemary, KRUPP Stefanie, KRUSE Freddy, KRUSE Katrina, KRUZINS Ed, KRUZINS Gillian, KRYMOVA Julia, KSENDZOVSKA Roksana, KU Allen, KU Hyo, KU Michael, KU Ester, KU Thomas, KU Veronica, KUAH Kim-Boo, KUAN Jiew Jin, KUAN Robert, KUBALCIK Milos, KUCHI Noriko, KUEHNER Geoff, KUENZEL Wieland, KUGATHASAN Naga, KUIPER Bernie, KUIPER Tina, KUIPERS Richard, KUITERS Rhonda, KUKOLJA Kristina, KUKRKA Mira, KULA-LEVY Seru, KULAKOFF Kathy, KULATUNGE Kumara, KULCHYCKI Eddy, KULINITSCH Nathan, KULLIK Wolfgang, KUMAR Jeevesh, KUMAR Kris, KUMAR Praveen, KUMAR Rajeev, KUMAR Kumar, KUMAR Ram, KUMAR Sarjit, KUMAR Savita, KUMAR Suba, KUMARALINGAM Shan, KUMARALINGAM Shanmugalingam, KUMARASINGHE Uttara, KUMCEVSKI Steve, KUMMERFELD Sarah, KUMPEL Hans, KUMRI Nora, KUNCZE Fred, KUND Maureen, KUNDATT James, KUNDE Cathy, KUNDE Christian, KUNDRUS-LITTLE Nadja, KUNDRUSLITTLE Nikki, KUNDU Kirit, KUNDU Tapan, KUNG Andrew, KUNG Eugene, KUNJO-KOKA Joyce, KUNOVEC Stan, KUNST Wendy, KUNSTANTINOV Orfey, KUNTZ Rebecca, KUNTZ Rozenn, KUNZ Anni, KUNZ Anneke, KUNZ Roberto, KUNZ Thomas, KUNZEL Wieland, KUNZELMANN Anna, KUO Angela, KUO Hsiu-Fen, KUOK Anna, KUPELIAN Liz, KUR Sandra, KURANGIL Irem, KURESHI Zahiruddin, KURIAN Mat, KURNIA Jeanette, KURNIAWAN Ferry, KURP Michelle, KURRLE Susan, KURT Sirma, KURTZ Megan, KURTZ Nev, KURUKULASURIYA Shanti, KURUKULASURIYA Nadia, KURUWITAGE-SILVA Shanthi, KUSABS Bill, KUSANO Naomi, KUSCHERT Trevor, KUSILEK Rebecca, KUSLLEK Elisabeth, KUSMANTO Utomo, KUSMIREK Mary, KUSNADI Edy, KUSNADI Steven, KUSS Adam, KUSTEDJO Hansen, KUSTER Nick, KUSTIAWAN Irwan, KUSTRA Frank, KUSTREBA Joanne, KUSUMA Ovyanty, KUTSCHEWSKI Christina, KUWAJIMA Natalie, KUYPERS Aziza, KUYULULU Warren, KUYYAMUDI Bhanu, KUZEK Andrew, KUZIOW Marie, KVANLI Benjamin, KVISLE Odd, KWA Ban-Keat, KWAAN Alex, KWAK Byung, KWAK Hyesun, KWAK In, KWAK Rira, KWAKWA Martin, KWAN Angela, KWAN Cecilia, KWAN Jodie, KWAN Louis, KWAN Louis, KWAN Soo, KWAN Tracey, KWANG Florence, KWEE Jensen, KWIATKOWSKA Margaret, KWIATKOWSKI Andrew, KWIATKOWSKI Aneta, KWIATKOWSKI Arek, KWIATKOWSKI Basia, KWOK Andrew, KWOK Anthony, KWOK Ben, KWOK Stephen, KWOK Lawson, KWOK Hiu, KWOK James, KWOK Joseph, KWOK Kenneth, KWOK Samuel, KWOK Sean, KWOK Wilson, KWOK Ying, KWON Grace, KWON Jong, KWON Andrew, KWON O'Chul, KWON Sodam, KWON Su, KWON Sun, KWONG Christopher, KWONG Fung, KWONG Patrick, KWONG Connie, KYD Allan, KYIET Lisa, KYLE Ian, KYLE Kyle, KYNOCH Cathy, KYOONG Anthony, KYOTANI Noriko, KYOUNG HEE Kim, KYPRIOTIS Anna, KYPRIOTIS Tim, KYRIACOU Andrew, KYRIACOU Helen, KYRIAKIDIS Nektaria, KYRIAKOPOULOS Martha, KYRIAZIS John, KYSA Tanya, KYSELOVA Natasha, KYTE-POWELL Craig, KYTZIA Regina, KYUSOJIN Coco.

L

LA Johnny, LA Nancy, LA Minh, LA Susan, LA BARRIE George, LA FERLA Susan, LA FONTAINE Graeme, LA FORCE Suen, LA MOTTA Jacinta, LA MOTTA Nick, LA ROCCA Tina, LA SCALA Nino, LA SPINA Lianna, LA TELLA Carla, LA TORRACA Roxanne, LAAJOKI Jaakko, LAAPER Marlies, LAAPER Niels, LABBOZZETTA Francesca, LABELLE Francis, LABOUR Louis, LAC Khuong, LACE Kim, LACE Vince, LACEY Leo, LACEY Alfred, LACEY Jamie, LACEY Jim, LACEY Nicole, LACEY Ron, LACEY Warwick, LACH Stephane, LACHMAIYA Vio, LACIN Ozan, LACK Brian, LACK Bruce, LACKEY Helen, LACKEY Ian, LACKEY John, LACKEY Wendy, LACKMANN Marisa, LACONI James, LACORCIA Michael, LACY Jeanette, LADANCHUK Lesley, LADD Penny, LADD Vonny, LADEWIG Allan, LADEWIG Rhonda, LAFFERTY Bill, LAFFIN Shereen, LAGANA Joseph, LAGERCHE Dee, LAGERLOW Terry, LAGINESTRA Fay, LAGOS Derani, LAGOS Maria, LAGOUDAKIS Maria, LAGUMBAY Randy, LAHER Goolam, LAHOUD Harry, LAHOUD Muna, LAI Amy, LAI Andrew, LAI Anthony, LAI Bento, LAI Donald, LAI Grace, LAI Kelvin, LAI Kellie, LAI Kevin, LAI Kevin, LAI Ricky, LAI Raymond, LAI Newton, LAI Paulo, LAI Kim, LAI Peter, LAI Rosalyn, LAI

Seng, LAI Sherman, LAI Sunny, LAI Steve, LAI Weslie, LAI Winifred, LAI Chris, LAI Darius, LAIDLAW Judy, LAIDLER Alison, LAINE Tuula, LAING Bev, LAING Rebecca, LAING Rod, LAING Shane, LAIRD Adele, LAIRD Kristin, LAIRD Michael, LAIRD Sue, LAIS Diana, LAK Anton, LAKE Aaron, LAKE Beverley, LAKE Nichola, LAKE Richard, LAKE Teleise, LAKHANI Preeya, LAKICEVIC Boris, LAKONAIVALU Wesley, LAKSANA Ratna, LAKSHMAN Asha, LAL Ravi, LAL Ron, LAL Slash, LALOR Michael, LALOR Ron, LALORPRIOR Bobbie, LAM Ada, LAM Andy, LAM Huyen, LAM Candy, LAM Kevin, LAM Leo, LAM Deborah, LAM Dennis, LAM Dominique, LAM Edmond, LAM Edward, LAM Eric, LAM Erin, LAM Esther, LAM Fan, LAM Gordon, LAM Henry, LAM Ho, LAM Hung, LAM Irene, LAM Justin, LAM Stephanie, LAM Candy, LAM Katharine, LAM Luong, LAM Lynda, LAM Vera, LAM Mark, LAM Michelle, LAM Nicholas, LAM Pauline, LAM Philip, LAM Kitty, LAM Purples, LAM Quan, LAM Rita, LAM Roselind, LAM Stephen, LAM Stephen, LAM Sue, LAM Susan, LAM Kim, LAM Tony, LAM Tuyet, LAM Van, LAM Vincent, LAM Yin, LAM SAM Cecillia, LAM SAM Eva, LAMA Raph, LAMARO Penny, LAMB Neville, LAMB Barbara, LAMB Claudia, LAMB Ian, LAMB Max, LAMB Merle, LAMBECK Marty, LAMBERT Adrian, LAMBERT Ashley, LAMBERT Tracey, LAMBERT Gordon, LAMBERT Hans, LAMBERT Helen, LAMBERT Jan, LAMBERT Joanne, LAMBERT Julia, LAMBERT Ken, LAMBERT Kenneth, LAMBERT Laurene, LAMBERT Margaret, LAMBERT Matthew, LAMBERT Raymond, LAMBERT Robyn, LAMBERT Sharyn, LAMBERT Tom, LAMBERT Wal, LAMBERT-FANTINI Helen, LAMBI Maria, LAMBLEY Kerry, LAMBORN Robert, LAMBROGLOU Connie, LAMEY Jen, LAMEY Lin, LAMEY Mick, LAMMERTS Desiree, LAMMEY Justine, LAMOND Fiona, LAMOND Greg, LAMOND Peter, LAMOND Phil, LAMONT Barry, LAMONT Bazza, LAMONT Dorothy, LAMONT Greg, LAMPARD Keri, LAMPHERE Reid, LAMPINEN Kaisa, LAMPL Cveta, LAMPRET Frank, LAMPRET Kathleen, LAMPRET Renee, LAMPSHIRE Karina, LAN Faye, LAN KAM Brad, LANCASTER Daniel, LANCASTER David, LANCASTER Heidi, LANCASTER Michael, LANCASTER Terry, LANCE FOLDEN Debra, LANCELEY Mike, LANCTOT Roby, LAND Carol-Anne, LAND Simon, LAND Victoria, LANDBECK Roger, LANDER Phillip, LANDERS Stephen, LANDON Gerard, LANDON Kevin, LANDON Rebecca, LANDOR David, LANDOR Denise, LANDOR Jenni, LANDRIGAN Marc, LANDSTRA Sonia, LANDY Al, LANDY Fiona, LANE Brendan, LANE Cheryl, LANE Helen, **LANE Jackie**, LANE Janice, LANE Jason, LANE Jason, LANE Jenny, LANE Leanne, LANE Mark, LANE Teresa, LANE Trish, LANE Phil, LANE Bec, LANE Robby, LANE Samuel, LANE Tim, LANEY Ian, LANEY Lisa, LANG Bruce, LANG Carole, LANG Cathy, LANG Debbie, LANG Debbie, LANG Des, LANG Elizabeth, LANG Gerri, LANG Jack, LANG Jan, LANG Jeff, LANGAN Gerard, LANGBEIN Lyn, LANGBEIN Sue, LANGBORNE John, LANGBRIDGE Eileen, LANGBY Peter, LANGDON Allison, LANGDON Julie, LANGDON Mark, LANGDON Phil, LANGDON Taryn, LANGE Kirsten, LANGE Sven, LANGENBERG Paul, LANGENEGGER Esther, LANGEVELD Marilyn, LANGEVOORT Marina, LANGFIELD Jan, LANGFORD Michele, LANGFORD Samantha, LANGFORD-BROWN Ian, LANGFORD-BROWN Jean, LANGFORD-BROWN Ross, LANGHANS Ron, LANGINS Larry, LANGLEY Cynthia, LANGLEY Eileen, LANGLEY Georgie, LANGLEY John, LANGLEY Michelle, LANGLEY Peter, LANGLOIS John, LANGRIDGE Jane, LANGRIDGE Narelle, LANGRIDGE Robert, LANGSHAW Brad, LANGTHORNE Peter, LANGTON Anita, LANGTON Steve, LANGTON Wendy, LANGWORTHY Alex, LANGWORTHY Ros, LANHAM Dianne, LANHAM Geoff, LANIGAN Barry, LANIGAN Margaret, LANIGAN Margaret, LANIGAN Petina, LANKSHEAR Scott, LANNAN Tony, LANSDOWN Peggy, LANSDOWN Trevor, LANSDOWN Vicky, LANSDOWNE Edward, LANSDOWNE Kath, LANTAY Nat, LANTE Roger, LANTO Saripoden, LANTS Viv, LANYON David, LANYON Megan, LANYON Sandra, LANZA Rosie, LANZONI Igor, LAO Anna, LAOSIRISERICHON Vichanee, LAPIERRE Fabrice, LAPINSKIMARGOVSKY Simona, LAPPAN Elke, LAPSHINOFF Ean, LAPSLEY Barbara, LARBALESTIER Frank, LARDEN Mal, LARDNER Alice, LARDNER Philip, LARGE Geoff, LARGE Ian, LARGE James, LARGE Norm, LARIA Mimma, LARK Karen, LARKIN Annabelle, LARKIN Cathy, LARKIN Col, **LARKIN Di**, LARKIN Garry, LARKIN Matt, LARKIN Neville, LARKIN Steve, LARKINS Peter, LARKINS Steve, LARKMAN Tracy, LARME John, LARNACH Clive, LAROUX Maxwell, **LARR Marcia**, LARSEN Ian, LARSEN Jeff, LARSEN Julie, LARSEN Suzanne, LARSSEN Astrid, LARTER Brian, LARVEN Erin, LARVEN John, LAS VEGAS Frederick, LASCELLES Wendy, LASH John, LASINKER Sravan, LASKA Wade, LASLETT Liz, LASPATZIS Antonia, LASSES Bill, LASSITER Denise, LASSO Gladys, LAST Dorothy, LAST Graeme, LAST Jack, LAST Jim, LAST Kirsty, LATA Rukeshma, LATCHMAN Latchman, LATE Alyssa, LATELLA Jane, LATHAM Clifford, LATHAM Frank, LATHAM Franz, LATHAM Jean, LATHAM Kate, LATHAM Linda, LATHERON Philip, LATHOUROS Marie, LATIF Adam, LATIF Nadeene, LATIF Wafik, LATIMER David, LATIMER Del, LATIMER Joanne, LATIMER Gordon, LATIMER Marie, LATIMER Mark, LATIMORE Liri, LATINO Rosanna, LATKICH Michael, LATKICH Tina, LATONA Sally, LATORRE-UGARTE Pablo, LATTA Robert, LATTA Warwick, LATTARI Liana, LATTER Ian, LATTER Kathie, LATTOUF Jason, LATTOUF Joseph, LAU Andy, LAU Andrew, LAU Belinda, LAU Ben, LAU Catherine, LAU Christine, LAU John, LAU Elim, LAU Frank, LAU Gloria, LAU Helen, LAU Janet, LA U Jennifer, LAU Joanne, LAU Joey, LAU Jonathan, LAU Juliet, LAU Kathleen, LAU Kwanman, LAU Martin, LAU Mark, LAU Mei, LAU Yvonne, LAU Michael, LAU Monica, LAU Nancy, LAU Natasha, LAU Nicholas, LAU Oliver, LAU Raymond, LAU Richard, LAU Roslyn, LAU Sam, LAU Peter, LAU William, LAU Terence, LAU Yee, LAU Samuel, LAU Alex, LAUBSCHER Luzanne, LAUCHT Willi, LAUDER Frank, LAUER Karen, LAUGHLAN Kyleigh, LAUGHLIN Bruce, LAUGHLIN Bruce, LAUGHLIN Sharon, LAUGHTON Cheryl, LAUGHTON Diana, LAUGHTON Dot, LAUGHTON Bob, LAUMUA Maryanne, LAUMUA Masalo, LAUNDERS David, LAUNDRY Kerrie, LAURA Laura, LAURANS Philippe, LAURENCE Jo, LAURENCE Judith, LAURENCE Jim, LAURIE Jim, LAURIE Debbie, LAURIE Emma, LAURIE MELISSA Richardson, LAURSEN Dave, LAUS Luke, LAUTERBACH Anne, LAUW Xiushan, LAUZON Majorie, LAVECKY George, LAVEE Helen, LAVELLE Brad, LAVENDER Dennis, LAVENDER Diane, LAVENDER Gladys, LAVER Brenton, LAVER Francis, LAVER Joel, LAVERACK John, LAVERCOMBE Simon, LAVERS Phyllis, LAVERTY Rebecca, LAVERTY Sharron, LAVERY Adam, LAVETA Andrea, LAVILLE Julie, LAVIN Gwen, LAVING Marilyn, LAVIS Andrea, LAVIS Carol, LAVOIE Mark, LAVORATO Joseph, LAVRENCIC Tony, LAVU Sai, LAW Adriana, LAW Alan, LAW Annie, LAW Michael, LAW Jeni, LAW Peter, LAW Stan, LAW Vivian, LAW Jacky, LAWANDOS Joy, LAWES Coral, LAWES Keith, LAWLER Brian, LAWLER Carolyn, LAWLER Dawn, LAWLER Judy, LAWLER Dean, LAWLER Michael, LAWLESS Kieran, LAWLOR Brian, LAWLOR Maree, LAWN Aub, LAWRANCE Neville, LAWRANCE Robert, LAWRENCE Angela, LAWRENCE Brian, LAWRENCE Christine, LAWRENCE Claire, LAWRENCE Darren, LAWRENCE David, LAWRENCE Lawrie, LAWRENCE David, LAWRENCE Gary, LAWRENCE Gleniss, LAWRENCE Jacqui, LAWRENCE Tim, LAWRENCE Josh, LAWRENCE Karin, LAWRENCE Kate, LAWRENCE Katie, LAWRENCE Lalanthi, LAWRENCE Laurie, LAWRENCE Lee-Anne, LAWRENCE Penelope, LAWRENCE Peta, LAWRENCE Prue, LAWRENCE Robin, LAWRENCE Rosalie, LAWRENCE Sarah, LAWRENCE Shane, LAWRENCE Stuart, LAWRENSON Lawrie, LAWRENTSCHUK Nathan, LAWREY Jacinta, LAWRIE Jo, LAWRIE Julia, LAWRIE Lisa, LAWRIE Bob, LAWRIE Roy, LAWRY Kris, LAWS Adam, LAWS Mary, LAWS Rob, LAWS Ron, LAWSON Aaron, LAWSON Denice, LAWSON Jenny, LAWSON Jill, LAWSON Leigh, LAWSON Lesley, LAWSON Malcolm, LAWSON Margaret, LAWSON Renee, LAWSON Roberta, LAWSON Robb, LAWSON Bob, LAWSON Sandra, LAWSON Shane, LAWSON Steve, LAWSON Stephanie, LAWSON Susan, LAWSON Tracey, LAWSON Tristan, LAWSON Yuki, LAWTHER Jennifer, LAWTHER Margaret, LAWTHER Tricia, LAWTHER Dave, LAWTON Bob, LAWTON Scott, LAWTON-WADE Dick, LAXTON MaryLouise, LAY Aaron, LAY Adolfo, LAY Edna, LAY Fernando, LAY Filomena, LAY Joanne, LAY Rose, LAY Anthony, LAYCOCK Ken, LAYCOCK Nancy, LAYTON Alan, LAYTON Kathleen, LAYZELL Mary, LAZAR Rose, LAZAR

Bill, LAZAREVIC Nada, LAZENBY Suzanne, LAZER Carol, LAZICH Alec, LAZORYZAK Lynette, LAZZARINI Robert, LE Anh, LE Anthony, LE Helen, LE Cathy, LE Duy, LE David, LE Hung, LE Inh, LE Lan-Hoa, LE Manle, LE Margaret, LE Andy, LE Nha, LE Peter, LE Tram, LE Quang, LE Tung, LE Victor, LE Vietlong, LE William, LE BAS Geoff, LE BOT Pierre, LE BOURDONNEC Kevin, LE BRETON Maggie, LE CLAIRE Laurie, LE CLERCQ Matthew, LE CLERCQ Shirley, LE CLERCQ Wal, LE COMTE Sally, LE GUEN Kerrie, LE GUEN Aniele, LE MARSENY Geoff, LE MOTTEE John, LE PAGE Ailsa, LE POER TRENCH Marcus, LE VESCONTE Michael, LEA Justine, LEA Steve, LEACH Anthea, LEACH Grace, LEACH Bob, LEACH Jen, LEACH Peta, LEACH Peter, LEADBITTER Michael, LEADER Alwyn, LEADER Anne, LEADER Keith, LEADER Wayne, LEAH Andrew, LEAH Bruce, LEAH Michael, LEAHEY Gary, LEAHY Elizabeth, LEAHY Geoff, LEAHY June, LEAHY Lily, LEAHY Sue, LEAKE Les, LEAN Craig, LEAN Diana, LEANEY Anthony, LEANG Amyl, LEANNE Johnson, LEARD Fiona, LEARHINAN Simon, LEARMONT Don, LEARMONT Joan, **LEARMONTH Jim**, LEARMONTH Judith, LEARNIHAN Mike, LEARY Anthony, LEARY Geoff, LEATHBRIDGE Bill, LEATHLEY David, LEATHLEY Forde, LEAVATT-BROWN Barry, LEAVER Allan, LEBEDEW Walter, LEBEUF Sylvain, LEBNAN Suzanne, LEBRETON Wendy, LEBRUN Ian, LECHER Geoffrey, LECHMINKA Tura, LECKIE Trish, LECKNING Clifford, LECLERC Sebastien, LECLERCQ Muriel, LEDBURY Sean, LEDDICK Liesa, LEDDY Adam, LEDDY Margaret, LEDERLE Melanie, LEDET Delphine, LEDGER Anne, LEDGER Charles, LEDGER Josh, LEDINGHAM Christine, LEDINIC Rose, LEDITSCHKE Fred, LEDO Kate, LEDWIDGE Ben, LEDWIDGE Donn, LEE Adrian, LEE Aerick, LEE Akiko, LEE Alexandra, LEE Alice, LEE Amy, LEE Andrew, LEE Annie, LEE Anne, LEE Anthony, LEE Arianne, LEE Arthur, LEE Astin, LEE Astrid, LEE Barbara, LEE Beckie, LEE Jules, LEE Boris, LEE Bryce, LEE Cameron, LEE Cameron, LEE Carol, LEE Cathie, LEE Catharine, LEE Catherine, LEE Celina, LEE Che, LEE Lee, LEE Jeffrey, LEE Chie-a, LEE Christine, LEE Christina, LEE Chris, LEE Ben, LEE Clive, LEE Colin, LEE Colette, LEE David, LEE David, LEE David, LEE Denise, LEE Don, LEE Tommy, LEE Donald, LEE Doreen, LEE Doreen, LEE Eddie, LEE Edward, LEE Ellen, LEE Eric, LEE Estelle, LEE Stephanie, LEE Andrea, LEE Faye, LEE Fjelda, LEE Florence, LEE Freda, LEE Fung, LEE Fung, LEE Lee, LEE Gary, LEE Garry, LEE Gene, LEE Gordon, LEE Gordon, LEE Grace, LEE Graham, LEE Mike, LEE Hae-Young, LEE Angela, LEE Heather, LEE Victor, LEE Hee, LEE Helen, LEE Jenny, LEE HungHui, LEE Hyeri, LEE Julianna, LEE Hyun, LEE Hyunji, LEE Caritas, LEE Igor, LEE Ivy, LEE Jacky, LEE Jack, LEE Joseph, LEE Janelle, LEE Jenny, LEE JeongHwan, LEE Jessica, LEE Jess, LEE Jessica, LEE Sun, LEE Teresa, LEE Ji, LEE Ji-Hwan, LEE Ji-hye, LEE Jin, LEE Jinhwan, LEE Jim, LEE Ryan, LEE Joanna, LEE Joel, LEE John, LEE John, LEE John, LEE Judith, LEE Judi, LEE Julianna, LEE John, LEE Jun, LEE Jenny, LEE Kenny, LEE Karyan, LEE Karen, LEE Kathryn, LEE Katrina, LEE Kathleen, LEE Kee, LEE Kerrie, LEE Keumran, LEE Kevin, LEE Alex, LEE Kim, LEE Eric, LEE King, LEE Kristy, LEE Eiston, LEE Kylie, LEE Christina, LEE Sharon, LEE KyungHee, LEE Kyung, LEE Laurence, LEE Leticia, LEE Linda, LEE Lisa, LEE Lok, LEE Loviner, LEE Gloria, LEE Maggie, LEE Marie, LEE May, LEE Jenny, LEE Mei, LEE Mei-Ching, LEE Melissa, LEE Michael, LEE Mike, LEE Mike, LEE Michelle, LEE Myung, LEE Narelle, LEE Steve, LEE Nick, LEE Nick, LEE Nichole, LEE Mui, LEE Ok, LEE Patricia, LEE PeiYu, LEE Peter, LEE Peta, LEE Phil, LEE Ray, LEE Richard, LEE Robert, LEE Robert, LEE Robert, LEE Robert, LEE Robert, LEE Ronald, LEE Rose, LEE Ruth, LEE Sang, LEE Sarah, LEE Susanna, LEE Sean, LEE Seeyan, LEE Janet, LEE Serena, LEE Seung-Hyun, LEE Seung, LEE Seung, LEE Shue, LEE Siew, LEE Simon, LEE Mary, LEE Stephen, LEE Su, LEE Sunny, LEE Susan, LEE Sue, LEE Sharon, LEE Tamara, LEE Tat, LEE Tedman, LEE Terry, LEE Terry, LEE Theresa, LEE Thong, LEE Tien, LEE Tim, LEE Tony, LEE Trisco, LEE Vanessa, LEE Veronica, LEE Vincent, LEE Virginia, LEE Wen-Kai, LEE Wendy, LEE Wendy, LEE William, LEE Yat, LEE Belinda, LEE Susana, LEE Young, LEE Young, LEE Gwyneth, LEE Karen, LEE Yvonne, LEE Hee, LEE Zenaida, LEE-BERNSTEIN Ron, LEECE Soph, LEECH Barbara, LEECH Fiona, LEECH Leonie, LEECHBURCH AUWERS Jenny, LEEDEN Katharine, LEEDEN Trevor, LEEDER Louise, LEEDER Ross, LEEDER Patricia, LEEDHAM Dion, LEEDHAM Leon, LEEDING Andrew, LEEMBRUGGEN Terri-Ann, LEEMEN Jill, LEEMEN Richard, LEEMING Rhonda, LEENDERS Peter, LEEPER Patricia, LEES Belinda, LEES Brett, LEES Colin, LEES Daniel, LEES Graham, LEES Greg, LEES Janice, LEES Jenny, LEES Pip, LEES Robyn, LEES Rod, LEESON Ben, LEESON Neryl, LEFEBVRE Justin, LEFFEL Bo, LEFLER Carey, LEGAL Hans, LEGARTEJA Nida, LEGASSICK Danielle, LEGAZ Peter, LEGER Mike, LEGG Jess, LEGG Kate, LEGGATT Cheryl-Ann, LEGGATT Rosemary, LEGGE Robin, LEGGETT Eric, LEGGO Joanne, LEGOWO Theo, LEGRAND Lyn, LEGRAND Pierre, LEHANE Lori, LEHMACHER Honor, LEHMAN John, LEHMANN Carole, LEHMANN John, LEHMANN Noel, LEHMANN Rose, LEHMANN Ursula, LEHOCZKY John, LEHR Elis, LEHRLE Alan, LEHRLE Barbara, LEHRLE Ric, LEI Paul, LEICESTER Robyn, LEICH Joseph, LEIDICH Gail, LEIFELS Mandy, LEIGH David, LEIGH Cindy, LEIGH Russell, LEIGHTON Elliot, LEIGHTON Josh, LEIGHTON Lois, LEIGHTON Sylvia, LEILUA Henrietta, LEINS Jim, LEIPOLD Vera, LEISER Bernadette, LEISHMAN Don, LEISHMAN Joan, LEISHMAN Kath, LEISHMAN Rob, LEISTNER Achim, LEITCH Cathy, LEITCH Jean, LEITCH Margaret, LEITCH Nicky, LEITCH Simon, LEITER Beverley, LEJINS Judy, LEJUS Olivier, LELBOFF Jillian, LELE Vinoo, LEMAIR Georgina, LEMAIRE Philip, LEMAITRE Philippe, LEMBACH Janet, LEMERAY Andre, LEMIN Trish, LEMKE Carmel, LEMME Maria, LEMMON Fiona, LEMOH Margaret, LEMON George, LEMON-SCOTT Candice, LEMOS Lurdes, LEMUS CARDONA Carmen, LENANE Dora, LENART Mary, LENARTIC Branko, LENDON Donna, LENE Sam, LENEHAN Annette, LENEHAN Ann, LENEHAN John, LENEHAN Trish, LENEHAN Paul, LENNAN John, LENNARD John, LENNE Brydan, LENNEY Val, LENNIE Walter, LENNON Diane, LENNON Jack, LENNON Judy, LENNON Judy, LENNON Katie, LENNON Kevin, LENNON Leo, LENNON Merv, LENNON Murray, LENNON Ray, LENNON Tai, LENNOX Jenny, LENNOX John, LENNOX Kevin, LENNOX Terri, LENON Joy, LENON Bob, LENTERN Kerry, LENTIN Dinaaz, LENTJES Chris, LENTJES Simon, LENTON Allen, LENTON Heather, LENTON Rob, LENZ Christopher, LENZO Tina, LEO Kenneth, LEO Robyn, LEON Gabby, LEONARD Don, LEONARD Nick, LEONARD Robin, LEONARD Sheila, LEONARDI Boediono, LEONARDS Robert, LEONE John, LEONELLO Heather, LEONG Benjamin, LEONG Freda, LEONG Esther, LEONG Nathan, LEONG Soon, LEONG Stanley, LEONG Sui, LEONG Wayne, LEONG Ming, LEONI Mark, LEOO Annie, LEOTA Leah, LEOUNAKIS Manny, LEOW Jo, LEPAGE Yvette, LEPAUX Corinne, LEPRINCE Elizabeth, LERKYINDEE Tippy, LEROY Bert, LESER Astrid, LESKE Amanda, LESLIE Albert, LESLIE Alice, LESLIE Greg, LESLIE Madeline, LESLIE Melissa, LESLIE Robbie, LESLIE Sam, LESLIE Steve, LESLIE Willie, LESLIGHT Ken, LESSARD Karine, LESSEY Robbie, LESSI Alana, LESTER Charlene, LETHAM Melissa, LETHEBY Al, LETHORN Perry, LETSON Kate, LETTAU Jennifer, LETTE Anneke, LETTE Janine, **LETTE Krys**, LEUNG Alan, LEUNG Andrew, LEUNG Ben, LEUNG Celina, LEUNG Charles, LEUNG Chein, LEUNG Simon, LEUNG Chi, LEUNG Ching, LEUNG Colin, LEUNG Colin, LEUNG Condy, LEUNG Denise, LEUNG Emily, LEUNG Florence, LEUNG Fred, LEUNG Ida, LEUNG Hon, LEUNG Jason, LEUNG Jeremy, LEUNG Joanna, LEUNG Joyce, LEUNG Ka, LEUNG Lai, LEUNG Luke, LEUNG Lydia, LEUNG Mark, LEUNG May, LEUNG Michael, LEUNG Pak, LEUNG Perlon, LEUNG Susanah, LEUNG Teresa, LEUNG Wendy, LEUNG Victor, LEUNG Vincent, LEUNG Wendy, LEUNG Yan, LEUNG Yuen, LEUNIG Geoff, LEUSDEN Brenda, LEUTHEN Jake, LEVANTROSSER Bill, LEVENE Amanda, LEVER Gwen, LEVER Kevin, LEVER Skye, LEVERTON Michael, LEVES Ian, LEVESCONTE James, LEVETT Kit, LEVIDO Kathryn, LEVIN Tuulikki, LEVIN Richard, LEVIN Sara, LEVIN Taryn, LEVINE Jason, LEVINE Judith, LEVIS Lou, LEVITIN Stan, LEVY Francois, LEVY Kevin, LEVY Malcolm, LEVY Suzanna, LEW Cecilia, LEW Peter, LEW-FATT Anita, LEW-FATT Seanne, LEWES Kris, LEWIN Mark, LEWINGTON Erin, LEWINSKI Antoni, LEWIS Alan, LEWIS Amanda, LEWIS Anna, LEWIS Anne, LEWIS Basil, LEWIS Benjamin, LEWIS Betty, LEWIS Bohdi, LEWIS Byron, LEWIS Carole, LEWIS Carli, LEWIS Charles, LEWIS Charles, LEWIS Darryl, LEWIS David, LEWIS David, LEWIS David, LEWIS Denise, LEWIS Doug, LEWIS Barrie, LEWIS Elise, LEWIS Felicity, LEWIS Gary, LEWIS Glen, LEWIS Gloria, LEWIS Grant, LEWIS Heidi,

LEWIS Jim, LEWIS Jane, LEWIS Jennifer, LEWIS John, LEWIS John, LEWIS Julie, LEWIS June, LEWIS Kanthi, LEWIS Kathryn, LEWIS Kev, LEWIS Leonne, LEWIS Mark, LEWIS Marie, LEWIS Matt, LEWIS Matthew, LEWIS Michelle,LEWIS Michael, LEWIS Moyra, LEWIS Neil, LEWIS Paul, LEWIS Peter, LEWIS Peter, LEWIS Phil, LEWIS Rae, LEWIS Robyn, LEWIS Bob, LEWIS Sandy, LEWIS Sean, LEWIS Shane, LEWIS Sylvia, LEWIS Terry, LEWIS Tracey, LEYENAAR Laurina, LEYGO Philip, LEYS Julie, LI Andrew, LI Bernard, LI Clare, LI Dan, LI Edward, LI Eric, LI Linda, LI Fiona, LI Gen, LI George, LI Tom, LI James, LI Ho, LI Jackie, LI Jane, LI Jenny, LI John, LI Judy, LI Carmen, LI Kevin, LI Irene, LI Lisa, LI Jessica, LI Michael, LI Ming, LI Snowave, LI Lily, LI Ping, LI Roger, LI Shu, LI Shujuan, LI Steven, LI Rossatti, LI Wei, LI Solomon, LI Eileen, LI Xiaogang, LI Xiao, LI Alan, LI Xuan, LI Yan, LI Lawrence, LI Kevin, LI Yong Bin, LI Katherine, LI Arlene, LI Zhen, LI Zhihao, LI Zhong, LIA Eddie, LIAN Katherine, LIAN Tsui-Lin, LIANG George, LIANG Simon, LIANG Sisy, LIANG Michael, LIANG Yan, LIANG Fannie, LIANG Ye, LIANTO Edy, LIAO Ben, LIAO Roy, LIAO Stephen, LIAO Tony, LIAO Xu, LIAROS Steven, LIASKOS Nafsika, LIBARDO Joel, LIBERATI Daniel, LIBTER David, LICHT Justin, LICURIA Robert, LIDDELL Corey, LIDDELL William, LIDDIARD Julian, LIDDICOAT Michael, LIDDLE Christine, LIDDLE David, LIDDY Karen, LIDDY Michael, LIDGARD Dave, LIDGARD Kate, LIDGARD Kay, LIDMAN Cassandra, LIDSTER Colin, LIE Emily, LIE Gretta, LIE Irene, LIE Jim, LIE Johan, LIE Jonathan, LIE Boz, LIE-REID Lin, LIEBHABER Joseph, LIEBOWITZ Sally, LIEBSON Celeste, LIEDTKE Gerlinde, LIEDTKE Kaye, LIEHR Malcolm, LIELL Carol, LIEN Jason, LIEN Tuyet, LIEPINS Avija, LIESER Norbert, LIESSMANN Jennifer, LIESSMANN Otto, LIEU Hue, LIEVERT Inge, LIEW Vincent, LIGAIUIU Sivoni, LIGGINS Vicki, LIGHT Andrew, LIGHT Erica, LIGHT Irwin, LIGHTFOOT Paddy, LIIMATAINEN Keijo, LIKOURESIS Toula, LILEY Jo, LILIAN Ruth, LILJA Nick, LILLEY Albert, LILLEY Duncan, LILLEY Penny, LILLEY Sue, LILLEYMAN Merrilyn, LILLEYMAN Peter, LILLICO Geoff, LILLIS Linda, LILLO Pablo, LILLYMAN Bec, LILLYWHITE Elsa, LILLYWHITE Peter, LIM Akin, LIM Bernard, LIM Bob, LIM Boon, LIM Cheryl, LIM Chiang, LIM Kristy, LIM Chris, LIM David, LIM Dewii, LIM Errol, LIM Gladys, LIM Ha, LIM Hock, LIM Huoy, LIM Vinty, LIM Irwin, LIM Jae, LIM Jeff, LIM Jenny, LIM Jia-Ying, LIM Jimn, LIM John, LIM Juliene, LIM Kanna, LIM Kayla, LIM Lee, LIM Meily, LIM June, LIM Michael, LIM Michael, LIM Pei-Ying, LIM Ping, LIM Rachel, LIM Robert, LIM Nicole, LIM Siveing, LIM Angela, LIM Susan, LIM Vey, LIM Victor, LIM Michelle, LIM Wen-hsien, LIMBREY Mike, LIMBREY Thomas, LIMBU Santosh, LIMEBEER Hiedi, LIMOND Wendy, LIMOR Shirley, LIMPUS Les, LIN Alan, LIN Beatrice, LIN Belle, LIN Bernard, LIN Bonnie, LIN Wallace, LIN Chi-Long, LIN David, LIN Fu, LIN Linda, LIN Jane, LIN Kenneth, LIN Karen, LIN Larry, LIN Pamela, LIN Roger, LIN Jenny, LIN Thomas, LIN Tina, LIN Wen-Hsien, LIN Xiao, LIN Ya, LIN Andrea, LIN Yuan, LIN Yuan, LIN Yvonne, LIN Zhen, LINCOLN Charles, LINCOLN Lesley, LINCOLNE Lorraine, LIND Dot, LIND Ted, LIND Kelly, LINDAO Miguel, LINDEMAN John, LINDEN Kerry-Ann, LINDEN Tracey, LINDENTHAL Hedi, LINDERMAN Shirley, LINDERMAN Wally, LINDERS Peggy, LINDFIELD SEAGER Neville, LINDFORS Rafaela, LINDHOLM Lorraine, LINDLEY Brooke, LINDLEY Robert, LINDOP Kirin, LINDORFF Barbara, LINDSAY Drew, LINDSAY Brianne, LINDSAY Cara, LINDSAY Chris, LINDSAY Christine, LINDSAY Danielle, LINDSAY Erin, LINDSAY Geoff, LINDSAY James, LINDSAY Jennifer, LINDSAY John, LINDSAY Jonathan, LINDSAY Kirsty, LINDSAY Najat, LINDSAY Richard, LINDSAY Steven, LINDSAY Warwick, LINDSAY Wayne, LINDSCHAU Lenore, LINDSELL Eric, LINDSET Hilde, LINDSLEY Carolyn, LINDSTROM Charles, LINEHAM Bev, LINES Angela, LINES Ken, LINFOOT David, LINGARD Jill, LINGLEY Jenny, LINHARES Marcos, LINK Claudius, LINK Raymond, LINKENBAGH Maria, LINKIO Pekka, LINKLATER Alan, LINKLATER Daniel, LINKLATER James, LINN David, LINN Jim, LINN Tiernan, LINNETT Amelia, LINNETT Nicholas, LINSELL Daniel, LINSLEY Peter, LINTON Alan, LINTON Sandy, LINTON Barry, LINTON Nikki, LIOBURY Norman, LIONDAS Vera, LIOW Karen, LIPARI Kerrie, LIPINSKI Mary, LIPINSKI CORLISS Linda, LIPLYN Annalee, LIPMANN Nicki, LIPPIATT Pat, LIPPIS Anne, LIPPIS Luigi, LIPSCH Jeroen, LIPSCOMBE Nicola, LIPSHAM Bernie, LIPSHAM Steve, LISAKKA Sharon, LISCHER Konstanze, LISTER Danielle, LISTER Jan, LISTO Alexander, LISTON Malcolm, LIT Wye, LITCHFIELD Heather, **LITCHFIELD Jim**, LITCHFIELD Suzie, LITCHFIELD Bill, LITHGOW Anne, LITRAS Peter, LITSON Andrew, LITT Sandra, LITTLE Allan, LITTLE Bruce, LITTLE Chris, LITTLE Chris, LITTLE Craig, LITTLE Frankie, LITTLE Gary, LITTLE Geoffrey, LITTLE Heidi, LITTLE James, LITTLE Judith, LITTLE Penny, LITTLE Bob, LITTLE Sam, LITTLE Victoria, LITTLE Vince, LITTLE William, LITTLECHILD Dennis, LITTLEJOHN Helen, LITTLER Duncan, LITTLER Susan, LITTLEWOOD Karen, LITTLEWOOD Pippa, LITWINOW Bec, LITZOW Troy, LIU Bo, LIU Brian, LIU Chirong, LIU Cho, LIU Cindy, LIU Dan, LIU Edgar, LIU Eugene, LIU Fang, LIU Fei, LIU Jeffrey, LIU William, LIU Hong, LIU Howard, LIU Michael, LIU Jiang, LIU Jack, LIU Johnny, LIU Kevin, LIU Kui, LIU Lisa, LIU Lucia, LIU Michelle, LIU Michael, LIU Michael, LIU Michael, LIU Min, LIU Muriel, LIU Lucia, LIU Raymnd, LIU Richard, LIU Richard, LIU Eva, LIU Sophia, LIU Ting-Ting, LIU Vanessa, LIU Wa, LIU Wai, LIU Wallace, LIU David, LIU Xiang, LIU Fiona, LIU Xiao, LIU Vicki, LIU Jasmine, LIU David, LIU Yuexin, LIU John, LIU Zhen, LIU Zhuo, LIU Jane, LIUS Irvie, LIVERSAGE Margaret, LIVERSEDGE Stefanie, LIVESEY Bill, LIVINGSTON Dennis, LIVINGSTON Fionnuala, LIVINGSTON Rhonda, LIVINGSTONE Jan, LIVINGSTONE Jeanette, LIVINGSTONE-MOLLER Elizabeth, LIYANAARACHCHI Sunethra, LIYANAGE Kit, LJUNGDAHL Lesley, LLAMBI Louis, LLAUDERES VALK Cristy, LLEDO Roland, LLEWELLYN Narissa, LLEWELLYN-SMITH G.R., LLORENTE Blanca, LLOYD Stephen, LLOYD Amanda, LLOYD Barry, LLOYD Barry, LLOYD Bazza, LLOYD Betsy, LLOYD David, LLOYD Dorothea, LLOYD Jeanie, LLOYD Esme, LLOYD Fred, LLOYD Gary, LLOYD Gillian, LLOYD Joan, LLOYD Kelly, LLOYD Matthew, LLOYD Mike, LLOYD Patrick, LLOYD Patti-Lynn, LLOYD Peter, **LLOYD Ray**, LLOYD Robert, LLOYD Robert, LLOYD Sarah, LLOYD Stephen, LLOYD Terry, LLOYD Terry, LLOYD Tim, LLOYD Tracey, LLOYD Wayne, LLOYD William, LO Peggy, LO Ai-I, LO Antony, LO David, LO Dennis, LO Eva, LO Fiona, LO Linda, LO Jennifer, LO Roanne, LO Kathrina, LO Kevin, LO Kin-Yat, LO Kwai, LO Lily, LO Macy, LO Taryn, LO Paul, LO Phillip, LO Sam, LO Shirley, LO Ronnie, LO Suzana, LO Irene, LO Willy, LO Winston, LO Annie, LO Yun-Feng, LO MONACO Mick, LO PO Simonetta, LO RICCO Roz, LO SURDO Lena, LO TAURO Tony, LOADER Wendy, LOADSMAN Leonie, LOADSMAN Leon, LOANE Alison, LOANEY Kylie, LOATS Keith, LOBASTOV Marina, LOBASTOV Natalie, LOBB Jill, LOBB Lawson, LOBBAN Marjorie, LOBO Glenn, LOBO Trevor, LOCHBIHLER Helen, LOCHER Susanne, LOCHUNAH Neel, LOCK Graham, LOCK Roger, LOCK Sarah, LOCK Trevor, LOCKE Anna, LOCKE Simon, LOCKE Belinda, LOCKE Christina, LOCKE Gary, LOCKE Jo-Anne, LOCKE Joan, LOCKE Kate, LOCKE Rachel, LOCKE Vicki, LOCKER John, LOCKERBIE Sheridan, LOCKET Tony, LOCKETT John, LOCKETT Pam, LOCKEY David, LOCKEY Lynne, LOCKHART Lauren, LOCKHART Rachael, LOCKIE Lucas, LOCKING Margaret, LOCKING Matthew, LOCKLEE Dave, LOCKLEY Peter, LOCKWOOD Erin, LOCKYER Jenny, LOCKYER Rita, LOCOCK Peter, LODGE Bill, LODGE Judith, LODIN Maggie, LOECKENHOFF Renee, LOEHR Kristen, LOEHRER Franziska, LOEL Amanda, LOEMKER Rabea, LOERSCH Alice, LOERSCH Helmut, LOESCHNER Conny, LOFTS Amanda, LOFTS Toni, LOFTUS Steve, LOGAN Andrew, LOGAN Andrew, LOGAN Barbara, LOGAN Carol, LOGAN Ian, LOGAN Jodie, LOGAN Lloyd, LOGAN Mary, LOGAN Marj, LOGAN Matthew, LOGAN Maureen, LOGAN Michele, LOGAN Richard, LOGAN Robert, LOGAN Ron, LOGAN Sandra, LOGAN Sarah, LOGAN Steve, LOGAN Steve, LOGAN-BELL Jim, LOGAN-BELL Christina, LOGOTHETIS Tom, LOGUE Joan, LOGUE Laurie, LOH Adrian, LOH Dennis, LOH Lyn, LOH Marianne, LOH Sin, LOH Wen, LOHIA Mona, LOHSE Dirk, LOI Glenn, LOIKO Kristin, LOITERTON Stephen, LOIZIDES Bill, LOIZOU Virginia, LOKANADAN Prasad, LOKE Chin-Ni, LOKE Jessica, LOKER Len, LOKI Va, LOKIC Amanda, LOMACA Constantin, LOMAS Alan, LOMAS Christine, LOMAS Pauline, LOMBARD Valerie, LOMBARDI Anthony, LOMBARDI Tony, LOMBARDO Franca, LOMBARDO Katrina, LOMBARDO Melissa, LOMBE Wayne, LOMMERSE Louise, LONARD Brian, LONARD Colin, LONDON Gary, LONERAGAN Anna, LONERAGAN Libby, LONERAGAN Robert, LONERGAN Karen, LONERGAN Michael, LONERGAN Noel, LONERGAN Rhonda,

LONERGAN Steve, LONEY Anthony, LONG Alf, LONG Brian, LONG David, LONG David, LONG Diana, LONG Heather, LONG Inta, LONG Jacki, LONG Jann, LONG Joan, LONG Mark, LONG Mike, LONG Nathan, LONG Peggy, LONG Robert, LONG Rosie, LONG Sunny, LONG Timothy, LONG Trevor, LONGA George, LONGBOTTOM Anthony, LONGES Alex, LONGFIELD Patrick, LONGHURST David, LONGHURST John, LONGLEY Wanda, LONGOBARDI Dianne, LONGRIDGE Jon, LONGWORTH Betty, LONGWORTH Renee, LONGWORTH David, LONNON Allan, LONNON Grant, LONSDALE Mick, LONT John, LOO Tee, LOO BUN Julie, LOOBY Mike, LOOK Henry, LOONEY Adrian, LOONG Louis, LOOTENS Betty, LOOTENS Jack, LOOYEN Amanda, LOPATICH Victor, LOPEDOTE Steve, LOPEZ Aileen, LOPEZ Barbye, LOPEZ Daniel, LOPEZ Dave, LOPEZ Karen, LOPEZ Karen, LOPEZ Luis, LOPEZ Miguel, LOPEZ Tunia, LOPEZ Zully, LOPEZ ARAGON Mario, LOPEZ DE D'AMICO Rosa, LOPEZ GARCIA Ruben, LOPEZ GARUA Ruben, LOPRESTI Frank, LOPRESTI Laura, LORBACH Caroline, LORBER Michael, LORD Brian, LORD Cheryl, LORD Dave, LORD Frederick, LORD Geoff, LORD Jerry, LORD Jennifer, LORD Byrom, LORD Kathryn, LORD Pam, LORD Penny, LORD Peter, LORD Roger, LORD Roslyn, LORENC Richard, LORENC Robert, LORENZ Michelle, LORENZ Peter, **LORENZIN Dennis**, LORENZIN Richard, LORENZO Mimma, LORGER Trish, LORGER Paul, LORIMER Coral, LORIMER Johno, LORIMER Peter, LORIMER Sarah, LORIZIO Bruno, LORQUET Marina, LORRIMER Harriet, LORSCHY Michelle, LOSEY Katherine, LOSS Alessia, LOTOCKI Sebastian, LOTORTO Robert, LOTT Ben, LOTT Charles, LOTT Colin, LOTT Patricia, LOTTY Dave, LOTZOF Ryan, LOU Jim, LOU Wing, LOUCAS Harry, LOUDON Annette, LOUDON Ray, LOUGHERY Frank, LOUGHHEAD Beau, LOUGHMAN Pam, LOUGHRAN Dave, LOUGHRIDGE Arthur, LOUIE Daniel, LOUIEJOHNSTON Mark, LOUKA Makram, LOUKAS Leo, LOUND Broni, LOUPATTY Marthin, LOUPIS Yasmine, LOURANDOS Vic, LOURIDAS Nicholas, LOVE Al ana, LOVE Bev, LOVE Eric, LOVE Greg, LOVE John, LOVE Greg, LOVE Kevin, LOVE Mardi, LOVE Paul, LOVE Philip, LOVE Rachel, LOVE Sonia, LOVEDAY Peter, LOVEGROVE Barry, LOVEGROVE Brett, LOVEGROVE Ian, LOVEGROVE Judy, LOVEGROVE Kay, LOVEJOY JP Don, LOVEKIN Shayne, LOVEKIN Terry, LOVELL Elise, LOVELL Fay, LOVELL Karen, LOVELL Lucy, LOVELL Lyn, LOVELL Peter, LOVELL Tanya, LOVELY Deborah, LOVELY Dennis, LOVELY Pip, LOVERIDGE Danny, LOVERIDGE John, LOVERIDGE Leslie, LOVETT Chris, LOVETT Matt, LOVETT Nathan, LOVETT Sean, LOVETT Allen, LOVI Noreen, LOVISON Stephen, LOW Andrew, LOW Cathy, LOW Debbie, LOW Florence, LOW Kathryn, LOW Lin, LOW Mary, LOW Michelle, LOW Phoenix, LOW Shu, LOW So-Siang, LOW Swang, LOW Hubert, LOW Tyron, LOW Wai, LOW Yin, LOWBEER Ilan, LOWDEN Robert, LOWDER Brian, LOWDER Kaitlyn, LOWDER Steve, LOWE Alan, LOWE Ari, LOWE Barbara, LOWE Beryl, LOWE Glen, LOWE Jim, LOWE Katrice, LOWE Kenny, LOWE Kylie, LOWE Lee, LOWE Margaret, LOWE Pamela, LOWE Gordon, LOWE Scott, LOWE Shirley, LOWE Steve, LOWE Stuart, LOWE Susan, LOWE Vicki, LOWE Vincent, LOWE Wendy, LOWE Bill, LOWENSTEIN Eric, LOWERY Edwin, LOWES Sandra, LOWES Julie, LOWES Julie, LOWINGER Paul, LOWLES Leesa, LOWNDES Christine, LOWNDES James, LOWNDES Parker, LOWNDES Lucy, LOWNDES Peter, LOWNDES Rob, LOWNDES Stuart, LOWNIE James, LOWRIE Adam, LOWRIE Virginia, LOWRY Mandy, LOWRY Cassandra, LOWRY Helen, LOWSON David, LOWY Michael, LOXLEY Nancee, LOXLEY Ron, LOXTON James, LOXTON Kylie, LOY Su, LOYER Angela, LOZADA Jeannette, LOZAN Katrina, LOZAN Peter, LOZANO Fabio, LOZANO Isabel, LOZANO PEREA Sandra, LU Ant, LU Belinda, LU Betty, LU Cheng, LU Ching, LU George, LU Hsin, LU Ivana, LU Jia, LU Karen, LU Ko-yi, LU Amy, LU Joy, LU Lily, LU Peter, LU Betty, LU Vivien, LU Wei, LU Wing, LU Xiao, LUBRANO Daniella, LUBUSKA Robin, LUC Hannah, LUC Lan, LUC Lu, LUCAS Brett, LUCAS Col, LUCAS David, LUCAS Debs, LUCAS Des, LUCAS Helene, LUCAS James, LUCAS Jeannine, LUCAS Judy, LUCAS Judy, LUCAS Kelly, LUCAS Kevin, LUCAS Maree, LUCAS Matt, LUCAS Myra, LUCAS Nikki, LUCAS Trish, LUCAS Peter, LUCAS Pete, LUCAS Phil, LUCAS Rebekah, LUCAS Rob, LUCAS Ruth, LUCAS Sue, LUCAS Valerie, LUCAS Wenda, LUCCHESI Fabio, LUCENA GOMEZ Fernando, LUCEV Brian, LUCEY Jennifer, LUCEY Philip, LUCHKO Zakhar, LUCIA Sestino, LUCIDON Amanda, LUCK Arthur, LUCK Graeme, LUCK Jan, LUCK Jenny, LUCK Paul, LUCK Penelope, LUCKETT Liz, LUCKETT David, LUCKHURST Tony, LUCKIE Frank, LUCKMAN Kris, LUCKOCK John, LUCKOCK Lauraine, LUCKRAFT Doug, LUCY Marianne, LUDEKENS AnneMarie, LUDEMANN John, LUDEMANN Jo, LUDER John, LUDER Ruby, LUDINGTON Herb, LUDLOW Tony, LUDLOW George, LUDOWYKE Danielle, LUDSKI Mark, LUDWELL Caroline, LUEY Tony, LUGG Malcolm, LUGG Nathan, **LUGSDIN Graham**, LUGTON Amanda, LUHRS Kylie, LUI Betty, LUI Carmen, LUI Gordon, LUI Ivan, LUI John, LUI Rosita, LUIDMANIS Maris, LUIK Aivi, LUITERS Keegan, LUK Ester, LUK Jack, LUK Lusy, LUK Milli, LUKABYO James, LUKE Adrian, LUKE Iris, LUKE Kevin, LUKE Margie, LUKE Peter, LUKE Ron, LUKE Shona, LUKER Daphne, LUKICH Diana, LUKINS David, LUKINS Warwick, LUKMAN Hengky, LUKMAN Herman, LUKOWSKI Marko, LUKS Matthew, LULAND Harold, LUM Alison, LUM Andrew, LUM Benjamin, LUM Carmen, LUM Justine, LUM Ming, LUM Peter, LUMI Carlos, LUMI Ricardo, LUMLEY John, LUMLEY Val, LUMSDAINE Elaine, LUMSDEN Bryce, LUMSDEN Jonathan, LUMSDEN Lisa, LUMSDEN Robyn, LUMSDEN Ross, LUMSDEN Suzanne, LUN David, LUN Jordan-Todd, LUN JoySimone, LUNA-ZAMORA Lidia, LUNARDI Bryce, LUNARO-GARCIA Laura, LUND Jenny, LUND Mandy, LUND Dennis, LUNDBERG Jack, LUNDBERG Neale, LUNG Mandy, LUNN Benjamin, **LUNN Mary**, LUNNAY James, LUNNON Barbara, LUNSFORD Roslyn, LUNSMANN Paul, LUO Becky, LUO Jimmy, LUONG Hieu, LUONG Judy, LUONG Chau, LUONG Richard, LUONG Thang, LUONG Tee, LUPTON Emma, LUPTON Greg, LUPTON Raymond, LUPTON Rebecca, LURIE Jane, LURIE Jeff, LUSCOMBE John, LUSCOMBE Tanna, LUSCOMBE Bill, LUSKEY Coralie, LUSKEY Jenna, LUSSICK John, LUSTHAUS Abbie, LUSTIG Linnea, LUSTMAN Renee, LUSTY Annette, LUSTY Sue, LUTFULLAHOGLU Ebru, LUTHER Wilson, LUTHERBORROW Elizabeth, LUTHERBORROW Jim, LUTTA Lisa, LUTTON Adrian, LUTTON Cherie, LUTTON George, LUTTRELL Anna, LUTTRELL Matt, LUTTRELL Tanya, LUTUI-PALMER Pele, LUTVEY Greg, LUTZE Nicole, LUU Minh, LUU Gary, LUU David, LUU Hai, LUU Hsiung, **LUU Nga**, LUU Julie, LUU Ivan, LUXFORD Hayley, LUXMOORE Sandra, LUXMOORE Wendy, LUXTON Garry, LUXTON Natalie, LUXTON Sally, LUYA Penny, LUZYNSKI Nelly, LWIN Kyi, LY Bang, LY Lee, LY Thia, LY Hieu, LY Hong, LY Hy, LY Jenny, LY Lisa, LY Maria, LY Meng, LY Thanh, LY Vien, LY Tri, LY Thomas, LY Vitthi, LY Vivian, LYALL Cathryn, LYALL Don, LYALL Geoff, LYALL Ian, LYALL Kay, LYALL Megan, LYALL Peter, LYCHO Tania, LYDDIETH Bradley, LYDEAMORE Murray, LYE Georgina, LYKOGIANNI Dimitra, LYLE Barbara, LYLE Ron, LYMBERY John, LYME Elaine, LYNAR Kathy, LYNCH Ness, LYNCH Andrew, LYNCH Ashleigh, LYNCH Carol, LYNCH Colleen, LYNCH David, LYNCH Eamonn, LYNCH Ellen, LYNCH Greg, LYNCH Janine, LYNCH Joe, LYNCH Maureen, LYNCH Nicole, LYNCH Paul, LYNCH Peter, LYNCH Rhonda, LYNCH Sydney, LYNDON Louise, LYNN Megan, LYNNE Amy, LYNSKEY Peter, LYNTON Anne, LYNTON Marj, LYNZAAT Liz, LYON Anne, LYON Donald, LYON Fiona, LYON Margaret, LYON Naomi, LYON Robyn, LYON Roderick, LYONS Damon, LYONS Dermot, LYONS Bobbie, LYONS Mary, LYONS Pat, LYONS Ray, LYONS Roley, LYONS Russell, LYONS Sandi, LYONS Terry, LYSLE Monika, LYTHGO Therese, LYTHGOE Fiona, LYTTON Sigrid.

M

M'SOULI Hassan, MA Benjamin, MA Fay, MA Genoveffa, MA Hok, MA Jack, MA Jessica, MA Alvin, MA Kamfai, MA Maggie, MA Malcolm, MA Matthew, MA Mabel, MA Casey, MA Patricia, MA Veronica, MA Santo, MA Kate, MAARBANI Allan, MAARBANI Wafa, MAARRAOUI Jamile, MAASTRICHT Monica, MABBUTT James, MABER Jane, MABER Jean, MABER Peter, MABERLY Kerry, MABEY Brenda, MACABENTA Ilynn, MACALPINE Barry, MACARTHUR Anneke, MACARTHUR Christine, MACARTHUR Kerryn, MACARTHUR Russell, MACARTHUR Steve, MACARTNEY Mark, MACARTNEY Shelley-Anne, MACAULAY Craig, MACAULAY Robin, MACAULAY Rob, MACBETH Irene, MACBRYDE Bruce, MACBRYDE Sandra, MACCALLUM James, MACCIOCCA David, MACCIOCCA Gaill, MACCOLL Pam, MACCOLL Rachel, MACCORQUODALE Don, MACCUBBIN Jane, MACDESSI Buddy, MACDONALD

Paddy, MACDONALD Alison, MACDONALD Amanda, MACDONALD Amy, MACDONALD Calli, MACDONALD Cate, MACDONALD David, MACDONALD Deborah, MACDONALD Deirdre, MACDONALD Heather, MACDONALD Iain, MACDONALD Ian, MACDONALD Jacqui, MACDONALD Jim, MACDONALD Jan, MACDONALD Kati, MACDONALD Llinos, MACDONALD Lynette, MACDONALD Malcom, MACDONALD Marnie, MACDONALD Pamela, MACDONALD Patricia, MACDONALD Patricia, MACDONALD Penny, MACDONALD Robin, MACDONALD Ros, MACDONALD Sarah, MACDONALD Somerled, MACDONALD Valerie, MACDONALD Yvonne, MACDUFF Cathy, MACEFIELD David, MACEY Leanne, MACEY Trevor, MACFARLANE Jane, MACFARLANE Ian, MACFARLANE Judy, MACFARLANE Michael, MACGEE Andrew, MACGIBBON John, MACGRAW Graeme, MACGREGOR Janeen, MACGREGOR Joy, MACHAALANI Roland, MACHADO Maddy, MACHADO Michel, MACHAIN Nelly, MACHEK Hana, MACHIDA Aya, MACHIDA Masaaki, MACHIELSE Leanne, MACHIN Alison, MACHIN John, MACHIN Scott, MACHON Robert, MACINANTE Joe, MACINNES Bill, MACINTOSH Anne, MACINTOSH Patty, MACINTYRE Sandra, MACK Carlos, MACK Jim, MACK Jarrett, MACK Lily, MACK Dick, MACKANDER Graham, MACKARELL Anne, MACKAWAY Jim, MACKAY Amber, MACKAY Ann, MACKAY Carol, MACKAY Cathy, MACKAY Debbie, MACKAY Helen, MACKAY Ian, MACKAY Jenifer, MACKAY Nathan, MACKAY Rosalie, MACKAY Tom, MACKAY Bill, MACKAY Linden, MACKEL Thomas, MACKELLAR Mon, MACKELLAR Yvonne, MACKEN Mary, MACKENZIE Alan, MACKENZIE Bruce, MACKENZIE Elizabeth, MACKENZIE Irene, MACKENZIE Josh, MACKENZIE Katrina, MACKENZIE Ken, MACKENZIE Kevin, MACKENZIE Margaret, MACKENZIE Michael, MACKENZIE Paul, MACKENZIE Robin, MACKENZIE Bob, MACKENZIE Ross, MACKENZIE Stephanie, MACKENZIE-BAIRD Stephanie, MACKENZIE-SNOWBALL Snow, MACKEY Amber, MACKEY David, MACKEY Devin, MACKEY Fiona, MACKEY Frances, MACKEY Julie, MACKEY Kaye, MACKEY Peter, MACKIE Brian, MACKIE Elizabeth, MACKIE James, MACKIE John, MACKIE Kristen, MACKIE Kristine, MACKIE Narelle, MACKIE Natalie, MACKIE Ralph, MACKIE Sylvia, MACKIEWICZ Joanna, MACKIEWICZ Judy, MACKILLOP John, MACKILLOP Clive, MACKINLAY Brett, MACKINLAY Robert, MACKINNON Ailsa, MACKINNON Chris, MACKINNON Tibby, MACKINNON Jan, MACKINNON Katherine, MACKINNON Sueanne, MACKINTOSH David, MACKINTOSH Peter, MACKNISH David, MACKOVA Jana, MACKOWIAK Robert, MACLACHLAN Jim, MACLACHLAN Stephanie, MACLAGAN Lorraine, MACLAREN Stewart, MACLAREN Christine, MACLAY John, MACLEAN Doug, MACLEAN Liz, MACLEAN Emily, MACLEAN Graeme, MACLEAN Helen, MACLEAN Ian, MACLEAN Jan, MACLEAN Jean, MACLEAN Kerry, MACLEAN Lesley, MACLEAN Sarah, MACLEAN Susanne, MACLENNAN Gary, MACLENNAN Kenneth, MACLENNAN Ray, MACLEOD Alan, MACLEOD Catriona, MACLEOD Ruth, MACLEOD Lew, MACLURCAN Charles, MACLURCAN Don, MACLURCAN John, MACMAHON Rohan, MACMANG James, MACMILLAN Tannis, MACMORRAN Irene, MACMORRAN Peter, MACNAUGHTON Andrew, MACNAUGHTON Dennis, MACNAUGHTON Rokelle, MACNEIL Angus, MACNEIL Kate, MACNEIL Fin, MACNEIL James, MACNEIL James, MACNEIL-BROWN Jessie, MACNICOL Christine, MACNISH Linda, MACOUSTRA Angus, MACPHAIL Blair, MACPHAIL Don, MACPHAIL Erica, MACPHAIL Mary, MACPHERSON Andrew, MACPHERSON Elizabeth, MACPHERSON Helen, MACPHERSON Ian, MACPHERSON Ian, MACPHERSON Jenny, MACPHERSON Judy, MACPHERSON Judy, MACPHERSON Sherman, MACPHERSON Ronald, MACPHERSON Rosalie, MACPHERSON Roslyn, MACPHILLAMY Jayne, MACRAE Annette, MACRAE Ian, MACREADY Elaine, MACREADY Barney, MACRI Adrian, MACRI Tony, MACRIS Steve, MACRONALD Helen, MACROW Jenny, MACSPORRAN Anne, MACSPORRAN David, MACWILLIAMS Emily, MADADI-REDDY Varun, MADAMS Marion, MADAR Madeleine, MADAY Kate, MADDAMS Paul, MADDEN Danielle, MADDEN Faith, MADDEN Jim, MADDEN Janet, MADDEN Joanna, MADDEN Kathey, MADDEN Ken, MADDEN Kristine, MADDEN Lee, MADDEN Margaret, MADDEN Mark, MADDEN Peter, MADDEN Phillip, MADDEN Shari, MADDISON Diane, MADDISON Guy, MADDOCK Anne, MADDOCK Dennis, MADDOCK Gaie, MADDOCKS Joe, MADDOX Alan, MADDOX Gail, MADDOX Linda, MADDREN Phil, MADER Tony, MADER Jana, MADEROVA Silvia, MADEY Brendon, MADGWICK Cliff, MADIGAN Aaron, MADIGAN June, MADIGAN Luke, MADIGAN Trish, MADIONA Anthony, MADKHUL Dakhylina, MADRID Elvira, MADSEN Joe, MADSEN Jason, MADSEN Paul, MADVIG Annette, MADVIG Penelope, MADYCKI Amy, MADYCKI Colleen, **MAE Lorraine**, MAEDA Natsu, MAGADAM Noosheen, MAGAGNINO Cathy, MAGANN Fred, MAGAREY Matthew, MAGDI Jason, MAGEE Patricia, MAGEE Valerie, MAGEN Ted, MAGILL Christina, MAGILL Margaret, MAGILL Mary, MAGILL Sang, MAGILL Val, MAGINNESS Grant, MAGLAMBAYAN Eleanor, MAGNER Rachel, MAGNER Sarah, MAGNO Nina, MAGNUS Eve, MAGNUSSON Bruce, MAGNUSSON David, MAGNUSSON Emma, MAGRAITH Matt, MAGRO Andy, MAGRO Judy, MAGUIRE Chris, MAGUIRE Denise, MAGUIRE Jim, MAGUIRE Dr, MAGUIRE John, MAGUIRE Maureen, MAGUIRE Mick, MAGUIRE Neil, MAGUIRE Pat, MAGUIRE Renee, MAGUIRE Ruth, MAGURREN Noelene, MAGWOOD Mandy, MAHAC Mark, MAHADEVAN Ram, MAHADEWA Bala, MAHAL Inderjit, MAHALINGAM Arivalakan, MAHANIDIS Theo, MAHANTY Nishith, MAHARAJ Danny, MAHBUB Abdul, MAHENDRAN Charmaine, MAHENDRAN Raj, MAHER Barry, MAHER Christen, MAHER Colin, MAHER Eamon, MAHER Gary, MAHER Garry, MAHER Helen, MAHER June, MAHER Ken, MAHER Kim, MAHER Laurie, MAHER Louise, MAHER Lyn, MAHER Lyn, MAHER Marlene, MAHER Maria, MAHER Margaret, MAHER Terry, MAHER Tim, MAHER Vicki, MAHFOUZ Mark, MAHITTIVANITCHA Premrudee, MAHITTIWANITCHA Prem, MAHMOOD Kashif, MAHMOUDI Shahla, MAHON Ann, MAHON Chris, MAHON Paul, MAHONE Derek, MAHONEY Cath, MAHONEY Isabel, MAHONEY Jude, MAHONY Ann, MAHONY Jessica, MAHONY Josh, MAHONY Mara, MAHONY Sam, MAHY Darin, MAHYUDDIN Abdillah, MAI Gordon, MAI Gunter, MAI Martin, MAI Bing, MAIDEN Bruce, MAIDEN Charlie, MAIDMENT Helen, MAIDMENT-HODGES Amanda, MAIER Heidi, MAIN Jo, MAIN Mora, MAIN Bob, MAINDONALD Paul, MAINEY Monique, MAINEY Bec, MAIR Bill, MAIRS Cassani, MAISANO Aggie, MAISEMA Vilame, MAITEM Ann, MAITEM Thelma, MAITLAND John, MAITLAND John, MAITLAND John, MAITRE Chris, MAIUOLO Frank, MAIZ Maria, MAIZEY Robyn, MAJAK Makur, MAJARIAN Aris, MAJIC Marion, MAJOR Ash, MAJOR Ken, MAJOR Leisha, MAJOR Paul, MAJOR Bob, MAJSTOROVIC Tina, MAJUMDAR Sam, MAJUMDAR Som, MAJZOUB Gada, MAJZOUB Sarah, MAK Cynthia, MAK Dorothy, MAK Witty, MAK Ken, MAK Grace, MAK Maria, MAK Paul, MAK Vivian, MAK Winnie, MAKALING Dennis, MAKAMAKA Sam, MAKARI Rosemary, MAKAUDE Sunil, MAKDISSI Michael, MAKEEV Fr, MAKEPEACE Narelle, MAKHLOUF Annette, MAKIN Kevin, MAKIN Lisa, MAKIN Sam, MAKKI Jamal, MAKKI Mohamed, MAKOHON Andrew, MAKRAS Phillip, MAKSIMOVIC Dani, MAKZOUME Dominique, MALADAY Dominique, MALAGODI Ligia, MALAKEDSUWAN Pattama, **MALANI Natasha**, MALAU Paul, MALBOURNE Karen, MALCHER Harry, MALCHER Helen, MALCOLM Alan, MALCOLM Angus, MALCOLM Byron, MALCOLM Roger, MALCOLM Sharon, MALCOLM William, MALE Brendan, MALECKAS Verona, MALECKY Julia, MALESPIN ROMERO Ana, MALETTA Raechela, MALEY Bruce, MALEY Dianne, MALHOTRA Parveen, MALIA Nang, MALIEPO Nai, MALIGAT Ronald, MALIK Azhar, MALIK Ihsan, MALIK Omar, MALIKARJUNA Fedilies, MALINEK Gary, MALINOWSKI Adam, MALKAN Rajiv, MALLADI Chandra, MALLAM Joel, MALLARD Alan, MALLARD Ben, MALLARD Wendy, MALLETT Gaenor, MALLETT Ron, MALLEY Bill, MALLIA Sam, MALLINSON Kay, MALLON Billie, MALLOUHI Katie, MALLOUK Richard, MALLOY Gerry, MALLY Louise, MALLY Wolfgang, MALLYON Russ, MALLYON Tracey, MALONE Brendan, MALONE John, MALONE Joy, MALONE Pat, MALONE Bob, MALONE Rosemarie, MALONE Terry, MALONEY Andrew, MALONEY Tony, MALONEY Bruce, MALONEY Christaan,

MALONEY Jack, MALONEY Kate, MALONEY Lauren, MALONEY Simone, MALOUF Jenny, MALOUF Lauren, MALOUF Morris, MALOUF Vic, MALOY Katie, MALP S Ken, MALTBY Connie, MALTBY Graham, MALTBY Helen, MALTBY Richard, MALTMAN Harry, MALUPO Matakaiongo, MALYON Dianna, MAMALOUKOS Pavlos, MAMALOUKOS Stephen, MAMMALITIE Martino, MAMO Christine, MAMO Donna, MAMOLEJO Rafael, MAMONE Chris, MAMONE Christine, MAMUCOD Lynne, MAMUN Abullah, MAN Anqi, MAN Veronica, MANAGO Rosalina, MANALO JosePierre, MANALO Marivic, MANALO Rey, MANCHANAYAKE Pramuk, MANCHANAYAKE Kavan, MAND Brendan, MANDALIOS Irene, MANDERS Veronica, MANDERSON Kathy, MANDERSON Suzanne, MANDIGMA Marilyn, MANDIK Rudi, MANDIKOS Freda, MANDIN Jennifer, MANDL Helen, MANDLA Reimund, MANDRELL Mark, MANEA Gabriella, MANEFIELD Barry, MANEFIELD Bruce, MANEFIELD Jennifer, MANEFIELD Patricia, MANERA Monique, MANESCU Ana, MANFIELD Josephine, MANG Jame, MANGA Gavin, MANGANO Janel, MANGANO Janice, MANGEL Kinga, MANGELSDORF Phillip, MANGHAM Brian, MANGION Stuart, MANGOLD Klaus, MANGONIS Andrew, MANGRAI Geraldine, MANGULABNAN ShaSha, MANGULABNAN Resurreccion, MANIA Karina, MANIAM Sofia, MANIC Eugeniu, MANILA Cornelio, MANINGO Willy, MANION John, MANIRAM Ana, MANIVONG Arri, MANLEY Krystyna, MANLEY Peter, MANLIK Jan, MANLY Dennis, MANN Gordon, MANN Corrine, MANN David, MANN Ian, MANN Judy, MANN Julia, MANN Kathleen, MANN Katherine, MANN Kelly, MANN Kevin, MANN Lucy, MANN Melissa, MANN Patrice, MANN Robert, MANN Sally, MANN Suetlana, MANN Terre, MANNA Tina, MANNERS Adele, MANNERS John, MANNERS Peter, MANNING Adrian, MANNING Albert, MANNING Alex, MANNING Annemarie, MANNING Broughton, MANNING Bruce, MANNING Grant, MANNING Alvin, MANNING Jessica, MANNING Leah, MANNING Stephen, MANNING Stephen, MANNING Valerie, MANNING Valda, MANNING Bill, MANNINO Roderick, MANNINO Rose, MANNION Jo, MANNION Moira, MANNIX Brian, MANNIX Robin, MANNIX Sarah, MANNY Madeleine, MANOLIADIS George, MANOLOPOULOS Toula, MANOLOPOULOS Pat, MANOTO Yasmin, MANOUKIAN Sarkis, MANSBERG Victor, MANSBRIDGE Allan, MANSELL Amanda, MANSELL Benjamin, MANSELL Warren, MANSER Sue, MANSERGH Nick, MANSFIELD Greg, MANSFIELD Heather, MANSFIELD James, MANSFIELD Jo, MANSFIELD Katrina, MANSFIELD Peter, MANSFIELD Sam, MANSFIELD Richard, MANSFIELD YOUNG Margaret, MANSKIE Tarryn, MANSON Jeanette, MANSON Neil, MANSON Owen, MANSON Pamela, MANSON Shireen, MANSOUR Shenouda, MANTARING Ricky, MANTEIT Matthew, MANTELL Peter, MANTERE Raila, MANTHEY Andrew, MANTINO Franco, MANTLE Roger, MANTLE William, MANTNANELI Ana, MANTON Chris, MANTON Colin, MANTON Glenn, MANTON Neil, MANTON Richard, MANTZIKOPOULOS Jim, MANU Ashwin, MANUEL Carlee, **MANUEL Judy**, **MANUEL Warren**, MANWARING Janene, MANYWEATHERS Jeannette, MANYWEATHERS Richmond, MANYWEATHERS William, MANZI David, MAO Cong, MAPA Roland, MAPAGU Maria, MAPLES Barry, MAPLESDEN David, MAPPERSON Rick, MAPPLEBECK Carole, MAR-YOUNG Cynthia, MARA Bebee, MARAGNA Nadia, MARALDO Nadine, MARANTZ Melissa, MARASCO Patricia, MARASHIAN Ahmad, MARASHIAN Tina, MARASIGAN Arjay, MARATHAKIS Margaret, MARATHAKIS Nick, MARATHAKIS Phillip, MARATHON Leo, MARC Amy, MARCANTELLI Alan, MARCELJA Claudia, MARCELLS George, MARCELO Jun, MARCELO Ray, MARCH Amanda, MARCH Lyn, MARCH Nick, MARCHEGIANI Christian, MARCHEI Alex, MARCHEI Carol, MARCHESANI Tammy, MARCHESE Mario, MARCHETTI Gina, MARCHETTO Leigh, MARCHINI Mick, MARCHIONE Bill, MARCHISELLA Sheila, MARCIANO Tina, MARCINIAK Alley, MARCINIAK Natasha, MARCO Patrick, MARCON Janice, MARCOS Steven, MARDANI Udi, MARDELL Katrina, MARDINI Zena, MARDO Gray, MARELIC Alex, MARETT Glenn, MAREVICH Elizabeth, MARGAN Sienna, MARGANSKI Leanne, MARGERISON Alan, MARGERISON Lyn, MARGERISON Phil, MARGETSON Claire, MARGETSON Samantha, MARGETTS Janette, MARGETTS Sandra, MARGO Gideon, MARGON Sandra, MARGRITZER Lou, MARIAN Irris, MARIAN Leigh, MARIC Ivan, MARIC Suzana, MARICH Andrej, MARICIC Zoran, MARIE Kylie, MARIELLA Francesca, MARIELLA Liliana, MARIN Cynthia, MARIN Liz, MARIN Fernando, MARIN Maria, MARIN-ULLOA Jessica, MARINACCIO Kerry, MARINER Heather, MARINO Frank, MARINO Odette, MARINOVIC Mila, MARIOTTI Serena, MARIS Liz, MARJANOVIC Betty, MARK Adam, MARK Corey, MARK Kai, MARKANDU Estelle, MARKER Tony, MARKEY Chris, MARKEY Claudia, MARKEY Edgar, MARKEY Mary, MARKEZIC Katrina, MARKEZIC Vega, MARKHAM Jacqui, MARKHAM Marilyn, MARKHAM Steve, MARKHAM Sue, MARKIE Bob, MARKIE Rose, MARKIEWICZ Joelle, MARKLEY John, MARKOTSIS Martin, MARKOULIS Clare, MARKOVIC Maja, MARKOVIC Sandra, MARKOVINA Lisa, MARKOVSKI Jim, MARKOVSKI Karon, MARKOVTZEV Sonia, MARKS Andrew, MARKS Fiona, MARKS Jason, MARKS Julie, MARKS Ruth, MARKS Sean, MARKS Tamara, MARKUS Susanne, MARLER Barry, MARLER Graham, MARLEY Dave, MARLIN Cynthia, MARLIN Darryl, MARLIN Pamela, MARLOW Len, MARM Chhayri, MARMION Kylie, MARNER Dara, MARNER Ray, MARNING Vaughn, MAROCCHINI Frank, MAROLIA Mitasha, MARONEY Frida, MARONEY Justine, MARONEY Mick, MARONEY Pauline, MARONEY Susie, MAROUN Lisa, MARQUARDT Tels, MARQUES Mauricio, MARQUETTE Julie, MARQUINEZ Laura, MARR Ric, MARR James, MARR Julia, MARR Kyle, MARR Mick, MARR Susan, MARRE John, MARREN Rowena, MARRINER Angie, MARRINGTON Shirley, MARRINGTON Janelle, MARRINGTON John, MARRIOTT Belinda, MARRIOTT Fran, MARRIOTT Lance, MARRIOTT Luana, MARRIOTT Nola, MARRIOTT Tess, MARROUN Joe, MARSDEN Jacqui, MARSDEN John, MARSDEN Sal, MARSDEN Sue, MARSELOS Colin, MARSH Christine, MARSH Gary, MARSH Ian, MARSH Lynne, MARSH Vicki, MARSH Wendy, MARSH Will, MARSHALL Anne, MARSHALL Belinda, MARSHALL Beverley, MARSHALL Brad, **MARSHALL Snow**, MARSHALL Bryony, MARSHALL Carlie, MARSHALL Carl, MARSHALL Charmaine, MARSHALL Chris, MARSHALL Daniel, MARSHALL Dorothy, MARSHALL Dreane, MARSHALL Evan, MARSHALL Grant, MARSHALL Ian, MARSHALL Jean, MARSHALL Jen, MARSHALL John, MARSHALL John, MARSHALL Karen, MARSHALL Kimberly, MARSHALL Kristy, MARSHALL Lloyd, MARSHALL Lucy, MARSHALL Margaret, MARSHALL Matt, MARSHALL Matthew, MARSHALL Melissa, MARSHALL Nick, MARSHALL Patricia, MARSHALL Peter, MARSHALL Suzanne, MARSHALL Ray, MARSHALL Bob, MARSHALL Bob, MARSHALL Russ, MARSHALL Sarah, MARSHALL Christopher, MARSHALL Steven, MARSHALL Sue, MARSHALL Sue, MARSHALL Tom, MARSHALL Valerie, MARSHALL Vic, MARSHALL Wayne, MARSHELINA Mira, MARSILLO Marco, MARSLAND Cameron, MARSOM Gary, MARSTERS Hongata, MARSTON David, MARSTON Helen, MARSTON-HILLIER Chris, MARSTON-HILLIER Judy, MARTELLI Paul, MARTENSSON Francis, MARTHICK Faye, MARTIGNAGO Telma, MARTIN Adam, MARTIN Alisha, MARTIN Al, MARTIN Anne, MARTIN Ann, MARTIN Barb, MARTIN Barb, MARTIN Campbell, MARTIN Carole, MARTIN Carmel, MARTIN Chris, MARTIN Chris, MARTIN Christine, MARTIN Clive, MARTIN Craig, MARTIN Crystal, MARTIN David, MARTIN Dawn, MARTIN Elinor, MARTIN Anne, MARTIN Friedel, MARTIN Geoff, MARTIN Geoff, MARTIN Geoff, MARTIN Gerard, MARTIN Gilmi, MARTIN Glenn, MARTIN Graham, MARTIN Helen, MARTIN Helen, MARTIN Ian, MARTIN Janice, MARTIN Jan, MARTIN Jared, MARTIN Jean, MARTIN Joan, MARTIN Joanne, MARTIN Jodie, MARTIN John, MARTIN John, MARTIN John, MARTIN John, MARTIN Joyce, MARTIN Joy, MARTIN Karen, MARTIN Keith, MARTIN Keith, MARTIN Ken, MARTIN Kev, MARTIN Kevin, MARTIN Kim, MARTIN Lisa, MARTIN Lola, MARTIN Lynette, MARTIN Marisa, MARTIN Michael, MARTIN Mike, MARTIN Neil, MARTIN Neil, MARTIN Nicola, MARTIN Nicholas, MARTIN Nola, MARTIN Owen, MARTIN Pam, MARTIN Pat, MARTIN Peter, MARTIN Peter, MARTIN Phillip, MARTIN

Ralea, MARTIN Rhonda, MARTIN John, MARTIN Ross, MARTIN Russell, MARTIN Rusty, MARTIN Ryan, MARTIN Sally, MARTIN Samantha, MARTIN John, MARTIN Steven, MARTIN Stewart, MARTIN Steph, MARTIN Steve, MARTIN Suezette, MARTIN Sue, MARTIN Sylvie, MARTIN Todd, MARTIN Veronica, MARTIN Vyvyan, MARTIN Warren, MARTIN Wendy, MARTIN Wendy, MARTIN William, MARTIN SKILTON Raquel, MARTINDALE Colin, MARTINELLI Peter, MARTINESI Anna, MARTINEZ Adriana, MARTINEZ Claudia, MARTINEZ Daniel, MARTINEZ Daysi, MARTINEZ Ebeneezer, MARTINEZ Erin, MARTINEZ Esmeralda, MARTINEZ Juan, MARTINEZ June, MARTINEZ Lester, MARTINEZ Lino, MARTINEZ Luz, MARTINEZ Margarita, MARTINEZ Maria, MARTINEZ Estela, MARTINEZ Raquel, MARTINEZ Ryan, MARTINEZ Susan, MARTINEZ Vicki, MARTINIELLO Frank, MARTINO Daniel, MARTINO Gina, MARTINS MONTEIRO Sonia, MARTINSEN Harold, MARTINSEN Jean, MARTINSONS Anita, MARTIR Dada, MARTIREZ Melanie, MARTIREZ Michelle, MARTISKIN Dianne, MARTON Alex, MARTON Sharron, MARTORANA Matt, MARTYN Janice, MARTYN Wendy, MARUO Hitomi, MARUSICH Nita, MARUYAMA Miki, MARVELL Kathleen, MARVELL Ken, MARVIN Ray, MARWAHA Geetika, MARYON Anne, MARZOCCHI Oriano, MARZULLI Janine, MASAWAN Paul, MASCARENHAS Carla, MASCARENHAS Godfrey, MASCARENHAS Robert, MASCARENHAS Yolanda, MASCERA Sam, MASCITTI-COSTANZO Roberta, MASCORD Adele, MASCORD Ken, MASCORD Kylie, MASCORD Paul, MASCORD Rosemary, MASCORD Shane, MASE Vaivi, MASEN Peter, MASENHELDER Trent, MASHFORD Judith, MASHFORD Margaret, MASHIACH Moty, MASHMAN Ruth, MASHMAN Stuart, MASI Tony, MASIELLO Angelo, MASINGA Masinga, MASKALL Jacqueline, MASKELL James, MASKELL Michael, MASKEY Sunil, MASKIELL Rosalind, MASLIC Dean, MASLIN Patricia, MASMANIDIS Theofilos, MASON Allan, MASON Mason, MASON Andrew, MASON Ian, MASON Barry, MASON Ben, MASON Beverley, MASON David, MASON Emma, MASON Tony, MASON Glen, MASON Gloria, MASON Grant, MASON Greg, MASON Jim, MASON Janice, MASON Jeanette, MASON John, MASON Kelly, MASON Kresta, MASON Lynne, MASON Lynette, MASON Nicki, MASON Trish, MASON Peter, MASON Peter, MASON Peter, MASON Richard, MASON Bob, MASON Robert, MASON Ron, MASON Steve, MASON Sue, MASON Terry, MASON Val, MASON Warren, MASON Wendy, MASON Wendy, MASOUD Eiva, MASPONS BOSCH Ramon, MASSE Pierre, MASSELLA-MAHONY Flavia, MASSENDER Brooke, MASSY-GREENE Jane, MASTERS June, MASTERS Barry, MASTERS Ian, MASTERS Janice, MASTERS John, MASTERS Kel, MASTERS Gina, MASTERS Rex, MASTERS Bob, MASTERS Sophie, MASTERS Wayde, MASTERS Wendy, MASTERSON Carolyn, MASTERSON John, MASTERSON Katherine, MASTERTON Julia, MASTORIDES Jackie, MASTROCOLLA Tatiana, MASTROGIANNOPOULOS Nick, MASTROIANNI Luciana, MASTROIENI Dom, MASUDA Nao, MASUHARA Yuko, MATALON Ginette, MATANOVIC Barbara, MATAR Tarek, MATCHETT Edward, MATCHETT Mark, MATEER Marian, MATEK Robert, MATEOS Marion, MATEOS Paul-Michael, **MATERNA Judith**, MATH Dala, MATHAI John, MATHAI Sarah, MATHER Diane, MATHER Jason, MATHER Judy, MATHER Ron, MATHERS Andrew, MATHERS David, MATHESON Bianca, MATHESON Deb, MATHESON Doug, MATHESON Ted, MATHESON Glenn, MATHESON Leon, MATHESON Marianne, MATHESON Terri, MATHEW Jennifer, MATHEW Usha, MATHEWS Allan, MATHEWS Ansel, MATHEWS Terry, MATHEWS Brenda, MATHEWS Kate, MATHEWS Katrina, MATHEWS Louise, MATHEWS Shane, MATHEWS Sharon, MATHEWS Susie, MATHIANG Abai, MATHIAS Gerry, MATHIAS David, MATHIASCH Vicki, MATHIESON Barbara, MATHIESON John, MATHIEU Philippe, MATHIEU Meagan, MATHIEUHARBROW Peta, MATHISON Beryl, MATHISON Julia, MATHUR Mukta, MATHUR Navin, MATHUR Neha, MATHY Aline, MATIS George, MATIUK Natalie, MATKOVICH Vinko, MATLEY Anne, MATLOUBI Michael, MATOLCSY Zoltan, MATON Glenys, MATSAS Fred, MATSUBARA Yoshi, MATSUDA Daishi, MATSUDA Yukiko, MATSUI Showhey, MATSUNAGA Josh, MATSUOKA Shoko, MATSUURA Eriko, MATSUZAWA Yuko, MATTAR Monica, MATTERN Robyn, MATTERN Sharyn, MATTERSON Brett, MATTES Ari, MATTES Bret, MATTES Judy, MATTES Penne, MATTES Phil, MATTES-HARRIS Amy, MATTESHARRIS Bryony, MATTESON Ron, MATTHEW Bryan, MATTHEW-STUBBS Jonathon, MATTHEWS Anna, MATTHEWS Bron, MATTHEWS Brooke, MATTHEWS Christine, MATTHEWS Clayton, MATTHEWS David, MATTHEWS David, MATTHEWS Emily, MATTHEWS Emma, MATTHEWS Frances, MATTHEWS Freda, MATTHEWS Johanna, MATTHEWS Keegan, MATTHEWS Ken, MATTHEWS Laura, MATTHEWS Lauren, MATTHEWS Leanne, MATTHEWS Maggie, MATTHEWS Meg, MATTHEWS Michelle, MATTHEWS Neita, MATTHEWS Pamela, MATTHEWS Pam, MATTHEWS Peter, MATTHEWS Peter, MATTHEWS Peter, MATTHEWS Peter, MATTHEWS Rebekah, MATTHEWS Robyn, MATTHEWS Robin, MATTHEWS Roy, MATTHEWS Sarah, MATTHEWS Serge,, MATTHEWS Siaan, MATTHEWS Sue, MATTHEWS Terry, MATTHEWS Therese, MATTHEWS Tonya, MATTHEWS Trevor, MATTHIAS Tarcisius, MATTHYSEN Paul, MATTI-GORGES Philemon, MATTICK Helen, MATTIUZZO Michael, MATTNER Kirsten, MATTS Bert, MATUS Gabby, MATUSCHKA Mary, MATUSKA Jules, MATWAY Julie, MATWIJOW Denise, MATYK Peter, MATZIE Raspy, MAUCH Vitor, MAUDE Bernard, MAUDE Helen, MAUDER Beate, MAUGERI Maria, MAUGHAN Geoff, MAUGHAN Geoffery, MAUNDER Danielle, MAUNDER Kate, MAUNDO Thitu, MAUNG Kyi, MAUNSELL Joyce, MAUNSELL Nicole, MAUNSELL Terry, MAUREEN Stanford, MAURER Klaus, MAURER Wayne, MAURICE Jon, MAURO Geraldine, MAURO Stuart, MAVOR Vicky, MAVRIK Poppy, MAVRITSKY Tania, MAVROFORA Vicki, MAVROMATIS Kristina, MAVROS Wendy, MAVROUDAKIS Dikaia, MAWBY Francis, MAWER Andrea, MAWER Bebe, MAWER Allen, MAWSON Ann, MAWSON Lyn, MAWSON Phil, MAWSON Steven, MAXFIELD Barbara, MAXIE Andrea, MAXWELL Carol, MAXWELL Catherine, MAXWELL Cathy, MAXWELL Ian, MAXWELL Jane, MAXWELL Kylie, MAXWELL Marie, MAXWELL Paul, MAXWELL Bob, MAXWELL Steph, MAXWELL Bill, MAXWELL-COGHLAN Peter, MAY Aileen, MAY Andrew, MAY Andrew, MAY Bruce, MAY Celia, MAY Cherie, MAY David, MAY Erica, MAY Francine, MAY Jayne, MAY Joyce, MAY Justin, MAY Lindsay, MAY Ray, MAY Greame, MAY Ruth, MAY Stephen, MAY Stuart, MAY Tony, MAY Wendy, MAYANOBE Yves, MAYBANK Paul, MAYBURY Barry, MAYBURY Muriel, MAYCOCK Dannielle, MAYCOCK Valda, MAYER Kim, MAYERS Carley, MAYFIELD Wendy, MAYGER Natasha, MAYHEW Angela, MAYHEW Barry, MAYHEW Claire, MAYHEW Helen, MAYHEW Melissa, MAYHEW Michele, MAYHEW Steve, MAYHEW Trevor, MAYNARD Jim, MAYNARD Keith, MAYNARD Paul, MAYNARD Bob, MAYNARD-LISTER Kerry, MAYNE Grahame, MAYNE Jenny, MAYNE Jonathan, MAYNE Lisa, MAYNE Lyndall, MAYNE Margaret, MAYNE Matthew, MAYNE Nicole, MAYO Betty, MAYO Jason, MAYO Nick, MAYR Jennifer, MAYR Josef, MAYR Manfred, MAZAR Maria-Sol, MAZENAUER Ern, MAZENCO Chris, MAZID Mazid, MAZUROVA Milena, MAZZANTI Lisa, **MAZZAROLI Louise**, MAZZERI Cecil, MAZZITELLI Anthony, MAZZOLANI John, MAZZON Stefania, MAZZONI Silver, MAZZUCCHELLI Alexander, MBA NCHAMA Sonia, MCADAM Leanne, MCADIE Cathy, MCALARY Graham, MCALARY Rock, MCALEER Donna, MCALEES Alex, MCALISTER Ray, MCALLAN Lesley, MCALLISON Kevin, MCALLISTER David, MCALLISTER Nicki, MCALOON Ronald, MCALPINE Amanda, MCALPINE Gordon, MCALPINE Peter, MCALPINE Phyllis, MCANDREW Barbara, MCANDREW Min, MCANDREW Robert, MCANELLY Don, MCAPPION Patrick, MCARDIE Margaret, MCARDLE Kirsty, MCARDLE Pete, MCARTHUR Jean, MCARTHUR Sheree, MCARTHUR Stephen, MCARTHUR Damien, MCASKILL Peter, MCAULEY Erica, MCAULEY Peter, MCAULEY Kaye, MCAULEY-WHITE Max, MCAULIFFE Alan, MCAULIFFE Leanne, MCAULIFFE Monica, MCAULLAY Susan, MCAUSLAND Enid, MCBREARTY Ruth, MCBRIARTY Laurel, MCBRIDE Peter, MCBRIDE Jay, MCBRIDE Jill, MCBRIDE Kris, MCBRIDE Lilian, MCBRIDE Peter, MCBRIDE Peter, MCBRIDE Ross, MCBRIDE Sharon,

MCBROOM Sweeper, MCBRYDE Daniela, MCBRYDE Mark, MCBURNIE Stephen, MCCABE Dorothy, MCCABE Bernadette, MCCABE Carole, MCCABE Cathy, MCCABE Clare, MCCABE Janice, MCCABE Jane, MCCABE Mark, MCCABE Tom, MCCAFFERTY Mary, MCCAFFERY Jenny, MCCAFFERY Megan, MCCAFFREY Frank, MCCALL Ben, MCCALLAN Tom, MCCALLION Stephen, MCCALLUM Ashley, MCCALLUM Jane, MCCALLUM John, MCCANN Tessa, MCCANN Damien, MCCANN Dianne, MCCANN Helen, MCCANN Jan, MCCANN Jean, MCCANN Nanette, MCCANN Rob, MCCANN Roy, MCCARDELL Rohan, MCCARROLL Lindy, MCCARROLL Nola, MCCARRON Hugh, MCCARRON Sam, MCCARRON Tania, MCCARTHY Fran, MCCARTHY Pat, MCCARTHY Ron, MCCARTHY Amanda, MCC RTHY Athol, MCCARTHY Ben, MCCARTHY Bernie, MCCARTHY Caryn, MCCARTHY Cathy, MCCARTHY Cheryl, MCCARTHY Courtney, MCCARTHY Daina, MCCARTHY Fiona, MCCARTHY Jim, MCCARTHY Jan, MCCARTHY Jo, MCCARTHY Kate, MCCARTHY Kevin, MCCARTHY Kirsten, MCCARTHY Raymond, MCCARTHY Robin, MCCARTHY Sarah, MCCARTHY Sophie, MCCARTHY Fred, MCCARTHY Travis, MCCARTHY Trevor, MCCARTHY Veronica, MCCARTHY Wayne, MCCARTNEY Bob, MCCARTY Mac, MCCASKIE Kylie, MCCATHY Roy, MCCAULEY Barbara, MCCAULEY Brian, MCCAULEY Jan, MCCAULEY Jo, MCCAULEY Richard, MCCAUSLAND Helen, MCCAUSLAND Nicole, MCCAWLEY Betty, MCCAWLEY Ken, MCCHEYNE Jason, MCCLAFFERTY Michelle, MCCLAREN Sean, MCCLARENCE Maureen, MCCLEAN Rebecca, **MCCLEAN Rowan**, MCCLEAN Tom, MCCLEAY Ken, MCCLELLAND Jan, MCCLELLAND Richard, MCCLELLAND Robert, MCCLELLAND Virginia, MCCLENAGHAN Anthony, MCCLENAHAN Pete, MCCLORY Fergus, MCCLORY Judy, MCCLOSKEY Bridget, MCCLOSKEY Mollie, MCCLOSKEY Neil, MCCLUAND Cindy, MCCLUER Bryan, MCCLUER Gale, MCCLUNG Angela, MCCLURE Anne, MCCLUSKEY Peter, MCCLUSKEY Ray, MCCLUSKIE Rachel, MCCLYMONT Jean, MCCOLL Katrina, MCCOLL Liza, MCCOLL Maxine, MCCOLL Phil, MCCOLLEY Paul, MCCOMBE Lee, MCCOMBIE Trish, MCCOMBS Kerry, MCCONACHIE Philip, MCCONACHY Diana, MCCONAGHEY Glenda, MCCONAGHEY Jim, MCCONCHIE Brenda, MCCONCHIE Rob, MCCONCHIE Vicki, MCCONCHIE Lisa, MCCONNELL Dean, MCCONNELL Lois, MCCONNELL Sian, MCCONNEY Simon, MCCONNOCHIE Pat, MCCONVILLE Martin, MCCONVILLE Maria, MCCOOK Lynne, MCCOOK Scott, MCCOOMBES Ray, MCCORD Bernadette, MCCORD Christopher, MCCORD Keith, MCCORKELLE Jennifer, MCCORMACK Barb, MCCORMACK Bob, MCCORMACK Dale, MCCORMACK Matt, MCCORMACK Susan, MCCORMACK Theresa, MCCORMICK Cheryl, MCCORMICK Grant, MCCORMICK Jo, MCCORMICK Rebecca, MCCORQUODALE Alexandra, MCCOSKER Jane, MCCOSKER Mike, **MCCOSKER Rick**, MCCOTTER Ken, MCCOTTER June, MCCOURT Jim, MCCOWAN June, MCCOY Damien, MCCOY Damian, MCCOY Joan, MCCOY Kathy, MCCOY Luke, MCCOY Mia, MCCOY Michelle, MCCRACKEN Hamish, MCCRACKEN Judy, MCCREANOR Sheila, MCCREANOR Audrey, MCCREDIE Dave, MCCREERY David, MCCROARY Sharon, MCCROHON Rosalie, MCCRONE Lisa, MCCRORY Pat, MCCRORY Paul, MCCUBBERY Phoebe, MCCUDDEN Pat, MCCUE John, MCCUISH Sandra, MCCULLAGH David, MCCULLAGH Karen, MCCULLAGH Maureen, MCCULLAGH Peta, MCCULLOCH John, MCCULLOCH Merrin, MCCULLOUGH Glenda, MCCULLOUGH Jim, MCCULLOUGH Sue, MCCULLY Bob, MCCUSKER Cristan, MCCUTCHEON John, MCCUTCHEON David, MCCUTCHEON Gina, MCCUTECHEON Amy, MCDADE Sanny, MCDANIEL Tom, MCDARRA Gracie, MCDAVITT Andy, MCDAVITT Belinda, MCDEED Julie, MCDERMID Edward, MCDERMID Judy, MCDERMID Ann, MCDERMOTT Reg, MCDERMOTT Andrew, MCDERMOTT Denise, MCDERMOTT Jeanie, MCDERMOTT John, MCDERMOTT John, MCDERMOTT Lesley, MCDERMOTT Margaret, MCDERMOTT Reg, MCDERMOTT Sue, MCDERMOTT Val, MCDERMOTT Wanda, MCDIARMID Helen, MCDIARMID Neill, MCDONAGH Dorothy, MCDONAGH Leigh, MCDONALD Alyssa, MCDONALD Bridie, MCDONALD Bronnie, MCDONALD Garry, MCDONALD John, MCDONALD Kev, MCDONALD Amy, MCDONALD Andrew, MCDONALD Andrew, MCDONALD Anita, MCDONALD Audrey, MCDONALD Beryl, MCDONALD Brad, MCDONALD Brian, MCDONALD Craig, MCDONALD Craig, MCDONALD Damien, MCDONALD Deborah, MCDONALD Dianne, MCDONALD Diana, MCDONALD Ted, MCDONALD Elise, MCDONALD Erin, MCDONALD Frank, MCDONALD Gaye, MCDONALD Gemma, MCDONALD Gillian, MCDONALD Glenn, MCDONALD Greg, MCDONALD Gwenda, MCDONALD Hugh, MCDONALD Ian, MCDONALD Janet, MCDONALD Jenna, MCDONALD Jodie, MCDONALD John, MCDONALD Julie, MCDONALD Kiara, MCDONALD Kirby, MCDONALD Laurie, MCDONALD Lindsay, MCDONALD Luke, MCDONALD Lyndal, MCDONALD Marilyn, MCDONALD Marlene, MCDONALD Michelle, MCDONALD Paquita, MCDONALD Pat, MCDONALD Patricia, MCDONALD Patti, MCDONALD Paul, MCDONALD Peter, MCDONALD Rob, MCDONALD Bob, MCDONALD Rosemary, MCDONALD Sara, MCDONALD Sharon, MCDONALD Shane, MCDONALD Steve, MCDONALD Stephen, MCDONALD Syd, MCDONALD Tony, MCDONALD Yoshiko, MCDONALD-KERR Campbell, MCDONALL Janet, MCDONALL Patricia, MCDONELL Alison, MCDONELL Angus, MCDONELL Anne-Marie, MCDONELL Colleen, MCDONELL Greg, MCDONELL Jill, MCDONELL Ryan, MCDONELL Yvonne, MCDONNEL Belinda, MCDONNELL Carmen, MCDONNELL Chris, MCDONNELL Chris, MCDONNELL Janice, MCDONNELL Janis, MCDONNELL Jody, MCDONNELL Rhonda, MCDONNELL Tom, MCDONOUGH Noel, MCDOUGALL Danni, MCDOUGALL Barbara, MCDOUGALL Catherine, MCDOUGALL David, MCDOUGALL Kirsty, MCDOUGALL Leanne, MCDOUGALL Peter, MCDOWELL Margaret, MCDOWELL Megan, MCEACHERN Roy, MCELDOWNEY John, MCELHINNEY Nikki, MCELHONE Ann, MCELROY Andy, MCENCROE Doreen, MCENCROE Plod, MCENEARNEY Helen, MCENIERY Helen, MCENTEE Tony, MCEVOY Margaret, MCEVOY Christina, MCEVOY David, MCEVOY Simon, MCEWAN Jemma, MCEWAN Robert, MCEWAN Warwick, MCEWAN-WATSON Lesley, MCEWEN Sue, MCEWEN Allan, MCEWEN Louise, MCEWIN Jenni, MCFADDEN Di, MCFADDEN Kev, MCFADDEN Anne, MCFADDEN Christy, MCFADYEN Cheryl, MCFADYEN Judy, MCFADYEN Kylie, MCFADYEN Lesley, MCFALL Arthur, MCFARLAND Brian, MCFARLAND Ian, MCFARLAND Tim, MCFARLAND Andrea, MCFARLAND Carolyn, MCFARLANE Ann, MCFARLANE Tony, MCFARLANE Grant, MCFARLANE Leslie, MCFARLANE Mark, MCFARLANE Penney, MCFARLANE Phil, MCFARLINE Damien, MCFAWN Vicki, MCGAIR Trevor, MCGANN Barbara, MCGANN Garry, MCGANN Susan, MCGARRAGHY Chris, MCGARRAGHY Rose, MCGARRIGLE Kyle, MCGARRY Joe, MCGAULLEY Paula, MCGAULLEY Paul, MCGAW Margie, MCGAW Wenz, MCGEACHIE William, MCGEE Jennie, MCGEE Phyllis, MCGEE Bill, MCGENNISKEN Brett, MCGEOWN Catherine, MCGETRICK Eoin, MCGETTIGAN Nikhil, MCGHEE Gary, MCGILL Peter, MCGILL Jodie, MCGILL Kirby, MCGILL Robyn, MCGILVRAY Tony, MCGILVRAY David, MCGILVRAY Neil, MCGILVRAY Richard, MCGILVRAY Val, MCGIMPSEY James, MCGINLAY Fiona, MCGINLEY Fiona, MCGINN Daphne, MCGINTY Grant, MCGIRR Clare, MCGIRR John, MCGIRR Murray, MCGIRR Thomas, MCGIVERN Jeanne, MCGLADE Peter, MCGLASHAN Lee, MCGLASHAN Paul, MCGLASHAN Reg, **MCGLINN Pam**, MCGLINN Ted, MCGLINN Margaret, MCGOLDRICK Gary, MCGORM Georgie, MCGOVERN Joy-Anne, **MCGOVERN Maureen**, MCGOVERN Merle, MCGOWAN Anne, MCGOWAN Graham, MCGOWAN Alan, MCGOWAN Danny, MCGOWAN Danielle, MCGOWAN Jessy, MCGOWAN Jillian, MCGOWAN John, MCGOWAN Kelly, MCGOWAN Les, MCGOWAN Nikki, MCGOWEN David, MCGOWEN Joanne, MCGOWN Ian, MCGOWN Kate, MCGOWN Max, MCGRADY Nik, MCGRADY Sally, MCGRANE Joy, MCGRANE Rob, MCGRATH Paul, MCGRATH Alfred, MCGRATH Barry, MCGRATH Brendan, MCGRATH Bruce, MCGRATH Carlene, MCGRATH Christine, MCGRATH Jim, MCGRATH Gina, MCGRATH Jacqueline, MCGRATH Jill, MCGRATH John, MCGRATH Leia, MCGRATH Lindsay, MCGRATH Luke, MCGRATH Lynda, MCGRATH Margot, MCGRATH John, MCGRATH Nic,

MCGRATH Pam, MCGRATH Frank, MCGRATH Paul, MCGRATH Paul, MCGRATH Peta, MCGRATH Philip, MCGRATH Sharon, MCGRATH Tim, MCGRATH Viv, MCGREGOR Ian, MCGREGOR Andrew, MCGREGOR Andrew, MCGREGOR Daniel, MCGREGOR David, MCGREGOR Gwen, MCGREGOR Richard, MCGREGOR Bob, MCGREGOR Sara, MCGRISKIN Greg, MCGRODER Gail, MCGRODER Gael, MCGROSKY Charles, MCGUFFICKE Terry, MCGUIGAN Wendy, MCGUIGAN Kerrie, MCGUIGGAN Phil, MCGUINESS Marie, MCGUINN Scott, MCGUINNESS Alistaire, MCGUINNESS Heidi, MCGUINNESS Terry, MCGUIRE Archibald, MCGUIRE Bernadette, MCGUIRE Greg, MCGUIRE Justin, MCGUIRE Michael, MCGUIRE Nessie, MCGUIRE Paddy, MCGUIRE Paul, MCGUIRE Peter, MCGUIRE Theresa, MCGURGAN Russell, MCHALE Frank, MCHALE Lynette, MCHARDIE Pam, MCHARDY Steve, MCHARG Amanda, MCHARG Charmaine, MCILLHATTON Coleen, MCILVEEN Stephen, MCILVEEN Bill, MCILVENIE Kylie, MCILVENIE Lisa, MCILWAINE Robert, MCILWAINE Sue, MCILWAINE Garry, MCILWRAITH Johnno, MCINDOE Daniel, MCINERNEY Marita, MCINERNEY Belinda, MCINERNEY Colin, MCINERNEY Garth, MCINERNEY John, MCINNES Ben, MCINNES Cameron, MCINNES Heather, MCINNES James, MCINNES Jennifer, MCINNES John, MCINNES Lorraine, MCINNES Mary, MCINNES Narelle, MCINNES Craig, MCINNES Robert, MCINNES Scott, MCINNES Terence, **MCINROY Margaret**, MCINTOSH Denis, MCINTOSH Elizabeth, MCINTOSH Allison, MCINTOSH Andrew, MCINTOSH Bernie, MCINTOSH Brent, MCINTOSH Bridget, MCINTOSH David, MCINTOSH Don, MCINTOSH Geoff, MCINTOSH Heather, MCINTOSH Ian, MCINTOSH Jane, MCINTOSH Joshua, MCINTOSH Julia, MCINTOSH Julie, MCINTOSH Kirrily, MCINTOSH Patti, MCINTOSH Peter, MCINTOSH Bob, MCINTOSH Russell, MCINTOSH Sarah, MCINTOSH Tom, MCINTYRE Gwen, MCINTYRE Heather, MCINTYRE Ken, MCINTYRE Alan, MCINTYRE Brian, MCINTYRE Cindy, MCINTYRE Davi , MCINTYRE David, MCINTYRE Donna, MCINTYRE Geoffrey, MCINTYRE Joan, MCINTYRE John, MCINTYRE Julia, MCINTYRE Lewis, MCINTYRE Lou, MCINTYRE Lyn, MCINTYRE Lynne, MCINTYRE Margaret, MCINTYRE Michael, MCINTYRE Nancie, MCINTYRE Neil, MCINTYRE Phil, MCINTYRE Sharon, MCINTYRE Stephen, MCINTYRE Steven, MCIVOR Denis, MCJANNETT Yvonne, MCKANE Kath, MCKAVANAGH Scott, MCKAY Angela, MCKAY Andrew, MCKAY Angus, MCKAY Angela, MCKAY Brett, MCKAY Brian, MCKAY Bruce, MCKAY Chelsea, MCKAY Denis, MCKAY Fitz, MCKAY Mac, MCKAY Janice, MCKAY Jennifer, MCKAY John, MCKAY Joshua, MCKAY Julie, MCKAY Karly, MCKAY Robin, MCKAY Margaret, MCKAY Fran, MCKAY Marnee, MCKAY Mark, MCKAY Rob, MCKAY John, MCKEAN Wendy, MCKECHNIE Hugh, MCKECHNIE Andrew, MCKECHNIE Leanne, MCKEE Susie, MCKEE Ilma, MCKEE Jackie, MCKEE Therese, MCKEE Steve, MCKEEN Suzanne, MCKEEVER Reg, MCKELL Jean, MCKELL William, MCKELLAR Lindsay, MCKELLAR Stuart, MCKELLEHER Helen, MCKELLEHER John, MCKELLEHER Lucretia, MCKELVEY David, MCKELVEY Scotty, MCKELVIE Ralph, MCKELVIE Lorraine, MCKELVIE Pippa, MCKENDRY Jason, MCKENDRY John, MCKENNA Hilton, MCKENNA Mathew, MCKENNA Michael, MCKENNA Nathan, MCKENNA Timothy, MCKENNY Bill, MCKENNY Amal, MCKENNY Francis, MCKENTY Graham, MCKENZIE Arthur, MCKENZIE Fred, MCKENZIE Alan, MCKENZIE Amy, MCKENZIE Andrew, MCKENZIE Tony, MCKENZIE Cameron, MCKENZIE Carolyn, MCKENZIE Cathrine, MCKENZIE Elizabeth, MCKENZIE Frances, MCKENZIE Gayle, MCKENZIE Gillian, MCKENZIE Giselle, MCKENZIE Helen, MCKENZIE Ian, MCKENZIE Horrie, MCKENZIE James, MCKENZIE Jeff, MCKENZIE Janine, MCKENZIE John, MCKENZIE Jonathon, MCKENZIE Judy, MCKENZIE Kathy, MCKENZIE Keith, MCKENZIE Kim, MCKENZIE Mark, MCKENZIE Margaret, MCKENZIE Matthew, MCKENZIE Pete, MCKENZIE Robyn, MCKEOGH Eileen, MCKEON Gabrielle, MCKEON Margaret, MCKEON Katherine, MCKEON Patricia, MCKEON Robyn, MCKEOWN Linda, MCKEOWN Prue, MCKERN Lisa, MCKERNAN Alec, MCKERNAN John, MCKERVEY Peter, MCKEVETT Garry, MCKIE Elisha, MCKIE Debbie, MCKIE Kristy, MCKIERNAN Lyn, MCKILLOP Allen, MCKILLOP Dave, MCKIM Betty, MCKINLAY Kevin, MCKINLEY Ilana, MCKINNEL Colin, MCKINNIS Geraldine, MCKINNON Annie, MCKINNON Clair, MCKINNON David, MCKINNON Gordon, MCKINNON Leanne, MCKINNON-PALMER Wesley, MCKISSICK Clare, MCKNOULTY Leanne, MCKOY Phil, MCKRAIG Janet, MCLACHLAN Alastair, MCLACHLAN Bruce, MCLACHLAN Marika, MCLACHLAN Melissa, MCLACHLAN Murray, MCLACHLAN Bobby, MCLAINE Sally, MCLANDERS Diane, MCLAREN Alison, MCLAREN Russell, MCLAREN Alicia, MCLAREN Allan, MCLAREN Deirdre, MCLAREN Ian, MCLAREN Jennifer, MCLAREN Judy, MCLAREN Margaret, MCLAREN Maureen, MCLAREN Peter, MCLAREN Shirley, MCLAREN Tom, MCLAUCHLAIN Ian, MCLAUCHLAN Brendon, MCLAUCHLAN Matt, MCLAUGHLAN Tony, MCLAUGHLAN Sarah, MCLAUGHLIN John, MCLAUGHLIN Cathy, MCLAUGHLIN Jane, MCLAUGHLIN Macca, MCLAUGHLIN Keith, MCLAUGHLIN Liam, MCLAUGHLIN Robin, MCLAUGHLIN Susan, MCLAY Andrew, MCLEAN David, MCLEAN Liz, MCLEAN Lyn, MCLEAN Trish, MCLEAN Bill, MCLEAN Angus, MCLEAN Barbara, MCLEAN Bebe, MCLEAN Cameron, MCLEAN Chrissy, MCLEAN Darren, MCLEAN Donald, MCLEAN Euan, MCLEAN Gary, MCLEAN Harry, MCLEAN Hayley, MCLEAN Jim, MCLEAN Jennifer, MCLEAN Jenny, MCLEAN Jack, MCLEAN John, MCLEAN Judy, MCLEAN Kate, MCLEAN Murray, MCLEAN Rob, **MCLEAN Robert**, MCLEAN Ross, MCLEAN Sheila, MCLEAN Stacey, MCLEAN Stephen, MCLEAN Stuart, MCLEAN Tom, MCLEAN Wendy, MCLEAN Xanthe, MCLEAN-MUTAGA Kate, MCLEISH Colin, MCLEISH Andrew, MCLEISH Diana, MCLELAND Linda, MCLELLAN Andy, MCLELLAN Patrick, MCLENNAN Dugald, MCLENNAN Amber, MCLENNAN Betty, MCLENNAN Cheryl, MCLENNAN Fiona, MCLENNAN Janet, MCLENNAN Katie, MCLENNAN Lesley, MCLENNAN Patricia, MCLENNAN Bill, MCLEOD Paola, MCLEOD Ann, MCLEOD Barbara, MCLEOD Belinda, MCLEOD Caroline, MCLEOD Colette, MCLEOD David, MCLEOD Felicity, MCLEOD Graeme, MCLEOD Grahame, MCLEOD Ian, MCLEOD Janelle, MCLEOD Lisa, MCLEOD Neil, MCLEOD Suzie, MCLERIE Bill, MCLIESH Paul, MCLOCHLAN Ashleigh, MCLOUGHLIN Andrew, MCLOUGHLIN John, MCLOUGHLIN Michelle, MCLOUGHLIN Steph, MCMAHON Kim, MCMAHON Aimee, MCMAHON Andrew, MCMAHON Annelisa, MCMAHON Belinda, MCMAHON Brendan, MCMAHON Carolyn, MCMAHON Estee, MCMAHON Gabrielle, MCMAHON Jennifer, **MCMAHON Judith**, MCMAHON Karolyn, MCMAHON Lee, MCMAHON Louise, MCMAHON Lyn, MCMAHON Marika, MCMAHON Maureen, MCMAHON Michael, MCMAHON Trish, MCMAHON Trish, MCMAHON Peter, MCMAHON Rod, MCMAHON Travis, MCMAHON Mac, MCMAHON Bill, MCMAHON William, MCMANUS Dorothy, MCMANUS Erin, MCMANUS June, MCMANUS Jacinta, MCMANUS Kate, MCMANUS Keith, MCMANUS Maile, MCMANUS Norman, MCMANUS Sam, MCMARTIN Malcolm, MCMARTIN Sonia, MCMASTER Annissa, MCMASTER Des, MCMASTER Kate, MCMASTER Rosanne, MCMASTER Stewart, MCMEEKIN Kevin, MCMENAMIN Scott, MCMENAMIN Claire, MCMENAMIN Hugh, MCMIKEN Donald, MCMILLAN Duncan, MCMILLAN Tina, MCMILLAN Amanda, MCMILLAN Barry, MCMILLAN Brett, MCMILLAN Bruce, MCMILLAN Debbie, MCMILLAN Greg, MCMILLAN James, MCMILLAN John, MCMILLAN Sue, MCMILLAN William, MCMILLEN Margaret, MCMONIGAL Damien, MCMONIGAL Pamela, MCMONIGAL Simone, MCMULLAN David, MCMULLEN Elfreda, MCMULLEN Eddie, MCMULLEN Georgie, MCMULLEN Sean, MCMULLIN Chuck, MCMURCHIE Marilyn, MCMURCHY Jim, MCMURRAY Lisa, MCMURRAY Robyn, MCMURTRIE Ian, MCMURTRY Matthew, MCNAB Anita, MCNAB Emma, MCNAB Larry, MCNABB Rachel, MCNAIR Gael, MCNAIR Stephen, MCNALLY Peter, MCNAMARA Brian, MCNAMARA Jane, MCNAMARA Joe, MCNAMARA Kathy, MCNAMARA Kim, MCNAMARA Anne, MCNAMARA Tony, MCNAMARA Denise, MCNAMARA Joe, MCNAMARA Julie, MCNAMARA Julie, MCNAMARA Kylie, MCNAMARA Lorraine, MCNAMARA Mark, MCNAMARA Neil, MCNAMARA Peter, MCNAMARA Shaun, MCNAMARA Shirley, MCNAMARA Simon, MCNAMARA Sonja, MCNAMARA Stacey,

MCNAMARA Tim, MCNAMARA Val, MCNAMARA Wendy, MCNAMEE Peter, MCNAMEE Sonya, MCNEIL Terry, MCNEIL Jac, MCNEIL Jason, MCNEILL Andy, MCNEILL Catherine, MCNEILL Karen, MCNEILL Marguerite, MCNEILLY Kevin, MCNEILLY Michelle, MCNICOL Adam, MCNIEL Marquerite, MCNIVEN Alec, MCNIVEN Jennie, MCNIVEN Margaret, MCNORTON Sara, MCNORTON Tricia, MCNULTY Carmel, MCNULTY John, MCONIE David, MCPHAIL David, MCPHEE Gaille, MCPHEE Glenys, MCPHEE Keith, MCPHEE Linda, MCPHERSON Faye, MCPHERSON Ailsa, MCPHERSON Fiona, MCPHERSON Hannah, MCPHERSON Kerstin, MCPHERSON Leah, MCPHERSON Lyndon, MCPHERSON Neil, MCPIKE Gary, MCQUEEN Marney, MCQUEEN Andrew, MCQUEEN Colette, MCQUEEN Duncan, MCQUEEN Peter, MCQUILLAN Carey, MCQUILLAN Kim, MCQUILLAN Lucy, MCQUILTY Neil, MCQUIRK Peter, MCRAE Chris, MCRAE Cob, MCRAE Lynne, MCRAE Pip, MCRAE Vic, MCREDIE Peter, MCSEVENY Emma, MCSHANE Maz, MCSHANE Marcia, MCSHANE Mavis, MCSORLEY Carol, MCSWAN Dick, MCSWEENEY Babs, MCSWEENEY Jim, MCSWEENEY Lyn, MCSWEENEY Majella, MCTAGGART Judith, MCVEAGH Melissa, MCVEAGH Robyn, MCVEIGH Gwendolyn, MCVEY Bruce, MCVEY Danny, MCWADE Julie, MCWATERS Rick, MCWATTERS Amy, MCWHIRTER Ron, MCWHIRTER-HART Gayle, MCWILLIAM Tristan, MCWILLIAMS Claire, MCWILLIAMS Peter, MEAD Annette, MEAD Kathy, MEAD Kerrie, MEAD Nick, MEAD Raymond, MEAD Stephen, MEAD Tom, MEADE Kristin, MEADE Olive, MEADE John, MEADER Chrys, MEADES Dick, MEADLEY Elmo, MEADOWS Barrie, MEADOWS Kay, MEADOWS Stacey, MEAGHER Eve, MEAGHER Marie, MEAGHER Pam, MEAGHER Paul, MEAGHER Simon, MEAKER Christopher, MEALING Adam, MEALING Allan, MEALING Suzanne, MEANEY Joy, MEARA Margie, MEARES James, MEARNS Tony, MEARNS Darryl, MEARS Kate, MECOLI Nadia, MECS Gabe, MEDCALF Carol, MEDCALF Heather, MEDCALF Rosemary, MEDCALF Taryn, MEDHURST James, MEDINA Alejandro, MEDINA Carlos, MEDINA Carmen, MEDINA Erika, MEDINA Francisco, MEDINA Max, MEDINA DE BARRY Lucina, MEDINA-VACC Sergio, MEDINACELLI Sophie, MEDIOLI Trish, MEDJUMURAC Jenny, MEDLEY Bruce, MEDLEY Denise, MEDLEY Jack, MEDLEY Merv, MEDULLA Linda, MEDWAY Kellie, MEE Emerson, MEE Stephen, MEE Zara, MEECH Sherilee, MEEHAN Aaron, MEEHAN Betty, MEEHAN Brooke, MEEHAN Janette, **MEEHAN Lisa**, MEEHAN Lyall, MEEHAN-BYRNE Macie, MEEK Chris, MEEK Graham, MEEK Paul, MEEKINGS Bruce, MEENY Chris, MEENY Steve, MEEPEM Mary, MEERS Carolyn, MEESRON-LEM Noi, MEEUWISSEN Greg, MEGALAA Hanaa, MEGARIANI Helen, MEGGITT Anthony, MEGGS Liza, MEGUMI Yoshie, MEGUYER Bob, MEHALSKI Kirsty, MEHARG Christine, MEHKARY Hassan, MEHL Kathryn, MEHMED Leanne, MEHMED Tony, MEHTA Dilip, MEHTA Gaurav, MEHTA Sonel, MEI Heng, MEIC Bozica, MEIER Daniel, MEIER Fabienne, MEIGAN Tom, MEIJER George, MEIJER Bill-Meijer, MEIKLE John, MEIKLEJOHN Gordon, MEINER Elizabeth, MEISELBACH Robert, MEISENHELTER Allan, MEISENHELTER Maggie, MEJIA Dario, MEJIA Theresa, MEKHAEL Amir, MEKHAIL Jeannette, MELAKA Ashraf, MELBOURNE Lance, MELBOURNE Paul, MELBOURNE Tim, MELDRUM Gus, MELDRUM Gordon, MELE Nino, MELEHAN Lauren, MELEHAN Patrick, MELEKA Michael, MELENDEZ Ces, MELHUISH Peter, MELIA Clarke, MELISSA MARIE Rollison, MELISSARI Jan, MELISSARI Leroy, MELIZZA Mari, MELLAN James, MELLEVISH Evan, MELLICK George, MELLIN Ella, MELLIN Gavin, MELLIS Darren, MELLON Barbara, MELLOR Andrew, MELLOR Cheryl, MELLOR Margaret, MELLOR Paul, MELLOR Thuy-Van, MELLOWES Kate, MELO Julio, MELOCCO Sophia, MELOV Mike, MELOV Sue, MELTON Alan, MELTZER Mark, MELTZER Rosemary, MELVERTON Karen, MELVILLE Tony, MELVILLE Kim, MELVILLE Michael, MELVILLE Therese, MELVILLE Val, MELVIN Nancie, MEN Joanna, MENADUE Brian, MENADUE Russel, MENCINSKY Yuri, MENDAY Tom, MENDELBAUM Daniel, MENDELS Tamara, MENDES Tony, MENDHAM Nathan, MENDHAM Noel, MENDOLA Marina, MENDOZA Jose, MENDOZA Rolando, MENDOZA Suz, MENDOZA ALDANA Georgina, MENEGUZZO Lou, MENELET Virginie, MENENDEZ Helen, MENESES Carolina, MENEZES Chris, MENEZES Flora, MENEZES Francisca, MENEZES Llana, MENEZES Nicole, MENEZES Olinda, MENG Mingwei, MENHART Barbara, MENHART Zdenkau, MENKE Felix, MENKENS Hans, MENOLOTTO Fabian, MENON Jaya, MENON Prasad, MENON Madhav, MENON Mohan, MENOS Phyllis, MENSER Lorraine, MENSFORTH Sheryl, MENTZING Chris, MENVIELLE Mark, MENZIES Charlotte, MENZIES Clare, MENZIES Dorothy, MENZIES Hugh, MENZIES Max, MENZIES Peter, MENZIES Susan, MENZIES Troy, MEO Rami, MEOLI Leanne, MEPPEM Eric, MERCADO Emmanuel, MERCE-VARELA Kay, MERCENE Nards, MERCER Bindi, MERCER Belinda, MERCER Dudley, MERCER Emma, MERCER Graham, MERCER Marilyn, MERCER Nic, MERCHANT Dean, MERCHANT Liz, MERCHANT Judy, MERCHANT Steve, MERCURI Alberto, MEREDITH Adrien, MEREDITH Tony, MEREDITH Denise, MEREDITH George, MEREDITH John, MEREDITH Keith, MEREDITH Michael, MEREDITH Olive, MEREDITH John, MERENA Peter, MERHI Stacey, MERIGAN Faye, MERITY Jenny, MERL Manfred, MERLINO Gary, MERLINO Joe, MERRELL Neville, MERRETT Doreen, **MERRETT Thorold**, MERRICK Jo-ann, MERRICK Melinda, MERRICK Michael, MERRIE Summer, MERRIGAN Lawrie, MERRILL Katherine, MERRIN Laura, MERRINGTON David, MERRINGTON Peter, MERRINGTON Rosemary, MERRINGTON Stephen, MERRITT Mavis, MERSON Jim, MERSON Leila, MERTON Anne, MERTON Peter, MERWIN Joshua, MESCH Martin, MESDAGHI Kourosh, MESDAGHI Sheereen, MESQUITA Mesquita, MESSENT Francoise, MESSER Helen, MESSER Shaun, MESSER Wayne, MESSINA Caterina, MESSINA Robert, MESSINBIRD Margie, MESSITER Brian, MESTANZA-ESPINOZA Johanna, METANOMSKI Evan, METAXAS Kaye, METCALF Arnold, METCALF Maiva-jean, METCALF Michaela, METCALFE Jason, METCALFE Nicole, METCALFE Rose, METCALFE Sacha, METCALFE Selwyn, METHAM Leigh, METHAM Wes, METLEDGE Matilda, METLEDGE Robyn, METSON Robin, METTNER Glenys, METZ Melanie, METZ Bob, METZELING Ralph, METZKE Kerry, METZNER Richard, MEUDELL Kristy, MEUNIER Gabriel, MEUNIER Jonathan, MEUNIER Serge, MEURA Aime, MEURA Simon, MEURANT Phil, MEURER Michael, MEURON Helen, MEURON Peter, MEURS Liliane, MEUSBURGER Frank, MEUSBURGER Margaret, MEUWISSEN Louise, MEVISSEN Amanda, MEW Colin, MEW-SUM Jenny, MEWING Kate, MEWING Patrick, MEWJORK Dick, MEWS Ewan, MEYER Abbie, MEYER Alex, MEYER Ashley, MEYER Berni, MEYER Bruce, MEYER Dirk, MEYER Ian, MEYER Jacoba, MEYER John, MEYER Michele, MEYER Roman, MEYER Tom, MEYER Tony, MEYER-GLEAVES Bianca, MEYER-GLEAVES Michael, MEYERS Elizabeth, MEYERS Gabbe, MEYERS Jenny, MEYERS Michelle, MEZA Fernando, MEZEI Peter, MEZENBERG CC, MEZRANI Ramy, MEZZINO Antonette, MHAJER Sabah, MIAHINEYSI Foad, MICALE Paul, MICALE Pete, MICALLEF Tony, MICALLEF Anthony, MICALLEF Belinda, MICALLEF Heelen, MICALLEF Jeff, MICALLEF Jocie, MICALLEF Mary, MICALLEF Marco, MICALLEF Monica, MICALLEF Pat, MICALLEF Paul, MICALLEF Sylvia, MICALOS Steve, MICCOLI Barbara, MICHAEL Anthea, MICHAEL Bruce, MICHAEL Dave, MICHAEL Edmund, MICHAEL Effie, MICHAEL Fiona, MICHAEL Hyam, MICHAEL Maria, MICHAEL Ngo, MICHAEL Nicholas, MICHAEL Peter, MICHAEL Margaret, MICHAEL Tisdell, MICHAEL Weston, MICHAELIS Al, MICHAELIS Hannah, MICHAELOPOULOS Chris, MICHAELS Katrina, MICHAELS Susan, MICHAILIDOU Marina, MICHALEWICZ Marek, MICHALOPOULOS Kenny, MICHEL Andy, MICHEL-VEIZAGA Herben, MICHELAKIS Michael, MICHELIN John, MICHELL John, MICHELL Margaret, MICHELMORE Bette, MICHELMORE Mary, MICHENER Camille, MICHIE Sue, MICHIELIN Sandra, MICHNIEWICZ Jan, MICKAN Katherine, MICKE Gina, MICKLE Kimberly, MICO David, MICOLICH George, MIDDLEBROOK Kevin, MIDDLETON Angie, MIDDLETON Craig, MIDDLETON David, MIDDLETON Janet, MIDDLETON John, MIDDLETON Kath, MIDDLETON Ken, MIDDLETON Leanne, MIDDLETON Bekk, MIDDLETON Ron, MIDDLETON Suloch, MIDDLETON Vikki, MIDSON Keith, MIDWINTER Tamara, MIECHEL Bree, MIEL Denise, MIELS Jan,

MIETLING Klaus, MIFSUD Deirdre, MIFSUD Kelly, MIFSUD Steve, MIFSUD Ronnie, MIFSUDGUERRA Juan, MIGAN Emily, MIGCHELS Hanneke, MIHAJLOVIC Veronica, MIHALIC John, MIHELAKIS Kiyoko, MIHNO Zina, MIHRSHAHI Aziz, MIJATOVIC Vesna, MIJAYA Sherly, MIKALAUSKAS Blanche, MIKALIC Ana, MIKALSEN Tone, MIKE David, MIKHAIL Camelia, MIKHAIL Kamal, MIKHAIL Mina, MIKHAILOV Leo, MIKHEEVA Tonia, MIKLOVIC Anthony, MIKULIC Ana, MIKULIC Marija, MILADINOVIC Boris, M!LAG Edwin, MILANOVA Nina, MILANOVIC Natalija, MILAZZO Wendie, MILBURN Peter, MILEHAM Neville, MILENKOVSKI William, MILES Amy, MILES Brian, MILES Cameron, MILES Claire, MILES Des, MILES Frank, MILES Helen, MILES Jess, MILES Kelvin, MILES Ray, MILES Richard, MILES Scott, MILES Shirley, MILES Simon, MILES Tracy, MILES Warren, MILFORD Sue, MILGATE Bradley, MILGATE Sandra, MILHAM Nic, MILINKOVIC Vesna, MILJEVIC Natasa, MILLA Elizabeth, MILLA Lorraine, MILLALONCO Astrid, MILLAN Ivette, MILLANTA Leonie, MILLAR Brian, MILLAR Liz, MILLAR Karin, MILLAR Luke, MILLAR Michelle, MILLAR Rachel, MILLAR Ray, MILLAR Bill, MILLAR Alistair, MILLARD Amanda, MILLARD Dawn, MILLARD Grant, MILLARD Jan, MILLARD Liz, MILLARD Nathalie, MILLARD Ray, MILLARD Rosemary, MILLBURN Frank, MILLE Charles,MILLER Abby, MILLER Gordon, MILLER Alfred, MILLER Andrew, MILLER Edwina, MILLER Ann, MILLER Tony, MILLER Audrey, MILLER Blake, MILLER Brett, MILLER Brenda, MILLER Brian, MILLER Bruce, MILLER Carol, MILLER Cec, MILLER Cherylene, MILLER Chris, MILLER Daniel, MILLER David, MILLER David, MILLER Donald, MILLER Erin, MILLER Frank, MILLER Garry, MILLER Genelle, MILLER George, MILLER Geoff, MILLER Glynis, MILLER Heather, MILLER Helen, MILLER Helene, MILLER Helen, MILLER Harry, MILLER Ian, MILLER Jan, MILLER Jayson, MILLER Jenny, MILLER Jess, MILLER John, MILLER Kate, MILLER Kay, MILLER Keith, MILLER Kelly, MILLER Keri, MILLER Kevin, MILLER Kevin, MILLER Kylie, MILLER Lyndsay, MILLER Mark, MILLER Michelle, MILLER Neil, MILLER Nick, MILLER Nicole, MILLER Patricia, MILLER Peter, MILLER Peter, MILLER Peter, MILLER Phillip, MILLER Rick, MILLER Rinky, MILLER Robert, MILLER Robyn, MILLER Ron, MILLER Ron, MILLER Sam, MILLER Stan, MILLER Stephen, MILLER Stuart, MILLER Stuart, MILLER Susan, MILLER Tracey, MILLER Vivienne, MILLER Bruce, MILLER Alan, MILLERCHIP Graham, MILLERD Margaret, MILLERSHIP Julian, MILLETT Brian, MILLICAN Helen, MILLICAN Wallace, MILLIGAN Cynthia, MILLIGAN Margaret, MILLIGAN Sarah, MILLIKEN Cathy, MILLIKEN Julie, MILLING Lisa, MILLMAN Beryl, MILLS Amity, MILLS Chris, MILLS Corrinne, MILLS Danny, MILLS David, MILLS Dennis, MILLS Di, MILLS Dorothy, MILLS Duncan, MILLS Emma, MILLS Fleur, MILLS Fran, MILLS Gary, MILLS Georgie, MILLS Greg, MILLS Hannah, MILLS Helen, MILLS Joanne, MILLS John, MILLS Kathryn, MILLS Kathryn, MILLS Kerry, MILLS Kirsten, MILLS Leanne, MILLS Lee, MILLS Leone, MILLS Linda, MILLS Lisa, MILLS Lyn, MILLS Marg, MILLS Margaret, MILLS Margaret, MILLS Melissa, MILLS Michael, MILLS Murray, MILLS Norm, MILLS Penny, MILLS Rob, MILLS Sarah-Jane, MILLS Suzi, MILLS Tracey, MILLS Tracy, MILLS Victor, MILLSOM Kelvin, MILLSOM Lyn, MILLSOM Lynne, MILLWARD Cate, MILNE Alan, MILNE Christine, MILNE Elizabeth, MILNE Eric, MILNE Geoff, MILNE Gladie, MILNE Gordon, MILNE John, MILNE Joni, MILNE Katrina, MILNE Les, MILNE Lucy, MILNE Marian, MILNE Stephenie, MILNE Theresa, MILNE Victoria, MILNER Bruce, MILNER Caroline, MILNER Cecily, MILNER Lisa, MILNER Mike, MILNER Keith, MILNER Paul, MILNER Sandy, MILOSEVIC George, MILSON Harvey, MILSON Kristy, MILTHORPE Pam, MILTON Eddie, MILTON Jon, MILTON Malcolm, MILTON Scott, MIMS Madeline, MIN Christina, MIN Min, MINA Michael, MINAHAN Ruth, MINALL Claire, MINBATIWALA Roxanne, MINCA Annette, MINCHENKO Jack, MINCHER Elizabeth, MINERS Heidi, MINETT Margaret, MINGS Sharon, MINGS SR Sam, MINJUNG Kim, MINNEY Harold, MINNOCK Shane, MINNS Leonie, MINNS Prue, MINODA Akiko, MINORS Joan, **MINSHALL Pamela**, MINTER Malcolm, MINTO Joe, MINTO Peter, MINTO Sean, MINTON Di, MINTU Abul, MINTY David, MIOK Vesna, MIR Ali, MIRABITO Maurie, MIRAGAIA PERRI Mariana, MIRAH James, MIRAN Michelle, MIRAN-KHAN Karim, MIRCESKI David, MIRIGLIANI Joe, MIRKAZEMI Lailani, MIRRA Andrea, MIRTSOPOULOS Lisa, MIRZA Dalia, MIRZA Tommy, MIRZABEGIAN Sera, MIRZAI Benes, MIRZARAZI Keshvar, MIRZAYAN Eric, MISAKI Yoshiko, MISAMER Annemarie, MISDOM Chris, MISDOM Sarah, MISDOM Tom, MISIRLI Deanna, MISIUS Hayley, MISKELL Rod, MISKELL Sharon, MISKOVIC Mila, MISON Bill, MISSEN Rodney, MISSON George, MISTRY Shirin, MITAI Raeanne, MITANI Yuka, MITCHEL MILNE Scott, MITCHELL Andrew, MITCHELL Tony, MITCHELL Ashleagh, MITCHELL Barb, MITCHELL Belinda, MITCHELL Ben, MITCHELL Brenda, MITCHELL Brett, MITCHELL Brett, MITCHELL Brian, MITCHELL Brooke, MITCHELL Christine, MITCHELL Chris, MITCHELL Chris, MITCHELL Christine, MITCHELL Coralie, MITCHELL Craig, MITCHELL David, MITCHELL David, MITCHELL David, MITCHELL David, MITCHELL Debbie, MITCHELL Debbie, MITCHELL Diane, MITCHELL Dominic, MITCHELL Donna, MITCHELL Don, MITCHELL Don, MITCHELL Donna, MITCHELL Duncan, MITCHELL Edward, MITCHELL Geoffrey, MITCHELL Glenn, MITCHELL Gordon, MITCHELL Graeme, **MITCHELL Graham**, MITCHELL Grant, MITCHELL Graeme, MITCHELL Heather, MITCHELL Helen, MITCHELL Janet, MITCHELL Jan, MITCHELL Jason, MITCHELL Jillian, MITCHELL Jo, MITCHELL John, MITCHELL Judith, MITCHELL Kirsten, MITCHELL Kylie, MITCHELL Lindsay, MITCHELL Lydia, MITCHELL Lynette, MITCHELL Marie, MITCHELL Maria, MITCHELL Mark, MITCHELL Mike, MITCHELL Nicolle, MITCHELL Paul, MITCHELL Lee, MITCHELL Perdi, MITCHELL Peter, MITCHELL Peter, MITCHELL Mitch, MITCHELL Reginald, MITCHELL Bob, MITCHELL Bob, MITCHELL Rodger, MITCHELL Sarah, **MITCHELL Sandy**, MITCHELL Scott, MITCHELL Shelley, MITCHELL Simone, MITCHELL Sonia, MITCHELL Steven, MITCHELL Stewart, MITCHELL Steve, MITCHELL Tamira, MITCHELL Tegan, MITCHELL Tommy, MITCHELL Thomas, MITCHELL Tim, MITCHELL Troy, MITCHELL Vicki, MITCHELL Wayne, MITCHELL Wendy, MITCHELL Yvonne, MITCHELL Zane, MITHIEUX Pat, MITIC Bob, MITRA Uday, MITRE Jo, MITRE Katina, MITRE Vana, MITREVSKI Robert, MITROPOULOS George, MITSAKIS Nadia, MITSUJI Takaaki, MITTAL Rajat, MITTAS Paul, MITTE Ravi, MIU Cindy, MIURA-HIGGS Yuko, MIYAGI Takahiro, MIYAKE Tama, MIYAMOTO Akiko, MIYAZAKI Koji, MIYAZATO Noriko, MIYAZAWA Tomoko, MIZZI Raymond, MO Jason, MO Sarah, MO Katherine, MOANA Betty, MOAR Bronwyn, MOAR Josie, MOAT Tony, MOATE Jodie, MOATE Steve, MOBBERLEY Carlene, MOBBS Dianne, MOCANCE Margaret, MOCELLIN Claude, MOCELLIN Este, MOCHER Yvonne, MOCTEZUMA Edgar, MODDE Alain, MODDE Ben, MODDEL Michael, MODESTO Rita, MODHIA Bhavin, MODICA Fred, MODRAK Kris, MOE Danielle, MOE Thet, MOEHEAD Diana, MOEHEAD Gavin, MOELLERS Joe, MOELLERS Shelley, MOEN John, MOES Kelly, MOFFAT Claudia, MOFFAT Diane, MOFFAT Elysha, MOFFAT Geoff, MOFFAT Kirsten, MOFFATT Carol, MOFFATT Drew, MOFFIT Marjorie, MOFFITT Adrian, MOFFITT Ben, MOFFITT Diane, MOFFITT Marj, MOFFITT Bob, MOGG Kathy, MOGG Lin, MOGGS Ian, MOHAMAD Mohamad, MOHAMAD Rima, MOHAMADIN El, MOHAMED Ayman, MOHAMED Moho, MOHAMED FAROOK Saleem, MOHAMMAD Asaduzzaman, MOHAMMAD Janed, MOHAMMADI Hossein, MOHAMMED Jameel, MOHAMMED Muns, MOHAMMEED Nadeem, MOHAMUD Said, MOHAN Ajit, MOHAN Bryson, MOHAN Kusum, MOHAN Lori, MOHAN Pal, MOHAN Sanjeev, MOHEBBI Fred, MOHINDRA Rakesh, MOHR Amanda, MOHRING Hella, MOIR Craig MOIR Lynne, MOIR Mike, MOIR Osanna, MOISO George, MOITIE Pam, MOK Charles, MOK Danny, MOK Etta, MOK Geoffrey, MOK Joshua, MOK Nick, MOK Ronald, MOK Silvia, MOK Stephen, MOKMARGANA Kumpul, MOKOTUPU Jaeneen, MOKRZYCKA Helen, MOL Sietske, MOLAN Gabrielle, MOLCHANOFF Cyril, MOLCHANOFF Peggy, MOLCHANOFF Peter, MOLDRICH Michael, MOLE Adrian, MOLE Ken, MOLE Les, MOLENAAR Mel, MOLENDA Martin, MOLESWORTH Paul, MOLIN Josefina, MOLINA Nora, MOLINEUX Narelle, MOLLENBECK Liz, MOLLER James, MOLLICA Luisa, MOLLICA Matt, MOLLOY Tony, MOLLOY Anthony, MOLLOY Bev, MOLLOY Bruce, MOLLOY Carol, MOLLOY Dennis, MOLLOY Janine, MOLLOY Margaret, MOLLOY Michael,

MOLLOY Noel, MOLLOY Rosie, MOLLOY Sandra, MOLLOY Bill, MOLLOY Yvonne, MOLNAR Liz, MOLNAR Penny, MOLNAR Steven, MOLONEY Anne, MOLONEY Brett, MOLONEY John-Paul, MOLONEY Wayne, MOLTINI Amelia, MOLYNEUX Greg, MOLYNEUX Greg, MOLYNEUX Joan, MOLYNEUX Maureen, MOMCILOVIC Alex, MONAEM Abdul, MONAGHAN John, MONAGHAN Bill, MONAHOS George, MONARDES Paula, MONCHGESANG Jenny, MONDEL Natasha, MONDEL Gina, MONDON Sandra, MONDS Karen, MONEA Princess, MONFORT Mark, MONG Daniel, MONG Jim, MONGAN Eleanor, MONGAN Kate, MONIKURA Celine, MONK Anne-Louise, MONK Geoff, MONK Jacquee, MONK Rachel, MONKLEY Veronica, MONKMAN Margaret, MONKMAN Tracy, MONKS Doreen, MONKS Ian, MONNIN Eric, MONOHAN John, MONOS John, MONOT Cole, MONOTTI Louise, MONROE Meredith, MONSIVAIS Darzee, MONSMA Corrie, MONTAGNER Luisa, MONTAGUE Jessica, MONTAGUE John, MONTAGUE Roz, MONTAGUE Steve, MONTAGUE-PHUA Lynn, MONTAIS Helen, MONTALBAN Maureen, MONTANARI Laraine, MONTANEZ Ana, MONTEIRO Oriana, MONTEITH Ian, MONTERO SOTO Miryam, MONTGOMERY Adrian, MONTGOMERY Beth, MONTGOMERY Cec, MONTGOMERY Chris, MONTGOMERY Debbie, MONTGOMERY Kathy, MONTGOMERY Geoff, MONTGOMERY James, MONTGOMERY John, MONTGOMERY Kaye, MONTGOMERY Tracy, MONTGOMERY Wendy, MONTIBELER Leanne, MONTONE Anthony, MONTOYA Maria-Rosa, MONTOYA-VAL Ryan, MONTOYA-VAL Scott, MONTY Monique, MOODIE Col, MOODLEY Shan, MOODLEY Nishlin, MOODLEY Steve, MOODY Andrew, MOODY Angus, MOODY Brian, MOODY David, MOODY Helen, MOODY Joyce, MOODY Ray, MOODY Dick, MOODY Sharyn, MOOIBROEK Karen, MOON Hee, MOON Hyuk, MOON Hyuck-Sang, MOON James, MOON Jason, MOON JiHee, MOON Julie-Anne, MOON Karen, MOON Kevin, MOON Lucas, MOON Ramona, MOON Robin, MOON Robert, MOONEY Belynda, MOONEY Greg, MOONEY Hedley, MOONEY Ingrid, MOONEY Kirsten, MOONEY Mary, MOONEY Myles, MOONEY Stuart, MOOPANAR Tezza, MOOR Elizabeth, MOOR James, MOOR Michael, MOOR William, MOORE Stuart, MOORE Adam, MOORE Aidan, MOORE Amanda, MOORE Amanda, MOORE David, MOORE Barry, MOORE Beryl, MOORE Bev, MOORE Brandon, MOORE Brett, MOORE Brian, MOORE Bruce, MOORE Caryn, MOORE Cath, MOORE Charlotte, MOORE Cheryl, MOORE Christian, MOORE Chris, MOORE Chris, MOORE Christine, MOORE David, MOORE Dave, MOORE David, MOORE David, MOORE Deanna, MOORE Diane, MOORE Ted, MOORE Elizabeth, MOORE Gemina, MOORE Glen, MOORE Heather, **MOORE Ivan**, MOORE Janice, MOORE Marie, **MOORE Joan**, MOORE Jo, MOORE John, MOORE John, MOORE John, MOORE June, MOORE Katharine, MOORE Katie, MOORE Kaye, MOORE Kay, MOORE Kaye, MOORE Ken, MOORE Krystina, MOORE Jelfs, MOORE Lee, MOORE Tom, MOORE Linda, MOORE Mandy, MOORE Marilyn, MOORE Marianne, MOORE Martin, MOORE Maureen, MOORE Mike, MOORE Micheal, MOORE Michael, MOORE Michelle, MOORE Michele, MOORE Nathaniel, MOORE Natalie, MOORE Nick, MOORE Nicola, MOORE Nicole, MOORE Tricia, MOORE Peter, MOORE Peter, MOORE Peter, MOORE Phil, MOORE Bob, MOORE Robert, MOORE Roy, MOORE Roger, MOORE Russell, MOORE Sarah, MOORE Stephanie, MOORE Steve, MOORE Steph, MOORE Stephen, MOORE Syd, MOORE Tim, MOORE Rick, MOORE Wayne, MOORE Wendy, MOORE Bill, MOORES Greg, MOORING Brian, MOORING Lorraine, MOOYAART Sue, MOR Gordon, MORABITO Christina, MORADI Pouria, MORAHAN John, MORAITIS Helen, MORALES Manuel, MORALES Nadia, MORALES Brigitte, MORALES MUNOZ Maria, MORALLEE David, MORAN Alan, MORAN Barbara, MORAN Beano, MORAN Dan, MORAN Elissa, MORAN Kristy, MORAN Michelle, MORAN Michael, MORAN Natalie, MORAN Paul, MORAN Rovert, MORAN Toni-Lee, MORAN Zelma, MORAND Brian, MORAND Vanessa, MORAND Wink, MORANTE Andrew, MORARTY Bec, MORAS STEPHENSON Karen, MORATH Tony, MORATH Gloria, MORCOM David, MORCOM Maureen, MORCOM Sarah, MORCOMBE Gerry, MOREAU Carol, MOREAU Vincent, MOREHOUSE Phillip, MOREHOUSE Win, MOREING Anna, MOREIRA Jefferson, MOREIRA Maria, MOREL Sandrine, MORENO Andres, MORENO Cynthia, MORENO Jorge, MOREY John, MORFITT Lorna, MORFOS Nick, MORGAN Alastair, MORGAN Amanda, MORGAN Andrew, MORGAN Anthony, MORGAN Barry, MORGAN Brian, MORGAN Cal, MORGAN Carly, MORGAN Carol, MORGAN Catherine, MORGAN Cheryl, MORGAN Claire, MORGAN David, MORGAN Dean, MORGAN Dennis, MORGAN Dennis, MORGAN Dot, MORGAN Gary, MORGAN Glenda, MORGAN Gordon, MORGAN Helen, MORGAN Ian, MORGAN Jan, MORGAN Janet, MORGAN Jeanette, MORGAN Jenny, MORGAN John, MORGAN Jonathan, MORGAN Juanita, MORGAN Julie, MORGAN Kathleen, MORGAN Laura, MORGAN Maggie, MORGAN Marilyn, MORGAN Narelle, MORGAN Nerys, MORGAN Neville, MORGAN Neville, MORGAN Philip, MORGAN Richard, MORGAN Robyn, MORGAN Roger, MORGAN Sam, MORGAN Scott, MORGAN Terry, MORGAN Tira, MORGAN Wayne, MORGAN William, MORGAN-KEITH Frances, MORGANS Anne, MORHEB Kamal, MORI Cristina, MORI Elizabeth, MORI Mark, MORIARTY Derek, MORIARTY Rick, MORIARTY Joanne, MORIARTY Kate, MORIARTY Kay, MORIARTY Sally, MORIARTY Timothy, MORICHIKA Hideo, MORING Ben, MORIOKA Akiko, MORISCO Matteo, MORISEY Daniel, MORISON Claire, MORISON Liz, MORISON Joan, MORISSET Edith, MORITA Masuyo, MORIYAMA Ayako, MORK Lisa, MORK Ray, MORLEY Tony, MORLEY Carolyn, MORLEY Diane, MORLEY Enid, MORLEY Gloria, MORLEY Stephen, MORLEY-HART Les, MORLING Jackie, MORONEY David, MORONEY Jenny, MORONEY Maurice, MORONEY Mike, MORONEY Pat, MOROZ Craigshain, MORPHETT Craig, MORPHETT Janice, MORPHETT John, MORPHETT Leonie, MORRALL Leanne, MORRELL Jane, MORRICE Esme, MORRICE Harry, MORRIS Anna, MORRIS Barbara, MORRIS Belinda, MORRIS Beth, MORRIS Brendan, MORRIS Carolyn, MORRIS Carole, MORRIS Chris, MORRIS Chris, MORRIS Chris, MORRIS Clare, MORRIS Clive, MORRIS Clinton, MORRIS Colin, MORRIS Darryl, MORRIS Daryl, MORRIS Denise, MORRIS Moose, MORRIS Diane, MORRIS Don, MORRIS Earle, MORRIS Eileen, MORRIS Fiona, MORRIS Geoff, MORRIS Geoff, MORRIS Graham, MORRIS Heather, MORRIS Helen, MORRIS Jenny, MORRIS Jennifer, MORRIS Jenny, MORRIS Jo, MORRIS John, MORRIS Josh, MORRIS Josie, MORRIS Joy, MORRIS Ken, MORRIS Ken, MORRIS Laura, MORRIS Lirel, MORRIS Mali, MORRIS Margaret, MORRIS Margaret, MORRIS Marie, MORRIS Mark, MORRIS Marilyn, MORRIS Max, MORRIS Noelle, MORRIS Pamela, MORRIS Paul, MORRIS Peta, MORRIS Roy, MORRIS Sharon, MORRIS Stephanie, MORRIS Susan, MORRIS Tracey, MORRIS Vic, MORRIS Virginia, MORRIS Yvonne, MORRIS-LEE Connie, MORRIS-SHAKESPEARE Pam, MORRISON Albert, MORRISON Molly, MORRISON Belinda, MORRISON Brian, MORRISON Chris, MORRISON Clarissa, MORRISON David, MORRISON David, MORRISON Denita, MORRISON Fiona, MORRISON Frank, MORRISON George, MORRISON Graeme, MORRISON Greg, MORRISON Heather, MORRISON Helen, MORRISON Ian, MORRISON John, MORRISON John, MORRISON Ken, MORRISON Ken, MORRISON Kirrilly, MORRISON Lisa, MORRISON Marty, MORRISON Meagan, MORRISON Pam, MORRISON Patricia, MORRISON Peter, MORRISON Becky, MORRISON Robyn, MORRISON Rowena, MORRISON Russell, MORRISON Shea, MORRISON Yvonne, MORRISSEY Fiona, MORRISSEY Gary, MORRISSEY Grant, MORRISSEY Joaney, MORRISSEY Norma, MORRISSY Barbara, MORROW Alan, MORROW Barbara, MORROW Col, MORROW Darrell, MORROW Georgina, MORROW Leah, MORROW Nicole, MORROW Paul, MORROW Philip, MORSHEDI Helal, MORSILLO Eddy, MORSINK Franel, MORSINK Theo, MORSINK-RYAN Fiona, MORSLEY Craig, MORSLEY Sheryl, MORSON Cross, MORSON Patricia, MORTAZAVI Azad, MORTAZAVI Sara, MORTENSEN Ronald, MORTIER Douglas, MORTIMER Claire, MORTIMER David, MORTIMER Joanne, MORTIMER Linda, MORTIMER Pauline, MORTIMER Vass, MORTIMER Wayne, MORTLEMAN Gordon, MORTLOCK Bryan, MORTLOCK David, MORTON Jim, MORTON Patricia, MORTON Trish, MORTON Sachiko, MORTON Simon, MORTON Zara, MORTON-EVANS Oliver, MOSCHETTI Andrew,

MOSCHITZ Cecelia, MOSCHOVAKIS Mary, MOSCOS George, MOSCROP Barry, MOSCROP Jen, MOSELEY Vivienne, MOSELY Ben, MOSES Mary, OSES Melanie, MOSES Robert, MOSHI Shamiram, MOSHONAS Maria, MOSKOS Antonia, MOSLEY David, MOSLEY Ray, MOSLEY Simon, MOSS Andrea, MOSS Andrew, MOSS David, MOSS Doug, MOSS Gary, MOSS Jeff, MOSS Justin, MOSS Keith, MOSS Kim, MOSS Mary, MOSS Margaret, MOSS Maureen, MOSS Fay, MOSS Prim, MOSS Ren, MOSS Ruth, MOSS Ted, MOSSE ROBINSON Matthew, MOSSEL Peter, MOSTAFAVI Flora, MOTHA John, MOTHERWELL Linda, MOTT Dixie, MOTT Russell, MOTT Sue, MOTTA Joanne, MOTTEE Lara, MOTTRAM Barbara, MOTTRAM Neil, MOTTRAM Sarah, MOTZ Sabine, MOUANGVONG Vieng, MOUAT Kristine, MOUATT Alan, MOUAWAD Amal, MOUBARAK Rosie, MOUJON Laurent, MOUK Whitlam, MOULARAS Helen, MOULD Colleen, MOULD Susan, MOULDEN Carol, MOULDER Eric, MOULDS Adam, MOULOS Alex, MOULTON John, MOUNIC Chris, MOUNIVONG Jamie, MOUNSEY Linda, MOUNT Jo, MOUNT Margaret, MOUNTFIELD Alana, MOUNTFORD Kay, MOURATIDIS Kerri, MOURELLE Judy, MOURRA Peter, MOUSLEY Sean, MOUSSA Omar, MOUSSA Vi, MOUSSEAU Kerri, MOUSTAFA Aziz, MOUTOU Danielle, MOUTRAY Ian, MOUTRIE Anne, MOUTZOURIS Yanna, MOWAT Alison, MOWBRAY Cassandra, MOWBRAY Lesley, MOWBRAY Mary, MOWBRAY Nic, MOWBRAY Olive, MOXHAM Amy, MOXHAM Ken, MOXHAM Philip, MOXON Bruce, MOXON Starr, MOY Michael, MOYA Carlos, MOYEEN Rashed, MOYES Ian, MOYES John, MOYES Josie, MOYES Jozefa, MOYES Peter, MOYES Sue, MOYLAN Mud, MOYLE Helen, MOYLE Leanne, MOYLE Sands, MOYNAHAN Barry, MOYNAHAN Dannielle, MOYNHAM Tony, MOYNIHAN John, MOYNIHAN Toni, MOYSE Eve, MOYSE John, MOYSEYENKO Demetri, MRAZ George, MRKOBRAD Mile, MRKOCI Josip, MRKOCI Lara, MROZ Natalia, MU Tony, MU June, MU Xiao, MUCKAN Kenny, MUDALIAR Lawrence, MUDDASANI Venugopalreddy, MUDGE Jayne, MUDGE Peta, MUEHLBERG Morrie, MUEHLBERG Sylvia, MUELLER Liz, MUELLER Jane, MUELLER Mark, MUELLER Teresa, MUENTE Maria, MUERS Robin, MUFALE Letty, MUFFET Cheryl, MUFFET Michael, MUFTI Hilal, MUGAMBWA Sanyu, MUGFORD Bruce, MUHAMMAD Rizky, MUHAMMAD Rizwan, MUHAN Janar, MUHARREM Mus, MUIR Colin, MUIR Glenys, MUIR Kathie, MUIR Lyn, MUIR Marg, MUIR Rowan, MUIR Sanjay, MUIR Sonia, MUIR Bill, MUIRHEAD Chris, MUKERJI Debu, MUKHERJEE Indrani, MUKHOPADHYAY Arun, MULA Rosemary, MULCAHY Annie, MULCAHY Ann, MULCAHY Leonie, MULCAHY Mary, MULCAIR David, MULCARE Patricia, MULCARE Philip, MULCHANDANI Milan, MULCHRONE Linda, MULD Ray, MULDER Gerry, MULDER Karen, MULDER Lyn, MULDOON Anna, MULDOON Coilin, MULDOON Faye, MULDOON Louise, MULDOON Nicholas, MULES Margaret, MULES Raymond, MULHARE Brian, MULHARE Merril, MULHEARN Jane, MULHEARN Paul, MULHEARN Ray, MULHEARN Val, MULHERON Mark, MULHOLLAND Bonnie, MULHOLLAND Emily, MULHOLLAND Jim, MULHOLLAND Jennye, MULHOLLAND Bill, MULIA Max, MULIANY Muliany, MULLA Sarfaraz, MULLANE Alyson, MULLANE Michael, MULLANE Rachel, MULLANEY Helen, MULLEN Johanna, MULLEN Kelly, MULLEN Robert, MULLER Alison, MULLER Bede, MULLER Charles, MULLER Heinz, MULLER Heidi, MULLER Ivy, MULLER Joanna, MULLER John, MULLER Lothar, MULLER Moya, MULLER Peter, MULLER Timothy, MULLEY Barbara, MULLEY Helen, MULLIGAN Rhonda, MULLIGAN Steve, MULLIGAN Terry, MULLINS Anne, MULLINS Bryan, MULLINS Elisha, MULLINS Marj, MULLINS Rachel, MULLINS Sebastian, MULQUEENEY Thomas, MULRINE Luke, MULVENNA Alleyne, MULVEY Allison, MULVIHILL Mike, MULYADI Linda, MUMBERSON Fay, MUMBY Lance, MUMFORD Karen, MUMFORD Peter, MUMFORD Wayne, MUN Al, MUNDAY Kevin, MUNDAY Trish, MUNDAY Warwick, MUNDELL Chris, MUNDRABY Dale, MUNDRATHI Laxmi, MUNDT Kellie, MUNDT Lyndal, MUNDY John, MUNGOVEN Greg, MUNKLEY Graham, MUNN Chrissie, MUNN Dulcie, MUNOZ Igor, MUNOZ Martha, MUNOZ Miguel, MUNRO Alison, MUNRO Allan, MUNRO Anne, MUNRO Di, MUNRO Ian, MUNRO Jim, MUNRO Jarrod, MUNRO Kathy, MUNRO Kylie, MUNRO Mal, MUNRO Michael, MUNRO Paul, MUNRO Rob, MUNRO Bob, MUNRO David, MUNRO Rochelle, MUNRO Stephen, MUNSELL Bronwyn, MUNTHREE Jerusha, MUNTON Wendy, MUNTZ Tara, MUNYARD Tricia, MURAKAMI Nana, MURALI Ranjit, MURAMOTO Takako, MURAOKA Ritsuko, MURAS Juliet, MURAS Les, MURAWSKI Egbert, MURAWSKI Timothy, MURCHISON Christine, MURCHISON Beth, MURDEN Marg, MURDOCCA Dianne, MURDOCH Ross, MURDOCH Michael, MURFET Ian, MURFET Lucy, MURFETT Sarah, MURGATROYD Arthur, MURILLO CAMUS Lydia, MURINCAKOVA Zaneta, MURN Kaoru, **MURNANE Lorraine**, MURNANE Stephanie, MURNIEKS Cassi, MURPHY Adam, MURPHY Adrian, MURPHY Alexia, MURPHY Andrew, MURPHY Andre, MURPHY Anna, MURPHY Anthony, MURPHY Bebe, MURPHY Beverley, MURPHY Brad, MURPHY Brendan, MURPHY Brian, MURPHY Bridie, MURPHY Brian, MURPHY Bronwyn, MURPHY Chris, MURPHY Chris, MURPHY Craig, MURPHY Darryl, MURPHY Dave, MURPHY Elaine, MURPHY Frank, MURPHY Garry, MURPHY Geoff, MURPHY Grahame, MURPHY Helen, MURPHY Helen, MURPHY Jeff, MURPHY Jennifer, MURPHY John, MURPHY Julie, MURPHY Julian, MURPHY Julia, MURPHY Justine, **MURPHY Kevin**, MURPHY Kim, MURPHY Leonie, MURPHY Linda, MURPHY Dennis, MURPHY Lorraine, MURPHY Lucinda, MURPHY Maryanne, MURPHY Mary, MURPHY Margot, MURPHY Maureen, MURPHY Michele, MURPHY Neil, MURPHY Pat, MURPHY Patrick, MURPHY Patrick, MURPHY Paul, MURPHY Paul, MURPHY Peter, MURPHY Peter, MURPHY Peter, MURPHY Peter, MURPHY Peter, MURPHY Rachel, MURPHY Raymond, MURPHY Regan, MURPHY Robyn, MURPHY Ron, MURPHY Scott, MURPHY Sharon, MURPHY Shireen, MURPHY Stephen, MURPHY Sue, MURPHY Sue, MURPHY Tara, MURPHY Terry, MURPHY Tim, MURPHY Tracie, MURPHY Virginia, MURRANT Jim, MURRAY Alison, MURRAY Alwyn, MURRAY Andrea, MURRAY Andrea, MURRAY Angus, MURRAY Anne, MURRAY Bree, MURRAY Barbara, MURRAY Brett, MURRAY Brent, MURRAY Bruce, MURRAY Carina, MURRAY Catherine, MURRAY Chris, MURRAY Chris, MURRAY Clare, MURRAY Col, MURRAY Murray, MURRAY Darren, MURRAY Doug, MURRAY Edward, MURRAY Fiona, MURRAY Gerard, MURRAY Graeme, MURRAY Gwen, MURRAY Howard, MURRAY Ian, MURRAY Ian, MURRAY Ian, MURRAY Ian, MURRAY Jacqui, MURRAY Jenny, MURRAY Jane, MURRAY Jeff, MURRAY John, MURRAY Judy, MURRAY Julie, MURRAY Julian, MURRAY June, MURRAY Kathy, MURRAY Kel, MURRAY Ken, MURRAY Linda, MURRAY Lisa, MURRAY Louise, MURRAY Lynda, MURRAY Mal, MURRAY Margaret, MURRAY Mary, MURRAY Maria, MURRAY Melissa, MURRAY Michael, MURRAY Neil, MURRAY Pat, MURRAY Peter, MURRAY Peter, MURRAY Phil, MURRAY Phil, MURRAY Rhonda, **MURRAY Rick**, MURRAY Ron, MURRAY Scot, MURRAY Sue, MURRAY Tom, MURRAY Tracy, MURRAY Warren, MURRAY Wendi, MURRAY Bill, MURRAY-LESLIE Babs, MURRAY-LESLIE Sarah, MURRELL Barbara, MURRELL Donna, MURRELL Gareth, MURRELL Ray, MURRELL Robert, MURTAGH Dave, MURTAGH Irene, MURTAGH Kristin, MURTHEN Sewa, MURTI Clyde, MURTI Reshmi, MURUET GARCIA Victor, MURUGESAN Anand, MURUGESAN Nithya, MURY Elizabeth, MUSA Azeena, MUSA Gerardo, MUSA Gerard, MUSA Josefina, MUSARRA Greg, MUSARRA Paul, MUSCARA Francesco, MUSCAT Edward, MUSCAT Maria, MUSCO Norman, MUSCROFT Geoff, MUSETH Bev, MUSGRAVE Anne, MUSGRAVE Celeste, MUSGRAVE Patrick, MUSGRAVE Rob, MUSGROVE Tim, MUSICO Antonino, MUSICO Natalie, MUSK Christine, MUSKER Doug, MUSSETT Amanda, MUSSO Ross, MUSSO Vince, MUSSON Cliff, MUSTAFA Ertay, MUSTAFA Zehra, MUSTO Ngaire, MUSTON Daniel, MUSTON Ed, MUSUMECI Silvana, MUTAGA Taxcete, MUTSUDDY Ankhi, MUTSUDDY Rupam, MUTTON Geoff, MUTTON Leisa, MUTTON Penell, MUTUA Alfred, MUTUA Anne, MUTUC John, MUYEN Lucienne, MUYEN Nico, MYALL Helen, MYATT Bronwyn, MYATT Eric, MYERS Amber, MYERS Anna, MYERS Toni, MYERS Barb, MYERS Kate, MYERS Chris, MYERS Craig, MYERS Gavin, MYERS Jacquie, MYERS Karen, MYERS Karen, **MYERS Miriam**, MYERS Paula, MYERS Terry, MYERS Bill, MYHRE-DAVIS Sharon, MYINT Joe, MYINT

Nicole, MYKYTIUK Bohdan, MYLAN Gordon, MYLAN Joan, MYLES Graham, MYLES Kelie, MYLES Teena, MYNDRESKOU Ivan, MYORS Karen, MYSORE Vanie, MYTHEN Tracey, MYTILINIOS Greg, MYTS Lynda.

N

NA Franz, NA Suzanna, NAAR David, NABARRO Ruth, NABI Asra, NABI Ajmal, NABKEY Renee, NACEY Kirsten, NADANAPATHAM Nada, NADARAJAH Sri, NADE Liz, NADEAK Taripar, NADEN Jeffrey, NADER Tony, NADYCZ Nic, NAFFA Maysoun, NAGAMMA Nagamma, NAGARAJ Chitra, NAGARAJ Poorima, NAGAYAMA Eriko, NAGEL Barrie, NAGEL Mark, NAGENDLA Rajarathnam, NAGIEL Peter, NAGORSKI Peter, NAGULESAPILLAI Thush, NAGY Anna, NAGY Janet, NAGY Maria, NAGY Bob, NAGY Scott, NAGY Tibor, NAHAS Mohamad, NAHLOUS Caroline, NAICKER Kris, NAIDOO Jay, NAIDOO Mandy, NAIDOO Suren, NAIDOO Sameera, NAIDOO Vasa, NAIDOO Yogeeta, NAIDU Arti, NAIDU Aruna, NAIDU Bala, NAIDU Nagaiya, NAIDU Omeson, NAIDU Ananda, NAIK Prashant, NAIL Gemma, NAIN VERA Claudia, NAIN VERA Ximena, NAIR Anand, NAIR Redika, NAIRN Glynis, NAIRN Merv, NAIRN Ryan, NAIRN Virginia, NAJJAR Sam, NAKAGAMI Shireen, NAKAMURA Kazumi, NAKANO Yumiko, NAKAO Marina, NAKASHIMA Michiko, NAKATA Shiho, NAKATANI Mikiyo, NAKATOMI Katsuhiro, NAKAYAMA Yumiko, NAKKOUR Charlie, NAKKOUR Emma, NAKKOUR Nancy, NALETIL IC Samantha, NALINVILAWAN Kamol, NALLETAMBY Jean-Claude, NALLY Margaret, NAM Nancy, NAMAN Helen, NAMASIVAYAM Nama, NAMBIAR Narendra, NAMEKAWA Yuko, NAN Beatrix, NAN Alice, NANAI Selepa, NANAYAKKARA Larshya, NANCE Starks, NAND Edrian, NANN Terry, NANSCAWEN Trevor, NAO Aisa, NAOROZ Pilloo, NAOROZ Spenta, NAPIER Fiona, NAPIER Kym, NAPIER Lachlan, NAPIER Lauren, NAPIER Michael, NAPIER Therese, NAPOLEONE Angela, NAPOLEONE Mario, NAPOLI Carmelina, NAPOLI Michael, NAPOLILUNA Sarah, NAPPER David, NAPPER Gaill, NAPPER Jodi, NAPPER John, NAPPER Tegan, NAPTHALI Amanda, NAQVI Mohsin, NARANG Megha, NARAYAN Hari, NARAYAN Satya, NARAYANAN Amundha, NARAYANAN Kavita, NARAYANAN Rashmi, NARDI Noelene, NARDI Todd, NARDO Sandra, NARDONE Linda, NARDONE Peter, NARITA Miwa, NASA Loretta, NASER Md., NASH Aaron, NASH Bernadette, NASH Colin, NASH Di, NASH Edd, NASH Greg, NASH Greg, NASH Jill, NASH Jack, NASH Leanne, NASH Pam, NASH Penelope, NASH Peter, NASH Peter, NASH Sarah, NASH Simon, NASH Sue, NASIO Ilalio, NASO Rosemary, **NASON Joy**, NASR Gassan, NASR John, NASSAR Daniel, NASSAU Alan, NASSIF Paula, NASSIM Jacob, NASSIR Neam, NASTASI Anne, NASTASI Robert, NASTASI Tony, NATAPRADJA Iwan, NATARAJAN Raja, NATAWARDAYA Helena, NATH Shirley, NATHAN Francis, NATHAN Hindi, NATHAN Ian, NATHING Gennady, NATHWANI Farida, NATOLI John, NATOLI Pinella, NATOLI Sharon, NATOUR Samar, NATSIS Basil, NATTRASS Cassandra, NATTRASS Stella, NAUDIN Helen, NAUGHTON Jan, NAUGHTON Patrick, NAUGHTON Lorraine, NAUMOVSKI Jovanco, NAUNTON Judy, NAUPAY IGREDA Frank, NAVARRO Julz, NAVARRO Torni, NAVARRO Vicen, NAVEA Peter, NAVEN Lynette, NAVIN Janice, NAVIN Sam, NAWALY Joseph, NAWAR John, NAY Jack, NAYANI Pradeep, **NAYLER Shane**, NAYLOR Adam, NAYLOR Andrew, NAYLOR Brian, NAYLOR Margi, NAYLOR Michelle, NAYLOR Ron, NAZARETH Gavin, NAZARIAN Araks, NAZARIAN Vanouhi, NDIAYE Omar, NEAL Ashley, NEAL Dean, NEAL Betty, NEAL Geoffrey, NEAL Hamish, NEAL Jodie, NEAL Les, NEAL Linda, NEAL Maggie, NEAL Margaret, NEAL Bluey, NEAL Sandy, NEAL Sue, NEALE Carol, NEALE David, NEALE Gavin, NEALE Kim, NEALON Michele, NEARY Carla, NEARY Natalie, NEAT Beverley, NEAVE Jesse, NED Huaifen, NEEDHAM Andrew, NEEDHAM Laurie, NEEDHAM Geoff, NEEDHAM John, NEEDHAM Matt, NEEDHAM Michael, NEEDHAM Sid, NEELY John, NEENAN Pam, NEETHLIING Louis, NEETHLING Louis, NEGISHI Miwa, NEGLINE Peter, NEGRI Richard, NEGRI Richard, NEGRO Andy, NEGUS Sharon, NEIL Alison, NEIL Amanda, NEIL Ben, NEIL Jennifer, NEIL Kirsten, NEIL Marina, NEIL Maureen, **NEIL Pat**, NEIL Perry, NEIL Sean, NEILAN Ed, NEILL Chris, NEILL Fiona, NEILL James, NEILL Merridee, NEILSEN Geoff, NEILSEN Stacey, NEILSEN Tyson, NEILSON Andrew, NEILSON Elly, NEILSON George, NEILSON Jennifer, NEILSON Joanne, NEILSON Bob, NEILSON Robert, NEILSON Stephen, NEJEDLIK John, NEJEDLIK John, NEKKENTI Rajiv, NELAN John, NELIS Barry, NELSON Ambrose, NELSON Anne, NELSON Ben, NELSON Chantelle, NELSON Gary, NELSON Glenn, NELSON Graeme, NELSON Jeff, NELSON Jennifer, NELSON Jenny, NELSON Jo, NELSON Joan, NELSON Joe, NELSON Julie, NELSON Karena, NELSON Lyn, NELSON Marjorie, NELSON Mark, NELSON Megan, NELSON Nan, NELSON Tricia, NELSON Peter, NELSON Peter, NELSON Philip, NELSON Shanta, NELSON Tanya, NELSON Tom, NELTHORPE Joel, NEMCOVA Lucie, NEMEC Tony, NEMES Carol, NEMES Josef, NEMESI Rossana, NEMET Paul, NEMETH Michael, NENKE Margaret, NEO Gu, NEOH Francis, NEOH Sooi, NEOH Swee, NERDAL Hal, NERI Rudy, NERTNEY Clive, NESPOR Wendy, NESS Kathleen, NESS Katie, NESVADARANI Behnaz, NETHERCOTT Agnes, NETHERY Craig, NETHERY David, NETI Priya, NETI Renuka, NETTHEIM Margot, NETTRANDER Kalle, NEUBAUER Ingrid, NEUBURGER Eric, NEUBURGER Karen, NEUCOM Colin, NEUMANN Ben, NEUMANN Katie, NEUMANN Michael, NEUMANN Nadine, NEUPANE Hari, NEUSS Katrina, NEVELL David, NEVILL Jackie, NEVILLE Alan, NEVILLE Anne, NEVILLE Barbara, NEVILLE Gary, NEVILLE Jan, NEVILLE Jennie, NEVILLE Ken, NEVILLE Keryn, NEVILLE Peter, NEVILLE Sharon, NEVIN Felicity, NEVIN Gene, NEW Alan, NEW David, NEW Keith, NEW Michael, NEWALL Barry, NEWBERRY Damian, NEWBERRY Margaret, NEWBERY Jennifer, NEWBERY Joyce, NEWBERY Robyn, NEWBIGIN Philippa, NEWCOMBE Kate, NEWCOMBE Virginia, NEWELL Jim, NEWELL Jodie, NEWELL Sharon, NEWEY Gill, NEWEY Bob, NEWFIELD Alla, NEWFIELD Val, NEWHAM Allison, NEWHAM Colin, NEWHAM Dannielle, NEWHAM Donna, NEWHAM Edwina, NEWHAM Mark, NEWHAM Murray, NEWHAM Raymond, NEWHAM Shane, NEWHAM Susan, NEWHAM Val, NEWHOUSE Ben, NEWHOUSE Dianne, NEWHOUSE Tracey, NEWLAND Henry, NEWLAND Jill, NEWLANDS Sally, NEWLINMAZARAKI Barbara, NEWLING Elizabeth, NEWLING Greg, NEWLING Joy, NEWLING Rob, NEWMAN Alan, NEWMAN Andrew, NEWMAN Carol, NEWMAN Damien, NEWMAN Daniel, NEWMAN Daniel, NEWMAN Deanna, NEWMAN Del, NEWMAN George, NEWMAN Glenn, NEWMAN Jo, NEWMAN Jo, NEWMAN Jocelyn, NEWMAN John, NEWMAN Kylie, NEWMAN Laurence, NEWMAN Lloyd, NEWMAN Malcolm, NEWMAN Margaret, NEWMAN Michelle, NEWMAN Mitch, NEWMAN Norma, NEWMAN Robert, NEWMAN Russell, NEWMAN Stephen, NEWMAN Tanya, NEWNHAM Greg, NEWNHAM Marijke, NEWNHAM Richie, NEWPORT Eric, NEWPORT Steve, NEWSAM Beatty, NEWSAM Chris, NEWSAM Peta, NEWSAM Sam, NEWSOME Sheralee, NEWTON Aaron, NEWTON Alex, NEWTON Anthea, NEWTON Chris, NEWTON Chris, NEWTON Glen, NEWTON Helen, NEWTON Irene, NEWTON Janice, NEWTON John, NEWTON Matt, NEWTON Rachel, NEWTON Steve, NEWTON Susan, NEWTON Tom, NEY Brenda, NEY Margaret, NEYLAN Rachel, NEYLE Deb, NG Agnes, NG Angela, NG Anthony, NG Antonio, NG Carmen, NG Cheng, NG David, NG Ee, NG Ellen, NG Erwin, NG Ho, NG Jacqui, NG Jason, NG Justin, NG Ka, NG Karen, NG Kenneth, NG Kit, NG Andy, NG Timmy, NG Elsie, NG Lynda, NG Marggie, NG Marie, NG Matthew, NG Michael, NG Michael, NG Alex, NG Mui, NG Annabella, NG Richard, NG Sen, NG Sylvia, NG Tzin, NG Victor, NG Vincent, NG Suzanne, NG Winnie, NG Winnie, NG Winnie, NG Dennis, NG Yye, NGAI Janice, NGAI Joyce, NGAI Robin, NGAI Virginia, NGALUAFE Josephine, NGAMSIRIVADHANA Jason, NGAMSUTTHI Dathipa, NGAN Carolyn, NGAN Jenny, NGAN Josephine, NGEOW Donna, NGHIEM Long, NGO Belinda, NGO Loc, NGO James, NGO Lisa, NGO Lyn, NGO Minh, NGO Mong, NGO Phillip, NGO Michael, NGO Tho, NGO Vivian, NGOC Chinh, NGOR William, NGOV Hong, NGOY Jessica, NGU Hui, NGUEMA Jose, NGURAH Ann, NGUY David, NGUY Bao, NGUYEN Tim, NGUYEN Anh, NGUYEN Anne, NGUYEN Ann, NGUYEN Anthy, NGUYEN Van, NGUYEN Wendy, NGUYEN Chinh, NGUYEN Chuc, NGUYEN Cu, NGUYEN Damson, NGUYEN Dang, NGUYEN Danny, NGUYEN Linh, NGUYEN David, NGUYEN Deon, NGUYEN Diem, NGUYEN Dominic, NGUYEN

DongChan, NGUYEN Duong, NGUYEN John, NGUYEN Tom, NGUYEN Duy, NGUYEN Ha, NGUYEN Hai, NGUYEN Helen, NGUYEN Hien, NGUYEN Ho, NGUYEN Scott, NGUYEN Hoang, NGUYEN Hong, NGUYEN Johnny, NGUYEN Hong, NGUYEN Jenny, NGUYEN John, NGUYEN Khui, NGUYEN Kim, NGUYEN Veronica, NGUYEN Kim, NGUYEN Kim, NGUYEN Kim, NGUYEN Lamy, NGUYEN William, NGUYEN Matthew, NGUYEN Minh, NGUYEN Minh, NGUYEN Paul, NGUYEN Phong, NGUYEN Phu, NGUYEN Anthony, NGUYEN Sarah, NGUYEN Tai, NGUYEN Thanh, NGUYEN San, NGUYEN Vicky, NGUYEN Linh, NGUYEN Tina, NGUYEN Tim, NGUYEN Toai, NGUYEN Trisha, NGUYEN Trang, NGUYEN Troy, NGUYEN Nathan, NGUYEN Truc, NGUYEN Huy, NGUYEN Tuyet, NGUYEN Kathy, NGUYEN Van, NGUYEN Vinh, NGUYEN Vu, NGUYEN DO Khanh, NGUYEN-LE Duc, NGUYER Vinh, NHAYNES Bradden-Lee, NHEULEONG Albert, NI Zezheng, NI CORRAIDH Rae, NIALL Nolene, NIAUX Estelle, NIBLETT Maurice, NICHOLAS Angela, NICHOLAS Barbara, NICHOLAS Bret, NICHOLAS Charles, NICHOLAS Cheronne, NICHOLAS Craig, NICHOLAS Di, NICHOLAS Emma, NICHOLAS John, NICHOLAS Katina, NICHOLAS Natasha, NICHOLAS Peter, NICHOLAS Tim, NICHOLL Tony, NICHOLL Vera, NICHOLLS Belinda, NICHOLLS Betty, NICHOLLS Brad, NICHOLLS Chris, NICHOLLS Corey, NICHOLLS Darren, NICHOLLS Darren, NICHOLLS David, NICHOLLS Gary, NICHOLLS Inia, NICHOLLS Kelly, NICHOLLS Leanne, NICHOLLS Mark, NICHOLLS Mitchell, NICHOLLS Tricia, NICHOLLS Scott, NICHOLLS Terry, NICHOLS Aaron, NICHOLS Andy, NICHOLS Austin, NICHOLS Gaylene, NICHOLS Joan, NICHOLS David, NICHOLS Kate, NICHOLS Kevin, NICHOLS Kim, NICHOLS Narelle, NICHOLS Nigel, NICHOLS Roy, NICHOLS Suzanne, NICHOLS Tim, NICHOLSON Alicia, NICHOLSON Brian, NICHOLSON Brooke, NICHOLSON Camille, NICHOLSON Craig, NICHOLSON Fiona, NICHOLSON Fran, NICHOLSON Heather, NICHOLSON Helen, NICHOLSON Jim, NICHOLSON June, NICHOLSON Kara, NICHOLSON Katie, NICHOLSON Kym, NICHOLSON Laurie, NICHOLSON Melina, NICHOLSON Peter, NICHOLSON Richard, NICHOLSON Bob, NICHOLSON Mike, NICHOLSON Robbi, NICHOLSON Rosemary, NICHOLSON Sandy, NICHOLSON Scott, NICHOLSON Sharyn, NICHOLSON Trevor, NICHOLSON Warwick, NICIAK Terry, NICITA Jennifer, NICITA Joanne, NICITA Lisa, NICKALLS Rob, NICKLESS Richard, NICKLIN Judy, NICKOLAS Margaret, NICKOLLS Lindsey, NICOL Tony, NICOL Barbara, NICOL David, NICOL Joan, NICOL Karen, NICOL Trevor, NICOLAI Virginia, NICOLAOU Chris, NICOLETTI Robert, NICOLL Amy, NICOLL Meryn, NICOLLS Jackie, NICOLOULIAS Joanna, NICOLSON Allison, NICOLSON Caroline, NICOLSON Melanie, NICOTRA Daniela, NICOTRA Elizabeth, NIELD Ashley, NIELD Erin, NIELSEN Ebbe, NIELSEN Erik, NIELSEN Hayley, NIELSEN Angus, NIELSEN Jim, NIELSEN Janne, NIELSEN Karen, NIELSEN Lucinda, NIELSEN Norma, NIELSEN Stuart, NIELSEN Susanne, NIELSEN Torben, NIELSON Janet, NIELSON Neils, NIEUWBOER Paula, NIEUWENDIJK Catherine, NIEUWENHUIZEN Katalin, NIEUWLAND Jack, NIEZABITOWSKI Teresa, NIGHTINGALE Jeannette, NIJMAN Jeanne, NIKFORIDES Panagiotis, NIKITIN Dennis, NIKKUNI Tomiko, NIKOLAKOPOULOS Constantine, NIKOLAKOPOULOS Helen, NIKOLAKOPOULOS Mary, NIKOLAOU Marina, NIKOLAS Margaret, NIKOLITSIS Tania, NIKOLOVA Vesna, NIKOLOVSKI Toni, NILAN Katie, NILAND Rhonda, NILON Catherine, NILON John, NILON Linda, NILON Nanette, NILON Stephen, NILON Sue, NILSON Peter, NILSSON Debbie, NILSSON Jasmine, NILSSON Sarah, NILSSON Sven, NILSSONHARDING Gisela, NIMCIW George, NIMMAGADDA Aruna, NIMMAGADDA Tejaswi, NIMMO Bich, NIMMO Doug, NINAN Vikram, NINAUS Greg, NINAUS Marta, NINAUS Niki, NINEDEK Alana, NING George, NINIO Mark, NINNESS Gordon, NIPPERESS Joe, NIPPERESS Jo, NIPPERESS Patricia, NIRMALANANDA Logan, NISBET Peter, NISBETT Joanne, NISCIOLI Paola, NISHIO Yoshimi, NISSEN Carole, NISTOR Dragosh, NISTOR Dora, NIU Xianwa, NIUKORE Sirea, NIUKORE Umutoru, NIUMATA Tina, NIVEN Carol, NIVEN David, NIVEN Michelle, NIX Erica, NIX Graham, NIXON Brian, NIXON Chris, NIXON Chris, NIXON David, NIXON Ross, NIXON Jaime, NIXON Jane, NIXON Jenny, NIXON Judy, NIXON Lorna, NIXON Malcolm, NOACK Scottie, NOAEEN Sumie, NOAKES Carol, NOAKES Liz, NOAKES Jennie, NOAKES Paula, NOAN Vivian, NOBBS Tony, NOBBS Margaret, NOBBS Pauline, NOBILO Jan, NOBLE Brian, NOBLE Colin, NOBLE Liz, NOBLE Fiona, NOBLE John, NOBLE Karen, NOBLE Marilyn, NOBLE Patricia, NOBLE Richard, NOBLE Rick, NOBLE Ruth, NOBLE Sharyn, NOBLETT Steph, NOCK Kenneth, NODA Kyoko, NOERGAARD Nicoline, NOESJIRWAN Alexandra, NOGUEIRA Lourdes, NOH Angi, NOHL Vanessa, NOIRJEAN Frederic, NOLAN Aaron, NOLAN Cathy, NOLAN Chris, NOLAN Fay, NOLAN Mick, NOLAN George, NOLAN Helen, NOLAN Joan, NOLAN John, NOLAN Kirsty, NOLAN Lyn, NOLAN Lynette, NOLAN Michael, NOLAN Michael, NOLAN Neville, NOLAN Stephen, NOLAN Terry, NOLDART Reece, NOLDUS Yves, NOLIMAIO Mark, NOMANI Azhar, NONAKA Kyoko, NOONAN Andrew, NOONAN Colleen, NOONAN Desmond, NOONAN Grace, NOONAN Isabelle, NOONAN Janette, NOONAN Jason, NOONAN Jen, NOONAN John, NOONAN Kirrily, NOONAN Maureen, NOONAN Paul, NOONAN Robyn, NOONE Jenny, NOOYEN Debra, NORBURY Sue, NORCOTT Lou, NORCROSS Ivy, NORDBAEK Lene, NORDEN Karen, NORDEN Steve, NORDIN Doug, NORDLAND Lene, NORE Chris, NOREIKS Robyn, NORGARD Chris, NORMAN Amy, NORMAN Edna, NORMAN Karen, NORMAN Mark, NORMAN Mary, N ORMAN Margaret, NORMAN Ross, NORMAN Rosa, NORONHA Ovina, NORONHA Roque, NORONHA Rowena, NORRIE Jan, NORRIE Mark, NORRIS Beverley, NORRIS Di, NORRIS Eric, NORRIS John, NORRIS John, NORRIS Peterson, NORRIS Julie, NORRIS Ken, NORRIS Mark, NORRIS Maree, NORRIS Nola, NORRIS Peter, NORRIS Roslyn, NORRIS Sarah, NORRIS Sharon, NORRIS Trent, NORRIS Val, NORRIS Warren, NORRIS Wendy, NORRIS-GRANT Sarah, NORRISS Denis, NORRISS Maree, NORSTEDT Helen, NORSWORTHY Vanessa, NORTH Christopher, NORTH Colin, NORTH David, NORTH George, NORTH Karen, NORTH Kim, NORTH Linda, NORTH Marjorie, NORTH Margaret, NORTH Ness, NORTHAGE Ivon, NORTHALL Tiffany, NORTHCOTT Suzanne, NORTHEND George, NORTHEY Pamela, NORTHEY Steve, NORTHOVER Sue, NORTHROP Kristy, NORTON Bill, NORTON Bryce, NORTON Elizabeth, NORTON Jeff, NORTON Ken, NORTON Len, NORTON Naree, NORTON Paul, NORTON Ross, NORTON Sam, NORUP Glen, NORWOOD Anthony, NORWOOD Sue, NOSAL Ana, NOSEDA Damian, NOSHIRO Naomi, NOSKE Bronwyn, NOSKE Graeme, NOSTI Darren, NOSWORTHY Pat, NOSWORTHY Syd, NOTARA Robert, NOTLEY Nancy, NOTLEY Ray, NOTT David, NOTT Keith, NOTT Naomi, NOTT Sharon, NOTT Stephen, NOU Kosol, NOU Dara, NOUH Muktar, NOVACEK Becky, NOVACEK Vlasta, NOVAK Daniel, NOVAK Rebecca, NOVAKOVIC Anna, NOVAKOVIC Mark, NOVAKOVIC Zoran, NOVELLY Peta, NOVOSEL Anne, NOVOSEL Martin, NOVY Michael, NOWAK Janina, NOWAK Jason, NOWAK Gimbert, NOWFAL Alan, NOWFEL Leone, NOWICKI Julie, NOWLAN Frank, NOWLAND Don, NOWLAND Donald, NOWLAND Graham, NOYCE Phil, NOZAKI Kazue, NP Bawk, NUGENT David, NUGENT Shane, NUGENT Yvonne, NUGHES Claude, NUINKA Michael, NUNAN Sally, NUNES Alexandre, NUNES Cosme, NUNES Miguel, NUNES Raquel, NUNEZ Carlos, NUNEZ Dods, NUNEZ Julie, NUNEZ FERNANDEZ Montserrat, NUNN Joslyn, NUNN Rod, NUNNARI Bianca, NUNNARI Frank, NUNURA Marcial, NUR Alam, NURKIC Sadin, NURMAN Michael, NUROO Ron, NURWISAH Ron, NUSKE Heloisa, NUSSER Heinz, NUTH Sreythet, NUTT Tyson, NUTTALL Colleen, NUTTALL Sue, NUTTALL Vicky, NYAMUSHI KAMEYA Olivier, NYDEGGER Christine, NYE Adrian, NYE Debbie, NYKL Edita, NYMAN Sue, NYSSEN Margaret, NYUNT Fred.

O

O'BRIEN Angela, O'BRIEN Bradley, O'BRIEN Carole, O'BRIEN Kitty, O'BRIEN Charles, O'BRIEN Cheryl, O'BRIEN Chris, O'BRIEN Christine, O'BRIEN Claire, O'BRIEN Conor, O'BRIEN Deb, O'BRIEN Dennis, O'BRIEN Don, O'BRIEN Elaine, O'BRIEN Emma, O'BRIEN Helen, O'BRIEN Jim, O'BRIEN Jim, O'BRIEN John, O'BRIEN John, O'BRIEN John, O'BRIEN John, O'BRIEN Kath, O'BRIEN Kathryn, O'BRIEN Kerryn, O'BRIEN Kristy, O'BRIEN Kylie-Ann, O'BRIEN Lorene, O'BRIEN Mark, O'BRIEN Mel, O'BRIEN Michelle, O'BRIEN Noel, O'BRIEN Patrick, O'BRIEN Patricia,

O'BRIEN Paul, O'BRIEN Paul, O'BRIEN Paul, O'BRIEN Robert, O'BRIEN Bob, O'BRIEN Ruth, O'BRIEN Sarina, O'BRIEN Sean, O'BRIEN Shannon, O'BRIEN Shannon, O'BRIEN Shawn, O'BRIEN Shirley, O'BRIEN Simone, O'BRIEN Stephen, O'BRIEN Sue, O'BRIEN Sue, O'BRIEN Terry, O'BRIEN Terry, O'BRIEN Valerie, O'BRYAN Paul, O'BYRNE Chris, O'CALLAGHAN Adam, O'CALLAGHAN Elizabeth, O'CALLAGHAN Renee, O'CALLAHAN Mike, O'CARROLL Debbie, O'CONNELL Anna, O'CONNELL Shaun, O'CONNELL Brendan, O'CONNELL Cathal, O'CONNELL Gregor y, O'CONNELL Jane, O'CONNELL John, O'CONNELL Ken, O'CONNELL Kerry, O'CONNELL Mary, O'CONNELL Mary, O'CONNELL Meredith, O'CONNELL Pat, O'CONNELL Paul, O'CONNELL Phyllis, O'CONNELL Terence, O'CONNELL Tom, O'CONNELL Violet, O'CONNOR AnneLouise, O'CONNOR Ann, O'CONNOR Barry, O'CONNOR Barbara, O'CONNOR Bernie, O'CONNOR Betty, O'CONNOR Brian, O'CONNOR Carole, O'CONNOR Carol, O'CONNOR Charlie, O'CONNOR Christine, O'CONNOR Darryl, O'CONNOR Des, O'CONNOR Diane, O'CONNOR Donna, O'CONNOR Glenda, O'CONNOR Helen, O'CONNOR Jessie, O'CONNOR Kate, O'CONNOR Kevin, O'CONNOR Larissa, O'CONNOR Elizabeth, O'CONNOR Christina, O'CONNOR Mary, O'CONNOR Margaret, O'CONNOR Rhonda, O'CONNOR Rob, O'CONNOR Sean, O'CONNOR Sue, O'DANIEL Bruce, O'DAY Tony, O'DEA Clarissa, O'DEA Dianne, O'DEA Jodie, O'DEA Kevin, O'DEA Leo, O'DEA Michelle, O'DEA Paul, O'DEA Bec, O'DEA Tamra, O'DELL Peter, O'DONAHUE Karen, O'DONNELL Brian, O'DONNELL Catherine, O'DONNELL Fiona, O'DONNELL Fran, O'DONNELL Jim, O'DONNELL Jamie, O'DONNELL Jan, O'DONNELL Jennifer, O 'DONNELL Jo, O'DONNELL John, O'DONNELL Kim, O'DONNELL Mike, O'DONNELL Paraic, O'DONNELL Rod, O'DONNELL Rodney, O'DONNELL Rosie, O'DONNELL Tracy, O'DONNELL Vanessa, O'DONNELL Bill, O'DONOGHUE Janette, O'DONOGHUE Carlie, O'DONOGHUE Paul, O'DONOGHUE Kirsten, O'DONOGHUE Maureen, O'DONOHUE Bridget, O'DONOVAN Anne, O'DRISCOLL Geraldene, O'DRISCOLL Neil, O'DWYER Frank, O'DWYER Odie, O'FARRELL John, O'FARRELL Maryanne, O'FLAHERTY Liam, O'FLAHERTY Molly, O'FLYNN Deirdre, O'FLYNN Julie, O'GORMAN Luke, O'GORMAN Paul, O'GRADY Doreen, O'GRADY Joyce, O'GRADY Keith, O'GRADY Louise, O'HAGAN Roslyn, O'HAGAN Suzanne, O'HAIRE Chris, O'HALLORAN Brendan, O'HALLORAN Rebeccah, O'HALLORAN Rosanne, O'HARA Dee, O'HARA Doreen, O'HARA Douglas, O'HARA Maureen, O'HARA Muriel, O'HARAE Kristin, O'HAZY Joy, O'HEARN Jim, O'HEHIR Bernadette, O'HEHIR Judy, O'KEEFE Barb, O'KEEFE Jai, O'KEEFE Claire, O'KEEFE Judy, O'KEEFE Nick, O'KEEFE Jill, O'KEEFE Stuart, O'KEEFFE Andrew, O'KEEFFE Cormac, O'KEEFFE Lori, O'KEEFFE Lyndal, O'KEEFFE Marilyn, O'KEE FFE Megan, O'KEEFFE Sandy, O'KELLY Cinderella, O'KELLY Neil, O'LACO Ramon, O'LEARY Retanne, O'LEARY John, O'LEARY Kay, O'LEARY Lauren, O'LEARY Melissa, O'LEARY Norrie, O'LOAN John, O'LOAN Vanessa, O'LOUGHLIN David, O'LOUGHLIN Helen, O'LOUGHLIN Jenny, O'LOUGHLIN Michelle, O'LOUGHLIN Stephen, O'LOUGHLIN Susan, O'MALEY James, O'MALLEY Christine, O'MALLEY Gillian, O'MALLEY Heather, O'MALLEY Sean, O'MALLEY Fay, O'MALLEY Michael, O'MALLEY Monica, O'MALLEY Stephanie, O'MARA Michael, O'MARA Ray, O'MEARA Damien, O'MEARA Fiona, O'MEARA Kelly, O'MEARA Lynne, O'MULLANE Bev, O'MULLANE Phil, O'NEIL Jason, O'NEIL Leah, O'NEIL Monica, O'NEIL Bronwyn, O'NEILL Andrew, O'NEILL Brian, O'NEILL Bron, O'NEILL Christine, O'NEILL Christine, O'NEILL Dianne, O'NEILL Don, O'NEILL Helene, O'NEILL Jackie, O'NEILL Janet, O'NEILL Janice, O'NEILL Joan, O'NEILL Louise, O'NEILL Mary, O'NEILL Marika, O'NEILL Matthew, O'NEILL Meghan, O'NEILL Nicholas, O'NEILL Peter, O'NEILL Peta, O'NEILL Roger, O'NEILL Russell, O'NEILL Terence, O'NEILL Tiffany, O'NEILL Virginia, O'REGAN Bridget, O'REGAN Geraldine, O'REGAN Kerry, O'REGAN Nick, O'REILLY Anthony, O'REILLY Cath, O'REILLY David, O'REILLY James, O'REILLY John, O'REILLY Lola, O'REILLY Louise, O'REILLY Monica, O'REILLY Phil, O'REILLY Shirley, O'RILEY Glen, O'RIORDAN Cameron, O'ROURKE Annie, O'ROURKE Barbara, O'ROURKE Christine, O'ROURKE Katy, O'ROURKE Siobhan, O'RYAN Phoebe, O'SHANNESSY Laurie, O'SHANNESSY Mark, O'SHEA Belinda, O'SHEA Colette, O'SHEA Graham, O'SHEA Helen, O'SHEA Joanna, O'SHEA John, O'SHEA Kevin, O'SHEA Michael, O'SHEA Wendy, O'SULLIVAN Barry, O'SULLIVAN Cherie, O'SULLIVAN Clare, O'SULLIVAN Eugene, O'SULLIVAN Hayley, O'SULLIVAN Heather, O'SULLIVAN Kathy, O'SULLIVAN Kerri-Ann, O'SULLIVAN Loretta, O'SULLIVAN Loretta, O'SULLIVAN Peter, O'SULLIVAN Rod, O'SULLIVAN Susie, O'SULLIVAN Tim, O'SULLIVAN Vince, O'TOOLE Fred, O'TOOLE Jennifer, O'TOOLE Roger, OAK Clare, OAKE Janice, OAKES Peter, OAKES Diana, OAKES Jason, OAKES Mark, OAKES Nancy, OAKES Norma, OAKESMOONEY Joy, OAKEY Helen, OAKEY Kim, OAKFORD Al, OAKLEY Jane, OAKLEY Kerryn, OAR David, OASTLER Jim, OATES Cathy, OATES Betty, OATES John, OATES Judy, OATS Heather, OATS Vicki, OBCHALANUKAN Pat, OBEIDAT Ekram, OBEREIGNER Carole, OBERG Tim, OBERMAN Mark, OBERMAN Paul, OBERMEYER Melanie, OBES David, OBRIEN Craig, OBRIEN Michael, OBRIEN Naomi, OCHOA Yanet, OCONNOR Judy, OCONNOR Paula, ODDIE Nola, ODDY Bruce, ODELL Kylie, ODGAARD Carolanne, ODISHO Nahreen, ODONNELL John, ODONNELL Megan, ODOUARD Irene, ODRI Steve, OELTJEN John, OELTJEN Trent, OETOMO Teddy, OFAMOONI Tila, OFFER Kevin, OFFICER Susan, OFFORD Pat, OFFORD Peter, OGAWA Mika, OGAWA Satoko, OGG Dianne, OGG Norma, OGIER Raychelle, OGILVIE Ian, OGILVY Corey, OGLE Doug, OGLE Gerry, OGLE Kirrily, OGULEV Vitaly, OGUNBOWALE Tony, OH Alex, OH Chris, OH Daniel, OH Hye, OH Jin, OH Jin, OH Judith, OH Jung, OH Nicole, OH Schola, OHARA Muriel, OHEHIR Jenny, OHL Justine, OHLMUS David, OHLMUS Fritsz, OHM Pat, OHM Young, OHN Margaret, OKAJIMA Naoko, OKAMOTO Miyako, OKARO Candice, OKAZAKI Hitomi, OKE Alicia, OKEEFE Ron, OKEIL Malika, OKI Mami, OKITA Kumiko, OKSUZ Shermin, OKUBO Takuji, OKUDA Yoko, OKULICZ Tony, OLAYA Luis, OLCZAK Martin, OLD Robert, OLDANO Anna, OLDFIELD Ryan, OLDHAM Sandy, OLDIS Meredith, OLDMEADOW Damian, OLDRIDGE Heidi, OLDS Fran, OLENDER Dianna, OLESEN Glenda, OLIVA Tony, OLIVARES Roxy, OLIVE Kerrie, OLIVE Lisa, OLIVEIRA Robert, OLIVER Ben, OLIVER Blake, OLIVER Brooke, OLIVER Janice, OLIVER Kerryanne, OLIVER May, OLIVER Owen, OLIVER Paul, OLIVER Peter, OLIVER Peter, OLIVER Suzie, OLIVERA Tony, OLIVIERI Carmine, OLIVIETA Luis, OLLE Dave, OLLE Phil, OLLERENSHAW Don, OLLERENSHAW Patricia, OLLEY Cheryl, OLLING Steve, OLMEDO Judy, OLMEDO Lawrence, OLMEDO Leigh, OLMOS Rosa, OLOFSSON Hampus, OLOFSSON Katarina, OLOFSSON HJORTH Anna, OLOUGHLIN Aiden, OLOUMI-YAZDI Haleh, OLSEN Ann, OLSEN Belinda, OLSEN Betty, OLSEN Chas, OLSEN Elaine, OLSEN Hans, OLSEN John, OLSEN Julie, OLSEN Karen, OLSEN Katherine, OLSEN Lestelle, OLSEN Torsten, OLSHEN Eryn, OLSON Belinda, OLSON Lynn, OLSON Rodney, OLSSEN Arrnott, OLSSON Murray, OLSSON David, OLSSON Liz, OLUWOYE Adi, OMALLEY Michael, OMAR Reema, OMARA Frank, OMOTE Tomoj, OMRAN Sherin, OMURA-DAVIS Atsuko, ONANA AWONO Aclhile, ONARI Hiroko, ONDERKOVA Jana, ONEILL Helen, ONEILL Lachlan, ONEILL Shannon, ONEILL Warren, ONG Charleen, ONG Damron, ONG Eng, ONG Sally, ONG Hup, ONG Justin, ONG Karen, ONG Ken, ONG Rubin, ONG Maryann, ONG Ron, ONG Inge, ONG Soo, ONG Soo, ONG Elizabeth, ONG James, ONGLEY Leane, ONGPIN Anna, ONIKUL Sophie, ONISHI Misato, ONO Karen, ONOFIA Naomi, ONORATO Dom, ONORATO Ray, ONUS Denise, ONUS Katrina, ONYEWUENYI Nonye, OO Aung, OO Maung, OO Myo, OOI Gavin, OOI Michaella, OOI Susan, OOI Toh, OOI Winston, OOMEN Chris, OON Ai, OON Millie, OOSTENDOR Mario, OOSTERHOFF Mark, OOSTERMAN Cathy, OPAZO Joseph, OPDENBROUW Cass, OPENA Erick, OPENSHAW Brian, OPETAIA Billy, OPHEL Kelly, OPIT Rita, OPITZ Adrian, OPPEGAARD Vicki, OPPIO Maree, OPPL Barbara, OR Jennifer, ORANGE Brad, ORBACH David, ORBEA Michael, ORCHARD Alex, ORCHARD Jesse, ORCHARD John, ORCHARD Olivia, ORCHARD Dick, ORCHARD Richard, ORCHIN Pam, ORCHISTON Debbie, ORDONEZ Luis, OREGAN Martina, ORELLANA Carlos, ORELLANA Patricia, ORESHKIN Paul, ORFANOS Liz, ORGAN Denise, ORGAN John, ORGAN Tom, ORKIN Bill, ORLAND Joseph, ORLAND Louisa, ORLANDI Anthony,

ORLANDO Belinda, ORLEY Oliver, ORLEY Vyvyan, ORLIK Hannah, ORLOVICH John, ORMAN Karen, ORMAN Linda, ORMES Garry, OROSZVARI Stephen, OROZCO Cesar, ORPHANIDES Michael, ORR Alan, ORR Alex, ORR Mel, ORRELL Jim, ORROCK George, ORSATTI Carla, ORTATO Rose, ORTEGA Guilleamo, ORTEGA Sonia, ORTEGA DEL RIO Viviana, ORTIZ Edson, ORTIZ George, ORTIZ Sonia, ORTIZ Yamila, ORTIZ MERUVIA Marcelo, ORTON Debbie, OSANAI-ANDERSON Fumiko, OSBORN Anthony, OSBORN Jay, OSBORN Paula, **OSBORNE Daryl**, OSBORNE Aussie, OSBORNE Hamish, OSBORNE Jason, OSBORNE Jodie, OSBORNE Julie, OSBORNE Les, OSBORNE Ricky, OSBORNE Ron, OSBORNE Toni, OSBORNE-NEWELL Janelle, OSBURG Chris, OSBURN Jay, OSCAR-TSCHIPAN Pasharina, OSGOOD Joy, OSGOOD Marian, OSHAUGHNESSY Lynne, OSLAND Darren, OSMA Raquel, OSMAN Margaret, OSMAN Tina, OSMOND Ben, OSMOND David, OSORIO Luis, OSS Jennifer, OST Andrew, OST Gaikim, OSTE Michael, OSTLER Greg, OSTOJIC Jonia, OSTRIC Milan, OSTROUMOV Vera, OSTROWSKI Caroline, OSTROWSKI Danien, OSTROWSKI Konrad, OSTROWSKY Oleh, OSTROZNY Voytek, OSULLIVAN Tony, OSULLIVAN Linda, OTA Fumiko, OTTAVIANI MORONI Eleonora, OTTAVIANO Joe, OTTAWAY Glenis, OTTE Tarren, OTTER Bernie, OTTEY John, OTTLEY Rosemary, OTTO Drosma, OTTO Edmund, OTTO Ray, OTTOMAR Joanne, OTTOSSON Maria, OTTOWAY Karen, OU Jing, OU John, OUDENRYN Len, OUDOMVILAY Danielle, OUMANSKI Michail, OUNG Sivinath, OUTRED Louise, OUTTERSIDE Joe, OUTTERSIDE Maura, OUTZEN Rina, OVAT Resan, OVCHINNIKOV Natasha, OVENDEN Rosemary, OVERALL Lisa, OVERDUIN Brooke, OVERDUIN Eldert, OVERDUIN Justils, OVERHALL Kerri-Lee, OVERMEIRE Steve, OVERTON Clarrie, OVERTON Denise, **OVERTON Dennis**, OVERTON Dorothy, OVERTON Karen, **OVERTON Kaye**, OVERTON Steve, OVERTON Billyo, OVSIENKO Gail, OWEN Annette, OWEN Ann, OWEN Tony, OWEN Barry, OWEN Bev, OWEN Beverley, OWEN Bruce, OWEN Cindi, OWEN Claire, OWEN Della, OWEN Diana, OWEN Edward, OWEN Gordon, OWEN Grant, OWEN Iris, OWEN Jay, OWEN John, OWEN John, OWEN John, OWEN Josh, OWEN Kim, OWEN Marilyn, OWEN Rell, OWEN Peter, OWEN Ronnie, OWEN Ruth, OWEN Sue, OWEN Sue, OWEN Bill, OWENS Barbara, OWENS Craig, OWENS Daniel, OWENS Dianne, OWENS Frank, OWENS Graham, OWENS Jim, OWENS Lawrie, OWENS Margaret, OWENS Margaret, OWENS Marion, OWENS Rosemary, OWENS Sonia, OWENS Stephen, OWENS Tracey, OWERS Jenny, OWERS Kirk, OWERS Westley, OWLES Wayne, OWSINSKI Adam, OWSINSKI Helena, OWUSU-AKYEAMPONG Julius, OWUSU-MENSAH Gladys, OXBORROW Ken, OXENFORD Pamela, OXENHAM Ashleigh, OXENHAM Don, OXENHAM Elaine, OXENHAM Skye, OXFORD Bruce, OXFORD Graeme, OXFORD Margaret, OXFORD Odette, OXFORD Sam, OXLEY Peter, OYAFUSO Wayne, OZAN Nermin, OZAN Yavuz, OZCAN Hatice, OZCAN Mustafa, OZDEMIR Hulusi, OZERS Linda, OZKAN Ibrahim, OZKOSE Salih, OZOLINS Alan, OZOLINS Amanda, OZOLS Edgars.

P

PA David, PAAR Eva, PACAREK Rose, PACE David, PACE Ivan, PACE Rod, PACHECO Janaina, PACHECO Manuel, PACHECO OLIVARES Rafael, PACI Sergio, PACK Sandra, PACKER Ben, PACKER Col, PACKER Denise, PACKER Jo, PACKER Marian, PACKER Meryl, PACKER Rex, PACKER Steve, PACKHAM Howard, PACKHAM Norah, PACKINGTON Stuart, PACKROSS Joern, PACZKOWSKI Margaret, PADDA Gurbal, PADDA Ravin, PADDA Santokh, PADDENBURG Trevor, PADDISON Donald, PADDOCK Bruce, PADDOCK Carol, PADE Allan, PADGETT John, PADILLA Emmanuel, PADILLA Nelson, PADOL Nick, PAECH Janiece, PAES Celene, PAEZ Andrea, PAGAN KariAnne, PAGANO Michael, PAGE Alison, PAGE Allan, PAGE Tony, PAGE Bron, PAGE Bryan, PAGE Carol, PAGE Donna, PAGE Gail, PAGE Genevieve, **PAGE Heather**, PAGE Heather, PAGE Ian, PAGE Jamie, PAGE James, PAGE Ken, PAGE Kevin, PAGE Lyn, PAGE Marianne, PAGE Meredith, PAGE Narelle, PAGE Nicole, PAGE Norma, PAGE Pam, PAGE Richard, PAGE Rodney, PAGE Rosemary, PAGE Sandra, PAGE Warwick, PAGE-SMITH Jodi, PAGET Denis, PAGNIN Damien, PAHLEY Graham, PAI Mel, PAIAU Fetalai, PAIGE Rhonda, PAILLARD Stephen, PAILLAT Edith, PAIN Anna, PAINE Justin, PAINE Jack, PAINE Reg, PAITSON Martha, PAIX Bruce, PAJTL Jamie, PAK Dominic, PAK Jean, PAK-KAI LI, PAKAKIS Michael, PAL Bethuel, PAL Deb, PAL Robyn, PAL Sanat, PAL Sat, PALACI Rafi, PALACIOS Claudia, PALACIOS James, PALACIOS JUGO Leopoldo, PALAMARA Joe, PALAMARA Janis, PALAMARCZUK Fiona, PALATINUS Janos, PALAVECINO Hernan, PALAYAN Pierre, PALAZZOLO Marianne, PALELLA Josephine, PALEMALA Subramaniam, PALEOHORITIS Effie, PALERMO Melissa, PALESE Raoul, PALET Andres, PALFREYMAN Andrew, PALFREYMAN Graham, PALFREYMAN Mike, PALIKMEY Omkar, PALLAS Ron, PALLAVUR NILAKANTAN Sankaran, PALLIER Lorraine, PALLISTER Ana, PALLISTER Matt, PALM Kathy, PALMA LOPEZ John, PALMANO Barbara, PALMER Barbara, PALMER Chris, PALMER Darren, PALMER Diane, PALMER Greg, PALMER Howard, PALMER Jennifer, PALMER Jess, PALMER Joan, PALMER Joy, PALMER Patrick, PALMER John, PALMER Kath, PALMER Kate, PALMER Ken, PALMER Ken, PALMER Leon, PALMER Les, PALMER Lucy, PALMER Lynne, PALMER Maria, PALMER Maria, PALMER Melissa, PALMER Mike, PALMER Moeva, PALMER Nathan, PALMER Neville, PALMER Peter, PALMER Ray, PALMER Ray, PALMER Rochelle, PALMER Sandra, PALMER Shane, PALMER Sue, PALMER Susanne, PALMER William, PALMER Bill, PALMER Ken, PALOMA Raul, PALU David, PALUZZANO Karyn, PALVAKIS Andrew, PAMAMULL Priya, PAMBOS Katrina, PAMBOS Mantalena, PAMELA Cornish, PAMP Maria, PAMPALIAN Lucy, PAMULA Irena, PAN An, PAN Irene, PAN Peter, PAN Wen, PAN Kyna, PANAGAKIS Aristidis, PANAGOPKA Jean, PANAGOPOULOS Peter, PANAPA Clayton, PANAYI Peter, PANAYI Stella, PANCHARATNAM Nerugini, PANCIA Maureen, PANDAY Abhaya, PANDEY Priyanka, PANDEY Ram, PANDEY Sameer, PANDOUSIS Maria, PANDOUSIS Peter, PANDYA Himansu, PANDYA Pradip, PANETTA Angela, PANETTA Antoinette, PANETTA Carlos, PANETTA Danielle, PANETTA Fay, PANETTA Michael, PANG Rosa, PANG David, PANG Frances, PANG Jermy, PANG Paulette, PANG Edwin, PANG Meng, PANG Wendy, PANG Lisa, PANGAS Brett, PANGCOG Lyn, PANGILINAN Lucy, PANICKAR Divya, PANIS Lotlot, PANJER Harry, PANKHURST Bob, PANOPOULOS John, PANOS George, PANOVRAKOU Christina, PANTA Chris, PANTANO Peter, PANTELAKAKIS Giannis, PANTELIC Dorothea, PANTELIDIS Harry, PANTENBURG Helen, PANTHER Al, PANTHER Jim, PAOLA John, PAOLONI Justin, PAOLUCCI Roberto, PAPA Christodoulos, PAPADOPOULOS Ally, PAPADOPOULOS Angela, PAPADOPOULOS Tony, PAPADOPOULOS Larry, PAPADOPOULOS Maria, PAPAIOANNOU Chris, PAPAJORGJI Lily, PAPAKOSTOPOULOU Zoi, PAPALIA Chris, PAPALIA Melissa, PAPAMICHALAKIS Kosta, PAPANASTASIOU Frederika, PAPANEK Juras, PAPANICOLAOU George, PAPANICOLAOU Theo, PAPARELLA Teresa, PAPAS Evan, PAPAS Meryl, PAPASAVAS Lazaros, PAPOULIS Foti, PAPPALARDO Alfina, PAPPALARDO Bob, PAPPAS Andy, PAPUSHEVA Ludmila, PAPWORTH Ian, PAPWORTH Nelly, PAPWORTH Stephen, PARADARIVAS Werner, PARADISE Sally, PARADISE Shirley, PARAFINA Reynand, PARALES Carol, PARAMONOV Victoria, PARARAJASINGHAM Shiranee, PARASHAR Alok, PARASHAR Kamini, PARASHAR Kapil, PARASKAKIS Emmamouel, PARASKEVOPOULUS Matthew, PARASS Alex, PARATA Amy, PARAVIA Margherita, PARBURY Anabel, PARDEDE Leanne, PARDON George, PAREDES Lourdes, PAREDES Olga, PAREEZER Narelle, PAREKH Devan, PAREKH Paresh, PARGALITI Tina, PARHAM Ruth, PARIKH Jitendra, PARINYAPARIWAT Supaluk, PARIS Remo, PARIS Justine, PARIS Maureen, PARIS Michael, PARISH Noel, PARK Andrew, PARK Charles, PARK Doug, PARK Kate, PARK Laura, PARK Helen, PARK Holy, PARK Hyo, PARK Hyunseok, PARK Janice, PARK Jeamin, PARK Jennifer, PARK Sunny, PARK Ji, PARK Ji-Hyoun, PARK Jihong, PARK Joanne, PARK Chan, PARK Eric, PARK Joohee, PARK Julie, PARK Jung, PARK Jungyeon, PARK Kyong, PARK Michelle, PARK Sarah, PARK Seromee, PARK Seung, PARK Soo-Joung, PARK Suckki, PARK Sun, PARK Wang-Kee, PARK Yoonmi, PARK Youmi, PARK Eric, PARKELLIOTT Adam, PARK-ELLIOTT Carole, PARKER Adri, PARKER Sandy, PARKER Amy, PARKER Chucky, PARKER Angela, PARKER Ann, PARKER Tony, PARKER Auvita, PARKER Beverley, PARKER

Brad, PARKER Carly, PARKER Chris, PARKER Darryl, PARKER David, PARKER David, PARKER James, PARKER Debbie, PARKER Douglas, PARKER Eamon, PARKER Evan, PARKER Fran, PARKER Alan, PARKER Frank, PARKER Frank, PARKER Garry, PARKER Garry, PARKER Geoffrey, PARKER Greg, PARKER Hannah, PARKER Helen, PARKER Irwin, PARKER Jacqui, PARKER James, PARKER Jennifer, PARKER Jill, PARKER John, PARKER John, PARKER Ted, PARKER Karen, PARKER Kate, PARKER Katie, PARKER Katherine, PARKER Kieren, PARKER Kirsty, PARKER Leonie, PARKER Len, PARKER Lynn, PARKER Lyn, PARKER Mal, PARKER Margaret, PARKER Melda, PARKER Michael, PARKER Michelle, PARKER Mitchell, PARKER Nikky, PARKER Nolan, PARKER Nyree, PARKER Odette, PARKER Pam, PARKER Pam, PARKER Pam, PARKER Patricia, PARKER Phil, PARKER Rhonda, PARKER Richard, PARKER Richard, PARKER Robert, PARKER Ross, PARKER Sandra, PARKER Shirley, PARKER William, PARKER-PRYCE Kalinya, PARKES Albert, PARKES Barry, PARKES Betty, PARKES Georgie, PARKIN Andrew, PARKIN Darrin, PARKIN Gary, PARKIN Michael, PARKIN Russell, PARKINS Graham, PARKINSON Carl, PARKINSON Marion, PARKINSON Michelle, PARKINSON Noel, PARKINSON Ross, PARKINSON Roy, PARKMAN Alecia, PARKS Allison, PARKS Cathy, PARKS Gloria, PARKS John, PARKS May, PARLE David, PARMAR Pramod, PARMAR Pukhraj, PARMAR Rahul, PARMENTER Mervyn, PARMINTER Christopher, PARNABY Jilliann, PARNELL Anne, PARNELL Brian, PARNELL Karen, PARNELL Lindsay, PARNELL Mel, PARNELL Rhonda, PARNHAM John, PARNHAM Karen, PARNIS Adam, PAROD Fernando, PARODI Elcira, PARODI Wilson, PAROUSIS Bill, PAROVEL Fulvio, PAROVEL Robert, PARR Keith, PARREY Annette, PARRIS Lyndall, PARRIS Richard, PARRISH Ange, PARRISH Christine, PARRISH Heather, PARRISH John, PARRISH Karen, PARRISH Linda, PARRON Sophie, PARROT Michelle, PARROTT Ian, PARROTT Lynne, PARROTT Mark, PARRY Alan, PARRY Amanda, PARRY Carolyn, PARRY Col, PARRY Ethel, PARRY Jessie, PARRY Lorne, PARRY Mavis, PARRY Merrilee, PARRY Nicolle, PARRY Rodney, PARRY Siarn, PARRY Stephen, PARRY Sue, PARRY Val, PARSEGHIAN Tanya, PARSELL Brian, PARSLOW Trev, PARSON Leonard, PAARSONS Alan, PARSONS Anne, PARSONS Brendon, PARSONS Carlicia, PARSONS Carole, PARSONS Catherine, PARSONS Col, PARSONS Damien, PARSONS David, PARSONS Donna, PARSONS Libby, PARSONS Evan, PARSONS Gary, PARSONS Graham, PARSONS Jackie, PARSONS Larissa, PARSONS Joanne, PARSONS Mary, PARSONS Michael, PARSONS Pat, PARSONS Phil, PARSONS Raymond, PARSONS Roger, PARSONS Russell, PARTANEN Melissa, PARTHA SARATHY Partha, PARTLIN Judith, PARTON Barry, PARTON Brian, PARTRIDGE John, PARTRIDGE Anne, PARTRIDGE Tony, PARTRIDGE Dot, PARTRIDGE Erin, PARTRIDGE Jennifer, PARTRIDGE John, PARTRIDGE Bob, PARTRIDGE Vanessa, PARTSAS Voula, PARVEZ Obaidul, PASCALE Angela, PASCALE Felix, PASCALE Lidia, PASCOE Carole, PASCOE Carolyn, PASCOE Gavin, PASCOE John, **PASCOE Juliet**, PASCOE Lesley, PASCOE Louise, PASCOE Marilyn, PASCOE Meryl, PASCOE Sandy, PASCUAL Petronila, PASFIELD Liz, PASFIELD John, PASHLEY Sophie, PASHOU Demi, PASLEY Jimmy, PASQUA Therese, PASQUARIELLO Maria, PASQUINI Marla, PASSA Passa, PASSADORE Marie, PASSANTE Jack, PASSEGGI Bernie, PASSEGGI Horacio, PASSFIELD Alicia, PASSIER Leanne, PASSLOW Emma, PASSMORE Chris, PASSMORE Frank, PASSMORE Ken, PASTRAS Kerryn, PASZKUDZKI George, PATAMANONT Chaovalit, PATARAMAS Decha, PATCHETT John, PATCHETT Leonard, **PATCHING Julius**, PATCHING Neil, PATE Bryan, PATE Dennis, PATE Harekrishna, PATEL Ashvin, PATEL Dipak, PATEL Gaurang, PATEL Ikebal, PATEL Niti, PATEL Shiraz, PATEL Zaved, PATEMAN David, PATEMAN Jillian, PATEMAN Tim, PATERSON Adam, PATERSON Amanda, PATERSON Brian, PATERSON Carol, PATERSON Caroline, PATERSON David, PATERSON Don, PATERSON Genevieve, PATERSON Gilly, PATERSON Gordon, PATERSON Greg, PATERSON Jim, PATERSON Jan, PATERSON Joelene, PATERSON Lauren, PATERSON Les, PATERSON Les, PATERSON Marilyn, PATERSON Marjorie, PATERSON Olive, PATERSON Rachael, PATERSON Robin, PATERSON Roger, PATERSON Scott, PATERSON Stuart, PATERSON Stuart, PATHAN Sana, PATHI Satish, PATHINATHER Lawrence, PATHMAN Vanita, PATHMANANDAVEL Malini, PATI Pati, PATIOLE Fetaitai, PATMAN Craig, PATMAN Val, PATON Ben, PATON Brooke, PATON Fi, PATON Jenni, PATON Jennifer, PATON Jodi, PATON Maria, PATON Marika, PATON Matthew, PATON Sue, PATON John, PATRICK Ben, PATRICK Benjamin, PATRICK Helen, PATRICK Jo, PATRICK Kym, PATRICK Rick, PATRIZI Rita, PATTEN Chris, PATTEN Govin, PATTERSON Adam, PATTERSON Alexander, PATTERSON Belinda, PATTERSON Deb, PATTERSON Denis, PATTERSON Doug, PATTERSON Fleur, PATTERSON Gavin, PATTERSON Jan, PATTERSON Jenny, PATTERSON Julia, PATTERSON Les, PATTERSON Marg, PATTERSON Noel, PATTERSON Noel, **PATTERSON Patricia**, PATTERSON Penny, PATTERSON Pete, PATTERSON Sam, PATTERSON Tania, PATTERSON Valerie, PATTERSON Wayne, PATTESON Christian, PATTI Mimmo, PATTI Vince, PATTIE Wayne, PATTIHES Evelyn, PATTINSON Kim, PATTINSON Tony, PATTIPEILOHY Herman, PATTISON Bruce, PATTISON Janine, PATTISON Josepine, PATTON Bruce, PATTON Christinne, PATTON Greg, PATTON Phil, PATTON Warren, PATWARY M, **PATZOLD Rick**, PAUL Ian, PAUL Audrey, PAUL Celeste, PAUL Col, PAUL Des, PAUL Wilson, PAUL Farey, PAUL George, PAUL Joseph, PAUL Robin, PAUL Robyn, PAULIDES George, PAULIDES Julie, PAULIN May-Lai, PAULING Peter, PAULIUKEVICIUS Katrina, PAULL Carol-Anne, PAULL Dianne, PAULL Karen, PAULL Dick, PAULL Zoe, PAULO Teel, PAUMER Karel, PAUNI Curtis, PAUNOVIC Peter, PAUW Josh, PAVANELLO Angelo, PAVANELLO Fabio, PAVER Jill, PAVER Rob, PAVEY Christopher, PAVEY Eric, PAVEY Joanne, PAVEY Kara, PAVINCICH Vin, PAVIOUR-SMITH Keryn, PAVISIC Nada, PAVITT Joan, PAVLOV Amelia, PAVLOV Laura, PAVONE Passafaro, PAWA Bill, PAWAR Shashank, PAWLICA Petr, PAWLOW Barbara, PAWSEY Maree, PAXTON Colin, PAXTON Kay, PAXTON Stella, PAYGET Fiona, PAYN Mike, PAYNE Alison, PAYNE Anne, PAYNE Arthur, PAYNE Audrey, PAYNE Brian, PAYNE Carolyn, PAYNE Ann, PAYNE Clive, PAYNE Craig, PAYNE Frank, PAYNE Gary, PAYNE Genelle, **PAYNE Gisella**, PAYNE Graeme, PAYNE Wendy, PAYNE Gwendoline, PAYNE Helen, PAYNE Jim, PAYNE John, PAYNE John, PAYNE Kathleen, **PAYNE Kathy**, PAYNE Katrina, PAYNE Leanne, PAYNE Michael, PAYNE Natalie, PAYNE Patricia, PAYNE Rebecca,PAYNE Sandy, PAYNE Scott, PAYNE Sharon, PAYNE Sue, PAYNE Terry, PAYNE Warren, PAYNTER Jim, PAYNTER Lorraine, PAYNTER Patricia, PAYTEN Robert, PAYTON Glenn, PAYZE Tash, PAZMINO Fabian, PAZMINO Franc, PAZOV Theodora, PEACH Craig, PEACH Rosanne, PEACHEY Bert, PEACHEY Alison, PEACHEY Peach, PEACHEY Peach, PEACHEY Barry, PEACOCK Andrew, PEACOCK Helen, PEACOCK Sally, PEADE Dan, PEAKE Bethany, PEAKE Carmel, PEAKE Narelle, PEAKE Pauline, PEARCE Andrew, PEARCE Brian, PEARCE Claire, PEARCE Gary, PEARCE Geoff, PEARCE Graydon, PEARCE Grace, PEARCE Heather, PEARCE Jarrem, PEARCE Jean, PEARCE Jodie, PEARCE Kelly, PEARCE Lauren, PEARCE Luke, PEARCE Michelle, PEARCE Murray, PEARCE Nicole, PEARCE Phil, PEARCE Beck, PEARCE Bob, PEARCE Robert, PEARCE Ron, PEARCE Ron, PEARCE Sally, PEARCE Steven, PEARCE Susan, PEARD Alexandra, PEARDON Larry, PEARMAN Martin, PEARN Jack, PEARSALL Felicity, PEARSALL Heather, PEARSALL Louise, PEARSON Adam, PEARSON Andrew, PEARSON Barbara, PEARSON Bradley, PEARSON David, PEARSON Debbie, PEARSON Heather, PEARSON Jim, PEARSON John, PEARSON Judy, PEARSON Kathie, PEARSON Les, PEARSON Lucille, PEARSON Masako, PEARSON Natalie, PEARSON Rachel, PEARSON Rebecca, PEARSON Scott, PEARSON Sheryl, PEART Darlene, PEASE Dianne, PEASLEY Nathan, PEASTON Juanita, PEAT Cliff, PEAT Michelle, PEBERDY Claire, PECH Joanne, PECK Brian, PECK Frank, PECK John, PECK Lyn, PECKHAM Colin, PECOTIC Elma, PECZEK Dariusz, PEDEN Karyn, PEDERSEN Arne, PEDERSEN Belinda, PEDERSEN Eric, PEDERSEN Tammie, PEDERSON Arne, PEDLER Cheree, PEDLER Sandra, PEDLEY Joan, PEDLEY Judy, PEDLEY Kate, PEDLEY-SMITH Merle, PEDLEY-SMITH Vanessa, PEDLOW Matthew, PEDRAM Sandra, PEDRANA Ross, PEDRETTI Tatiana, PEEK John, PEEK Kaz, PEEK Ronald, PEEK

Tom, PEEL Adrian, PEEL Barbara, PEEL Cliff, PEEL Damien, PEEL Danielle, PEEL Michael, PEEL Steven, PEERANARONG Chairat, PEFFERINI John, PEFFERINI Sandra, PEGG Claudia, PEGG Danielle, PEGRUM Julie, PEGRUM Reg, PEI Lei, PEI Sulesa, PEI Bob, PEIME David, PEIRCE Tony, PEIRCE Kerry, PEITSAHO Mika, PEJKOVIC John, PEKA Hayden, PEKLER Christian, PELAEZ Dennis, PELANTAKIS Nikos, PELAYO Ma., PELED Nir, PELEKANOS Rebecca, PELJO Kal, PELL Brendan, PELL Jeff, PELLAERS Marianne, PELLEGRINI Emil, PELLEGRINO Irene, PELLEN Steve, PELLERIN Luc, PELLETIER Di, PELLEW Louise, PELLICO-URRUTIA Alberto, PELLIZZARI Elizabeth, PELLIZZON Belinda, PELLY Fiona, PELTOLA David, PEMBER Max, PEMBERTON Elizabeth, PEMBERTON Garry, PEMBERTON Katie, PEMBLE Gwen, PEMBROKE Elaine, PENA Ron, PENA MAYEN Dolores, PENBERTHY Francine, PENBERTHY Wal, PENDALL Stan, PENDER Dave, PENDER Dennis, PENDER Fiona, PENDER Jan, PENDER Richard, PENDERED Robert, PENDERGAST Brendan, PENDERGAST Kevin, PENDERGAST Maureen, PENDLEBURY Diane, PENDLEBURY Kay, PENDLEBURY Philby, PENDLEBURY Renee, PENFOLD Gary, PENFOLD Philippa, PENG Jimmy, PENG Kay, PENGEL Liset, PENGILLY Anita, PENGILLY Bill, PENHALL Diana, PENHALL Lorraine, PENI Marty, PENI Reg, PENKOV Michael, PENN Chris, PENNA Pietro, PENNEFATHER Kath, PENNEFATHER Goldie, PENNEFATHER Graham, PENNEKAMP Maryolein, PENNEY Ian, PENNEY Kate, PENNEY Lisa, PENNINGER John, PENNINGS Richard, PENNINGTON Brian, PENNINGTON Sharon, PENNY Chris, PENNY Doug, PENNY John, PENNY John, PENNY Shannon, PENROSE Danny, **PENROSE Jim**, PENROSE Bill, PENROSE-HERBERT Lisa, PENSINI Alf, PENTECOST Martin, PENTELA Sreekanth, PENTY Ann, PEOPLES Angela, PEPE Veronica, PEPLER Rhonda, PEPLOE Dick, PEPPAS John, PEPPER Glenn, PEPPER Jenny, PEPPERALL George, PEPPERELL Betty, PEPPERELL Betty, PEPPERELL Martine, PEPPERELL Roland, PEPPINCK Brad, PERALTA Mabe, PERCIVAL Anthony, PERCY Kristen, PERCY Nathan, PERCY Paula, PERCY Shannon, PERDON Angela, PEREDERIY Maryna, PEREDES Mario, PEREIRA Alyson, PEREIRA Anna, PEREIRA Aylmer, PEREIRA David, PEREIRA Gabriela, PEREIRA Garth, PEREIRA Jennifer, PEREIRA John, PEREIRA Julio, PEREIRA Nathan, PEREIRA Randolph, PEREIRA Shanna, PEREIRA Yolanda, PEREL Rob, PERELMAN Mike, PERERA Chandi, PERERA Cliford, PERERA Panagodage, PERERA Perera, PEREYRA Nelly, PEREYRA Percy, PEREZ Bric, PEREZ Cristina, PEREZ Tina, PEREZ Mark, PEREZ Oscar, PEREZ MINOZ Luis, PERFECT Benjamin, PERGOLA Sam, PERI Josene, PERIC Ljubomir, PERIC Fr, PERICH Sen, PERIZZOLO Amanda, PERKIN Danny, PERKIN Margaret, PERKINS Bindi, PERKINS David, PERKINS Tim, PERKINS Di, PERKINS Jim, PERKINS John, PERKINS Kevin, PERKINS Kim, PERKINS Leanne, PERKINS Lianne, PERKINS Linda, PERKINS Lisa, PERKINS Marette, PERKINS Monique, PERKINS Pat, PERKINS Paul, PERKINS Randall, PERKINS Sue, PERKINS Vickie, PERKISS Steve, PERKS Warwick, PERL Judith, PERLSTEIN Philip, PERNICE Sal, PERONACE Donna, PERONCHIK Bob, PERONI Steven, PERRAM Jenny, PERRE Marianna, PERRETT Robert, PERRETT Rosemary, PERRI Ian, PERRIER Cedric, PERRIMAN Jim, PERRIMAN Matt, PERRIN Andrew, PERRIN Helen, PERRIN Judy, PERRIN Kate, PERRIN Kate, PERROTT Bruce, PERROTT David, PERROTT Marg, PERROTT Margo, PERROTT Pat, PERROW Caroline, PERROW Lorraine, PERRY Annette, PERRY Bronwyn, PERRY Tim, PERRY Chris, PERRY Don, PERRY John, PERRY John, PERRY Judy, PERRY Justin, PERRY Ken, PERRY Kim, PERRY Lisa, PERRY Melinda, PERRY Michael, PERRY Michael, PERRY Michael, PERRY Monica, PERRY Ralph, PERRY Ron, PERRY Ross, PERRY Shane, PERRYBOLT Pat, PERRYMAN Thomas, PERSOHN Annette, PERSON Claude, PERSSON Katarina, PERSSON Lisa, PERT Terry-Ann, PERTOSI Sue, PERTZEL Gail, PERUMAL Anthony, PERVAN Nicola, PERYMAN John, PESCATELLO Heather, PESCHKE Horst, PESLE John, PESSANHA Guilherme, PESUDOVS Konrad, PETALE Ozden, PETAN John, PETCH Beverley, PETCH Pauline, PETCH Richard, PETCHELL Michael, PETER Peter, PETER Rodney, PETER Zita, PETER KOK HENG Nah, PETERIE Carolyn, PETERMAN Anthony, PETERMAN Nicole, PETERS Carol, PETERS Alan, PETERS Angelique, PETERS Anthony, PETERS Betty, PETERS Barry, PETERS Bronwyn, PETERS Chris, PETERS Connie, PETERS Dave, PETERS Deborah, PETERS Donna, PETERS Eddie, PETERS Glenn, PETERS Gregory, PETERS Ian, PETERS Jan, PETERS Jenny, PETERS Jill, PETERS Joan, PETERS Kim, PETERS George, PETERS Lynda, PETERS Mary, PETERS Noel, PETERS Peter, PETERS Phillip, PETERS Robin, PETERS Simone, PETERS Sonya, PETERS Troy, PETERS Vanessa, PETERS Wilma, PETERS Bill, PETERSSMITH Raymond, PETERSEN Bev, PETERSEN Carolynne, PETERSEN Helen, PETERSEN Jenny, PETERSEN Kathryn, PETERSEN Ken, PETERSEN Kim, PETERSEN Ruby, PETERSON Alex, PETERSON Catherine, PETERSON Chantelle, PETERSON Chris, PETERSON Elaine, PETERSON Jillian, PETERSON Jillian, PETERSON Kate, PETERSON Kerrie, PETERSON Meredith, PETERSON Peter, PETERSON Richard, PETERSON Ron, PETERSON Trevor, **PETERSON Wayne**, PETERSSON Sylvia, PETHERBRIDGE Peter, PETHERBY Roslyn, PETHYBRIDGE Raymond, PETIDIS Theo, PETITCOLIN Giselle, PETITFILS Anne-Marie, PETKOV Adriana, PETKOVICH Julia, PETKOVICH Renee, PETKOVICH Sue, PETKUS Johnathon, PETRAKIS Con, PETRANKER Joshua, PETRANKER Robert, PETRENKO Victor, PETRESKI Debbie, PETRIE Gail, PETRIE Helen, PETRIKAS Chris, PETRIKAS Dick, PETRIKAS Judy, **PETROCCO Andrea**, PETROFF Heidi, PETRONI Sam, PETROPOULOS Chris, PETRORO Tom, PETROSILLO Patricia, PETROTTA Daniel, PETROVA Diana, PETROVIC Elaine, PETROVIC Maria, PETROVSKA Kata, PETROW Carol/Cass, PETROW Carol, PETRUCCI Rosetta, PETRUS Kristina, PETRYSHEN Tom, PETTERSEN Ashley, PETTERSEN Dulcie, PETTERSEN Bob, PETTERSONO'BRIEN Annie, PETTIFER Veronica, PETTIFORD Colleen, PETTIFORD Sheridan, PETTIGREW Larry, PETTIT Jackie, PETTIT Jonathon, PETTITT Doris, PETUKH Sam, PETZOLD Volker, PEYSER Pete, PEZET Owen, PEZZANO Anthony, PEZZANO Joanna, PFAU Naomi, PFEIL Uwe, PFIEL Ray, PFITZENMEIER Wendy, PFITZNER Jodi, PHABMIXAY Thana, PHABOUTDY Jamie, PHADKE Anjali, PHADKE Sangita, PHAM Anna, PHAM Duy, PHAM Helene, PHAM Hilp, PHAM Hung, PHAM Johnny, PHAM Joseph, PHAM Minh, PHAM Myle, PHAM My, PHAM My, PHAM Vinh, PHAM Thanh, PHAM Diep, PHAM Kathy, PHAM Kim, PHAM Hanh, PHAM Thi, PHAM Chi, PHAM Van-Dong, **PHAM-VU Yumi**, PHAN Kha, PHAN Nguyet, PHAN Phuong, PHAN Qui, PHAN Tan, PHAN Thi, PHAN Thu, PHAN Xuan, PHEGAN Ali, PHELAN Amy, PHELAN Evan, PHELAN Jennifer, PHELAN Kerry, PHELAN Lyn, PHELAN Sandra, PHELPS George, PHELPS Jason, PHELPS Judy, PHELPS Matthew, PHI Duc, PHILBROOK Bill, PHILIP Corey, PHILIP John, PHILIP Pamela, PHILIPPE MarieClaude, PHILIPPSOHN Sharon, PHILIPS Romilda, PHILIPSON Debbie, PHILISTIN John, PHILLEMORE Cec, PHILLIPPS Jo, PHILLIPPS Sasha, PHILLIPS Phil, PHILLIPS Alexis, PHILLIPS Allison, PHILLIPS Andrew, PHILLIPS Barry, PHILLIPS Bas, PHILLIPS Brad, PHILLIPS Carole, PHILLIPS Catherine, PHILLIPS Bill, PHILLIPS Charles, PHILLIPS Charles, PHILLIPS Craig, PHILLIPS David, PHILLIPS Diana, PHILLIPS Di, PHILLIPS Liz, PHILLIPS Ernie, PHILLIPS Ron, PHILLIPS Helen, PHILLIPS James, PHILLIPS Jean, PHILLIPS Jeff, PHILLIPS Jeffrey, PHILLIPS Jenny, PHILLIPS Keith, PHILLIPS Kevin, PHILLIPS Kevin, PHILLIPS Lee, PHILLIPS Leonie, PHILLIPS Lynne, PHILLIPS Marnie, PHILLIPS Megan, PHILLIPS Michelle, PHILLIPS Michael, PHILLIPS Patricia, PHILLIPS Paul, PHILLIPS Rod, PHILLIPS Ron, PHILLIPS Rosemary, PHILLIPS Sheryn, PHILLIPS Sheryn, PHILLIPS Shelley, PHILLIPS Stuart, PHILLIPS Violeta, PHILLIPS Bill, PHILLIPS Winston, PHILLIPS-GALL Rhonda, PHILLLIP Nevine, PHILLPOT Diane, PHILLPOTT Jim, PHILLPOTT Margaret, PHILLPOTT Neita, PHILLPOTT Warwick, PHILP Craig, PHILP Peter, PHILPOTT Mary, PHILPS Barry, PHILPS Bruce, PHIMLEUT Touttou, PHINN Gai, PHINN Bill, PHIPPS Dale, PHIPPS Jo, PHIPPS Jon, PHIPPS Steve, PHO T C, PHO Trinh, PHOEBUS Sally, PHOUTHAVONG Sonesay, PHUA Albin, PHUA Rowena, PHUAH Ivan, PHUNG Karen, PHUNG Mary, PHUONG Anthony, PHUONG Selina, PHUONG Patrick, PHYTHIAN Ray, PHYTHIAN Val, PIATEK Anita, PIAZZA Angelo, PIAZZANO Mattia, PICCIONE Anne, PICCLES John, PICCOLO David, PICCOLRUAZ Isabella, PICHEL-SMACZNY Sylvia, PICHON Nikki, PICK Blair, PICKARD Alissia, PICKARD Craig, PICKERING Glen, PICKERING Josie, PICKERING Katrina, PICKERING Paul,

PICKERING Wayne, PICKERING Scott, PICKERING Steve, PICKERING Stephen, PICKERING Susan, PICKERING Trevor, PICKERING Vicky, PICKERS Georgina, PICKERSGILL Arthur, PICKERSGILL Brian, PICKETT Gerry, PICKETT Gordon, PICKFORD Jon, PICKFORD Ray, PICKLES Warren, PICKUP Adrian, PICKUP Brian, PICKUP Martin, PICKUP Nicole, PICKUP Robert, PICTON Teo, PICTON Ruth, PIDGEON Merilyn, PIDOUX Beth, PIDOUX Peter, PIEFKE Michael, PIERCE Cheryl, PIERCE David, PIERCE Jeremy, PIERCE Patricia, PIERES Ron, PIEROTTI Tanya, PIERRE Isabelle, PIETRUSZEWSKI Mark, PIETSCH Jo, PIFFARELLI Maureen, PIGGIN Anthony, PIGGIN Mel, PIGGOT Amy, PIGNA Lisa, PIGNATARO Anthony, PIGOT Doug, PIGOTT Peter, PIGRAM Peter, PIHLAK Olav, PIHLAK Vella, PIKE Alex, PIKE Lisa, PIKE Anne, PIKE Chris, PIKE David, PIKE Donya, PIKE Graeme, PIKE Lesley, PIKE Melanie, PIKE Simon, PIKIS Harry, PILBROW Daniel, PILE John, PILE Mike, PILICHOWSKI Adam, PILIMON Tony, PILISKIC Darko, PILKINGTON Joanne, PILKINGTON Joy, PILKINGTON Melissa, PILKINGTON Pauline, PILLAI Annette, PILLAI Anu, PILLAI Joy, PILLAI Nathan, PILLAY Maheshni, PILLER Tracy, PILLING Melanie, PILLON Rosi, PILLONI Annette, PILTZ William, PIMENTEL Precious, PIMM Sharon, PINARD Greg, PINAZZA Adrian, PINCH Jean, PINCH Beth, PINCOTT John, PINDER Andrew, PINDER Doug, PINE William, PINEDA Benjamin, PINES Michael, PINHEIRO Marcia, PINHEY Annette, PINHO Daniella, PINI Albert, PINI Lorraine, PINK David, PINKERTON Carol, PINKERTON Micaela, PINKEWICH Marie, PINNERUP Lisbet, PINOCHET Astrid, PINOCHET Jaime, PINTAINHO Tinho, PINTAINHO William, PINTER Dean, PINTO Elsa, PINTO Grace, PINTO Rene, PINTO Renata, PINTOS Claude, PINZONE Josephine, PINZONE Mary, PIOCH Jill, PIONKA Maggie, PIORKOWSKI Daniel, PIPER Janine, PIPER Joe, PIPER Marilyn, PIPER Tom, PIPERIDIS Jim, PIPITONE Maria, PIRIE Alex, PIRIE Amanda, PIRIE Bryan, PIRIE David, PIRIE Judy, PIRIE Stuart, PIRKEBNER Marie, PIRLO Katrina, PIRO Jon, PIROZZI Jill, PIRRECA Belinda, PIRRELLO Maria, PISANI Grant, PISANI Sam, PISK Karen, PISUTPIBOONVONG Demy, PITAKTOMORN Jakrit, PITCHER Brad, PITIYAARACHCHI Omali, PITMAN Alicia, PITMAN-SMITH Erica, PITSIS Chris, PITT Alison, PITT Frank, PITT Gordon, PITT Michael, PITT Robert, PITTAWAY Barbara, PITTAWAY Judy, PITTAWAY Miffy, PITTAWAY Ryan, PITTMAN Brenton, PITTMAN Helen, **PITTMAN Henry**, PITTMAN Jackie, PITTMAN Mick, PITTMAN Yvonne, PITTOCK Doug, PITTOCK John, PITTS Theresa, PIVETTA Eduardo, PIWARI Jack, PIZZUTI Anthony, PIZZUTI Laurie, PLACEK Janina, PLACIDO Fernando, PLACING Kaye, PLAIL Janelle, PLAINE-LEPINE Iris, PLAISTED Fiona, PLANNER John, PLANT Alan, PLANT Jane, PLANT Kelly, PLANT Lucy, PLANT Pat, PLANTEN Glenda, PLASHCHIK Natasha, PLASKITT Marilyn, PLASKITT Richard, PLASTO Dawn, PLATEL Tiffany, PLATER Merrick, PLATH Sue, PLATIL Francis, PLATT Elaine, PLATT Eza, PLATT Keith, PLATT Laurie-Ann, PLATT Nancy, PLATT-HEPWORTH David, PLATUS Louis, PLAUDE Marian, PLAYFAIR Judy, PLAYFORD Anne, PLAYFORD Wendy, PLAYLE Brett, PLAZAS John, **PLEDGER Helen**, PLEDGER Tom, PLEDGER Venus, PLEDGER Paul, PLEITER Yvonne, PLENO Mel, PLEWS Dawn, PLIM Lydia, PLIOPLIS Clio, PLOCIENNIK Lara, PLOHL Matthew, PLOSKODNIAK Oleh, PLOWES Lindsay, PLOWMAN Anne, PLOWMAN John, PLOWMAN Lyn, PLOWMAN Ray, PLUCKNETT Barry, PLUCKNETT Jenni, PLUG Joanne, PLUMB Laura, PLUMB Leah, PLUMB Noel, PLUMBE Robert, PLUMMER Cate, PLUMMER Greg, PLUMMER Jenny, PLUMMER Kaye, PLUMMER Rodney, PLUMRIDGE Frank, PLUNGKLANG Kob, PLUNKETT Don, PO Ilyn, PO Kannika, POBJIE Brenton, POCEPKO Vadims, POCEPKO Vadim, POCHE Brenda, POCHE Fred, POCKNALL Noelle, POCOCK Benjamin, POCOCK Jean, POCOCK Stoddart, PODBURY Maurie, PODDATOORU Amarnath, PODGER Ian, PODGORNIK Max, PODGORSKA Paulina, PODMORE Bruce, PODMORE Duncan, PODMORE Naomi, PODOLSKAYA Yana, POE Gwen, POE Howell, POH Eddy, POHIO Riki, POHL Rudi, POHLMANN Jennine, POHORILLE Ralph, POI Chuk, POIGNAND Martina, POINTING Greg, POINTING Judith, POINTING Phyllis, POINTNER Ann, POINTON Bryan, POISEL Tim, POK June, POKORNY Adrian, POKORNY Peter, POL Lori, POLAK Aaron, POLAK Abbie, POLAK Gaye, POLCZYNSKI Jan, POLDEN Joe, POLE Bronwyn, POLEC Liz, POLETTO Dario, POLICARPIO John, POLICARPIO Myke, POLINESS Edmund, POLITIS Lyn, POLITO Teresa, POLJAK Mira, POLJAK Ve sna, POLKINGHORNE Neil, POLKINGHORNE Nevis, POLKINGHORNE Rodger, POLL Annemiek, POLL Kees, POLLACK Tessa, POLLACK Thomas, POLLAK Andrew, POLLAK Susannah, POLLARD Andy, POLLARD Beverley, **POLLARD Emma**, POLLARD Emily, POLLARD John, POLLARD Kate, POLLARD Sherelle, POLLETT Jo, POLLICINA Helen, POLLITT John, POLLITT Thomas, POLLOCK Belinda, POLLOCK Brent, POLLOCK Bruce, POLLOCK David, POLLOCK Dave, POLLOCK Jasmin, **POLLOCK Judy**, POLLOCK Maree, POLLOCK Ross, POLLOK Ann, POLMANTEER Gary, POLONYI John, POLS Roger, POLUAKAN Toar, POLYA Daniel, POLYANOVSKYI Sasha, POLYBLANK Lisa, POLYDOROPOULOS Nikos, POMARE Tony, POMERING Graham, POMEROY Gregory, POMMEREL Naomi, PONDER Penny, PONG Dennis, PONG Alice, PONGNUKRAWSIRI Yuwadee, PONGSAGONOPDOL Nick, PONTELLO Kristen, PONTES Gizelle, PONTI Marcel, PONTIFEX Tony, PONTIKIS Peter, **PONTONI Felicity**, POOK David, POOK Helen, POOLE Peter, POOLE Bill, POOLE Bev, POOLE Carol, POOLE Gregory, POOLE Jillian, POOLE Lisa, POOLE Maurie, POOLE Patricia, POOLE Sandra, POOLEY Michael, POOLMAN Grant, POON A da, POON Bruce, POON Charles, POON Poon, POON Claudine, POON Janine, POON Jennifer, POON Matthew, POON Patrick, POON Richard, POON Stephen, POON Winnie, POOTS Jeff, POP Alin, POPCHEFF Kathy, POPE Brian, POPE Brian, POPE Charles, POPE Charles, POPE Keith, POPESCU Alina, POPESCU Gabriel, POPIC Kathy, POPLE Geoff, POPOVIC Helena, POPPELIERS Erwin, POPPITT Caryl, POR Paula, PORCH Ben, PORCU Edilia, PORDAGE Harry, PORDEL Abbas, PORGES Kate, PORGES Stuart, PORITERS Larissa, PORITERS Nicholas, PORMAN Noeline, PORROVECCHIO Naomi, PORTA Ester, PORTA CUBAS Gonzalo, PORTAIL Jean-Jacques, PORTAS Teresa, PORTCH Terry, PORTELA Matias, PORTELLI Darren, PORTELLI Jason, PORTELLI Joseph, PORTEOUS Ian, PORTER Mandy, PORTER Ann, PORTER Carol, PORTER Chris, PORTER Christine, PORTER Daniel, PORTER Ernest, PORTER Harry, PORTER Janet, PORTER John, PORTER John, PORTER John, PORTER Kerry, PORTER Kerrie, PORTER Kim, PORTER Kirsten, PORTER Lesley, PORTER Leslie, PORTER Lionel, PORTER Lynda, PORTER Norma, PORTER Ronald, PORTER Sally, PORTER Sharon, PORTER Warwick, PORTER Zoe, PORTNOY Eddy, PORTOLESI Elizabeth, PORTOLESI Linda, PORZSOLT Vivienne, POSA Michelle, POSADAS Gally, POSPICHAL Pavel, POSPISHIL Jason, POST John, POSTHOORN Rachael, POSTHUMA Stephen, POSTLE Byron, POSTLE Frank, POSTOSH Paul, POTE James, POTHIN Daphne, POTOCKA Dot, POTTEN Keith, **POTTEN Rita**, POTTER Andrew, POTTER Det, POTTER Douglas, POTTER Neil, POTTER Jackie, POTTER Jenny, POTTER Jessie, POTTER Les, POTTER Marg, POTTER Melissa, POTTER Rosemary, POTTER Tom, POTTER Lance, POTTHAST Silke, POTTIER Peggy, POTTINGER John, POTTINGER Kylie, POTTS Alison, POTTS Christopher, POTTS Gary, POTTS Henry, POTTS David, POTTS Kerry, POTTS Kylie, POTTS Leanne, POTTS Lesley, POUDOV Genn, POULADI Hamid, POULADI Reza, POULLOS Anthea, POULOS Olga, POULSEN Katrina, POULTER Cassandra, POULTER Georgina, POULTER Rudolf, POULTER Tracey, POULTON Blair, POULTON Mick, POULTON Michael, POULTON Sharon, POULTON Victor, POUNARTZIS Mia, POUNCEY Leigh, POUNCEY Patsy, POUPART John, POURPOURAS Teresa, POUS Patricia, POUSINI Samiuela, POVEY Amy, POVEY Sheila, POVIS Victoria, POWANI Poonah, POWDERLY John, POWDERLY Mark, POWELL Adam, POWELL Alan, POWELL Anne, POWELL Barbara, POWELL Mouse, POWELL Brendan, POWELL Brian, POWELL Chas, POWELL Bob, POWELL Denise, POWELL Diana, POWELL Donna, POWELL Georgina, POWELL Gerard, POWELL Glenn, POWELL Glenis, POWELL Ian, POWELL Ian, POWELL Jan, POWELL Jason, POWELL John, POWELL Juliet, POWELL Keith, POWELL Kerry, POWELL Kylie, POWELL Len, POWELL Lisa, POWELL Lyn, POWELL Marcelle, POWELL Raymond, POWELL Bob, POWELL Robert, POWELL Miku, POWELL Sean, POWELL Sue, POWELL Will, POWER Chrissy, POWER David, POWER Fran, POWER Gary, POWER Gretel, POWER Kelly, POWER Laurie, POWER Lynette, POWER Michelle, POWER Michelle, POWER Peter, POWER Rhiannon, POWER

Stephen, POWER Willhameena, POWERS Karen, POWERS Karen, POWERS Larry, POWERS Maureen, POWIS Michael, POWLES David, POWLES Bob, POWNALL Wendy, POWNALL Bill, POWRIE Toni, POYNER Sue, POYNTER Jo, POYNTER Marian, POYNTING Michael, POYNTON Daniel, POZARIK Lee, POZARIK Michael, POZNIAK Roslyn, POZNIAK Sheldon, POZZATO Margareta, POZZATO Ray, POZZATO Theresa, POZZINI Jeri, PRACY Jan, PRACY John, PRADELLA Alan, PRADHAN Kuldeep, PRADHAN Pooja, PRADHAN Pravin, PRADHAN Samir, PRADHAN Esspee, PRADO Brett, PRADO Rocio, PRAKASH Anantha, PRAKASH Andrew, PRANANTO Dessy, PRANCE Shannon, PRASAD Abe, PRASAD Babita, PRASAD Nalini, PRASAD Richard, PRASAD Ritesh, PRASAD Stephen, PRASAD Steve, PRASAD Sujit, PRASAD Vince, PRASAD Vinay, PRASAI Chandra, PRASETHYO Jenly, PRATAP Hamesh, PRATAP Raj, PRATER Adam, PRATER Jenny, PRATHEES Kan, PRATT Angela, PRATT Doug, PRATT Elizabeth, PRATT Frances, PRATT Kylie, PRATT Narelle, PRATTEN Tony, PRATTEN Jo, PRAVICA Milena, PRAWIRA Stan, PRECIANS Jan, PREECE Harry, PREECE Pauline, PREEDY Shirley, PREHN Eileen, PREINER Anita, PRELL Sue, PREMACHANDRA Hasanthi, PREMACHANDRA Iran, PRENDERGAST Doug, PRENDERGAST-WHITE Mary, PRENSKY Isaac, PRENTICE Andrew, PRENTICE Jon, PRENTICE Meg, PRENTICE Rob, PRENTICE Tamara, PRERAD Dragana, PRESBURY Fred, PRESBURY Gregory, PRESBURY John, PRESBURY Steve, PRESCOTT Ellen, PRESCOTT Jean, PRESCOTT Paul, PRESCOTT-SMITH Ian, PRESILSKA Betty, PRESLAND Daniel, PRESLAND Terry, PRESLEY Laura, PRESS Maurice, PRESS Peter, PRESSLEY Lynne, PRESSLEY Marjorie, PRESTIPINO David, PRESTON Bette, PRESTON Chris, PRESTON Chris, PRESTON Glen, PRESTON Jason, PRESTON John, PRESTON Kate, PRESTON Katie, PRESTON Ros, PRESTON Sam, PRESTON Timothy, PRESTON Trevor, PRESTON-STANLEY Bev, PRESUTTI Mario, PRETTY David, PREUSS Karl, PREVITERA Peter, PREVOST Valerie, PREWER Barbara, PRICE Carole, PRICE Charlene, PRICE Dale, PRICE Kristina, PRICE Erlinda, PRICE Gary, PRICE Jackie, PRICE James, PRICE Jane, PRICE Jilly, PRICE John, PRICE Jack, PRICE Karen, PRICE Keith, PRICE Keith, PRICE Ken, PRICE Lionel, PRICE Mal, PRICE Marilee, PRICE Martin, PRICE Michelle, PRICE Nigel, PRICE Peter, PRICE Petrina, PRICE Robyn, PRICE Rochelle, PRICE Sandy, PRICHARD Bec, PRICHARD Robert, PRICHARD Stephen, PRIDAY Julie, PRIDDIN Kerri, PRIDDLE Daniele, PRIDDLE Graham, PRIDDLE Teresa, PRIDDLE Bill, PRIDE Belinda, PRIDE Robyn, PRIDEAUX Brian, PRIDEAUX Graham, PRIEST Tony, PRIEST Bernice, PRIEST Edwina, PRIEST Ian, PRIESTLEY Liz, PRIESTLEY Gary, PRIESTLEY Helen, PRIESTLY Beverly, PRIESTNALL Brian, PRIETO Andrea, PRIETO Jose, PRIETO Louie, PRIMAVERA Anthony, PRIME Emma, PRINCE Greg, PRINCE Kirsty, PRINCE Nathan, PRINCE Robyn, PRINCEKERNER Chris, PRINCIPE Ernie, PRINCIPE Maria, PRINEAS James, PRINGLE Janine, PRINGLE Michelle, PRINGLE Bill, PRIOR Alan, PRIOR Deborah, PRIOR Joanne, PRIOR Mervyn, PRIOR Simon, PRISCOLIN Luigi, PRITCHARD Barbara, PRITCHARD Carolyn, PRITCHARD Brother, PRITCHARD Kip, PRITCHARD Dennis, PRITCHARD Elva, PRITCHARD Kay, PRITCHARD Geoff, PRITCHARD Michelle, PRITCHARD Owen, PRITCHARD Rose, PRITCHETT Gray, PRITZLER Emma, PRIVETT Rowen, PRO Manuel, PROANO Kavina, PROBST Kathryn, PROCTER John, PROCTER Marie, PROCTER Sash, PROCTOR David, PRODANOVICH Jim, PROESTOS Andreas, PROFFITT Wendy, PROIETTO Emilia, PROIETTO Melinda, PROKES Ludek, PROLOV Jul ie, PROSS Kay, PROSSER Leanne, PROSSER Bill, PROTAS Kestas, PROTIC Joanne, PROTIC Phyllis, PROTT Fiona, PROTTKEYS Janey, PROUD Elaine, PROUD Garth, PROUD Pat, PROUDFOOT David, PROUDFOOT Ross, PROUDFOOT Sue, PROUDLOCK Adam, PROUDLOCK Steve, PROUDMAN Louise, PROULX Michael, PROUSIS Andy, PROUT Neil, PROUTEN Mish, PROUTING Beverley, PROUTSOS Anthony, PROUTSOS Tessie, PROVAN Margaret, PROVENCHER-STOTT Johanne, PROVIANS Marilyn, PROWSE Cathy, PROWSE Dawn, PROWSE John, PROWSE Roxanne, PRUDAMES Fran, PRUNSTER Richard, PRUSCINO Michael, PRUSSNER Barb, PRUTHI Gaurav, PRUYN Tim, PRYDE Betty, PRYDE Howard, PRYKE Mark, PRYOR Cherylyn, PRYOR Geoff, PRYOR Lindsay, PRYOR Mark, PRYTZ Sherrel, PSAILA Tracey, PSALTIS Pennie, PSATHAS Dimos, PSOMAS Thomas, PSYHOGIOS Bill, PTASZNIK Ronnie, PTOLEMY Mike, PUCCI Belinda, PUCHER Mick, PUCHETA Juan, PUCKERIDGE Diana, PUDADERA Richard, PUDDICOMBE Sandra, PUDUGRAMAM Vishy, PUECHBERTY Rene, PUENTE-TREVINO Jimena, PUGGIONI Maurice, PUGH Sue, PUGIN Belinda, PUGSLEY Michelle, PUGSLEY Rose, PULFORD Mandy, PULLAN Lindsay, PULLAR Imogen, PULLEN Alan, PULLEN Ken, PULLEN Lauren, PULLEN Michaela, PULLEY Les, PULLIN Ian, PULLIN Jim, PULLIN Prudence, PULLINGER Megan, PULLMAN Jaroslav, PULVANO Fab, PUMGUMARN Muanfan, PUN Alvin, PUN Hong, PUN Peter, PUN Yu, PUNCH Greg, PUNI Anisha, PUNSALAN Ernie, PUNZALAN Sylvia, PURBA Endo, PURBA Daniel, PURCELL Adam, PURCELL Adam, PURCELL Christine, PURCELL Danielle, PURCELL Denice, PURCELL Jennifer, PURCELL Joan, PURCELL John, PURCELL Kate, PURCELL Lyn, PURCELL Martin, PURCELL Oonagh, **PURCELL Patrick**, PURCELL Ray, PURCELL Rob, PURCELL Sylvia, PURCELL Bill, PURCHIARONI Antonello, PURDIE Christine, PURDIE Sue, PURDON Tony, PURDY Jenny, PURDY John, PURDY John, PURDY Judy, PURDY Robert, PUREAU Maui,PURIC Sanela, PURKIS Marie, PURKIS Andrew, PURKIS Stephen, PURNELL Anna, PURNELL Graham, PURNELL Sam, PURNELL-JONES Jacqueline, PURNOMO Lourence, PURNOMO Shianto, PURSELL Gerard, PURSELL Rob, PURSER Lisa, PURTLE Brian, PURVIS Bronwyn, PURVIS Colleen, PURVIS Paul, PUTHA Vidyadhararao, PUTHANVEETIL Subash, PUTLAND Lorraine, PUTLAND Mark, PUTS Peter, PUTT Jenny, PUVANENDIRANATHAN Pradesha, PUZ Keterina, PUZ Sergio, PYBUS Pamela, PYE Carolyn, PYE David, PYE Don, PYE Dudley, PYE Glad, PYE Glenys, PYE Jim, PYE Laurie, PYE Noel, PYKE Bruce, PYKE Maxine, PYKE Rona, PYM Andrew, PYM Margy, PYM Tomas, PYNE Carole, PYNE Gordon, PYNE Keith, PYRGIOTIS Jim.

Q

QI Joe, QIAN Sammy, QIAN Wen, QIAN William, QIU Chaojie, QIU Julie, QIU Yun, QUACH David, QUACH Ha, QUACH Linda, QUACH Tien, QUADE Samantha, QUADRACCIA Giulia, QUAGLIA Alfredo, QUAGLIO Emerson, QUAH Tora, QUAN Bing, QUAN Willie, QUANCE Tony, QUARANTA Nicky, QUARANTINO Kathryn, QUARATINO Corinne, QUARATINO Kat, QUARLES Sallie, QUARRIER Diane, QUARRY Neville, QUARTERMAINE Deanne, QUARTLY Annette, QUARTLY Brian, QUARTLY Helen, QUARTLY Isabelle, QUARTLY Kathlene, QUARTLY Margaret, QUARTLY Peter, QUASS Beryl, QUATTROMANI Alec, QUATTROMANI Jenny, QUAY Mark, QUAYLE Amanda, QUAYLE Doug, QUEEN Kevin, QUEHENBERGER Magdalena, QUEK Yen, QUELCH Beryl, QUELCH Hugh, QUERALT Veronica, QUERIN Peter, QUERIPEL Nathan, QUEZADA Patricia, QUEZADA Robinson, QUICK Barbara, QUICK Brian, QUICK Doug, QUICK Kevin, QUICK Lauren, QUICK Mary, QUICK Pam, QUICK Shayne, QUICKENDEN Kate, QUIGG David, QUIGG Phillip, QUIGGIN Rachelle, QUIGLEY Paul, QUILICHINI Veronique, QUILKEY Chris, QUILL Mary, QUIMM Michelle, QUINLAN Mike, QUINLIN Diane, QUINLIN Jennifer, QUINLIVAN Brendan, QUINLIVAN Trish, QUINN Alice, QUINN Andrew, QUINN Angela, QUINN Barbara, QUINN Dale, QUINN Geoff, QUINN Kenneth, QUINN Lesleigh, QUINN Madeline, QUINN Mal, QUINN Margaret, QUINN Mark, QUINN Michelle, QUINN Paul, QUINN Paul, QUINN Sally, QUINN Shannan, QUINN Stephaanie, QUINN Steve, QUINN Terry, QUINN Tracey, QUINON Hermie, QUINTAL Aimee, QUINTAL John, QUINTANA Priscilla, QUINTAO Aida, QUINTERO Miguel, QUINTO Maria, QUINTON Graham, QUINTON Shawn, QUIREY Lydia, QUIRK Darrell, QUIRK Elaine, QUIRK Geoff, QUIRK Koley, QUIRK Marilyn, QUIRK Mark, QUIRK Peter, QUIRK Peter, QUIRK Steven, QUIRK Tom, QUIROZ Lucia, QUIROZ Siluana, QUISPE Linda, QUISPES GARAY Stephanie, QUIZON Arvine, QUODLING Amelia, QUON Merlane, QUYYUM Raid.

R

RAAD Mariam, RAAM Robbie, RAASCHOU Suncha, RABBITT Annette, RABBITT Mick, RABER Genna, RABONE Laura, RACHED Rima, RACHID CARROLL Tania, RACHMAT Denny, RACKEL Garry, RACKLYEFT Rex, RACKLYEFT Trevor, RACO Rita, RADAKOVICH

Zlata, RADBURN Bill, RADCLIFFE Janelle, RADCLIFFE Tessa, RADECKI Michael, RADER Marc, RADFORD Alison, RADFORD Anita, RADFORD Ann, RADFORD Toby, RADFORD Erin, RADFORD Gill, RADFORD Ian, **RADFORD Ingrid**, RADFORD Margaret, RADFORD Michelle, RADFORD Nathan, RADFORD Philip, RADFORD Steve, RADFORD Tim, RADHAKRISHNAN Bhuvana, RADLEY Elizabeth, RADLOFF Cheryl, RADNAI Leslie, RADNIDGE Sandra, RADO Paul, RADO William, RADONYI Peter, RADOVANOVIC Tony, RAE Alicia, RAE Cheryl, RAE Doug, RAE Douglas, RAE Garry, RAE Ian, RAE Ian, RAE Janet, RAE Judy, RAE Judith, RAE Katherine, RAE Les, RAE Trish, RAE Mary, RAE Michelle, RAEBURN Peg, RAFAEL Marcelle, RAFANELLI Val, RAFAUD Clint, RAFFAELE CJ, RAFFAELE Renato, RAFFAELE Tina, RAFFERTY Naomi, RAFFERTY Peter, RAFFERTY Peter, RAFFLE Marg, RAFFLE Sara, RAFIEE Sia, RAFTER Nicki, RAFTER Steven, RAFTERY Adrian, RAFTERY Mary, RAFTERY Michael, **RAFTY Tony**, RAGGATT Donald, RAGGATT Margaret, RAGGIO Carlos, RAGHAVAN Arundathi, RAGOZZINO Madeline, RAGUNATHAN Ragu, RAGUZ Angela, RAGUZ Jad, RAHAMAN Mohammed, RAHARDJA Henny, RAHLF Frank, RAHMAN Janet, RAHMAN Anowar, RAHMAN Md, RAHMAN Mohammad, RAHMAN Mohammod, RAHMANIAFOOSI Venus, RAHTMZADEH Kash, RAI Van, RAIMOND Rita, RAIMOND Bill, RAINBOW Elizabeth, RAINBOW Georgina, RAINE Jim, RAINE Wendy, RAINES David, RAINES Kevin, RAINEY Irene, RAINNIE Graham, RAINSFORD Lyn, RAINSFORD Suzanne, RAINSTRICK Paul, RAISON Stephanie, RAITALA Marilyn, RAJ Isaac, RAJ Kushal, RAJ Malini, RAJ Yatishna, RAJADURAI Edilbert, RAJAGOPALAN Ragu, RAJAKUMAR Pras, RAJAN Sarojini, RAJAN Nathan, RAJARATNAM Rema, RAJARATNAM Shankari, RAJASHEKAR Nataraja, RAJASINGAM Pushpavathy, RAJBANSHI Anil, RAJBHANDARI Siru, RAJESH Kovoori, RAJIC Anthony, RAJKUMAR Raddi, RAJKUMAR Rubini, RAJPUT Sana, RAJU John, RAJU Julie, RAJU Shirley, RAJU Sudha, RAKOWSKI Mark, RALEVSKI David, RALPH Belinda, RALPH George, RALPH Warren, RALPH Wendy, RALPH Yuko, RALSTON Robert, RALULU Asenaca, RALUMU Ini, RAM Monica, RAM Ritesh, RAMADANI Seide, RAMAGE George, RAMAGE Gerard, RAMAGE Terry, RAMAGE William, RAMAMURTHY Vijay, RAMAN Neel, RAMAN Raghu, RAMANAN Dinesh, RAMANATHAN Ram, RAMAS Dave, RAMASUNDARA Yohan, RAMASWAMY Kannan, RAMAY Ali-Ramay, RAMDANE Ramdane, RAMERMAN Johan, RAMETTA John, RAMIREZ Carla, RAMIREZ Dolores, RAMIREZ Gene, RAMIREZ Roy, RAMJAN Owen, RAMLI SHIMIZU Thomas, RAMLU Shri, RAMOS German, RAMOS Inti, RAMOS Matthew, RAMOS Melany, RAMOS Nelida, RAMOS Omar, RAMOS Richard, RAMOS Suzy, RAMSAY Amanda, RAMSAY Andrew, RAMSAY Catherine, RAMSAY Elisabeth, RAMSAY Florence, RAMSAY Gaynor, RAMSAY Heather, RAMSAY Ian, RAMSAY Nicola, RAMSAY Shelley, RAMSDALE Bill, RAMSDEN Lizi, RAMSER John, RAMUS Peter, RANA Neetal, RANASINGHE Dashika, RANASINGHE Eranga, RANAURO Chris, RAND Alma, RAND Molly, RAND Barry, RANDALL Clem, RANDALL Dean, RANDALL Dianne, RANDALL Jennifer, RANDALL Lucy, RANDALL Margaret, RANDALL Martin, RANDALL Sara, RANDALL-SMITH Leanne, RANDENI KADUPITIGE Sunil, RANDLE Fiona, RANDLE Greg, RANDS Virginia, RANFORD Deanne, RANFORD Tania, RANGANATHAN Shreya, RANGANATHAN Nicky, RANGER Maurie, RANGHUNA Lisa, RANGIAH Dalziel, RANGIHUNA Letitia, RANGOTT Lewis, RANKEN Hamish, RANKIN Bernie, RANKIN Clyde, RANKIN Jill, RANKIN Karen, RANKIN Lucinda, RANKIN Maria, RANKIN Philip, RANKIN Roy, RANKIN Roy, RANKIN-STUBBINGS Eril, RANKINE Jim, RANKINS Anne, RANKMORE Jasmine, RANKMORE Mark, RANN Nancy, RANN Nayomi, RANNARD Tony, RANNARD Gwen, RANNARD Bill, RANSE Brian, RANSLEY Darren, RANSLEY Richard, RANSOM Michael, RANSOME Sarah, RAO Siddhartha, RAPAEA Lynda, RAPAEA Rhonda, RAPER Lee, RAPER Ray, RAPER Simon, RAPHAEL Bo, RAPHAEL Eddie, RAPKE Paul, RAPLEY Irene, RAPP Peter, RASANAYAGAM Shivani, RASCHHOFER Erika, RASCHILLA Frances, RASHED Polina, RASHEED Rubina, RASHID Mohammad, RASIAH Rajan, RASIKA Fernando, RASKA Robert, RASKOVIC Slavica, RASMUS Brad, RASMUSSEN Carmel, RASMUSSEN Jennifer, RASMUSSEN Lorna, RASMUSSEN Renee, RASO Carlos, RASPANTI Carmelo, RASTOCIC Senko, RASULO Ilaria, RATCLIFF Rosalie, RATCLIFF Trevor, RATCLIFFE Beverley, RATCLIFFE Cindie, RATCLIFFE Danny, RATCLIFFE Donald, RATCLIFFE Lynell, RATCLIFFE Tricia, RATCLIFFE Peter, RATCLIFFE Ron, RATCLIFFE Sara, RATCLIFFE Sarah, RATCLIFFE Walter, RATHBONE Neil, RATHJEN Tracy, RATI Vickie, RATJENS Wallace, RATNAKUMAR Karthiga, RATTIGAN Daniel, RATTRAY Olivia, RATTRAY Philip, RATTRAYWOOD Susan, RATU Joseya, RAU Werner, RAVAGNANI Mattia, RAVANNACK James, RAVEENDRAKUMAR Ravi, RAVEENDRAN Ragul, RAVESE Vince, RAVESI Tanya, RAVIOLOS Emmanuel, RAVN Kim, RAVN Kurt, RAWANDUZY Hasan, RAWLINGS Kelly, RAWLINS Tony, RAWLINSON Pat, RAWNSLEY Matthew, RAWSON Carolyn, RAWSON Geoff, RAWSON Kerenna, RAWSTHORNE David, RAY Ahn, RAY Damien, RAY David, RAY Kenneth, RAY Leigh, RAY Nicole, RAY Tony, RAY Steve, RAYA Chedi, RAYA Monica, RAYMENT Alistair, RAYMENT Barbara, RAYMENT Leigh, RAYMOND Arthur, RAYMOND Dave, RAYMOND David, RAYMOND Deirdre, RAYMOND Jen, RAYMOND Jill, RAYMOND John, RAYMOND John, RAYMOND Katherine, RAYMOND Kim, RAYMOND Lauraine, RAYMOND Thalia, RAYNER Angela, RAYNER Cathy, RAYNER Dawn, RAYNER Denise, RAYNER Dennis, RAYNER Diianne, RAYNER Don, RAYNER Jennifer, RAYNER Joy, RAYNER Laurie, RAYNER Len, RAYNER Marc, RAYNER Matthew, RAYNER Ruth, RAYNER Scott, RAYNER Wendy, RAYNES Lewis, RAYON Marry, RAYWARD Forster, RAZEK Roasette, RAZEY Janet, RAZI Homaira, RAZZINO Robert, RE Tony, REA Alan, REA Amanda, REA Jim, REA Jenny, REA John, REA Judy, REA Lorraine, **REA Russell**, REABURN Ken, READ Peter, READ Georgia, READ Glenn, READ Jeanne, READ John, READ John, READ Kerrie, READ Kim, READ Mark, READ Rose, READ Shirley, READ Susannah, READ Tara, READE Lisa, READE Sue, READE Tom, READFORD Sharon, READMAN Bill, READY Deidre, REAGAN Kate, REAL Bruce, REALI Michael, REARDON Elaine, REARDON Fiona, REARDON Margo, REASON Matthew, REAY David, REAY Jo, REAY Marilyn, REAY Noel, REAY Ronnie, REBANO Susan, REBBECK Trudy, REBELLO Tanya, REBERGER Brian, REBOREDO Anna, REBROVS Andrew, RECENO Gali, RECKE Conny, REDAELLI Evelyn, REDAELLI Rae, REDAELLI Rae, REDDAN Kerrie, REDDEN Glen, REDDINGTON John, REDDY Dheeraj, REDDY Jenni, REDDY Kamini, REDDY Lila, REDDY Pradnya, REDDY Sath, REDDY Shivanjani, REDFERN Harry, REDFERN Julie, REDFORD Brian, REDFORD Carol, REDGROVE John, REDIMERIO Evelyn, REDMAN Darleen, REDMAN Dave, REDMAN Dawn, REDMAN Helen, REDMAN Jason, REDMAN Joelene, REDMAN Joy, REDMAN Mark, REDMAN Maureen, REDMAN Meredith, REDMAN CARPENTER Amanda, REDMAYNE Max, REDMAYNE Ronald, REDMOND Andrew, REDMOND Michael, REDPATH Colin, REDPATH Oliver, REDWIN Bev, REDWOOD Sean, REE John, REECE Jo, REECE Bill, REED Al, REED Alison, REED Allen, REED Barbara, REED Darken, REED Greg, REED Jeff, REED Ken, REED Kevin, REED Kevin, REED Nick, REED Patrick, REED Walter, REEDMAN Peter, REEDS Jo, REEDY Bev, REEDY James, REES Beverley, REES Daniel, REES Dave, REES Deborah, REES Doug, REES Geoff, REES Ivor, REES Jenny, REES Kate, REES Kelly, REES Lois, REES Narelle, REES Peter, REES Rebecca, REES Roberta, REES Rochelle, REES Trevor, REES-DAVIES Maureen, REETZ Linda, REEVE Maureen, REEVE Max, REEVE Vicki, **REEVES Alison**, REEVES Ann, REEVES David, REEVES Glen, REEVES Graeme, REEVES Jim, REEVES Kaye, REEVES Margaret, REEVES Trish, REEVES Peter, REEVES Robyn, REEVES Quentin, REGAN Brian, REGAN Emma, REGAN John, REGAN Leonard, REGAN Lori, REGAN Mark, REGGIANI Aldo, REGLIN Bob, REGNIS Jeff, **REGOS Tatiana**, REHAN Aditi, REHAUT Marie, REHDER Sandro, REIBEL Jodie, REICHARDT David, REICHMANN Monique, REID Adam, REID Adam, REID Ross, REID Allan, REID Arthur, REID Arthur, REID Barry, REID Belinda, REID Beverley, REID Bobby, REID Catriona, REID Colin, REID David, REID David, REID David, REID Deidre, REID Diane, REID Elise, REID Fay, REID Glenys, REID Gregory, REID Heather, REID Henry, REID James, REID Jan, REID Jan, REID Jennifer, REID Jodie, REID John, REID John, REID Kay, REID Kirsty, REID Kristin, REID Kristy, REID

Lily, REID Luke, REID Margaret, REID Marlene, REID Melissa, REID Nicola, REID Nicole, REID Nikki, REID Norma, REID Trisha , REID Paul, REID Paul, REID Bob, REID Bruce, REID Robyn, REID Ross, REID Sarah, **REID Teresa**, REID Bill, REID CALLEJA Irene, REIFENSTEIN Michael, REILLY Diana, REILLY Marty, REILLY Mark, REILLY Michael, REILLY Norl, REILLY Valerie, REIM Kirsten, REIMANN Marianne, REIMER Bev, REIN Jeannette, REIN Kathy, REINEKER John, REINER Peter, REINERS Brian, REINFELD Heidi, REIS Leigh, REISGYS Jurate, REISSIS Nick, REITANO Alfred, REITANO Cathy, REITER Heinz, REITER Paul, REITH Michael, REJLICH Vitold, RELPH Andy, RELUNIA Jun, RELUNIA Nimfa, REMBISZ Kathy, REMINIS Emma, REMINSKA Z Janina, REN Daxing, REN Yan, RENATA Trevor, RENDALL Jan, RENDALL Tamara, RENDEL Philippa, RENDELL Cindy, RENDELL Denice, RENDLE Valerie, RENDULIC Adam, RENDULIC Lynette, RENDULIC Mark, RENE Anthony, RENEKER Gary, RENHAM Dilys, RENN Andy, RENN Cynthia, RENNES Debbie, RENNES Emily, RENNES Jonathan, RENNIE David, RENNIE Elaine, RENNIE Elizabeth, RENNIE Michael, RENNIE Patsy, RENNIE Peter, RENNIE Rosalind, RENOTTE Carol, RENOUF Coral, RENOUF Jamie, RENSHAW Kylie, RENSHAW Robert, RENTON Anne, RENTON Beryl, RENTON John, RENTON Vivienne, RENTON Lara, RENTSCH Joylene, REPETI George, REPORTER Zareer, RERECIC Dario, RESTUCCIA Linda, RETAMAL Marisol, RETTIE Debra, RETTIG Kasia, REUTER Xavier, REVELL Kelly, REVELL Robyn, REVET Elaine, REVILLE Dianne, REVILLE Michael, REVSON George, REW David, REWALD Betty, REWELL Cate, REYES Daniel, REYES Efren, REYES Jason, REYES Joe, REYES Leanne, REYES Nelson, REYES Rey, REYES Ryan, REYES Yolanda, REYESGONZALEZ Ramon, REYMENT Don, REYMENT Joyce, REYN Mick, REYNALDO Lobarbio, REYNARD David, REYNAUD Ben, REYNES WILLIAMS Agnes, REYNOLDS Adrian, REYNOLDS Alex, REYNOLDS Al, REYNOLDS Allan, REYNOLDS Anisah, REYNOLDS Ben, REYNOLDS Bindi, REYNOLDS Brian, REYNOLDS Carole, REYNOLDS Chris, REYNOLDS Debra, REYNOLDS Ern, REYNOLDS Grant, REYNOLDS Margaret, REYNOLDS Margaret, REYNOLDS Matthew, REYNOLDS Moira, REYNOLDS Neil, REYNOLDS Rachel, REYNOLDS Ron, REYNOLDS Shaun, REYNOLDS Shirley, REYNOLDS Sue-Ann, REYNOLDS Tara, REYNOLDS Carrol, REYNOLDS Wayne, REYNOLDS Zac, REZEK Jennifer, REZEL Nuwan, RHEAD Julia, RHEAD Philip, RHEAD Simon, RHEINBERGER James, RHEINBERGER Marie, RHEUBEN Ross, RHIND John, RHODES Louise, RHODES Paul, RHODES Paul, RHODES Robert, RHONE Levi, RHONE Merrick, RHYS-JONES Katie, RHYSJONES Sally, RIAKOS Megan, RIAKOS Stacy, RIAKOS Suzanne, RIBBONS Jeffrey, RIBBONS Mark, RIBEIRO Hugo, RIBEIRO Jill, RIBEIRO Lisa, RIBOLDI John, RICARD Jean, RICARDO Helena, RICCARDI Danielle, RICE Alan, RICE Bernard, RICE Don, RICE Herb, RICE Jim, RICE Joan, RICE Joyce, RICE Selina, RICEPUTI Brigitte, RICH Brian, RICH Daniel, RICH Victor, RICHARD Carolyne, RICHARD Caroline, RICHARD Joel, RICHARD Nick, RICHARD-EVAN Iain, RICHARDS Adam, RICHARDS Mick, RICHARDS Anne, RICHARDS Anna, RICHARDS Benita, RICHARDS Brad, RICHARDS Brent, RICHARDS Brian, RICHARDS Bryn, RICHARDS Cameron, RICHARDS Rosemarie, RICHARDS Craig, RICHARDS Daniel, RICHARDS Dianne, RICHARDS Douglas, RICHARDS Liz, RICHARDS Graeme, RICHARDS Jacqui, RICHARDS Jodie, RICHARDS Kevin, RICHARDS Kim, RICHARDS Lou, RICHARDS Maria, RICHARDS Marnie Jayne, RICHARDS Nada, RICHARDS Peter, RICHARDS Peter, RICHARDS Rachel, RICHARDS Bob, RICHARDS Sarah, RICHARDS Simon, RICHARDS Steven, RICHARDS Suzanne, RICHARDS Terry, RICHARDS Vicky, RICHARDS Bill, RICHARDS-PUGH Bob, RICHARDSON Amanda-Jane, RICHARDSON Barrie, RICHARDSON Brian, RICHARDSON Carol, RICHARDSON Charles, RICHARDSON Richo, RICHARDSON Daryl, RICHARDSON Debbie, RICHARDSON Debbie, RICHARDSON Denis, RICHARDSON Don, RICHARDSON Doreen, RICHARDSON Elica-Jane, RICHARDSON Vic, RICHARDSON Frank, RICHARDSON Frank, RICHARDSON Francis, RICHARDSON Gary, RICHARDSON Graeme, RICHARDSON Graham, RICHARDSON Helen, RICHARDSON Holly, RICHARDSON Jamie, RICHARDSON Jocelyn, **RICHARDSON John**, RICHARDSON John, RICHARDSON John, RICHARDSON Jo, RICHARDSON Julie, RICHARDSON Karen, RICHARDSON Linda, RICHARDSON Luke, RICHARDSON Mark, RICHARDSON Melissa, RICHARDSON Murray, RICHARDSON Murray, RICHARDSON Nichole, **RICHARDSON Pamella**, RICHARDSON Pam, RICHARDSON Peter, RICHARDSON Rob, RICHARDSON Rod, RICHARDSON Sarah, RICHARDSON Sheridan, RICHARDSON Skye, RICHARDSON Tegan, RICHARDSON Tracey, RICHARDSON Viean, RICHARDSON Vivien, RICHARDSON Warwick, RICHARDSON Bill, RICHENS Amy, RICHENS Bruce, RICHENS George, RICHENS Michelle, RICHENS Roger, RICHES Grant, RICHES David, RICHES Judith, RICHES Bob, RICHES Suzanne, RICHES Terence, RICHES Tiffany, RICHES Warren, RICHMOND Coralie, RICHMOND Michael, RICHMOND Michael, RICHMOND Ron, RICHTER Adonna, RICHTER John, RICHTER Ron, RICKABY Philip, RICKARD Bruce, RICKARD Carol, RICKARD Gill, RICKARD James, RICKARD Jane, RICKARD Jillian, RICKARD John, RICKARD Scott, RICKARD Tim, RICKARD Trudy, RICKARD Veronica, RICKARDS Craig, RICKARDS Nat, RICKERSEY Alexandria, RICKERSEY Arthur, RICKERSEY John, RICKETTS Colin, RICKETTS Di, RICKETTS Gerry, RICKS Dulcie, RICKWOOD Anne, RICKWOOD Neil, RICKWOOD Peter, RIDANI MaryAnne, RIDDELL Gavin, RIDDELL Matthew, RIDDEN Helen, RIDDEN Pam, RIDDLE Rick, RIDDLE Jan, RIDDLE Sheridan, RIDEOUT Chris, RIDER Isabelle, RIDER Shirley , RIDGE Terry, RIDGES Marjorie, RIDGEWELL David, RIDGEWELL Samantha, RIDGLEY Kirstin, RIDGWAY Emma, RIDGWAY Kylie, RIDING Hannah, RIDLEY Belinda, RIDLEY David, RIDLEY Jann, RIDLEY Peter, RIDOUTT Patricia, RIDTHIPRASART Ruamporn, RIECHERS Trinette, RIECKMANN Marianne, RIED Ross, RIEDEL Mark, RIEDIGER Kellie-Anne, RIEDL Helen, RIEDLING Audrey, RIEDLING Les, RIEDRICH Nadine, RIENECKER Stewart, RIENZNER Martina, RIEPER Lyn, RIESCO Susana, RIESE Gregor, RIESSEN Heide, RIETDYK Bill, RIETHMULLER Drew, RIETVELD Mon, RIFFEL John, RIFKIN Julian, RIGBY Lina, RIGBY Owen, RIGBY Stan, RIGBY Stephen, RIGBY Thel, RIGBY Bill, RIGG John, RIGGIO Richard, RIGGS Nora, RIGGS Tricia, RIGGS Ronald, RIGHETTI Christine, RIGNEY Alan, RIGNEY Luke, RIGO Gilma, RIGO Michael, RIGONALLI Sandra, RIGONI Eda, RIGOPOULOS Rigas, RIHANI Robyn, RIIK David, RIISE Kristin, RIJAL Umesh, RIKARD-BELL Maggie, RILEY Lexie, RILEY Amy, RILEY Barry, RILEY Chris, RILEY Chris, RILEY Colin, RILEY Dennis, RILEY Dimity, RILEY Fiona, RILEY Gert, RILEY Irene, RILEY Jo, RILEY Judy, RILEY Kim, RILEY Leanne, **RILEY Len**, RILEY Martin, RILEY Nicole, RILEY Nigel, RILEY Norma, RILEY Roger, RILEY Rosemary, RILEY Shauna, **RILEY Wendy**, RILEY William, RILEY Winnie, RIMBAULT Marie, RIMMER Alan, RIMMER Ian, RIMMER Matthew, RIMMER Nicole, RIMON Rhonda, RIMPHONGUEN Kannika, RINDFLEISH Adam, RINDFLEISH Barry, RINDFLEISH Belinda, RINDFLEISH Scott, RINDFLEISH Sue, RINGLAND Andrew, RINGROSE Barry, RINGROSE Michael, RINOT Ruth, RINTALA Beverly, RIOLO Alex, RIOLO Max, RIORDAN Andrew, RIORDAN Frances, RIORDAN Hazel, RIOS Isabel, RIOS Heberto, RIPIA Wik, RIPLEY Pauline, RIPLEY Vanya, RIPPON Paul, RIPPON Steve, RISBRIDGER Susanne, RISBY Janelle, RISCO Gloria, RISI Pierre, RISSMAN Lu, RISTEVSKI Basil, RISTEVSKI Valentina, RISTICH Dragan, RISTOM Barbara, RISTOVSKA Olivija, RISTUCCIA Cecily, RISTUCCIA Tom, RISTUCCIA John, RITAR June, RITAR Karl, RITCHARD David, RITCHARD Louise, RITCHARD Robert, RITCHIE Bruce, RITCHIE Ceri, RITCHIE Doug, RITCHIE Fi, RITCHIE Jude, RITCHIE Katie, RITCHIE Nancy, RITCHIE Paul, RITCHIE Ruth, RITCHIE Sarah, RITCHIE Shane, RITCHINGS Marilyn, RITORTO Daniela, RITOSSA Claudio, RITSON Kerry, RITTER Andrew, RITTER Gordon, RITTERMAN Danielle, RITTIDECH Tong, RITZER Pauline, RITZROW Mike, **RIVERO Esther**, RIVERO Shirley, RIVEROS Andrea, RIVEROS Andrea, RIVEROS Hugo, RIVERS Allan, RIVERS Collette, RIVERS John, RIVERS Robert, RIX Jean, RIXON Emelia, RIXON Jodi, RIXON Sherri, RIXON Sue, RIZAL Yosep, RIZK Bill, RIZK Phyllis, RIZKALLA Bishoi, RIZZARDINI Michelle, RIZZI Claudette, RIZZO Peter, RIZZO Peter, RO Scarlet, ROACH Alan, ROACH Carol, ROACH Catrina, ROACH Elaine, ROACH Wilcock, ROACH Joan, ROACH John, ROACH Karen, ROACH Bob, ROAC Vanessa, ROACH Wes, ROACHE John, ROAQUIN Virginia, ROAST Gayle, ROBATI Naea, ROBB Ben, ROBB Berice, ROBB Janice, ROBB Raymond,

ROBB Bruce, ROBBINS Caleb, ROBBINS Holly, ROBBINS Margaret, ROBBINS Peter, ROBBINS Scott, ROBENS Barry, ROBENS Carolyn, ROBERSON Hal, ROBERSTON Denzil, ROBERT Geller, ROBERT Olsen, ROBERTS Randall, ROBERTS Alison, ROBERTS Mandy, ROBERTS Amy, ROBERTS Andrew, ROBERTS Ann, ROBERTS Arthur, ROBERTS Barry, ROBERTS Beverley, ROBERTS Cheryl, ROBERTS Chris, ROBERTS Chris, ROBERTS Chris, ROBERTS Cresenciana, ROBERTS David, ROBERTS Dave, ROBERTS Denise, ROBERTS Don, ROBERTS Douglas, ROBERTS Joyce, ROBERTS Alaine, ROBERTS Erin, ROBERTS Faye, ROBERTS Garry, ROBERTS Glen, ROBERTS Graham, ROBERTS Greg, ROBERTS Hayley, ROBERTS Jim, ROBERTS Harry, ROBERTS Jim, ROBERTS Jane, ROBERTS Jan, ROBERTS Jason, ROBERTS Jeffrey, ROBERTS Jeremy, ROBERTS John, ROBERTS John, ROBERTS Judith, ROBERTS Kathy, ROBERTS Kelly, ROBERTS Kerrie, ROBERTS Kerry, ROBERTS Kylie, ROBERTS Leanne, ROBERTS Lindy, ROBERTS Luke, ROBERTS Marilyn, ROBERTS Mark, ROBERTS Mari-Ann, ROBERTS Michael, ROBERTS Nicole, ROBERTS Nick, ROBERTS Noel, ROBERTS Peter, ROBERTS Peter, ROBERTS Roger, ROBERTS Ros, ROBERTS ScottAntony, ROBERTS Scott, ROBERTS Simone, ROBERTS Steve, ROBERTS Stephen, ROBERTS Susan, ROBERTS Suzanne, ROBERTS Trevor, ROBERTS Val, ROBERTS Zoe, ROBERTS-THOMSON Adam, ROBERTSON Amy, ROBERTSON Angela, ROBERTSON Carolyn, ROBERTSON Christine, ROBERTSON Christine, ROBERTSON David, ROBERTSON Dennis, ROBERTSON Denzil, ROBERTSON Douglas, ROBERTSON Doug, ROBERTSON Douglas, ROBERTSON Gordon, ROBERTSON Grant, ROBERTSON Jarrod, ROBERTSON Jean, ROBERTSON Jennifer, ROBERTSON Jill, ROBERTSON John, ROBERTSON John, ROBERTSON John, ROBERTSON John, ROBERTSON Judith, ROBERTSON Julie, ROBERTSON June, ROBERTSON Kate, ROBERTSON Kellie, ROBERTSON Kim, ROBERTSON Leonie, ROBERTSON Lynette, ROBERTSON Malcolm, ROBERTSON Mandy, ROBERTSON Mark, ROBERTSON Mel, ROBERTSON Merrilyn, **ROBERTSON Nancy**, ROBERTSON Neil, ROBERTSON Nicole, ROBERTSON Nicholas, ROBERTSON Patrick, ROBERTSON Paul, ROBERTSON Phil, ROBERTSON Ray, ROBERTSON Rodger, ROBERTSON Shane, ROBERTSON Bill, ROBERTSON Tim, ROBERTSON Val, ROBERTSON Vicki, ROBERTSON Winsome, ROBEY Neale, ROBEY Senja, ROBICHAUX Samantha, ROBILLIARD Claire, ROBILLIARD Katrina, ROBINS Ben, ROBINS Elizabeth, ROBINS Beth, ROBINS Jeremy, ROBINS Laurie, ROBINS Martine, ROBINS Maureen, ROBINS Melissa, ROBINS Owen, ROBINS Trish, ROBINS Sarah, ROBINS Sonia, ROBINSON Alan, ROBINSON Alice, ROBINSON Mandy, ROBINSON Amy, ROBINSON Andrew, ROBINSON Anne, ROBINSON Anna, ROBINSON Anne, ROBINSON Brian, ROBINSON Brooke, ROBINSON Brooke, ROBINSON Carl, ROBINSON Catherine, ROBINSON Cec, ROBINSON Chris, ROBINSON Chris, ROBINSON Christine, ROBINSON Clem, ROBINSON Col, ROBINSON Dean, ROBINSON Dean, ROBINSON Debbie, ROBINSON Denis, ROBINSON Di, ROBINSON Donna, ROBINSON Mal, ROBINSON Liz, ROBINSON Evelyn, ROBINSON Frances, ROBINSON Glenda, ROBINSON Gordon, ROBINSON Iain, ROBINSON Ian, ROBINSON Ian, ROBINSON Jane, ROBINSON Joan, ROBINSON Robbo, ROBINSON John, ROBINSON Karryne, ROBINSON Kathy, ROBINSON Kate, ROBINSON Katy, ROBINSON Kelly, ROBINSON Leigh, ROBINSON Ken, ROBINSON Kim, ROBINSON Kim, ROBINSON Linda, ROBINSON Lorena, ROBINSON Luke, ROBINSON M.Shirley, ROBINSON Mark, ROBINSON Margot, ROBINSON Michele, ROBINSON Nicholas, ROBINSON Olive, ROBINSON Paul, ROBINSON Peter, ROBINSON Peta, ROBINSON Peter, ROBINSON Phil, ROBINSON Phil, ROBINSON Garth, ROBINSON Robyn, ROBINSON Ron, ROBINSON Roy, ROBINSON Scott, ROBINSON Scott, ROBINSON Sharon, ROBINSON Shane, ROBINSON Shane, ROBINSON Shiralee, ROBINSON Tara, ROBINSON Trevor, ROBINSON Troy, ROBINSON Vincent, ROBINSON Irene, ROBINSON William, ROBINSONOBST Charlie, ROBINSON-OBST Fay, ROBISON Raymond, ROBLES Mario, ROBLES CABRERA Rafael, ROBSHAW Maureen, ROBSON Carol, ROBSON Courtney, ROBSON Erika, ROBSON Wal, ROBSON Riv, ROBSON Hugh, ROBSON Janete, ROBSON John, **ROBSON Maurya**, ROBSON Peter, ROBSON Stan, ROBSON Tom, ROBY Howard, ROCA George, ROCCA Christine, ROCCO Mario, ROCH Marie, ROCHA Meggan, ROCHA Sandra, ROCHE Alan, ROCHE Anita, ROCHE Brad, ROCHE Cathy, ROCHE Colin, ROCHE Kathy, ROCHE Kelvin, ROCHE Michele, ROCHE Pam, ROCHE Tom, ROCHECOUSTE Claire, ROCHECOUSTE Janick, ROCHELLI Mario, ROCHETA Simone, ROCHFORT Chris, ROCHNA Roxanne, ROCHOW Laura, ROCK Sue, ROCKS Brian, RODAN Lisa, RODARO Vitt, RODDA Adele, RODDA Steve, RODEN Tony, RODEN Peta, RODEN Tom, RODEWIJK Helen, RODGER Angela, RODGER Arthur, RODGER Irene, RODGER James, RODGER Sue, RODGERS Bryan, RODGERS Kate, RODGERS Crystal, RODGERS Edward, RODGERS Kerry, RODGERS Lesley, RODGERS Mary, RODGERS Richard, RODGERS Wayne, RODIER Darryn, RODIER Robyn, RODIONOFF Paul, RODITIS Chris, RODNEY Anna, RODRAKSA Natthinee, RODRIGUES Bev, RODRIGUES Juanita, RODRIGUES Marina, RODRIGUES Melanie, RODRIGUES Natasha, RODRIGUES Sandra, RODRIGUES Sophie, RODRIGUES Valeria, RODRIGUES Victorino, RODRIGUESVAZ Yvonne, RODRIGUEZ Gus, RODRIGUEZ Christopher, RODRIGUEZ Erika, RODRIGUEZ Fab, RODRIGUEZ Fernando, RODRIGUEZ Gil, RODRIGUEZ Jo, RODRIGUEZ Manuel, RODRIGUEZ GONZALEZ Elish, RODRIGUEZ GONZALEZ Elizabeth, RODRIGUEZ-VALVENY Pilar, RODWELL David, RODZIEWICZ Kerry, ROE Alan, ROE Jamie, ROE John, ROE Bek, ROE Keith, ROE Wendy, ROEBUCK Paul, ROEDER Gayle, ROEDIGER Anita, ROEDIGER Rosemary, ROEGER Veronica, ROES Robert, ROEST Leesh, ROETS Hilda, ROFAIL Tony, ROFE Kenneth, ROFE Rosalie, ROFFE Kevin, ROFFEY Arthur, ROFFEY Michelle, ROGAN Haidee, ROGAN Juila, ROGER Greg, ROGER Lin, ROGER BARTLEY Roger, ROGERS Brenda, ROGERS Caroline, ROGERS Pat, ROGERS Col, ROGERS Colin, ROGERS Dale, ROGERS Daphne, ROGERS Eric, ROGERS Fran, ROGERS Fred, ROGERS Gill, ROGERS Hayley, ROGERS Harry, ROGERS Ian, ROGERS Janet, ROGERS Paul, ROGERS Jonette, ROGERS Kerrie, ROGERS Kym, ROGERS Linda, ROGERS Margaret, ROGERS Merv, ROGERS Neil, ROGERS Peter, ROGERS Rebecca, ROGERS Richard, ROGERS Stephanie, ROGERS Stuart, ROGERS Vivienne, ROGERSON Bruce, ROGERSON Jean, ROGERSON Len, ROGERSON Terence, ROGERSON Ula, ROGULSKI Bart, ROH Grace, ROHANA Helda, ROHDE Sarah, ROHR Angela, ROHRMULLER Lutz, ROJAS Bruni, ROJAS Iris, ROJAS Omar, ROJAS Thelma, ROJAS BADENAS Sue, ROJAS CORTEZ Pedro, ROJO Doug, ROKITZKI Martin, ROKOBULI Bill, ROLAND Karin, ROLDAN JosePaolo, ROLE Lina, ROLES Quincy, ROLFE Christine, ROLFE Jennifer, ROLFE John, ROLFO Alex, ROLINSON Dennis, ROLL Desmond, ROLLAND Claude, ROLLAND-MCKENZIE Corinne, ROLLES Donna, ROLLESTON Denny, ROLLESTON Graeme, ROLLINS Douglas, ROLLO Antonia, ROLLS Chris, ROLPH Dallas, ROMAIN David, ROMAN Ana, ROMANO Anthony, ROMANO Chiara, ROMANO Denis, ROMANOV Elaine, ROMANOV Victor, ROMANOVSKI Levko, **ROMARI Gail**, ROMASZKO Emma, ROMEO Frank, ROMEO George, ROMEO Remy, ROMEO Sam, ROMERO Hugo, ROMITI Maria, ROMOW Alex, RONALDS John, RONAN John, RONAN Craig, RONCA Frank, RONG Shirley, RONSISVALLE Terri, ROOHAN Pamela, ROOKE Andy, ROOKE Simon, ROOKES Neil, ROONEY Kieran, ROONEY Tania, ROONGROTE Rungsarid, ROOPE Jeanne, ROOS Norman, ROOSMALECOCQ Ellen, ROOSMALE-COCQ Selina, ROOT Christopher, ROOTS Sue, ROOTSEY Les, ROPER Kay, ROPER Olga, ROPER Peter, ROPER Suzanne, ROPER-TYLER Ainsley, ROPERTI Catherine, ROQUE Anto nio, RORRISON Elisabeth, ROS Somy, ROSA Margaret, ROSA Charmaine, ROSA Steve, ROSALES Bobby, ROSALES Bancie, ROSALES Freddie, ROSARIO Eric, ROSARIO Prisca, ROSARIO Rod, ROSATI Annie, ROSATO Michael, ROSBERG Des, ROSCOE Denis, ROSCOE Ian, ROSE Acacia, ROSE Andrew, ROSE Anna, ROSE Ben, ROSE Caroline, ROSE Cathy, ROSE Chris, ROSE Doug, ROSE Elaine, ROSE Helen, ROSE Irene, ROSE Jeff, ROSE Kate, ROSE Linda, ROSE Louise, ROSE Matthew, ROSE Michelle, ROSE Murray, ROSE Neville, ROSE Norma, ROSE Paul, ROSE Penny, ROSE Peter, ROSE Lee, ROSE Simon, ROSE Stan, ROSE Steve, ROSE Suzanne, ROSE Terri, ROSEBERY Dot, ROSEBY Nigel,

ROSEBY Rebecca, ROSEN Bess, ROSEN Derek, ROSEN Ernie, ROSEN Faye, ROSEN John, ROSEN Jolyon, ROSEN Sandra, ROSENBERG SveEllen, ROSENFELD Aline, ROSENHECK Renee, ROSENTHAL Juleen, ROSENTHAL Leola, ROSENTRETER Roger, ROSENVALD Tracie, ROSER Alison, ROSER Barbara, ROSER Katrina, ROSER Melissa, ROSETTENSTEIN Gavin, ROSETTENSTEIN Lauren, ROSEVEAR Cheryl, **ROSEVEAR Kerry**, ROSEWARNE Joanne, ROSEWARNE Laura, ROSEWARNE Wendell, ROSEWELL Diana, ROSISNANYI Tamara, ROSNER Joanne, ROSOLEN Grahame, ROSOLEN Ron, ROSON Jacqueline, ROSON Jonathan, ROSON Jay, ROSPERICH Lee, ROSS Drew, ROSS Andrew, ROSS Angus, ROSS Anita, ROSS Annette, ROSS Anthea, ROSS Barry, ROSS Brett, ROSS Cameron, ROSS Charles, ROSS Coralie, ROSS David, ROSS Doreen, ROSS Doug, ROSS Gordon, ROSS Halina, ROSS Hazel, ROSS Ian, ROSS Isabel, ROSS John, ROSS Jordan, ROSS Karryne, ROSS Kate, ROSS Kaylene, ROSS Lila, ROSS Linda, ROSS Lyn, ROSS Mark, ROSS Mark, ROSS Merle, ROSS Morris, ROSS Pauline, ROSS Phil, R OSS Ralph, ROSS Bec, ROSS Rita, ROSS Roz, ROSS Sharon, ROSS Shantala, ROSS Stephen, ROSS Steven, ROSS Sue, ROSS Tali, ROSS Terry, ROSS Tom, ROSS-EDWARDS Bobbie, ROSSENDELL Irene, ROSSETTO Veronica, ROSSI Colleen, ROSSI Eleonora, ROSSI Felicia, ROSSI Irene, ROSSI Sue, ROSSI Suzanne, ROSSIDES Matenia, ROSSIE Katie, ROSSIE Rebecca, ROSSIGNOL Serge, ROSSITER Amy, ROSSITER Lynette, ROSSITER Mark, ROSSITER Steve, ROSTEDT Anne, ROTH Lenny, ROTH Mark, ROTH Nicole, ROTHBERG Jackie, ROTHBERG Lea, ROTHE Mary, ROTHENBERGER Frank, ROTHERHAM Jean, ROTHERHAM Robyn, ROTHERY John, ROTHFIELD Daniel, ROTHMORE Paul, ROTHWELL Adam, ROTHWELL Barry, ROTHWELL Deryck, ROTHWELL Diana, ROTHWELL Ellis, ROTHWELL Gill, ROTHWELL Vera, ROTT Trish, ROTT Torsten, ROTTER Elke, ROTTMANN Sabine, ROUBOS Henk, ROUCH Anne, ROUDENKO Marie, ROUECHE Viviane, ROUEN Andrew, ROUEN Heather, ROUEN Terry, ROUFOGALIS Jim, ROUGHAN Kathryn, ROULSTONE Bruce, ROUMANDUS Ray, ROUMANOUS Therese, ROUMIEH Nasser, ROUND Julie, ROURKE John, ROUSE Jan, ROUSSEL Catherin e, ROUTLEY Kaye, ROVERE Michael, ROVERE Roger, ROVIRA Vicky, ROW Elizabeth, ROW Francis, ROWAN Bruce, ROWAN Michael, ROWAN Rhonda, ROWAN Shaun, ROWE Amy, ROWE Stacey, ROWE Annette, ROWE Bruce, ROWE Carolyn, ROWE Christy, ROWE David, ROWE Gregory, ROWE Heather, ROWE Helen, ROWE Jane, ROWE Jemma, ROWE Lesley, ROWE Michael, ROWE Michael, ROWE Nora, ROWE Phillip, ROWE Rodney, ROWE Sandra, ROWE Bruce, ROWE Vivianne, ROWED Jan, ROWELL Geoff, ROWELL John, ROWEN Louise, ROWLAND Tony, ROWLAND Barbara, ROWLAND David, ROWLAND Derek, ROWLAND Gail, ROWLAND Ian, ROWLAND Margaret, ROWLAND-SMITH Judy, ROWLANDS Taffy, ROWLANDS Pam, ROWLANDS Peter, ROWLATT Mike, ROWLES Rhonda, ROWLEY Anne, ROWLEY Craig, ROWLEY Dean, ROWLEY Jeanie, ROWLEY Ken, ROWLEY Mick, ROWLEY Dianne, ROWLEY Ron, ROWLEY Stephanie, ROWLEY-BATES Meg, ROWLEYBATES Peter, ROWLING Julie, ROWLING Ron, ROWLINGS Donna, ROWSELL Tiesh, ROXBERRY John, ROXBURGH Jane, ROXIN Joachim, ROY Alan, ROY Barry, ROY Bim, ROY Claudette, ROY Heather, ROY Jason, ROY June, ROY Peter, ROY Ray, ROY Stephane, ROYCE Brian, ROYCROFT Clarke, ROYCROFT Julie, ROYCROFT Vicki, ROYE Michael, ROYLANCE Sam, ROYLE Christopher, ROYLE Em, ROYSTON Karen, ROYSTON Paul, ROZARIO Peter, ROZARIO Philip, ROZE Magdalena, ROZEN Richard, ROZENBERG Maurie, RUAN Dina, RUAN Zi, RUBBERT Danielle, RUBBERT Danielle, RUBBI Jean, RUBENS Bernard, RUBENSSON Caroline, RUBIE Howard, RUBIN Helen, RUBIN Tany, RUBINIC Wilma, RUBINO Annelies, RUBY James, RUCKIAT Jarinya, RUDA Taraq, RUDD Emily, RUDD Heather, RUDD James, RUDD Jono, RUDD Jonathon, RUDD Lee, RUDD Meagan, RUDDER Brian, RUDDER Terry, RUDDUCK Brad, RUDESKI Ace, RUDKO Elizabeth, RUDMAN Sandra, RUDY Heather, RUDZKI Nick, RUEDIN Claire, RUFF Brett, RUFF Darla, RUFF Thornel, RUFLE Frank, RUGGERI Maria, RUGGIERO Ralph, RUGLESS Lorinda, RUHL Cameron, RUHLE Helen, RUHLE Pat, RUHOTAS Annette, RUI LIN Wang, RUIG Jill, RUISI Annie, RUIZ Adrian, RUIZ Alvaro, RUIZ DE GAMBOA Antonieta, RUIZ RUIZ David, RUKOMEYE Omar, RUKUMAGADAN Jana, RULE Amanda, RULE Catherine, RULE Christine, RULE Kerrie, RULE Pamela, RUMBLE Garry, RUMBLE Louise, RUMBLE Rhonda, RUMBLE Val, RUMI Catherine, RUMMER Jodie, RUMMERY Liz, RUMP Paulus, RUMPEL Tess, RUMPHORST Michelle, RUMSEY Amy, RUMSEY Barbara, RUMSEY Libby, RUMSEY Marie, RUNDELL Shirley, RUNDLE David, RUNHAM Jan, RUNHAM Jim, RUPA Roksana, RUPERTO John, RUPOLO Caterina, RUPRECHT Rhonda, RUPRECHT Ron, RUSCH Peter, RUSCHIN Vicki, RUSCOE Virginia, RUSH Horace, RUSHAN Don, RUSHEN Barbara, RUSHTON Mark, RUSHTON Ron, RUSHWORTH Geoffrey, RUSHWORTH Julie, RUSHWORTH Sarah, RUSKIN Kim, RUSSEK Andrew, RUSSELL Angry, RUSSELL Don, RUSSELL Alistair, RUSSELL Andrea, RUSSELL Angela, RUSSELL Barry, RUSSELL Cassandra, RUSSELL Colin, RUSSELL Deborah, RUSSELL Bruce, RUSSELL Dot, RUSSELL Edward, RUSSELL Eleanor, RUSSELL Elfrieda, RUSSELL Anne, RUSSELL Ellen, RUSSELL Fiona, RUSSELL Glenys, RUSSELL Gordon, RUSSELL Graham, RUSSELL Iain, RUSSELL Ian, RUSSELL Irene, RUSSELL Jim, RUSSELL Jim, RUSSELL Jan, RUSSELL John, RUSSELL John, RUSSELL Julie, RUSSELL Ken, RUSSELL Laurel, RU SSELL Lesley, RUSSELL Marnie, RUSSELL Mark, RUSSELL Michael, RUSSELL Michelle, RUSSELL Neil, RUSSELL Nicole, RUSSELL Norah, RUSSELL Norm, RUSSELL Noria, RUSSELL Peter, RUSSELL Raeleen, RUSSELL Ron, RUSSELL Rose, RUSSELL Scott, RUSSELL Simon, RUSSELL Susan, RUSSELL Vince, RUSSELL Vivienne, RUSSELL-STONE Rod, RUSSELLE Leigh, RUSSETT Helen, RUSSO Isabella, RUSSO Kate, RUSSO Tresma, RUSSO Vince, RUST Phil, RUSTANDAR Emil, RUSTON Steve, RUSTON Stephen, RUSTON Yvonne, RUTH Lois, RUTH Nadja, RUTHERFORD Barry, RUTHERFORD Deidre, RUTHERFORD Donna, RUTHERFORD Jane, RUTHERFORD Lenore, RUTHERFORD Lory, RUTHERFORD Rhoda, RUTHVEN Ron, RUTLEDGE Belinda, RUTLEDGE Brad, RUTLEDGE Bruce, RUTSTEIN Debbie, RUTTEN Bob, RUTTEN TRISH Trish, RUTTER Arthur, RUTTER Barry, RUTTER Carolyn, RUTTER Dj, RUTTER David, RUTTER Elaine, RUTTER Bette, RUTTER Holly, RUTTER Jennie, RUTTER Mostyn, RUTTER Stanley, RUTTER Terence, RUTTER Wayne, RUTTYN Tony, RUWOLDT Janine, RUXTON John, RUXTON Margaret, RUZDIC Rasim, RYALL Yvonne, RYAN Alison, RYAN Al ison, RYAN Alison, RYAN Myra, RYAN Athena, RYAN Ruth, RYAN Bridget, RYAN Bronwyn, RYAN Bruce, RYAN Bruce, RYAN Carmen, RYAN Catherine, RYAN Catherine, RYAN Ciaran, RYAN Colleen, RYAN Cynthia, RYAN David, RYAN David, RYAN Debbie, RYAN Den, RYAN Diane, RYAN Elise, RYAN Emma, RYAN Errol, RYAN Fiona, RYAN Gerard, RYAN Graham, RYAN Jim, RYAN Jim, RYAN Jill, RYAN Joan, RYAN Joanna, RYAN Joan, RYAN John, RYAN Jon, RYAN Judy, RYAN Kathy, RYAN Ken, RYAN Kerry, RYAN Kev, RYAN Kim, RYAN Linda, RYAN Mark, RYAN Merilyn, RYAN Michael, RYAN Michele, RYAN Natasha, RYAN Nerissa, RYAN Nev, RYAN Paul, RYAN Pauline, RYAN Paul, RYAN Peter, RYAN Peter, RYAN Pete, RYAN Rob, RYAN Sally, RYAN Shirley, RYAN Sue, RYAN Sue, RYAN Suzanne, RYAN Tracey, RYAN Virginia, RYAN Wendy, RYBALKA Jacque, RYBECK Dionne, RYBICKI Paul, RYBIYAKOV Alexey, RYDER Alana, RYDER Glenn, RYDER Mike, RYELAND Terry, RYKEN Paul, RYLAND Ian, RYLEY Derrick, RYMAN Marlene, RYMER Alana, RYMER Chris, RYMER Kylie, RYMER Mark, RYMILL Skye, RYNEHART Aaron, RYOU Caecilia , RYOU Nakyong, RYU Byeong, RYU Chae-Mun, RYU Sarah, RYU Shin-Ae.

S

SA Maung, SA Zoya, SAAD Joanne, SAAD Sam, SAAD Tony, SAADAT Michael, SAADE Charbel, SAADE Sid, SAADEH Fadia, SAADEH Jason, SAADIEH Jalal, SABA Jackie, SABA Mary-Anne, SABA Sam, SABALLA Rey, SABAPATHY Elvis, SABARETNAM Mayu, SABATER Sebastian, SABBAGH Claudette, SABETI Naysan, SABIC Dusanka, SABINE Susannah, SABINES Nadia, SABISTON David, SABLOK Vinod, SABRA Nick, SABRY Rhania, SACCO George, SACCO Joanne, SACHINWALLA Capt, SACHINWALLA Toos, SACHS Adam, SACHS Bianca, SACHSE George, SACKS Paul, SACKS Saundra, SADAYAPPAN Karthik, SADEK Ahmad, SADIKOT Moiz, SADLER Graeme, SADLER Kim, SADLER Pam, SADLER Patricia, SADLER Rob, SADNI Kylie-Anne, SADOW Frank, SAE-JONG Theerawat, SAE-LIEO Akapon, SAELIEO

Kee-Shaun, SAE-LIEO Leon, SAEED Tahir, SAEED Tahir, SAEGUSA Rika, SAENZ Carolina, SAEZ-NIETO Emilia, SAFANIEV Marc, SAFARI Michael, SAFE Joynes, SAFI Suzie, SAFOUR Joseph, SAFRO David, SAFRO Mark, SAFWAN Adnan, SAGE Diana, SAGGI Jaspal, SAGGUS Kellie, SAGGUS Maureen, SAGGUS Tracy, SAGNA Moussa, SAGRILLO Valentina, S AHAN Erinc, SAHARA-KHAN Lisa, SAHAROFF Slav, SAHIB Alicia, SAHIN Kaan, SAHLIN Camilla, SAHLOS Sophie, SAIBA Pornsupa, SAID Joe, SAID Louise, SAIFY Dianne, SAILER Jill, SAILLARD Steve, SAINI Dave, SAINSBERY Matt, SAINSBURY Kim, SAINSBURY Neville, SAINT Bridget, SAINT Micaela, SAISON Francis, SAITO Ai, SAITO Akiko, SAITO Masayo, SAITO Yasu, SAJINOVIC Mila, SAJJAMONGKOL Apiradee, SAKAMOTO Naoko, SAKARIA Jai, SAKATA Eri, SAKATA Manabu, SAKATSIE Toli, SAKELLARIS Nina, SAKER Claire, SAKEY Michelle, SAKEY Russell, SAKKUAKULWONG Chetta, SAKR George, SAKUL-THANASAKDI Kanda, SAKURA Tadahiro, SAKURAI Issei, SALA Frauke, SALADRAU Kitty, SALAJ Kim, SALAMA Wally, SALAMEH Rabee, SALAMON Andi, SALAMON Sara, SALAMONSEN Fumiko, SALAT Cornelia, SALATINI Michael, SALAVERRY Renee, SALEH Anumart, SALEH Ashraf, SALEH Danielle, SALEH Hassan, SALEH Nicole, SALEH Sayed, SALEH Khodr, SALEKIN Sirajus, SALEM Allira, SALEM Asad, SALEM Dianna, SALEM Janet, SALEM Mohammed, SALEM Suzana, SALEME Bernadette, SALENGA Fely, SALES Fred, SALHANI Maurice, SALIB Juan, SALIB Madeleine, SALIBA John, SALIBA Katherine, SALIER Maureen, SALIER Peter, SALIER Simone, SALIM Keiko, SALIM Saheed, SALIPUR Milos, SALLAN Meinrado, SALLES JR Jorge, SALLES SR Jorge, SALLING Jennifer, SALLIS Geoff, SALMON Darren, SALMON Ted, SALMON Jason, SALMON Judy, SALMON Kerrie, SALMON Lynette, SALMON Tess, SALMON Rob, SALMON Bob, SALNA Joy, SALOKHE Amar, SALPETER Barbara, SALT Jason, SALT Zoe, SALTANOVSKI Maxim, SALTER Claire, SALTER David, SALTER Dave, SALTER Gabriella, SALTER Jeremy, SALTER Marj, SALTER Mary, SALTISSI David, SALTMARSH Leon, SALTWELL Janelle, SALUNKE Netaji, SALVA Thierry, SALVADOR Denise, SALVAGE Sue, SALVATORE Tore, SALVETER Philipp, SALVO Paul, SALY Joy, SALY Leo, SALZKE Dean, SALZKE Noel, SALZMANN Valerie, SAM Roland, SAMANEK Yue, SAMARANAYAKE Mahendra, SAMARGHANDI Syd, SAMARJIA Tony, SAMBO Keith, SAMIMI Nina, SAMIOS Chris, SAMMELLS Bob, SAMMON Linda, SAMMONS John, SAMMUT Cathie, SAMMUT John, SAMMUT Kerry, SAMMUT Margaret, SAMOJLOWICZ Annette, SAMOJLOWICZ Te d, SAMOSIR Marisi, SAMOUELIAN Caroline, SAMPATHKUMAR Minnie, SAMPEDRO Javier, SAMPEDRO Michael, SAMPSON Annette, SAMPSON Brian, SAMPSON Michael, SAMPSON Rachel, SAMPSON Becky, SAMPSON Ross, SAMS Ernest, SAMS Sue, SAMSELY Maureen, SAMSON Stephen, SAMUEL Glenn, SAMUEL Nyorie, SAMUEL Thekla, SAMUELS Alan, SAMUELS Colin, SAMUELS Lyndon, SAMUELS Marion, SAMUYA Michelle, SAN PEDRO-LOYOLA Randolph, SANABRIA Roberto, SANANIKONE Phra-Mangkone, SANBURG Gemma, SANCANIN Dragan, SANCATALDO Frank, SANCHEZ Alexis, SANCHEZ Carmen, SANCHEZ Elki, SANCHEZ Guy, SANCHEZ Jon, SANCHEZ Jose, SANCHEZ Lupe, SANCHEZ Pedro, SANCHEZ Tomas, SANCHEZ ARROYO Carlos, SANCHEZ PEREZ Francisco, SANCHEZ QUINTAS Manuel, SANCHI Viviane, SANDBERG Carole, SANDBERG Christina, SANDBROOK-SCOTT Linda, SANDELL Ray, SANDEMAN Merrilee, SANDER Tania, SANDERCO Brett, SANDERCOCK Kerri, SANDERS Barbara, SANDERS Caroline, SANDERS George, SANDERS Janet, SANDERS Joanne, SANDERS Linda, SANDERS Mal-Malcolm, SANDERS Marg, SANDERS Margaret, SANDERS Tricia, SANDERS Pa ul, SANDERSON Alan, SANDERSON Cecilia, SANDERSON Gail, SANDERSON George, SANDERSON Helen, SANDERSON Margaret, SANDERSON Patricia, SANDERSON Bill, SANDERSON-EDMUNDS Don, SANDHU Simran, SANDIE Caroline, SANDIE Margaret, SANDILANDS Bill, SANDISON Robyne, SANDISON Bill, SANDLANT Travis, SANDO Grace, SANDONA Benedetto, SANDONIS Ana, SANDOVAL Claude, SANDOVAL Jaime, SANDOVAL Rene, SANDS Joan, SANDS Raelene, SANDS Stephen, SANDS Stephen, SANDS Victoria, SANDY Robert, SANELLI Lily, SANFORD Richard, SANGDAE Cha, SANGER Diane, SANGER Jurgen, SANGER Paul, SANGUE Diana, SANGWELL Pauline, SANHUEZA Elba, SANHUEZA Jorge, SANHUEZA Vanessa, SANNEY Frank, SANO Federica, SANPRADITH Pavadee, SANPRADITH Preeyada, SANSON Gordon, SANSON Pat, SANTA CRUZ John, SANTACATTERINA Diane, SANTAMARIA Elissa, SANTAMARIA Katherine, SANTAMARIA Tomas, SANTANA Miguel, SANTHANAH Santee, SANTI Oscar, SANTIAGO Lorenzo, SANTIAGO Pedro, SANTILLAN Nida, SANTILLAN Richard, SANTLEBEN Kate, SANTOLIN Adrian, SANTONI Margaret, SANTOS Aimee, SANTOS Ann, SAN TOS Manny, SANTOS Henry, SANTOS Jose, SANTOS Kathy, SANTOS Louise, SANTOS Marlene, SANTOS Nenita, SANTOS Nieves, SANTOS Beck, SANTOS E FONSECA Conseicao, SANTOSO Hendra, SANTOSO Raymond, SANTOSO Sujudi, SANTOSO Yongkie, SANZARI Leanne, SAOUSHKIN Rose, SAPINA Diana, SAPINA Zvonimir, SAPRE Anil, SAPSFORD Pamela, SARA Judy, SARACENO Angela, SARAH Liv, **SARANDIS Claire**, SARANGAYA Antonio, SARAVANJA Drago, SARDELIC Ljubica, SARFUDIN Riaz, SARGANT Darryn, SARGEANT Alan, SARGEANT Barbara, SARGEANT Estherann, SARGEANT Dick, SARGEANT Rex, SARGENT Amy, SARGENT Diana, SARGENT Emma, SARGENT Graeme, SARGENT Jeff, SARGENT Kathryn, SARGENT Maureen, SARGENT Olivia, SARICH Bronwyn, SARKEALA Hanna, SARKIS Mona, SARNELLI Ciro, SARRIS Sophia, SARWAR Abu, SASAKI Akemi, SASAKI Etsuo, SASSALL Darren, SATER George, SATHASIVAM Nalayini, SATHE Priyanka, SATKUNARAJAH Bala, SATKUNARAJAH Paul, SATKUWARAJAH Bala, SATO Atsuko, SATO Tomomi, SATO Yuko, SATORRE Ariel, SATTAR Abdus, SATTIN Jean, SATTIN Rebecca, SATTLER Louise, SATYA Shabir, SA U Michael, SAUCIS Nick, SAUER Henry, SAUL Jared, SAUL Jeff, SAUL John, SAUL Kylie, SAUL Lyn, SAULE John, SAULS Karen, SAUMWEBER Fyonn, SAUNDARARAJAN Santhanam, SAUNDERS Charlie, SAUNDERS David, SAUNDERS David, SAUNDERS Ted, SAUNDERS Elaine, SAUNDERS Liz, SAUNDERS Eric, SAUNDERS Glenn, SAUNDERS Graham, SAUNDERS Helen, SAUNDERS Jacqueline, SAUNDERS Jeni, SAUNDERS Jo, SAUNDERS Judy, SAUNDERS Kellie, SAUNDERS Ken, SAUNDERS Narrelle, SAUNDERS Norm, SAUNDERS Peter, SAUNDERS Peta, SAUNDERS Gina, SAUNDERS Ronald, SAUNDERS Rosalie, SAUNDERS Susan, SAUNDERS Tim, SAUSA Eva, SAVAGE Craig, SAVAGE Daniel, SAVAGE Del, SAVAGE Elise, SAVAGE Greg, SAVAGE Nicole, SAVAGE Tom, SAVAS Erol, SAVELAINEN Katrina, SAVERIMUTTU Dunstan, SAVIDGE Kerri, SAVIDGE Kim, SAVIDIS Tom, SAVIDIS Faye, SAVILLE Caroline, SAVILLE Greg, SAVILLE Katrina, SAVILLE Les, SAVILLE Michele, SAVILLE Pat, SAVILLE Bob, SAVILLE Wendy, SAVITSKY Vadim, SAVONA Joe, SAVOULIAN Sonia, SAVVA Conrad, SAVVA Georgina, SAVVA Mark, SAVVAS Helen, SAVVAS Vicki, SAW Sui, SAWAGA SHIRA Takanobu, SAWAKI Hee-Jin, SAWAKI Shungo, SAWAKID Nadiem, SAWAN Maha, SAWANG Tien, SAWATT Vicky, SAWCZYN Genia, SAWHNEY Aushima, SAWICKI Hubert, SAWKINS Margaret, SAWOHYN Dawn, SAWROOP Vishav, SAWYER Bridget, SAWYER Kevin, SAWYER Margaret, SAWYER Michael, SAXBY Carole, SAXBY Shane, SAXBY Tim, SAXBY Valda, SAXELBY Warren, SAXENA Sonia, SAYASANE Rattasinh, SAYCE Nancy, SAYCON Rolando, SAYED Shazly, SAYEGH Gaston, SAYER Anne, SAYERS Albert, SAYERS Ann, SAYERS Yvonne, SAYERS Rob, SAYERS Wayne, SAYRAFI Kinan, SAYSANA Sandrine, SAYWELL Christine, SAYWELL Garry, SAYWELL Lyn, SAZONOVA Nadia, SAZONOVA Valya, SBRESNI Dominic, SCALA Pauline, SCALLY Lorna, SCALZI Linda, SCAMAKAS George, SCAMAKAS Pamela, SCAMMELL Bernadette, SCANDRETT Michelle, SCANLAN Anthony, SCANLAN Mous, SCANLAN Roberta, SCANLAN Bill, SCANLON Bruce, SCANLON Keith, SCANLON Lee, SCANLON Virginia, SCARABOTTO FERRARI Sylvia, SCARBOROUGH Bronwyn, SCARBOROUGH Robert, SCARDIGNO Phil, SCARF MarieLouise, SCARFE Rona, SCARLETT Jane, SCARLETT Jack, SCARR G raham, SCARR Helen, SCARR Val, SCASCIGHINI Jack, SCATTINI Jennifer, SCATURCHIO Adrian, SCHACHT Joy, SCHAEFER Kim, **SCHAEFER Linda**,

SCHAEFER Peter, SCHAER Daniel, SCHAFER Cathy, SCHAFER Charmaine, SCHAFER Lindy, SCHAFER Rolf, SCHAFFER Garry, SCHAFFERIUS Doreen, SCHAFFLER Jean, **SCHAFTER Monique**, SCHAHINGER Jennie, SCHALCHLIN Grant, SCHALCHLIN Nicole, SCHALCHLIN Tanya, SCHALK Julie, SCHALK Kaylene, SCHAN Halyna, SCHAPER Katie, SCHAPIRO Mike, SCHARF Hans, SCHARRER Klaus, SCHARRER Rose, SCHATTIGER Maria, SCHATZ Julie, SCHAUDINN Gaby, SCHAUMBERG Timothy, SCHEELE Fleur, SCHEIJVEN Johannes, SCHEINBERG Carol, SCHELL Irene, SCHELL Paul, SCHELLACK Joel, SCHEMBRI Gina, SCHEMBRI Mark, SCHEMBRI Michael, SCHEMBRI Robert, SCHEMBRI Ryan, SCHEMBRI Sonia, SCHEMBRI Suzanne, SCHEMBRI Viv, SCHENSCHER Luke, SCHERER Inoe, SCHERPENISSE Joanne, SCHERRER Michele, SCHETTER Mike, SCHETTLER Klaus, SCHEU Peter, SCHEURMANN Alex, SCHILF Elaine, SCHILHANECK Michael, SCHILLER Ziggy, SCHILLING Launa, SCHILLING Natasha, SCHILLING Tim, SCHILPZAND Julius, SCHILT Maria, SCHINKEL Dennis, SCHIPANO Sandra, SCHIRMER Elizabeth, SCHIRMER Kym, SCHLAFRIG Uri, SCHLEGEL Christopher, SCHLEGEL Clement, SCHLICHTE Karl, SCHLICK Hans, SCHLOSS Gary, SCHLOSS Joan, SCHLOTHAUER Steve, SCHMID Carl, SCHMID Robyn, SCHMIDT Barb, SCHMIDT Chris, SCHMIDT Daniel, SCHMIDT Janet, SCHMIDT Paul, SCHMIDT Petra, SCHMIDT Rod, SCHMIDT Sandra, SCHMIDT Stephan, SCHMITT Herbert, SCHMITT Margaret, SCHMITT Michelle, SCHMUTTER Trent, SCHNECK Mirjam, SCHNEIDER David, SCHNEIDER Ken, SCHNEIDER Sue, SCHNEIDER Tim, SCHOBEL Petra, SCHODDE Stuy, SCHODDE Virginia, SCHOEBERL Rene, SCHOENFELD Tom, SCHOETZ Fritz, SCHOETZ Petra, SCHOFIELD Alex, SCHOFIELD Amy, SCHOFIELD Elizabeth, SCHOFIELD Ken, SCHOFIELD Peter, SCHOFIELD Sharon, SCHOFIELD Bill, SCHOKKER Elaine, SCHOKKER Franz, SCHOKMAN Sonia, SCHOLES Colin, SCHOLES David, SCHOLES Rebecca, SCHOLES Warwick, SCHOLL JR Ed, SCHOLTEN Mark, SCHOLTEN Vicki, SCHOLTENS James, SCHOLZ Nicole, SCHOLZ Sue, SCHONNING Katharina, SCHOOLING Demelza, SCHOOTS Tom, SCHORNIK OW Tamara, SCHRADER Conrad, SCHRAM Jo, SCHRAM Robyn, SCHREIBER Pauline, SCHREURS Hugh, SCHRODER Ashley, SCHRODER Jenny, SCHRODER Mark, SCHRODER Mary, SCHRODER Michelle, SCHRODER Neil, SCHRODER Wim, SCHRODTER Leanne, SCHROEDER Alfred, SCHUBERT Lillian, SCHUBERT Ralph, SCHUBERTH Garry, SCHUBERTH Michael, SCHUCK Joy, **SCHUCK Lynette**, SCHUCK Ron, SCHUDDEBOOM Inge, SCHUETT Rudy, SCHULMAN Jeff, SCHULTER Vivien, SCHULTIES Darren, SCHULTIES John, SCHULTZ Helmut, SCHULTZ Jamie, SCHULTZ Kelli, SCHULTZ Konrad, SCHULTZ Sharon, SCHULZ Anthony, SCHULZ David, SCHULZ Emma, SCHULZ Isabel, SCHULZ Jennifer, SCHULZ Judy, SCHULZ Nicole, SCHULZ Paul, SCHULZ Penelope, SCHULZE Danielle, SCHULZE Roslyn, SCHULZE Sonja, SCHUMACHER David, SCHUMACHER John, SCHUMACHER Kylie, SCHUMACHER Lorraine, SCHUMACHER Martin, SCHUMACHER Melva, SCHUMACHER Sarah, SCHURCH Dominic, SCHURCH Peter, SCHUSTER Astrid, SCHUTTE Felix, SCHUTZ Tracey, SCHWAB Andre, SCHWAB Jeanette, SCHWAB John, SCHWAB Leslie, SCHWAB Lynette, SCHWAB Trevor, SCHWARCZ Micheal, SCHWARTZ Jerry, SCHWA RTZ Robyn, SCHWARZ Annabelle, SCHWARZ David, SCHWARZ Kym, SCHWARZE Allan, SCHWEBEL Les, SCHWEIGHOFFER Matt, SCHWERDT Raelene, SCIBERRAS Emanuel, SCIBERRAS Jo, SCIBERRAS Joe, SCIBILIO Charlie, SCICLHNA Tom, SCICLUNA Elizabeth, SCICLUNA Michelle, SCIGLITANO Angie, SCINTO Carmen, SCIORTINO Wayne, SCIOSCI Beatrice, SCIOTTO Peter, SCIVETTI Dominic, **SCLAVOS Cleopatra**, SCNEIDER Uwe, SCOBELL Beverley, SCOBIE David, SCOBIE Jenny, SCOBIE Peter, SCOBIE Peter, SCOBLE Astrida, SCOBLE Murray, SCODELLARO Adriana, SCOLLAY Kym, SCOLLON James, SCOLTOCK Carol, SCOMPARIM Luciana, SCOPPA Billie, SCOPPA Joseph, SCORSE Anna, SCORSE Fred, SCORZELLI David, SCORZELLI Frank, SCOTHERN Angela, SCOTHERN Karen, SCOTLAND Andrew, SCOTLAND Jill, SCOTLAND John, SCOTNEY Todd, SCOTT Amelia, SCOTT Angela, SCOTT Anja, SCOTT Anne, SCOTT Tony, SCOTT Tony, SCOTT Arthur, SCOTT Barbara, SCOTT Betty, SCOTT Cameron, SCOTT Carla, SCOTT Caroline, SCOTT Carolle, SCOTT Caroline, SCOTT Cathy, SCOTT Chloe, SCOTT Darren, SCOTT David, SCOTT Donald, SCOTT Elizabeth, SCOTT Emma, SC OTT Evelyn, SCOTT Fiona, SCOTT Fred, SCOTT Geoff, SCOTT Scotty, SCOTT Graham, SCOTT Greg, SCOTT Hazel, SCOTT Jeff, SCOTT Joel, SCOTT Joy, SCOTT Julian, SCOTT Juliet, SCOTT Karen, SCOTT Kylie, SCOTT Lisa, SCOTT Marie, SCOTT Melissa, SCOTT Michael, SCOTT Neville, SCOTT Pat, SCOTT Paul, SCOTT Paul, SCOTT Paul, SCOTT Penny, SCOTT Peter, SCOTT Peta, SCOTT Philip, SCOTT Rachel, SCOTT Ray, SCOTT Raymond, SCOTT Rex, SCOTT Rhonda, SCOTT Robyn, SCOTT Rodney, SCOTT Rohan, SCOTT Sarah, SCOTT Stephen, SCOTT Stuart, SCOTT Susan, SCOTT Susan, SCOTT Suzanne, SCOTT Thomas, SCOTT Tim, SCOTT Tracey, SCOTT Wayne, SCOTT Wendy, SCOTT-STEVENSON Iain, SCOTTING Andrew, SCOTTON Matthew, SCOTTS Linden, SCOTTS Marion, SCOWCROFT Jacqui, SCOWCROFT Steve, SCREEN Jennifer, SCRIVEN Bryce, SCROGIE David, SCUDERI Ross, SCULLARD Trish, SCULLARD Warwick, SCULLEY Debbie, SCULLIN Avis, SCULLIN Fran, SCULLION John, SCULLY Jim, SCULLY Joann, SCULLY Laurel, SCULLY Michael, SCULLY Rosemary, SCULTHORPE Celina, SCUTTER Marilyn, SCUTTS Kay, SCUTTS Miche I, SCUTTS Peter, SEACH Yolanda, SEAGE Nathan, SEAL Danielle, SEAL Ian, SEAMAN Alan, SEAMAN Donna, SEAMONS Kathryn, SEAN Simon, SEANIGER Di, SEARANT Julie, SEARLE David, SEARLE Dawn, SEARLE Kingsley, SEARLE Pearl, SEARLE Bob, SEARLE Roy, SEARLE Tracey, SEARLE Warren, SEARS Chris, SEARS Frances, SEARS Kerry, SEARSON Barry, SEARSON Patrick, SEARY Dianne, SEARY Nick, SEARY Ray, SEATON Beryl, SEATON Shona, SEAY Bill, SEBARATNAM Tony, SEBASTIAN Isabel, SEBBAG Raphael, SEBBENS Matt, SEBEL Janny, SEBERRY Rosemary, SECCOMBE Alexander, SEDAGHATI Hazhir, SEDDON Geoffrey, SEDDON Judy, SEDDON Lisa, SEDER Vera, SEDGMAN Craig, SEDGMAN Derek, SEDGMAN Rebecca, SEDGWICK Vince, SEDLAK Jan, SEDMAK Frank, SEE Alex, SEE Rod, SEEBECK Alex, SEEDSMAN Andrew, SEEGERS Gavin, SEELAN Thava, SEELIGER Manfred, SEEMANN Seemann, SEERS Margaret, SEERUTHUN Yves, SEET Clairie, SEETO Alison, SEETO Belinda, SEETO Chris, SEETO Karen, SEETO Myron, SEETO Roger, SEETO Yvette, SEGAL Leslie, SEGAL Sidney, SEGALLA Elio, SEGALLA Janice, SEGERS Beryl, SE GERS Michelin, SEGGIE Noel, SEGHERS Larisa, SEGOVIA Carolina, SEGREDOS Peter, SEGURA Berta, SEGURA Mireia, SEI Elisabeth, SEIDL Edmond, SEIGERT Sharon, SEILER Judith, SEILER Michael, SEINOR Bill, SEK Michael, SEK Sokhon, SEKHON Harry, SEKUL Nicholas, SEKULES Peter, SEKULICH Alice, SELBY David, SELBY Fay, SELBY Fay, SELBY Mal, SELBY Paula, SELBY Steve, SELFE Paul, SELIG Bridget, SELIGMAN Pete, SELIM Emile, SELINGER Eric, SELKIRK Elizabeth, SELL Gavin, SELL Oliver, SELLANES Eber, SELLAR David, SELLARS Anthony, SELLARS Julie, SELLARS Kara, SELLARS Oliver, SELLEN Clive, SELLER Eva, SELLERS Adele, SELLERS Ann, SELLERS Katherine, SELLS Merrill, SELMES Craig, SELMES Samantha, SELVAGE Gayle, SELVAKUMAR Shelvaraj, SELVANAYAGAM Samanthi, SELVARAJAH Karthi, SELVARAJAH Kavitha, SELVARATNAM Vino, SELVATICO Sonya, SELWAY Denise, SELWAY Mal, SELWOOD Bruce, SELWOOD Bob, SELWOOD Tim, SEM Michelle, SEM Gwen, SEMAAN Linda, SEMMENS Gresta, SEMMENS John, SEMMENS Leonie, SEMMENS Sally, SEMRANI Fred, SEN Tung, SENADEERA Janesh, SE NARATNE Jagath, SENCHENKO Andrew, SENCHENKO Michael, SENDRA Ferdy, SENESE Carmelina, SENF Megan, SENG Sally, SENGMANEE Annie, SENGMANEE Karen, SENGSTOCK Bevan, SENIOR Anike, SENIOR Jason, SENIOR Kathy, SENIOR Lesley, SENIOR Vicki, SENIOR Wayne, SENKER Chris, SENN Rolf, SENN Veronika, SENTANA Alex, SENTAS Leah, SENTINELLA Mimi, SEO Chang, SEO Christine, SEO Grace, SEO Reno, SEO Simone, SEO Holly, SEPASSPOUR Manny, SEPPALA Jaana, SEPPALA Sam, SEPPELT Pamela, SEPPONEN Juha, SEQUEIRA Juliette, SEQUEN Serge, SER Danii, SERAFIN Belinda, SERAPHIM Andrea, SERAZIO Pablo, SERCOMBE Dorothy, SERETIS Rick, SERGAS Michelle, SERGEANT Peter, SERGI Joe, SERGIS Ste la, SERGYOS Romani,

SERMSITTIPORM Jen, SERNIG Kieran, SERNIG Norbert, SERNIO Pina, SERPA Jose, SERRA Imelda, SERRANO Marcos, SERRET Daniel, SERRY Brent, SESTA Linda, SESTIC Helen, SETCHELL Greg, SETHI Rajiv, SETHI Sumit, SETHI Sumintra, SETHIA Vineet, SETHNA Beheruz, SETHNA Madhavi, SETIABUDY Alfred, SETIAWAN Agus, SETIAWAN Armand, SETIAWAN Hansen, SETIAWAN Diana, SETIAWAN Anita, SETIONAGO Marilyn, SETIONAGO Tina, SETON Fran, SETON Mike, SETRAKIAN Henry, SETTAPRASERT Aksorn, SETZ Karen, SEVA Sukumar, SEVARES Zully, SEVE Malama, SEVELLE Karin, SEVENOAKS Ron, SEVIL John, SEVIL Katie, SEVILLA Ernie, SEWARD Hugh, SEWARD Peter, SEWARD Robert, SEWARD Veronica, SEWELL Brett, SEWELL Damon, SEWELL Mark, SEXTON Diane, SEXTON Meryl, SEXTON-FINCK Durrielle, SEYMOUR Cathy, SEYMOUR Denise, SEYMOUR Liz, SEYMOUR Frank, SEYMOUR Joan, SEYMOUR Judy, SEYMOUR Kristy, SEYMOUR Mary, SEYMOUR Mike, SEYMOUR Vanessa, SEYMOUR Wayne, SEYNER Colin, SEZUN Gregory, SFIRSE Marisa, SHACKLE Nicki, SHACKLETON Lyn, SHACKLOCK Fay, SHADDICK Kim, SHADDOCK Betty, SHADDOCK Perry, SHADE Judith, SHADILY Christine, SHADWELL Pam, SHAFIK Henry, SHAFIQUE Kamran, SHAGAEV Jahangir, SHAGRIN Anne, SHAGRIN Ilana, SHAGRIN Jess, SHAH Jaismit, SHAH Parsh, SHAH Parshv, SHAH Ravi, SHAH Sid, SHAH Uday, SHAH Zankhna, SHAH MD Ehsan, SHAHKHAN Zulfi, SHAHANI Roger, SHAHEED Shamsun, SHAHHO Stella, SHAHID Imran, SHAHPOOR Ally, SHAI-HEE Darren, SHAKER Ahmed, SHAKESPEAR Peter, SHAKESPEAR Phil, SHAKESPEAR Susan, SHAKESPEARE Dave, SHAKESPEARE Merril, SHALDIN Dian, SHALIAPIN Frederick, SHALLCROSS Rhonda, SHAMGAR Rosy, SHAMMU Nizar, SHAMRAKOV Maria, SHAMRAKOV Sveta, SHAN Guoliang, SHAN June, SHANAHAN Madeleine, SHANAHAN Mary, SHANAHAN Marienne, SHANAHAN Terry, SHAND Lil, SHANDLEY Leigh, SHANE Vikki, SHANG Li, SHANKAR Shankar, SHANKELTON Ernie, SHANKS Jocelyn, SHANMUGAN Prashanth, SHANMUGANATHAN Thila, SHANMUGANATHEN Jaya, SHANNON Gabrielle, SHANNON Barbara, SHANNON Doug, SHANNON Frances, SHANNON John, SHANNON Maree, SHANNON Veronica, SHANNOS Chris, SHAPIEVSKY Nina, SHAPIRA Deborah , SHAPIRO Anthony, SHAPIRO Susy, SHARAN Sanjana, SHARDA Anupam, SHARIAT Ali, SHARIFF Shanaaz, SHARKEY Cecelia, SHARKEY Michael, SHARMA Chirag, SHARMA Chitra, SHARMA Hari, SHARMA Kallol, SHARMA Mituri, SHARMA Nigel, SHARMA Parveen, SHARMA Sonia, SHARMA Virendra, SHARMA Yogesh, SHARMAN Fay, SHARMAN Matthew, SHARMAN Michael, SHARP Alice, SHARP Arthur, SHARP Bruce, SHARP Dane, SHARP Geoffrey, SHARP Gillian, **SHARP Jeanette**, SHARP Jodie, SHARP Ken, SHARP Linda, SHARP Gae, SHARP Patrick, SHARP Peter, SHARPE Anthony, SHARPE Geoff, **SHARPE Marg**, SHARPE Sue, SHARPIN Mike, SHARPLES Warwick, SHARROCK Andrew, SHARROCK Coral, SHARROCK Robin, SHARROCK Skey, SHARRY Joan, SHARRY Leo, SHARWOOD Catherine, SHAW Allan, SHAW Andrea, SHAW Barry, SHAW Bart, SHAW Hudson, SHAW Christine, SHAW David, SHAW Dean, SHAW Georgie, SHAW Elaine, SHAW Emma, SHAW Fergus, SHAW Gary, SHAW Harry, SHAW Helen, SHAW Jacqui, SHAW Jenny, SHAW Jo, SHAW Joan, SHAW Joy, SHAW Judy, SHAW Ken, SHAW Lara, SHAW Rae, SHAW Tricia, SHAW Tony, SHAW Robert, SHAW Sam, SHAW Shirley, SHAW Steve, SHAW Stephen, SHAW Stirling, SHAW Sue, SHAW Verline, SHAW Wendy, SHAW William, SHAW Yvette, SHAW-McGUINESS Hayley, SHAWDON, Anik, SHAWL Tony, SHAWYER Kathy, SHAYEB Jamileh, SHAYEB Mary, SHEA Beverley, SHEAHAN Jeanette, SHEAHAN Trevor, SHEAN Bob, SHEAN Warwick, SHEARER Annetta, SHEARER Brian, SHEARER Samantha, SHEARGOLD El, SHEAERGOLD Glen, SHEARGOLD Leanne, SHEARGOLD Pam, SHEARING Garry, SHEARMAN Bruce, SHEARMAN Kasey, SHEARMAN Zoe, SHEARS Andrew, SHERY Patricia, SHEATHER Carmel, SHEATHER Max, SHEATHER Michelle, SHEATHER Nick, SHEDDON Carly, SHEED Chris, SHEEDY Michael, SHEEHAN Peter, SHEEHY Peter, SHEEHY Wayne, SHEEKEY Robbie, SHEELY Ray, SHEEN Thomas, SHEER Holly, SHEERAN Freya, SHEFFIELD Ian, SHEFFIELD Jennifer, SHEH Raymond, SHELBOURNE Beverley, SHELDON Paul, SHELDON Raymond, SHELDON Richard, SHELL Deryk, SHELL Natalie, SHELLEY Corrina, SHELLEY Maureen, SHELLEY Bill, SHELTON Ann, SHELTON Brian, SHELTON Debbie, SHELTON Mavis, SHELTON Nathan, SHELTON Robin, SHEN Echo, SHEN Guang-Yuan, SHEN Hai, SHEN Jane, SHEN Thomas, SHEN Wei, SHENODA Marcleno, SHENSTONE Bain, SHENTON Chris, SHEOREY Manisha, SHEPHARD Darrell, SHEPHARD Dianne, SHEPHARD Marie, SHEPHARD Wendy, SHEPHERD Tony, SHEPHERD Catalina, SHEPHERD Cathy, SHEPHERD Chris, SHEPHERD Dan, SHEPHERD Graeme, SHEPHERD Helen, SHEPHERD Ian, **SHEPHERD Janet**, SHEPHERD Janelle, SHEPHERD Jenny, SHEPHERD Jules, SHEPHERD Ken, SHEPHERD Kristy, SHEPHERD Leisal, SHEPHERD Meegan, SHEPHERD Melissa, SHEPHERD Pauline, SHEPHERD Bob, SHEPHERD Todd, SHEPHERD Tracey, SHEPHERD Zolly, SHEPHERDSON Barry, SHEPHERDSON Helen, SHEPPARD Dave, SHEPPARD David, SHEPPARD Dawn, SHEPPARD Elwyn, SHEPPARD Kate, SHEPPARD Lola, SHEPPARD Louise, SHEPPARD Michael, SHEPPARD Russel, SHEPPARD Stan, SHEPPARD Vic, SHEPPARD Wendy, SHEPPEARD Greg, SHER Misha, SHER Tamara, SHERANZEY Said, SHERBAKOV Gennady, SHERBURD Troy, SHERIDAN Brett, SHERIDAN Camilla, SHERIDAN Clare, SHERIDAN David, SHERIDAN John, SHERIDAN Melissa, SHERIDAN Bob, SHERIDAN Robert, SHERIFF Zeenath, SHERINGHAM Lach, SHERLOCK Des, SHERLOCK Sam, SHERMAN Andrew, SHERMAN Halina, SHERMAN Kyla, SHERMAN Russell, SHERN Peter, SHERPA Pam, SHERRAH Heather, SHERRARD Nigel, SHERRELL Sophie, SHERRIFF Amanda, SHERRIFF Crystal, SHERRIFF Joanne, SHERRINGHAM Keith, SHERRINGHAM Peter, SHERRY Ben, SHERRY Lisa, SHERRY Eugene, SHERRY Peter, SHERWIN Maria, SHERWIN Pete, SHERWIN Rod, SHERWOOD Sascha, SHERWOOD Ted, SHERWOOD Carry, SHERWOOD Kate, SHERWOOD Maray, SHERWOOD Robert, SHERWOOD Troy, SHEUNG Andrew, SHEWAN Anthony, SHEWAN Luke, SHEWRY Libby, SHI Ban, SHI Ji, SHI Jun, SHI Lin, SHI Liping, SHI Wan, SHI Wen, SHI Peter, SHI Xiaoyan, SHI Yali, SHI Jenny, SHICHIYAMATANI Shinsuke, SHIDIAK Louis, SHIEH Nina, SHIEL Paul, SHIELDS Alan, SHIELDS Donna, SHIELDS Graham, SHIELDS Judy, SHIELDS Lynne, SHIELDS Patricia, SHIELDS Bob, SHIELDS Roslyn, SHIELDS Sue, SHIELL Harry, SHIELS Daph, SHIELS Jenny, SHIELS Roger, SHIH Sean, SHILLABEER Evan, SHILLABEER Warren, SHILLIDAY John, SHILLING Genine, SHILLITO Sophie, SHIM Sun, SHIMA Sayuri, SHIMELD Mac, SHIMELD Stuart, SHIMIZU Emi, SHIMIZU Reiko, SHIMIZU Kako, SHIMMIN Sue, SHIMOMOTO Yoshi, SHIN Hyun, SHIN Hyun-Ju, SHIN James, SHIN Charlie, SHIN Jim, SHIN Jung, SHIN Menae, SHIN Norman, SHIN Philip, SHIN Sang, SHIN Soon, SHIN Theresa, SHIN Youn, SHINE Brendan, SHINE Brigid, SHINE Terri, SHINMURA Midori, SHINN Dorothy, SHINODA Emi, SHINOUDA Fadip, SHIOIRI Masumi, SHIOZAWA Harry, SHIPHAM Ash, SHIPLEY Barry, SHIPLEY Douglas, SHIPP Garry, SHIPP Gregory, SHIPTON Christine, SHIPTON Craig, SHIPTON Masue, SHIPWAY Caroline, SHIRAZI Mahmoud, SHIRAZIAN Majid, SHIRAZIAN Mitsuko, SHIRDON Don, SHIRLEY Anna, SHIRLEY Caroline, SHIRLING Diana, SHIRREFS Pauline, SHISHKOV Tony, SHIU Joe, SHLEEF Reem, SHMAIT Abz, SCMARYAN Anastasia, SHMIGEL Peter, SHNAIDER Roman, SHNIER Ron, SHOARD Dorothy, SHOEMARK Richard, SHOESMITH Gary, SHOLL Peter, SHONE Peter, SHONO Yuri, SHOOLBREAD Angela, SHOOTER Leanne, SHOOTER Neville, SHOPAULUK Kas, SHOR Michael, SHORE Katinka, SHORT Adrian, SHORT Chris, SHORT David, SHORT Debbie, SHORT Elizabeth, SHORT Kim, SHORT Lyn, SHORT Marienne, SHORT Mark, SHORT Melanie, SHORT Neville, SHORT Nev, SHORT Peter, SHORT Richard, SHORT Robyn, SHORT Stephen, SHORT Stephen, SHORTALL Alan, SHORTEN Brett, SHORTER Barbara, SHORTER Mike, SHORTER Sally, SHORTHOUSE Philippa, SHORTLAND Harris, SHORTLAND John, SHOTTON Peter, SHOUKRALLAH Rifaat, SHOULDER Julia, SHPARLINSKI Irina, SHREAD John, SHREEVASTAV Dinesh, SHREEVE Lisa, SHREEVE Nat, SHRESTHA Antoinetter, SHRESTHA Kiran, SHRESTHA Megh, SHRESTHA Praphulla, SHRESTHA Raz, SHRESTHA Rhuee, SHRESTHA Shiva, SHUE Shieh-Yin, SHUE Yen, SHUKLA Arvind,

SHUKLA Avi, SHUKLA Kiran, SHUKLA Raj, SHUKLA Vijay, SHULMAN Lauren, SHUM Hubert, SHUM Carol, SHUMACK Lenus, SHUMACK Trevor, SHUMMEN Robyn, SHUNKER Sharon, SHURETY Andrew, SHUTE Graham, SHUTE Julie, SHUTE Nereda, SHUTTLEWOOD Geoff, SHY ti Alexander, SHYING Malcolm, SIA Billie, SIACKHASONE Voravong, SIAMBATON Henny, SIAPKAS Kostantinos, SIAR Tom, SIBAL Somesh, SIBILLIN Anthony, SIBIO John, SICAT Erick, SICE Ed, SICE Ollie, SICHEL Michael, SICILIANO Carol, SID Allan, SIDARI Laurance, SIDDIQI Tariq, SIDDIQUI Ashher, SIDDIQUI Kashif, SIDDIQUI Sultan, SIDDIQUI Amir, SIDEBOTTOM Cedric, SIDELL Samantha, SIDGREAVES Gini, SIDHOM Eddie, SIDHU Palvinder, SIDHU Param, SIDI Albert, SIDMAN Kevin, SIDNEY Di, SIDNEY Michael, SIDRAK Laura, **SIEBEN Inge**, SIEBERT Mark, SIECK Cornelia, SIECZKO Jarek, SIECZKO Paulina, SIEGERS Hans, SIEGERT Julie, SIELY Virginia, SIEMIATKOWSKI Margaret, SIEN Serena, SIENCZUK Richard, SIEPMANN Dot, SIERINK Arnold, SIERRA Marianella, SIETSMA Kor, SIEUR Jean, SIEW Ai, SIEW Vivien, SIFRI Mimmy, SIGALA Giuliana, SIGGINS Lorna, SIGGINS Ray, SIGMONT Charles, SIGURDSSON Jo, SIJABAT Bona, SIKAIS Sandra, SIKAIS Viktor, SILACCI Greg, SILBERSCHNEIDER Max, SILBERY Lyndall, SILCOCK Colin, SILK Aniko, SILK Di, SILK Peter, SILK Rod, SILLAR Geoff, SILLICK Vola, **SILLINCE David**, SILLIS Debbie, SILLIS Judy, SILOM Karen, SILOOY Benita, SILOOY Melinda, SILSBY Patricia, SILVA Andrea, SILVA Bernie, SILVA Carlos, SILVA Maria, SILVA Sonia, SILVA Suzanne, SILVA Tom, SILVEIRA Anabela, SILVER Liz, SILVERI Antonio, SILVERLOCK Blair, SILVERS Nadia, SILVERWOOD Mary, SILVESTER Garry, SILVESTRI Claudio, SILVESTRO Phil, SILVEY Bernie, SILVOLLI Rob, SILVY Kevin, SIM Sue, SIM Boon, SIM Gary, SIM Grace, SIM Joanne, SIM Joanne, SIM Rebecca, SIM Bob, SIM Royston, SIM Sim, SIM Swee, SIM-SING Beatrice, SIMAI Bernie, SIMALLA Alain, SIMANJUNTAK Elyna, SIMANOWSKY Halina, SIMANOWSKY J Bill, **SIMCOX Lisa**, SIMENSEN Vibeke, SIMISTER Peta, SIMMONDS Simi, SIMMONDS Donna-Maree, SIMMONDS Jackie, SIMMONDS Jan, SIMMONDS Kellie, SIMMONDS Robin, SIMMONS Cherine, SIMMONS Neil, SIMMONS Ted, SIMMONS Liz, SIMMONS Emily, SIMMONS Gary, SIMMONS Jim, SIMMONS Lynn, SIMMONS Robert, SIMMONS Susan, SIMMONS Tina, SIMMS Amy, SIMMS Carolyn, SIMMS Gerard, SIMMS Irene, SIMMS Lamar, SIMMS Terry, SIMMS Michael, SIMMS Phil, SIMMS Robyn, SIMMS Toni, SIMOES SILVA Socorro, SIMON Jill, SIMON Simonian, SIMON Leonie, SIMON Louise, SIMONDS Shelly, SIMONIAN Albert, SIMONOVSKI Steve, SIMONS Joshua, SIMONS Pete, SIMONS Rob, SIMPFENDORFER Clair, SIMPFENDORFER Ralph, SIMPFENDORFER Sue, SIMPLE John, SIMPSON Adam, SIMPSON Alex, SIMPSON Allan, SIMPSON Alma, SIMPSON Belinda, SIMPSON Brenda, SIMPSON Brian, SIMPSON Brian, SIMPSON Campbell, SIMPSON Charlotte, SIMPSON Bob, SIMPSON Clive, SIMPSON Craig, SIMPSON Danielle, SIMPSON Darren, SIMPSON Dawn, SIMPSON Deby, SIMPSON Dianne, SIMPSON Dode, SIMPSON Douglas, SIMPSON Elicia, SIMPSON Fiona, SIMPSON Grant, SIMPSON Grahame, SIMPSON Gwen, SIMPSON Harley, SIMPSON Herb, SIMPSON Ian, SIMPSON James, SIMPSON Jim, SIMPSON Jim, SIMPSON Jim, SIMPSON Jim, SIMPSON Janet, SIMPSON John, SIMPSON John, SIMPSON Judy, SIMPSON Judy, SIMPSON Karen, **SIMPSON Lea**, SIMPSON Lisa, SIMPSON Lynette, SIMPSON Margaret, SIMPSON Matthew, SIMPSON Michelle, SIMPSON Narelle, SIMPSON Nita, SIMPSON Norma, SIMPSON Phil, SIMPSON Rachel, SIMPSON Robin, SIMPSON Robert, SIMPSON Bob, SIMPSON Scott, SIMPSON Scott, SIMPSON Wallace, SIMPSON Wayne, SIMPSON Wendy, SIMPSON Yvonne, SIMPSON Benjamin, SIMS Cherie, SIMS Garry, SIMS Jean, SIMS Maureen, SIMS Bob, SIMSIRI Soraya, SIMSON Alan, SIN Chung, SIN Do, SIN Karen, SINBANDHIT Lena, SINCLAIR Andy, SINCLAIR Gus, SINCLAIR McCourt, SINCLAIR Barbara, SINCLAIR Cameron, SINCLAIR Clyde, SINCLAIR Diana, SINCLAIR Jim, SINCLAIR Jonine, SINCLAIR Judy, SINCLAIR Ken, SINCLAIR Margaret, SINCLAIR Lyn, SINCLAIR Maxine, SINCLAIR Megan, SINCLAIR Michael, SINCLAIR Monica, SINCLAIR Peta, SINCLAIR Pete, SINCLAIR Robert, SINCLAIR Sarah, SINCLAIR Sharon, SINCLAIR Toby, SINCLAIR Bill, SINCLAIR-SMITH Clive, SINCOCK Bruce, SINDONE Pina, SINDONE Tino, SINFIELD Graham, SINFIELD Ian, SINFIELD Ross, SING Claudia, SING TJ, SINGER Kate, SINGER David, SINGER Karina, SINGER Lois, SINGERMAN Deborah, SINGH Jit, SINGH Amarpreed, SINGH Amarjit, SINGH Aruinder, SINGH Bachittar, SINGH Baldev, SINGH Balwinder, SINGH Lucky, SINGH Bobby, SINGH Davinder, SINGH Gurdial, SINGH Gurinder, SINGH Harpreet, SINGH Harmeek, SINGH Jaspal, SINGH Joe, SINGH Judy, SINGH Karanjeet, SINGH Kusum, SINGH Mahendra, SINGH Navkamal, SINGH Peter, SINGH Param, SINGH Prabh, SINGH Priva, SINGH Rachel, SINGH Sikander, SINGH Surinder, SINGH Sue, **SINGH Zahin**, SINGH Zinga, SINGLA Amit, SINGLE Alan, SINGLE Deb, SINGLE Margaret, SINGLETON Allan, SINGLETON Diane, SINGLETON Helen, SINGLETON Julie, SINGLETON Bill, SINGLETON Mavis, SINGLETON Natasha, SINGLETON Patricia, SINGLINE Chris, SINHA Marie, SINHA Neena, SINICINS George, SINISKA Alain, SINTHORNCHAIKUL Will, SIOSTROM Ron, SIOW Alexander, SIOW Ediie, SIOW Howard, SIR Sedat, SIRETT Leeson, SIRI Inko, SIRIPUN Sarawut, SIRIWANIJ Wareewan, SIRNA Sam, SIRYANI Lisa, SISKOVIC Henrik, SISMANOGLO Aylin, SISMANOGLU Berna, SISMANOGLU Turner, SISMEY Alan, SISSIAN Meg, SIT Brendan, SITCHEFF Thea, SITNIKOSKA Lalita, SITTAMDALAM Kadir, SIU Aaron, SIU Ben, SIU Sunny, SIU Clement, SIU George, SIU Michael, SIU Ronald, SIU Steven, SIVA Ken, SIVABALAN Ramesh, SIVAGNANAM Cumaran, SIVALOGARAJAH Jeevika, SIVANATHAN Dhakshmi, SIVANESAN Sivakanthan, SIVARAJAH Gayathri, SIVARAJAH Piriyandan, SIVASUPRAMANIAM Devaranie, SIVIOUR Debbie, SIVKOVA Marina, SIWAK Wayne, SIZGORIC Edi, SJARIEF Jacqueline, SKAGERFALT Pat, SKAIFE Lorraine, SKAINES Fay, SKAMP Erin, SKANDAKUMARAN Erambamoorthy, SKAPINKER Vicki, SKARDON Ken, SKAROS Andriana, SKEE Lesley, SKEEN Bruce, SKEGG Charlotte, SKEHAN John, SKEHAN Margaeret, SKELLETT Matt, SKELLON Pauline, SKELLY Justin, SKELTON Dorothea, SKELTON Ellis, SKELTON Kylie, SKELTON Marc, SKELTON Mark, SKENNAR Karyn, SKERMAN Yang, SKETCHLEY Tina, SKEWES Washington, SKIADAS Toula, SKIBINSKI Kaz, SKILBECK Michael, SKILBECK Wendy, SKIMIN Richard, SKINNER Arthur, SKINNER Cheryl, SKINNER David, SKINNER Jan, SKINNER Jeffrey, SKINNER John, SKINNER Leisa, SKINNER Marc, SKINNER Rod, SKINNER Rosemary, SKINNER Sara, SKINNER Sue, SKINNER Violeta, SKINNER Vivienne, SKIPPER Gert, SKIPPER Tony, SKLAVOUNOS Harry, SKOBELKIN-MULCAIR Olga, SKOMBA Bob, SKORNIAKOFF George, SKOUGAREVSKY Alexandra, SKOUGAREVSKY Andrei, SKOWRONSKI Emma, SKRABAK Joseph, SKRANDIES Darren, SKRIBINS Norma, SKRIBINS Walter, SKRINNIKOFF Vicotr, SKRYBIN Oleg, SKULANDER Gary, SKULANDER Nick, SKULANDER Thomas, Zac, SKUSE Dave, SKUTHORP Lucy, SKUTHORPE Jim, SKY Leanne, SKYRING Merril, SLACK David, SLACK Ella, SLACK Annie, SLADE Carol, SLADE David, SLADE Graeme, SLADE Jack, SLADE Les, SLADE Lloyd, SLADE Lynette, SLADE Ron, SLADEK Ruth, SLAGER Anne, SLANIC Sandra, SLARKE Eileen, SLARKE Noel, SLARP Colin, SLATER Barry, SLATER Debbie, SLATER Gay, SLATER Hayley, SLATER Ian, SLATER Lena, SLATER Nigel, SLATER Dick, SLATER Sonya, SLATER Valli, SLATER Susan, SLATTER Doug, SLATTERY Bernie, SLATTERY Genevieve, SLATTERY Heather, SLATTERY James, SLATTERY Jack, SLATTERY Julie, SLATTERY Trish, SLAVICH Irene, SLAVIN Chris, SLAVOVA Stani, SLEDGE Barry, SLEDGE Jose, SLEE Mike, SLEEMAN Anthony, SLEEMAN Pat, SLEEP Anne, SLEEP Joel, SLEFENDORFAS Albert, SLEIMAN Joe, SLEIMAN Nola, SLEIMAN William, SLEMBEK Ingrid, SLEMMERMANN Nev, SLEVISON Ann-Marie, SLIM Monique, SLINEY Gwenda, SLINGER Robert, SLITERIS Daina, SLITERIS Viktor, SLIWINSKA Katrin, SLIWINSKI Janina, SLOAN Helen, SLOAN Leola, SLOAN Bob, SLOAN Scott, SLOAN Sharon, SLOANE Allan, SLOANE Des, SLOANE Liz, SLOCOMBE Hayley, SLOUGH-SCHORZMANN Terri, SLOWIK Tony, SLUITER Dirk, SLUNSKY Steve, SLY Wayne, SMALDON Gillian, **SMALL Brenden**, SMALL Brian, SMALL Elaine, SMALL Grahame, SMALL Karen, SMALL Keith, SMALL Les, SMALL Mark, SMALL

June, SMALL Michelle, SMALL Tricia, SMALL Pauline, SMALLCOMBE Kim, SMALLHORNE Chris, SMALLMAN Peter, SMALLWOOD Barry, SMALLWOOD Roney, SMAREGLIA Gabriella, SMART Atsuko, SMART Carmel, SMART Cathy, SMART Dave, SMART Denis, SMART George, SMART Ian, SMART Joy, SMART Philip, SMART Richard, SMART Stephen, SMEALIE Phil, SMEDES Jonathan, SMEDLEY Alan, SMEE Ray, SMETHURST David, SMIALKOWSKI Anna, SMID George, SMIDLERS Julie, SMILESKI Chris, SMILEY Doug, SMILJANIC Harry, SMIRNIS Mary, SMIT John, SMITH Adam, SMITH Adam, SMITH Adrian, SMITH Adrian, SMITH Alan, SMITH Alan, SMITH Alan, SMITH Alex, SMITH Alison, SMITH Lorraine, SMITH Andrew, SMITH Angelita, SMITH Angela, SMITH Ann, SMITH Annette, SMITH Annie, SMITH Anne, SMITH Tony, SMITH Tony, SMITH Ashley, SMITH Barbara, SMITH Barbara, SMITH Barbara, SMITH Belinda, SMITH Ben, SMITH Benjamin, SMITH Benjamin, SMITH Benjamin, SMITH Bernadette, SMITH Betty, SMITH Bradley, SMITH Brett, SMITH Brenda, SMITH Brett, SMITH Brianna, SMITH Brian, SMITH Brian, SMITH Bronwyn, SMITH Bruce, SMITH Bruce, SMITH SMITH Cameron, SMITH Carlene, SMITH Carole, SMITH Carey, SMITH Carolyn, SMITH Carmen, SMITH Carole, SMITH Carmel, SMITH Cara, SMITH Carol, SMITH Carmel, SMITH Charlie, SMITH Cherry, SMITH Cheryl, SMITH Chris, SMITH Tina, SMITH Chris, SMITH Chris, SMITH Chris, SMITH Christina, SMITH Chuck, SMITH Clive, SMITH Clive, SMITH Clif, SMITH Colin, SMITH Colin, SMITH Colin, SMITH Colleen, SMITH Daniel, SMITH Daniel, SMITH Dan, SMITH Dane, SMITH Daryl, SMITH David, SMITH Dave, SMITH David, SMITH David, SMITH David, SMITH David, SMITH David, SMITH David, SMITH Davia, SMITH David, SMITH Dawn, SMITH Debbie, SMITH Debbie, SMITH Denise, SMITH Donna, SMITH Don, SMITH Donald, SMITH Don, SMITH Dorelle, SMITH Doug, SMITH Duncan, SMITH Dyan, SMITH Ray, SMITH Elaine, SMITH Liz, SMITH Betty, SMITH Liz, SMITH Libby, SMITH Beth, SMITH Emily, SMITH Emma, SMITH Eric, SMITH Ros, SMITH Faye, SMITH Finley, SMITH Fiona, SMITH Frank, SMITH Frank, SMITH Frederick, SMITH G. Keith, SMITH Gai, SMITH Gail, SMITH Gary, SMITH Gary, SMITH Gary, SMITH Garry, SMITH Garon, SMITH Geoff, SMITH Geoff, SMITH George, SMITH Geoffrey, SMITH George, SMITH Gordon, SMITH Graeme, **SMITH Grant**, SMITH Graham, SMITH Graham, SMITH Grant, SMITH Greg, SMITH Greg, SMITH Gwen Heather, SMITH Heidi, SMITH Helen, SMITH Howard, SMITH Howard, SMITH Ian, SMITH Ian, SMITH Ian, SMITH Jacqui, SMITH Jacqueline, SMITH Jim, SMITH Jim, SMITH James, SMITH James, SMITH Jim, SMITH Jim, SMITH Janet, SMITH Janice, SMITH Jan, SMITH Janene, SMITH Janet, SMITH Janelle, SMITH Jason, SMITH Jason, SMITH Jeanne, SMITH Jean, SMITH Jeff, SMITH Jeff, SMITH Jennifer, SMITH Jenny, SMITH Jenny, SMITH Jenny, SMITH Jeremy, SMITH Joan, SMITH Jo, SMITH Jody, SMITH Jodie, SMITH Jodie, SMITH John, SMITH John, SMITH John, SMITH Joy, SMITH Joy, SMITH Joy, SMITH J.R, SMITH Julie, SMITH Julie, SMITH Julie, SMITH Julie, SMITH Julie, SMITH Julie, SMITH June, SMITH Karen, SMITH Kathryn, SMITH Katrina, SMITH Kathleen, SMITH Kate, SMITH Kelvin, SMITH Ken, SMITH Ken, SMITH Ken, SMITH Ken, SMITH Kenneth, SMITH Kerry, SMITH Keryn, SMITH Kirilly, SMITH Kristine, SMITH Chris, SMITH Kristy, SMITH Lauren, SMITH Laurie, SMITH Leonie, SMITH Leon, SMITH Leon, SMITH Leticia, SMITH Lindsay, SMITH Lindsay, SMITH Lisa, SMITH Lisa, SMITH Lisa, SMITH Lorraine, SMITH Louise, SMITH Louise, SMITH Louise, SMITH Lyn, SMITH Majella, SMITH Mal, SMITH Marg, SMITH Martine, SMITH Margaret, SMITH Marg, SMITH Maree, SMITH Marion, SMITH Mary, SMITH Mary, SMITH Mark, SMITH Margaret, SMITH Marie, SMITH Margaret, SMITH Matt, SMITH Maureen, SMITH Max, SMITH Megan, SMITH Melanie, SMITH Melinda, SMITH Melinda, SMITH Mercia, SMITH Micheal, SMITH Michael, SMITH Mike, SMITH Mike, SMITH Michael, SMITH Michael, SMITH Michele, SMITH Michael, SMITH Micheal, SMITH Migel, SMITH Milton, SMITH Monty, SMITH Myra, SMITH Narelle, SMITH Nathan, SMITH Neal, SMITH Neil, SMITH Neil, SMITH Nick, SMITH Nicole, SMITH Nick, SMITH Nicole, SMITH Nicola, SMITH Nigel, SMITH Noelene, SMITH Noeline, SMITH Noel, SMITH Norma, SMITH Norm, SMITH Pamela, SMITH Jan, SMITH Pam, SMITH Pat, SMITH Pauline, **SMITH Paul**, SMITH Paul, SMITH Pauline, SMITH Peter, SMITH Peter, SMITH Peta, SMITH Peter, SMITH Peter, SMITH Peter, SMITH Peter, SMITH Peter, SMITH Peter, SMITH Phil, SMITH Rachel, SMITH Rach, SMITH Randall, SMITH Raylene, SMITH Rebecca, SMITH Becky, SMITH Rebecca, SMITH Rebekah, SMITH Rebecca, SMITH Bruce, SMITH Rhae, SMITH Richard, SMITH Robin, SMITH Robyne, SMITH Rob, SMITH Rob, SMITH Robyn, SMITH Robyn, SMITH Rob, SMITH Robert, SMITH Rod, SMITH Rod, SMITH Ron, SMITH Rosanne, SMITH Ross, SMITH Ross, SMITH Rossalyn, SMITH Rowland, SMITH Russell, SMITH Ruth, SMITH Ryan, SMITH Sally, SMITH Sally, SMITH Sandra, SMITH Sandy, SMITH Sarah, SMITH Sharyn, SMITH Shelley, SMITH Shelley, SMITH Shirley, SMITH Stacey, SMITH Stephen, SMITH Stephen, SMITH Steve, SMITH Steve, SMITH Stephen, SMITH Stuart, SMITH Sue, SMITH Sue, SMITH Sue, SMITH Tamara, SMITH Tamara, SMITH Tania, SMITH Tanya, SMITH Terry, SMITH Tim, SMITH Trent, SMITH Trevor, SMITH Valerie, SMITH Verlei, SMITH Walter, SMITH Warwick, SMITH Warwick, SMITH Warwick, SMITH Warren, SMITH Warren, SMITH Wayne, SMITH Wez, SMITH Kent, SMITH William, SMITH Yvonne, SMITH Yvonne, SMITH-EXTON Alyson, SMITH-GANDER Craig, SMITH-HILL Elke, SMITH-WHITE Rosalind, SMITHERS Barry, SMITHERS Dianne, SMITHERS Dotti, SMITHERS Julian, SMITHERS Penny, SMITHSON Lisa, SMITHSON Rosemary, SMITS Bill, SMIYIELSKI Silvio, SMOKER Les, SMOLLEN Paul, SMOLONOGOV Tanya, SMOOTHY Kate, SMUK Joanne, SMUK Mark, SMUK Tracy, SMYTH Brett, SMYTH Brian, SMYTH Coralie, SMYTH Courtney, SMYTH David, SMYTH John, SMYTH Denise, SMYTH Greg, SMYTH Kate, SMYTH Lyn, SMYTH Margaret, SMYTH Sarah, SMYTHE Laurane, SMYTHE Michael, SMYTHE Trent, SMYTHE Wendy, SNAPE Dan, SNASHALL Carol, SNEDDEN Paul, SNEDDON Catherine, SNEDDON Denise, SNEDDON Greg, SNEDDON Jacky, SNEDDON Rhonda, SNELL Dulcey, SNELL Ian, SNELL Stephen, SNELLGROVE Tracy, SNELLING Michael, SNG Ying, SNIJDERS Peter, SNODGRASS Bill, SNOW Debbie, SNOW Marisa, SNOW Rod, SNOWDEN John, SNOWDEN Norm, SNOWDEN Renate, SNOWDEN Rene, SNOXALL Jason, SNYDER Jack, SNYDER Kim, SO Andrew, SO Austen, SO Clement, SO Jacqueline, SO Jennifer, SO Joseph, SO Jung, SO Kenneth, SO Kwong, SO Monica, SO Norman, SO Su, SO Wai, SO Yoo-Bin, SO Mike, SOMAN Simon, SOADY Gabrielle, SOADY Sandra, SOAMES David, SOAN Nancy, SOANE Mick, SOANS Glynnis, SOANS Rosh, SOARES Lila, SOARES Mark, SOBEY Karen, SOBEY Tom, SOBKOWSKI Chantelle, SOBOL Amy, SOCHA Joel, SODBINOW George, SODEN Ron, SODERBORG Tom, SOE Thu, SOE MYA MAUNG John, SOEB Md, SOEKARNO Frank, SOELAIMAN Rudi, SOETJIONO Sofi, SOFIOS Patricia, SOFIOU Voula, SOFTLEY Barbara, SOFTLEY Don, SOGARI Carlos, SOGHOMONIAN Shant, SOH Bee, SOH Jeffrey, SOH John, SOH Wan, SOHEL Abu, SOHN Cheonhee, SOHN Renate, SOHN Young, SOININEN Pentti, SOK Hoeun, SOKAC Andrew, SOKCEVIC Susana, SOKOL Robyn, SOLANAKIS Harry, SOLANO Joseph, SOLAR Jack, SOLAR Marcelo, SOLARI Cassandra, SOLBERG Lew, SOLDATIC Fred, SOLE Pamela, SOLER Eugene, SOLIGO Narelle, SOLIGO Vilma, SOLIMAN Adel, SOLIMAN F. Ed, SOLIMAN Fiedi, SOLIMAN Maryatta, SOLIS Cesar, SOLIS Enrique, SOLIS William, SOLLARS Dawn, SOLLING Jenny, SOLLOM Robyn, SOLMAN Jim, SOLMAN Sue, SOLOMON Lina, SOLOMON Jenny, SOLOMON John, SOLOMON John, SOLOMON Kathy, SOLOMON Peter, SOLOMON Richard, SOLOMON Ross, SOLOMON Simone, SOLOMON Steven, SOLOMONS David, SOLOMONS Ian, SOLOMONS Reji, SOLOMONS Bill, SOLOWIJ Yaros, SOLTA Glenda, SOLTAN Ihab, SOLTI Lisa, SOMBATTHEERA Chattrakul, SOMERS Dave/David, SOMERS Tam, SOMERVAILLE Hannah, SOMERVILLE Adam, SOMERVILLE Daniel, SOMERVILLE Fiona, SOMERVILLE Iain, SOMERVILLE Ian, SOMMER Hans, SOMMER Jenny, SOMMER Jurg, SOMMERVILLE alan, SOMPORNKIAT Mos, SON Abel, SON Jae, SON Joo-Young, SON Sook, SONCINI Al, SONCINI Lidia, SONDEREGGER Doris, SONDERGAARD Lars, SONE Koji, SONEJI Keith, SONG Adrian, SONG Byeoung, SONG Chang, SONG Jai, SONG Jai, SONG Jee, SONG Joon, SONG Min, SONG David, SONG

Romy, SONG Seil, SONG Emily, SONG Wendy, SONI Kulbir, SONI Sudhir, SONKAEW Uthit, SONNANTE Marino, SONNE Jill, SONNET Brett, SONNLEITNER Stefanie, SONTER Aileen, SONTER Amanda, SONTER Grahame, SONTER Lynn, SOO Bonnie, SOO Carmen, SOO Choi, SOO Edmond, SOO Anne, SOO Hwa, SOO Kair, SOO Kenneth, SOO Kevin, SOO Millie, SOO Sherlyn, SOOKNAH Stephanie, SOON Julie, SOON Kim, SOON Serena, SOOVOROFF Ken, SOOYEON Liu, SOPER Lachlan, SOPHIOS Chris, SOPHOCLEOUS Andreas, SOPHOCLEOUS Peter, SOPRU Caraine, SORBAN David, SOBELLO Fab, SORECA Frank, SORENSEN Bjarte, SORENSEN Debbie, SORGESE Alex, SORGINA Julianna, SORI Steve, SORIA Rachel, SORIA Lina, SORIAL Andrea, SORIANO Arvin, SORIE Elsie, SORLIE Else, SOROHAN Brian, SORRAGHAN Jenni, SORRAINE Denise, SORRAINE Edward, SORRENTI Janette, SORRENTI Phylis, SORTWELL Tory, SOSA Ignacio, SOSA Ladis, SOSA-RAFFO Maria, SOSTAREC Marija, SOTHERAN Dianne, SOTHERAN Frank, SOTHERAN Steve, SOTNEAM Ken, SOTO Nilda, SOTO Victor, SOTO QUEZADA Monica, SOUKIE Moussa, SOUKOULIS Sue, SOULBY Cliff, SOULSBY David, SOURRIS Georgia, SOURRY Nick, SOUTER Flenn, SOUTER Jay, SOUTER Nicole, SOUTH Denise, SOUTH Dave, SOUTHAM Patrick, SOUTHBY Chris, SOUTHEREN Ray, SOUTHERN Jane, SOUTHERN Lyn, SOUTHERTON Cherri, SOUTHWELL Geoff, SOUTHWELL Leza, SOUTHWELL Margaret, SOUTHWELL Megan, SOUTHWELL Michael, SOUTHWELL Paul, SOUTHWELL Wayne, SOUTHWICK Ian, SOUTHWICK Mette, SOUTO Victor, SOUVANNASING Theresa, SOUVOROVA Tania, SOUZA CRUZ Iva, SOV Lisa, SOWA Gregory, SOWARD Greg, SOWDEN John, SOWONJA Maxine, SOWRY Rob, SOWTER Rosy, SOWTER Trent, SPAANS Jennifer, SPACKMAN Spacky, SPACKMAN Jez, SPAGNOLETTI Tony, SPAIN Catherine, SPAIN Michie, SPALDING Jane, SPALTMAN Vivienne, SPANIOL Lucy, SPANKIE Robbie, SPARGO Verity, SPARGO Viv, SPARHAM Ernie, SPARKES Laurie, SPARKES Lyn, SPARKES Naomi, SPARKS Christa, SPARKS Gillian, SPARKS Sharon, SPARLING Bonnie, SPARLING Dennis, SPASARO Melinda, SPAUL Marie, SPAULL Bevan, SPEAKE Bronwyn, SPEARE Peter, SPEARS Barbara, SPEARS Peter, SPEARDS Ed, SPECK Dale, SPECK Steven, SPEECHLAY Merilyn, SPEECHLAY Therese, SPEECHLEY John, SPEECHLEY Lea, SPEECHLY Edna, SPEECHLY Keith, SPEED Brihony, SPEEDY Robert, SPEER Marg, SPEER Bob, SPEERING Carla, SPEERING Santa, SPEIRS Louise, SPEIRS Vanessa, SPEK Will, SPELLMANN Oliver, SPENCE Barbara, SPENCE Dana, SPENCE Greg, SPENCE Margaret, SPENCE Racheal, SPENCE Renee, SPENCER Alex, SPENCER Anne, SPENCER Brian, SPENCER Cam, SPENCER Caroll, SPENCER David, SPENCER Dianne, SPENCER Di, SPENCER Gerlinde, SPENCER Hugh, SPENCER Ian, SPENCER James, SPENCER Jennie, SPENCER John, SPENCER John, SPENCER Julie, SPENCER K, SPENCER Kate, SPENCER Kate, SPENCER Kate, SPENCER Kirsten, SPENCER Paul, SPENCER Peggy, SPENCER Rosemary, SPENCER Samantha, SPENCER Sandra, SPENCER Su, SPENCER Tessa, SPENCER Tinnile, SPENCER Allan, SPENNE Renee, SPERANDEO Roberta, SPERANDO Vincent, SPETCH Luke, SPETS Amy, SPICE Luke SPICER Isabel, SPICER Jude, SPICER Matt, SPIER Helen, SPIER Margaret, SPIER Sharon, SPIERIG Marianne, SPIERINGS Martin, SPIERS Jim, SPIES Jillian, SPIES John, SPIES Lorraine, SPIEWAK Richard, SPIGHT Ann, SPIKE Michelle, SPILIOPOULOS Chris, SPILLANE Jenny, SPILLANE Pip, SPILLER Alec SPILLER Vanessa SPILSTEAD Barry, SPINAZE Janet, SPINAZE Patricia, SPINAZE Pauline, SPINKS Allan, SPINKS Colin, SPINKS Dale, SPINKS Jeremy, SPINKS Ann, SPINKS Rob, SPINKS Shane, SPINNER Shaz, SPIRA Suzie, SPIRO Robin, SPIROPOULOS Eugenia, SPITERI Ben, SPITHILL Arthur, SPITTLE Nancy, SPOHR Brunni, SPOKAS Romanta, SPONG Alison, SPONG Frank, SPONG Timothy, SPOONER Tim, SPORNE Mal, SPOTSWOOD Nathan, SPOTSWOOD Wendy, SPRAGUE Paul, SPRAINGER Maree, SPRAINGER Neil, SPRALJA Susan, SPRANZ Wolfgang, SPRATLIN Margaret, SPRATT Lyn, SPRAY Gillian, SPRENGER Peter, SPRIGG Jill, SPRING Eric, SPRING George, SPRING Mary, SPRING Pat, SPRINGALL Matt, SPRINGLE Lyn, SPRINGTHORPE Josephine, SPRING THORPE Margot, SPROGIS Karl, SPROULE Joe, SPROULE Emma, SPROULE Mark, SPROULE Marg, SPRY Robert, SPULAK Liz, SPURGEON Jim, SPURLING Maureen, SPURRS Rob, SPURWAY Keith, SPURWAY Margaret, SPYROU George, SQUAIR Mandy, SQUARDRITO Tina, SQUIBB Greg, SQUIBB Tricia, SQUIER Andre, SQUILLARI Trish, SQUIRES Amanda, SQUIRES Bruce, SQUIRES Cheryl, SQUIRES Christene, SQUIRES Melanie, SQUIRES Peter, SQUIRES Robert, SQUIRES Rodney, SRACEK Martin, SREEDHARAN Sheamala, SRI GANESHWARAN Abhi, SRI RANJAN Hillary, SRIBALAN Jana, SRIBHADUNG Prasart, SRIKHANTA Rangan, SRIMANONUKUL Sumolchat, SRIMANONUKUN Kamon, SRINIVAS Usha, SRINIVASAN Meera, SRINIVASAN Richard, SRINIVASAN Uma, SRINIVASAN Veda, SRIPARASHARA Rishikesh, SRUHAN Lea, SSALADRAU Kitty, ST BAKER Diane, ST CLAIR Donna, ST CLAIR Sophie, ST GEORGE Lourdes, ST JOHN Juanita, ST JOHN COX Tara, ST LEON Sonja, ST QUINTIN Jenny, ST VINCENT Steffie, ST VINCENT WELCH Kathryn, ST. CLAIR Katerine, ST. FLOUR Alain, ST. JOHN John, STAAL Neil, STAAL Shari, STACE Allan, STACE Sue, STACEY Alan, STACEY Fiona, STACEY Jacinta, STACEY John, STACEY Lionel, STACEY Mike, STACEY Phil, STACHAN Gary, STACK Susanne, STACKPOOL Amanda, STACY Roy, STACY Miriam, STADIOLIUKAS Antanas, STAFA Sue, STAFFORD Annette, STAFFORD Ted, STAFFORD Kerry, STAFFORD Lorraine, STAFFORD Victor, STAFFORD-SMITH Keith, STAGG Adrian, STAGG Andrea, STAGG Anthony, STAGG Danielle, STAHMER Gail, STAIB, Jenny, STAIB Jennifer, STAIB Ken, STAIKOS Spyros, STAINER Janine, STAINES Bart, STAINES Elyssa, STAINES Maggie, STAINES Melissa, STAINES Michele, STAIT Davina, STAKES David, STALDER Mavis, STALDER Norm, STALEY Brooke, STALKER Joan, STAMATAKOS Jim, STAMATELAKY Watchie, STAMATELLIS Mary, STAMATELOS Nick, STAMBOULAKIS Kathy, STAMBOULAKIS Theona, STAMMEL Robert, STAMOS Jo, STAMP Andrew, STANAWAY Gayle, STANBOROUGH Bronwyn, STANBRIDGE Nancy, STANBRIDGE Sallyanne, STANBURY Ian, STANBURY Janette, STANBURY Nick, STANDEN Dave, STANDEN Greg, STANDEN Fullback, STANDEN Kev, STANDERWICK Skye, STANDISH Rowan, STANEK Bob, STANEKE Carolyn, STANFIELD Alison, STANFORD Andrew, STANFORD Bradley, STANFORD Carmel, STANFORD Donna, STANFORD Edwin, STANFORD Elaine, **STANFORD Gaynor**, STANFORD Sorrow, STANFORD Viva, STANHAM Mark, STANILAND Kelly, STANIS Sandra, STANISLAS Cindi, STANKEVICIUS Christine, STANKOVIC Sasha, STANLAKE Myrna, STANLEY Andrea, STANLEY Bruce, STANLEY Carolyn, STANLEY Christine, STANLEY Debbie, STANLEY Emma, STANLEY Graeme, STANLEY Harry, STANLEY John, STANLEY Kate, STANLEY Larissa, STANLEY Lucille, STANLEY Mary, STANLEY Melinda, STANLEY Richard, STANLEY Bob, STANLEY Rod, STANLEY Roger, STANLEY June, STANLEY Tom, STANLEY Tony, STANMORE Geoff, STANNARD Alan, STANNARD Lauren, STANSFIELD Belinda, STANSFIELD Ian, STANSHALL Sandra, STANTON Barry, STANTON Breta, STANTON Cameron, STANTON Chris, STANTON Dot, STANTON Julianne, STANTON Kathy, STANTON Mark, STANTON Neil, STANTON Norm, STANTON Rae, STANTON Rebecca, STANTON Robert, STANTON Terry, STANTON Wendy, STANTON Yvette, STANWELL Brian, STANWELL Karlv, STANWELL Kristy, STANYER Ted, STAPLES Bryan, STAPLES Finny, STAPLES Ken, STAPLETON Kevin, STAPLETON Luanne, STAPLETON Nicolle, STAPLETON Therese, STAPLEY Kris, STAR Sam, STARCEVIC Mary-Louise, STAREY James, STARK Carole, STARK David, STARK Julia, STARK Laurie, STARK Louise, STARK Nichol, STARK Sharon, STARK Stan, STARKEY Clive, STARKEY Ian, STARKEY Joanne, STARKEY Margo, STARKEY Viv, STARLING Leanne, STARMER Sean, STARR Debra, STARR Edith, STARR Mark, STARR Sarah, STASA Helen, STATHAM Hugh, STATON Natalie, STATZENKO George, STAUB Ronnie, STAUGHTON Ann, STAUNTON Ann, STAUNTON Graeme, STAUNTON Robyn, STAUNTON Robyn, STAUNTON Tonina, STAV Brett, STAVELEY Maisie, STAVELEY Ray, STAVENHAGEN Chris, STAVREFF Sonia, STAVRETIS Bill, STAVROULAKIS Nicholas, STAYT Jason, STAZIC Don, STEAD Heather, STEAD Kerry, STEAD Peter, STEAD Wendy, STEADMAN Helen, STEARNS Patrick, STEDMAN Glen, STEDMAN Tracy, STEED

Dianne, STEED Sarah, STEEDMAN Brenda, STEEDMAN Michael, STEEL Alex, STEEL Bron, STEEL David, STEEL Graeme, STEEL Grahame, STEEL Joan, STEELL Judy, STEEL Kate, STEEL Ken, STEEL Max, STEEL Melinda, STEEL Murray, STEEL Richard, STEEL Robbie, STEEL Vicki, STEELE Allen, STEELE Bronwyn, STEELE Paul, STEELE Deborah, STEELE Fiona, **STEELE Jeremy**, STEELE Julienne, STEELE Lyn, STEELE Margaret, STEELE Matt, STEELE Michelle, STEELE Peter, STEELE Steve, STEELL Elizabeth, STEELL Nance, STEELL Bill, STEEN Robert, STEENHOUWER Herman, STEENSON Peter, STEER Barbara, STEER Erica, STEER Sharon, STEERS Robert, STEFAN Benvenuto, **STEFANO Nicole**, STEFANOPOULOS Steve, STEFANOV Jane, STEFANOVIC Vicki, STEFANOWICZ Leon, STEFANSON Dominic, STEFFENSEN Judy, STEGGINK Catherine, STEGGLES Margaret, STEH LY Gerard, STEIGMANN John, STEIGRAD Stephen, STEIN Miriam, STEIN Phil, STEIN Richard, STEINER Enid, STEINHOFF John, STELZER Megan, STENDER Hilda, STENGEL Angela, STENHOUSE Brett, STENHOUSE Christopher, STENING Carol, STENNING Tricia, STENOS Bill, STENT Jeryl, STENT Norman, STENTON Julia, STEPANEK Paul, STEPHAN Ryan, STEPHEN Barry, STEPHEN Margaret, STEPHENS Anna, STEPHENS Chas, STEPHENS Charles, STEPHENS Clare, STEPHENS Daniel, STEPHENS David, STEPHENS Dave, STEPHENS Dave, STEPHENS David, STEPHENS Deborah, STEPHENS Frank, STEPHENS Harry, STEPHENS Janet, STEPHENS Jan, STEPHENS Jean, STEPHENS John, STEPHENS Junene, STEPHENS Karen, STEPHENS Kate, STEPHENS Kathy, STEPHENS Kim, STEPHENS Len, STEPHENS Martin, STEPHENS Margaret, STEPHENS Peter, STEPHENS Bob, STEPHENS Sara, STEPHENS Tanya, STEPHENS Trudy, STEPHENS Steve, STEPHENSON Gerry, STEPHENSON Ian, STEPHENSON Irene, STEPHENSON Joan, STEPHENSON Judy, STEPHENSON Kellie, STEPHENSON Lesley, STEPHENSON Lyn, STEPHENSON Bob, STEPHENSON Ross, STEPHENSON Tom, STEPINSKI Teresa, STEPKOVITCH Betty, STEPNIEWSKI Joe, STERK Bronte, STERKI Hanny, STERLAND Ron, STERLING Jackie, STERLING Stuart, STERN Estelle, STERN Jack, STERN Jacob, STERN Jason, STERN Terry, STERNBERG Sue, STERNFELD Dan, STEVANOVSKI Jim, STEVE Koh, STEVEN Ursula, STEVENS Alan, STEVENS Alex, STEVENS Alison, STEVENS Arthur, STEVENS Brian, STEVENS Carol, STEVENS Catherine, STEVENS Daniel, STEVENS Darrel, STEVENS David, STEVENS Derek, STEVENS Libby, STEVENS Helen, STEVENS Jan, STEVENS Janet, STEVENS Jane, STEVENS Jane, STEVENS Jenny, STEVENS Jeremy, STEVENS Joe, STEVENS Kylie, STEVENS Lana, STEVENS Leigh, STEVENS Lew, STEVENS Liam, STEVENS Lisa, STEVENS Lisa, STEVENS Martell, STEVENS Melissa, STEVENS Mick, STEVENS Pat, STEVENS Penelope, STEVENS Peter, STEVENS Prue, STEVENS Raymond, STEVENS Ronald, STEVENS Rosie, **STEVENS Ros**, STEVENS Steve, STEVENS Roy, STEVENSON Andrew, STEVENSON Barry, STEVENSON Emma, STEVENSON Ian, STEVENSON Ian, STEVENSON James, STEVENSON Jean, STEVENSON Arthur, STEVENSON John, STEVENSON John, STEVENSON Ann, STEVENSON Kylie, STEVENSON Margaret, STEVENSON Martha, STEVENSON Matt, STEVENSON Mike, STEVENSON Nancye, STEVENSON Peter, STEVENSON Ralph, STEVENSON Ronald, STEVENSON Val, STEVENSON Victoria, STEVER Brian, STEVIC Matt, STEWARD Chris, STEWARD Kass, STEWARD Rob, STEWARD Steve, STEWART Alison, STEWART Allison, STEWART Bedelia, STEWART Beverley, STEWART Beverley, STEWART Beverly, STEWART Richard, STEWART Dane, STEWART Darren, STEWART David, STEWART David, STEWART Des, STEWART Diana, STEWART Diane, STEWART Doug, STEWART Elizabeth, STEWART Fiona, STEWART Frances, STEWART Garry, STEWART Gordon, STEWART Helen, STEWART James, STEWART Janette, STEWART Jennifer, STEWART Joanne, STEWART Joan, STEWART John, STEWART John, STEWART Kelly, STEWART Keryn, STEWART Kerrie, STEWART Kimber, STEWART Lauren, STEWART Lyn, STEWART Lyndsay, STEWART Margaret, STEWART Marion, STEWART Margaret, STEWART Matthew, STEWART Maxine, STEWART Michael, STEWART Pamela, STEWART Penny, STEWART Peter, STEWART Richard, STEWART Ric, STEWART Gay, STEWART Roland, STEWART Sean, STEWART Sonja, STEWART Sue, STEWART Terry, STEWART Vicki, STEWART Wendy, STEWART-HUNTER Sally, STIBBS Gaynor, STIBBS Lillian, STICHTER Margaret, STICKLAND Amanda, STICKLAND Tlaloc, STICKLER Paul, STICPEWICH David, STIEBEL Paul, STIEL Andrew, STIEL Ben, STIEL Hilary, STIFFLE Gail, STIGLIANO Joan, STIGWOOD Tanya, STILGOE Joan, STILGOE Ralph, STILIANOU Bakarevic, STILL Don, STILLMAN Kelvin, STILLMAN Kristine, STILSBY Annette, STIMITSIOTIS Marian, STIMSON Chris, STIMSON Irene, STIMSON Norma, STIMSON John, STINSON Carol, STINSON Chris, STINSON Judy, STINSON Julie, STIRLING Donna, STIRLING Janet, STIRLING Lindsay, STIRLING Tom, STITT Dianne, STITT Jai, STITT John, STIVENSON Bob, STOBART Caroline, STOBAUS Ron, STOBIE Michelle, STOCK Dawn, STOCK Lurline, STOCK Raymond, STOCKERT Lori, STOCKFORD Mila, STOCKFORD Vanessa, STOCKHAM Sara, STOCKLEY Tony, STOCKS Robyn, STOCKTON Cath, STOCKWELL Alan, STOCKWELL Dot, STOCKWELL Jane, STODDARD Tionette, STOECKEL Katie, STOFFELS Flik, STOFFELS Jake, STOJANOVIC Boris, STOJANOVIC Milena, STOJANOVIC Bill, STOJANOVIC Vera, STOJANOVSKI Nick, STOKELL Marion, STOKER Trevor, STOKES Adam, STOKES Tony, STOKES Barry, STOKES Bev, STOKES Chris, STOKES Colleen, STOKES David, STOKES Debra, STOKES Jim, STOKES Jane, STOKES Jon, STOKES Margaret, STOKES Mike, STOKES Bob, STOKES Shirley, STOLIAR Richard, STOLJAR Larissa, STOLL Heather, STOLL Narelle, STONE Belinda, STONE Ted, STONE Graeme, STONE Jutta, STONE Ken, STONE Kristy, STONE Lonnie, STONE Matt, STONE Michael, STONE Michael, STONE Mitchell, STONE Nicole, STONE Paul, STONE Pip, STONE Rene, STONE Dick, STONE Rick, STONE Sandra, STONE Sylvia, STONE Vanessa, STONE Stoney, STONEBRAKER Rick, STONEHAM Marilyn, STONEHOUSE Alan, STONEMAN Jenny, STONEY Carrie, STORAKER Morten, STORER Bill, STORES Leonie, STOREY Liz, STOREY Fe, STOREY Julna, STOREY Syd, STOREY Michael, STOREY Syd, STOREY Wayne, STORK Bill, STORKEY Craig, STORMANNS Christa, STORR Ann, STORRAR Stuart, STORRAR Lyn, STORY Randy, STOTT James, STOTT Jenny, STOTT Marty, STOTT Paul, STOTT Rae, STOTT Shirley, STOURNARAS Harri, STOVOLD Maria, STOW Barry, STOWERS Ray, STOWERS Teina, STOYEF Simeon, STRAATSMA John, STRACEY Doug, STRACHAN Alan, STRACHAN Cecilia, STRACHAN James, STRACKE Terry, STRAHAN Karin, STRAHAN Tania, STRAIN Susie, STRALOW George, STRALOW Jean, STRALOW Maurie, STRANG Colin, STRANG Rainie, STRANG Sarah, STRANG Stephanie, STRANGE Norm, STRANGER Jane, STRANGER Ken, STRANGIO Nino, STRASSBERG Catherine, STRASSBERG Fred, STRATFORD Andrew, STRATFORD Barbara, STRATFORD Claire, STRATHDEE Gordon, STRATHDEE Marlene, STRATTON Alan, STRATTON Frank, STRATTON Lyn, STRATTON Sharon, STRAUCH Ron, STRAWBRIDGE Michelle, STREADER Allyson, STREBER Verena, STREET John, STREET Judy, STREET Neville, STREET Philip, STREET Skye, STREETER Anne, STREETER Daniel, STREETER George, STREETER Kathleen, STREETING Sean, STREICHLER David, STREIM Brigitte, STREITBERGER Vanessa, STREMPEL Liz, STREMPEL Robert, STRETTON Bob, STRETTON-MORGAN Ian, STRICKLAND Adam, STRICKLAND Tony, STRICKLAND Joel, STRICKLAND Pamela, STRICKLAND Junior, STRIDE Julie, STRIDE Yvonne, STRIE Janina, STRINGER Arthur, STRINGER Dorothy, STRINGER Lindi, STRINGER Shane, STRINGFELLOW Michael, STRINGFELLOW Michelle, STRITT BURK Carmen, STRODE Cec, STROGYLOS Andrew, STRONG Annie, STRONG Ben, STRONG Bridget, STRONG Tony, STRONG Kim, STRONG Rosie, STROUD Arlene, STROUD Peter, STROUD Elaine, STRUCK Charles, STRUCK John, STRUDWICK Avis, STRUIK Emma, STRUK Peter, STRUMENDO Olivo, STRUYVE Mitchell, STRZELECKI George, STUART Alissa, STUART Bronwyn, STUART Gilda, STUART Mark, STUART Steve, STUART Susan, STUART Tim, STUART Timothy, STUART-DUFF John, STUART-MUIRK Alec, STUART-SMITH David, STUBBINGS Josh, STUBBINGS Kate, STUBBINGS Steve, STUBBINGS Sue, STUBBINGTON David, STUBBINGTON Sheila, STUBBS Jenny, STUBBS Jo, STUBBS Narelle, STUBBS David, STUBBS Philip, STUBBS

Rachel, STUBBS Robert, STUBBS Sue, STUBBS Therese, STUBBS Bill, STUBBS-MILLS Nicola, STUBENRAUCH Fred, STUBING Kathy, STUCKEY John, STUCKEY Marietje, STUCKEY Robert, STUDDERT Jack, STUDHOLME Brett, STUECKELBERGER Andre, STUMP Lyn, STUNDEN Kaye, STURCH Rodney, STUREVSKI Cynthia, STURGEON Bradley, STURGESS Ellen, STURGISS Iris, STURMAN Nick, STURROCK Rob, STURROCK Valda, STURZ June, STUTCHBURY Robyn, STUTE Steve, STUTO Alfio, STYAN Tony, STYAN Helen, STYLES Ian, STYLES Marilyn, STYLES Melissa, STYLIANOU Andrea, STYLIANOU Christina, SU Amanda, SU Cynthia, SU Ricky, SU Kevin, SU Paul, SU Rupert, SU Sophia, SU Tina, SU Tony, SU Yi, SU William, SU Daniel, SU Xin, SUAN Theresa, SUARDIAZ Francisco, SUAREZ Cristina, SUAREZ Rhoemell, SUBAR Nicker, SUBBARAM Sundar, SUBRAMANI Selvi, SUBRAMANIAN Kabilan, SUBRAMANIAN Deepa, SUCCARIE Nabeel, SUCHOVSKY Jan, SUCHOWERSKA Natalka, SUCHOWERSKYJ Jurij, SUCIC Nandy, SUDDIR Abhishek, SUDHAKARAN Raj, SUDHOLZ Peter, SUDIRO Bruno, SUDLOW Anna, SUDSANGUAN Paula, SUE Dianna, SUE SEE Brett, SUEN Judy, SUEN Yvonne, SUGAR Fay, SUGAR Graham, SUGGATE Arthur, SUGIMOTO Chiharu, SUGIMURA Chiyori, SUGPATAN Jose, SUGUMARAN Joshua, SUHARTA Ferdy, SUHOOD Feroni, SUJANTO i, SUJECKI Mark, SUJENTO Sujento, SUJITNO John, SUKAN Ismet, SUKIRNO Joe, SUKKAR Elias, SULIGON Carlos, SULLIVAN Alan, SULLIVAN Allan, SULLIVAN Amy, SULLIVAN Annaleisha, SULLIVAN Bruce, SULLIVAN Debbie, SULLIVAN Des, SULLIVAN Diana, SULLIVAN Fiona, SULLIVAN Fred, SULLIVAN Genia, **SULLIVAN Geoff**, SULLIVAN Glen, SULLIVAN Jan, SULLIVAN Jason, SULLIVAN Jill, SULLIVAN John, SULLIVAN Liam, SULLIVAN Lynne, SULLIVAN Michael, SULLIVAN Michael, SULLIVAN Nellie, SULLIVAN Pam, SULLIVAN Bob, SULLIVAN Travis, SULLY Peter, SULTAN Mahmoud, SULTAN Shadi, SULTANA Anthony, SULTANA Michelle, SULTANA Tracy-Lee, SULTANA William, SULU Joyce, SUMABON Jonah, SUMARYONO Ony, SUMELJ Anthony, SUMIDA Midori, SUMMER Roxanne, SUMMERBELL Debby, SUMMERELL Patricia, SUMMERFIELD Imee, SUMMERFIELD Kerry, SUMMERFIELD Simon, SUMMERHAYES Norrie, SUMMERS Allan, SUMMERS Amanda, SUMMERS Faye, SUMMERS Frank, SUMMERS Harry, SUMMERS Janine, SUMMERS Lorrae, SUMMERS Paul, SUMMERS Sally, SUMMERSCALES Chris, SUMMERSIDE Tanya, SUMMERSON Kevin, SUMMERTON Laura, SUMMONS Glen, SUMNER Julia, SUMNER Michelle, SUMNER Roy, SUMNER-POTTS Wendy, SUMNERS Ruth, SUMPTER Cath, SUMPTON Katie, SUN Andrew, SUN Charles, SUN Chong, SUN Di, SUN Jessie, SUN Winnie, SUN Richard, SUN Timothy, SUN Yang, SUN Youngmee, SUN Yun, SUNARTO Levicia, SUNDERLAND Pauline, SUNDQVIST Max, SUNG Hwa, SUNG Jay, SUNG Louise, SUNG William, SUNGA Mariette, SUNTHANKAR Upala, SUNTHARAMOORTHY Sutharsan, SUOS Emi, SUOS John, SUPAARMORAKUL Punnada, SUPANDI David, SUPHERS Tab, SUPPIAH Muthu, SUPRIADI Ahmad, SURANINGDIAH Sophie, SURANSKY Mark, SURAPANENI Sree, SURAVILAS Teraset, SURBEY Elizabeth, SURE VENKATA Suresh, SURGEON Geoff, SURGEON Jennifer, SURIYAARACHCHI Devinda, SURIYANTO Suriyanto, SURJAN Erik, SURMAN-SMITH Robert, SUROPRAJITNO Arion, SURREY Martin, SURTEES Ron, SURTI Amita, SURYA Raj, SURYOBROTO Suryo, SUSAN John, SUSANTO Daniel, SUSANTY Sri, SUSKA Ches, SUSKA Troy, SUSKA Val, SUSNJA Maria, SUSTAR Tony, SUTANTIO Shirley, SUTANTO Arwin, SUTCLIFFE Ann, SUTCLIFFE Bryce, SUTCLIFFE Daryl, SUTCLIFFE Jodie, SUTER Belinda, SUTER Paul, SUTERS Tony, SUTERS Jane, SUTHERLAND Andrew, SUTHERLAND Anthea, SUTHERLAND Barbara, SUTHERLAND Beverley, SUTHERLAND Brad, SUTHERLAND Brian, SUTHERLAND Hilda, SUTHERLAND James, SUTHERLAND Janet, SUTHERLAND Jennie, SUTHERLAND Karen, SUTHERLAND Patricia, SUTHERLAND Rebecca, SUTHERLAND Ryan, **SUTHERN John**, SUTHERN Megan, SUTHERS Don, SUTIONO Felix, SUTOPO Evelin, SUTTIE Pam, SUTTLE Robin, SUTTON Angela, SUTTON Angela, SUTTON Cameron, SUTTON Carole, SUTTON Casey, SUTTON Christopher Joh, SUTTON Debbie, SUTTON Dianne, SUTTON Garry, SUTTON Gary, SUTTON Gayl, SUTTON Gerard, SUTTON Graeme, SUTTON Helen, SUTTON Janice, SUTTON Jenny, SUTTON John, SUTTON John, SUTTON Julie, SUTTON Kaaren, SUTTON Lorraine, SUTTON Matthew, SUTTON Mette, SUTTON Morag, SUTTON Paul, SUTTON Peter, SUTTON Pete, SUTTON Richard, SUTTON Tonia, SUTTON Vonnie, SUVAJASUWAN Voraphong, SUWANDEJ Sasipa, SUZANNE DOROTHEA Jessop, SUZUKI Kumiko, SUZUKI Mariko, SUZUKI Naomi, SUZUKI Reiko, SUZUKI Sawako, SVACHA Halinka, S VAGELLI Carlo, SVALINA Marianne, SVED Peter, SVENSEN Graham, SVENSEN Kari, SVENSON Audrey, SVENSON Dane, SVENSSON Lina, SVOBODA Kristen, SWADLING Chris, SWADLING Mark, SWADLING Tova, SWAIN Lorraine, SWAKER Narissa, SWALES Alan, SWAN Barbara, SWAN Darren, SWAN Megan, SWAN Robert, SWAN Stephen, SWAN Bill, SWANBROUGH Lynne, SWANE Glenn, SWANE Ron, SWANENBERG Robert, SWANK Tammy, SWANN Tui, SWANN Margaret, SWANN Dick, SWANSON Aurora, SWANSON Dorothy, SWANSON Leanne, SWANSON Marisa, SWANSON Anna, SWANTON Sandy, SWASBRICK Bronwyn, SWAYSLAND Clive, SWE Carole, SWEATMAN Daniel, SWEATMAN Les, SWEBBS Annemarie, SWEENEY Aram, SWEENEY Bren, SWEENEY Cherylene, SWEENEY Clive, SWEENEY Jess, SWEENEY Marten, SWEENEY Paul, SWEENEY Joe, SWEENEY Steve, SWEENEY Sue, SWEENEY Therese, SWEENY Carole, SWEENY Gail, SWEENY John, SWEENY Peter, SWEETEN Maureen, SWEETLAND John, SWENSEN Karen, SWENSON Marsha, SWETZ Debra, SWIECKIHALABURA Jakub, SWIFT Gary, SWIFT Glenn, SWIFT Lisa, SWIFT Michael, SWINBURN Elizabeth, SWINDELLS Mandy, SWINTON Stuart, SWITZER Joan, SWYSTUN Allan, SWYSTUN Kat, SY Raph, SYAHAILATUA Augy, SYDENHAM Kim, SYDES Belinda, SYDNEY Sarah, SYDNEY-SMITH Brett, SYED Jim, SYED KHAJA Imran, SYKES Clifford, SYKES Diane, SYKES Jack, SYKES Les, SYKES Matthew, SYKES Bob, SYKES Sharon, SYKORA Jiri, SYKORA Karel, SYLESTER Patricia, SYLVESTER David, **SYLVESTER Kay**, SYLVESTRE Ann, SYME Jan, SYME Jenice, SYMES Murray, SYMONDS Mavis, SYMONS Beryl, SYMONS Brian, SYMONS Ian, SYMONS June, SYMONS Lisa, SYMONS Melanie, SYMONS Merv, SYMONS Mike, SYMONS Peter, SYMONS Sandra, SYMONS Suellen, SYMONS Warwick, SYNNOTT Alethea, SYNNOTT David, SYRATT Jenna, SYROM Philip, SYRON Don, SYVERSEN Jan, SZABO Lajos, SZABO Stephen, SZALAY Suzie, SZALOKI Deb, SZE Kenny, SZEKELY Steve, SZENTKUTI Catherine, SZEPS Josh, SZERDA Kornel, SZETO Jeffrey, SZETU Matthew, SZILAGYI Attila, SZITTNER Kalman, SZOMOR Laszlo, SZUCS Frank, SZUDEJ Lester, SZUKALSKI Mirtha, SZWANENFELD Henry, SZYCZEW Alex, SZYDA Steve, SZYFER Reanna, SZYMANSKI Marek.

T

TA Anne, TA Kimberly, TA Ten, TABACMAN Ana, TABARES Claudia, TABARES Nora, TABATA Kaori, TABE Mandy, TABET Ray, TABONE Joe, TABRETT Scott, TABRETT Shaun, TABUCANON Suzette, TABUKI Toshiro, TACHIBANA Tak, TADACHI Mac, TADDEO Barbara, TADESSE Zed, TADROS Deborah, TAFF George, TAFFA Carmelita, TAFFA Peter, **TAFTHENDRY Senta**, TAGG Alana, TAGGART Cheryl, TAGGART Janet, TAGGART Sally, TAGGART Sue, TAGUE Lynn, TAGUE Jeremy, TAHERI Ali, TAHU Mabel, TAI Jenny, TAI Kai, TAI Jee, TAI Nicholas, TAI Yi-Wen, TAIG Kylie, TAIT Alan, TAIT Alistair, TAIT Carole, TAIT Kaemi, TAIT Lisa, TAIT Merrilyn, TAIT Michelle, TAIT Noel, TAIT Norm, TAIT Bob, TAITO Osea, TAJUDDIN Ayu, TAKABAYASHI Misaki, TAKACS David, TAKADA Yuko, TAKAHASHI Aki, TAKAHASHI Hideko, TAKAHASHI Takashi, TAKAHASHI Yumi, TAKASAKI Yumiko, TAKAYAMA Hiroko, TAKEDA Kinuyo, TAKEDA Mitsko, TAKEKAWA Hiroko, TAKKEN Maki, TAKLA Amir, TALANOA Hala, TALBOT Annette, TALBOT Jane, TALBOT Karyn, TALBOT Lee, TALBOT Mark, TALBOT Micheal, TALBOT Stephen, TALEVICH Stephen, TALEVSKI Ilija, TALIANA Ron, TALIANGIS Michael, TALL Gary, TALLENTIRE Liz, TALLIS David, TALTY Curry, TALTY Doug, TAM Anthony, TAM Betty, TAM Carrie, TAM Chelsea, TAM Chi, TAM Clement, TAM Daisy, TAM Diahann, TAM Eric, TAM Fiona, TAM Henry, TAM Henry, TAM Ho, TAM Janette, TAM Janet, TAM Jenny, TAM Kevin, TAM Kwok, TAM Ricky, TAM Olivia, TAM Patrick, TAM Pauline, TAM Kenneth, TAM Titus, TAM

Virginia, TAM Wendy, TAMA Sarah, TAMAYO Billy, TAMAYO Bobby, TAMBA Emi, TAMBASCO Belinda, TAMBOTO Anna, TAME Noel, TAME JP Noelena, TAMER Joseph, TAMHANE Jaideep, TAMMEKAND Arnold, TAMPI Vijay, TAMPIN Alan, TAMPLIN Adrian, TAMSSEN Elizabeth, TAN Agustin, TAN Aun, TAN Ava, TAN Bee, TAN Bee, TAN Bel, TAN Chen, TAN Cheng, TAN Cindy, TAN Emma, TAN Esther, TAN Franciscus, TAN Harianto, TAN Hiram, TAN Lynn, TAN Jessica, TAN John/ Johnny, TAN Jonathan, TAN Josh, TAN Julian, TAN June, TAN Justin, TAN Coco, TAN Kwan-Tjo, TAN Li, TAN Lucy, TAN Luz, TAN Megan, TAN Pan, TAN Paul, TAN Ping, TAN Raymond, TAN Sheh-Wan, TAN Sok, TAN Soon, TAN Stuart, TAN Susan, TAN Swee, TAN Yenny, TAN Teewoon, TAN Tom, TAN Wil, TAN Yik, TAN Yong, TANAKA Katsu, TANAKA Mari, TANAKA Miki, TANAKA Ryuichi, TANASE Ellina, TANAULI Zafar, TANCEROVA Simona, TANCRED Jeanette, TANCRED Madeleine, TANCRED Wes, TANDON Manjari, TANDON Neha, TANDON Pallavi, TANG Amanda, TANG Andrew, TANG BenYuan, TANG Tom, TANG Choi, TANG Choi, TANG Cindy, TANG Davina, TANG Dorothy, TANG Gabrielle, TANG Gloria, TANG Gordon, TANG Green, TANG Henry, TANG Ivy, TANG Judy, TANG Karen, TANG Kristy, TANG Lawrence, TANG Linda, TANG Maggie, TANG Mary, TANG Michelina, TANG Mui, TANG Kwok, TANG Sam, TANG Shaying, TANG Stanley, TANG Susan, TANG Sylvia, TANG Tiffany, TANG Tony, TANG Tung, TANG Vanessa, TANG Agnes, TANG Yong, TANG Yu, TANG Yu, TANGNEY Yvonne, TANGWONGCHAI Pithcha, TANKALA Kishore, TANKARD Christine, TANKS Earl, TANNEBRING Keren, TANNER Alan, TANNER David, TANNER Lyn, TANNER Fred, TANNER Graham, TANNER Judy, TANNER Keith, TANNER Marina, TANNER Marshal, TANNER Rebecca, TANNER Robert, TANNER Victoria, TANNER Yvonne, TANNOUS George, TANNOUS Leonarda, TANNOUS Nicolas, TANNOUS Peter, TANOU Etienne, TANSWELL Ken, TANSWELL Nell, TANSWELL Peter, TANTI Rob, TANTINI Ossie, TANTRUM Mel, TAO Adeline, TAORMINA Joe, TAPAITAU JR, TAPIA Alicia, TAPIA Blanca, TAPIA Fernando, TAPIA Vladimir, TAPIAFABRES Alejandra, TAPNER John, TAPP Raice, TAPPER Anne, TAPPER John, TAPPLY Simon, TAPPOURAS Niki, TAPSCOTT Judith, TARANEC Natalie, TARANTO Paul, TARASENKO David, TARBOTTON Leanne, TARBOTTON Leon, TARBOX Fran, TARBOX Simon, TARBOX Steve, TARCAN Ilie, TARDENT Greg, TARDENT Timothy, TARDIANI Greig, TARDREW Gordon, TARGETT Meg, TARIGA Joy, TARIQ Omar, TARJAN George, TARKANYI Zoltan, TARLING John, TARLINTON Brian, TARLINTON Ted, TARLINTON Gen, TARLINTON Kaye, TARR Anthony, TARR Claire, TARRAN David, TARRAN Sarah, TARRANT Aleisha, TARRANT Heather, TARRANT Michael, TART John, TARTAKOVER Emily, TARUA Liasi, TASAKA Satako, TASESKA Natasha, TASEVSKI Mick, TASKER Barry, TASKER Catherine, TASKER Jenny, TASKER Kye, TASKER Maryann, TASKIN Sam, TASSELL Helen, TASSELL John, TASSONE Nerina, TASSONE Ralph, TAT Tu, TATAM Pauline, TATAWIDJAJA Rauni, TATE Gayle, TATE Lauren, TATE Marcus, TATE Sally, TATE Shannon, TATHAM Linda, TATSU Mio, TATTAM Anne, TATTAM Danielle, TATTERS Richard, TATTERSALL Dave, TATTERSALL Kylie, TATTERSALL Rod, TATTERSALL Bill, TATTERSELL George, TATTON Ben, TATTON Benjamin, TATULLI Ben, TAUEKI Bradley, TAUFA Mele, TAULU Jimmy, TAUMALOLO Chief, TAUSCHEK Richard, TAVENDER Peter, TAVENER Stirling, TAVERNER Jane, TAVLU Matt, TAW David, TAWADROUS Germine, TAWIL Hanade, TAXALI Naresh, TAY Herman, TAY Roxana, TAYA Mitsuyo, TAYAR Margaret, TAYCO Patrick, TAYLOR Alissa, TAYLOR Alison, TAYLOR Joy, TAYLOR Ania, TAYLOR Ann, TAYLOR Anne, TAYLOR Ann, TAYLOR Ben, TAYLOR Beryl, TAYLOR Bev, TAYLOR Bev, TAYLOR Brian, TAYLOR Brian, TAYLOR Bronwyn, TAYLOR Bronwyn, TAYLOR Carlie, TAYLOR Carolyn, TAYLOR Kate, TAYLOR Cathy, TAYLOR Chris, TAYLOR Christopher, TAYLOR Clive, TAYLOR David, TAYLOR David, TAYLOR Doug, TAYLOR Robert, TAYLOR Libby, TAYLOR Elizabeth, TAYLOR Errol, TAYLOR Eve, TAYLOR Frances, TAYLOR Gerry, TAYLOR Gillian, TAYLOR Graham, TAYLOR Graham, TAYLOR Heather, TAYLOR Helen, TAYLOR Helen, TAYLOR Helene, TAYLOR Jack, TAYLOR Jane, TAYLOR Jan, TAYLOR Janene, TAYLOR Janette, TAYLOR Janet, TAYLOR Jan, TAYLOR Jane, TAYLOR Janine, TAYLOR Jasmine, TAYLOR Jean, TAYLOR Jeff, TAYLOR Jeffrey, TAYLOR Jenette, TAYLOR Jennifer, TAYLOR Jill, TAYLOR Jill, TAYLOR Joan, TAYLOR Keith, TAYLOR John, TAYLOR John, TAYLOR Judy, TAYLOR Judith, TAYLOR Julie, TAYLOR Justin, TAYLOR Karen, TAYLOR Karen, TAYLOR Katie, TAYLOR Katie, TAYLOR Ken, TAYLOR Kenneth, TAYLOR Kerry, TAYLOR Kerry, TAYLOR Kevin, TAYLOR Kim, TAYLOR Kim, TAYLOR Kristy, TAYLOR Lesley, TAYLOR Lesley, TAYLOR Lissanthea, TAYLOR Taylor, TAYLOR Lyn, TAYLOR Lynne, TAYLOR Margaret, TAYLOR Maris, TAYLOR Margaret, TAYLOR Marlene, TAYLOR Martin, TAYLOR Michael, TAYLOR Michael, TAYLOR Nada, TAYLOR Niccole, TAYLOR Noel, TAYLOR Norma, TAYLOR Norm, TAYLOR Owen, TAYLOR Paul, TAYLOR Peter, TAYLOR Peter, TAYLOR Peter, TAYLOR Peter, TAYLOR Philip, TAYLOR Rach, TAYLOR Raelene, TAYLOR Raye, TAYLOR Becky, TAYLOR Rees, TAYLOR Reg, TAYLOR Bob, TAYLOR Robbie, TAYLOR Bob, TAYLOR Bob, TAYLOR Rohan, TAYLOR Ron, TAYLOR Ron, TAYLOR Ron, TAYLOR Rose, TAYLOR Ross, TAYLOR Sandy, TAYLOR Sarah, TAYLOR Scott, TAYLOR Scott, TAYLOR Sharon, TAYLOR Simon, TAYLOR Stephen, TAYLOR Stephen, TAYLOR Stephen, TAYLOR Stuart, TAYLOR Suzy, TAYLOR Tammie, TAYLOR Tracy, TAYLOR Tracey, TAYLOR Trudy, TAYLOR Vickie, TAYLOR Viva, TAYLOR Wayne, TAYLOR Wendy, TAYLOR Wendy, TAYLOR Bill, TAYLOR Yvette, TAYLOR Harry, TAYLOR-CANNON Lew, TAYLORCANNON Sabrina, TAZAWA Mary, TCHAN Mike, TCHERNIN Serge, TCHIRTCHENKO Helen, TCHORLIAN Albert, TCHORLIAN Marie, TCHOU Nancy, TDHADLI Kiran, TE Meng, TE HAARA Rina, TE KOWHAI Toni, TEAGLE Phil, TEAGUE Julie, TEAGUE Lex, TEAKLE Brian, TEAKLE John, TEAL Margaret, TEAL Johanna, TEALE Graham, TEALE Katy, TEAOTAI Louisa, TEARLE Gary, TEARLE Lorraine, TEASDALE Scott, TEASDALE Steven, TEASDALE Tony, TEASDEL Annaliesse, TEASDELL Shane, TEASEL Robert, TEBB Nigel, TEBBUTT Niall, TEDJA Connie, TEE Yen, TEELAND Elizabeth, TEEUW Cor, TEGG Anne, TEH Christine, TEH Conway, TEH David, TEH Francis, TEH Cindy, TEH Jason, TEH Karen, TEH Peck, TEH Ray, TEH E-Xian, TEH Zulfaa, TEHAN Phil, TEHEUHEU Susan, TEHLIWEC Vikki, TEHUPURING Michael, TEIDEMAN Tony, TEKKATTE Shantha, TELEBRICO Jhun, TELEKI Ana, TELFER Anne, TELFER Jordan, TELFER Nathan, TELFER-DUNNE Caz, TELFORD Mal, TELFORD Melissa, TELFORD Ian, TELLOGLOU Stratis, TEMBY Kiera, TEMPLAR Graham, TEMPLE Michael, TEMPLE Simon, TEMPLEMAN JP Barry, TEMPLETON Graham, TEMPLETON Graeme, TEMPLETON Joy, TEMURCUOGLU Eddie, TEN Rose, TENAGLIA Sally, TENCH Edwina, TENEDORA Remy, TENG John, TENHUNEN Tiina, TENORIO Annabelle, TEO Margaret, TEO Seng, TEO Shirley, TEO Siew, TEO Doris, TEODORO Katrina, TEODOROWYCH Boris, TEOH Choon, TEOH Christopher, TEOH Clara, TEOH Huey, TEOH Mei, TEOH Tiong, TEOH Yi-Kwan, TEOH Yun, TEOH Zee, TEPPER Glenn, TER-WIEL Sheridan, TERAUDS Imants, TERAUDS Mara, TERECHOVS Mark, TEREMI Ilon , TERESZKUN Julie, TERLICH John, TERMINELLO Joe, TERP Jane, TERPCOU Chris, TERPOS Christopher, TERPSTRA Jon, TERRACINI Mark, TERRANTROY Debbie, TERRAVECCHIA Susan, TERRELL Lesley, TERRENCE EDWARD Terrence, TERREY Lyn, TERRILL Peter, TERRONE Adriana, TERRY Gillian, TERRY Linda, TERRY Regan, TESHIGAHARA Takako, TESORIERO Cecilia, TESORIERO John, TESORIERO Leanne, TESORIERO Maria, TESTA Louise, TESTER Cheree, TESTER Luke, TESTER Ross, TESTROW Jodie, TETLEY Andrew, TETLEY Maryanne, TETT Allison, TEUBEN Bernard, TEUDT Rick, TEULILO Ana, TEULON Judy, TEULON Michael, TEVER Jo, TEW Jenny, TEWES Billy, TEYCHENNE Kristine, THA Khin, THACKER Glenn, THACKERAY Brian, THACKERAY Ken, THACKRAY Belinda, THACKWRAY Helen, THADANI Chandru, THAI Gia, THAI Phuc, THAI Jason, THAIN Eddy, THAKKAR Rupa, THAKKER Maulik, THAKUR Sumit, THALER Kurt, THAM Nicholas, THANABALASINGAM Nirmalan, THANAKRISHNAN Krish, THANE Gill, THANE Sharon, THANGASAMY Udaya, THANH Lisa, THANKACHAN Elizabeth, THANKI Ketan, THANN Petra, THANN Valerie, THANT Janette, THAPA Naresh, THARION Joe, THARMARAJAH Skanda, THATCHER Maggy, THATCHER Michele, THATCHER Patricia, THAUNG Jerry, THE Fiona, THE Owen, THEAKER Gwenda, THEBRIDGE Carl, THEIN Aung, THEIN Nyan, THEIVENDRARAJAH Raj,

THEKKINIYIL Venu, THELANDER Charlotte, THELMO Bennett, THEMSEN Kirsten, THEMSEN Nick, THEOHAROUS Maria,THEOPHANOU George, THEOS Sofie, THEUMA Mark, THEVASEELAN Stephen, THEVENET Marie, THEWLIS Yvonne, THIBAULT Jean-Luc, THIBAUX Maurice, THIDA Tun, THIEL Christy, THIELE Angela, THIELE Gigi, THIELE Rosemarie, THIELE Sam, THIENTOSAPOL Audrey, THIES Bec, THIESON Jennifer, THIESON Leonard, THILLAINATHAN Mythili, THIMM Wendy, THINN Yin, THINNAKONE Ernie, THIRUCHITTAMPALAM Dharini, THIRY Leah, THISTLETHWAITE Alyssa, THISTLETHWAITE Liz, THISTLETHWAITE Pamela, THISTLETON Garrick, THISTLETON John, THISTLETON Shelley, THIXTON Elspeth, THIXTON John, THODAY Belinda, THODE Stephen, THOEUNG Toro, THOM Jeanette, THOM John, THOMAS Alex, THOMAS Allan, THOMAS Andrew, THOMAS Andrew, THOMAS Anthony, THOMAS Audrey, THOMAS Bev, THOMAS Brett, THOMAS Brian, THOMAS Candy, THOMAS Carol, THOMAS Carol, THOMAS Craig, THOMAS Craig, THOMAS David, THOMAS David, THOMAS Debe, THOMAS Des, THOMAS Diana, THOMAS Di, THOMAS Doug, THOMAS John, THOMAS Emily, THOMAS Evan, THOMAS Libby, THOMAS Garth, THOMAS George, THOMAS Geoff, THOMAS Geradine, THOMAS Graham, THOMAS Heather, THOMAS Hendi, THOMAS Ian, THOMAS Ian,THOMAS Ian, THOMAS Ian, THOMAS Ian, THOMAS Jim, THOMAS Jan, THOMAS Jenny, THOMAS Jerry, THOMAS Joan, THOMAS Jodi, THOMAS John, THOMAS Anne, THOMAS Jon, THOMAS Joe, THOMAS Julia, THOMAS Julie, THOMAS Kate, THOMAS Ken, THOMAS Kevin, THOMAS Kevin, THOMAS Leanne, THOMAS Linda, THOMAS Lyn, THOMAS Lynne, THOMAS Lyn, THOMAS Lyne, THOMAS Ann, THOMAS Mark, THOMAS Myrna, THOMAS Norma, THOMAS Trish, THOMAS Patty, THOMAS Paul, THOMAS Pauline, THOMAS Peter, THOMAS Phillippa, THOMAS Phil, THOMAS Phillip, THOMAS Rachel, THOMAS Rani, THOMAS Rick, THOMAS Richard, THOMAS Bob, THOMAS Ron, THOMAS Ross, THOMAS Sharni, THOMAS Shirley, THOMAS Stan, THOMAS Stephen, THOMAS Stephen, THOMAS Susan, THOMAS Sue, THOMAS Sue, THOMAS Susan, THOMAS Sue, THOMAS Tina, THOMAS Vanessa, THOMAS Wayne, THOMAS Wayne, THOMAS Wil, THOMAS Arthur, THOMAS ROBIN Connah, THOMASMARSH Erin, THOMAS-TROPHIMES Christophe, THOMASON Ron, THOMLINSON Len, THOMMEN Edmond, THOMMEN Gaby, THOMPSON Alan, THOMPSON Alex, THOMPSON Alisa, THOMPSON Alison, THOMPSON Allan, THOMPSON Allan, THOMPSON Ange, THOMPSON Angela, THOMPSON Bart, THOMPSON Bev, THOMPSON Campbell, THOMPSON Carol, THOMPSON Cec, THOMPSON Hedley, THOMPSON Chris, THOMPSON Chris, THOMPSON Colleen, THOMPSON Colleen, THOMPSON Col, THOMPSON Col,

THOMPSON Colin, THOMPSON Daisy, THOMPSON Kawika, THOMPSON David, THOMPSON Dawn, THOMPSON Debbie, THOMPSON Denis, THOMPSON Derek, THOMPSON Dianne, THOMPSON Emily, THOMPSON Emma, THOMPSON Emma, THOMPSON Frances, THOMPSON Gabrielle, THOMPSON Gaye, THOMPSON Geoff, THOMPSON Graham, THOMPSON Graeme, THOMPSON Heather, THOMPSON Jackie, THOMPSON James, THOMPSON Jeffrey, THOMPSON Jenny, THOMPSON Jeremy, THOMPSON Jocelyn, THOMPSON Jodie, THOMPSON Scott, THOMPSON Joy, THOMPSON Judy, THOMPSON Karen, THOMPSON Kate, THOMPSON Kat, THOMPSON Keith, THOMPSON Kerry, THOMPSON Kevin, THOMPSON Laurel, THOMPSON Leanne, THOMPSON Lorna, THOMPSON Betty, THOMPSON Luke, THOMPSON Majorie, THOMPSON Mark, THOMPSON Margaret, THOMPSON Matthew, THOMPSON Maureen, THOMPSON Michael, THOMPSON Michael, THOMPSON Myrtha, THOMPSON Neil, THOMPSON Nicole, THOMPSON Niko, THOMPSON Patricia, THOMPSON Peter, THOMPSON Phelan, THOMPSON Philip, THOMPSON Philip, THOMPSON Phyl, THOMPSON Raels, THOMPSON Ray, THOMPSON Rhonda, THOMPSON Rhonda, THOMPSON Thommo, THOMPSON Rick, THOMPSON Bob, THOMPSON Robyn, THOMPSON Rodney, THOMPSON Ross, THOMPSON Ryan, THOMPSON Sarah, THOMPSON Shevaun, THOMPSON Terry, THOMPSON Trevor, THOMPSON Trevor, THOMPSON Valerie, THOMPSON Vanessa, THOMPSON Vicki, THOMS Steven, THOMSEN Brent, THOMSEN Lyn, THOMSEN Peter, THOMSON Anne, THOMSON Anthony, THOMSON Robb, THOMSON Tommo, THOMSON Carina, THOMSON Craig, THOMSON Dorothy, THOMSON Elizabeth, THOMSON Jo, THOMSON Graeme, THOMSON Helen, THOMSON Helen, THOMSON Holly, THOMSON Jack, THOMSON Jaie, THOMSON Jane, THOMSON Jeffrey, THOMSON Jennifer, THOMSON Jennie, THOMSON Jenni, THOMSON Jill, THOMSON Craig, THOMSON Kate, THOMSON Larry, THOMSON Lindsay, THOMSON Mary, THOMSON Marie, THOMSON Martin, THOMSON Myra, THOMSON Peter, THOMSON Peter, THOMSON Rob, THOMSON Roslyn, THOMSON Roslyn, THOMSON Shona, THOMSON Steve, THOMSON Theodore, THOMSON Warwick, THOMSON Wendy, THOMSON-HICKS Andrea, THONFELD Eva, THOO Chee, THORBURN David, THORDARSON Pall, THORLEY Chris, THORLEY Meg, THORN Anne, THORN Brooke, THORN Nicole, THORN Pat, THORN Torie, THORNBER Di, THORNBLOM Christina, THORNE Glenys, THORNE Jason, THORNE John, THORNE Margaret, THORNE Michael, THORNE Michael, THORNE Peter, THORNE Sandie, THORNE Tim, THORNETT Richard, THORNTHWAITE Melissa, THORNTON Lex, THORNTON Barry, THORNTON Campbell, THORNTON Carly, THORNTON Des,

THORNTON Donald, THORNTON Jennifer, THORNTON June, THORNTON Margaret, THORNTON Kirrily, THORNTON Lee, THORNTON Mel, THORNTON Meredith, THORNTON Stuart, THORNTON Sally, THORNTON Suzanne, THORNTON Tammy, THORNTON Tim, THOROGOOD Doug, THOROGOOD Janette, THORPE Ian, THORPE Karyn, THORPE Kenneth, THORPE Malissa, THORPE Mark, THORPE Marion, THORPE Neil, THORPE Bob, THORPE Robert, THORPE Roy, THORPE Spencer, THORPE Thomas, THORSEN Betina, THREADGOLD Mariska, THREADGOLD Mark, THREDGOLD Jenny, THRELFALL Carolyn, THRELFALL Elwyn, THRIMURTHULA Santosh, THRUM Emma, THUEMLING Bernnard, THURAISWAMY Siva, THURBON Scott, THURECHT AnneMaree, THURECHT Brian, THURECHT Judy, THURECHT Rita, THURLING Barry, THURLING Dale, THURLOW Harry, THURLOW Jason, THURLOW Pamela, THURLOW Ray, THURSTON Linda, THURTELL Karen, THURTELL Melissa, THWIN Albert, THYRD Belinda, THYRD Debbie, THYREGOD Vagn, TIAN Evelyn, TIAN Ju-Ping, TIAN Rochelle, TIAN Shaung, TIAN Xue, TIANG Susan, TIBBS David, TIBERI Michael, TIBONI Roberta, TICKELL Lynne, TICKLE Brooke, TICKLE Damien, TICKLE Sharon, TICKNER Kerrie, TICKNER Peta, TIDSWELL Kerry, TIEMAN Sabrina, TIERMAN Irene, TIERMAN Neil, TIERNEY Anne, TIERNEY Ann, TIERNEY Don, TIERNEY Johneen, TIERNEY Liam, TIERNEY Rebecca, TIEU Thihue, TIGANI Raff, TIGHE Barb, TIGHE Brian, TIGHE Richard, TIGHE Susanne, TILDEN Geoff, TILDEN Patrick, TILDEN Richard, TILDSLEY Ken, TILDSLEY Margaret, TILIA Daniel, TILL Joy, TILL Suzi , TILLER Denise, TILLER Hans, TILLETT Megan, TILLEY Alex, TILLEY Benjamin, TILLEY Leana, TILLEY Mitchell, TILLMAN Bronwyn, TILLOTT Janine, TILO Dorzie, TILSED Tracey, TILSTED Poul, TIMAR Frank, TIMBRELL Nicole, TIMBS Fran, TIMBS George, TIMBURY Kristy, TIMMINS Maureen, TIMMINS Pat, TIMMINS Pete, TIMMINS Robyn, TIMMINS Ross, TIMMINS Sally, TIMMINS Sylvia, TIMMONS Peter, TIMMONY Velella, TIMMS Denis, TIMMS Ian, TIMMS Mark, TIMMS Robyn, TIMONERA Pant, TIMOTHY Elizabeth, TIMOTHY George, TIMTCHEV Ivan, TINDALL Allan, TINDALL Jaine, TINDALL Ron, TINDIGLIA Steve, TING Hoi, TING Philip, TING Tony, TING-KONG Chris, TINGLE Greg, TINK Kay, TINNER Alan, TINNER Kathie, TINSLEY Scott, TIONG John, TIONG Siew, TIOSECO Anna, TIPANI Terena, TIPLER Carol, TIPLER John, TIPPAYAWAT Jean, TIPPETT Graham, TIPPETT Justin, TIPPETT Sandie, TIPTON Ron, TIPTON Sue, TIRADO Marcelo, TIRADOS Rudy, TIRANDA Era, TIRCHETT JR Saviour, TIRICOVSKI Diana, TIRTA Fransiskus, TIRUMALASETTI Raghuram, TISCHLER Sue, TISDALE Michelle, TISDALL Nena, TISIOT Karine, TISSINGTON Colin, TISSINGTON Rhondda, TITMUS Leah, TITMUSS Amy, TITMUSS Angela, TITMUSS Kathy, TITO Rana, TITTELBACH Karen, TITTERTON Anne, TITTERTON Phillip, TIVA Dors, TIVER John, TIVOLI George, TIZZONE Piera, TJAHJA

Francisca, TJAHJAKUSUMA Sofie, TJAN Angelin, TJEN Julie, TJENDRA Rudy, TJEUW JR Michael, TJHIN Darius, TJOA Caroline, TJOA Cathy, TJOENO Lusy, TJOPUTRA Erwin, TJORE Ketil, TO David, TO Hung, TO Karen, TO Kelvin, TO Kelvin, TO Edmond, TO Trinh, TOBIN Leo, TOBIN Lorna, TOBIN Maurice, TOBIN Michael, TOBIN Pauline, TOBOREK DJ, TODA Anthea, TODD Alan, TODD Fiona, TODD Fiona, TODD Ian, TODD Joan, TODD Julie, TODD Ken, TODD Melissa, TODD Myra, TODD Peter, TODD Philip, TODD Roslyn, TODD Ruth, TODDIE Bruce, TODDYWALLA Adil, TODHUNTER Garry, TODHUNTER Geoff, TOEDT Ellie, TOFLER Maree, TOFT Per, TOGNOLINI Lisa, TOH Jason, TOH Jono, TOH Justin, TOH Sandra, TOH Shyann, TOHI Dj, TOHILL Anne, TOHNAI Tsutomu, TOIVANEN Nea, TOIVONEN Dennis, TOIVONEN Kolin, TOIVONEN Trevor, TOKARCZYK Ted, TOKARZ Anni e, TOKARZ Jim, TOKAZU Miyuki, TOKCAN Kerim, TOLAND Brian, TOLEDO Ernie, TOLEMAN John, TOLENTINO Athaleya, TOLHURST Anthony, TOLHURST Brian, TOLHURST Lynne, TOLHURST Ray, TOLL Mick, TOLLEFSEN Glenda, TOLLEY-RISCH Fiona, TOLMIE Barrie, TOLMIE Wayne, TOLNAY Judit, TOLONE Ugo, TOLUK Melek, TOMA Judy, TOMA Younan, TOMAC Val, TOMAN Debbie, TOMAN Greg, TOMAN-MONDEGUER Francoise, TOMAS Jorge, TOMAS Katrina, TOMASETTI David, TOMASI Louisa, TOMASSINI Oriella, TOMAZOS Emmanuel, TOMCZYK Teresa, TOMEI Donato, TOMEK Margaret, TOMELDEN-SEGGIE Thelma, TOMES Marc, TOMIC Michael, TOMIC Tom, TOMKINS Carolyn, TOMKINS Cynthia, TOMKINS David, TOMKINS Jenny, TOMKINS Sally, TOMLIN Dale, TOMLIN David, TOMLIN Raymond, TOMLIN Roger, TOMLINSON Ann, TOMLINSON Ian, TOMLINSON Julie, TOMLINSON Nick, TOMLINSON Peter, TOMLYN Maureen, TOMPKINS Helga, TOMPSON Margaret, TOMPSON Norrazalishah, TOMS Keleigh, TOMS Ricky, TOMSU Frank, TON David, TON Sheila, TONDI Peter, TONECHAI Nadine, TONG Zeng, TONG Chris, TONG Keith, TONG Elvan, TONG Hong, TONG Lilian, TONG Mandy, TONG Michael, TONG Sam, TONG Tiffany, TONG Winnie, TONG Gigi, TONG Yuen, TONGE Duck, TONKIN Anne, TONKIN Brenden, TONKIN Cassi, TONKIN Connie, TONKIN Geoff, TONKIN Helen, TONKIN Shannon, TONO Iwen, TOO Henry, TOOBY Arthur, TOOGOOD Ann, TOOGOOD Jim, TOOHEY Helen, TOOHEY Iain, TOOHEY Michel, TOOHEY-MICHELIS Anne, TOOLE Rebecca, TOOLIN Mal, TOOLIN Stuart, TOOMBS Keith, TOOMEY Yvonne, TOON Danielle, TOONEN Hubert, TOOTH Patricia, TOPALOV Louise, TOPFER Corinne, TOPHAM Helen, TOPLIS Colin, **TOPLIS Ralph**, TOPOR Helen, TOPOR Krystyna, TOPORSTANLEY Sacha, TOPP Damian, TOPP Karen, TOPP Nikki, TOPP Shirley, TOPS Sebastian, TORDA Phylliz, TOREY Brett, TORMEY Rachel, TORNIAINEN Paivi, TORNYA Susie, TOROK Andrew, TOROK Stephen, TORPY Gerry, TORRE Edgar, TORRECILLA Ben, TORREGZOSA ITURBIDE Paula, TORRES Irene, TORRES Margaret, TORRES Millie, TORRES Mercedes, TORRES Rafael, TORRES Rod, TORRESAN Paula, TORRINGTON Hayley, TORTORA Roberta, TORY Bruce, TOSH Philippa, TOSTI Andrew, TOSUN Filiz, TOTH Joe, TOTH Les, TOTH Magdalena, TOTH Michael, TOTH Wendy, TOTOEVA Luba, TOTTEN Richard, TOTTLE Lisa, TOUCHARD Chris, TOUCHARD Linda, TOUGH Julian, TOUHILL Fiona, TOULEMONDE Clement, TOULMIN Lindsay, TOUMA Pam, TOUMA Sandra, TOURNAS Vaya, TOURNAY Nathan, TOURNIER Keith, TOURTAS John, TOUT Mark, TOUZELL Di, TOVAR Natalia, TOW Glenda, TOW Thel, TOWART Barbara, TOWELL Graham, TOWELL Judy, TOWELL Stephen, TOWELL Val, TOWERS Barrie, TOWERS Chris, TOWERS John, TOWERS Terry, TOWEY Eddie, TOWEY Val, TOWHIDI Nasser, TOWLE Alana, TOWLE Malcolm, TOWLE Paul, TOWMA Shamiran, TOWN Russell, TOWNE Sam, TOWNEND David, TOWNEND Sarah, TOWNER Rosemary, TOWNER Steve, TOWNSEND Alan, TOWNSEND Albert, TOWNSEND Barry, TOWNSEND Cathie, TOWNSEND Cathy, TOWNSEND Colin, TOWNSEND David, TOWNSEND Dean, TOWNSEND Denise, TOWNSEND Don, TOWNSEND Liz, TOWNSEND Bette, TOWNSEND Glenn, TOWNSEND Graeme, TOWNSEND James, TOWNSEND John, TOWNSEND Katie, TOWNSEND Lawrie, TOWNSEND Leone, TOWNSEND Marion, TOWNSEND Narelle, TOWNSEND Pat, TOWNSEND Paul, TOWNSEND Phil, TOWNSEND Sue, TOWNSEND Hawea, TOWNSEND Hendy, TOWNSHEND Cora, TOYOKAWA Michiko, TOZER Cathie, TOZER Nicole, TOZER Rhiannon, TOZZI Anna, TRABINGER Kerry, TRACEY Jane, TRACEY Lisa, TRACHSLER Doris, TRACY Penny, TRACY Robert, TRAD Rachid, TRAEGER Mark, TRAFALSKI Clare, TRAGOS Irene, TRAIKOGLOU Panayiotis, TRAILL Alison, TRAINOR Sean, TRAJKOVSKI Peter, TRAJKOVSKI Peter, TRAJKOVSKI Tatiana, TRAKOSAS Penny, TRAM Helen, TRAM Jimmy, TRAM Anh, TRAN Peter, TRAN Angela, TRAN Anne, TRAN Anthony, TRAN Cam, TRAN Dao, TRAN Dao, TRAN Diana, TRAN Diana, TRAN Minh, TRAN Edward, TRAN Giang, TRAN Hang, TRAN Hieu, TRAN Hien, TRAN Hung, TRAN Phong, TRAN Johnny, TRAN Yen, TRAN Kiet, TRAN Lily, TRAN Lily, TRAN Linh, TRAN Manh, TRAN Maria, TRAN Mark, TRAN Maurice, TRAN Minh, TRAN Nicole, TRAN Sheng, TRAN Sophia, TRAN Stephanie, TRAN Sylvie, TRAN Tam, TRAN Thuy, TRAN Trang, TRAN Trong, TRAN Tuyen, TRAN Uy, TRAN Van, TRAN Wendy, TRAN William, TRAN Vonnie, TRANBY Henry, TRANTER Ben, TRANTER Steve, TRAPP Barry, TRAPP Marie, TRATCH Robert, TRAUNTNE R Lisa, TRAURIG Steve, TRAVERS Luke, TRAVERS Pippa, TRAVERS Vicki, TRAVERS Wendy, TRAVIS Philip, TREACEY David, TREACEY Kelly, TREACY Daniel, TREACY Denise, TREACY Paula, TREBLE Bill, TREDGET Claire, TREDINNICK Lee, TREDREA Ledly, TREES Ronald, TREFZGER Andreas, TREGEAR Gregg, TREGEAR Noel, TREGONING Gayle, TREGURTHA Ros, TREHAN Raj, TREHARNE David, TREHARNE Jeanine, TREHEARNE Zara, TREICHEL Jurgen, TRELEAVEN Janey, TRELOAR Jenny, TRELOAR Kate, TRELOAR Lynne, TRELOAR Michelle, TRELOUR Paul, TRELOUR Val, TREMAIN Ian, TREMAINE David, TREMBATH Donna, TREMBATH Lea, TREMBATH Murray, TREMBLAY Karine, TRENEAR Jill, TRENERRY Bruce, TRENERRY Edith, TRENKOVSKI Nick, TRENKOVSKI Valentina, TRENT Karin, TRENT Rogerson, TRENTHAM Storm, TRETHEWEY Dawn, TRETHEWY Christopher, TREUR Linda, **TREVANION Maureen**, TREVARTHEN Jan, TREVASCUS Terry, TREVASKIS Fraser, TREVASKIS Michael, TREVASKIS Peter, TREVASKIS Peter, TREVENA Scott, TREVETHAN Kerry, TREVILLION Stephen, TREVISAN Nara, TREVITT Jan, TREVORROW Barry, TREW Sandra, TREZISE Cyndy, TRIANTAFYLLOU William, TRIBBECK Danni, TRICKETT Doreen, TRICKETT Ron, TRIFFETT Don, TRIFILO Adrian, TRIGG John, TRIGGS Jessica, TRIGGS Rebecca, TRIGGS Ruth, TRIGLIA Donna, TRIHEY Tim, TRIJASSON Leniac, TRIM Gene, TRIM Gregory, TRIMARCHI Gerry, TRIMBOLI Domenic, TRIMBOLI Jay, TRINCA Michael, TRINDALL Dot, TRINDALL Raelene, TRINDER Norman, TRINDER Rob, TRINDER Robyn, TRINH David, TRINH Kim, TRINH Quynh, TRINH Thai, TRINH Thuy, TRINH To-Nu, TRINH Wendy, TRINH Vanita, TRINIDAD Adele, TRINIDAD Michael, TRINKS John, TRIOLO Frances, TRIONFO HuiHsin, TRIPICIANO Gino, TRIPODI Beverley, TRIPODI Matthew, TRIPODY John, TRIPOLONE Sam, TRIPP Steven, TRIPP Steve, TRIST Les, TRITON Sara, TRITSINIOTIS Eleni, TRIVEDI Chetan, TRIVEDI Maulik, TRIVEDI Rashmi, TRNKA Milos, TROAKE Paul, TROATH Sue, TROCHE Oscar, TROEDEL Martin, TROFYMOWYCH Delaine, TROMPF Leisel, TRONC Nicole, TRONQUET Monique, TRONSON Mark, TROODE Christopher, TROPE Jonathan, TROSETH Silje, TROSSER Jann, TROTH Mark, TROTHE Adrian, TROTTER Inge, TROTTER-CALLEJA Lynette, TROUNCE Don, TROUNCE Nancy, TROUNCE Robert, TROUSDALE Susan, TROVATO Cristina, TROVATO Daniel, TROVATO Vince, TROW Rodney, TROW Ron, TROWER Jo, TROXELL Christopher, TROY Alan, TROY Effie, TROY Jeff, TROY Terry, TROY Wally, TRUANT Sarah, TRUBKA Marcella, TRUBKA Michael, TRUMAN Judy, TRUMPOLD Ursula, TRUONG Alex, TRUONG Christine, TRUONG Huey, TRUONG Jasmyne, TRUONG Leanne, TRUONG Lee, TRUONG Minnie, TRUONG Nancy, TRUONG Phoebe, TRUSCOTT Tobby, TRUSCOTT Danielle, TRUSCOTT Betty, TRUSKETT Joan, TRUSKETT Phil, TRUSSLER Michael, TRUSWELL Jo, TRUSWELL John, TRUSWELL Rick, TRUSWELL Trudie, TRY Lesley, TRYERS Emma, TRYFONOPOULOS Dimitrios, TRYFONOPOULOS Souzi, TRZOPEK Greg, TSACOS Christie-Lee, TSAGLAKIS Stephanie, TSAI Nicole, TSAI Fen, TSAKANOV Serge, TSAKONAS Frances, TSALANIDIS Joseph, TSANG Christine, TSANG Connie,

TSANG David, TSANG Eugene, TSANG Fai, TSANG Jo, TSANG Sosan, TSANG Bob, TSANG Winnie, TSATSARONIS James, TSE Alex, TSE Eurosia, TSE Kelvin, TSE Kylie, TSE Jesse, TSE Quincy, TSE Clarissa, TSE Lily, TSE Wil, TSE Mary, TSE SHEUNG CHEONG Jason, TSEKENIS Peter, TSEMBELIS Zoi, TSENG Chih-Wei, TSENG Chih, TSIANTARLIS Les, TSIKRIKIS Steven, TSIM Charles, TSIM Shin, TSIMBLER Leonid, TSIOUGOS Angela, TSIPOURAS Wayne, TSIRBAS Tsirbas, TSIRIMIAGOS Jim, TSIROS John, TSIROS Paul, TSO Ben, TSO Sophia, TSO Hoi, TSO Lorna, TSO Paul, TSOBAWIKAS Tony, TSOI Ellen, TSOI Justin, TSOLAKIS Michael, TSOLAKIS Phyllis, TSOTSOS Nick, TSOUNIS Helen, TSUI Amy, TSUI Danny, TSUI Eric, TSUI John, TSUI Kit, TSUI Penny, TSUI Yi, TSUL Kimmy, TSZ-WING NG Wayne, TSZYU Boris, TSZYU Kostya, TU Jing, TU Lebinh, TU Mylinh, TUAZON Irene, TUBMAN Charles, TUBMAN Phillip,TUCH Michelle, TUCK Lin, TUCK Pam, TUCKER Anne, TUCKER Bev, TUCKER Bronwyn, TUCKER Bruce, TUCKER Craig, TUCKER Cynthia, TUCKER James, TUCKER Jane, TUCKER Jenny, TUCKER Ken, TUCKER Neil, TUCKER Penny, TUCKER Sharon, TUCKER Steve, TUCKER Stuart, TUCKER Vicki, TUCKER Vivienne, TUCKETT Mandy, TUCKETT Shan, TUDGE Denise, TUDORIN Nara, TUENNECKE Rainer, TUERO Joe, TUFFLEY Jill, TUFT Darrell, TUFUGA Siliva, TUGWELL Denise, TUGWELL Elizabeth, TUGWELL Heidi, TUGWELL Holly, TUHIN Darius, TUIDIA Sol, TUILAU Bai, TUISORISORI-CHAMBAULT Ottui, TUKA Ana, TULIC Frank, TULIC Lisa, TULLEY Anne, TULLOCH Jean, TULLOCH Graeme, TULLOCH Joy, TULLOCH Ross, TULLOH Louise, TULLY Bob, TULLY Tom, TULLY Warren, TUMBER Maria, TUN Thida, TUNBRIDGE Daren, TUNBRIDGE Dave, TUNBRIDGE Max, TUNBRIDGE Peter, TUNCDORUK Handan, TUNCHON Dave, TUNG Connie, TUNG Nancy, TUNG Terry, TUNG Wilfred, TUNKS Lee, TUNNEY Patrick, TUNSTALL Amanda, TUPPIN Amy, TUREK Angela, TURK Ryan, TURLAND Fran, TURLEY Carolyn, TURLEY Marion, TURMANIS Juris, TURNBULL Aaron, TURNBULL Alice, TURNBULL Allison, TURNBULL Ann, TURNBULL Danielle, TURNBULL Dennis, TURNBULL Don, TURNBULL Liz, TURNBULL Elspeth, TURNBULL Graeme, TURNBULL Ian, TURNBULL Jenny, TURNBULL Jill, TURNBULL Justine, TURNBULL Nev, TURNBULL Richard, TURNBULL Dick, TURNBULL Robert, TURNBULL Sam, TURNBULL Sue, TURNBULL Tom, TURNBULL Angela, TURNBULL-MOODY Kate, TURNER Allen, TURNER Annerie, TURNER Ann, TURNER Ann, TURNER Mark, TURNER Belinda, TURNER Brett, TURNER Bryce, TURNER Chantal, TURNER Cherie, TURNER Clive, TURNER Dan, TURNER David, TURNER Deirdre, TURNER Deidre, TURNER Valerie, TURNER Maureen, TURNER Elaine, TURNER Elenore, TURNER Elizabeth, TURNER Elizabeth, TURNER Evelyn, TURNER Glen, TURNER Gordon, TURNER Helen, TURNER Irene, TURNER Arab, TURNER Jane, TURNER Jill, TURNER Jo, TURNER Joan, TURNER Jocelyn, TURNER Judith, TURNER Justine, TURNER Kathleen, TURNER Kathryn, TURNER Kellie, TURNER Kim, TURNER Kirsty, TURNER Kylie, TURNER Lew, TURNER Lorraine, TURNER Lorraine, TURNER Louise, TURNER Lyn, TURNER Marion, TURNER Michael, TURNER Michael, TURNER Michaela, TURNER Michelle, TURNER Michael, TURNER Miranda, TURNER Murray, TURNER Nev, TURNER Dave, TURNER Nicole, TURNER Norma, TURNER Patricia, TURNER Paul, TURNER Pauline, TURNER Petrina, TURNER Peter, TURNER Randel, TURNER Reysan, TURNER Ron, TURNER Suzanne, TURNER Tammy, TURNER Thais, TURNER Toby, TURNER Tracey, TURNER Violet, TURNER-DAVIS Susan, TURNEY Pam, TURNIP Mohan, TURNNIDGE-KENWORTHY Emma, TURRA Marco, TURRI Marc, TURTIAINEN Jarkko, TURTON Chris, TURTON Geoff, TUSLER Steve, TUTISAI JC, TUTOKA Mohelagi, TUTSCH Tom, TUTT Gary, TUTTLE John, TUTTLEBEE Glenda, TUTTLEBEE Wendy, TUTTY John, TUTUAFU Delphine, TUTUK Kudret, TUTUNOA Lisaberth, TUXFORD Beula, TUXFORD Charles, TUZOVIC Gordana, TWADDELL Scott, TWEDDLE Ron, TWEEDDALE Katrina, TWEEDIE Charles, TWEMLOW Cassandra, TWIDELL Sara, TWIGG Judy, TWISS Janette, TWISS Simone, TWITE Christopher, TWOMEY Anthony, TWOMEY Mark, TY Christine, TYACK Paul, TYACKE Elizabeth, TYACKE Philip, TYAS Heather, TYDEMAN Bob, TYE Dennis, TYE Elinor, TYE Ivan, TYE Pam, TYERS Kristy, TYGIELSKI Carol, TYLER Debbie, TYLER Georgia, TYLER John, TYLER Judith, TYLER Kathleen, TYLER Nita, TYLER Shawn, TYLER Stuart, TYMKIW Karl, TYMOC Peter, TYMOSZUK Pablo, TYNDALE-BISCOE Simon, TYNDALL David, TYNDALL Kate, TYNE Jodi, TYRIKOS Sam, TYRRELL Graham, TYRRELL John, TYRRELL Markham, TYRRELL Berti, TYSON Millie, TYSON Janelle, TYSON Lorraine, TYSON Trish, TYSON Sara, TYSSEN Alison, TZANNES Fay, TZAVARAS Annette, TZIGERAS Athena, TZIMOS Tassos.

U

U Kevin, UBALDE Adrian, UBRIHIEN Ashley, UCHIDA Chi, UCHIYAMA Jun, UCHIYAMA Lumi, UCHIYAMA Yukari, UDA Kanae, UDAGAWA Jun, UDDIN Mayen, UDDIN Ritu, UDOVICIC John, UDOVICIC Louise, UEBEL Chris, UEBEL Ian, UEDA Tomomi, UEMURA Ted, UENO Hiromi, UENOYAMA Masae, UGOALAH Nick, UHLHORN Nadine, UHRIG Debbie, UHRWEISS Benedek, UJHELYI Babette, UJSZASZI Tom, ULATKO Maja, ULIBARRI Vicki, ULJEVIC Wilson, ULLMAN Alysa, ULLMAN Jen, ULLMAN Mark, ULLOA Abdon, ULLOA Catrin, ULPH Annette, ULRICK Craig, ULRIK Paul, ULUTAS Aytac, UMALI Edmund, UMANSKY Albert, UMAR Bhatti, UMEZU Hiromi, UNDERHILL Geoff, UNDERWOOD Jenny, UNDERWOOD Kath, UNDERWOOD Margaret, UNFERDORBEN Frank, UNG Simon, UNG Peter, UNGAR David, UNGER Elizabeth, UNGLIK Harry, UNICOMB Barry, UNSWORTH Adi, UNSWORTH Mark, UNTHANK Shirley, UNWIN Alison, UNWIN Carol, UPFILL Frank, UPHAM Rose, UPHILL Ron, UPPAL Zesh, UPRETY Rajendra, UPRETY Sunil, UPTON Alec, UPTON Kellie, UPTON Ken, UPTON Susan, URANKIT Elwarin, URBAN Dave, URBANCIC Frank, URBANSKI Richard, URBEN Urby, URCH Ian, URE Mark, URE Shauna, UREN Sandra, URETA Julia, URH Mary, URIBE Vanessa, URIBE HENAO Gustavo, URMENETA Elsa, UROE Lilly, URQUHART Lance, URQUHART Michelle, URQUHART Narrelle, URQUHART Rob, URQUHART Sarah, URREA Eliseo, URSINO Dominic, URWIN Kelly, URWIN Steve, USHER Glenn, USHER Helen, USHER Jayne, USOV Belinda, USSHER Bryan, USUI Masatoshi, UTHOF Dean, UTICK Ray, UTRIA-COUTISSON Ines, UYANIK Adem, UYTENGSU Glenndon, UZUN-GRUEL Jeannine.

V

VAAFUSUAGA Saunoa, VACCARELLA Anne, VACCARELLA Michael, VADALA Roslyn, VADIVELOO Yoges, VAGO Anderson, VAHAVIOLOS Diane, VAILE George, VAINS Annette, VAINS Greg, VAISHYA Sharad, VAITAFE Rauva, VAKALIWALIWA Susana, VALACAS Michael, VALAREZO Sara, VALCIC Sonja, VALE Charles, VALE Hollis, VALE Joselyn, VALENCIA Cristina, VALENCIA Meg, VALENTE Teresa, VALENTI Joe, VALENTINE Chris, VALENTINE Dom, VALENTINE Justine, VALENTINE Megan, VALENTINE Pamela, VALENTINE Trent, VALENTINE FLINT Angie, VALENZUELA Linda, VALENZUELA Marcia, VALERA Arturo, VALERI Julie, VALERI Walter, VALIOS Dimitrios, VALKA Marie, VALKAI Frank, VALKENBURG Maria-Louise, VALL Fran, VALLAK Jodi, VALLANCE Brent, VALLANCE John, VALLAYDAM Marlon, VALLER Joan, VALLETTA Joe, VALLIAR Kadir, VALLONE Javier, VALSAMAKIS Con, VALSAMIS Steven, VALVIS Anthony, VAMVALELLIS Desie, VAN Can, VAN Samantha, VAN Soon, VAN ALTENA Ian, VAN ARENDONK Janet, VAN ASTEN Frank, VAN BAAST Gerry, VAN BAVEL Anton, VAN BOCKEL Adriana, VAN BODEGRAVEN Helen, VAN BREE Betsy, VAN BRUGGE Chiaki, VAN CAMP Monique, VAN COEVORDEN Danielle, VAN DAM Helen, VAN DE HOEK Jane, VAN DE HOEK Peter, VAN DE WALL Toni, VAN DE WATER Rudy, VAN DE WEYER Eric, VAN DE WEYER Sharni, VAN DEN BERG Andre, VAN DEN BERG Paulus, VAN DEN BOK Sally, VAN DEN HEUVEL Helma, VAN DEN HOEK Joanna, VAN DEN NIEUWENHUIZEN Norbert, VAN DEN TILLAART Janine, VAN DER ARK Mark, VAN DER ENDE Estelle, VAN DER HORN Bernard, VAN DER HURK Robb, VAN DER KAMP Anna, **VAN DER LINDEN Julia**, VAN DER PADT Veronica, VAN DER STRUIK Bernice, VAN DER VLIET Len, VAN DER WAGEN Merilynn, VAN DER WALL Jilska, VAN DER WALL Lucy, VAN DER WALLEN Marty, VAN DER WALT Stephan, VAN DER WOODE Willy, VAN DER WOUDE Ria, VAN DIJK Ria, VAN DONGEN John, VAN DONGEN Wendy, VAN DORT Barbara, VAN DRUTEN-KARS Ieris, VAN DULLEMEN Cathy, VAN DYK Liz, VAN DYKE Phoenix, VAN ERP Harm, VAN ESSEN Andrew, VAN EWIJK

Denise, VAN GELDER Herman, VAN GELDER Mick, VAN GELDER Max, VAN GENDER Ellie, VAN GOOL Martin, VAN GRAFHORST Sandra, VAN GRINSVEN Lisa, VAN GROESEN Lesley, VAN HAM John, VAN HERP Shane, VAN HERTEN Geoff, VAN HOLLAND Simon, VAN HOLST PELLEKAAN Sheila, VAN HOMRIGH Pam, VAN HOVE Marquita, VAN HUNNIK Jas, VAN KEMPEN Aart, VAN LEEUWEN Tigh, VAN LOO Capucine, VAN LUYN Carol, VAN MAGILL Brian, VAN MEGEN Sue, VAN MENS Augustina, VAN MEYGAARDEN Tiny, VAN MEYGAARDEN Rob, VAN NEIJENHOFF Paul, VAN NETTEN Anna, VAN NETTEN Jacobus, VAN NIEKERK Dawn, VAN NUS John, VAN NUS Tricia, VAN OORT Edith, VAN OPSTAL Piet, VAN OYEN Bill, VAN PUTTEN Kirsty, VAN REESCH Paul, VAN ROOY Wilhelmina, VAN SCHAICK Esther, VAN TIL Dick, VAN ULET Irene, VAN VOORTHUIZEN Ellen, VAN VREUMINGEN Yolanda, VAN VUGT Hans, VAN VUGT Rossella, VAN WELY Brad, VAN WESSEL Cath, VAN WESSEL Rob, VAN WYCK Helen, VAN-DE-LEY Darren, VAN-DER-LEY Gwenda, VAN-DER-LEY Kylie, VAN-DERLEY Mathew, VANBREUGEL Deborah, VANCE Ben, VANCE Brooke, VANCE Gregory, **VANCE Johanna**, VANCE Kevin, VANDAM Fiona, VANDEBURGT Gary, VANDEN BERG Jason, VANDEN BERGH Damien, VANDEN HOGEN Anne, VANDENBERG Renee, VANDERBURG Ingrid, VANDERJAGT Hans, VANDERKEILEN Anthony, VANDERLINDEN Ronald, VANDERNENT Tim, VANDERPUTT Tanya, VANDERSLUYS Judy, VANDERSTOK Joanne, VANDERTUUK Tony, VANDERVAERE Maurice, VANDERVELDE Michael, VANDERVLIST Kylie, VANDERWERT Glenn, VANDERWOUDE Ben, VANDERZWET Roz, VANDEWATER Melissa, VANDYKE Yvonne, VANE-TEMPEST Susanne, VANGHEL Marjory, VANHOFF John, VANHOFF Jenny, VANHOFF Kathleen, VANJOUR Wendelynn, VANKUYK Jack, VANNECK Jane, VANO Jorge, VANYAI Simon, VAPORIS Micki, VARAGNOLO Giordana, VARCOE Christine, VARCOE-COCKS Julie, VARDANEGA Primo, VARELA Elisa, VARGA David, VARGA Keith, VARGA Terri, VARGAS Gus, VARIGOS Greg, VARIPATIS Constantine, VARJAVANDI James, VARLOW Lauren, VARLOW Megan, VARNERIN Ingrid, VARNEY Marty, VARNIER Flora, VARNS David, VARRENTI Jeanette, VARSHNEY Ajay, VARSHNEY Kavita, VARSHNEY Savita, VARTANIAN Serge, VARTULI Bruno, VARTULI Sue, VARTULI Susan, VASARHELYI Lara, VASCONEZ Amparo, VASIC Bart, VASIC Vesna, VASIL Koula, VASIL Peter, VASILIADES Anthony, VASILIADES George, VASILIKOU Alexia, VASISTA Anna, VASISTA Esh, VASITTAPAPAT Nootjarin, VASQUEZ Frank, VASS Alex, VASS George, VASS Joe, VASSALL Val, VASSALLO Amanda, VASSALLO Chris, VASSALLO Indu, VASSALLO Joe, VASSALLO Lilian, VASSALLO Bill, VASSILACOS Deborah, VASSILEVSKA Jiva, VASSILI Kevin, VASSILI Peter, VASSILIADIS Helen, VASSILIEFF Michael, VASSILIOU Peter, VASWANI Ross, VAUDAT Payvand, VAUGHAN Angie, VAUGHAN Catherine, VAUGHAN Di, VAUGHAN Peter, VAUGHAN Jeanette, VAUGHAN Joan, VAUGHAN John, VAUGHAN Peter, VAUGHAN Michele, VAUGHAN Naomi, VAUGHAN Patricia, VAUGHAN Robin, VAUGHAN Ron, VAUGHAN Ron, VAUGHN Ros, VAUSE Glen, VAUX Susan, VAY Christine, VAYANI Harris, VAZ Amanda, VAZ Wally, VAZENIOS Nick, VAZOURAS Kon, VAZOURAS Sonia, VAZQUEZ-RECIO Luis, VEAL Nicky, VEALE Brenton, VEALE Jane, VEASEY Jackie, VEATER Lawrence, VECELLIO Tony, VECELLIO Judy, VECOVSKI Paul, VEDI Aditi, VEECH Anna, VEECH Renee, VEEDER Candace, VEENSTRA Alan, VEENSTRA Peter, VEERABANGSA Roshmin, VEERABANGSA Sudeshini, VEERAGANTI DEV Jaya, VEGA Edith, VEGA Gus, VEGA Inger, VEGA Jaime, VEGA Red, VEGA Rodigo, VEGA Vlaudin, VEGA Vrelo, VEGA Vriduar, VEGA Vromel, VEIDELIS Leia, VEIGA Susana, VEIGLI Dave, VEIL Claude, VEINBERG Nicola, VEITCH Christopher, VEITCH Danuta, VELARDE John, VELASCO Erlinda, VELASCO Virginia, VELASQUEZ Blanca, VELAYUTHAM Selvi, VELAZQUEZ DECIGA Hugo, VELEZ Carlos, VELI Mustafa, VELICKOVICH Svetlana, VELING Trent, VELIZ Walter, VELJOVIC Dejan, VELKOSKI Ivan, VELKOVSKI Petar, VELLA Amanda, VELLA Annette, VELLA Ann, VELLA Frank, VELLA Jan, VELLA Marg, VELLA Michael, VELLA Paul, VELLA Samuel, VELLA Thomas, VELOSO FERNANDEZ Jose, VELTMEYER Perry, VENDY Willi, VENGETAS Anu, VENHAUS Toni, VENIS Jim, VENKATESH Manju, VENKATESHWASAA RAO Gargipati, VENN Michael, VENNING Damien, VENNING Tom, VENTER Mark, VENTURA Imeldo, VENTURA Mary, VENTURA Sab, VENTURA Silvio, VENTURINI Carlos, VENTURINI Micah, VENTURINO Michelle, VERAART Sonja, VERCO David, VERCO Jane, VERDEC Louise, VERDICH Madeleine, VERDOORN Gerry, VERDUIN Nettie, VERE Walter, VEREY Carolyn, VEREY George, VEREY Kim, VEREY Roberta, VERGARA Julia, VERGARA Magdalena, VERGARA Manuel, VERGARA Millie, VERGELIUS Pamela, VERGHIOS Michael, VERGHIS Jackie, VERGHIS Mich, VERHAGEN Amanda, VERHAGEN Meredith, VERHEYEN Paul, VERHOEVEN Hans, VERMESGABOS Andras, VERMEULEN Ilse, VERMEULEN Klaartje, VERNIERS Hans, VERNON Benjamin, VERNON James, VERNON Kaye, VERNON Kellie, VERNON Kim, VERNON Pamela, VERNON Pamela, VERON Sheree, VERON Zac, VERRAN Murray, VERRELL Paul, VERRIER Bert, VERROCCHIO Illaria, VERROS Helene, VERRY Cathy, VERSTAPPEN Dianne, VERSTEEGH Ronald, VERSTEGEN Betty, VERSTEGEN Peter, VERVELD Bernard, VERVLIET Erik, VERWEY Kristen, VERWEY Sheridan, VERZELETTI Lew, VERZOSA Ricardo, VESELINOVIC Marko, VESIC John, VEVERKA Narelle, VEZER Inge, VI Michael, VIAL Andrew, VIAL Margaret, VIAPIANA Danny, VIAPIANA Hector, VIAPIANA Trish, VIBERT Lester, VICARS John, VICARS Sandra, VICARY Sandra, VICENTE Carlos, VICHUR Suresh, VICK Lesley, VICKERS Christine, VICKERS Damien, VICKERS Wayne, VICKERS Graeme, VICKERS Grub, VICKERS Kirsty, VICKERS Mem, VICKERS Herrin, VICKERSTAFF Jin, VICKERY Glenn, VICKERY Jade, VICKRESS Frank, VICTOR Prekesh, VIDA Kathy, VIDAL Adriana, VIDAL Mario, VIDLER Elizabeth, VIDLER Peter, VIDLER Margaret, VIDMAR Maria, VIDMAR Sarah, VIDMAR Silvana, VIDONI Julio, VIDONI Silvana, VIEGAS Kathryn, VIEIRA Angelica, VIEIRA Paulo, VIERBOOM Jenny, VIG Balvinder, VIGAR Glenn, VIGLIENZONE Rudi, VIGLINO Robert, VIJAYAKUMAR Vidhyu, VIJEYARASA Ramona, VIK Chris, VIK Vlado, VILA Pablo, VILE Darren, VILE Jenni, VILLA Anthony, VILLAESCUSA Mario, VILLALBA LADINO Anibal, VILLANUEVA Erlinda, VILLANYI George, VILLARAN Julia, VILLAREAL Dan, VILLARROYA Dee, VILLASENOR-AGUILAR Hector, VILLAZON Victoria, VILLEGAS Rey, VILLIERS Steven, VINALL Greg, VINCE Bill, VINCENT Bronwyn, VINCENT Catherine, VINCENT Geoffrey, VINCENT Margaret, VINCENT Patrick, VINCENT Prue, VINCENT Ron, VINCENT Sohail, VINCENT Tamara, VINCENTI Richard, VINCENTY Lydia, VINCENZI John, VINE Steve, VINE Suzie, VINE Wayne, VINER Chris, VINER-SMITH Chris, VINES Barry, VINEY Natalie, VINING Ben, VINING Mark, VINK Alison, VINK Stephen, VINKO Shara, VINNER Georgiy, VINNER Georgiy, VINOD Edward, VINSON Shannon, VINTILA Iris, VINTILA Meta, VINTON Robert, VIRAG Katalin, VIRGONA Jess, VIRGONA Justine, VIRGONA Michelle, VIRGONA Stephen, VIRIYARAMPO Phra, VIRTUE Jacob, VISCAINO QUINTANA Sonia, VISCIONE Joe, VISENTINI Paul, VISI John, VISIONE Doug, VISIONE James, VISSER Kathryn, VISWANATH Aravind, VISWANATHAN Murali, VISWANATHAN Shehara, VITO Elena, VITTOR D avid, VITZTHUM Anette, VIVAS Edgar, VIVIANI Iain, VIZCAINO LOSA Susan, VIZUETE Saturnino, VIZY Priscilla, VLACHOUTSIKOS Iris, VLAHOPOULOS Peter, VLAHOS Evangelos, VLASICH Sue, VLATKOVIC Nino, VLIETSTRA John, VLIETSTRA Jo, VLISMAS Mischa, VO An, VO Henry, VO Giao, VO Tan, VO Thi, VO Paul, VO Tuan, VOGEL Peter, VOGELMANN Karen, VOGES Neville, VOGES Stella, VOGLER Andrew, VOGT Louise, VOGT Michele, VOICU Nelu, VOIGT Sarah, VOIGT Shane, VOIGTLANDER Anja, VOIKIN LAMBERTH Lorna, VOLEK Zdenek, VOLKERTS Dorothy, VOLKLAND Gerry, VOLKLAND Gisela, VOLKOV Veronica, VOLLER Jon, VOLLER Lyndal, VOLONAKIS Mina, VOLPATO Julie, VOMACKA Frank, VON BUELOW Malte, VON CERVA Ivan, VON KONIGSMARK Andrew, VON KONIGSMARK John, VON SUMMER Hollis, VONDRA Peter, VONG William, VONHOFF Bart, VORA Aftab, VORK Anita, VORLICEK Simon, VOROBIEFF Pete, VORONOVA Taisia, VORREITER Franz, VOS Maggie, VOSGERAU Detlev, VOSPER Adele, VOSPER Dione, VOSS Rose, VOSU Alida, VOTANO Joe, VOULANAS Nick, VOUT Jenny, VOUT Judy, VOYSEY Michael, VOZILA Olivia, VOZZO Stephen, VRABAC Nick, VRAGALIS Nick, VRANA Erik, VRANICH Bruno, VREKE Ben, VRINS Daniel, VROEGH Esther, VROOMBOUT Frank, VROOMBOUT Ruth, VRTKOVSKI Peter, VU

Anne, VUCIC Margie, VUJICIC Damian, VUKALOVICH Douglas, VUKASOVIC Matthew, VULAONO Lopeti, VULETIC Marjan, VULETICH Nada, VUMBACA Ross, VUONG Chiton, VUONG Eileen, VUONG Jenny, VUTUKURI Satya, VUU Tu, VYDEN Sarah, VYSE Jocelyn, VYSE Maureen, VYSMA Wendy, VYTHEESWARAN Malar, VYTIACO Jerome.

W

WAALDER Roger, WACH Isabelle, WACHER Henry, WACHMAN Diane, WACHMAN Stanley, WACHTER Anke, WADA Junji, WADAS Jenny, WADDELL Gary, WADDELL Heather, WADDELL Jason, WADDELL Myf, WADDELL Sandi, WADDELL Tanya, WADDINGTON Gordon, WADDINGTON Janine, WADE Andrew, WADE Anita, WADE Annette, WADE Brian, WADE Catherine, WADE Lauren, WADE-FERRELL Glen, WADEFERRELL Peter, WADEMAN Barry, WADEY John, WADHAM Yvonne, WADHAWAN Anil, WADLEY Colleen, WADLEY James, WADSWORTH Damien, WADSWORTH Glenn, WADSWORTH Pam, WAEGELING Carl, WAEGER Sandra, WAETFORD Charles, WAGENAAR HUMMELINCK Petra, WAGG Noel, WAGHORNE Cielo, WAGNER Amy, WAGNER Beryl, WAGNER Hannelore, WAGNER Jenny, WAGNER Lorraine, WAGNER Nikkie, WAGNER Peter, WAGNER-PASQUIER Anthony, WAGSTAFF Allen, WAGSTAFF Anne, WAGSTAFF Jane, WAHEDI Matinn, WAHL Carol, WAHLBERG Keith, WAHLSTROM Anna, WAI Susu, WAI-TOE Maung, WAI-TOE Nila, WAIGHT Darrell, WAINOHU Christina, WAINWRIGHT Jan, WAITE Jeremy, WAITE John, WAITE Steven, WAITHMAN Anne, WAITING Brian, WAJON Ria, WAJSWELNER Henry, WAKABAYASHI Yuko, WAKE Terry, WAKEFIELD Margaret, WAKEFIELD James, WAKEFIELD Jo, WAKEFIELD John, WAKEFIELD John, WAKEFORD Anne, WAKEHAM David, WAKELING Sara, WAKELY Greg, WAKEMAN Susanne, WAKERLEY Estelle, WAKIM Bass, WAKIM Donna, WAKIM Paul, WALDA Maurice, WALDECK Kym, WALDEN Nicole, WALDMANN Nicholas, WALDOCK Margaret, WALDON Lance, WALDRON Alan, WALDRON Diane, WALDRON Jack, WALDRON Liz, WALDRON Mike, WALDRON Nina, WALDRON Robyn, WALES Brodie, WALES Jayne, WALES Ken, WALES Ray, WALEY Pat, WALFORD Ron, WALI Manizha, WALI Pary, **WALK Noeline**, **WALKER Agnes**, WALKER Albert, WALKER Andrew, WALKER Andrew, WALKER Angus, WALKER Anne, WALKER Anne, WALKER Arch, WALKER Bruce, WALKER Carol, WALKER Clare, WALKER Darren, WALKER David, WALKER David, WALKER Debbie, WALKER Neil, WALKER Di, WALKER Dolly, WALKER Don, WALKER Liz, WALKER Ellen, WALKER Joy, WALKER Emily, WALKER Gary, WALKER Glenn, WALKER Harry, WALKER Helen, WALKER Lindsay, WALKER Janet, WALKER Jason, WALKER Jeff, WALKER Jenifer, WALKER Joanne, WALKER Jo, WALKER Johnnie, WALKER John, WALKER John, WALKER John, WALKER John, WALKER John, WALKER Karen, WALKER Karen, WALKER Karan, WALKER Kev, WALKER Larry, WALKER Lee, WALKER Les, WALKER Lindsay, WALKER Linda, WALKER Lisa, WALKER Lois, WALKER Lynette, WALKER Anne, WALKER Martin, WALKER Marjie, WALKER May, WALKER Matthew, WALKER Matt, WALKER Megan, WALKER Michael, WALKER Natalie, WALKER Neroli, WALKER Pam, WALKER Pam, WALKER Pam, WALKER Peter, WALKER Peter, WALKER Phil, WALKER Rhonda, WALKER Robin, WALKER Neil, WALKER Bob, WALKER Ross, WALKER Rowena, WALKER Sam, WALKER Sam, WALKER Sharon, WALKER Shirley, WALKER Stanley, WALKER Shirley, WALKER Sue, WALKER Terry, WALKER Tom, WALKER Tim, WALKER Tony, WALKER Trudy, WALKER Veronica, WALKER Mena, WALKER-HARRIS Jan, WALKER-SMITH Harry, WALKERDEN Crystal, WALKINSHAW Mary, WALKLING Peter, WALKOM Michael, WALL Anne, WALL Tony, WALL Doreen, WALL Frank, WALL John, WALL John, WALL Judith, WALL Kate, WALL David, WALL Stan, WALLACE Ness, WALLACE Alan, WALLACE Beverley, WALLACE Cameron, WALLACE Catherine, WALLACE Colette, WALLACE Georgina, WALLACE Greg, WALLACE Ian, WALLACE Irene, WALLACE Jan, WALLACE Jeannie, WALLACE Jenny, WALLACE John, WALLACE Jack, WALLACE Kerry, WALLACE Margaret, WALLACE Michael, WALLACE Paula, WALLACE Rachael, WALLACE Rebecca, WALLACE Rod, WALLACE Sarah-Jayne, WALLACE Sarah, WALLACE Susan, WALLACE Bill, WALLBRIDGE Alan, WALLEN Bob, WALLER Cheryl, WALLER Frank, WALLER Jay, WALLER Vicki, WALLEY Jan, WALLGREN John, WALLIN Judith, WALLIN Trevor, WALLING Sarah, WALLINGTON Kathleen, WALLINGTON Natasha, WALLIS Andrew, WALLIS Andrew, WALLIS Chris, WALLIS David, WALLIS Jill, WALLIS Karen, WALLIS Ken, WALLIS Lorraine, WALLIS Lorraine, WALLIS Ngaire, WALLIS Nicky, WALLIS Shari, WALLIS Stephen, WALLISH Lena, WALLMAN Joyce, WALLWORK Darren, WALLWORK Jason, WALMSLEY Ashley, WALMSLEY Belinda, WALMSLEY Greig, WALMSLEY Stephen, WALPOLE Sharyn, WALRUT Bernard, WALSH Alan, WALSH Alan, WALSH Alice, WALSH Andrew, WALSH Anthony, WALSH Tony, WALSH Audrey, WALSH Brian, WALSH Caroline, WALSH Cathy, WALSH Clare, WALSH Clare, WALSH Danielle, WALSH Darren, WALSH Emily, WALSH Helen, WALSH Jack, WALSH Jacqui, WALSH Jim, WALSH Jim, WALSH James, WALSH Jason, WALSH Jo, WALSH Joy, WALSH Karen, WALSH Katie, WALSH Joye, WALSH Kerrie, WALSH Laurel, WALSH Leanne, WALSH Leith, WALSH Linda, WALSH Lisette, WALSH Marilyn, WALSH Michael, WALSH Noelene, WALSH Patty, WALSH Peter, WALSH Peter, WALSH Sean, WALSH Shirley, WALSH Stuart, WALSH Susan, WALSH Terry, WALSH Toni, WALSHAM John, WALSHAW Nathan, WALSHE David, WALTER Cecile, WALTER Emma, WALTER Gloria, WALTER Janelle, WALTER Jodee, WALTER Korabelnikoff, WALTER Sue, WALTERS Albert, WALTERS Barbara, WALTERS Brian, WALTERS Charley, WALTERS Chantal, WALTERS Denis, WALTERS Dixie, WALTERS Wally, WALTERS Glenda, WALTERS John, WALTERS Jo, WALTERS Katrina, WALTERS Khris, WALTERS Kristy, WALTERS Kylie, WALTERS Matthew, WALTERS Patricia, WALTERS Rebecca, WALTERS Stan, WALTERS Teresa, WALTERS Reed, WALTHER Jane, WALTHER John, WALTHEW Kate, WALTHO Shelley, WALTON Ann, WALTON Daniel, WALTON Darren, WALTON Gaille, WALTON Gillian, WALTON Judy, WALTON Michael, WALTON Naomi, WALTON Peter, WALTON Sally, WALTON Steve, WALTON Stephen, WALTON Toni, WALZEL Stefan, WAN Amy, WAN Bonny, WAN Kim, WAN K, WAN Ethan, WAN Stephen, WAN Susan, WANG Alice, WANG Alvin, WANG Angela, WANG Bernie, WANG Bing, WANG Ben, WANG Judy, WANG Buyang, WANG Charles, WANG Alex, WANG Chunxun, WANG David, WANG Dong, WANG Emyo, WANG Eric, WANG George, WANG Gui, WANG Jia, WANG Jian, WANG Charles, WANG Kang, WANG Karen, WANG Liang, WANG Lijie, WANG Louis, WANG Mathee, WANG Michael, WANG Mo, WANG Nancy, WANG Ni, WANG Rui, WANG Sharon, WANG Susan, WANG Tong, WANG Tracy, WANG Wen, WANG Wei, WANG Wendy, WANG Tony, WANG Wendy, WANG Michelle, WANG Emma, WANG Xiaomin, WANG Xwe, WANG Ya, WANG Yan-Feng, WANG Alma, WANG Yi, WANG Ying, WANG Jerry, WANG Zhi, WANG Zhi, WANGTAKO Susanna, WANKE Aaron, WANNAN Terry, WANSTALL Ross, WANT Paul, WAPLES Catherine, WAQQAS Waqqas, WARBRICK Graham, WARBURTON Aaron, WARBURTON Lydia, WARBURTON Richard, WARBY John, WARBY John, WARBY Margaret, WARD Michael, WARD Allan, WARD Amanda, WARD Amanda, WARD Barry, WARD Barrie, WARD Carolyn, WARD Cait, WARD Chris, WARD Craig, WARD David, WARD David, WARD Dianne, WARD Emma, WARD Emma, WARD Frank, WARD Gillian, WARD Grahame, WARD Greg, WARD Greg, WARD Warren, WARD Jan, **WARD John**, WARD John, WARD John, WARD John, WARD John, WARD Judy, WARD Katherine, WARD Kenrick, WARD Kylie, WARD Lew, WARD Luke, WARD Malcolm, WARD Mark, WARD Mark, WARD Marie, WARD Maryanne, WARD Mark, WARD Max, WARD Megan, WARD Meryl, WARD Norma, WARD Pam, WARD Ray, WARD Ray, WARD Rhonda, WARD Bob, WARD Steve, WARD Tim, WARD Tim, WARD Wendy, WARD William, WARD William, WARD Yvonne, WARDELL Lena, WARDELLJOHNSON Ian, WARDELL-JOHNSON Trisha, WARDEN Isobel, WARDEN Ross, WARDEN Stuart, WARDILL Steven, WARDLAW Anne, WARDLE Aaron, WARDLE Penny, WARDMAN Ian, WARDROBE Brad, WARDROP Michael, WARDROP Tim, WARE Doug, WARE Francoise, WARE Hermoine,

WARE Joel, WARE Phillip, WARE Simon, WARE Steve, WARE Susan, WAREHAM Paul, WARES Pip, WARGENAU Maryska, WARHOLM Arild, WARHURST Trish, WARING Sam, WARK Matthew, WARK Michelle, WARK Pam, WARLOW George, WARLTERS Ian, WARMAN Lesley, WARN Gisela, WARN Janelle, WARN Joyce, WARN Pat, WARN Steve, WARNCKEN Jack, WARNE David, WARNE Ralph, WARNEKE Fiona, WARNEKE Heather, WARNEKE Kathy, WARNEKE Ken, WARNER Ashley, WARNER Brad, WARNER Brett, WARNER Brian, WARNER Craig, WARNER Darlene, WARNER David, WARNER Dinah, WARNER Doug, WARNER Jan, WARNER John, WARNER John, WARNER Justine, WARNER Les, WARNER Maggie, WARNER Marion, WARNER Narelle, WARNER Petrina, WARNER Sarah, WARNES Caroline, WARNOCK Damo, WARNOCK Natalie, WARR Colleen, WARR Fred, WARR Gayle, WARR Poppy, WARRAND James, WARRAND Juliet, WARRELL Matthew, WARREN Amanda, WARREN Chris, WARREN David, WARREN Fiona, WARREN Hayley, WARREN Jackie, WARREN Jasmin, WARREN Jennifer, WARREN Jennifer, WARREN John, WARREN John, WARREN John, WARREN Judi, WARREN Kate, WARREN Kate, WARREN Kathleen, WARREN Kate, WARREN Kim, WARREN Leon, WARR EN Luke, WARREN Elizabeth, WARREN Mitsuyo, WARREN Peter, WARREN Phil, WARREN Raelene, WARREN Rick, WARREN Richard, WARREN Richard, WARREN Robert, WARREN Ron, WARREN Ron, WARREN Price, WARREN Sarah, WARRICK Del, WARRILOW Jane, WARRILOW Peter, WARRINGTON Ann, WARSITO Wally, WARTON Aileen, WARTON Gail, WARTON Pamela, WARWAR Alex, WARWICK Brian, WARWICK David, WARWICK Mary, WARWICK Petrina, WARWICK Ross, WARWICKER Shirley, WASHINGTON Bobby, WASHINGTON Dorothy, WASHINGTON Mick, WASHINGTON Regina, WASHINGTON Bob, WASHINGTON Sarah, WASHINGTON Terry, WASILEWICZ Gosia, WASLEY Harry, WASON Liz, WASS Craig, WASS Anne, WASSALL Dave, WASSEF Kamal, WASSEF Lillian, WASSELL Jim, WASSERMAN Sue, WASSILENKO Neil, WASSON Em, WASSON Jenna, WASTELL Nyree, WATANABE Kaoru, WATANABE Makiko, WATCH Linda, WATCHORN Doug, WATERHOUSE Helen, WATERHOUSE Kim, WATERMAN Kay, WATERS Annette, WATERS Cheryl, WATERS David, WATERS Grant, WATERS Helen, WATERS Joel, WATERS Lesley, WATERS Monique, WATERS Pat, WATERSON Beverley, WATERSON Heather, WATERSON Laurie, WATERSON Nyree, WATERWORTH Eric, WATERWORTH Mark, WATHERSTON Rory, WATHLE Albert, WATKEYS Rachael, WATKINS Barb, WATKINS Gail, WATKINS Julie, WATKINS Kevin, WATKINS Kim, WATKINS Noele, WATKINS Robert, WATKINS Ron, WATKINS Susan, WATKINS Tanya, **WATKINS Wayne**, WATKINSON Ross, WATLING Colin, WATLING Sandra, WATMAN Allan, WATMORE Lisa, WATSFORD John, WATSON Adrian, WATSON Lex, WATSON Alli, WATSON Amanda, WATSON Ann, WATSON Aroha, WATSON Ben, WATSON Bev, WATSON Carolyn, WATSON Carmel, WATSON Cheryl, WATSON Chloe, WATSON Chris, WATSON Clinton, WATSON Daniel, WATSON Wato, WATSON Deborah, WATSON Dianne, WATSON Ted, WATSON Ehetere, WATSON Fiona, WATSON Geoff, WATSON Glenn, WATSON Gloria, WATSON Graeme, WATSON Hazel, WATSON Helen, WATSON Helen, WATSON Helen, WATSON Hugh, WATSON Hugh, WATSON Jim, WATSON James, WATSON Jayne, WATSON Jeannie, WATSON Jenny, WATSON Joann, WATSON John, WATSON John, WATSON Joshua, WATSON Joy, WATSON Judy, WATSON Justin, WATSON Kathiy, WATSON Katrina, WATSON Ken, WATSON Kevin, WATSON Lee, WATSON Leone, WATSON Luke, WATSON Lyndall, WATSON Mark, WATSON Mardi, WATSON Maureen, WATSON Max, WATSON Michelle, WATSON Nancy, WATSON Neale, WATSON Pat, WATSON Pat, WATSON Paul, WATSON Penny, WATSON Peter, WATSON Raelene, WATSON Renelle, WATSON Richard, WATSON Richard, WATSON Ricky, WATSON Robert, WATSON Rod, WATSON Sarah, WATSON Irene, WATSON Toby, WATSON Tory, WATSON Warren, WATSON Wayne, WATT Alastair, WATT Alexander, WATT Brian, WATT Chris, WATT David, WATT Deanna, WATT Elizabeth, WATT Graeme, WATT John, WATT John, WATT Judy, WATT Margaret, WATT Melinda, WATT Nat, WATT Reg, WATT Siobhan, WATT Suze, **WATT Wendell**, WATTERS Mark, WATTERS Sidney, WATTON Cheryl, WATTON Laura, WATTON Les, WATTS Barbara, WATTS Danni, WATTS Graeme, WATTS Jeanie, WATTS Kath, WATTS Maggie, WATTS Philip, WATTS Ralph, WATTS Richard, WATTS Bob, WATTS Ross, WATTS Victor, WATTS Will, WAUGH Andrew, WAUGH Ashleigh, WAUGH Dave, WAUGH Naomi, WAUGH Pauline, WAUGH Rex, WAWN Geoff, WAWN John, **WAY Felicity**, WAY John, WAY Mike, WAY Norman, WAY Beck, WAYGOOD Jenny, WAYLEN David, WAYLING Sharyn, WAYNE Ian, WAYNE Laima, WAYPER Murray, WAYTHE Sian, WEAKLEY Val, WEALE Brad, WEALE Suzie, WEAR Lee, WEARIN Raymond, WEARNE Bruce, WEARNE Keith, WEARNE Sylvette, WEATHERALL David, WEATHERBURN Tracy, WEATHERLY Henny, WEATHERSTONE Anthony, WEAVER Charlie, WEAVER Jeffrey, WEAVER Nicole, WEAVER Prue, WEAVING Geoff, WEBB Alan, WEBB Alan, WEBB Andrew, WEBB Arthur, WEBB Barry, WEBB Beryl, WEBB Betty, WEBB Cassy, WEBB David, WEBB Drew, WEBB Georgina, WEBB Gloria, WEBB Webby, WEBB Greg, WEBB Heidi, WEBB Jenny, WEBB Judy, WEBB Kate, WEBB Kerrie, WEBB Loz, WEBB Lawrie, WEBB Leonie, WEBB Lorraine, WEBB Margaret, WEBB Martin, WEBB Melissa, WEBB Melanie, WEBB Michael, **WEBB Monika**, WEBB Pat, WEBB Paul, WEBB Phil, WEBB Richard, WEBB Ronald, WEBB Sally, WEBB Terry, WEBB Tokiko, WEBB Val, WEBB Vanessa, WEBB Warren, WEBBER Andrew, WEBBER Caroline, WEBBER Dianne, WEBBER Karen, WEBBER Susan, WEBBER Sue, WEBBER Suzanne, WEBER Brett, WEBER Danielle, WEBER Ollie, WEBER Pascal, WEBER Robbie, WEBER Shaun, WEBER Yvette, WEBSTER Amanda, WEBSTER Andrew, WEBSTER Angie, WEBSTER Athol, WEBSTER Chris, WEBSTER Des, WEBSTER Gai, WEBSTER Helen, WEBSTER Irene, WEBSTER Jennie, WEBSTER Jonathan, WEBSTER Kevin, WEBSTER Kieran, WEBSTER Lodie, WEBSTER Marilyn, WEBSTER Michael, WEBSTER Natalie, WEBSTER Peter, WEBSTER Ron, WEBSTER Sara, WEBSTER Sue, WEBSTER Veronica, WEBSTER Vicki, WEBSTER Bill, WEDDING Tracy, WEDEMEIJER Harry, WEDES Debbie, WEDES Rhyees, WEDESWEILER Craig, WEDGWOOD Ray, WEDMAIER Barry, WEE Daryl, WEED Chris, WEEDEN Gail, WEEDON Jackie, WEEDON Mark, WEEKES Barry, WEEKES Jo, WEEKES Ken, WEEKES Mi, WEEKES Nigel, WEEKES Pat, WEEKES Shelley, WEEKES Mrs., WEEKS Denise, WEEKS Greg, WEEKS John, WEEKS Paul, WEEKS Richard, WEEKS Scott, WEERAKOON Thilini, WEGNER Kim, WEHLMANN Cordula, WEHNER Gerd, WEHNER Helen, WEHNER Margaret, WEHR Daniel, WEHR Dayle, WEHR Malcolm, WEHRLE Lucinda, WEI Diana, WEI Tina, WEIBERLE Jenny, WEICKHARDT John, WEIDNER Ronald, WEIER Keith, WEIGH Maree, WEIJERS Willy, WEILING Charles, WEININGER Edith, WEINSTEIN Beth, WEINSTOCKDRORY Sagit, WEIR Alan, WEIR Barry, WEIR Josh, WEIR Michael, WEIR Pat, WEIR Roger, WEIR Sarah, WEIR Stephen, WEISHEIT Matt, WEISMANTEL Sharon, WEISMANTEL Bill, WEISS Anne, WEISS Margaret, WEISS Renate, WEISSKE Georg, WEISSKE Veronica, WELCH April, WELCH Jenny, WELCH John, WELCH Rick, WELDEN Diane, WELDEN Kerri, WELDEN Bob, WELDON Beris, WELFARE Matthew, WELFORD Jimmy, WELFORD Mike, WELHAM Warren, WELKE Jeff, WELLER Peter, WELLER David, WELLER Timothy, WELLFARE Judith, WELLFARE Judy, WELLHAM Katie, WELLINGS Ben, WELLINGS Elli, WELLINGS Lindsay, WELLINGS Matthew, WELLINGS Matt, WELLINGS Ross, WELLINGS Vanessa, WELLINGTON Nina, WELLINGTON Phillip, WELLINS Helen, WELLMAN Wayne, WELLS Alisha, WELLS Andrew, WELLS Cindy, WELLS Irene, WELLS Jason, WELLS John, WELLS Kerry, WELLS Margaret, WELLS Matt, WELLS Robyn, WELLS Bob, WELLS Ron, WELLS Sally, WELLS Serena, WELLS Stephen, WELLS Stefanie, WELLS Sue, WELLS Tania, WELLS Bill, WELSBY Stan, WELSCH Erika, WELSH Anthony, WELSH Bindy, WELSH Caroline, WELSH Deane, WELSH Greg, WELSH Louise, WELSH Nelma, WELSH Nicole, WELSH Richard, WELSH Teena, WELTON Jenny, WEMYSS Josephine, WEMYSS Mark, WEN Wendy, WENBAN Neville, WENDAFRASH Yodit, WENDELBORN Tracy, WENDT Baden, WENDT Glenn, WENDY Wei, WENG Charles, WENG Xing-Tai, WENGOBORSKI Klaus, WENMAN Alice,

WENMAN Chris, WENMAN Jim, WENSOR Ken, WENTLAND Lynn, WENTWORTH Annie, WENTWORTH Laurel, WENTZEL Karl, WERCHON Carl, WERE Wellesley, WERE Michael, **WERLE Theodora**, WERNDURFF Beate, WERNER Helmut, WERNER Kimball, WERNER Michael, WESLEY Lynch, WESLEY Michelle, WESSEL Bill, WESSELING Karen, WESSLER Bob, WEST Adam, WEST Alisha, WEST Allan, WEST Bev, WEST Brian, WEST Bryan, WEST Carol, WEST Cassie, WEST Cathy, WEST Westy, WEST David, WEST David, WEST Donna, WEST Gayl, WEST Geoff, WEST Heather, WEST Linda, WEST Jacky, WEST Jaden, WEST Jason, WEST Jeanette, WEST John, WEST Laurie, WEST Lyn, WEST Margaret, WEST Mike, WEST Rita, WEST Ron, WEST Sue, WEST Wen, WESTAWAY David, WESTAWAY Rebecca, WESTBURY Craig, WESTBURY Lynne, WESTELL Cherie, WESTERHOF Jan, WESTERLAND Ann, WESTERMAN Janet, WESTERWELLER John, WESTFALLEN David, WESTLEY Cathy, WESTLING David, WESTMACOTT Barb, WESTMACOTT Bob, WESTON Adam, WESTON Anthony, WESTON Barry, WESTON Christina, WESTON Garry, WESTON Judith, WESTON Mel, WESTON Quinton, WESTON Terri, WESTREN Ann, WESTREN Don, WESTWOOD Barbara, WESTWOOD Carolyn, WESTWOOD Dick, WESTWORTH Di, WETSTEYN Hans, WETTASINGHE Amali, WETTON Harry, WETZEL Deborah, WEXSELBLATT Christian, WEYLAND Bernie, WEYMARK Nicole, WEYNEN Nicky, WHAITE Anne, WHALAN Barry, WHALAN Janece, WHALAN Jeff, WHALAN Jeni, WHALAN Kevin, WHALAN Kim, WHALE Wendy, WHAN Greg, WHANT Brian, WHARRIE Philip, WHARTON Kerry, WHARTON Scott, WHARTON Susie, WHATHAM Don, WHATHAM Fiona, WHATMAN Ian, WHATMAN Rachel, WHATMAN Sarah, WHATSON Elena, WHEALY John, WHEALY Nicholas, WHEALY Tricia, WHEATE Rhys, WHEATLEY Brian, WHEATLEY Wendy, WHEATLEY Ian, WHEATLEY Janelle, WHEATLEY Jennifer, WHEATLEY Mark, WHEATLEY Murray, WHEATLEY Susie WHEBLE Anne, WHEELAHAN Dan, WHEELER Bernie, WHEELER Cathleen, WHEELER Charles, WHEELER Claire, WHEELER Danielle, WHEELER David, WHEELER Helen, WHEELER John, WHEELER Julie, WHEELER Keith, WHEELER Ladd, WHEELER Lauren, WHEELER Lexie, WHEELER Paul, WHEELER Ross, WHEELER Sid, WHEELER Terry, WHEELER Jane, WHEELER Bill, WHEELWRIGHT Danielle, WHEEN Steve, WHEILDON Jeanette, WHELAN Tony, WHELAN Benedict, WHELAN Bernard, WHELAN Debra, WHELAN Gerard, WHELAN Jenny, WHELAN Julia, WHELAN Mike, WHELAN Noel, WHELAN Paul, WHELAN Shane, WHELAN Steve, WHELDON Winnie, WHELLUM Scott, WHELPTON Cathy, WHETTON Meryl, WHIGHAM Laura, WHIGHT Margaret, **WHILES Ernie**, WHILEY Nick, WHILLAS Andrew, WHILLAS Craig, WHIPOY Ferris, WHIRISKEY Kathy, WHISH-WILSON Donna, WHISSON Ross, WHITAKER Alfred, WHITAKER Bianca, WHITAKER Denise, WHITAKER Dorothy, WHITAKER Phil, WHITAKER Suzie, WHITBOURN Ian, WHITBY Alex, WHITBY James, WHITBY Monica, WHITE Adrian, WHITE Adrienne, WHITE Alan, WHITE Alan, WHITE Alanna, WHITE Allan, WHITE Angela, WHITE Anna, WHITE Annie, WHITE Arthur, WHITE Barbara, WHITE Brian, WHITE Bronwyn, WHITE Bruce, WHITE Bruce, WHITE Bruce, WHITE Carol, WHITE Chris, WHITE Chris, WHITE Christine, WHITE Christine, WHITE Christopher, WHITE Col, WHITE Craig, WHITE Daimer, WHITE Dale, WHITE Danielle, WHITE Darren, WHITE David, WHITE Debbie, WHITE Debbie, WHITE Del, WHITE Jerry, WHITE Donna, WHITE Doffy, WHITE Doug, WHITE Doug, WHITE Ted, WHITE Elissa, WHITE Elizabeth, WHITE Eric, WHITE Eric, WHITE Estelle, WHITE Fiona, WHITE Fran, WHITE Fran, WHITE Gary, WHITE Gavan, WHITE Gloria, WHITE Gordon, WHITE Greg, WHITE Gwen, WHITE Helen, WHITE Honor, WHITE Hugh, WHITE Ian, WHITE Ian, WHITE Ian, WHITE Jackie, WHITE Jacquie, WHITE Janet, WHITE Jan, WHITE Joanne, WHITE John, WHITE Joyce, WHITE Judi, WHITE Judy, WHITE Katie, WHITE Kathryn, WHITE Keith, **WHITE Ken**, WHITE Kevin, WHITE Kristine, WHITE Lance, WHITE Lana, WHITE Laura, WHITE Laurie, WHITE Leanne, WHITE Lee, WHITE Lindy, WHITE Lynne, WHITE Lynn, WHITE Margaret, WHITE Maurie, WHITE Maurice, WHITE Mim, WHITE Monica, WHITE Nat, WHITE Nerida, WHITE Neville, WHITE Patricia, WHITE Tric, WHITE Pat, WHITE Patricia, WHITE Paul, WHITE Paul, WHITE Peter, WHITE Pete, WHITE Peter, WHITE Rachael, WHITE Rhonda, WHITE Rick, WHITE Bob, WHITE Robert, WHITE Rohan, WHITE Ron, WHITE Ron, WHITE Serena, WHITE Sheila, WHITE Stephen, WHITE Stewart, WHITE Stewart, WHITE Susan, WHITE Susan, WHITE Suzanne, WHITE Tarina, WHITE Tobias, WHITE Vanessa, WHITE Warren, WHITE Wendy, WHITE Wendy, WHITE Bill, WHITE Bill, WHITE Yumi, WHITE Yvonne, WHITEFIELD Jenny, WHITEFIELD Vince, WHITEFORD Ian, WHITEFORD Jess, WHITEFORD Rhys, WHITEHEAD Amber, WHITEHEAD Catherine, WHITEHEAD Jim, WHITEHEAD Kathy, WHITEHEAD Rob, WHITEHEAD Terry, WHITEHILL Bill, WHITEHOUSE Micky, WHITEHOUSE Graham, WHITEHOUSE Joseph, WHITEHOUSE Susan, WHITELAKE Robyn, WHITELAW Melanie, WHITELAW Stewart, WHITELAW Sue, WHITELUM Shirley-Anne, WHITEMAN Barry, WHITEMAN Karen, WHITEMAN Trish, WHITEMAN Robert, WHITEOAK Kristy, WHITESIDE Duncan, WHITESIDE Andrew, WHITESIDE Linda, WHITFELD Betsey, WHITFELD Roger, WHITFIELD Judith, WHITFIELD Michelle, WHITFIELD Robyn, WHITFIELD Vivien, WHITFORD Deslee, WHITFORD Dot, WHITFORD Joe, WHITHAM Sue, WHITICKER Helen, WHITING Chris, WHITING Dennis, WHITING Graeme, WHITING Julian, WHITING Ken, WHITING Len, WHITING Peter, WHITING Yvonne, WHITLA Cecily, WHITLEN Doug, WHITLEY Robin, WHITMORE Kim, WHITMORE Murray, WHITNALL Vicki, WHITNEY Leeanne, WHITNEY Trevor, WHITNOSE Smith, WHITSON Narelle, WHITTAKER Colin, WHITTAKER Ted, WHITTAKER Evelyn, WHITTAKER Glenn, WHITTAKER Hugh, WHITTAKER Joy, WHITTAKER Mary, WHITTAKER Bob, WHITTAKER Sam, WHITTAM Kylie, WHITTEMORE Matthew, WHITTET B enjamin, WHITTINGTON Peter, WHITTLE Jonathon, WHITTLE Rowena, WHITTLES Anna, WHITTON Diane, WHITTON Julie, WHITTON Trish, WHITTY Jason, WHITWELL Jacqui, WHOLOHAN Burt, WHYBROW Anthony, WHYTCROSS Ted, WHYTE Alice, WHYTE Cheriden, WHYTE Don, WHYTE Emma, WHYTE Greg, WHYTE Jason, WHYTE Julia, WHYTE Lyn, WHYTE Mary, WHYTE Roger, WHYTE Bill, WIBAWA Enrico, WIBBERLEY Tyne, WIBBERLEY Yasmin, WICHT Shirlee, WICKE Christopher, WICKENS-CAMPBELL Linda, WICKHAM Jenny, WICKHAM Jon, WICKHAM Zoe, WICKREMASINGHE Srimal, WICKS Donna, WICKS Annie, WICKS Helen, WICKS Larry, WICKS Michelle, WICKS Peter, WICKS Sheron, WICKSTROM Wayne, WIDER Bruno, WIDIYARINI Rosa, WIDJAJA Adelina, WIDJAJA Emily, WIDJAJA Rika, WIDJAYA Hubert, WIDMER Andi, WIDMER Rick, WIEBKE Warnken, WIECHMAN Max, WIECKMANN Cathy, WIEDEN Teisha, WIEDMAN Danny, WIEGAND Dominique, WIEGMANN Gloria, WIELAND Karina, WIELAND Lyn, WIELGOSZ Meg, WIEMER Barbara, WIENER Horst, WIERZBICKA Magdalena, WIERZBICKI Anna, WIESE Jenny, WIESMEIER Torsten, WIESSNER Tina-Louise, WIGG Aaron, WIGG Alison, WIGG Glenda, WIGGINS Bev, WIGGINS David, WIGGINS John, WIGGINS Kate, WIGLEY John, WIGNARAJAH Devika, WIGNEY Laurie, WIGNEY Paul, WIGREN Johanna, WIJEYASINGHE Kusum, WIJOYO Eka, WIJRDEMAN Susan, WIKA Maren, WILBERFORCE James, WILBERS Barbara, WILBERS John, WILCHER Dennis, WILCOCK Darrell, WILCOCKSON Jenny, WILCOX Chris, WILCOX Darren, WILCOX Gary, WILCOX Joan, WILCOX Paul, WILCOX Susan, WILCOX Wendy, WILCOXON Tara, WILCOXON Tracy, WILD Emily, WILD Ivan, WILD Laurie, WILD Rebecca, WILD Robyn, WILD Tanya, WILD Victoria, WILDBLOOD Angus, WILDE Clare, WILDE Dez, WILDE John, WILDE Kaylene, WILDE Les, WILDEN Marie, WILDER Herbert, WILDER Judith, WILDIN Mavis, WILDING Sandra, WILE Naomi, WILE Robyn, WILES Lianna, WILESMITH Angela, WILEY Tyler, WILHELM Sophie, WILKES Chris, WILKES Garry, WILKES Jon, WILKES Peter, WILKIE Alex, WILKIE David, WILKIE Terry, WILKIN Alan, WILKIN Emily, WILKINS Anne, WILKINS Barbara, WILKINS Bev, WILKINS Heather, WILKINS Judy, WILKINS Mark, WILKINS Ron, WILKINSON Marita, WILKINSON Barry, WILKINSON Belinda, WILKINSON Bev, WILKINSON Bruce, WILKINSON Bryan, WILKINSON Camilla, WILKINSON Cecilia,

WILKINSON Col, WILKINSON Denis, WILKINSON Gail, WILKINSON Gary, WILKINSON Hayley, WILKINSON Helen, WILKINSON Jessica, WILKINSON Judy, WILKINSON Kathleen, WILKINSON Lachlan, WILKINSON Leslie, WILKINSON Marc, WILKINSON Pamela, WILKINSON Trish, WILKINSON Phil, WILKINSON Lin, WILKS Alan, WILKS Arthur, WILKS Trish, WILKS Paul, WILL Naomi, WILL Tricia, WILLARD Barry, WILLARD Glenn, WILLARD Kelly, WILLARD Renate, WILLARD Rex, WILLARD Ronald, WILLARD Samantha, WILLCOCKS John, WILLCOCKSON Donna, WILLCOX Elizabeth, WILLCOX Pat, WILLEMS Erwin, WILLEMS Lembit, WILLER Jenny, WILLER Steve, WILLET Scott, WILLETT Annette, WILLETT Cathy, WILLETT Geoff, WILLETT Janelle, WILLIAMS Aileen, WILLIAMS Alex, WILLIAMS Alice, WILLIAMS Allan, WILLIAMS Allison, WILLIAMS Allan, WILLIAMS Amanda, WILLIAMS Amanda, WILLIAMS Andrew, WILLIAMS Anita, WILLIAMS Anne, WILLIAMS Anne, WILLIAMS Anne, WILLIAMS Annette, WILLIAMS Barbara, WILLIAMS Belinda, WILLIAMS Brenda, WILLIAMS Brett, WILLIAMS Brian, WILLIAMS Carla, WILLIAMS Carli, WILLIAMS Cathy, WILLIAMS Cheryl, WILLIAMS Chris, WILLIAMS Clare, WILLIAMS Craig, WILLIAMS Daphne, WILLIAMS Darrell, WILLIAMS Darrell, WILLIAMS David, WILLIAMS Debra, WILLIAMS Donald, **WILLIAMS Dorothy**, WILLIAMS Dorothy, WILLIAMS Doug, WILLIAMS Dru, WILLIAMS Elizabeth, WILLIAMS Emina, WILLIAMS Emma, WILLIAMS Fiona, WILLIAMS Fiona, WILLIAMS Garry, WILLIAMS Gareth, WILLIAMS Gaven, WILLIAMS Geoff, WILLIAMS Geoffrey, WILLIAMS Geoff, WILLIAMS Glenn, WILLIAMS Glenn, WILLIAMS Graham, WILLIAMS Greg, WILLIAMS Howie, WILLIAMS Ian, WILLIAMS Ion, WILLIAMS Jim, WILLIAMS James, WILLIAMS Jamie, WILLIAMS James, WILLIAMS Janet, WILLIAMS Jane, WILLIAMS Jan, WILLIAMS Jan, WILLIAMS Jean, WILLIAMS Jen, WILLIAMS Jenny, WILLIAMS Jody, WILLIAMS John, WILLIAMS Judy, WILLIAMS Jules, WILLIAMS Julian, WILLIAMS Julie, WILLIAMS Karen, WILLIAMS Karen, WILLIAMS Karen, WILLIAMS Karen, WILLIAMS Kathryn, WILLIAMS Kellie, WILLIAMS Kelsy, WILLIAMS Kerry, WILLIAMS Kevin, WILLIAMS Kris, WILLIAMS Kylie, WILLIAMS Larry, WILLIAMS Leanne, WILLIAMS Leslie, WILLIAMS Linda, WILLIAMS John, WILLIAMS Lyn, WILLIAMS Lynn, WILLIAMS Martin, WILLIAMS Margaret, WILLIAMS Peg, WILLIAMS Marli, WILLIAMS Mark, WILLIAMS Mark, WILLIAMS Marion, WILLIAMS Margaret, WILLIAMS Mark, WILLIAMS Matt, WILLIAMS Matthew, WILLIAMS Matthew, WILLIAMS Maxine, WILLIAMS Melissa, WILLIAMS Melissa, WILLIAMS Mike, WILLIAMS Michelle, WILLIAMS Mike, WILLIAMS Michelle, WILLIAMS Nicholas, WILLIAMS Nicole, WILLIAMS Nic, WILLIAMS Milton,

WILLIAMS Norm, WILLIAMS Owen, WILLIAMS Pam, WILLIAMS Trish, WILLIAMS Patrick, WILLIAMS Patricia, WILLIAMS Peter, WILLIAMS Peter, WILLIAMS Peter, WILLIAMS Peter, WILLIAMS Phil, WILLIAMS Phillip, WILLIAMS Ray, WILLIAMS Rebecca, WILLIAMS Rebekah, WILLIAMS Rhonda, WILLIAMS Rick, WILLIAMS Lindsay, WILLIAMS Bob, WILLIAMS Robyn, WILLIAMS Robert, WILLIAMS Robert, WILLIAMS Robert, WILLIAMS Rodger, WILLIAMS Ronald, WILLIAMS Ronald, WILLIAMS Rosemary, WILLIAMS Roz, WILLIAMS Roy, WILLIAMS Sally, WILLIAMS Sam, WILLIAMS Vicki, WILLIAMS Sarah, WILLIAMS Scott, WILLIAMS Scott, WILLIAMS Selwyn, WILLIAMS Sharon, WILLIAMS Shirley, WILLIAMS Sonya, WILLIAMS Stan, WILLIAMS Steve, WILLIAMS Steve, WILLIAMS Sue, WILLIAMS Suzanne, WILLIAMS Syd, WILLIAMS Terry, WILLIAMS Tim, WILLIAMS Tony, WILLIAMS Tracey, WILLIAMS Ronnie, WILLIAMS Wayne, WILLIAMS Wayne, WILLIAMS Wayne, WILLIAMS Wendy, WILLIAMS Wendy, WILLIAMS Ray, WILLIAMS SNR Jeff, WILLIAMSON Annette, WILLIAMSON Barbara, WILLIAMSON Elaine, WILLIAMSON Geoffrey, WILLIAMSON Grace, WILLIAMSON John, WILLIAMSON Jeff, WILLIAMSON Joe, WILLIAMSON Karynne, WILLIAMSON Katrina, WILLIAMSON Keith, WILLIAMSON Les, WILLIAMSON Linda, WILLIAMSON Lynette, WILLIAMSON Marjorie, WILLIAMSON Tina, WILLIAMSON Muriel, WILLIAMSON Nancye, WILLIAMSON Nathan, WILLIAMSON Rob, WILLIAMSON Shirley, WILLIAMSON Sue, WILLIAMSON Susan, WILLIAMSON Yvonne, WILLICK Suzanne, WILLILAMS Judy, WILLIMOTT Andrew, WILLIMOTT Peter, WILLINGE Donna, WILLINGTON Jill, WILLINGTON Tennille, WILLIS John, WILLIS Allie, WILLIS Anna, WILLIS Bruce, WILLIS Darren, WILLIS David, WILLIS Deborah, WILLIS Don, WILLIS Pat, WILLIS Elsa, WILLIS Erika, WILLIS David, WILLIS Heather, WILLIS Helen, WILLIS Jen, WILLIS John, WILLIS Katrina, WILLIS Ken, WILLIS Kim, WILLIS Neil, WILLIS Rachael, WILLIS Ray, WILLIS Rebecca, WILLIS Richard, WILLIS Dick, WILLIS Bob, WILLIS Sarah, WILLIS Scott, WILLIS Val, WILLIS Woranuch, WILLMETTE Rob, WILLMORE Renee, WILLMOT Krysteena, WILLMOT Yvonne, WILLMOTT Gloria, WILLMOTT Joanna, WILLMOTT Lionel, WILLOCK Lisa, WILLOTT Steve, WILLOUGHBY Allan, WILLOUGHBY Ann, WILLOUGHBY Celia, WILLOUGHBY Judy, WILLOUGHBY June, WILLOUGHBY Ken, WILLOUGHBY Margaret, WILLOUGHBY Paul, WILLOUGHBY Bob, WILLS Craig, WILLS Joy, WILLS Simon, WILLS Stephen, WILLSHER David, WILLSHIRE Dennis, WILLSHIRE Barbara, WILLSON David, WILLSON Lyn, WILLSON Melinda, WILMANN Ron, WILMOTT Brian, WILMSHURST Cheryl, WILMSHURST John, WILSHIRE Tony, WILSMORE Gary, WILSON Albert, WILSON Alex, WILSON John, WILSON Alyssa, WILSON Amber, WILSON Amy, WILSON Anna, WILSON Ann, WILSON AnnJane,

WILSON Anthony, WILSON Ted, WILSON Barry, WILSON Belinda, WILSON Bernadette, WILSON Beverley, WILSON Brian, WILSON Carl, WILSON Carly, WILSON Cec, WILSON Cedric, WILSON Charles, WILSON Cheryl, WILSON Chris, WILSON Christopher, WILSON Clairemarie, WILSON Claire, WILSON Cliff, WILSON Craig, WILSON Danielle, WILSON Darren, WILSON Darryl, WILSON David, WILSON Deanna, WILSON Dianne, WILSON Dianne, WILSON Eddie, WILSON Ross, WILSON Elizabeth, WILSON Elizabeth, WILSON Betty, WILSON Elsie, WILSON Fiona, WILSON Fiona, WILSON Garry, WILSON Geoff, WILSON Graham, WILSON Graham, WILSON Heath, WILSON Helen, WILSON Ian, WILSON Jackie, WILSON Jade, WILSON Jim, WILSON Jan, WILSON Jane, WILSON Jane, WILSON Jane, WILSON Janette, WILSON Jane, WILSON Jill, WILSON Jo, WILSON Joan, WILSON Joel, WILSON John, WILSON John, WILSON Judy, WILSON Judy, WILSON Karen, WILSON Katrina, WILSON Kath, WILSON Kathryn, WILSON Keith, WILSON Ken, WILSON Kerry, WILSON Kerryn, WILSON Kevin, WILSON evin, WILSON Kim, WILSON Kimberley, WILSON Kristy, WILSON Kylie, WILSON Lancew, WILSON Lauren, WILSON Leo, WILSON Leonie, WILSON Leslie, WILSON Lyn, WILSON Lou, WILSON Lynda, WILSON Lynn, WILSON Lyndall, WILSON Mandy, WILSON Margaret, WILSON Maggie, WILSON Marjorie, WILSON Marilyn, WILSON Mary, WILSON Margaret, WILSON Marilyn, WILSON Marilyn, WILSON Margaret, WILSON Mark, WILSON Mary, WILSON Margaret, WILSON Meg, WILSON Margaret, WILSON Margaret, WILSON Matthew, WILSON Megan, WILSON Melissa, WILSON Melissa, WILSON Narelle, WILSON Nerrelle, WILSON Nick, WILSON Noel, WILSON Paea, WILSON Patricia, WILSON Patricia, WILSON Paul, WILSON Penny, WILSON Peter, WILSON Stuart, WILSON Peter, WILSON Rach, WILSON Rebecca, WILSON Rebecca, WILSON Rhonda, WILSON Ricky, WILSON Ris, WILSON Bruce, WILSON Barry, WILSON Robert, WILSON Robyn, WILSON Ron, WILSON Ross, WILSON Rosemary, WILSON Russell, WILSON Samuel, WILSON Sandra, WILSON Sandra, WILSON Sheenagh, WILSON Sonya, WILSON Steve, WILSON Campbell, WILSON Sue, WILSON Terry, WILSON Tiaki, WILSON Val, WILSON Victor, WILSON Yvette, WILSON Zydia, WILTON Bron, WILTON Jeff, WILTON John, WILTON John, WILTON Pat, WILTSHIRE Belinda, WILTSHIRE Cliff, WILTSHIRE Ken, WILTSHIRE Les, WILTSHIRE Marlene, WILTSHIRE Matt, WILTSHIRE Myrene, WIMBLE Barbara, WIMPENNY Ian, WIN Win, WINARCZYK Dianne, WINARTO Win, WINCH Russell, WINCHESTER Gary, WINCHESTER Gaye, WINCHESTER Paul, WINCHESTER Rodney, WINCKLE Graham, WIND Ralph, WINDEBANK Russell, WINDHOLZ Kim, WINDLE Jacqui, WINDLE John, WINDLE Ruth, WINDLEY Beth, WINDOWS Deanna, WINDRED Norm, WINDSCHUTTEL Bob, WINDSOR Gunapala, WINDSOR Kenneth, WINDSOR Kenneth,

WINDSOR Melissa, WINDSOR Ray, WINDYBANK Ann, WINE Del, WINEBERG Sharyn, WINER Charles, WINES Barbara, WINES Bob, WINFIELD Philip, WING George, WING Jacinda, WING Phillip, WING KEE Percy, WINGFIELD DIGBY Andrew, WINKELMANN David, WINKLER Adelheid, WINKLER Allan, WINKLER David, WINKLER Eleanor, WINKLER Katina, WINKLER Marion, WINKLEY Nikki, WINKWORTH Sue, WINLAW Jen, WINLEY Max, WINN Robyn, WINN Thiri, WINNALL John, WINNALL Marion, WINNETT Jason, WINNIE Adrian, WINOTO Thea, WINROW Colin, WINROW Mavis, WINROW Rosalie, **WINSLADE Natalie**, WINSLET Teneil, WINSOR Hughie, WINSOR Lorraine, WINSOR Shirley, WINSTON-SHAFER Cathy, WINTER Bernard, WINTER Dianne, WINTER Jill, WINTER Kevin, WINTER Len, WINTER Maria, WINTER Sally, WINTER Susan, WINTER Reid, WINTER-STIENEN Johanna, WINTERS Kathryn, WINTERS Lesley, WINTERS Phillip, WINTERS Ross, WINTERTON Andrew, WINTLE Bob, WINTON Gai, WINTON Les, WINTON Shirley, WINTON Paige, **WINTON-BROWN Tim**, WINWOOD Kane, WINWOOD-SMITH Maree, WINWOOD-SMITH Ray, WINYARD David, WIOGO Johan, WIRIANSKI Mark, WIRIANTO Charles, WIRTH Peter, WIRZ Pacofrancesco, WISBEY Loren, WISCHER Rachael, WISDOM Craig, WISE Al, WISE Bryan, WISE Jodee, WISE John, WISE Bill, WISEMAN Adam, WISEMAN Brian, WISEMAN Debbie, WISEMAN Heather, WISEMAN Keith, WISEMAN Margaret, WISEMAN Max, WISEMAN Nicole, WISHART Brad, WISSAM George, WITANOWSKI Mark, WITEHIRA Mereana, WITHALL Kevin, WITHANEACHI Daya, WITHELL John, WITHERBY Ray, WITHERS Desley, WITHERS John, WITHERS Karlene, WITHERS Marnie, WITHERS Marilyn, WITHERS Suzy, WITHNALL Joanne, WITHNELL Faith, WITJES Louke, WITKOP Peter, WITT Flea, WITT Geoffrey, WITT Jody, WITT Ray, WITT Sheila, WITTEN Neville, WITTER Wendi, WITTEY Gregory, WITTRIEN Bob, WITTS Andrew, WITTSTROM Susanne, WITTWER Hans, WITTWER Naree, WIXON Diane, WIZBICKI Ewa, WIZBICKI Jan, WO Jeffrey, WODECKI Nilda, WODIANICKY-HEILER Nick, WOELMS Ricardo, WOELZ Keren, WOHLWEND Diane, WOJCIECHOWSKI Waldemar, WOJCIK Grace, WOJTOWYEZ Mary, WOJTYNSKI Stan, WOLAVER Nicholas, WOLF David, WOLF Wolfie, WOLFENDEN Cheryl, WOLFENDEN Elmer, WOLFF Kimberley, WOLFRAM Astrid, WOLFSOHN Ali, WOLFSON Asher, WOLFSON Chloe, WOLKE Michael, WOLLAGE Ann, WOLSTENHOLME Shaun, WOLTRING Beatrice, WOMERSLEY Bee, **WOMSLEY Garry**, WON Alex, WON Kwang-Yeon, WON Margaret, WONG Aaron, WONG Ada, WONG Alan, WONG Alex, WONG Alex, WONG Alison, WONG Alice, WONG Allan, WONG Arthur, WONG Belinda, WONG Bradley, WONG Cai, WONG Carissa, WONG Carol, WONG Charles, WONG Chaudie, WONG Christine, WONG Alex, WONG Darren, WONG David, WONG Dennis, WONG Dennis, **WONG Desmond**, WONG Doris, WONG Eddie, WONG Eddy, WONG Edwin, WONG Elaine, WONG Emily, WONG Ernest, WONG Esther, WONG Eugene, WONG Fiona, WONG Flora, WONG Boris, WONG Angela, WONG Grace, WONG Henry, WONG Richard, WONG Jess, WONG Isaac, WONG Ivy, WONG Jackie, WONG James, WONG Jason, WONG Jason, WONG Jeremy, WONG Jess, WONG Jess, WONG Joan, WONG Joanna, WONG Johnny, WONG Jonathan, WONG Joe, WONG Judy, WONG Justin, WONG Kan, WONG Karina, WONG Kathlen, WONG Ken, WONG Keuh, WONG Kevin, WONG Kevin, WONG Ki, WONG Kit-Tsun, WONG Lai, WONG Lucia, WONG Maggie, WONG Man, WONG Margie, WONG Matt, WONG Merrill, WONG Mike, WONG Ngai, WONG Nicole, WONG Pat, WONG Pauline, WONG Peng, WONG Priscilla, WONG Joelle, WONG Raymond, WONG Rosemary, WONG Sally, WONG Sara, WONG Shirley, WONG Simon, WONG Stephanie, WONG Venus, WONG Sun, WONG Sylvia, WONG Ken, WONG Thomas, WONG Tinny, WONG Michael, WONG Vicky, WONG Vincent, WONG Vincent, WONG Viola, WONG Jennifer, WONG Patrick, WONG Andrew, WONG Wing, WONG Sherry, WONG Ingrid, WONG Zoe, WONG Yvonne, WONG NAM Chris, WONG WING KEE Christopher, WONG YUEN KOOK Charles, WONGSOWIDJOJO Sutomo, WONSON Daniel, WONSON Stacey, WONSON Trevor, WOO Anthony, WOO Derek, WOO Karen, WOO Kyoung, WOO Grace, WOO Riberza, WOO Sam, WOO Andrew, WOO Warren, WOOD Adam, WOOD Andrew, WOOD Brad, WOOD Brian, WOOD Brian, WOOD Brooke, WOOD Bruce, WOOD Cameron, WOOD Catherine, WOOD Chris, WOOD David, WOOD Dave, WOOD David, WOOD David, WOOD Di, WOOD Donald, WOOD Elizabeth, WOOD Elliott, WOOD Emma, WOOD Fran, WOOD Gabrielle, WOOD Pek, WOOD Gnarie, WOOD Doug, WOOD Graham, WOOD Helen, WOOD James, WOOD Jim, WOOD James, WOOD Jane, WOOD Jeanie, WOOD Joanne, WOOD John, WOOD Kathy, WOOD Kelly, WOOD Kim, WOOD Lawrence, WOOD Leanne, WOOD Len, WOOD Linda, WOOD Lorraine, WOOD Lyall, WOOD Matt, WOOD Michael, WOOD Mike, WOOD Michael, WOOD Monica, WOOD Nicholas, WOOD Phill, WOOD Pam, WOOD Paula, WOOD Peter, WOOD Bob, WOOD Robert, WOOD Robert, WOOD Russell, WOOD Sandy, WOOD Sara, WOOD Sharyn, WOOD Sherelle, WOOD Stephanie, WOOD Steve, WOOD Stuart, WOODBURN Andrew, WOODBURN Denny, WOODBURN James, WOODBURY Keith, WOODBURY Ray, WOODCOCK Alan, WOODCOCK David, WOODCOCK Keith, WOODCOCK Leslie, WOODCOCK Marylin, WOODCOCK Max, WOODEN Jody, WOODEN Kay, WOODEN Kerry, WOODEN Simone, WOODFIELD Nicole, WOODFORD Athol, WOODFORD Norm, WOODGATE Matt, WOODGATE Robyn, WOODHAMS Anne, WOODHAMS Elizabeth, WOODHAMS Nick, WOODHART Maryann, WOODHEAD Mark, WOODHOUSE Elke, WOODHOUSE Garry, WOODHOUSE Mark, WOODHOUSE Jeffrey, WOODHOUSE Michelle, WOODHOUSE Susan, WOODLEIGH Frank, WOODLEY Christopher, WOODLEY Diana, WOODLEY Jill, WOODLEY John, WOODLEY Yok, WOODMAN Andrew, WOODMORE Peter, WOODROFFE Libby, WOODROW Michael, WOODROW Jo, WOODRUFF Peter, WOODS Alan, WOODS Andrew, WOODS Bonnie, WOODS Brett, WOODS Carol, WOODS Carmel, WOODS Claire, WOODS Daryl, WOODS David, WOODS Libby, WOODS Elizabeth, WOODS Fiona, WOODS Frances, WOODS Graeme, WOODS Greg, WOODS Jacinta, WOODS Janeen, WOODS Jan, WOODS Jennifer, WOODS John, WOODS Karen, WOODS Kristen, WOODS Michael, WOODS Paul, WOODS Ray, WOODS Rob, WOODS Rod, WOODS Rodney, WOODS Steven, WOODS Tim, WOODSIDE Elizabeth, WOODWARD Betty, WOODWARD Des, WOODWARD Diana, WOODWARD Emily, WOODWARD Graham, WOODWARD Janis, WOODWARD John, WOODWARD Leonard, WOODWARD Phil, WOODWARD Rex, WOODWARD Bob, WOODWARD Sue, WOODWARD Sue, WOODWARD Taya, WOODWARD Todd, WOOLAGE Bob, WOOLARD Adrian, WOOLBANK Felicity, WOOLCOCK Neta, WOOLCOTT Sophie, WOOLDRIDGE Tony, WOOLDRIDGE Barry, WOOLDRIDGE Margaret, WOOLDRIDGE Maureen, WOOLFE Barry, WOOLFE Jenny, WOOLFE Trevor, WOOLFENDEN Christine, WOOLFSON Liz, WOOLLARD Jann, WOOLLARD Shylee, WOOLLEY Brendan, WOOLLEY Ian, WOOLLEY Jim, WOOLLEY Jo, WOOLLEY Peter, WOOLMAN Sandy, WOOLMER Barb, WOOLMER John, WOOLNER Peter, WOOLTERTON Tricia, WOON Judy, WOOSNAM Denise, WORAKUL Loy, WORBOYS Beryl, WORBS Carol, WORGER Benjamin, WORKER Julie, WORLAND Jacinta, WORLEY April, WORLEY Esme, WORMALD Jo, WORMLEATON Cheryl, WORNER Matt, WORNER Troy, WORONCZAK Matt, WORRALL Ross, WORRALL Lesley, WORRELL Jim, WORRELL Karen, WORSLEY Belinda, WORSLEY Neil, WORT Kay, WORTENDYKE Krista, WORTH Gregory, WORTH Lesley, WO RTH Nat, WORTH Pippa, WORTHINGTON Andrew, WORTHINGTON Tony, WORTHINGTON Roger, WORTON Sandra, WOSIK John, WOTHERSPOON Jaime, WOTHERSPOON Ronald, WOULFE Steve, WRAGG Paul, WRAIGHT Joanne, WRATHALL Andrew, WRATHALL Helen, WRATHALL Jill, WRATTEN Kylie, WRAY Maureen, WRAY Bob, WREN Chris, WREN Dorothy, WREN Dick, WRENCH Garry, WRICE Brian, WRIGHT Alanna, WRIGHT Alan, WRIGHT Alex, WRIGHT Alison, WRIGHT John, WRIGHT Amanda, WRIGHT Anne, WRIGHT Arthur, WRIGHT Barbara, WRIGHT Beryl, WRIGHT Bev, WRIGHT Bruce, WRIGHT Caroline, WRIGHT Christina, WRIGHT Christa, WRIGHT Chris, WRIGHT Claire, WRIGHT Peter, WRIGHT Col, WRIGHT Diane, WRIGHT Liz, WRIGHT Gary, WRIGHT Alan, WRIGHT Jane, WRIGHT Jeff, WRIGHT Anne, WRIGHT Joanne, WRIGHT John, WRIGHT John,

WRIGHT John, WRIGHT John, WRIGHT Kate, WRIGHT Katherine, WRIGHT Keven, WRIGHT Kristopher, WRIGHT Marilyn, WRIGHT Marcus, WRIGHT Marg, WRIGHT Melinda, WRIGHT Nell, WRIGHT Nicky, WRIGHT Nicole, WRIGHT Nigel, WRIGHT Rex, WRIGHT Robert, WRIGHT Roberta, WRIGHT Steve, WRIGHT Sue, WRIGHT Sue, WRIGHT Tim, WRIGHT Vicki, WRIGHT Wayne, WRIGHT-SMITH John, WRIGHTMAN Tony, WRIGHTSON Les, WRIGHTSON Val, WRIGLEY Patricia, WRIGLEY Colin, WRIGLEY Peter, WROE Noreen, WU Alice, WU Amy, WU Andrew, WU Anna, WU Bao, WU Charlie, WU Doughuan, WU Emily, WU Yvonne, WU Feng, WU William, WU Jannie, WU Jenny, WU Jen, WU James, WU Jie, WU Jonathan, WU Irene, WU Redknapp, WU Li, WU Louisa, WU Jing, WU Lei, WU Lydia, WU Mark, WU Marina, WU Michael, WU Catherine, WU Min, WU Nancy, WU Paul, WU Philip, WU Kenny, WU Shirley, WU Vicky, WU Steven, WU Thomas, WU Tina, WU Tina, WU Wei, WU Wendy, WU Xiao, WU Xiaoling, WU Xinxi, **WU Ying**, WU Youping, WU Yu, WU Annie, WU Yuheng, WUEST Norm, WULFF Julia, WULFF Mark, WULFF Melissa, WULFF Paul, WULFF JENSEN Kirsten, WURR Karen, WURTH Peter, WUTTHIKRAIKRIANG Anong, WUU Philip, WYATT Alf, WYATT Barbara, WYATT Cameron, WYATT Don, WYATT Elaine, WYATT Gregory, WYATT Judy, WYATT Roy, WYBORN David, WYCHERLEY Rosemary, WYER Geraldine, WYER Paul, WYETH Jeanette, WYKANAK Domonic, WYKES Glenn, WYLD Ben, WYLD Justine, WYLDE Katelynn, WYLDE Paul, WYLDE-BROWNE Carol, **WYLDEBROWNE Ross**, WYLES Barbara, WYLIE Cathie, WYLIE Liz, WYLIE Geraldine, WYLIE Hellen, WYLIE Jeni, WYLLIE Ian, WYMAN Baz, WYMAN John, WYNDHAM Clara, WYNDHAM Michael, WYNER Joshua, WYNN Arthur, WYNN Bruce, WYNN David, WYNNE Kellie, WYNNE Kerry, WYNNE Leon, WYNNE Michael, WYNNE Patricia, WYNNE Patrick, WYNTER Steven, WYSE Rebecca, WYSMANDAVIDSON Veona, WYTHES Claudia, WYTON Barry.

X

XAVIER Catherine, XAVIER Tiago, XAVIER Yolanda, XIAO Mandy, XIAO Ping, XIAO Zhen, XIAO MIN Xu, XIE Maggie, XIE Li, XIE Yi, XIE Sarah, XIN Ronald, XIN Tuo, XING Chunhua, XIONG Xiong, XIONG Xay, XU Alan, XU Alicia, XU Bailey, XU Bei, XU Betty, XU Gerry, XU Sophie, XU Jenny, XU Lin, XU Ming, XU Min, XU Peng, XU Ping, XU Wei, XU Linda, XU Rena, XU Xiaomin, XU Xu, XU Yanyan, XU Angela, XUE Hui, XUE Lin, XUE Cherie, XUEREB Carmen.

Y

YABSLEY David, YABSLEY John, YABSLEY Louise, YACOUB Jack, YADAV Asha, YADAV Krishna, YADAV Pankaj, YAGANEGI Ed, YAGHI Sam, YAGHOBIAN-AZARI Tanya, YAGOUB Thoria, YAHIAOUI Fatna, YAHL Kylie, YAKAN Arzu, YAKO George, YALAKI Erhan, YALDA Sarkis, YALDALOO Nina, YALDEN Mike, YALLOURIS Nick, YAM Kin, YAMAGUCHI Sonomi, YAMAMOTO Etsuko, YAMAMOTO Kai, YAMAMOTO Mika, YAMAMOTO Sarah, YAMAMOTO Takeshi, YAMAN Efe, YAMANA Mariko, YAMAZAKI Chieko, YAMAZAKI Tomomi, YAN Josie, YAN Kim, YAN Rachel, YAN Ray, YAN Stanley, YAN Wei, YANATCHKOVA Viara, YANDELL James, YANG Ai, YANG Kathy, YANG Jenny, YANG Chang, YANG Dae, YANG Eric, YANG Joseph, YANG Eleanor, YANG Jesse, YANG Kwong, YANG Maggie, YANG Su, YANG Shun, YANG Stephen, YANG Thierry, YANG Vivian, YANG Sylvia, YANG Arthur, YANG Yubin, YAO Yao, YAO Shih-Ern, YAP Carmen, YAP Chee, YAP Edgardo, YAP Pek, YAP Sarah, YAP Melanie, YAPOUDJIAN Arek, YAPP Ivan, YAPP Jonathan, YARDIN Sybil, YARNOLD Wendy, YARRINGTON June, YASAN Fisun, YASUDA Fuki, YASUGI Yumiko, YATA Mariko, YATA Yukiko, YATES Bruce, YATES Carole, YATES Carol, YATES June, YATES Gordon, YATES Kathleen, YATES Kevin, YATES Luke, YATES Marie, YATES Maureen, YATES Max, YATES Peta, YATES Mal, YATES Samuel, YAU Ivan, YAU Wen, YAVUZ Sukru, YAW Adrian, YAXLEY Louise, YAZBECK Taminy, YE Hong, YE Hua, YE Holly, YE Melissa, YE Xiao, YE Ziming, YEADON Max, YEAP Ming, YEAROT Taly, YEATES Amelia, YEATES Del, YEATES Robynne, YEATS Carolyn, YEATS Sarah, YEE Allan, YEE Darren, YEE Eleanor, YEE James, YEE Larry, YEE Sandra, YEH Karina, YELDA Samia, YELDHAM Mireille, YELISTRATOV Valeriy, YEN Edward, YEN Jackie, YEN Peter, YEN TJ, YENDLE Corrine, YENG Boh, YENNE Carleen-Violet, YENSON Brendon, YEO Tony, YEO Josephine, YEO Janelle, YEO Jonathan, YEO Karen, YEO Kim, YEO Kyung-Mi, YEO Loy, YEO Michelle, YEO Misun, YEO Myeong, YEO Khuan, YEO Steve, YEO Steven, YEOH Ean, YEOH Pak, YEOH Thomas, YEOW Peter, YESMIN Sohela, YEUNG Anthony, YEUNG Betty, YEUNG Christine, YEUNG Chun, YEUNG David, YEUNG Henry, YEUNG Sarm, YEUNG Irene, YEUNG Jasmine, YEUNG John, YEUNG JIn, YEUNG Carrie, YEUNG Melissa, YEUNG Josephine, YEUNG Orsino, YEUNG Victoria, YEUNG Vita, YEUNG Jamilla, YEUNG Winnie, YEW Ann, YEW Ming, YEWDALL Shelley, YI Frank, YI Peter, YI Jai-Cheol, YI Suzy, YI Tin, YI Yu, YIANNAKOPOULOS Fay, YIK Elaine, YILMAZ Kutsal, YILMAZ Yalcin, YIM Jessie, YIM Candy, YIM Charles, YIN Daniel, YIN Paul, YIN Sammi, YIN Whye, YIN PING Cheah, YING Cheng, YING Frank, YING Yvonne, YIP Anne, YIP Carol, YIP Caroline, YIP Christina, YIP Danny, YIP Hung, YIP Joy, YIP Keith, YIP Moh, YIP Robin, YIP Samantha, YIP Sarah, YIT Sovan, YIU Chung, YIU Paul, YIU Johnny, YIU SZE CHENG Judy, YOCK Rachael, YOLE David, YOLLAND Rose, YONEMORI Ayako, YONEYAMA June, YONG James, YONG Set, YONG Set, YONG So, YONGE Warwick, YONGIL Cho, YOO Clara, YOO Donna, YOO Moon, YOO Sunny, YOON Andy, YOON Joosung, YOON Hannah, YOON Mook, YOON Min, YOONG William, YOONG Yvonne, YORK Dave, YORKE Steve, YORKSTON Emily, YORMAZ Ozi, YOSHIDA Junko, YOSHIMATSU Saori, YOSHIMURA Tokuko, YOSHIYAMA KazukO, YOU Carol, YOU Steven, YOUDALE Margaret, YOUELL Gaylene, YOUKHANA Benjamin, YOUL Phillip, YOUN Michael, YOUN Jerry, YOUN Roo, YOUNAN Christine, YOUNAN-SEDRAK Michael, YOUNG Alex, YOUNG Allan, YOUNG Barry, YOUNG Bronwen, YOUNG Cameron, YOUNG Carmel, YOUNG Cathy, YOUNG Charlie, YOUNG Martin, YOUNG Cherie, YOUNG Colleen, YOUNG Cynthia, YOUNG Dawn, YOUNG Dawin, YOUNG Denise, YOUNG Dianne, YOUNG Douglas, YOUNG Eric, YOUNG Fiona, YOUNG Gabrielle, YOUNG George, YOUNG Geoff, YOUNG Gloria, YOUNG Hayden, YOUNG Helen, YOUNG Herry, YOUNG Jenny, YOUNG Jeff, YOUNG Jo, YOUNG Joan, YOUNG Jocelyn, YOUNG John, YOUNG Karen, YOUNG Kate, YOUNG Kathryn, YOUNG Katrina, YOUNG Kelly, YOUNG Kenneth, YOUNG Kirsty, YOUNG Lawrence, YOUNG Leanna, YOUNG Len, YOUNG Lisa, YOUNG Lorraine, YOUNG Luke, YOUNG Margaret, YOUNG Marie, YOUNG Mary, YOUNG Maureen, YOUNG Merrilyn, YOUNG Michael, YOUNG Nikki, YOUNG Pam, YOUNG Pamela, YOUNG Paul, YOUNG Peter, YOUNG Peter, YOUNG Rachel, YOUNG Bob, YOUNG Robyn, YOUNG Bob, YOUNG Ross, YOUNG Shaun, YOUNG Shannon, YOUNG Soowan, YOUNG Stacie, YOUNG Steve, YOUNG Steven, YOUNG Steven, YOUNG Sue, YOUNG Susan, YOUNG Teresa, YOUNG Tina, YOUNG Vicki, YOUNG Virginia, YOUNGMAN Anne, YOUNIE John, YOUSIF Farouk, YOUSIF Jamil, YOUSSEF Dominic, YOUSSEF Jannet, YOUSSEF Ziad, YOUSUF Yousuf, YOW Philippe, YU Alisun, YU Bernard, YU Helen, YU Alicia, YU Jin, YU Joyce, YU Jun, YU Kathy, YU Peter, YU Sally, YU Tsai-Ying, YU Virginia, YU Vivienne, YU Xueqin, YU Michael, YU Yi, YU Bridgett, YUAN Jun, YUAN Amy, YUE Connie, YUEN Alice, YUEN Ben, YUEN William, YUEN Thomas, YUEN Christine, YUEN Joyce, YUEN Patrick, YUEN Angie, YUEN Regina, YUEN Syd, YULE Iain, YULI Yulianti, YULIANTO Linda, YUN Chi, YUN Choung, YUN Daniel, YUN David, YUN Mi, YUN Myung, YUN Deborah, YUNG Carli, YUNG Esther, YUNUS Fadzil.

Z

ZABAKS Kerrie, ZABAT Buddy, ZABOLOTNY Valentina, ZABORSZKY Alex, ZACCAK Lynda, ZACCARDO Don, ZACHARIAH Geniene, ZACHOU Theodora, ZACHULSKI Clare, ZADRAVEC Stefan, ZADRO Elio, ZAFFER Abu, ZAFIROPOULOS Peter, ZAGAME Kathy, ZAGAMI Clare, ZAGAR Barbara, ZAGHAM Rabiya, ZAGON George, ZAGORA George, ZAGORODNYUK Dennis, ZAHAR Pandora, ZAHARY Lizz, ZAHN Marilyn, ZAHOS Helen, ZAHOS Peter, ZAHR Hannan, ZAI Darren, ZAID Alex, ZAIDI Syed, ZAIKA Boris, ZAINI Giusseppe, ZAITOUNI Joe, ZAKARIAN Avo, ZAKI Mike, ZAKIS Allegra, ZAKIS Constantine, ZAKLAMA Reem, ZAKNICH Zak, ZAKOUT Feras, ZALDARRIAGA Jeraz, ZALEWSKI Michael, ZAMAN S.m., ZAMBELLI Frances, ZAMBOLT Andrea, ZAMECNIK Pavel, ZAMMIT Tony, ZAMMIT Carmel, ZAMMIT Catherine,

ZAMMIT Charlie, ZAMMIT Charles, ZAMMIT Diane, ZAMMIT Eddy, ZAMMIT Justin, ZAMMIT Lew, ZAMMIT Marisa, ZAMMIT Michael, ZAMMIT Ted, ZAMORA Octavio, ZAMPIERO Nicolas, ZANOLLA Danny, ZANTEY Effie, ZANTOS Penny, ZANTOS Steve, ZAOUD Khaled, ZAOUD Sam, ZAPANTA Bobby, ZAPPALA Phillip, ZAPPALA Yvonne, ZAPPIA Antonio, ZAPPIA Dom, ZAPPIA Elisabetta, ZARANTONELLO Claude, ZARB Jerry, ZARB Koryn, ZARIFA George, ZARIFA Marc, ZARIN Michele, ZARKOVIC Durad, ZARRA Nikki, ZARTH Adam, ZARZECKI Kari, ZASLAVSKY Alex, ZASLAVSKY Len, ZAUBZER Pat, ZAVISKA Monika, ZAWISZ Marzena, ZBARAS Olga, ZBIKOWSKI-SPENCE Lisa, ZDANOWICZ-MUCHLADO Victor, ZDOLSEK Maja, ZDRAVKOVIC Nina, ZEA Emilia, ZEA Roxanna, ZEARO Emil, ZEBEC Denis, ZEC Anthony, ZECHNER Gunter, ZECKENDORF Helen, ZEED Ibrahim, ZEED Yunus, ZEIDAN Malek, ZEIN Tarek, ZEINI Caroline, ZEITZ Gavin, ZEITZ Keiko, ZEKIC Peter, ZELAZOWSKI George, ZELENOVIC Jelena, ZELENY Jo, ZELEZETSKII Igor, ZELJKOVIC Dragan, ZELKA Lukas, ZELL Marg, ZELL Max, ZELUNZUK Carni, ZEMAN Anita, ZENG GuangZhao, ZENG Louise, ZENG Victor, ZENULI Nancy, ZEON Andrew, ZEPINIC Violeta, ZERAFA Don, ZERBES Rolf, ZERBINI Romi, ZERVAAS Mark, ZERVOS Amanda, ZHAI Ken, ZHAI Xue, ZHAN Ying, ZHANG Sam, ZHANG Chen, ZHANG Chunhui, ZHANG Ding, ZHANG Dongmo, ZHANG Fan, ZHANG Gao, ZHANG Hong, ZHANG Hua, ZHANG Jenny, ZHANG Winston, ZHANG Linda, ZHANG Jie-Chuan, ZHANG Jing, ZHANG Gary, ZHANG Allen, ZHANG Janson, ZHANG Li, ZHANG Li, ZHANG Lily, ZHANG John, ZHANG Lucy, ZHANG Sharon, ZHANG Sharon, ZHANG Ting-Liang, ZHANG Ury, ZHANG Weimin, ZHANG Weiyi, ZHANG Wei, ZHANG Erica, ZHANG Xiaolu, ZHANG Xun, ZHANG Yi, ZHANG Yi, ZHANG Ingrid, ZHANG Yin, ZHANG Ying, ZHANG James, ZHAO Alan, ZHAO Andrew, ZHAO Henry, ZHAO Zhao, ZHAO Holly, ZHAO Hui, ZHAO Jen, ZHAO Lucy, ZHAO Michael, ZHAO Ping, ZHAO Sue, ZHAO Shirley, ZHAO Xing, ZHENG Christina, ZHENG Connie, ZHENG Hailan, ZHENG Lin, ZHENG Michael, ZHENG Zeni, ZHENG Richard, ZHENG Shitao, ZHENG Ann, ZHENG Wing, ZHENG Jason, ZHONG Lichan, ZHONG Wen, ZHOU Warren, ZHOU Bob, ZHU Christina, ZHU Di, ZHU Hong, ZHU Hui, ZHU JJason, ZHU Judy, ZHU Samuel, ZHU Song-Bo, ZHU Charles, ZHU Wei-Zhong, ZHU Jessie, ZHU Yany, ZHU Yuen, ZHU Eric, ZHUGE Kevin, ZIEGLER Stuart, ZIEGLER Ziggy, ZIELAZO Michelle, ZIETZ Jenny, ZIKPI Philip, ZIKRIA Lavon, ZIKRIA Wais, ZIMERMANN Al, ZIMMERMANN Nigel, ZIMMWEMANN Heinz, ZINDEL Thomas, ZINKE Heinz, ZIRAH Alexis, ZIRPS Michael, ZITNAKOVA Martina, ZITO Lynette, ZIVKOVIC Alexa, ZIVKOVIC Tanja, ZLOBINE Kirill, ZMUDA Mark, ZOABI Ghassan, ZOBONOS Paul, ZODINS Kate, ZOELLNER Holger, ZOGOPOULOS Chris, ZOLBOOT Itgel, ZONG Judy, ZONIES Janet, ZONNEVELD Kay, ZORAS Joanne, ZORIC Alex, ZOU Harry, ZRILIC Jim, ZRINSKI Groz, ZUBKOV Dinah, ZUDINS Eddie, ZUGEC Natalie, ZUHAIR Mohamed, ZUMBRENNEN David, ZUMSTEIN Martin, ZUNDANS Mark, ZUNG STRIBELL Martin, ZUNGAR Joelmon, ZURAK John, ZUSAK Helmut, ZVERINOVA Kristina, ZVIRBLIS Kathy, ZWATRZKA Nelly, ZWECK David, ZWECK Tamara, ZWEGERS Denysse, ZYBRANDS John, ZYDENBOS Tom, ZYGADLO Ken, ZYLSTRA Warren.

VOLUNTEER ORGANISATIONS

Sydney 2000 Olympic Volunteers Social Club
The Unofficial Website of the Sydney 2000 Olympic Volunteers

http://communities.ninemsn.com.au/sydneyolympicvolunteers

This site is dedicated to furthering friendships and contacts fostered during the Olympics. You'll find lists of upcoming social events, photo albums, prizes to be won and discussion and chat rooms.

VOLUNTEER REFERRAL CENTRES

These organisations will help you find opportunities to share in the rewards of volunteering. They can also refer you to numerous regional and suburban organisations.

AUSTRALIAN CAPITAL TERRITORY
Volunteering ACT
PO Box 48
Belconnen ACT 2616
Ph: 02 6251 4060
Fax: 02 6251 4161

NEW SOUTH WALES
Volunteering NSW
Level 2, 228 Pitt Street
Sydney NSW 2000
Ph: 02 9261 3600
Fax: 02 9261 4033
www.volunteering.com.au

NORTHERN TERRITORY
Volunteering NT
Level 4, Darwin Central
21 Knuckey Street
Darwin NT 0800
Ph: 08 8981 3405
Fax: 08 8941 0279

QUEENSLAND
Volunteering Queensland
333 Adelaide Street
Brisbane QLD 4000
Ph: 07 3229 9700
Fax: 07 3229 2392
www.volunteeringqueensland.org.au

SOUTH AUSTRALIA
Volunteering South Australia
1st Floor, 220 Victoria Square
Adelaide SA 5000
Ph: 08 8221 7177
Fax: 08 8221 7188
www.volunteeringsa.org.au

TASMANIA
Volunteering Tasmania
18 Goulburn Street
Hobart TAS 7000
Ph: 03 6231 5550
Fax: 03 6234 4113
Email: volunteering.tasmania@tassie.net.au

VICTORIA
Volunteering Victoria
4th Floor, 247 Flinders Lane
Melbourne VIC 3000
Ph: 03 9650 5541
Fax: 03 9650 8868
Email: volunteer@infoxchange.net.au

WESTERN AUSTRALIA
Volunteering Western Australia
City West Lotteries House
2 Delhi Street
West Perth WA 6005
Ph: 08 9420 7288
Fax: 08 9420 7289
Email: community@volunteer.org.au
www.volunteer.org.au